REFORMATION MARRIAGE

*The Husband and Wife Relationship in the
Theology of Luther and Calvin*

REFORMATION MARRIAGE

*The Husband and Wife Relationship in the
Theology of Luther and Calvin*

Michael Parsons

WIPF & STOCK · Eugene, Oregon

Wipf and Stock Publishers
199 W 8th Ave, Suite 3
Eugene, OR 97401

Reformation Marriage
The Husband and Wife Relationship in
the Theology of Luther and Calvin
By Parsons, Michael
Copyright©2005 by Parsons, Michael
ISBN 13: 978-1-61097-633-6
Publication date 8/2/2011
Previously published by Rutherford House, 2005

To my wife, Becky,
and to our children, Christopher and Katy.

Thank you. Through you all, I am constantly
reminded of the Lord's goodness and grace.

CONTENTS

Foreword	ix
Acknowledgements	xi
Abbreviations	xiii

I	**INTRODUCTION**	1
	1. Recent Scholarship	1
	Luther	8
	Calvin	23
	2. The Approach of the Present Study	37
	Introduction	37
	Method of Enquiry	41
II	**THE MARRIAGE TRADITION**	49
	3. Augustine on Marriage	49
	The Significance of *ordo*	52
	Marriage in the Divine Purpose	56
	Hierarchy and Mutual Friendship	59
	Sexuality within Marriage	67
	Conclusion	73
	4. Medieval Marriage	77
	Medieval Insistence on Order	80
	Sexual Ambivalence	87
	Excursus: Aquinas on Marriage	91
	Conclusion	100
III	**MARRIAGE IN LUTHER**	103
	5. Marriage and the Temporal Kingdom	103
	The Two Kingdoms	105
	Marriage as Worldly Vocation	134
	Conclusion	138

	6. Marriage as Vocation	141
	Marriage before God	142
	Traditional Reasons for Marrying	159
	Excursus: Luther's Reluctance to Marry	173
	Conclusion	177
	7. Luther, Hierarchy and Mutual Love	179
	Luther's Biblical Exposition	179
	A Fixed Patriarchy with Mutuality	197
	Excursus: Luther's Marriage	203
	Conclusion	207
IV	**MARRIAGE IN CALVIN**	213
	8. Marriage and Divine Order	213
	Calvin, Order and Marriage	215
	Hierarchy in Social Relations	226
	The Preservation of Order	231
	Conclusion	251
	9. The Nature of Marriage	256
	Marriage in the *ordo creationis*	257
	Traditional Reasons for Marrying	265
	Conclusion	288
	10. Calvin, Hierarchy and Mutual Love	292
	Calvin's Biblical Exposition	292
	Conclusion	333
V	**REFLECTION**	336
	11. Luther, Calvin and Marriage	336
	Summary	340
	The Significance of the Study	349
Bibliography		353
Indexes		376

FOREWORD

Luther and Calvin continue to attract attention, particularly within the Protestant tradition, and this is right and proper given their role in shaping the Reformation. While both of them offered the world fresh ideas that were to stimulate thought for centuries, they were men of their times, shaping their thoughts within the context of their circumstances and the ideas that were prevalent in their communities. Not least is this so in what they had to say about marriage and in particular the place of women in the relationship.

Yet there is a need for more careful thought and an ongoing examination of what their ideas were on such matters and this is precisely what this book gives us, a careful and fair account of what the Reformers believed about such things. In this major work on the subject, the Reformers' thoughts are examined and the results are compared with those of others with an interest in the field. Yet simply to describe this book in this way is only to scratch the surface. This is a book that is not limited to those with historical interests. The concerns go beyond that. It is a book that raises issues that are of particular interest at the present time. It is a book about Christian ethics arising from the views of these two great Christian thinkers.

To describe both Luther and Calvin as reformers ought not to hide the fact that in some significant ways they held quite different views. Their differences in theology are well documented but there is also the possibility that they differed in their views on the outworking of the Christian faith, not least about the marriage relationship. In recent years questions of contemporary importance have been raised about their views. For example, given that their views were patriarchal, did they have room for ideas of mutual love? For some of us, one surprising tendency in recent times has been the suggestion that Calvin wanted to see more freedom and equality for women. It is a question that clearly is of considerable interest in contemporary society.

Here is a new and significant contribution to our understanding of such matters, firmly placed within the context of the thinking of two of the most important and influential Protestant thinkers. It provides a fascinating glimpse into the ways in which our wider thinking influences us in the manner that we see the specific issues of our relationship with others.

Colin Brown
Former Academic Registrar
Spurgeon's College, London
March, 2005

ACKNOWLEDGEMENTS

Although the end product is entirely my own – warts and all – many people in different ways have helped to shape this book. I gratefully acknowledge that help here.

The idea of the study was given me by Harold Rowdon, formerly of London Bible College, who suggested in his typically enthusiastic manner that I should turn a short article that I had drafted into a much larger piece of research. This I did – changing my views in the process.

The present book is a revised version of my doctoral thesis, completed in 1996. The British Academy was good enough to give me a generous studentship. That allowed the work to be done fulltime, which was a blessing. I am very thankful to my two supervisors at Spurgeon's College, London. Colin Brown and John Colwell were always encouraging, knowledgeable and critical in good measure. I am particularly grateful to Colin for writing the foreword of this work.

I am immensely grateful to my two examiners, Professor J. B. Torrance and Principal E. ap Nefydd Roberts, for their generous comments and stimulating discussion of the work's central ideas. It was Professor Torrance who encouraged me towards publication.

Others too have been a real encouragement along the way. The concerned interest, stimulating conversation and friendship of Derek Tidball, Principal of London School of Theology, and Keith Jones, Rector of the International Baptist Theological Seminary, Prague, were very much appreciated. Paul Fiddes, Principal of Regent's Park College, Oxford, offered the College's resources and helpful advice. I am grateful, too, for the help given to me by the staff of the Bodleian Library, Oxford. Haydn Nelson generously looked at the whole manuscript, proofreading and helpfully commenting throughout. Chris and Lynn White did a great deal of work sorting out the bibliography. I am grateful, too, for the help afforded by David Wright and particularly Lynn Quigley of Rutherford House.

In a very tangible way, this study is not only the work of academic pursuit. It has also been a work of faith. I am particularly grateful to my wife, Becky, who shared the vision and supported me so fully. Above all I am truly grateful to the Lord who set me on a path and caused me to persevere to the end. My prayer is that this work brings glory to him and causes others to fashion their lives on his love and grace in Christ.

Michael Parsons
The Baptist Theological College
Perth, Western Australia

ABBREVIATIONS

ABQ	*American Baptist Quarterly*
AHR	*American History Review*
AKG	*Archiv für Kulturgeschichte*
ARG	*Archiv für Reformationsgeschichte*
ASW	*Augustine: Selected Works* in P. Schaff, *A Select Library of the Nicene and Post Nicene Fathers*, volumes 1-8 (The Christian Literature Company, Buffalo, 1886)
Aug	*Augustiniana*
BHPF	*Bulletin de l'Histoire du Protestantisme Français*
BT	*The Banner of Truth Magazine*
CD	Karl Barth, *Church Dogmatics*, volumes 1-4 (T&T Clark, Edinburgh, 1936-1977)
CH	*Church History*
Ch	*Churchman*
CHist	*Christian History*
CNTC	*Calvin's New Testament Commentaries*, volumes 1-12, D. Torrance / T. F. Torrance, (eds), (Eerdmans, Grand Rapids, 1957-1970)
CO	*Ioannis Calvini, Opera quae supersunt omnia* in G. Baum / E. Cunitz / E. Ruess (eds), *Corpus Reformatorum* (Brunswick and Berlin, Schwetschke and Filium, 1863-1900)
CTJ	*Calvin Theological Journal*
CTQ	*Concordia Theological Quarterly*
CTS	Calvin Translation Society
DH	*Der deutsche Hugenott*
Farley	B. W. Farley (trans.), J. Calvin, *Sermons on the Ten Commandments* (Baker Book House, Grand Rapids, 1980)
GH	*Gender and History*
HeyJ	*Heythrop Journal*
HJ	*Historical Journal*
HTR	*Harvard Theological Review*
Inst	F. L. Battles (trans.), J. Calvin, *The Institutes of the Christian Religion* (Westminster, Philadelphia, 1960)
Int	*Interpretation*
JCR	*Journal of Christian Reconstruction*
JECS	*Journal of Early Christian Studies*
JFH	*Journal of Family History*

JFSR	*Journal for Feminist Studies in Religion*
JHI	*Journal of the History of Ideas*
JIH	*Journal of Interdisciplinary History*
JMF	*Journal of Marriage and the Family*
JMH	*Journal of Medieval History*
JPT	*Journal of Psychology and Theology*
JRH	*Journal of Religious History*
JSH	*Journal of Social History*
JTS	*Journal of Theological Studies*
Kelly	D. Kelly (trans.), J. Calvin, *Sermons on 2 Samuel, 1-13* (Banner of Truth Trust, Edinburgh, 1992)
LCC22	*Calvin's Theological Treatises*, J. K. S. Reid (ed.), Library of Christian Classics, volume 22 (Westminster, Philadelphia, 1964)
LQ	*Lutheran Quarterly*
LW	Martin Luther, *Luther's Works*, volumes 1-55 [American Edition] (Concordia, St. Louis / Westminster, Philadelphia, 1958-86)
MQR	*Mennonite Quarterly Review*
MSBodl.740	*Calvin's Sermons upon Genesis*, D. Raguenier (trans.) [1559], The Bodleian Library, Oxford.
OS	*Johannis Calvini Opera Selecta*, volumes 1-5, P. Barth / W. Niesel (eds), (Chr. Kaiser, Munich, 1929-1952)
PL	*Patrologiae cursus completus, series Latina*, J. P. Migne (ed.), (Paris, 1886)
PP	*Past and Present*
REA	*Revue des Études Augustiniennes*
REB	Revised English Bible (Cambridge University Press, Cambridge / Oxford University Press, Oxford, 1989)
RHPR	*Revue d'Histoire et de Philosophie Religieuses*
RJ	*Reformed Journal*
RL	*Religion in Life*
RPW	*The Reformed and Presbyterian World*
RRef	*La Revue Réformée*
RTAM	*Recherches de Théologie Ancienne et Médiévale*
RUB	*Revue de l'Université de Bruxelles*
SBET	*Scottish Bulletin of Evangelical Theology*
SCH	*Studies in Church History*
SCJ	*Sixteenth Century Journal*
TrinJ	*Trinity Journal*
VE	*Vox Evangelica*
WA	*D. Martin Luthers Werke: Kritische Gesamtausgabe* (Hermann Böhlaus Nachfolger, Weimar, 1883-1987)

WA Br.	Martin Luther. *D. Martin Luthers Werke. Briefwechsel* (Hermann Böhlaus Nachfolger, Weimar, 1930-48)
WA Tr.	Martin Luther. *D. Martin Luthers Werke. Tischreden* (Hermann Böhlaus Nachfolger, Weimar, 1912-21)
WHR	*Women's History Review*
WTJ	*Westminster Theological Journal*

Abbreviations of Augustine's works:

CD	*Contra duas epistolas Pelagianorum ad Bonifacium Papam*
CF	*Contra Faustum Manichaeum*
DBC	*De bono coniugali*
DC	*De continentia*
DCD	*De civitate Dei*
DCR	*De catechizandis rudibus*
DDoC	*De doctrina christiana*
DGnI	*De Genesi ad litteram liber imperfectus*
DGnM	*De Genesi contra Manichaeos*
DGrC	*De gratia Christi, et peccato originali*
DGrL	*De gratia et libero arbitrio*
DME	*De moribus ecclesiae catholicae et de moribus Manichaeorum*
DNB	*De natura boni contra Manichaeos*
DNG	*De natura et gratia*
DNu	*De nuptiis et concupiscentia*
DPM	*De peccatorum meritis et remissione et de baptismo parvulorum*
DSO	*De sermone Domini in monte*
DSL	*De spiritu et littera*
DSV	*De sancta virginitate*
DT	*De Trinitate*
DVR	*De vera religione*
En	*Enchiridion ad Laurentium de fide, spe, caritate*
EnP	*Enarrationes in Psalmos*
EXG	*Expositio Epistulae ad Galatas*
J	*In Epistulam Joannis ad Parthos tractatus X*
JE	*In Joannis evangelium tractatus CXXIV*

Unless otherwise stated the British and Foreign Bible Society's second edition of the Greek New Testament and the Revised English Bible translation of the Old and New Testaments have been employed throughout this study.

I INTRODUCTION

CHAPTER 1

RECENT SCHOLARSHIP

[B]y the grace of God, everyone declares that it is something good and holy to live with one's wife in harmony and peace.[1]

Martin Luther's words, written late in his life, reveal the self-conscious progress that he believed to have been made in the area of marriage during and as a result of his reforming ministry. Calvin could have echoed Luther's sentiment; although, no doubt, he would have done so without the confident optimism of his older colleague.

Marriage became central to both reformers' doctrinal application – almost a social gauge of the acceptance of reformational ideas, beginning with ministers and permeating to the people. Certainly, it is difficult to exaggerate the social importance of the reformers' conviction that the clergy should be married. Steven Ozment concludes that no institutional change instigated by the Reformation was 'more conducive to new social alterations than the marriage of protestant clergy'. He continues, 'The reformers argued theologically and attempted to demonstrate by their lives the superiority of a married over a celibate clergy. In doing so they extolled as few before them the virtues of marriage and family life.'[2] Calvin's personal reticence notwithstanding, this was no less true of him than of Luther.

---

[1] *Comm. Gen.* 2:22, LW 1.135 [WA 42.101]. See also, LW 47.52 [WA 30². 317]; *Tischreden* [2867ᵇ] Jan. 2, 1533, LW 54.177 [WA Tr. 3.40].

[2] S. Ozment, *The Age of Reform. 1250-1550* (Yale University Press, New

If this is true of the clergy, it is paralleled in the congregations. Despite recent scholarly doubt on the subject, if Luther's social teaching had effect at all, it is generally agreed that the place at which it most influenced the lives of the people was the familial sphere.[3] That is, the reformer's social impact on the masses, the populace (*Gemeinde*), was felt most strongly in this area of domestic and family life.[4] Although certainly exaggerating the point, Bainton suggests that, in practice, the home was the *only* sphere in which Lutheranism achieved any revolution in attitude.[5] Certainly, Luther was conscious of the potential

---

Haven, 1980), 381. See M. Bucer, 'The Restoration of Lawful Ordination' (1549) in D. F. Wright (ed.), *Common Places* (Sutton Courtenay Press, Appleford, 1972), 265-6 as a later example of the development of this positive attitude. The Protestant reformers were not unique in arguing for a married clergy, of course. Erasmus consistently argued for the marriage of priests *within* the church. See L. E. Halkin, *Erasmus, A Critical Biography* (Blackwell, Oxford, 1994), 168, 179.

[3] See S. M. Johnson, 'Luther's Reformation and (Un)holy Matrimony', *JFH* 17 (1992), 271-88. Though claiming that the degree of *actual* change resulting from Luther's praise of the family as an institution proves difficult to discern, Johnson's conclusion is that there was little enduring change in attitude and behaviour. She argues this from information on household climate, the divorce rate, the social role of women and child-rearing practices and education in this period. Certainly, it is difficult to evaluate the effect of religious or philosophical ideas on human behaviour or to measure the dissemination of an idea into a given population (278). Therefore, any desire to exaggerate the impact of the reformers' teaching should, at least, be tempered by this consideration. See also M. Lienhard, 'La Réforme de Luther et l'Europe: Succès ou Échec?' *RHPR* 75 (1995), 113-21.

[4] See, for example, W. von Loewenich, *Martin Luther: The Man and his Work* (Augsburg, Minneapolis, 1986), 292; M. U. Chrisman, *Strasbourg and the Reform* (Yale University Press, New Haven, 1967), 292; I. D. K. Siggins, *Luther* (Oliver and Boyd, Edinburgh, 1972), 148; E. O. James, *Marriage and Society* (Hutchinson, London, 1952), 125; O. A. Piper, *The Christian Interpretation of Sex* (Nisbet, London, 1942), 22; J. K. Yost, 'The Reformation Defense of Clerical Marriage in the Reigns of Henry VIII and Edward VI', *CH* 7 (1981), 152-65.

[5] R. Bainton, *The Reformation of the Sixteenth Century* (Hodder and Stoughton, London, 1963), 256. G. Strauss, *Luther's House of Learning* (Johns Hopkins University, Baltimore, 1978) is generally credited with beginning the recent debate concerning the alleged failure of the Lutheran reform to change the populace in a social way. See, particularly, 299-308. The fact is that there *was* a degree of indifference, but also a moderate degree of outward conformity to the evangelical church. Luther was more realistic (or cynical) than is often portrayed, believing that, in reality, it would be impossible to gather enough real Christians in Germany to create even one congregation (WA 19.72-5) - cited by B. Tolley, *Pastors and Parishioners in Württemburg During the Late*

influence of his teaching and the weight of responsibility that he carried, both as an instructor and as an example.

Similarly, John Calvin makes much of the concept of marriage as a constant focus of his didactic application. Though there are no occasional pieces on the subject, as in Luther's *corpus*, and only a few specific references to marriage and the husband-wife relationship in the *Institutes*, his commentary material and particularly his sermons are peppered with reference and instruction on the subject. In these, he sets about the task of exhortation and encouragement – to explain, to concretize the Word of God to the edification of his listeners. McGrath emphasizes that generally Calvin shows a 'relentless drive to relate theory and practice'.[6] His sermons bring the theology of the *Institutes* and the exegesis of the commentaries into the lives of the people, they seek to make the Bible *familière* to everyone – not only to the academics, but also to the unlearned. In a characteristic remark from a sermon on Job, Calvin states that God

> wants not only to instruct learned clergy [*les grands clercs*] and people who are very subtle and have been trained in school, but wishes to accommodate to even the roughest common people [*les plus rudes idiots qui soyent*].[7]

It is hardly surprising that he often focuses application on the idea of marriage; after all, marriage was *the* basic, common vocation of those who listened to him.

Perhaps it should be observed at the beginning that to write on Luther's and Calvin's understanding of marriage and, specifically, of the structure and dynamic of the relationship between the spouses is almost inevitably to be tempted to slant that study in the direction of wives in the conjugal arrangement. There are, at least, two reasons for this.

Reformation (Stanford University Press, Stanford, 1995), 116 and 173, fn. 7. See also chapter 5, particularly 87-102.

[6] A. E. McGrath, *A Life of John Calvin* (Blackwell, Oxford, 1993), 220. See B. Armstrong, '*Duplex cognitio Dei*, Or the Problem and Relation of Structure, Form and Purpose in Calvin's Theology' in E. A. McKee / B. Armstrong (eds), *Probing the Reformed Tradition* (Westminster/John Knox, Louisville, 1989), 142. He is correct in saying that, 'Calvin simply does not understand theology to be partly theoretical and partly practical. It is always at once practical and edifying.'

[7] *Serm.* Job 1:6-8 [CO 33.63].

First, the reformers' hierarchicalism has continued to come under fire in recent years – both by those who reveal only a superficial understanding of the concept[8] and, more significantly, by scholars of a liberationist persuasion who see the wife as unfairly downtrodden by a subordinationist patriarchy.[9] Understandably, they argue that male dominance is reflective of a deficient teaching on marriage and that the whole situation should be redressed. Any study of the reformers' view of the marriage structure should take these criticisms into account for they form part of the present, ongoing debate. In doing so, a close examination of what Luther and Calvin *meant* by their hierarchicalism will necessarily highlight the position of wives in order to address that criticism.

Second, the upsurge of recent interest in feminist studies in a wide variety of disciplines necessitates a realistic and balanced approach to the study of marriage in the past. Too often historical or theological examination has been conducted by men and has appeared to be written in favour of men – women have often simply been ignored. It has too often been assumed that gender difference counts for nothing and that, at best, women have merely adopted their husband's or father's experience.[10] In fairness, as we shall see, both Luther and Calvin generally attempt to speak to both the husband *and* the wife in their application of biblical texts and this present study will seek to reflect this.

So, why focus, specifically, on Luther and Calvin? Apart from what many are still finding to be the inherent historical

---

[8] See for example L. Hodgkinson, *Unholy Matrimony – The Case for Abolishing Marriage* (Columbus, London, 1988), particularly 53, 124.

[9] See the bibliographical details under, K. Armstrong (1986); R. R. Ruether (1974, 1979, 1983, 1988); M. S. Behrens (1973); M. Wiesner (1978, 1988); P. K. Jewett (1976); and others in the text following.

[10] See M. W. Wiesner, 'Beyond Women and the Family: Towards a Gender Analysis of the Reformation', *SCJ* 18 (1987), 311-22. She observes that three approaches have generally been attempted – to ignore women, to document men's opinions about women, and to focus on exceptional women. The present thesis seeks to document the reformers' opinions about women in the marriage relationship. P. Matheson, *Argula von Grumbach. A Woman's Voice in the Reformation* (T&T Clark, Edinburgh, 1995), is a recent and very good example of the last approach. Similarly, S. M. Stuard, 'The chase after theory. Considering medieval women', *GH* 4 (1992), 135-46; J. M. Bennett, 'Feminism and History', *GH* 1 (1989), 251-72; A. Burton, '"History" is Now: feminist theory and the production of historical feminisms', *WHR* 1 (1992), 25-38.

fascination of the two reformers, the most obvious general reason for a continued interest in them is that they both stand at the head of living, continuing, significant, ecclesiastical traditions. In addition, much of Western societal thought and politics owes its shape, in part, to the influence of the Reformation – it is an important stage in the continuum of theological exploration and ethical application of the gospel.[11] More specifically, our concept of marriage and ideas of the status and roles of both spouses derive, as much as anything, from biblical attitudes and understanding, reinforced (perhaps construed) by a long line of interpretive thinkers from the Early Church, the Fathers, through the diversity of medieval formulation and the biblicized dogma of the Protestant Reformation, and on. In other words, the Reformation is a critical and influential stage in the continuum of theological and social understanding. This is clear from citing one major contemporary example. The marital theology of Karl Barth[12] is regularly seen as a post-critical attempt to continue the main outlines of reformational understanding on the subject, particularly, in relation to the wife's status.[13] Merry Wiesner's remark is characteristic: 'Barth is, of course, simply putting Luther in twentieth-century terms. The image [of women] is the same.'[14] A similar conclusion is sometimes reached with the

---

[11] See J. L. Thompson, *Calvin and the Daughters of Sarah* (Librairie Droz, Geneva, 1992), 1-2.

[12] See P. S. Fiddes, 'The Status of Woman in the Thought of Karl Barth' in J. M. Soskice (ed.), *After Eve* (Collins, London, 1990), 138-55. See also, P. K. Jewett, *Man as Male and Female* (Eerdmans, Grand Rapids, 1976), 37-46, 69-85; J. A. Romero, 'The Protestant Principle: A Woman's-eye View of Barth and Tillich' in R. R. Ruether (ed.), *Religion and Sexism* (Simon and Schuster, New York, 1974), 319-40; R. R. Ruether, *Sexism and God-Talk* (SCM, London, 1983), 95-9; M. W. Y. Wan, 'Authentic Humanity in the Theology of Paul Tillich and Karl Barth' (unpublished doctoral thesis, Oxford University, 1984). For Barth's own theology, see the following specifically, *CD* III/1, 290, 301-6, 326-7; III/2, 292-3, 309-21; III/4, 150, 163, 172-6.

[13] S. L. Paul, 'Patriarchal Anthropology: Spiritual Equality / Natural Subordination', *Ex Auditu* 13 (1997), 120-22, speaks of Barth's position as 'the modern statement of the reformed tradition'.

[14] M. Wiesner, 'Luther and Women: The Death of Two Marys' in J. Obelkevich / L. Roper / R. Samuel (eds), *Disciplines of Faith* (Routledge and Kegan Paul, London, 1987), 308. See also R. R. Ruether, *Women-Church: Theology and Practice* (Harper and Row, San Francisco, 1988), 138-9; idem, *Sexism and God-Talk* (SCM, London, 1983), 95-9; M. Daly, *Beyond God the Father* (Women's Press, London, 1986), 19, 22; Romero, art. cit., 319-40. See also,

caveat that Barth seeks to do this while insisting on the woman's difference, *not* her inferiority.[15]

Another reason behind studying the marriage relationship in Luther and Calvin is that, though a great deal of work is being written on their views on women in general,[16] relatively little major study of their doctrine of marriage is currently available. Lazareth's work, *Luther on the Christian Home* (1960), is somewhat dated and confessional, as is Cocke's later essay.[17] André Biéler's *L'homme et la femme* (1961),[18] though invaluable, only briefly touches on Calvin's understanding of marriage in a much wider context. In more recent years, one or two works have singled out the marital aspect of their theology. Baldwin's article, 'Marriage in Calvin's Sermons', for example, is exceptional but merely suggestive of the important subject matter. Van der Walt's, in comparison, is lengthy but covers too much material in general terms.[19] So, there is a lack of thoroughly researched material on the subject of marriage and the husband-wife relationship in the teaching of either Luther or Calvin, though, at the same time, many scholars comment on and/or criticize their

---

E. C. McLaughlin, 'Equality of Souls, Inequality of Sexes: Women in Medieval Theology' in R. R. Ruether (ed.), *Religion and Sexism* (Simon and Schuster, New York, 1974), 259.

[15] See, for example, Jewett, op. cit., 69-85.

[16] See biographical details on the following notable examples: Behrens (1973); Blaisdell (1982, 1985, 1988); Bratt (1976); de Boer (1976); Douglass (1974, 1984, 1985); Karant-Nunn (1982, 1986); Potter (1986); Thompson (1988, 1992); Wiesner (1987); Zophy (1985).

[17] W. H. Lazareth, *Luther on the Christian Home* (Muhlenburg, Philadelphia, 1960). This followed his research thesis, 'Testimony of Faith, The Genesis of Luther's Marriage Ethic seen against the background of his Early Theological Development. 1517-1525' (unpublished doctoral thesis, Columbia University, 1958). See also, W. E. Cocke, 'Luther's View of Marriage and Family', *RL* 42 (1973), 103-16.

[18] A. Biéler, *L'homme et la femme dans la morale calviniste* (Labor et Fides, Geneva, 1961).

[19] C. M. Baldwin, 'Marriage in Calvin's Sermons' in R. V. Schnucker (ed.), *Calviniana: Ideas and Influence of Jean Calvin* (SCJ Publishers, Kirksville, 1988), 121-9; B. J. van der Walt, 'Woman and Marriage: In the Middle Ages, in Calvin and in our own time' in idem, (ed.), *John Calvin's Institutes: His Opus Magnum* (Potchefstroom University for Christian Higher Education, Potchefstroom, 1986), 184-238. Clearly, there is also reference to the marriage relationship in more general works on Luther, Calvin and on the Reformation period, itself. These will be noted in the appropriate footnotes.

views. Therefore, there is a need to present a thorough, critical study of the theology of the marriage relationship in Luther and Calvin.[20]

A third reason for examining Luther and Calvin on the marital structure and relationship is simply, but importantly, because some of the questions that reformational theology sought to address have not gone away – they are of contemporary significance.[21] It is here that we get to the *raison d'être* of the present thesis. Within the current debate on women's issues, there seems to be a deepening awareness of the importance of researching historical, relational models in order to ground present thinking in concrete and substantive thought. Certainly, recent feminist and liberationist writers have not been slow to return to the period of Protestant Reformation and to the societal/familial principles espoused by the reformers to elucidate such concepts as patriarchy or hierarchy. The period has been used for diverse reasons. Some seek to demonstrate the deficiency of the ideas; some to employ them to sharpen the argument against what are discerned to be unfair and unequal power-relations between the sexes;[22] or yet others in order to further clarify the egalitarian nature of the gospel, together with a call for a re-assertion of that core-truth; and so on.

As this might suggest, there has always been a wide variety of responses to Luther's and Calvin's teaching on the husband and wife relationship. As we will see below, the common approach has been to read the reformers as traditional in their thinking, maintaining the *status quo* as far as the marriage arrangement is concerned, and perhaps only slightly modifying the relationship

---

[20] See V. N. Olsen, *The New Testament Logia on Divorce. A study of their Interpretation from Erasmus to Milton* (Mohr, Tübingen, 1971); C. W. Pfeiffer, 'Heinrich Bullinger and Marriage' (unpublished doctoral thesis, St Louis University, 1981); H. J. Selderhuis, *Marriage and Divorce in the Thought of Martin Bucer* (Thomas Jefferson University Press, Kirksville, 1999).

[21] See B. T. Adeney, *Strange Virtues* (Apollos, Leicester, 1995), 31, 192-219.

[22] The phrase 'unequal power-relations' is from K. Zappone, 'Is there a Feminist Ethic?' in S. Freyne (ed.), *Ethics and the Christian* (Columba Press, Blackrock, 1991), 113. See also, C. Heyward, 'Notes on Historical Grounding: Beyond Sexual Essentialism' in J. B. Nelson / S. P. Longfellow (eds), *Sexuality and the Sacred* (Mowbray, London, 1994), 9-18. Heyward's comment is useful: 'We cannot comprehend the meaning of sexuality from a historical perspective without viewing its place in the context of power relations between genders' (14). See, J. B. Nelson, *The Intimate Connection* (Westminster Press, Philadelphia, 1988), 89-111.

between the husband and wife with an emphasis on love and companionship. The latter is usually more credited to Calvin than to Luther. However, both are generally linked in this way and, therefore, a modicum of improvement is attributed to each. Beside this there are two more or less extreme positions. On the one hand, there are those who, for one reason or another, see the ethical teaching of the reformers as demeaning and as damaging to the wife. This generally stems from what is perceived to be either negative reformational views of sex or, simply, the reformers' continuance of unequal power-relations upheld by social structure. On the other hand, some writers would want to read Calvin, in particular, as suggestive of an openness to change the status and role of wives, and therefore as at least theoretically improving their lot a great deal. However, this more positive stance is attributed to Calvin, not to Luther as such – though he too has his (mostly confessional) supporters.

Obviously, this is an artificial categorisation and somewhat oversimplified, but initially it may be helpful to sacrifice complexity as a starting point to the present examination. In simple terms, then, what we find is a sliding scale of response and reaction to the reformers' views on the husband-wife relationship. Calvin, generally, gets a better press; but both are to be found at each point of the scale. A closer examination of that scholarly opinion will now form the basis and background of the thesis, for it is important to view the debate before presenting our own thesis. As each reformer will be presented separately in the main text, each will now be outlined individually before we turn, briefly, to a clear demarcation of the subject matter, a statement of the primary source material employed and the proposed methodology, in the next chapter.

LUTHER

A Modified Traditionalism

Blaisdell's essay, 'The Matrix of Reform: Women in the Lutheran and Calvinist Movements', epitomizes the position of those who see Luther's marital teaching as traditional, but who read there a slight modification in its emphasis.[23] They stress the conventional character of his understanding of the marriage relationship and, particularly, of the position of the wife. Together with this, they pinpoint a generally qualified, innovative shift in perspective.

Blaisdell maintains that both Luther and Calvin were clearly influenced by the ideas of the late medieval church and of their own society: 'Both, therefore, interpreted Scripture and wrote from social, economic, political and religious assumptions and prejudices of their times.'[24] Her stress, then, is that Luther's teaching on the man-woman relationship, sexuality and marriage is 'notably conservative'.[25] He believed women to be inferior to men and accepted the hierarchical system of his day in which the husband ruled, the wife obeyed. The woman's purpose in life is that of procreation, companionship and the management of the household. Because of her responsibility in the original sin and the consequent curse she is also to be an antidote for the lust of her husband. Basically, therefore, in this Luther was a man of his time.

However, Blaisdell indicates a parallel and concurrent level of innovation and 'a shift of thought about marriage away from the traditional' in the ethical teaching of the Reformer.[26] This, she says, is discernible in Luther because he stresses the need for love and companionship in marriage, which he pictures as a concept approaching that of partnership. He seems to emphasize a crucial emotional contentment. Luther also teaches that sexual intercourse is pleasurable and good, not merely for the purpose

---

[23] C. J. Blaisdell, 'The Matrix of Reform: Women in the Lutheran and Calvinist Movements' in R. L. Greaves (ed.), *Triumph Over Silence* (Greenwood Press, Westport, 1985), 13-44.

[24] Ibid., 14.

[25] Ibid., 14. See also, 19.

[26] Ibid., 17. Luther and Calvin 'straddled tradition and innovation in their attitudes towards the female role' (36). In a similar way, others underline the traditional in Luther's ideas while stressing a slight shift from accepted thought. See, for example, V. H. H. Green, *Luther and the Reformation* (Batsford, London, 1964), 14, 140; J. W. Zophy, 'We must have the Dear Ladies: Martin Luther and Women' in K. C. Sessions / P. N. Bebb (eds), *Pietas et Societas* (SCJ Publishers, Kirksville, 1985), 141-50; R. E. O. White, *The Changing Continuity of Christian Ethics* (Paternoster, Exeter, 1981), vol.2, 171-3; E. Storkey, *What's Right with Feminism?* (SPCK, London, 1985), 122. On Luther's letters to women, see M. Arnold, *Les femmes dans la correspondance de Luther* (Université de France, Paris, 1998).

of procreation. Marriage is no longer seen simply as a remedy for sexual incontinence, but something far more positive for both the husband and the wife. Because the family is posited as the centre of both church and society, the status of women's *work* is raised by Luther. So, although Luther 'remained rooted in the principles of patriarchy',[27] his familial ethics accorded greater respect for women in their roles as wives and mothers. These roles gained new prestige and importance, but with no noticeable improvement in the women's status and position as women *per se*.

Karant-Nunn emphasizes these points in an influential article, published a couple of years later than Blaisdell's work, in which she illustrates the ideas from the concrete example of the city of Zwickau.[28] Again, she describes the Reformer with both the terms 'traditional' and 'innovative'. As did his contemporaries, Luther regarded women 'as lesser creatures than men, given to impulse, governed by emotion, incapable of profound thought, and wholly unsuitable for public responsibility'.[29] However, according to Karant-Nunn, what Luther added was new prestige for the bond of marriage itself, and greater dignity for the wife in her role as wife. She says of the Reformer, 'His teachings constituted no revolution but a change in emphasis. He cultivated and nurtured a tree of wedlock that was already sufficiently healthy.'[30]

Another writer of some note is worth mentioning here. While retaining the somewhat uneasy balance between the traditional and the innovative in Luther's explicit teaching, I. D. K. Siggins faces the problem and its resolution from a different angle altogether.[31] He admits that, in practice, the Reformer probably encouraged the process of the reduction of women to 'an instrumental and ancillary function' but emphasizes that what Luther *intended* was quite the reverse. He had hoped to encourage respect for women, especially in contrast to the

---

[27] Ibid., 20.

[28] S. C. Karant-Nunn, 'The Transmission of Luther's Teachings on Women and Matrimony. The Case of Zwickau', *ARG* 77 (1986), 31-46.

[29] Ibid., 31.

[30] Ibid., 45. See idem, 'Continuity and Change: Some Effects of the Reformation on the Women of Zwickau', *SCJ* 12 (1982), 17-42. See also, E. Fuchs, *Sexual Desire and Love* (James Clarke, Cambridge, 1983), 145.

[31] I. D. K. Siggins, 'Luther's Mother Margarethe', *HTR* 71 (1978), 125-50.

contemporary scorn and ridicule heaped on women as worthless. Though Luther makes reference to this intention in the context of his opposition to contemporary disdain,[32] Siggins takes this evidence as read and examines another area to illustrate his thesis. He admits that Luther was bound by traditional thinking and attitude – what he calls the Reformer's 'severely limited horizons'.[33] But he sees in his imagery signs of genuine appreciation and value of women.

Siggins claims that images crowding around the exercise of faith in Christ maintain a healthy balance between 'feminine' and 'masculine' metaphorical language – on the one hand, brood-hen, jewel, inexhaustible fountain of living water (images of intimacy and nurture) and, on the other hand, slayer of sin, devourer of death, victor, leader, guide, lord of creation. The writer concludes that Luther felt no inconsistency in this use of imagery[34] and that here we find the Reformer's genuine respect and approbation for women which, nevertheless, did not clearly surface in his practical, social teaching on marriage and the husband-wife relationship.[35]

Though they cover a wide variety of opinions on other matters, on the issue of Luther's perception of marriage and its effect on women these writers stress Luther's adherence to the traditional understanding and hierarchical marital structure. They do this while, at the same time, pointing out a slight modification of, and improvement in, the status and the role of the wife within that structure. The significance of this group of

---

[32] See, for example, *The Estate of Marriage*, LW 45.36 [WA 10².293]; *Comm. Gen.* 24:35-44, LW 4.289-91 [WA 43.343-4].

[33] Art. cit., 147.

[34] Ibid., 148-50.

[35] It is worth pointing out that, though Siggins may be correct to stress Luther's *intention* to approve of women, there *is* a great deal of ambiguity in the Reformer's work. At times he defends women against the slights of men as we have noted, but often he speaks as his contemporaries were wont to do. See, for example, *Comm. Isa.* 3:16-26, LW 16.47-9 [WA 31².33-4]; *Comm. 1 Pet.* 3:1-6, LW 30.91 [WA 12.345]; *Comm. 1 Tim.* 3:11, LW 28.298 [WA 26.61]; *Comm. Tit.* 2:3, LW 29.53 [WA 25.43]. Neither does Siggins mention adverse female imagery, as when Luther uses the concept of uncleanness of a woman in menstruation as an image of the believer's former righteousness, which is unclean before God – *Comm. Gal.* 2:16 (1519), LW 17.220 [WA 2.490]; and to stress woman's place in the home, the image of the wife as a nail driven into the wall – *Comm. Gen.* 3:16, LW 1.202-3 [WA 42.151].

scholars is that they posit both traditionalism and development, however slight. The next group focus on the former without giving credence to the latter. This is largely because they begin from a liberationist position, themselves, and some read Luther negatively from the outset.

Destructive of the Wife's Status

In order to move outwards from the centre of the sliding scale that was formerly conceived, we need now to take a brief look at those who see Luther's teaching as negative.

Many have examined Luther's familial ethics and have concluded that he short-changes women as women *per se*, even if it may be conceded that he raises the perception of the roles of wife and mother, both by his teaching and by his own marital example. However, his continued ambivalence on the subject of women and their status and the ambiguous, problematic quality of much of his writing allows (perhaps, invites) critical comment from those who major on this side of the ambivalence. These are largely scholars who have their own theological-ethical foundations within a liberationist or a feminist perspective and who emphasize different aspects of the reformer's teaching. That is, they begin from an assumed conclusion that women must be liberated from medieval patriarchalism – seen as permeating culture and attitudes even to the present day – and that anything that prevents progress is innately destructive. Some are harsher than others as they explicate their criticism. Generally, there are two basic, but overlapping, emphases in their approach. Some hold that the core problem of Luther's teaching is a sexual one, others, that it lies in the concept of hierarchical power.

He retains traditional sexual negativity
It is often pointed out that medieval theologians and moralists were deeply concerned with the sexual element in marriage. Their concern sometimes reached the point of obsession. Following the traditional line through both Jerome and Augustine they generally condemned sex for pleasure alone, seeing it, at best, as a means of procreation, and, otherwise, as an antidote for sin and lust. The complaint that scholars level at Luther, then, is that he maintains these unenlightened views of sexuality. They say that he does not modify understanding of women in this area but that

he retains the negative attitude towards sex within marriage.[36] Had he rectified thinking on this subject, he might have genuinely elevated the role of wife from being that which is used by man to a more egalitarian, companionate idea and social practice. Therefore, he might have gained more respect for wives generally, and pointed the church and society towards a greater freedom and equality for women. These writers lament the fact that he did not.

Paul Lehmann makes this point. He says that the Reformation, in general, and Luther, in particular, 'was mistakenly in accord with the tradition of Christian ethical thought in its failure to break out of the stranglehold of negativity which regarded marriage as the legitimization of the sexual act and the precarious guardian both of continence and of social stability and health where sexuality was involved'.[37]

Similarly, in her book, *The Gospel According to Woman*,[38] Karen Armstrong claims that Luther followed Augustine too closely with a negative, unbiblical attitude towards sexuality. She speaks of Augustinian sexual disgust and neurosis as the foundation of the Reformer's teaching.[39] It appears that this is the exceptionally narrow basis from which Armstrong criticizes Luther's social ethics in the area of the husband-wife relationship. Accordingly, Luther is said to have had no time at all for sexual intercourse – it is merely sinful, even within marriage. She states that Luther teaches that the only reason that God made woman was to have her husband's children, to populate the world and, consequently, to people the kingdom of heaven: 'It didn't matter what effect this might have on women. ...There was no other way

---

[36] However, for a contrasting view, see L. A. Brundage, *Love, Sex and Christian Society in Medieval Europe* (University of Chicago Press, Chicago, 1987), 552; Fuchs, op. cit., 157-63.

[37] P. L. Lehmann, *Ethics in a Christian Context* (SCM, London, 1963), 136. See, generally, 134-6.

[38] K. Armstrong, *The Gospel According to Woman* (Elm Tree Publishers, London, 1986).

[39] Ibid., 30-31. A similar conclusion is put more constructively by Margaret Farley, 'Sexual Ethics' in Nelson / Longfellow (eds), op. cit., 54-67. She says that Luther (and Calvin) 'shared Augustine's pessimistic view of fallen nature in which human sexual desire is no longer ordered as it should be within the complex structure of the human personality' (63).

a woman could help man.'[40] Luther, apparently, sees the husband and the wife as two separate individuals inhabiting two separate worlds. There is no room for intimacy between them: no love, no equality, no togetherness. In fact, the wife is kept as a prisoner in her husband's home, 'in a state of deprivation'.[41] Armstrong makes Luther's concept of a vocation seem like a trap from which a wife cannot escape.[42] This sort of comment places the wife's subjection more especially within the limited area of the genital act of sexuality and of the Reformer's apparent disgust of it.

His patriarchalism is 'a sanctified tyranny'[43]

Liberationist scholarship has suggested that Reformation theology advocates a hierarchical structure between unequals in which wives are unfairly dominated by their husbands. It claims that marriage, as defined by the reformers, was contractual rather than consensual. Whether or not this is a strictly correct reading, the perception is that of a mutual but not a reciprocal relationship between husband and wife in which the husband rules and the wife obeys. The result of this was the destruction of any possibility of seeing women as entirely equal to men and as having genuine worth *in society* – although, of course, they retained their spiritual worth and equality before God, in Christ. The question that has been posed is whether or not woman's spiritual equality should have entailed a correlative political and social equality.

This is related to the reformer's retention of sexual negativity in the sense that that is seen, generally, as the base line of inequality: woman was made for man and in particular to satisfy his sexual need and to alleviate his sexual conscience. From this perspective, Rosemary Ruether stresses that, within the patriarchal context women's bodies were *owned* by their

---

[40] Ibid., 62. R. Miles, *The Women's History of the World* (Michael Joseph, London, 1988), 77, adopts a similar tone and draws similar conclusions: 'In the grand design of the monotheistic male, woman was no more than a machine to make babies, with neither the need nor the right to be anything else.' See also 91, 203.

[41] Armstrong, op. cit., 275.

[42] Ibid., 273, 279. See also, A. Alvarez, *Life After Marriage* (Macmillan, London, 1982), 123.

[43] A. Primavesi, *From Apocalypse to Genesis* (Burns and Oates, Tunbridge Wells, 1991), 100.

husbands – indeed, 'their wombs and ovaries belong to their husbands who impregnate them; to priests and doctors who make the rules of birth and death'.[44]

Many look more generally at what they perceive to be a patriarchal dominance and control in every area of a woman's life. Patriarchy, they claim, is based on power and, inherently, at the root there are inequality, subordination and dependence – all to the detriment of women, of course.[45] Whereas others seek to understand the reformers as improving the lot of women (even if only slightly),[46] this group of writers would largely define the traditional, patriarchal line of theological reasoning as the anti-sexual, anti-female, anti-sensuality heritage of Christianity[47] to which Luther and others assented.

In this context, two scholars merit particular comment. Over 20 years ago, M. S. Behrens wrote a research thesis on the subject with the title, 'Martin Luther's View of Women' (1973), and more recently Merry Wiesner (1987) has presented an interesting article from a different angle which comes to similar conclusions. Both of these works have been influential in a negative and a critical

---

[44] R. R. Ruether, *Women-Church*, 71: 'Pope, patriarchs and prelate join hands in fraternal alliance over the prone body of woman.' See also, idem, *Sexism and God-Talk*, 17; Jewett, op. cit., 66-7,131-2.

[45] See D. Gittins, *The Family in Question* (Macmillan, Basingstoke, 1985), 35, 58, where she defines the term *paterfamilias* as, in many respects, simply male dominance based on power. See also L. Kreiger, 'The Idea of Authority in the West', *AHR* 82 (1977), 253; C. Jordan, *Renaissance Feminism* (Cornell University Press, Ithaca, 1990), 5-24; L. Stone, *The Family, Sex and Marriage in England. 1500-1800* (Penguin Books, Harmondsworth, 1979), 111; G. Lerner, *The Creation of Patriarchy* (OUP, Oxford, 1986), 172-3; M. Daly, *Beyond God the Father* (Woman's Press, London, 1986), 3, 22, 127; A. E. Carr, *Transforming Grace* (Harper and Row, San Francisco, 1990), 98; M. Grey, *Redeeming the Dream* (SPCK, London, 1989) 12; R. Dowsett, 'Womanhood and Feminism', *SBET* 10 (1992), 80-93.

[46] See chapter 5, 'Marriage and the Temporal Kingdom'.

[47] B. W. Harrison, 'Human Sexuality and Mutuality' in J. L. Weidman (ed.), *Christian Feminism* (Harper and Row, San Francisco, 1984), 144. She continues, 'The reformers ... embraced marriage almost as a duty. ... I would add that it had to be, for if men must marry women whom they view as deficient in humanity, the external rule of "duty" necessarily must be invoked.' See 141-57. Also, Primavesi, op. cit., 100, 215; L. Isherwood / D. McEwan, *Introducing Feminist Theology* (Sheffield Academic Press, Sheffield, 1993), 49; P. M. Doyle, 'Women and Religion: Psychological and Cultural Implications' in Ruether (ed.), *Religion and Sexism*, 31.

way.⁴⁸ From this negative side of reading Luther, these two scholars stand out as the most significant for the purposes of our present study. Chapters 5-7 (in seeking to allow weight to both ends of the Reformer's ambiguity) will argue a more positive overall understanding.

In her introduction Behrens states her underlying assumption that, while not original in this, Luther transmits the idea of woman's inherent evil and inferiority in an intense and emotively powerful way. She claims that 'he gathers the most negative strands of the medieval concept of woman, weaves them with a sick and patronising chivalry, and presents the fabric as woman's being-in-the-world'.⁴⁹ Then, dividing her study into two parts, she deals with Luther's view of natural woman (as creature) and his view of social woman (in relationship). Behrens concludes that Luther teaches that woman is naturally physically weak, morally deficient, emotionally unstable and mentally lacking. Because this opinion is held there exists a dominant-dependent aspect to male-female relationships generally – the woman relying on the man, the man in turn patronizing and tolerating the woman.⁵⁰ In her analysis of Luther's teaching regarding woman in society (that is, particularly married woman in the society of her home) Behrens emphasizes that the Reformer's justification for woman's existence is for the sole purpose of procreation. In that context, woman is seen merely as an instrument or a tool of God. Luther's tendency is to regard woman as a mechanism with a function to perform rather than as a human being with a life to be lived.⁵¹ Woman is to be made use of in curtailing man's sexual lust and is good for little else. Behrens' critical work leads her to the conclusion that Luther had

---

⁴⁸ M. S. Behrens, 'Martin Luther's View of Women' (unpublished Masters thesis, North Texas State University, 1973); M. Wiesner, 'Luther and Women: The Death of Two Marys' in J. Obelkevich / L. Roper / R. Samuel (eds), *Disciplines of Faith* (Routledge and Kegan Paul, London, 1987), 295-308.

⁴⁹ Behrens, op. cit., 13. She says that 'the idea that woman is evil is implicit in Luther's interpretation' (17). This charge is made repeatedly throughout the thesis, though as it stands, it is unfounded: 4, 8, 11, 12, 16, 35, 40, 52, 118, 121, and so on.

⁵⁰ Ibid., 29, 33. Similarly, Isherwood / McEwan, op. cit., 49-50, speak of Luther's contempt for women.

⁵¹ Ibid., 54. Later she says that 'the inordinate emphasis upon woman as an instrument of procreation does at least mutely hint that except for this boon woman would not be worth saving' (100).

'a deep and pervasive negativity toward woman. He had to accept the presence of woman in the world, but he did not do it joyfully or positively.' And again she states that 'it would be difficult to over-emphasize the *totality* of Luther's negativity toward women'.[52] A cursory glance at this thesis reveals its antithetical bias and exaggeration to which we will return in examining Luther.

Behrens' harsh treatment of Luther's views regarding women has been reiterated by Merry Wiesner, who tackles the problem from an altogether different perspective. She is concerned, not with what the Reformer explicitly says, but with the way he expresses what he says. That is, Wiesner's concern is with the imagery that Luther employs as he comments on women. She begins with the premise that Luther taught that women's subjection to men is, in fact, inherent in and intrinsic to their natural makeup and was present from their creation, and that the only way in which a woman could fulfil God's calling was through marriage and motherhood. For Luther, the ideal woman is said to be Martha carrying out the daily household tasks and chores, rather than her sister, Mary, listening to and trying to understand the teaching of Jesus.[53] In this there is said to be a real reduction of the female ideal from a heavenly, spiritual one to an earthy, housebound one – particularly as it seems to correspond with his lessening of the role of the Virgin Mary herself. Woman, other than as the ideal, is depicted in a belittling manner.

Wiesner takes some of the more derogatory images that Luther employs and turns them to what would appear to be her own purpose. For instance, she singles out the degrading comment that the 'woman is like a nail, driven into the wall. ... She sits at home.'[54] Again, she quotes Luther: 'All women know the art to catch and hold a man by crying, lying and persuasion, turning his head and perverting him. ... [I]t is often more difficult

---

[52] Ibid., 67, 69 – emphasis added.

[53] It is unfair of Wiesner to drive a wedge between these two sisters. They epitomise two aspects of life – temporal and spiritual. Luther's comments on Martha need to be seen in the context of his teaching that, though managing the house *is* an important work, it will not attain the goal of righteousness, nor of salvation: indeed, it is necessarily a *limited* (a this-worldly) use of things. See, for example, *Comm. John* 7:28-9, LW 23.247 [WA 33.392]; *Comm. Gal.* 2:20 (1535), LW 26.173 [WA 40^1.292]; *Comm. 1 Pet.* 3:1-6, LW 30.88 [WA 12.242].

[54] LW 1.202-3 [WA 42.151] – art. cit., 299.

for him to withstand such enticements than to resist his own lust.⁵⁵ Wiesner's rather exaggerated conclusion is that Luther's intention is to say that all women 'share the qualities of a prostitute to some degree'. On Luther's favourite epithet for human reason ('the devil's whore'), Wiesner similarly concludes that '*by extension* all women who attempt to act reasonably may also be seen to be whores of the devil'.⁵⁶

Her overall opinion is that Luther's imagery is harsh and that a de-emphasis on the feminine qualities of God, Christ and the Church, for example, adds weight to this. She admits that Luther does employ maternal and nurturing images, yet her general conclusion is that, though a masculine emphasis and preoccupation – together with a lessening of 'feminine' qualities in religion – did not originate with Luther, he gave it new ammunition and, therefore, can be charged with lowering the status of women and of maintaining and bolstering up the *status quo* regarding their subjection.⁵⁷

Interestingly, Wiesner's work reveals one of the central problems in the feminist critique of Luther and, oddly, it is a problem shared with those, on the other end of the scale, who would champion him. She fails to account for the deeply ambiguous and contradictory nature of Luther's contribution to

---

⁵⁵ *Tischreden*, WA Tr. 4 [4786]. See *Comm. Gen.* 39:7-10, LW 7.76.

⁵⁶ Art. cit., 301, 302 – emphasis added. The full quotation is interesting in the context of Wiesner's conclusion: 'Usury, drunkenness, adultery and murder can all be detected and understood by the world as sinful. But when the devil's bride, reason, the petty prostitute, enters into the picture and wishes to be clever, what she says is accepted at once as if she were the voice of the Holy Ghost. ... She is surely the devil's chief whore' (Wiesner's own translation of *D. Martin Luthers Sämtliche Werke* (Erlangen & Frankfort, 1826-57) 16.142). Wiesner's extension of the Reformer's thought does not do justice to his intention, which is clearly limited to a description of how subtle reason is. If anything, the significance lies in the fact that he uses the imagery of 'whore' and 'prostitute', rather than that of 'woman'.

⁵⁷ Ibid., 303-4. J. D. Douglass, 'Calvin's use of Metaphorical Language for God: God as Enemy and God as Mother', *ARG* 77 (1988), 126-40, in seeking to sharpen understanding of Calvin's use of female imagery by comparison with Luther's, concludes (with regard to Luther) that he was conscious both of female imagery in the Bible and of the fact that it would edify his congregation. However, her point is that he did not allow that imagery to become part of his own theological thinking. See also Siggins, art. cit., 150, for a somewhat contradictory conclusion, as noted above.

the subject of women and, especially, women in relation to men.[58] The paradoxical stance is apparent in the imagery Luther uses – both imagery to describe women themselves *and* female imagery employed to represent spiritual reality and religious institutions.

This is not the place to develop this idea, but it is worth noting at this point. Luther's 'feminine' imagery for God must carry significant weight in the balance of his statements. Through these metaphors he helps his readers and those to whom he preached to feel both the motherly and the paternal care of God towards them. In his commentary on Genesis, for instance, he explicitly says that, 'God depicts Himself to us in the form of a woman and a mother.' And, again, the Word of God is depicted as the uterus and womb of God by which 'we are fashioned and borne'.[59] It may be complained that Luther is merely using the image of the woman's *task* and is not genuinely concerned with her *as a woman*. But that is to miss the point on two accounts. First, the Reformer does not separate the person and the task in that way – for him, they are one. Second, he wishes to show God's constant and intimate care and he chooses to do so by employing female imagery. Luther can also use daring female imagery as he does when he teaches on the hiddenness of the church in close fellowship with God: 'God does not want the world to know when he sleeps with his bride.'[60]

All in all, then, Wiesner's critical comments need to be tempered with a more balanced view of the Reformer's attitude towards women. The difficulty with contradictions and paradoxes

---

[58] See L. Roper, *The Holy Household* (Clarendon, Oxford, 1989), 1, 72; M. E. Hayter, 'The New Eve in Christ. The Use and Abuse of the Bible in the Debate about Women's Ministry' (unpublished doctoral thesis, Oxford University, 1985), 171. It must also be said that Wiesner seems mistaken about several important issues – that Luther teaches that women's sex drive is much stronger than men's (299); that he lays all the responsibility for the Fall on Eve, alone (300); that the Reformer belittles his wife's efforts to understand or to learn (300). At best, Luther is ambiguous on these issues; therefore, the converse of these ideas may also be important in Luther's writing, to which the present study will return below.

[59] *Comm. Gen.* 43:11-14, LW 7.325 [WA 44.541]; *Comm. Isa.* 46:4, LW 17.139 [WA 3.370-71], respectively. See also *Comm. Zeph.* 3:18, LW 18.363 [WA 13.509]; *Comm. Isa.* 49:15, LW 17.183-4 [WA 31^2.404-6]; LW 45.43 [WA 10^2.298].

[60] '*Denn Got wil die welt nichtt* [sic] *lassen wissen, wenn er bei seiner braut schlafft*' (WA 17^2.501) – quoted by T. George, *Theology of the Reformers* (Broadman, Nashville, 1988), 89.

is that they can give ample ammunition to both ends of the scale, while neither end does justice to Luther's intentions. The central assumption and conclusion from these negative scholars is that Luther does not challenge the dominant-subordinate pattern of relationship between husband and wife, in which woman's full humanity is seen to be either denied or distorted in some way. C. Jordan sees the idea current in the early sixteenth century as follows: 'Because woman was initially made from the side of man to be his *helper*, and afterward, in her postlapsarian state, ordered to be his *subject*, she was doubly underprivileged.' The manner of her creation from Adam revealed an ontological inferiority, the consequent punishment for her sin revealed a political or social subordination.[61] Luther, then, is accused of remaining within the *status quo* as if it were an invariable law of nature and religion. Rather, the liberationist writers say that he should have questioned it on the authority of the gospel which gives freedom to both men *and* women, on the basis of Galatians 3:28.[62]

In contrast to the situation in Calvin scholarship, the discussion of Luther's familial ethics and of his views regarding the husband-wife relationship and the individual worth of women *per se* shows little genuine, open and non-defensive dialogue between those who hold a more positive view and those who do not. Perhaps this is due as much to the lack of apparent space to manoeuvre in the Reformer's teaching as to the dogmatic, and sometimes polarized, stance of those who write on the subject. Perhaps Luther's contradictory statements give too much scope for contrapositions and not enough for synthesis, as we have observed above.

In opposition to those who criticize Luther's teaching, there have always been those writers who speak uncritically of Luther's views on marriage and the husband-wife relationship. They need not detain us here.[63] In reality, these attempts have helped neither

---

[61] Jordan, op. cit., 22 – emphasis original.

[62] 'There is no such thing as ... male and female; for you are all one person in Christ Jesus.'

[63] Wiesner, art. cit., 295, lists K. Bücher, *Die Frauenfrage in Mittelalter* (Tübingen, 1910); W. Kamerou, *Die Reformation und die Ehe* (Verein für Reformationsgeschichte, 1892); E. Ahme, 'Wertung und Bedeutung der Frau bei Martin Luther' in *Luther*, volume 35, 295-6. See also E. G. Schwiebert, *Luther and his Times* (Concordia, St Louis, 1950), 581-602; Lazareth, op. cit. (1960), vii; E. Simon, *Luther Alive* (Hodder and Stoughton, London, 1968); Cocke, art. cit.

our understanding of the dynamics and ethical difficulties involved in Luther's patriarchalism, nor the academic endeavour to relate that hierarchicalism to what Scripture, theology or experience may reveal about the fundamental nature of man and woman and the essence of marriage.

Quantitatively, the extent of Luther's influence is generally agreed upon. But what is clearly more open to question and discussion is exactly *how* Luther's teaching influenced people – that is its 'qualitative' measure. Therefore, before turning in a similar way to recent writing on Calvin, there are a number of relevant conclusions and consequent questions that can be drawn from the summary of scholarly opinion given above. Asking these questions, now, will highlight some of the specific problems involved in examining Luther on marriage and will also alert us to similar lines of enquiry in studying Calvin's marital ethics.

Not surprisingly, each of the writers outlined has placed Luther's thought squarely in the traditional ideas of his day and of the preceding Christian centuries. Basically, his teaching belongs to medieval theology and morality, informed by patristic writing and contemporary opinion. When scholars specify a major influence, Augustine is the name that they underline. Luther, therefore, holds to and teaches a hierarchicalist and patriarchal social arrangement within the household. The husband is the head of the household, the wife his inferior and subordinate help. The question raised is whether Luther retains a low view of the wife by seeming, on the whole, to condone this pattern of relationships, or whether there is, in his writing, that which raises the woman's worth and ultimately militates against the very structure that he upholds. That is, does he really shift the perception of marriage in woman's favour, even if only slightly, as some would suggest – say, by stressing the concepts of companionship and mutual love, for example? It should be noted, of course, that even at its best, no-one attributes to Luther latent liberationist thought, as they do regarding Calvin.

(1973); J. H. Alexander, 'Katherine von Bora, wife of Luther' in *Ladies of the Reformation* (Gospel Standard Strict Baptist Trust, Harpenden, 1978), 75-86; D. MacCuish, *Luther and His Katie* (Christian Focus Publications, Fearn, 1999); S. Ozment, *Protestants: The Birth of a Revolution* (Image Books, London, 1993), 151-68.

Several of the writers reviewed above have pointed out that, within the traditional structure, Luther raises the standing and prestige of the *role* of woman as wife and mother, but not the *status* of woman, in and of herself. That is, the work of wives is seen to be important before God who has called them to it, but are the women themselves of worth or value in Luther's scheme of things? Can we divide the woman from her vocational duty (or, indeed, the man from his), or are they so inextricably bound in the thought of the Reformer that to see one is to see the other?

Another line of enquiry concerns the idea of equality between the man and his wife. There is a consensus among writers that Luther holds to an equality between the sexes, but not an agreement on how to define that equality, or at what point that equality came to be. Some hold that Luther teaches that men and women are equal at creation, but not after the Fall. Others suggest that equality of the sexes occurs only in Christ – that is, there is an intrinsic inequality between men and women which pervades history from the very beginning, but which is translated into spiritual parity on their coming to Christ. These ideas, themselves, stir questions about his view of marriage. Is Eve the equal of Adam at their creation or not? Are the husband and wife equal in the context of marriage? How can the couple be equal spiritually but not socially within temporal structures, such as the household? Is this a clear example of sexist dualism?[64] Is this attitude appropriate in the light of the liberating nature of the gospel that is supposed to give freedom to all?

Several writers have argued that Luther innovates in the area of partnership and companionship within the marriage relationship. Naturally, the question arises: if Luther emphasizes the primacy of a companionate male-female couple as the basic unit of society, how does he correlate this with his belief in a hierarchical order within that relationship? Indeed, is it possible to hold both positions? Will the 'tyranny' of the one abolish the intimacy of the other? Is a companionate expression of the marital relationship viable in Luther's theology, given his

---

[64] The phrase, 'sexist dualism' is from T. M. Eugene, 'While Love is Unfashionable...' in Nelson / Longfellow (eds), op. cit., 107. Eugene, usefully, defines it as 'the systematic subordination of women in church and society, within relationships between males and females, as well as within linguistic patterns and thought formulations by which women are dominated'. See also, J. B. Nelson, *Embodiment* (SPCK, London, 1979), chapter 3.

apparently negative views on the sexual and procreative aspects of marriage? On the other hand, it must be asked whether Luther qualifies the detrimental comments of his thinking in any convincing or effective way.

Lastly, implied in the liberationist critique is that Luther uses eisegesis in his commentary and sermons on Scripture. In our examination, then, his theology of marriage and the conjugal relationship will be placed alongside his exposition of the relevant biblical passages in order to see whether his theological and societal presuppositions preclude any possibility of a genuine move towards a biblical egalitarianism. In question form: does he work from Scripture as the governing foundation for his doctrine, or from society (as the determinative factor) to scriptural exegesis?

CALVIN

To return to the image of the sliding scale (which we previously employed), a similar pattern of response emerges on examination of scholarly writing on Calvin's thought on marriage. Again, we discern three basic positions – but, again, this oversimplifies for the sake of initial clarity. The central position maintains that the Reformer simply altered the traditional view, in a strictly limited way, by an emphasis on mutual love. Then, there appear two polarized theses. One argues that Calvin's teaching is detrimental to the status of the woman as wife, the other, that his ideas are suggestive of greater freedom for the woman and are, on that basis, of positive value for a reassessment of the hierarchical structure in which the wife is dominated. This last, positive, approach to Calvin is markedly different from anything to date in Lutheran studies[65] – as will be shown below. We turn, therefore, to a brief survey and examination of these positions, keeping in

---

[65] However, as with Luther, there are still writers who read Calvin uncritically at this point. As noted above, Biéler, *L'homme et la femme*, 36, 44, 80, 148, etc., holds that there is no real contradiction between hierarchy and equality in Calvin's thought. See, also, R. Mancha, 'The Woman's Authority: Calvin to Edwards' *JCR* 6 (1979-80), 86-98; E. Stickleberger, *John Calvin* (T&T Clark, Edinburgh, 1959); Alexander, op. cit., 87-98.

A Modified Traditionalism

W. F. Graham represents writers who believe that Calvin stayed firmly within the traditional view of marriage – a view inherited from and through the teaching of the Middle Ages. By implication, this would mean that the Reformer accepts the medieval tendency to think in hierarchical terms, and believes that the head of the household is the man and that the wife owes him complete obedience. Graham holds that within Calvin's teaching there is a mutual regard and basic equality that was inherent in creation, lost in the Fall and reconstituted in Christ. However, as he assesses Calvin's contribution to marital ethics, he claims that we do not 'see much more than a slight softening of certain traditional patterns and a tendency towards equalizing the position of the woman. Calvin's influence on the common life was more in the line of modernising the traditional than in its revolution.'[66] So, according to Graham, there *is* change, but it is merely superficial and not structural.

In an essay alluded to earlier, Blaisdell reaches similar conclusions. She says that neither Luther nor Calvin brought about 'any major changes in attitude towards women or the roles permitted them in the early modern period'.[67] This was because the reformers were men of their time and their time was not conducive to fundamental change at this point. So Calvin, for example, continued the strong patriarchal strain – women were to be subordinate, men to have the supremacy in societal relationships. The highest female vocation was that of wife – serving the husband, raising his children. 'We find little that is

---

[66] W. F. Graham, *The Constructive Revolutionary* (John Knox, Richmond, 1971), 153.

[67] C. J. Blaisdell, 'The Matrix of Reform...', 35. See also, idem, 'Calvin's Letters to Women: The Courting of Ladies in High Places', *SCJ* 13 (1982), 67-85; idem, 'Calvin's and Loyola's Letters to Women' in Schnucker (ed.), op. cit., 235-53. See also, F. W. Barton, *Calvin and the Duchess* (Westminster / John Knox, Louisville, 1989), 30; Dowsett, art. cit., 80-93.

new ... on women, sexuality, the relationship between the sexes, and marriage.'[68]

While agreeing with Blaisdell, Mary Potter starts from a different premise. She begins her examination with an admission that there is an apparent contradiction in Calvin's teaching on the husband-wife relationship.[69] She recognizes that there is a radical equality between man and woman from, what she calls, the perspective of the *cognitio Dei* – that is, before God. Yet, she also discovers an innate inferiority of women from the perspective of the *cognitio hominis* – that is, before mankind. There is *both* a gender-equality *and* a gender-hierarchy in what she considers to be Calvin's three crucial theological areas of creation, fallenness and redemption. For Potter, this is not altogether contradictory, nor does it reveal a tendency to seek fundamental change in women's status. Rather, Calvin employs two distinct perspectives: *cognitio Dei* and *cognitio hominis*. She comments:

> The perspective of *cognitio Dei* is an absolute perspective, from which all things appear equal. ... The perspective of *cognitio hominis*, however, is a relative perspective. From the temporal perspective of human beings in the world, all persons appear as part of an inviolable, graded hierarchy in which male persons are superior and female persons are inferior.[70]

Despite the fact that Potter believes that this represents an advance over 'the single, hierarchical perspective that patriarchal Christianity had practised in the past',[71] in reality, it produced only a superficial adjustment to its structure or practice, *not* a full reformation. According to Potter, then, this 'secures the bolts on the doors of the patriarchal prison for women'.[72]

---

[68] Ibid., 28,14. See also, W. J. Bouwsma, *John Calvin: A Sixteenth Century Portrait* (OUP, New York, 1988), 53-4, 138, 233; Baldwin, art. cit., 121-9.

[69] M. Potter, 'Gender Equality and Gender Hierarchy in Calvin's Theology', *Signs* 2 (1986), 725-39.

[70] Ibid., 731. One problem with Potter's idea is that it appears to divide too stringently between the spiritual (God's perspective) and the temporal (mankind's perspective). Calvin teaches that the temporal is *God's* ordering of society and, therefore, it must reflect God's perspective, in some way. See also, her later work (under her married name, Engel), *John Calvin's Perspectival Anthropology* (Scholars Press, Decatur, 1988), 56-60, 160.

[71] Ibid., 736.

[72] Ibid., 738.

Destructive of the Wife's Status

If in this way Potter is able to suggest a small improvement in the status of women, while maintaining an overall negative conclusion on Calvin's understanding of the man-woman relationship, it is not altogether surprising that other liberationist writers take up the idea that Calvin did not, fundamentally, move marital ethics out of the Middle Ages. In fact, several accuse him of sexism.

Rosemary Ruether and Paul Jewett could be cited in this regard. More recently, Karen Armstrong has taken up the challenge in dogmatic terms.[73] Initially, she claims that Calvin was the first Christian theologian to speak favourably of women and that 'with Calvin we are very much nearer to the christianization of marriage as an integral part of the Christian life'.[74] To back this positive assertion, she states that Calvin taught that woman was created to be a companion to man and that marriage was instituted by God precisely for that companionship – that is, not merely in order to procreate, as previous generations had believed. Despite these positive aspects to the reformer's teaching, Armstrong sees as the more significant idea, and finally the more damaging, Calvin's insistence that the woman's role as a companion was limited by definition and actually confined to the area of domesticity. This was an idea that ultimately embedded the Reformer firmly in the concepts and concrete practice of the Middle Ages. Together with this, Armstrong argues that Calvin (with his 'anti-sexual neurosis'[75]) has little time for sexual relations because 'he carried [Augustine's] negative attitudes towards sexuality and marriage right into the heart of the Reformation'.[76]

Other writers have come to a similar position[77] – and one would have to say that there is some truth in this general

---

[73] See, for example, R. R. Ruether, *Mary, the Feminine Face of the Church* (SCM, London, 1979), 61; Jewett, op. cit., 66; Armstrong, op. cit. For generally negative portraits of Calvin, see R. Stauffer, *The Humanity of Calvin* (Abingdon, Nashville, 1971), chapter 11.

[74] Armstrong, op. cit., 273.

[75] Ibid., 278.

[76] Ibid., 25.

[77] See, for example, Stone, op. cit., 104-6; A. P. Coudert, 'The Myth of Improved Status of Protestant Women: The Case of the Witchcraze' in J. R. Brink / A. P. Coudert / M. C. Horowitz (eds), *The Politics of Gender in Early Modern*

conclusion. Calvin did not revolutionize Christian thinking on marriage and the husband-wife relationship, any more than Luther had. That much is clear from a cursory reading of his work. The concept of hierarchical structure and rank, which Calvin upholds, is rooted in the medieval idea of society and marriage. The apparent mistrust of sex can be traced back to an attitude that permeated medieval writing on the subject and the subordination of women is also crucial to both the Middle Ages and the Reformation period.

However, increasingly, there has arisen the need to question an apparent implication in Calvin's *corpus* that more freedom for women is a real possibility, and that is precisely what the final group of writers seeks to do.

Calvin a Latent Liberationist

Biéler, Bratt and de Boer

The early work by Biéler is important, indeed seminal in this area. He stresses that Calvin teaches a definite equality between man and woman, but also a clear subordination of the wife to the husband in domestic and public relations. Although, at first sight, this seems contradictory, Biéler states that it is not ambiguous, nor inconsistent. He says that 'functional subordination ... does not really run counter to the egalitarian statements'.[78] This differentiation and complementarity are defined by the two phrases, 'egalité fondamentale, diversité fonctionelle'.[79] That is, as Biéler explains, ontologically as creatures of God and spiritually as children of God, the two sexes are entirely equal. Yet, in terms of their social and, particularly, their familial status, they are not equal, having been set in a hierarchical structure from the

---

Europe (SCJ Publishers, Kirksville, 1989), 61-89; R. Miles, *The Rites of Man* (Grafton, London, 1991), 122-9; Lerner, op. cit., 172-3, 183; Jewett, op. cit., 67, 131-2; G. Harkness, *Women in Church and Society* (Abingdon, Nashville, 1958), 83; R. Stauffer, *Dieu, la création et la providence dans la prédiction de Calvin* (Lang, Berne, 1978).

[78] A. Biéler, *L'homme et la femme*, 36-7. [Part of this monograph was translated as 'Man and Woman in Calvin's Ethic', *RPW* 27 (1963), 357-63, and as 'Mann und Frau in Calvins Ethik', *DH* 28 (1964), 69-74.]

[79] Ibid., 76.

beginning. He sees the question of subordination as one of external, political order.

It is important to notice that Biéler holds that Calvin, though working within a traditional, hierarchical framework, *at least in principle*, did not exclude the changes which a new age would be able to effect in the status of women and, therefore, changes in the relational structure of the family at the husband-wife level. He says that 'it is important, however, to emphasize that, in Calvin's view, social inequality of married people was a contingent fact, historically conditioned and politically determined, whereas their spiritual equality was inherent and unchangeable'.[80] He also notes that Calvin teaches a mutuality of the sexes from creation itself.[81]

Biéler's work is significant because it seems to have provided the basis for future elaboration. It is, particularly, his assertion that, for Calvin, relational structures between the sexes in the political-social realm are subject to modification according to circumstance (being evolutionary by nature) that has precipitated a great deal of theological writing in the area. Two suggestive essays of the 1970s should be noted before we move to what is perhaps the main development of Biéler's ideas.

The first is by J. H. Bratt[82] in which he states his thesis: 'Calvin posited a qualified but definite subordination of woman and a qualified but definite supremacy of man in the structure of human relationships as ordained and established by God.'[83] Largely arguing from the reformer's commentary and sermons on Paul's first letter to the Corinthians, he suggests that Calvin held to 'a normative pattern' of relationships based on the creational law of nature which gave the prerogative for authority and leadership to man. The woman's responsibility was that of being a helper in a subordinate and inferior role. Bratt admits that there is a threefold equality – in common humanness, in the sharing of a common salvation and in conjugal rights and privileges. The point remains that 'hierarchical arrangement in Calvin's

---

[80] Ibid., 80.

[81] Ibid., 36-9, 99.

[82] J. H. Bratt, 'The Role and Status of Woman in the Writings of Calvin' in P. de Klerk (ed.), *Renaissance, Reformation and Resurgence* (Calvin Theological Seminary, Grand Rapids, 1976), 1-17.

[83] Ibid., 1.

estimation is to be permanently binding. It permits of no alteration, modification, or cancellation'.[84]

Given this unpromising and apparently uncompromising thesis, the significant thing to notice here is that Bratt suggests that there is evidence that Calvin, himself, was hesitant in his comments on the Corinthian correspondence because he wondered whether Paul's instructions were normative for the church or whether this was 'a localism and an *ad hoc* situation'. Bratt continues, 'Perhaps we can go no further than to say that in Calvin's estimation the passages of 1 Corinthians, so frequently marshalled in favour of the traditional view, are *not necessarily indicative of a timeless principle.*'[85] At the crucial point of decision, Calvin seems to remember the created order (understood from Genesis 2) and shuts the door he had momentarily left ajar. But it is that suggestive moment of hesitation, pinpointed by Bratt, on which others have also focused. Perhaps an argument can still be raised for Calvin's liberationist tendency.[86]

The second essay, published in the same year, re-opens the door apparently slammed shut by Calvin and asserts more

---

[84] Ibid., 9.

[85] Ibid., 11 – emphasis added.

[86] The term 'liberationist' in this context should be defined. By it, we mean someone who, by their writing and/or their practice, shows a concern for the improvement of the status of women: that is, someone who is not content with the *status quo* in this area. It means less than the term 'feminist' which, though anachronistic (strictly speaking), has become the word for those of the same period of Renaissance culture who actively sought the improvement of women's status: see, for example, its use in Jordan, op. cit.; B. Gottlieb, 'The Problem of Feminism in the Fifteenth Century' in J. Kirshner / S. F. Wemple (eds), *Women of the Medieval World* (Blackwell, Oxford, 1987), 337-64; J. Kelly, 'Early Feminist Theory and the *Querelle des Femmes*: 1400-1789', *Signs* 8 (1982), 4-28; Halkin, op. cit., 192; Bennett, art. cit., 251. The protracted debate over woman's superiority or inferiority (*Querelle des femmes*) was both pan-European and transgeneric. It is precisely this debate which goes some way to defining what present writers term 'feminists' of the Renaissance period. Jordan, op. cit., 249-50, says of it, 'Equality in principle is constantly celebrated in feminist literature of the period, however qualified it may be in particular cases. Equality, in practice, by contrast, is mourned as a concept whose time has not yet come.' See also, 308. Also, Kelly, art. cit., 4-28; M. P. Fleischer, '"Are Women Human?" The Debate of 1595 between Valens Acidalius and Simon Gediccus', *SCJ* 11 (1981), 107-21.

definitely what Bratt only implied.[87] In this article de Boer agrees that Calvin's views on women were basically traditional.[88] However, the essay outlines possible feminist influences on Calvin – Marguerite de Valois, Cornelius Agrippa,[89] Katherine Zell.

Despite this possibility, it is clear to de Boer that the Reformer's preconceived ideas show through his commentaries and sermons on Paul's letters to the Corinthian church. He comments,

> For Calvin, the man is not subject to the woman – such would be an upsetting of the created order. The man is the head, leader, ruler; he holds a superior position. The woman is to serve him, obey him and be his lesser help. Calvin is confident that this is the very order of creation.

He adds, 'He noted how little the creation account itself supports him on this.'[90] Again, the writer admits areas of equality – he lists a shared humanity, a sharing of the image of God, a sharing too of the authority that parents have jointly over their children and an equality in the related matter of divorce.

Having said this, however, de Boer argues that Calvin does leave 'open doors for modification' in the way that he seems to relativize the apostle's argument at certain points. He says that the general tendency of Calvin is to see the Corinthian passages as arising from particular situations of disorderliness within the congregation and to conclude, therefore, that the injunctions are not universal. It is merely the ordering of outward things (*ordinem istum in rebus externis*) or the setting right of the propriety that is, itself, closely linked with cultural conditioning and customs. The essay concludes, however, that Calvin's thought

---

[87] W. P. de Boer, 'Calvin on the Role of Women' in D. E. Holwerda (ed.), *Exploring the Heritage of John Calvin* (Baker, Grand Rapids, 1976), 236-72.

[88] Ibid., 236.

[89] Though de Boer does not actually quote from these authors, Miles, op. cit., 110, quotes Agrippa from *Of the Nobility and Superiority of the Female Sex* (1505), as follows: 'Adam means Earth: Eve stands for Life: *ergo*, Adam is the product of nature, and Eve the creation of God. Adam was admitted to the Paradise for the sole purpose that Eve might be created.' However, it is very difficult to see how such a teaching could influence Calvin with his strictly hierarchical theory of the man-woman relationship.

[90] Ibid., 245.

was too controlled by the idea of a fixed, created, hierarchical order to allow him to follow through his own suspicions. Apparently, at this point Calvin regularly recalls the created order, 'And suddenly all thoughts of flexibility, adjustment, adaptation to the times vanish into thin air.'[91]

We see from these two scholars that there *may be* a case for arguing a potential for openness and change in Calvin's thought, but they suggest that his understanding of created order is a weight too heavy to drag into new possibilities. It is that which becomes his governing doctrine in this area. Bratt argues that the hierarchical arrangement, so frequently expressed by Calvin, allows no alteration, and the door, temptingly left open for a brief spell, slams closed. De Boer, on the other hand, reasons that, though Calvin is consistent in his hierarchical teaching, he is, nevertheless, uneasy at times and adjusts Scripture to suit his own view.

Jane Dempsey Douglass

One of the more significant writers for the purposes of this present study is Jane Dempsey Douglass. What she has more recently sought to do is to take the apparent contradictions and qualifications in Calvin's writing and to see him struggling with a liberationist tendency which is held in tension with his more traditional thinking. She has written some very cogent work on the subject, much of which develops ideas already nascent, perhaps, in the two former essays just reviewed.[92] Like Bratt and de Boer, she begins with the traditional elements in Calvin's thought. She places Calvin's teaching squarely in the context of traditional religious teaching, 'hardly going beyond Augustine', for example, 'in his assertion of the equality of the spouses in the sexual relationship, in conjugal rights to protect marital fidelity'.[93] Calvin continues the patristic and scholastic tradition of distinguishing between a spiritual equality and an inequality in

---

[91] Ibid., 264.

[92] J. D. Douglass, 'Women and the Continental Reformation' in Ruether, R. R. (ed.), *Religion and Sexism* (Simon and Schuster, New York, 1974), 292-318; idem, 'Christian Freedom: What Calvin Learned at the School of Women', *CH* 53 (1984), 155-73; idem, *Women, Freedom and Calvin* (Westminster Press, Philadelphia, 1985) and the related article, 'Calvin's use of Metaphorical Language for God: God as Enemy and God as Mother', *ARG* 77 (1988), 126-40.

[93] *Women, Freedom and Calvin*, 79.

the world. There is a pervasive belief in woman's inferiority permeating the Reformer's work.

In her early essay (1974) Douglass lists twelve relevant theological insights that she believes helped the reformers to develop a new doctrine of marriage. Some of them are more relevant to Calvin than others. These would include the following: there are no valid distinctions between 'commands' and 'counsels', there is no greater merit in celibacy above the married state, the family is the most important context in which faith and obedience to God is to be exercised, *all* believers bear a priestly responsibility for the ministry of prayer,[94] marriage is to be appreciated as a means of procreation (although, obviously, it remains a remedy against sin and a legitimate means of having children).[95] In her later essay (1984) Douglass seeks to show that Calvin was influenced by the liberationist thinkers of his day.[96]

---

[94] Though the idea of the priesthood of all believers was important in other areas, it has yet to be shown to have had any influence on the reformers' doctrine of marriage or their ideas of the social relationship between man and woman. See J. R. Crawford, 'Calvin and the priesthood of all believers' *SJT* 21 (1968), 145-56; J. S. Whale, *The Protestant Tradition* (CUP, Cambridge, 1955), 152. See, in Calvin's work, *Comm. 1 Pet.* 2:5-9 [CO 55.233-41]; *Comm. Rom.* 15:16 [CO 49.276]; *Comm. Col.* 2:14 [CO 52.107]; *Comms. 1 Cor.* 3:16 [CO 49.358]; 4:19 [CO 49.375]; *Comm. Ps* 113 [CO 32.177-9].

[95] Douglass, 'Women and the Continental Reformation', 293-302. Thompson, *Calvin and the Daughters of Sarah*, 8, extracts these as the most pertinent to Calvin's theology and, correctly, adds the fact that marriage was seen by the reformers as a creational institution, not a sacrament of the church. This brought it outside of the church's jurisdiction and under the authority of the state.

[96] We noted that de Boer had done this in his earlier work. In 'Christian Freedom...' (1984), 167-71, Douglass cites Cornelius Agrippa, Marguerite de Valois, Marguerite de Angoulême and also, interestingly, the women who preached in Geneva before Calvin's own arrival - e.g. Claudine Levet, Marie Dentière. See also, *Women, Freedom and Calvin*, 68-72, 83-4. Her conclusion in the article, 'Calvin's use of Metaphorical Language...' 139, is significant; she believes that there 'is some reason to believe Calvin hears the arguments of women writers of his day who aggressively defend women's rights and who at least sometimes themselves use female imagery for God.' Two problems with Douglass' argument, at this point, appear to be that she does not take time to prove Calvin's dependence, and, in any case, it is far easier to demonstrate some connection, than to establish any actual influence on the Reformer's theology or practice. This is certainly Thompson's conclusion on the matter - op. cit. 25, 31-63.

The area of analysis that Douglass particularly develops is the concept of order as it impinges on Calvin's thinking regarding relational ethics. She believes that though order is perhaps a central, governing theological motif for Calvin it is *not* to be conceived as static and finished. She emphasizes that the importance of the concept is not strict arrangement but, rather, the *intention* of that order. Divine ordering of the cosmos is mirrored by man's arrangement of society. Just as God's creative and providential ordering progresses in human history, so 'human order is the result of human governance (*politia*) which must adapt to changing circumstances'.[97] She says that 'conformity to the order of nature ... is not an absolute command: it must always take into account God's *purpose* for that order'.[98]

The Reformer puts the subject of woman's subordination into the realm of human order. Here, it is open to evolution, to change and modification within social progress and development - in varying forms, in different ages and cultures. Accordingly, because of our limited perspective on things and because God only rarely inverts natural order anyway, the order of nature appears to us to be reliable and consistent. It is for this reason that Douglass sees fit to qualify Calvin's meaning of his much-used word, 'inviolable'. She writes, 'It appears that what he calls the inviolable order of men ruling over women is inviolable only in the sense that women should not presumptuously seek an office which is not theirs. God is quite free to violate that order.'[99] Her conclusion is that 'Calvin is genuinely open to exceptions to the normal rule of woman's subordination.'[100]

If the rule of nature is not in any absolute sense a norm for determining the moral behaviour of Christians, as this development might imply, why does Calvin not move in the direction of real freedom from social bondage in his practical exhortation? Douglass appears to suggest two possible reasons. First, Calvin was afraid of social upheaval in Geneva. He sought to keep a moderate balance between the two extremes of radicalism

---

[97] 'Christian Freedom...', 156.

[98] *Women, Freedom and Calvin*, 29 - emphasis added. See also, 36-40. See 'Christian Freedom...' 155.

[99] Ibid., 57; also, 29, 36, 40, 42.

[100] Ibid., 104-5. Thompson, op. cit., 22, does not exaggerate when he refers to Douglass' conclusion as implying that Calvin was a 'latent feminist' (also, 269).

and catholicism. Second, after the initial flush of reforming enthusiasm died down, it was part of the institutionalisation of the church that things began to take on form. Part of this was Calvin's expectation of women resuming the role of subjection.[101]

Douglass' writing has certainly advanced the initial thesis. Some of her conclusions are worth briefly restating at this point. First, though there is a widespread assumption that Calvin is extremely negative regarding women and holds to their subjection, Douglass says that Calvin evidences little positive support for the traditional general subordination of women.[102] Second, the Reformer's view of divine order, rather than being of a fixed kind, is an arrangement which changes according to the purposes of God in a given community and time. There is, therefore, no reason to suppose that Calvin viewed marital hierarchy as permanently binding on every age or culture.[103] Third, Douglass concludes that the main change that takes place in Calvin's teaching on the husband-wife relationship is a shift of priority. That shift takes it away from its procreative and remedial aspect towards mutual love and respect. She holds that though Calvin taught that patriarchal marriage is a blessing of God, it needs to be humanized.[104] This represents a significant development from views held in the Middle Ages.[105]

Whereas the central group of writers looks upon Calvin as positive, but as little more than traditional in his ethical thinking on the husband-wife relationship, and the second reads his theology extremely negatively, this group follows Biéler's lead and sees the Reformer in a much more favourable light. For those concerned, there are hints that Calvin, consciously or at least in

---

[101] See, 'Christian Freedom...', 166, 169-73.

[102] Ibid., 165. Also, *Women, Freedom and Calvin*, 63.

[103] *Women, Freedom and Calvin*, chapter 1.

[104] Ibid., 86.

[105] Others have written from a similar standpoint, but have not materially advanced the thesis. See, particularly, van der Walt, art. cit., 184-238; N. L. Roelker, 'The Appeal of Calvinism to French Noblewomen in the Sixteenth Century', *JIH* 2 (1972), 391-418; idem, 'The Role of Noblewomen in the French Reformation', *ARG* 63 (1972), 168-95. H. H. Eßer, 'Zur Anthropologie Calvins: Menschenwürde-Imago Dei zwischen humanistischen und theologischen Ansatz' in H.-G. Geyer, et al., (eds), *Wenn nicht jetzt, wann dann?* (Neukirchener, 1983), 269-81, claims that Calvin's commitment to women's dignity is seen in his refusal to deny the image of God to women. But as Thompson (op. cit., 104) points out this was not a distinctive of the Reformer's thought.

principle, moved the concept of women's freedom forward in this social area. Even though he rarely speaks of practical change, he is projected as a 'liberationist' in varying degrees.

Though the approaches outlined are different in their basic conclusions, there are several points to be made. First, as with Luther, Calvin is held to be traditional in his presuppositions concerning the relative status of man and woman. Again, Augustine is usually singled out as the major, post-biblical influence on Calvin's marital and sexual teaching. Second, many of the writers reviewed have pointed out the central importance of the concept of order in Calvin's ethical thought. The Reformer's idea of an ordered universe, reflected in an ordered community, is significant to his thinking on familial relations in which hierarchical structures play such a part. Basically, marriage is one of the social hierarchies – the man is the head, the woman is his inferior help. The question is variously answered as to whether the Reformer viewed this structure to be static or as contingent upon social circumstance and custom. Is it 'inviolable' in any definitive sense, or is it culturally bound? Again, does he seek to alleviate the woman's lot in a patriarchal society (even if only in principle), or does he justify the inequality? Is there any real, concrete evidence of his changing the perception of marital relationships from that which was taught in, say, the Middle Ages?

Third, there is a consensus that Calvin *does* hold a view of the equality of the sexes, but no agreement of the nature of that equality, nor any satisfactory theory as to how he holds both equality and hierarchy together, without compromising either. Fourth, several writers argue that Calvin brings preconceived ideas to his exposition of Scripture, or that he expounds passages to suit his own purpose. It needs to be asked whether Calvin's theological view of order, for instance, and that of woman's role in society come as clearly from the biblical text as he assumes. Do they colour his exposition of key biblical passages on the roles of husband and wife?

The preceding survey has given an outline of the work that has been done on Luther and Calvin in the area of their respective views on women and their understanding of the husband-wife relationship. We have also tabled some of the questions that have been raised, but which have not, necessarily, been satisfactorily or consistently answered. Clearly, though there has been a great deal of study on the reformers in these and related subjects, there is a good deal left to clarify. Indeed, in placing Luther together with Calvin in the way that we have suggests something of the demarcation and focus of the present study, to which we turn in chapter 2.

CHAPTER 2

THE APPROACH OF THE PRESENT STUDY

INTRODUCTION

Having surveyed recent scholarship on Luther's and Calvin's understanding of the marital relationship, what we have found is that generally, in the past, scholars have placed them together in such a way as to imply that their understanding is similar enough to warrant no acute division between them. They are both said to hold to a conventional hierarchical structure, they both teach that the husband is the superior head and that the wife is the subordinate helper, they both teach that their views are biblically based, and so on. As we have noted, both Reformers have been given credit for a new emphasis on love and mutual respect – though, in practice, Calvin often gets the better press. However, little real or significant change from the established position is attributed to either. Perhaps there has been a slight modification in attitude, but no actual advance from the medieval position.

In contrast, there have always been those who have looked negatively at the Reformers' theology of marriage and have accused them of demeaning women in the tradition of Western misogyny. This has been increasingly so with the relatively recent advent of liberationist writers on the subject, as Armstrong, Wiesner, Jewett, and others demonstrate. For them, either Luther or Calvin, or both, fall down on the twin areas of negativity towards sexual relations (even within marriage) and patriarchy or an unequal power structure within that relationship.

Also, the survey has indicated a relatively new perspective on Calvin, which sees his theology as insinuating at least an openness to change in the status of women. It has taken some time to take seriously some of Biéler's ideas, but gradually since the 1970s more writers have made the point. With Jane Douglass, this argument has taken on greater force and an urgency to see Calvin in this role. Her analysis of Calvin's view of order must now be taken into account. However, a significant side effect of this is that a wedge is necessarily driven between the reformers. Because no such development has ensued in Luther studies, he is still, at best, only given the role of advancing marital ideas a superficial amount. It is argued by some, however, that Calvin was actually a latent feminist.

This ideological polarisation between Luther and Calvin in the area of man-woman relationships is an unsatisfactory development, simply because it is fundamentally unrealistic. John Thompson's work makes this clear – at least, from the perspective of Calvin's writing.[1] He begins his research thesis by stating that Calvin's theology is both a mixture of hierarchical teaching and a real concern for the dignity of women. He was not a great innovator, although with Calvin marriage did change from being, merely, respectable to being 'religiously significant' as a vocation or a divine office.[2]

Thompson pursues a comparison between Calvin and his predecessors and contemporaries with a focus on two problems: namely, Calvin's ambivalence between hierarchical theory and egalitarian dignity, and his possible openness to real change. His findings are specific. First, Calvin is, generally, to be found in the conservative mainstream of biblical commentators in this area of thought. Second, Douglass' theory of genuine openness (Calvin as an innovator in the theology of gender status and roles) is insupportable. According to Thompson, 'Calvin proves significantly less open to women in exceptional (read "leadership") roles than many of his predecessors and fellow

---

[1] See his published doctoral thesis, *John Calvin and the Daughters of Sarah* (Librarie Droz, Geneva, 1992) and the related article, '"*Creata ad Imaginem Dei, Licet Secundo Gradu*": Woman as the Image of God According to John Calvin', *HTR* 81 (1988), 125-44.

[2] *John Calvin and the Daughters of Sarah*, 15, 7. See also, T. M. Safley, *Let No Man Put Asunder* (SCJ Publishers, Kirksville, 1984), 30.

commentators and there is almost nothing in Calvin which is without precedent.'³

Thompson argues that Calvin was not influenced by the writers of the *querelle des femmes* or by women he knew personally,⁴ nor was he innovative in his views concerning women in regular roles, nor in his theory of women in exceptional roles.⁵ On this basis, Thompson believes that Douglass' thesis is not viable. Calvin is found to display 'a thorough solidarity with the patriarchal and hierarchical views of his predecessors and contemporaries'.⁶ Thompson's final sentences are worth quoting: 'But is Calvin genuinely open to change in women's public roles? That is, outside of emergency circumstances, and this side of heaven? Regrettably, no – not at all.'⁷

Again, in his related essay on the Reformer's understanding of the *imago Dei* in relation to women Thompson confirms an equality-hierarchy juxtaposition in Calvin's thought and denies Douglass' conclusion that Calvin displays a genuine openness to change.⁸ Rather, Thompson plays down the significance of the concept of inequality to show that, for Calvin, it was of little consequence.

> In comparison with the truth of the spiritual and eternal equality of man and woman, the hierarchical relationship between the sexes in the present life is clearly a matter of small importance, destined to pass away. Likewise, compared with the doctrines of salvation, the concrete experiences of woman's subjection are themselves virtually trivial matters.⁹

---

³ Ibid., 24-5.

⁴ Thompson deals, specifically, with the possible influence of Agrippa, Marguerite de Navarre, Dentière, Levet, Postel and Katherine Zell (ibid., 35-59). His conclusion is worth quoting here: '[M]ost (if not all) of the prowoman humanist writers who were Calvin's contemporaries and who may have influenced Calvin's views were also figures with whom Calvin had grounds for serious disagreement over other matters of religion and theology' (47; see also, 48, 62).

⁵ Ibid., 65-226.

⁶ Ibid., 277.

⁷ Ibid., 280. Insofar as Thompson's thesis impinges on the subject of man-woman relationship (principally, within the ecclesiastical context) its reasoning and conclusions are important to the present study.

⁸ Thompson, art. cit., 104, 121.

⁹ Ibid., 141.

Obviously, some would not agree with Thompson's perspective. Yet, if he has not actually reversed the direction of Calvin studies in this area, Thompson clearly seems to have taken it back to the drawing board.

We have insisted, above, that driving a wedge between Luther and Calvin in their teaching on the man-woman relationship is unrealistic and, therefore, unsatisfactory. As far as Calvin's exegesis of the passages is concerned, Thompson's work adequately shows this to be the case. The present study proposes to complement Thompson's research. The distinct difference is that the present thesis examines a similar, but not the same, subject area from a different focus. That is, more specifically, the study examines Luther and Calvin comparatively against a general understanding of the tradition in which they stand. It examines the area of marriage and the husband-wife relationship, not so much women in ecclesiastical and exceptional roles. And it seeks to do so from a broad theological, not so much simply an exegetical, perspective. However, the present writer responds to Douglass' (and to liberationist) conclusions in a similarly sceptical manner to that of Thompson, but, generally, from a wider, doctrinal base.

Whereas Thompson draws his conclusions directly from Calvin's exegesis in relation to that of his contemporaries and predecessors, we draw ours from an examination of Luther's and Calvin's social theology. We employ their exegesis to verify what we have discovered in general terms to demonstrate that theology as it pervades and shapes the reformers' exegesis and to give further nuance to our findings.

The contention of the present thesis is that this potential polarisation of the two Reformers is unsatisfactory for at least two reasons. *First, it is the theological framework in which they locate their view of marriage which shapes their understanding.* Their respective frameworks preclude any genuine possibility that either reformer could give more real, concrete freedom to wives within the strictly hierarchical structure they adopt. It will be shown below that Luther's understanding of the marital relationship falls within his teaching on the temporal kingdom in which marriage is a divinely appointed vocation. As such, it becomes an institution by which God maintains hierarchical order between the husband and wife in which, by definition, the woman is inferior to her husband. The location of marriage in

Calvin's thinking on social order is just as restrictive. Against what he sees to be the anarchic potential of sin, he maintains a hierarchical arrangement between the spouses. For both Reformers, their theology of social order and its purpose shapes their perception of marriage and, thus, excludes the possibility of structural change. We argue that this has not been sufficiently recognized by those who reason otherwise.

Second, the supposed difference between Luther and Calvin in the area of marital relationships is a misunderstanding or a myth. The teaching of Calvin on marriage is as fundamentally traditional as that of Luther. Apart from relatively insignificant differences they both hold to a similar understanding of the husband-wife relationship. The fact that they both stress conjugal love and companionship is actually reflective of traditional Augustinian-medieval views on the relationship. It is not innovative in any creditable way. Apart from the most negative writers, the conventional understanding of marriage sought to soften a strict hierarchicalism through emphasis on friendship and mutuality – yet it remained a strict hierarchicalism. Those who argue that the reformers advanced perception in this area appear to read the Reformers too positively and the tradition too pessimistically. They underline the negative strand of Augustinian teaching without taking note of its qualifying opposite. Any attempt to suggest that Calvin's views are more 'enlightened' fails to take into account that a detailed examination of their respective teaching shows Calvin to be as reticent as Luther to move from conventional thinking. Indeed, it could be argued that Luther's application of the ideas shows him, on a personal level, to be *more likely* so to move. However, neither suggests a perceptible change in the status or roles of wives.

THE METHOD OF ENQUIRY

Most, if not all, suggest that Luther and Calvin follow traditional thinking in their views of marriage and of the relationship structure within that institution. As we have noticed, some accuse the Reformers of inherited negativity. Others speak of the improvement of the whole concept of marriage, and of the wife's status in particular. This gives the starting point to the study. Chapter 3 will examine the teaching of Augustine on marriage and chapter 4, briefly, looks at medieval understanding and practice. It will be found that, generally, reading of Augustine has been too negative. Though he holds to a hierarchical arrangement in marriage, the teaching *is* qualified by an emphasis on mutual respect and Christian love. The medieval period is characterized and complicated by diversity, but the same ideas permeate ecclesiastical and theological teaching of the time.

The main body of the book, then, turns to Luther and Calvin. Though we are aware of Höpfl's warning, in respect of Calvin study, against massing random quotations from works of unequal length and from different periods,[10] we have chosen to use a broad basis of examination. There are several reasons for this. First, there is a present, general recognition of the need to broaden the base for a reading in the Reformer's work. David Steinmetz has recently stated that, 'It is now common for Calvin scholars to assert that Calvin cannot be understood from the *Institutes* alone. All of his writings ... contribute to a right understanding of the man and his thought, and none can be omitted without real loss.'[11] What is helpful in Höpfl's comment is that it cautions against 'random' quotations being 'massed'. Safeguards against this have been implemented in the present approach. Our intention has been to avoid distortion by reading Calvin's words within their wider context. Any quotation will assume that. Also, it will be found that the final chapter on each Reformer's exegesis will act as a gauge on the accuracy of the previous presentation. Höpfl's warning also makes us aware of the danger of missing development in the writing of Luther or Calvin by mismatching chronologically indiscriminate

---

[10] H. Höpfl, *The Christian Polity of John Calvin* (CUP, Cambridge, 1985), 3.

[11] D. Steinmetz, *Calvin in Context* (OUP, Oxford, 1995), vii. See also, J. McNutt, 'Martin Luther as Human Being: Reflections from a Distance', *Ch* 108 (1994), 265-70; T. H. L. Parker, *Calvin. An Introduction to his Thought* (Geoffrey Chapman, London, 1995), ix, 1. Both, R. White, 'Women and the Teaching Office According to Calvin', *SJT* 47 (1994), 495 and earlier, R. Stauffer, *Dieu, la création et la providence dans la prédication de Calvin* (Lang, Berne, 1978), 303-6, emphasize the significance of Calvin's writing other than the *Institutes*. W. J. Bouwsma, *John Calvin. A Sixteenth Century Portrait* (OUP, New York, 1988) is a recent, paradigmatic example of a broadly based study on Calvin; as is D. E. Tamburello, *Union with Christ. John Calvin and the Mysticism of St. Bernard* (Westminster / John Knox, Louisville, 1994).

quotations. In fact, it is generally agreed that there is very little development in the area of their understanding of the marital relationship. This has been found to be the case. What little progress there is will be alluded to in the text.

Our second reason for having a broad base in the reformers' work is because the theology of marriage is not an end in itself. It is teaching to be applied to the concreteness of life. It is important that use is made of those works in which that theology is given as advice or in exhortation. Therefore, a wide variety of works become relevant – although, clearly, they are not all of equal importance. Therefore, for example, Luther's treatises and sermons on marriage and his commentaries are important and they cover an extensive chronological span of the Reformer's thinking.[12] Together with these primary texts, other genres will be referred to, largely as clarification and application of his theological ideas. Luther's sermons are important,[13] as are his

---

[12] *A Sermon on the Estate of Marriage* (1519), LW 44.7-14 [WA 2.166-71]; *The Estate of Marriage* (1522), LW 45.17-49 [WA 10².275-304]; *On Marriage Matters* (1530), LW 46.265-320 [WA 30³.205-48]; Sermon preached at the wedding of Sigismund von Lindenau (1545), LW 51.357-67 [WA 49.797-805]; *Comm. 1 Cor.* (1523), LW 28.1-56 [WA 12.88-142]; *Comm. 1 Pet.* (1523-24), LW 30.3-145 [WA 12.249-399]; *Comm. 1 Tim.* (1527-28), LW 28.217-384 [WA 26.1-120]; *Comm. Gal.* (1519 and 1535), LW 26 and 27.11-152 [WA 40¹]; *Comm. Gen.* (1535-45), LW 1-8 [WA 42-4]. Luther's commentary on Genesis, *In Primum Librum Mose Enarrationes*, is particularly important as the Reformer's mature work. The accounts of the betrothals and marriages of the patriarchs give Luther occasion to open out the subject of the husband-wife relationship and to discuss it. This work is almost an episodic treatise on marriage, the spouses' relationship and the vocational roles and responsibilities of each partner.

[13] The importance of Luther's preaching is amply argued by scholars. See, for example, W. Sparn, 'Preaching and the Course of the Reformation' in H. Robinson-Hammerstein (ed.), *The Transmission of Ideas in the Lutheran Reformation* (Irish Academic Press, Dublin, 1989), 173-83 and, in the same volume, H. Robinson-Hammerstein, 'Luther and the Laity', 11-46. See also Y. Ishida, 'Luther the Pastor' in C. Lindberg (ed.), *Piety, Politics and Ethics* (SCJ Publishers, Kirksville, 1984), 27-37; J. Kittelson, 'Successes and Failures in the German Reformation: The Report from Strasbourg', *ARG* 73 (1982), 153-74. If, as R. W. Scribner argues in *The German Reformation* (Humanities Press, Atlantic Highlands, NJ, 1986), 20, literacy in Germany was as low as 4%-5%, the sermon was forced to be a significant conveyor of Reformed ideas. See *Comm. Gen.* 4:8, LW 1.272 [WA 42.201]; *The Bondage of the Will*, LW 33.52 [WA 18.626]; preface to *Comm. Hab.* LW 19.153 [WA 13.351]; preface to *Comm. Deut.* LW 9.6 [WA 14.499].

letters and Table-Talk.¹⁴ His life-experience (*Lebenswelt*) and his relationship to his wife, Katherine, testify to his own social understanding in this area. Use will be made of each of these genres though primary attention will be given to his major works.¹⁵

Unlike Luther, Calvin wrote no occasional pieces outlining his views on marriage. However, as far as Calvin is concerned six distinct sources may be discerned.¹⁶ The *Institutes* are the primary resource for his religious thought, though there is little specific reference to marriage and the conjugal relationship. His commentaries are secondary, but important, nonetheless.¹⁷

---

¹⁴ Luther's letters (1507-46) are found in LW 48-50 [WA Br. 1-12] and his Table-Talk (*Tischreden*) in LW 54 [WA Tr. 1-6; WA 48.365-719]. Also, W. Hazlett (trans.), *Table Talk* (Fount, London, 1995). Perhaps, the best commendation for the use of the Table-Talk comes from Luther, himself: 'Discourses are the real condiments of foods ... since godly conversations refresh the hearts, arouse faith, kindle love, and instruct in many ways' (*Comm. Gen.* 18:9, LW 3.200 [WA 43.18]).

¹⁵ Unless otherwise indicated, we refer to Luther's work in both the English translation, *Luther's Works* (American Edition), 55 volumes (Concordia, St Louis / Fortress, Philadelphia, 1955-86) and the German edition, *D. Martin Luthers Werke: Kritische Gesamtausgabe* (Herman Böhlaus Nachfolger, Weimar, 1883-1987), cited throughout as LW and WA, respectively. Generally we have followed the American Edition, departing from it only rarely.

¹⁶ Unless otherwise indicated we refer to Calvin's work in the *Corpus Reformatorum* edition, G. Baum / E. Cunitz / E. Reuss (eds), *Ioannis Calvini quae supersunt omnia* (Schwetschke et Filium, Brunsvigae, 1863-1900), cited as CO throughout. For Calvin's *Institutes* we have used the Latin edition in P. Barth / D. Scheuner (eds), *Johannis Calvini Opera Selecta* (Chr. Kaiser, Monachii in Aedibus, 1952), together with the French edition J. D. Benoît (ed.), *Institution de la Religion Chrestienne* (J. Vrin, Paris, 1957), cited throughout as OS and Benoît, respectively. Generally, we have followed the translation by F. L. Battles, *Institutes of the Christian Religion* (Westminster Press, Philadelphia, 1960). In regard to Calvin's sermons, commentaries and so on, we have been helped in translation as indicated by the English and French editions and translations in the bibliography, generally accepting them unless there seemed good reason to depart from them.

¹⁷ The nature of the complex relationship between the *Institutes* and Calvin's commentaries determines the importance of the latter. See Steinmetz, op. cit., 14. As Parker, op. cit., 4-10, points out, as its purpose developed the *Institutes* was not meant to be a complete work, in itself, but rather supportive and instrumental *loci communes* which enabled Calvin to condense his comments on Scripture without need of lengthy digression. See CO 1.255-6, cited by Parker, ibid., 7. Parker says, 'The writing of the *Institutio*, therefore, is tied firmly not only to Scripture but also to the author's commentaries on Scripture.' The writing of the *Institutes* does not negate the significance of the

Together with these his sermons,[18] tracts, treatises, letters[19] and liturgical and catechismal writings will also be brought into the discussion as far as they help to further our understanding of the matter. Use will be made of each of these sources, but primary theological attention will be given to the *Institutes*.

Third, a good deal of attention has been given to single passages or to imagery in the Reformer's writing, but, though useful, it has generally brought little overall clarification. It is a contention underlying the following chapters that thorough, discursive deliberation is best done from a general to a particular focus. That is, in beginning with a broad canvas of the Reformers' writing to introduce their theological context of marriage and, then, in particularising their teaching on marriage, the examination of their exegesis stands a better chance of being in line with the *total* and *overall* perspective of their understanding. In order to follow this line of reasoning chapter 5 outlines Luther's theological-ethical concept of vocation within his teaching on the two kingdoms of God's rule. It does so because the first task is to establish the wider context of Luther's teaching on marriage. This will provide a context by which we can gauge the governing limitations with which he defines the husband-wife relationship. We find that the vocation of marriage is part of God's temporal realm and, as such, it is an aspect of his ordering and control of society. This is an order for both believer and

---

commentaries. Thus, for example, speaking of *Inst* I.xiv.1-2, Parker notices that there is no detailed exposition of Gen.1-2 at this point. He adds, 'No doubt we are meant to read the relevant parts of Calvin's commentary on Genesis, which had appeared five years before this *Institutio*' (ibid., 36). This is a feature that will be taken into account in the present book.

[18] The importance of Calvin's sermons is attested by many writers. See, for example, T. H. L. Parker, *Calvin's Preaching* (T&T Clark, Edinburgh, 1992), 89, 118; G. M. Sumner, 'The Style of John Calvin's Sermons 1549-60' (unpublished BLitt dissertation, University of Oxford, 1976), 78-80, 251-3; M. Anderson, 'John Calvin: Biblical Preacher (1539-1564)', *SJT* (1989), 167-81; D. Fischer, 'L'élément historique dans la prédication de Calvin', *RHPR* (1984), 365-86; C. M. Baldwin, 'Marriage in Calvin's Sermons' in R. V. Schnucker (ed.), *Calviniana: Ideas and Influence of Jean Calvin* (SCJ Publishers, Kirksville, 1988), 121-9; B. W. Farley, 'John Calvin's Sermons on the Ten Commandments' (unpublished doctoral thesis, Union Theological Seminary, Richmond, 1976), 123, 162. See also, *Inst* IV.i.1, 5; IV.iii.1-14; *Comm. Phil*.1:23-4 [CO 53.18-9].

[19] See J. D. Benoît, 'Calvin the Letter Writer' in G. E. Duffield (ed.), *John Calvin* (The Sutton Courtenay Press, Appleford, 1966), 67-101.

unbeliever alike, in which unequal-relations is a fundamental characteristic.

The following chapter elaborates Luther's understanding of marriage within this theological context. It discovers a creational logic about Luther's ideas and a conventional teaching on the three purposes for marriage: the desire for sex, the procreation of children, and companionship. His understanding of these and their outworking is seen to be largely determined by the overall context of vocation within the temporal kingdom and God's purpose for that realm. A brief examination of his own reasons for marriage shows that the characteristics that Luther espouses are, perhaps, more flexible in practice than they appear in writing. Chapter 7 takes a closer look at the Reformer's thought with an exposition of aspects of his exegesis of the major biblical passages on the subject. This chapter highlights the theological and ethical ideas of his teaching on marriage as they appear in his detailed writing on the texts. It shows that Luther often has presuppositions that inform the text and even surface as the primary teaching. This is so even if, at times, they are not that clearly important in the Scripture;[20] or sometimes they become emphasized contrary to the intention of the biblical writer.[21]

The overall conclusion of the three chapters on Luther is that he upholds conventional teaching and that he reaffirms it by his understanding of the reality of the secular kingdom and of vocation within it. This is seen in his theology of marriage and the husband-wife relationship, and again, clearly, in the way that that works out in the exposition of scriptural passages. However, it is also apparent that Luther reveals a positive attitude towards women and sexual contact – an attitude not always recognized or appreciated by his critics. Nevertheless, Luther's theology *will not allow him* to posit any freedom for wives within this arrangement. His definition of temporal reality prohibits any movement in that direction.

Chapters 8-10 turn to a similar study of Calvin. This is in order to see how alike they are in their understanding of the husband-wife relationship, to evaluate any possible development from one to the other and to discern if there is room for any

---

[20] See, for example, on Genesis 1-3.
[21] See, for example, on 1 Peter.

optimism that Calvin leaves doors open for women's domestic liberation.

The task of a starting point is found to be easier for a study of Calvin. Many have suggested the concept of order (*ordo*) as a determining factor in his ethics. Indeed, this is the case and it dovetails with the preceding chapters on Luther. Again, Calvin's understanding of marriage is discovered to be set in the wider concept of God's intention for societal relationships in which divine order is to be maintained. Calvin is obsessed with order in society. For him, this is an order that combats the inroads of sin and social chaos, an order which upholds God's hierarchical structuring of society and, importantly for this thesis, the marital arrangement in which traditional ideas are retained. The chapter concludes with some preliminary arguments against Douglass' suggestions, on the grounds that they do not do justice to Calvin's strict concept of patriarchal order in the community.

Chapter 9 narrows the focus in order to elucidate Calvin's understanding of marriage and the husband-wife relationship within the broader theological framework outlined in the previous chapter. It is shown that as Calvin comments on the three conventional reasons for getting married his application is, partly, determined by the need to stabilize society, that is, to maintain order. For example, a significant conclusion, though not the only one, is that his teaching on companionship does not stress the importance of companionship, *per se*, but the importance of companionship with the purpose of remedying sexual lust and for having children in a legitimate way. In other words, what may seem on the surface to be a development from traditional teaching is merely a means to the same end. In fact, it is not far removed from conventional thinking. Calvin's concern is for order and societal peace, not so much the genuine, mutual sociability of the couple.

Chapter 10 parallels the final chapter on Luther and presents an examination of Calvin's exegesis of biblical passages seeking to reveal in what way the Reformer employs his theological assumptions in his reading of Scripture. Again, as with Luther, Calvin sometimes emphasizes his own agenda, not always that of the biblical writer. Ultimately, he is interested in the outworking of a strictly ordered, hierarchical structure of marriage. His theological understanding of the vocational nature of marriage *will not permit* a more liberated reading of the text.

The concluding chapter recapitulates and shows in what significant ways Luther and Calvin are traditional and similar in their thinking on the subject of marriage. The attempt by Douglass and others to exonerate Calvin as a man who sought a real freedom for women (and, thereby elevating Calvin above many of his contemporaries, including Luther), though in many ways attractive, will be shown to be over-optimistic and ultimately unfounded. The present work will show this to be the case in two important ways. First, a thorough examination of their teaching on marriage will reveal that, in this area, Luther and Calvin cannot be separated in any significant way. Luther and Calvin stand or fall together, as it were. Though there *are* differences in attitude, emphasis and nuance, the hierarchical outline of the husband-wife relationship is singularly conventional and equivalent. Second, Calvin's understanding of the husband-wife relationship will be shown to be determined largely by his obsession with a fixed order in society. There is nothing in his approach to the ethics of marriage that will satisfactorily divorce his teaching from that of Luther.

II THE MARRIAGE TRADITION

CHAPTER 3

AUGUSTINE ON MARRIAGE

As we have noted above, those writers who either suggest that the Reformers modify a tradition or who complain that they are trapped within that tradition point to Augustine as the major post-biblical influence upon them. Certainly, he is the most important and influential patristic author to write on sexual matters. Amongst his many works he wrote two expressly on marriage – *De Bono coniugali* and *De nuptiis et concupiscientia*[1] – and others abound with reference to the subject.[2] Though not accepted *in toto*, much of what he wrote became standard

---

[1] *De bono coniugali* (401), PL 40.373-96; *De nuptiis et concupiscientia* (418-20), PL 40.451-86, abbreviated as *DBC* and *DNu*, respectively. Unless otherwise indicated we have employed the Latin text of Augustine's works in J. P. Migne (ed.), *Patrologiae cursus completus* (Faculties Catholiques, Lille, 1952), vols 32-46, abbreviated as PL throughout. We have also used *Sancti Augustini* in *Corpus Christianorum* (Typographi Brepols Editiores Pontificii, Turnholt, 1967) vols 27-50ª and, in translation, *Augustine: Selected Works* in P Schaff, (ed.), *A Select Library of the Nicene and Post Nicene Fathers*, vols 1-8 (The Christian Literature Company, Buffalo,1886) – the latter cited throughout as ASW.

[2] Chapter 2 argued for the advantage gained in employing diverse and various sources from the Reformers' works in order to show not only the theology but also the application and, where possible, the practice of their ideas. It is therefore interesting to note that B. D. Shaw, 'The Family in Late Antiquity – the Experience of Augustine', *PP* 115 (1987), 5-6, states this preference in regard to Augustine, *specifically on this subject of family relationships*. See also, M. T. Clark, *Augustine* (Chapman, London, 1994), 120.

premises for the Middle Ages and beyond. In this context, Brundage speaks of Augustine as 'the one whose views have most fundamentally influenced subsequent ideas'.[3] Whether that influence is considered to be positive or not depends largely on the perspective of the critic – though no-one reads Augustine as anything more consistent than ambivalent on the subject of marriage. There are those who would defend him against misogyny, but it is worth noting that most of these would interpret his thinking as moderate only in comparison to that of his contemporaries.[4] This is understandable as a cursory reading of the exaggerated pessimism of Jerome[5] or even the milder thought of Ambrose shows.[6] Nevertheless, van Bavel has recently spoken more positively of Augustine as opening new perspectives and of instigating further evolution by his emphasis on marital love and conjugal friendship.[7]

In contrast, many scholars would read Augustine as clearly negative in his understanding of marriage.[8] One such writer is

---

[3] J. A. Brundage, *Law, Sex and Christian Society in Medieval Europe* (University of Chicago Press, Chicago, 1987), 80. See also, C. Brooke, *The Medieval Idea of Marriage* (OUP, Oxford 1991), 61-2; D. Nineham, *Christianity Medieval and Modern* (SCM, London, 1993), 19.

[4] See, particularly, K. E. Børresen, *Subordination and Equivalence: The Nature and Role of Woman in Augustine and Thomas Aquinas* (University Press of America, Washington, 1981), 94-156. Also, R. J. McGowen, 'Augustine's Spiritual Equality: The Allegory of Man and Woman with regard to *Imago Dei*', *REA* 33 (1987), 255-64; P. Brown, *Augustine of Hippo* (Faber, London, 1967), 390; Clark, op. cit., 127; S. L. Paul, 'Patriarchal Anthropology: Spiritual Equality / Natural Subordination', *Ex Audito* 13 (1997), particularly, 114-16.

[5] A sustained analysis of Jerome's thought is beyond the scope of this chapter. But see, for example, his letter to Eustochium and his work, *Against Jovinian*, extracted in E. Amt, *Women's Lives in Medieval Europe* (Routledge, New York, 1993), extracts 23-6 and in G. G. Coulton, *Life in the Middle Ages* (CUP, Cambridge, 1967), vol. 4, 5-28. See also, P. Brown, *The Body and Society. Men, Women and Sexual Renunciation in Early Christianity* (Faber, London, 1990), 366-86, 399-400; Brundage, op. cit., 82-5; S. D. Driver, 'The Development of Jerome's Views on the Ascetic Life', *RTAM* 62 (1995), 44-70; V. Burrus, 'The Heretical Woman as Symbol in Alexander, Athanasius, Epiphanius, and Jerome', *HTR* 84 (1991), particularly 243-6.

[6] See, particularly, *De institutione virginis* (PL 16.319-47), *De virginibus* (PL 16.197-243) and *Exhortatio virginitatis* (PL 16.347-79). Also, Brown, *The Body and Society*, 341-65; F. Bottomley, *Attitudes to the Body in Western Christendom* (Lepus, London, 1979), 65-71. Contra, F. Heer, *The Medieval World* (Cardinal, London, 1962), 318.

[7] J. van Bavel, 'Augustine's View of Women', *Augustiniana* 39 (1989), 5-53.

[8] See, for example, H. A. Deane, *The Political and Social Ideas of St*

Rosemary Ruether who has given, perhaps, the most scathing detraction of Augustine's views to date. She argues forcefully that Augustine's theology of woman stems from an androcentric understanding of the *imago Dei* in which woman, taken by herself, is not incorporated. Woman partakes of the image only in conjunction with the man. Taken from Adam, Eve symbolizes the corporeal side of man, leaving Adam to symbolize the spiritual dimension. Ruether says that it is this that determines Augustine's 'double definition of woman, as submissive body in the order of nature and "revolting" body in the order of sin...'. She continues,

> But he thinks that what she thus symbolizes, in the eye of male perception, is also what she is in her female nature! It never occurs to him that defining woman as something other than what she is, and placing her in subjection in the order of nature *from the perspective of the male visual impression of her as a 'body'* is nothing else than an expression, in the male himself, of that disorder of sin, and thus, in no way a stance for the definition.[9]

Ruether argues that Augustine's androcentric perspective is presupposed but never questioned as it ought to be. On this basis, Augustine is said to have viewed conjugal sexual intercourse as depersonal and unfeeling.

Our purpose in commenting on these opposite interpretations of Augustine's teaching on marriage (or man and woman, more generally) is to show that scholarship is as divided in its understanding of Augustine in this area as it is on the Reformers. This should alert us to the fact that on the basis of selective quotation either position is possible and, probably, that there is some truth in both. Or, to put this another way: perhaps Augustine is as ambivalent as the Reformers on the topic of the husband-wife relationship. Indeed, his ambivalence, itself,

---

Augustine (Columbia, New York, 1966), 54-5; R. Miles, *The Women's History of the World* (Michael Joseph, London, 1988), 68, 97; K. Armstrong, *The Gospel According to Woman* (Elm Tree Books, London, 1996), 7, 30-31.

[9] R. R. Ruether, 'Misogynism and Virginal Feminism in the Fathers of the Church' in idem, (ed.), *Religion and Sexism* (Simon and Schuster, New York, 1974), 157, 158 respectively – emphasis original. She says that 'woman is not really seen as a self-sufficient, whole person with equal honor, as the image of God in her own right, but is seen, ethically, as dangerous to the male' (156-7).

became a characteristic of the Middle Ages and of subsequent generations.

It is not feasible, nor desirable, here to undertake a complete review of Augustine's teaching on marriage in order to weigh up the contrasting interpretations. However, they will be taken into account in the following pages. Of necessity, the aim of this chapter is limited but its purpose is significant for the subsequent argument. Its intention is to summarize Augustine's understanding, particularly concentrating on those elements which find parallels in the Medieval period and in the *corpus* of Luther and of Calvin. This ought to add to our perception of the Reformers' continuance in and their divergence from traditional teaching. This in turn should allow us to evaluate what is distinctive about their theology at this point and whether, particularly Calvin, shows any demonstrably innovative thought in permitting women domestic equality, as is sometimes suggested.

We will discover, at least, two things. First, though Luther and Calvin follow Augustine closely in basics, in emphasis they soften his more negative stress on sexuality. Second, both Reformers (Calvin more obviously) maintain Augustine's strict teaching on the importance of hierarchical order – a teaching which, it will be argued, precludes any real shift towards a domestic liberation of women.

THE SIGNIFICANCE OF *ORDO*

Bottomley's opinion is correct: 'It is difficult to emphasize sufficiently the centrality of the notion of order in Augustine's thought. It affects his thinking on almost every topic.'[10] This is a significant point, both as it relates to Augustine's own understanding of marriage and because it is paralleled by the Reformers' later teaching.

There is, for Augustine, a divinely established, hierarchical order of the universe. He insists that all order is of God[11] –

---

[10] Bottomley, op. cit., 90. Also, E. Osborn, *Ethical Patterns in Early Christian Thought* (CUP, Cambridge, 1976), 181.

[11] '*Omnis ordo a Deo est*' – DVR 41.77.

creation, itself, is a manifestation of that order in the material world. Mankind's task, then, is to ensure that social order conforms to the eternal *ordo* as much as is possible, post-Fall, so that everything is perfectly ordered. For this to be accomplished they must maintain their appropriate place, performing the corresponding function.[12]

In relation to humanity, Augustine insists that their original condition was ordered and harmonious both in themselves as created, and with each other socially. In respect to themselves there was internal and external harmony. Their paradisal condition was essentially marked by integrity, wholeness and order. This meant, for example, that their soul was the master of their body.[13] If individual order is important to Augustine's marital ethics, so too is his teaching that mankind's nature is fundamentally social not solitary. As created, a harmonious social existence is natural to humanity and a desire for such is inherent in their makeup:

> By the very laws of his nature man is, so to speak, forced into social relationships and peace [*societatem pacemque*] with other men, so far as is possible.[14]

Personal order and societal tendency conjoin in Adam and Eve, for though at the beginning there *was* sexual differentiation, there existed unity in that duality.[15] Augustine posits this relationship

---

[12] DCD 19.13, '*Ordo est parium dispariumque rerum sua cuique loca tribuens dispositio.*' The following longer quotation is a helpful indication of the comprehensiveness of Augustine's teaching on order: 'The peace of the body, then, consists in the duly proportioned arrangement of its parts. The peace of the irrational soul is the harmonious repose of the appetites, and that of the rational soul the harmony of knowledge and action. The peace of body and soul is the well-ordered and harmonious life and health of the living creature. Peace between man and God is the well-ordered obedience of faith to eternal law. Peace between man and man is well-ordered concord. Domestic peace is the well-ordered obedience of faith between those of the family who rule and those who obey. Civil peace is a similar concord among citizens. The peace of the celestial city is perfectly ordered and harmonious enjoyment of God, and of one another in God. *The peace of all things is the tranquility of order*' (DCD 19.13 – emphasis added).

[13] See DPM 2.36; DNu 2.59 [xxxv], (ASW 5.308).

[14] DCD 19.12. See also, DBC 1.1, 8.8; DCD 12.21, 27; 19.5.

[15] Bottomley, op. cit., 91.

as the primary, paradigmatic, natural bond in human society[16] and so the union of husband and wife (*copula, copulatio*) becomes the irreducible unit within the natural order and the household (*domus*) becomes an extension of that.[17]

The family is situated, in Augustine's thought, in the *civitas terrena* as opposed to the *civitas Dei*. It is numbered among temporal blessings, together with health, possessions, honour, wife, friends, peace and so on. Though the subject of the two cities is important in its own right, its significance for the present study lies in the location of marriage in the earthly city, for that has something to say about Augustine's attitude towards it.[18] The cities (two groups of people – *duo genera hominum*) are defined in terms of the ultimate motivation of their members:

> The two cities were created by two kinds of love: the earthly city was created by self-love reaching the point of contempt for God, the Heavenly City by the love of God carried as far as contempt of self.[19]

This, in effect, describes two loyalties within human conflict. Temporal blessings are not to be preferred to heavenly[20] – people should not be entranced by them, nor attached to them. Nevertheless, they are to be used, in order 'to arrive at the full enjoyment of the spiritual', for the sake of attaining eternal life, as well as to foster peace between men and between men and women in present social existence.[21] In this context, family is an institution that engenders earthly peace after the disruption of sin's entrance into the world.[22]

As for Luther and Calvin, so for Augustine. There is a clear and important link between order in the family and civic order in the community. The former establishes and maintains order in the latter; the latter fosters an ordered context in which the former flourishes. Notice, though, Augustine's order is intrinsically hierarchical.

---

[16] It is significant that he begins at this point in *De bono coniugali*, 1.1. See also, *DCD* 12.22, 19.12; *EnP* 14.9.
[17] *DCD* 15.16. See Shaw, art. cit., 11.
[18] See *J* 2.8; *EnP* 61.8, 65.2-3, 99.4; *DCD* 1.13, 2.21, 11.1, 14.28, 15.1, 18.54.
[19] *DCD* 14.28.
[20] *EnP* 138.18; *JE* 40.10.
[21] See *DDoc* 1.22; *DCD* 19.16.
[22] *De ordine* 1.9.27. See also, *DCD* 19.17, 20, 26; *DME* 13.22.

> The union of male and female is the seedbed, so to speak, from which the city must grow. ... [I]t follows clearly enough that domestic peace serves civic peace, that is, that the ordered agreement of command and obedience among those who live together in a household serves the ordered agreement of command and obedience among citizens.[23]

Therefore, Christians are to pursue this peace and to maintain it through the institutions that promote it. Indeed, 'the whole use ... of things temporal has a reference to this result of earthly peace'.[24]

Augustine stresses the pursuance of peace or harmony for he has a continual, grim awareness of the proximity of disorder, disruption and disintegration. He says, 'There is, owing to the defects that have entered our nature, not to the constitution of our nature, a certain *necessary* tendency to sin.'[25] The resultant disorder is, in fact, part of the judgement of God.[26] Societal peace and order is, at best, precarious.

To summarize, Augustine's ethical thinking rests on the foundation of an eternal order that has been drastically upset by the Edenic sin. Man and woman, created to correspond – both individually and socially – to the primal order were made to live in social harmony with others, but find that sin has largely ruined that possibility. Now, by his providential working God, who is recreating mankind and re-establishing order through the *civitas Dei*, demands that Christians work as much as is possible towards maintaining order and peace through the institutions that they have been given in the *civitas terrena* – principally, through the household and through government. It is specifically to the former that we now turn.

---

[23] *DCD* 15.16. See also, *DCD* 19.13; E. Pagels, 'The Politics of Paradise: Augustine's Exegesis of Genesis 1-3 versus that of John Chrysostom', *HTR* 78 (1985), 85.

[24] *DCD* 19.14.

[25] *DNG* 79 [lxvi], (ASW 5.149) – emphasis added. Elsewhere he says, 'There is, therefore, in us lust of sin, which must not be suffered to reign; there are its desires, which we must not obey, lest obeying it reign over us' – *DC* 8. See also, his letter to Jerome on James 2:10 (ASW I.537-8); *Confessiones* 8.8.15; *DSD* 1.12.33; *En* 45; *DCD* 21.15. Interestingly, Augustine employs the image of sickness to depict sinfulness – a metaphor that the Reformers were later to use in the context of their understanding of marriage as a remedy against sin – *DC* 18.

[26] *DCD* 14.15.

MARRIAGE IN THE DIVINE PURPOSE

Augustine's foundational assertion concerning marriage is that the institution is essentially good[27] – though it is second best to celibacy.[28] The goodness of marriage needs to be his premise, for to say otherwise would be to bring into doubt both the goodness of God, who instituted marriage in creating Adam and Eve, and the good of the natural sociability of mankind. Marriage existed before sin,[29] the prelapsarian relationship between Adam and Eve is clearly a prototype for later marriage unions.[30] It would also be to cast suspicion over what Augustine sees as the good of marriage:

> Marriage, therefore, is a good in all things which are proper to the married state. And there are three: it is the ordained means of procreation, it is the guarantee [*fides*] of chastity, it is the bond of union [*conubii sacramentum*].[31]

Of the three, legitimate procreation generally takes priority – marriage was instituted for this reason. Theoretically, at least, this was the case before the Fall; Adam and Eve were made physically different with this in view.[32] The command to be fruitful and to increase, therefore, was given previous to sin's entrance, 'in order that the procreation of children might be recognized as part of the glory of marriage and not of the punishment of sin'.[33]

---

[27] This is often repeated in Augustine's *corpus*. See, for example, *DBC* 3; *Sermones* 304.3.2, 354.4.4. Because of the polemical nature of his work, he asserts this also by stating the negative: marriage is not an evil – *DBC* 8 11, 18; *DBV* 14; *DSV* 18; or that the evil entailed in marriage is a result of sin, not inherent – *DGrC* 2.42 [xxxvii] (ASW 5.252).

[28] See *De sancti virginitate*, PL 40.397-428; *DME* 1.30.63, 35.77-8; *DNu* 1.5; *DC* 1.

[29] *DGrC* 2.40 [xxxv] (ASW 5.251).

[30] *DBC* 1.1; *DNu* 1.8, 1.10 (ASW 5.266, 267); *CD* 1.9.

[31] *DGrC* [xxxiv] (ASW 5.251). See also, *DGrC* 2.42 (ASW 5.252); *DBC* 31; *DNu* 1.19 [xvii] (ASW 5.271),1.23 [xxi] (ASW 5.273).

[32] This is almost commonplace in Augustine's works. See, for example, *DBC* 19.22; *DNu* 1.16 [xiv] (ASW 5.270), 2.13 (ASW 5.287), 2.39 (ASW 5.300); *CF* 19.26, 22.47; *DME* 1.30.63, 2.18.65; *Serm* 1 (ASW 6.22.253). See also, L. Cahill, *Between the Sexes* (Fortress, Philadelphia, 1985), 113.

[33] *DCD* 14.22; 14.21, respectively. See also, *DGrC* 2.40 [xxxv] (ASW 5.251); *DC* 27.

Having stated that Augustine prioritizes procreation in this way, it should be noted that at times he does so with another end in view. In *De bono coniugali* he divides life's blessings into two categories: those which are good for their own sake and those which are necessary as a means to an end. In the former he includes wisdom, health, friendship; in the latter, learning, meat, drink, sleep, marriage, sexual intercourse. He illustrates this by juxtaposing marriage and friendship in the following way. He says that marriage is necessary, 'for the sake of friendship ... for hence subsists the propagation of the human kind, *wherein friendly fellowship is a great good*'.[34] He goes on to say that in the beginning it was necessary to marry in order to propagate, with the purpose of having children and of increasing friendship. However, now (that is, after Christ) there are enough people with whom to live in community and so the necessity for this reason is, largely, past. Having children, then, is never an end in itself – they are born for friendship with others (primarily, to have fellowship with God, through regeneration).[35] It is, partly, this emphasis on mutual friendship that van Bavel highlights as innovative – particularly as it permeates Augustine's teaching on the marital relationship itself.[36] This is a major theme to which we return below. However, at this point, it is a useful reminder to notice that, for Augustine, procreation always implies more than merely producing children. That procreation is a good of marriage also obliges both parents to raise the children thus born in the fear and the hope of God, 'with co-operation, with wholesome teaching, and earnest prayer'.[37]

The second good of marriage is the 'guarantee of chastity'. That is, after the Fall marriage became a remedy against fornication and extra-marital sexual sin.[38] Through marriage, sex is brought into an honest use, 'in order that out of the evil of lust the marriage union may bring to pass some good'. He says, 'For

---

[34] *DBC* 9 – emphasis added.

[35] *DSV* 6, 9. See *DBC* 17; *DNu* 1.14 [xiii] (ASW 5.269). Also, van Bavel, art. cit., 49.

[36] van Bavel, art. cit., 5-53.

[37] *DSV* 12. Also, *DBC* 22; *DNu* 1.5 [iv] (ASW 5.265), 1.20 [xviii] – 22 [xx] (ASW 5.272-3); *DSV* 24.

[38] See *DGrL* 8; *DBC* 10. Also, T. J. Bigham / A. T. Mollegen, 'The Christian Ethic' in R. W. Battenhouse (ed.), *Companion to the Study of St Augustine* (OUP, New York, 1955), 391.

this reason are they married, that lust being brought under a lawful bond, should not float at large without form and loose.'[39] The language here is significant. Marriage is a 'lawful bond' – legitimizing the sexual union between husband and wife, wherein pardon is procured, sin is covered and the disruptive forces of humanity's lust are restricted and contained.[40] His striking use of imagery depicting potential lack of control is evident again (as is a certain reticence, even on the subject of legitimate sexual intercourse itself) in *De bono viduitatis*. He writes that

> to be engaged in the begetting of children, not after the fashion of dogs by promiscuous use of females, but by honest order of marriage, is not an affliction such as we are able to blame in a man.[41]

Elsewhere, he says,

> The good, then, of marriage lies not in the passion of desire, but in a certain legitimate and honourable measure in using that passion, appropriate to the propagation of children, not the gratification of lust.[42]

So, marriage makes a good use of an evil thing when the spouses are able to restrain their concupiscence by the constraints of matrimony.[43]

The third good inherent in marriage is that of its sacramental nature. By this, Augustine indicates that, 'The content of the sacrament [*res sacramenti*] is ... the indestructibility of the conjugal bond by which the human union reflects the union of Christ and his Church.'[44] He does not, thereby, indicate a

---

[39] *DBC* 3, 5, respectively.

[40] See also, *DBC* 11; *DNu* 1.16 [xiv] (ASW 270), 1.18 [xvi] (ASW 5.271). Both men and women need to find 'relief in their [sexual] infirmity' – *Serm* 1 (ASW 6.25.254-5).

[41] *DBV* 11. See also, *DGrC* 2.38 [xxxiii] (ASW 5.250); *Serm* 1 (ASW 6.25.254-5).

[42] *DPM* 1.57.

[43] On the subject of concupiscence see G. W. Schlabach, '"Love is the Head of the Soul": The Grammar of Continence in Augustine's Doctrine of Christian Love', *JECS* 6 (1998), 59-92. The writer stresses that the idea of concupiscence did not simply grow out of a crude preoccupation with sexuality, but from a complex analysis of the sources of all human behaviour (59).

[44] Børresen, op. cit., 106.

conveying of saving grace or the like but, rather, that the indissolubility of the marital covenant reflects the nature of the relationship between Christ and his Church[45] –'the marriage fellowship of faith ... cannot be dissolved'.[46]

The three aspects of the good of marriage will become theological premises in succeeding generations and are prominent in the thinking of both Luther and Calvin in the sixteenth century.[47] They imply both marital relationship, generally, and sexual relationship as an intrinsic part of that union. It is to these that we now turn.

HIERARCHY AND MUTUAL FRIENDSHIP

The relationship between the husband and wife derives its character from a wider structure. It is important to repeat that in Augustine's thought the universal *ordo* is inherently hierarchical. This is so on a 'cosmic' level and then is reflected in the civic and the domestic realms. Augustine speaks of the latter as the 'primitive order of peace', *viz*, man is subject to Christ, woman is subject to man.[48] In this arrangement, the wife has to be obedient, humble and peace-keeping.[49]

Clearly, spiritual freedom in Christ does not materially affect the arrangement. The following is Augustine's comment on Galatians 3:28.

> Although the differences between nations, life situations *and sexes* are abolished by the unity of faith, yet these differences remain in existence with our mortal relationships [*conversatione mortali*] with one another, because our body is still dead because of sin (Rom. 8:10). On our way through this life, we have to keep this order [*ordinem*].[50]

---

[45] *DNu* 2.23 [xxi] (ASW 5.273); *DBC* 31.

[46] *DBC* 5.

[47] See chapters 6 and 9 of the present study.

[48] '...ac sic in pristinam pacem atque ordinem et uir Christo et mulier uiro subicitur'– *DSD* 1.12.34.

[49] *DBC* 11; *DNu* 1.10 [ix] (ASW 5.267) – citing 1 Cor. 11:3, Col. 3:18, 1 Pet. 3:6; *Sermones* 51.11.18; *EnP* 143.6.

[50] *Expositio Epistulae ad Galatas* [*EXG*] 28 (emphasis added). Gal. 3:28,

This dismissal of any social levelling resulting from the grace of God in the gospel is later reflected in the Reformers' interpretation of Galatians 3:28 but, in the latter case, on the grounds that the gospel does not alter social order because it has been divinely fixed. At this particular juncture, however, Augustine seems to suggest that social hierarchy is the result of sin but that it ought to be respected anyway, simply on the grounds that it is present reality. Van Bavel seems to accept this passage as Augustine's definitive teaching on the matter.[51] The conclusion thus drawn is that 'Augustine's refusal to consider the subjection of one human being to another as something natural, and his view of faith as the abolition of such subordination' is a positive contribution. However, this seems to be an over-optimistic interpretation of the passage. At best, Augustine appears to allow only *theoretically* for the abolition of any hierarchical distinction. In practical terms, it seems to make no difference at all – it is retained. In fact, on the whole and more often than not, he sees hierarchical structure as 'natural' in the sense of being inherent in created existence or of being founded on an antecedent superiority[52] – as do Luther and Calvin. In any event, he thereby promotes a *status quo* of social hierarchy.[53]

Augustine's familial hierarchicalism is uncompromising. For him, the primal state of Adam and Eve implied and continues to demand hierarchy. It was part of God's intention and original order.[54] In this arrangement, of course, the Lord submits the female to the male – the latter rules, the former obeys.[55] In *De continentia*, Augustine outlines the logic of it in the following way:

> The Apostle (Paul) has made known to us three particular unions, Christ and the Church, husband and wife, spirit and flesh. ... All the things are good when in them [some people] set over by way of pre-

---

'There is no such thing as ... *male* or *female*, for you are all one person in Christ Jesus' (*REB* – emphasis added).

[51] van Bavel, art. cit., 13-14.
[52] Pagels, art. cit., 85-6.
[53] See Børresen, op. cit., 94; Brown, *The Body and Society*, 400.
[54] *DGnL* 9.59.
[55] *DGnL* 8.23.44; *DGnM* 1.19.30; *Serm* Jn 6:55 (ASW 6.2.505); *DCD* 19.12; *Confessiones* 1.2.17. See also, Børresen, op. cit., 62.

eminence, [and others] made subject in a becoming manner, observe the beauty of order.[56]

The consequence of this is that the man must follow Christ's example, the woman the man's.[57] This is intrinsic to Augustine's androcentric perspective in which the woman is defined against the man – he is the supreme *exemplum* of humanity. Børresen concludes, 'the existence of woman is ordained for that of man, her state of life is defined by her relationship with him'.[58]

Though the husband-wife hierarchical structure originates in creation, it degenerates into a kind of servitude (*servitutem*), for the wife at least,[59] as a consequence of and the punishment for the Fall. That which was voluntary is now mandatory – a punishment on the woman.[60] The resultant dynamic of the relationship makes domestic order precarious – both want to control. Augustine's intention is to stress male authority (*imperare, imperium*) and dominance – which, however, the man has to establish and maintain. Shaw illustrates this, saying that, 'If a husband won and the woman was subdued to his *dominium*, there reigned a *pax recta* in the household; if not and the woman dominated, a *pax perversa*.' However, in theory, the husband's control was near total: 'Wives were not permitted so much as to dispense alms or to change their clothes without their husband's permission.'[61] The character of the rule, thus delineated, will include coercion and

---

[56] *DC* 23.

[57] *DCR* 18. Interestingly, part of this arrangement is that the man must take on 'the office of the Episcopate' in his own household in order 'to take care how his household believe, that none of them fall into heresy' – *Serm* Matt. 25:24 (ASW 6.1.406). Luther and Calvin later employ the same image for the *paterfamilias* in similar contexts.

[58] Børresen, op. cit., 93.

[59] It should be noticed, perhaps, that in one place, at least, Augustine speaks of 'mutual servitude'; but the reference is to sexual mutuality, as the context makes clear – DBC 6.6.

[60] *DGnL* 11.37.50. Pagels, art. cit., 85-6, interpreting Augustine, says, 'God himself reinforced the husband's authority over his wife, placing divine sanction upon the social, legal and economic machinery of male domination.' See also, Børresen, op. cit., 62.

[61] Shaw, art. cit., 28 – he cites *Epistulae* 262.4-9. See also, G. Gould, 'Women in the Writings of the Fathers: Language, Belief and Reality' in W. J. Sheils / D. Wood (eds), *Women in the Church* (Blackwell, Oxford 1990), 1-13. Also, *EnP* 143.6.

punishment, for (like society itself) the family has a tendency to become disordered by sin.[62]

Nevertheless, to a limited extent Augustine's teaching on male dominance is softened by emphases on service and friendship. For example, he explains the relationship in the following passage:

> This is the origin of domestic peace, or well-ordered concord of those in the family who rule and those who obey. For *they who care for the rest rule* – the husband the wife ... and they who are cared for obey – the women their husbands... .[63] But in the family of the just man who lives by faith ... *even those who rule serve those whom they seem to command.*[64]

He goes on to explain this in a way that will be closely paralleled by Calvin, in particular:[65] Husbands do not rule because they love power or authority, but 'because they love mercy'.[66] Together with ruling, defined as service, comes a stress on mutual love. That is, within the household hierarchical authority is balanced by a 'counter-ideology of love'.[67] He speaks of a man's wife as his darling (*cara*), partner (*coniunx*) and household slave (*famula*).[68]

In patristic thought, generally, *caritas* functions as a cohesive force in the community.[69] Certainly, in Augustine the concept of

---

[62] *DCD* 19.16, 12.1.

[63] He adds, 'the parents the children, the masters the servants' and 'the children their parents, the servants their masters', respectively.

[64] *DCD* 19.14 – emphases added.

[65] See Calvin on the concept of mutual subjection in chapter 10.

[66] Previously, quoting 1 Tim. 5:8 (concerning providing for one's own household), Augustine has said that the household is the man's primary care, 'for the law of nature and of society gives him readier access to them and *greater opportunity of serving them*' – *DCD* 19.14 (emphasis added). See also, *DCD* 19.15-16; *EnP* 124.7-8. R. A. Marcus, *Saeculum: History and Society in the Theology of St Augustine* (CUP, Cambridge, 1970), 197-8, suggests that in Augustine's thought care is defined in terms of authority: 'to guide is to exercise authority (*imperant enim qui consulunt*) ... to be guided is to obey (*obediunt autem quibus consulitur*)'.

[67] The phrase is Shaw's – art. cit., 18.

[68] *EnP* 143.6 – cited by Shaw, art. cit., 32. Augustine also says that the husband is the head of the wife, 'through sincere love [*sed sinceri amoris legibus praeficis*]' – *DME* 1.30.63.

[69] D. Herlihy, *Women Family and Society in Medieval Europe* (Berghahn Books, Providence, 1995), 121. Herlihy suggests that the progressive weakening

caritas is central to his ethical ideas and, specifically, to his understanding of the relationship between the husband and wife. Consistent with the foundational idea of *ordo* in Augustine's thought, *caritas,* itself, has to be ordered.[70] The husband has to love his wife before anyone else (except God, of course, who always takes the precedence). Nevertheless, wives take priority over neighbours and enemies![71]

Employing a New Testament image, Augustine insists in the same way that men love their own bodies, so they must love their wives, who, in turn, should reciprocate that love.[72] He speaks of 'loving affection' (*affectus dilectionis*) between spouses and bases it on the undergirding notion of Eve's creation from Adam:

> [T]he fact that woman was made for the man from his own side, shows us clearly how affectionate [*cara*] should be the union of husband and wife.[73]

Marital love is to be selfless, seeking to please the other partner,[74] inclusive of a sense of loyalty and solidarity,[75] a mutual service of sustaining (*excipiendae*) one another's weakness,[76] and the wife's love (in particular, but not exclusively) is to be consoling.[77] However, this is not necessarily to be interpreted as implying mutual affection for the sake of companionship alone. There is a salient point that would seem to compromise that judgement. By

---

of paternal authority in Roman times demanded the strengthening of domestic affection as another form of bonding in the household.

[70] '...ille autem juste et sancte vivet qui ordinatam dilectionem habet' – *DDoc* 1.27.28. See also, *DGrL* 15.31; *J* 8.10; *Epistulae* 137.5.17; *Soliloquia* 1.13.22; *De Ordine* 83.35; *JE* 41.8.8. Also, Clark, op. cit., 42; Bigham, art. cit., 371-97; Osborn, op. cit., 174-5.

[71] *Confessiones* 4.9.14; *Serm* Matt. 22:2 (ASW 6.10.398); *EnP* 56.16.

[72] *DDoc* 1.25.26; *CF* 19.26; *DCD* 22.17; *DME* 2.18.65; *DSD* 1.15.42. At *DME* 1.30.63, Augustine repeats the idea that men have authority over their wives, 'not to mock the weaker sex, but in the laws of unfeigned love'. Also, *DSV* 55; *DBC* 1.1.

[73] *DCD* 12.28. See also, *DCD* 14.22, 21.26; *DBC* 1.1, 3.3; *DGnM* 2.12.17.

[74] See *DBC* 3.3; *DGnL* 11.42; *DBV* 8.11; letter to Possidius, Bishop of Calama [245] (ASW 1.587-8).

[75] Augustine remarks that Adam fell into sin because of his love for Eve. He had eaten with her *amicali benevolentia* (out of the nature of a friend). See *DGnL* 11.42; *DCD* 14.11; *DBC* 7.7. Also, Brown, *The Body and Society*, 402.

[76] *DBC* 6. Augustine seems to have sexual weakness in mind.

[77] *EnP* 35.5.

this we refer to the fact that, at times, Augustine's emphasis seems to be on making a go of what is manifestly considered second best.

For instance, he stresses that if the divine intention had been primarily to create a companion for the man, then God would have supplied another man – not a woman:

> If it was company and good conversation that Adam needed, it would have been much better arranged to have two men together, as friends, not a man and a woman.[78]

On the basis of this passage, Børresen analyses Augustine's perspective on Genesis 2:18-24, stating that the text raises two significant questions for him. First, what is the purpose of woman's creation? Second, what is the significance of the way her body is formed? Børresen's conclusion is that Augustine cannot find any other reason for Eve's specific existence than that she is a passive help to Adam in the work of procreation.[79] This is borne out by his comments on Genesis 1:27-28 in *De nuptiis et concupiscientia*, in which he states that the woman was provided by God, specifically, for child-bearing.[80]

This appears to be where a woman's value mostly lies. It is not so much on the possibility of companionship, but rather that she is capable of helping her husband to procreate – though it should be noted that Augustine, occasionally, emphasizes that the husband, too, has the duty to have children with his wife.[81] The difference between these is that this is *not* where Augustine places the man's intrinsic worth in the manner that he seems to with reference to the wife. What emerges, then, is that, in Augustine's view, conjugal companionship is always significantly between a superior and an inferior. It would be better for the husband to be with another man as a companion, if that was the divine priority. But, because it is not, he needs to tolerate friendship with his wife. Thus, in softening his hierarchical teaching by a secondary stress on marital love and friendship, in effect, he comes full circle because that teaching is so heavily qualified by implications of inferiority on the woman's part in the crucial area of created

---

[78] *DGnL* 9.5.9. See also, *DGnL* 9.7.11-12; *DGrC* 2.40 [xxxv] (ASW 5.251).
[79] Børresen, op. cit., 17.
[80] *DNu* 2.12 (ASW 5.287).
[81] See, for example, *DBC* 6.

sociability. This connotation of woman's inferiority is reinforced in other areas of Augustine's thought – yet to a large extent his writing remains ambivalent. However, some of these areas will be seen as particularly significant to our study.

First, for instance, although the *imago Dei* fundamentally resides in the *rationalis mens*,[82] both man and woman possess the image through creation[83] and both experience its renewal through grace.[84] In this sense, the husband and wife are spiritual equals. The problem arises, however, when Augustine seeks to conform Paul's teaching (1 Corinthians 11:7) with that of Genesis in formulating an account of the *imago Dei*. Here, again, the woman is shown to be the inferior of the man:

> When woman is assigned as a helpmate, which pertains to her alone, she is not the image of God; however, what pertains to man alone is the image of God, just as fully and completely as when he is joined with the woman.[85]

On the basis of this passage, van Bavel's conclusion that the ground for woman's inferiority is actually social, seems reasonable. However, the situation is more complex than that because Augustine would say that woman is created with the purpose of being a helpmate to the man. That is her role by creation and it signifies something of the fixed social order imposed on created reality. According to Augustine, even in this woman remains intrinsically inferior. It is true that she (together with her husband) possesses the image of God, but that is heavily

---

[82] The word 'although' in this sentence conveys a perceived problem in Augustine's thinking at this point, for the woman came to be regarded as representing irrational, passionate and sexual aspects of the human composite, yet retains possession of the image of God – see, particularly, *DGnM* 2.11.15, 2.14.21. Also, *DT* 12.7.10; *J* 8.6; *DCD* 12.23 *DGNL* 12.6-14; *Epistulae* 243.10 and Gould, art. cit., 10; Brown, *Augustine*, 205. This is in line with Greek thought in which woman is associated with the body and man with the mind – see, for example, Aristotle, *Politics* 1.5.

[83] *EnP* 48.2, 96.12; *DGnL* 9.3.6.

[84] Though, in his earlier works (e.g. *DGnL* 6.27.28), Augustine teaches that the image is entirely lost by the Fall, he later corrected this, saying that it was merely deformed and in need of reforming – see *Retractiones* 2.50; *De Spiritu et Littera*, 48.

[85] *DT* 12.7.10 – quoted by McGowen, art. cit., 258. See also, H. Somers, 'Image de Dieu: Les Sources de l'exégèse augustinienne', *REA* 7 (1961), 105-25.

qualified in the androcentrically weighted, social outworking of her married life.[86]

Børresen is helpful at this point. She shows that because in woman there exists a duality between *homo exterior* and *homo interior*, she possesses the *imago Dei* in her rational soul, but does not reflect that image on a bodily level (in so far as she is *femina*). 'When woman, therefore, fulfils her function of being man's helpmeet, a function she carries out on a bodily level, she is not the image of God.'[87] We see, then, that the inferiority of the female, in fact, is closely bound up with bodily inferiority.

Augustine also suggests that the woman's subjection is due to the fact that she is the weaker sex. She is said to be weaker physically (*infirmior*), in needing support (*imbecillior*), in her frailty (*fragilitas*), and having a more delicate constitution (*delicatior*).[88] However, according to van Bavel, there is only one instance where he refers to her as intellectually inferior:

> There is a natural order among beings [*ordo naturalis in hominibus*]: *wives* have to serve their husbands ... the weaker intellect serves the stronger intellect. The person who prevails intellectually should have a greater dominance. This is a question of justice in all forms of dominance and servitude.[89]

Augustine's general teaching is better summed up in the following quotation from his *Confessiones:* 'In her mind, regarding intellectual understanding, the woman certainly possesses a nature equal to that of the man.'[90] The contradiction in the two passages highlights the problem of reading Augustine on this subject. Nevertheless, his predominant thought seems to be that women are *not* intellectually inferior. And, in fact, when

---

[86] It is the androcentrism of Augustine's interpretation that Ruether, art. cit., argues so forcefully against – as noted above. Speaking of the same problem in different terms, Børresen, op. cit., 31, concludes that, 'In both cases, whether subjection is based upon the difference of her *conformatio* or on her position as helper (*adjutorium*), the inferiority of woman is linked to her sex, *homo exterior*.'

[87] Ibid., 28 (see 27-9). Also, *DGnL* 3.22, 6.7.

[88] Van Bavel, art. cit., 7-9, See also, *DME* 1.30.63; *DCD* 22.24.

[89] *Quaest. in Hept. CCL* 33.59 – quoted more fully by van Bavel, art. cit., 8. See also, *DCD* 19.14.16; *Epistulae* 104.2.7, 130.6.12, 133.2, 138.2.14.

[90] '...*quae haberet quidem in mente rationalis intellegentiae parem naturem*' – *Confessiones* 13.32.47. Contra, Gould, art. cit., 7.

addressing the moral strengths of the male and female, Augustine singles out the latter as generally showing greater self-control and marital faithfulness and the former as warranting the stronger reproaches.[91]

It is clear that Augustine sees woman as inferior to man. He bases this on what he sees to be God's intention in creation, on her constitution and on her social function as wife and mother. These three are closely interrelated in Augustine's theology. It is also apparent that Augustine sees much good in woman and wishes to posit her equality in terms of the possession of the *imago Dei* (in some ambiguous way), her renewal by divine grace and her mutual obligations and rights in the conjugal sphere.[92] There is, however, a great deal of ambivalence because of the dual stress on both subordination and equivalence – two components of his anthropology that Augustine holds together in tension. However, nowhere is tension more apparent than in the area of the sexual relationship of marriage.

SEXUALITY WITHIN MARRIAGE

No other aspect of Augustine's teaching on the relationship between the husband and wife attracts so much criticism as that of his understanding of the sexual element in marriage. Most scholars point out his obsession with sexual lust,[93] while some draw attention to what they see as his own personal struggles or, even, inadequate psychological development. Though moderate,

---

[91] Van Bavel, art. cit., 16 – citing *Sermones* 9.12, 132.2.2, *DVR* 41.78 and *Sermones* 224.3.3, 392.4.4-5, respectively. See also, Serm John 6.55 (ASW 6.505). He is also aware of the double standards imposed by Roman divorce law and defends women against its discriminatory bias – *Sermones* 9.4, 153.5.6, 392.4-6.

[92] Brundage, op. cit., 93, speaks of this as follows: 'The marital debt created a parity of rights and obligations between the spouses. Each had an equal right to demand that it be paid; each had an equal obligation to comply with the other's demands. Equality of the sexes in marriage meant equality in the marriage-bed, but not outside of it.' See also, van Bavel, art. cit., 11, who cites *Sermones* 51.13.22.

[93] See, for example, Bottomley, op. cit., 81-96; P. Lehmann, 'The Anti-Pelagian Writings' in Battenhouse (ed.), op. cit., 221, Brooke, op. cit., 56; Deane, op. cit., 54; H. Chadwick, *Augustine* (OUP, Oxford, 1986), 90; Brown, *The Body, and Society*, 387.

Brundage is, perhaps, somewhat typical. He says that Augustine's tendency to isolate sex, treating it as evil, 'presumably mirrored his own feeling, when he was contemplating marriage himself, that he was a slave to lust. The feeling, in turn, seems to have been based upon disgust at his own sexual cravings and desires.'[94] The viability of this judgement is supported by Augustine's own comments. For example, he writes retrospectively in a later work that 'the madness of raging lust exercised its supreme dominion over me'.[95]

The significance of this aspect of his thought is twofold. First, Augustine takes his own negative sexual experience as indicative of Adam's post-fallen experience and therefore as indicative for *all* sexual experience. Second, the resultant construal of sexual experience is dominated by the conflict between what Augustine sees as an essentially good created order and the evil consequences of sin that permeate human activity at this point of sexual relationship and contact. This conflict, as Børresen notes, becomes the principal theme in Augustine's teaching on marriage.[96] The conflict is apparent in a passage from an early work in which Augustine exhorts the husband

> to love the creature of God whom he desires to be transformed and renewed; but to hate the corruptible and mortal conjugal connection and sexual intercourse [*odisse autem coniunctionem copulationemque corruptibilem atque mortalem*] – that is, to love in her what is characteristic of a human being, to hate in her what belongs to her as a wife (*DSD* 1.15.41).

---

[94] Brundage, op. cit., 90. In fact Augustine does not single out sex, or even sexual lust, as evil. He certainly speaks of it predominantly, but as merely one of the few basic drives of sinful man – together with the lust for power, or domination and covetousness, for example – *DNu* 2.36 [xxi] (ASW 5.297); Deane, op. cit., 44-5. However, on the main point, see also, Pagels, art. cit., 76; Brown, *Augustine*, 390; idem, *The Body and Society*, 387; Rowe, op. cit., 82; and more cynically, Ruether, art. cit., 150-78; Armstrong, op. cit., 30-31. Conversely, S. Dowell, *They Two Shall be One: Monogamy in History and Religion* (Collins, London, 1990), 92-3, in disagreeing with this conclusion, suggests that the problem lies in the theology and culture which Augustine inherited. In fact, it is probably the case that Augustine's neurosis (for that is what it appears) was fed by contemporary cultural and theological assumptions related to sexuality and gender.

[95] *Confessiones* 2.2.3. See also, 6.16.25.

[96] Børresen, op. cit., 111-12.

However, it would be quite wrong to take such thought as the *formative* idea behind Augustine's teaching on the marital sexual relationship. While it is true that Augustine is highly suspicious of the sexual act, he is so because of the flaw in humanity (*concupiscentia carnis*) which appears to drive them towards the flesh and away from the spirit. Yet, even within his negative understanding of sexuality, Augustine stresses the fundamentally good nature of Adam and Eve's physicality – a goodness that still permeates the nature of marriage and of sexual intercourse, though, now, spoiled by sin. This is an emphasis that appears often and is understandably missed by most writers on the subject.

The idea that marriage and the sexual act are intrinsically good is a necessary theological corollary following Augustine's assertion of the goodness both of God and of his creation (including humanity).[97] From the former perspective, he claims that procreation is a corroborative work between God, the Creator, and the married couple[98] – it cannot be envisaged, in itself, as *entirely* sinful. From the latter perspective, Augustine affirms the full physicality and sociability of Adam and Eve – they are the paradigm for succeeding generations.[99] Though Augustine's teaching in this area is complicated in that his own understanding developed,[100] it is clear that he concludes that Adam and Eve were set in Eden to found a *populus*. Sexual

---

[97] See, for example, *DNu* 1.4 (ASW 5.264): '[T]he soul and the body, and all the natural endowments which are implanted in the soul and the body, *even in the persons of sinful men,* are still gifts of God; for it is God who made them, and not they themselves' (emphasis added). See also, *DNu* 2.36 [xxi] (ASW 5.298), 53 [xxxi] (ASW 5.305); *DBC* 22, 27; *DNG* 65 [lv] (ASW 5.144); EnP 9, 10; *DCD* 13.16, 19.18.

[98] *DCD* 22.24; *DNu* 2.12 (ASW 5.287), 2.26 (ASW 5.293), 2.29 (ASW 5.294-5), 2.35-6 [xx-xxi] (ASW 5.297-8). Augustine states that God *could* give progeny without human intercourse taking place (*DBC* 2) This seems to safeguard the notion of divine capability while, at the same time, recognizing the divine intention in present conjugal experience.

[99] *DGNL* 9.6. 10; *DBC* 2.2.

[100] In his earlier work (e.g. *DGnM*,1.19.30) he says that Adam and Eve would not have procreated and that the blessings mentioned are to be spiritually interpreted. However, later, in *DBC* 2.2, he suggests two possibilities: either Adam and Eve would have procreated by God's power alone or by carnal procreation. And later, (e.g. *DGnL* 9.3, 9, 10, 11; *DNu* 2.37 [xxii] (ASW 5.298); *DCD* 14.17, 21; *Retractiones* 1.9.2, 1.11.8) he speaks of innocent sexual intercourse under the domination of the rational will.

impulse and virility were divinely appointed; indeed, at that time sexual members were not suggestive of shame as (according to Augustine) they are today. Rather, they deserved to be 'commended and praised as the work of God'.[101]

Significantly, even coitus, *per se,* is said to be good, not evil: 'The connubial embrace ... as intended for the procreation of children, *considered in itself simply,* and without reference to fornication, *is good and right ... the embrace is not, after all, a sin in itself.*'[102] It is noticeable that Augustine stipulates legitimate sexual intercourse (that is, inside the bounds of marriage) and with the intention to procreate. However, the point is that he can and does teach that sexual intercourse, in itself, is not sinful. Elsewhere, he repeats this important, basic idea: 'necessary sexual intercourse for begetting *is free from blame*'.[103] That this more positive judgement is relatively rare and that it is clouded by Augustine's greater emphasis on and obsession with the sinful concomitants of the act, should not cause us to forget its underlying theological and ethical importance.

However, the moral criterion for judging sexual intercourse is not its origin, nor its intrinsic nature, but whether or not it conforms to its main purpose – that of creating offspring (*proles*):[104]

> The union, then, of male and female *for the purpose of procreation* is the natural good of marriage. But he makes a bad use of this good who uses it bestially so that *his intention* is on the gratification of lust, instead of the desire of offspring.[105]

That is, it is without sin if a married couple have sexual intercourse with the intention of having children. However, if they have intercourse for pleasure (providing there is no attempt at contraception) there is venial sin which, nevertheless, marriage 'covers' and excuses. He says,

---

[101] *CD* 1.31; *DNu* 2.14 [v] (ASW 5.288), respectively.

[102] *DGrC* 2.43 (ASW 5.253) – emphases added.

[103] *DBC* 11. See also, *DNu* 1.13 (ASW 5.269), 2.39 [xxiv] (ASW 5.300).

[104] Børresen, op. cit., 114. She cites *DBC* 3.3; *DNu* 1.4.5. Augustine says that 'the ornament of marriage is the chastity of begetting' (*DBC* 14).

[105] *DNu* 1.5 [iv] (ASW 5.265) – emphases added.

> Carnal concupiscence ... must not be ascribed to marriage: it is only to be tolerated in marriage. It is not a good which comes out of the essence of marriage, but an evil which is the accident of original sin.[106]

A lengthy passage from *De nuptiis et concupiscientia* outlines Augustine's recurrent ideas on this matter:

> [W]henever it comes to the actual process of generation, the very embrace which is lawful and honourable cannot be effected without the ardour of lust, so as to be able to accomplish that which appertains to the use of reason and not of lust. Now, this ardour, whether following or preceding the will, does somehow, by a power of its own, move the members which cannot be moved simply by the will, and in this manner it shows itself not to be a servant of a will that commands it, but rather to be the punishment of a will which disobeys it. It shows, moreover, that it must be excited, not by a free choice, but by a certain seductive stimulus, and that on this very account it produces shame.[107]

Several things are worth briefly noting. First, Augustine emphasizes the fundamental goodness of sexual intercourse. That is his starting point, as we have observed. Second, such is the nature of the postlapsarian sinfulness of men and women that the sexual act cannot be performed without sin attaching to it.[108] Third, he draws a definite dichotomy between reason and lust, or the will and the emotion – a dichotomy that lies at the heart of his obsession with sexual matters. Though in paradisal condition, the motion of the body would have been 'quietly discharged, undisturbed by lustful passion',[109] lust (which is, itself, passed on by generation[110]) has now usurped the power of the will; desire has escaped the mind's control.[111] This spells personal and,

---

[106] *DNu* 1.19 [xvii] (ASW 5.271). Earlier he had said, 'Marriage makes pardonable that which does not essentially appertain to itself' – *DNu* 1.16 [xiv] (ASW 5.270). See also, *DBV* 5; *DGrC* 2.43 (ASW 5.253); *CD* 1.33; *DBC* 11, 12; *DPM* 2.43, 45.

[107] *DNu* 1.27 [xxiv] (ASW 5.275).

[108] *Serm* 1 (ASW 6.21.253); *DBC* 6.

[109] *DGrC* 2.41 [xxxvi] (ASW 5.252). Also, *DNu* 2.53 [xxxi] (ASW 5.305); *DCD* 14.23, 24.

[110] *DNU* 1.25 [xxiii] (ASW 5.274).

[111] See *DCD* 14.20; *DC* 29; *DNu* 1.7 [vi] (ASW 5.266). Also, Bottomley, op. cit., 81–96; Brown, *The Body and Society*, 406, 416; van Bavel, art. cit., 33–4. The

almost inevitably, social disorder. Fourth, for Augustine, the rupture between what man was in Eden and what he became after the Fall is clearly seen in the independent shameless movement (*impudens motus*)[112] of the sexual organs. Fifth, he mentions punishment and shame [113] – punishment for the autonomous turning of man's will from God, shame (also, in itself, a punishment) because of the conspicuousness of the member's activity.

Augustine says that marriage has 'a diseased condition about it'.[114] Yet, he is not entirely pessimistic: he retains eschatological hope of healing and renewal. 'Although [lust's] guilt is now taken away, it still remains until our entire infirmity be healed by the advancing renewal of our inner man.' Until that time men and women must overcome lust by the fear of God, 'moderating, and in a certain way limiting ... and ordering ... within fixed limits its unquiet and inordinate motion.'[115] The 'fixed limits' are evidently defined by legitimate marriage and the intention to procreate.

---

following passage seems to indicate Augustine's own experience – he says that sexual lust, 'not only takes possession of the whole body and outward members, but also makes itself felt within, and moves the whole man with a passion in which mental emotion is mingled with bodily appetite, so that the pleasure which results is the greatest of all bodily pleasures. So possessing indeed is this pleasure, that at the moment of time in which it is consummated, all mental activity is suspended' (*DCD* 14.16).

[112] *DCD* 13.24.

[113] *DCD* 14.17; *Sermones* 51.3.4; *EnP* 70.1. See also, Brown, *Augustine*, 388-9: '[I]t was a permanent punishment, it was presented as a permanent tendency ... imprisoning a man in the sexual element of his imagination.' Augustine's significant comment reads, '[T]he devil inflicted a heavy wound, not indeed on marriage itself but on man and woman by whom marriage is made, by prevailing on them to disobey God, ... a sin which is requited in the course of the divine judgement by the reciprocal disobedience of man's own members' [*DNu* 2.54 (ASW 5.305)]. Augustine interprets the idea that the eyes of Adam and Eve were opened (Gen. 3:7) as indicative of sexual shame. See, for example, *DGnL* 9.11.19, 11.32.42; *DCD* 14.17-19. Brown, op. cit., 422, says, 'In Augustine's mind, sexuality served one, strictly delimited purpose: it spoke, with terrible precision, of one single, decisive event within the soul. It echoed in the body the unalterable consequence of mankind's first sin.' He concludes, 'It was a drastically limited vision of a complex phenomenon.' See also, *DNu* 2.59 [xxxv] (ASW 5.308); *DPM* 2.36; *DCD* 14.18.

[114] *DNu* 2.55 [xxxiii] (ASW 5.306).

[115] *DNu* 1.28 [xxv] (ASW 5.275), *DSV* 34, *DC* 27, respectively. Also, *DBC* 34; *DNu* 1.9 [viii] (ASW 5.267).

Within these boundaries, Augustine reluctantly exhorts husbands and wives to 'descend to [sexual intercourse] with regret'.[116]

CONCLUSION

The major areas of Augustine's teaching on the husband and wife relationship – most relevant to the present study – are three in number. Delineated more fully above, they may be summarised as follows.

1. In grounding his understanding of created reality in the hierarchical concept of *ordo,* Augustine determines that mankind's domestic arrangement (as reflective of the wider structure) will be hierarchical by nature. Because the husband and wife relationship is posited as the irreducible unit within natural order, that relationship is both intrinsically hierarchical and fixed. The husband is the authoritative head of the household; the wife is to be obedient to him. And, though Augustine does not identify sin with disorder, the relationship is very strong. To go against the divinely established hierarchical order would be to sin. A necessity is laid upon both spouses to establish in concrete experience and to maintain a patriarchal, marital order.

Clearly, if Augustine's teaching at this point was to be closely followed by Luther and Calvin (and we shall argue that it is) then their traditionalism would, theologically, preclude any possibility of innovative teaching on the domestic liberation of women. Potentially, this modification would only be possible if either Reformer was to alter the Augustinian perception *of ordo* in his own theology. Contemporary revisionists would reason in this way. Douglass and others seek to show that in Calvin, at least, *ordo* is a contingent fact, not an immutable one.[117]

What we will argue is that, for two reasons, Calvin's theology of order dismisses any chance of a more liberated understanding of the wife's status and position. The first is simply that his teaching on the marriage relationship is, arguably, so close to

---

[116] *Serm* 1 (ASW 6.25.254).

[117] Revisionist ideas are summarised in chapters 1 and 8 of the present study.

Luther's (who remains strictly Augustinian on this point) that to show anything new in Calvin's view would necessitate demonstrating a clear divergence in the Reformers' opinions. This, however, is not the case. The second is that Calvin, himself, employs the concept of order in a way that suggests immutability. The revisionist assertion of contingency does not hold up under the weight of the evidence. In fact, to reason otherwise is to interpret Calvin over-optimistically and fails to take into account the intransigence of his theology of order.

2. At the base of Augustine's teaching on the husband-wife relationship appears to be an androcentrism which permeates his thinking. Of course, this appears to be implicit in the concept of conjugal hierarchy in which man's superiority and his wife's inferiority are manifested in terms of authority (*viz*, power) and of responsibility.

It might be argued that Augustine demonstrates an egalitarian view of women in certain aspects of his teaching. Indeed, this is true of his understanding of woman's possession of the *imago Dei* (but, only ambiguously), of her intellectual capabilities, of the wife's conjugal rights and duties and in the fact that God renews her in Christ as he does man. However, undergirding his construal of woman there remains a concept of her innate inferiority. She is so by divine intention, because of her constitution and because of her roles as wife and mother.

This is most obviously seen in Augustine's insistence that it is the man who is the *exemplum* of humanity, and not the woman. She follows him as he does Christ. Her punishment is a mandatory servitude to her husband. This is unaffected by the liberty brought about by the gospel of Christ. As we have seen, Augustine is willing only for a theoretical abolition of the differences between the sexes. In practice, the *ordo* has to remain – the woman stays in the lower relational position.

We noticed, too, that though Augustine counters the idea of the husband's authority by a double emphasis on service and friendship, he apparently does so somewhat reluctantly. Eve was created, not for companionship, but for procreation.

In our examination of Luther and Calvin it will be noticed that they argue from a similarly androcentric position. Essentially Augustinian in character (though differently nuanced), their thinking on the husband-wife relationship portrays the same ambivalence as Augustine on the question of the equality of the woman. Fundamentally, the wife is inferior to her husband and, though both Reformers seek to soften that teaching by an emphasis on conjugal love, the husband remains humanity's *exemplum* and the wife retains the duty of following him in a subservient manner. Again, it will be argued that this is not the sort of theological basis for either Reformer to innovate with the concept of a greater liberty for women. Indeed, they do not. And it is their theological and ethical understanding of the marital relationship that precludes them from doing so.

3. On the face of it, Augustine's three good purposes of marriage would appear to be conducive to an understanding of equality in the conjugal relationship. God's intentions for marriage are said to be the procreation of children, the guarantee of chastity and the indissolubility of the union – all of which might appear to imply mutuality in relationship. However, such are the assumptions concerning sin which undergird these that Augustine's construal of the marriage relationship never surpasses the idea of mutual obligation in the marital bed. A laudable stress on friendship is spoiled both by his teaching that man-to-man companionship is to be preferred to that of man-to-woman and by his obsession with sin attaching to sexual intercourse, even within marriage.

Even though he insists that sexual union is good and proper, by emphasizing the evil accompanying it Augustine effectively fails to discover a way of articulating the fact that sexual intercourse signifies and enhances the marital relationship. Indeed, for Augustine, coitus is, at best, the means to the end of procreation or it is nothing but concupiscential. Ruether is correct in her assessment:

> Sex is thereby conceived of as narrowly as possible, as either impersonally instrumental or carnally masturbatory, with no role left for the expression of a personal love relationship as a legitimate purpose of sex.[118]

---

[118] R. R. Ruether, 'Misogynism and Virginal Feminism in the Fathers of the Church' in idem, (ed.), *Religion and Sexism* (Simon and Schuster, New York, 1974), 166. See also, the following, who concur with that judgement: Rowe, op. cit., 97, 103 (fn. 127); Brown, *The Body and Society*, 402; E. Fuchs, *Sexual Desire and Love* (James Clarke, Cambridge, 1983), 117.

Examination of the Reformers' teaching will indicate an Augustinian stress on the sinfulness necessarily entailed in sexual intercourse, but, perhaps, more emphasis (certainly, in Luther) on the willing grace of God which covers that sin.

Despite some misgivings, both Luther and Calvin appear to understand the relationship between the husband and wife as more positive and the possibility of genuine companionship as more likely. The next chapter selectively outlines the continuance of Augustine's basic teaching on marriage through the lengthy period of the Middle Ages.

CHAPTER 4

MEDIEVAL MARRIAGE[1]

There has been a helpful growth in significant scholarly work on the understanding of the Middle Ages, both on the subject of marriage, itself, and on the status and place of women in medieval society.[2] Some of this is extremely specific.[3] A realistic conclusion that appears increasingly common in the literature is that there is no single, monolithic understanding of marriage, either throughout the thousand years period as a whole, or even

---

[1] Because of the nature and broad scope of the first half of the present chapter we will be largely dependent on secondary literature to give an overview of the subject.

[2] For an overview of medieval marriage see D. Herlihy, 'The Making of the Medieval Family: Symmetry, Structure and Sentiment', *JFH* 8 (1983), 116-30; idem, *Medieval Households* (Harvard University Press, Harvard, 1985); idem, *Women, Family and Society in Medieval Europe* (Berghahn, Providence, 1995); P. Delhaye, 'The Development of the Medieval Church's Teaching on Marriage', *Concilium* 5 (1970), 83-8; F. Gies / J. Gies, *Marriage and the Family in the Middle Ages* (Harper and Row, New York, 1987); J. A. Brundage, *Law, Sex and Christian Society in Medieval Europe* (University of Chicago Press, Chicago, 1987); C. Brooke, *The Medieval Idea of Marriage* (OUP, Oxford, 1991); G. Duby, *Love and Marriage in the Middle Ages* (Polity, Chicago, 1994). On the place and status of women see E. C. McLaughlin, 'Equity of Souls, Inequality of Sexes: Woman in Medieval Theology' in R. R. Ruether (ed.), *Religion and Sexism* (Simon and Schuster, New York, 1974), 213-66; F. Gies / J. Gies, *Women in the Middle Ages* (Harper Perennial, New York, 1978); K. E. Børresen, *Subordination and Equivalence* (University Press of America, Washington, 1981), 158-295; D. Webb, 'Woman and Home: The Domestic Setting of Medieval Spirituality' in W. J. Sheils / D. Wood (eds), *Women in the Church* (Blackwell, Oxford, 1990), 159-73. Note also the primary material translated and extracted in E. Amt, *Women's Lives in Medieval Europe. A Source Book* (Routledge, New York, 1993).

[3] See, for example, J. M. Bennett's detailed examination of the social standing of women in the village of Brigstock, *Women in the Medieval English Countryside* (OUP, Oxford, 1989).

across Europe at a given time. This means that the picture confronting us is one of diversity and complexity. Naturally, there was development, both in understanding and in social experience during this time – though viewed over the entire period, the concepts of marriage and family 'appear in some respects almost static by comparison with the changes that have shaped and shaken them since'.[4] Two such significant developments, that form a backdrop to the Reformers' own cognizance and experience of marriage, are worth singling out in an introductory manner.

The first has to do with the structure and the internal-dynamic nature of the family. 'Within families, strong emotional bonds were ... taking form, based on particular conceptions of domestic roles, of the functions and contributions to the common life of father, mother and children.'[5] The emerging medieval family did not lack familial affection as has sometimes been supposed – though the social unit was organised on a strictly hierarchical and patriarchal pattern. Implicit in Herhily's words is the idea that affection operates across strongly defined social callings. As we have observed, this concept is explicit in Augustine's writing, with his twin stress on friendship and service. It is also present, later, in the thinking of both Luther and Calvin. Within this development of strong familial affection, there was a gradual transformation in the concept of the marital relationship from the contractual (a matter of family alliance and property exchange, where duties are mutual, but not reciprocal) to the personal or consensual (a matter of mutual consent and physical union).

The second development to note is the Church's acquisition of exclusive control over marital concerns[6] – a control that the

---

[4] Gies / Gies, *Marriage and Family in the Middle Ages*, 295.

[5] Herhily, art. cit., 129. The growth of familial affection is one of three characteristics that Herhily discerns in the development of the medieval family. The others are its largely comparable and commensurable composition (symmetry) and its particular structure. See also, idem, 'The Family and Religious Ideologies in Medieval Europe' in *Women, Family and Society in Medieval Europe*, 154-73, particularly, 162-72; idem, *Medieval Households*, 56-62, 78, 143-4; Gies / Gies, op. cit., 297; idem, *Women in the Middle Ages*, 34-6.

[6] Brooke, *The Medieval Idea of Marriage*, 127, argues that, 'By slow stages the Church became more active, more involved. To point to an exact date when the Church assumed competence in marriage suits is impossible.' Brooke

Reformers would later question and erode by their insistence that marriage is fundamentally a temporal matter. Together with this acquisition, there arose a determined attempt to define and enforce the Church's law of marriage. Previously, the Church had sought to be influential in these matters, but the law had remained secular. Nevertheless, the Church was insisting that marriage was to be monogamous[7] and indissoluble as early as the eighth and ninth centuries. However, the mid- and late Middle Ages appear to be crucial. During this period, theologians and canonists defined with new specificity what marriage was, who could and could not marry, and so on. It sought a clear and enforceable definition of what marriage comprised. Together with this, canon law replaced secular codes. Nonetheless, within the Church's own concrete example, there seems to have been an ambiguous message concerning the marriage of its clergy. Since the fourth century the clergy had been able to marry by custom (but not, however, by law), but from the eleventh century on, celibacy was demanded of them. Significantly, Brundage points out that there is ample documentary evidence to suggest that by the late Middle Ages clerical incontinence had become a scandal in many parts of Europe.[8]

Against the background of these two major (but gradual) developments and the acknowledgement of the diverse and complicated situation, generally, this present chapter can do no more than sketch a few relevant ideas. Unfortunately, in discussing the concept of the marital relationship over such a long and diverse period of time we stand a chance of being in some way or other fairly inaccurate. There is a real danger of generalizing too much and missing the specifics. However, within the whole thesis, this chapter has a restricted role. That is, its limited purpose is to relate something of the medieval Church's attachment to Augustinian emphases concerning marriage, and

---

himself points to cases as early as the ninth and tenth centuries, but argues that it was rare before the twelfth. Contra, Delhaye, art. cit., 83.

[7] It is worth noting that, though monogamy was the ideal set for marriage, 'Monogamous *mating* was conspicuously absent throughout the Middle Ages' - L. Betzig, 'Medieval Monogamy', *JFH* 20 (1995), 205 - original emphasis. See 181-216. See also, Duby, *Love and Marriage in the Middle Ages*, 9; Gies / Gies, *Marriage and the Family in the Middle Ages*, 53; Herhily, 'Did Women have a Renaissance?' in *Women, Family and Society*, 47.

[8] Brundage, op. cit., 536.

the husband and wife relationship in particular. If Luther and Calvin are to be examined against a tradition, then the tradition, forefronted by Augustine, needs to be described (however briefly) and shown to continue up until the Reformers' ministry in order to evaluate their continuance of it.

The three crucial, general areas that were discerned in Augustine's understanding – areas of the importance of order, of sexual negativity and of androcentrism – will be delineated in the following survey. The latter will be seen to be implicit throughout the other two. Following the general survey, the thought of Thomas Aquinas will be summarised as specifically exemplifying the general mainstream ideas and (importantly) the ambivalence of the period.

MEDIEVAL INSISTENCE ON ORDER

One of the significant ideas behind Augustine's understanding of marriage is his emphasis on an ordered universe and the necessity of ordered social and domestic structures. This patristic stress on *ordo*, so prominent in Augustine, continued in the succeeding centuries. In this, the medieval period fully accepted the ordered nature of reality, both on a 'cosmic' and on a societal level.[9] The divisions within the latter, for instance, were regarded as being religious in origin and in character; that is, they were believed to be rooted in the divine intention – their basic arrangement having been given at the time of the creation. The primal structure simply reflected the way things inherently were. Significantly, the God-given ordering of reality was inherently hierarchical. The whole ordering of the universe made that apparent and, in reflecting it, social order was to be hierarchical in its outworking.

---

[9] See, particularly, D. Nineham, *Christianity Medieval and Modern* (SCM, London, 1993), chapter 13. See also, J. Huizinga, *The Waning of the Middle Ages* (Penguin, Harmondsworth, 1955), 56-66; D. Hay, *The Medieval Centuries* (Methuen, London, 1964), 31-57; C. Brooke, *The Structure of Medieval Society* (Thames and Hudson, London, 1971), 73-116; R. Brooke / C. Brooke, *Popular Religion in the Middle Ages* (Thames and Hudson, London, 1985), 47-56; B. Hamilton, *Religion in the Medieval West* (Edward Arnold, London, 1986), 87-95.

This had, at least, two important implications. First, because the hierarchy was directly attributable to God, many regarded the divisions as absolutely immutable. As these had not been created by people or society itself, they simply could not be changed. Within that immutable arrangement, the individual's freedom lay in fulfilling their responsibilities circumscribed by the vocation or status in which they found themselves. In this sense, the concept of society in the Middle Ages is generally static, not dynamic. Above all, it seeks to maintain the *status quo*. Southern comments that hierarchical stability was the dominant aim of (at least) the last two centuries of the medieval period.[10]

The second implication is that the notion of *inaequalitas* was seen to be an essential principle of reality and, as Nineham points out, '[T]here were strong reactions against even the slightest suggestion of mitigating it.'[11] Generally, the medieval theologians did not lose sight of verses such as Galatians 3:28, with their potential for an egalitarian understanding – but in following Augustine (and others), they taught that all were fundamentally equal by nature (being created in the *imago Dei*), but not so within the social *ordo*. 'From God downwards all beings descended in an order of being which was also an order of value.'[12]

'Orders' or 'estates' within this hierarchical arrangement (such as matrimony, itself) represented divine institutions: that is, social elements of God's creation.[13] By definition, then, their structure was to be unchangeable and the vocational relationships within them were necessarily hierarchical. As we observed of Augustine's thought, so too in medieval ideas. Those

---

[10] R. W. Southern, *Western Society and the Church in the Middle Ages* (Hodder and Stoughton, London, 1970), 247.

[11] Nineham, op. cit., 146.

[12] Ibid., 23. V. H. H. Green, *Luther and the Reformation* (Batsford, London, 1964), 15, says of the Middle Ages that lordship and hierarchy, 'so abundantly obvious on earth and so inescapable, was an expression of the revealed truth behind all creation.'

[13] Obviously, in such a diverse age there were those – such as the Cathars and others – who repudiated marriage altogether. See, particularly, M. Lambert, *Medieval Heresy* (Blackwell, Oxford, 1994), 17-29, 55-6, 107. See also, P. Biller, 'The Common Woman in the Western Churches in the 13th and Early 14th Centuries' in Sheils / Woods (eds), op. cit., 127-57; U. Wiethaus, 'Sexuality, Gender, and the Body in Late Medieval Women's Spirituality', *JFSR* 7 (1991), 35-52.

in the higher relational positions (e.g. husbands) were higher both in order of being *and in order of value* from those in lower relational positions (e.g. wives, children, servants) –although the husband's power was, perhaps, less absolute than that of the old Roman *paterfamilias*.[14] Nevertheless, man was considered the sole authority in society and in the family; wives were seen to be both intrinsically and socially inferior to their male counterparts.

In speaking generally of the medieval period, R. A. Houlbrooke comments, 'In the *official image* of marriage sustained by a male-dominated society, woman was the subordinate partner.'[15] This thought is exemplified in Gratian's *Decretum*, for instance: 'The woman has no power, but in everything she is subject to the control of her husband.'[16] In a word, the husband is her 'lord' (*dominus*). Indeed, from her particular and detailed enquiry, Bennett concludes that, 'femaleness (itself) was largely defined by the submissiveness expected of wives'.[17] Much of the writing of the period bears this out. For example, the manual written by the *Ménagier* of Paris (1392) commands his wife to be obedient, gentle, amicable and peaceable. She is threatened that if she does not persevere in these virtues she will be put down, 'even as Lucifer was'.[18] This, of course, implies that the sin of pride is the motivating force behind any attempt to reverse accepted status and roles. Wives from the Old Testament – Sarah, Rebecca, Ruth and so on – serve as examples of virtuous and obedient women.[19]

It is interesting to note, though, that together with a demand for obedience and submission there is implicit respect and love towards the *Ménagier's* wife:

---

[14] See Gies / Gies, *Marriage and the Family in the Middle Ages*, 59.

[15] R. A. Houlbrooke, *The English Family 1450-1700* (Longman, London, 1984), 118 – emphasis added.

[16] '*Nulla est mulieris potestas, sed in omnibus uiri dominio subsit*' (Rubric to C.33q5cl7) – quoted by Brundage, op. cit., 255, fn. 158.

[17] Bennett, op. cit., 141. She also suggests, therefore, that the subordination of women was 'rooted neither in government nor economy, but rather in the household' (198).

[18] An abridged translation is found in Amt, op. cit., 317-30 – from which quotations are given. It is also found in E. Power, *Medieval People* (Methuen, London, 1929), 85-110.

[19] Ibid., 319. See a similar example in Geoffrey de la Tour-Landry's, *Book of the Knight of the Tower* (1371) – extracted in G. G. Coulton, *Life in the Middle Ages* (CUP, Cambridge, 1967), 2.114-15.

[B]y doing what I have said you will cause him [the husband] to miss you all the time and have his heart with you and your loving service, and he will shun all other houses, all other women, all other services and households.[20]

Within the confines of her domestic vocation as wife, she is also given a great deal of responsibility: managing the household, gardening, choosing servants and tradesmen, and the like. But, we notice that it is *a delegated responsibility*.[21] Certainly, in terms of the spiritual well-being of the family and its devotional practices, the husband had the authoritative oversight.[22]

However, one clear, but unfortunate, outworking of male dominance in the period was the abuse of wives who refused to comply or of those who simply failed, for whatever reason, to reach the required standard.[23] This seems to have been true of all strata of society.[24] Again, many of the documents suggest that hierarchical subordination should be strictly enforced. For instance,

> A man may chastise his wife and beat her for her correction; for she is of his household, and therefore the lord (*dominus*) may chastise his own, as it is written in Gratian's *Decretum*... .[25]

Of interest, here, is the fact that maltreatment or punishment is justified, in societal terms, on the suppositional basis of the wife's lower status in her husband's household and, in theoretical terms, on the basis of the weight of Gratian's authority.[26]

---

[20] Ibid., 322.

[21] Ibid., 319-20. He speaks of her, in this context, as 'sovereign mistress of the household' (329).

[22] See Webb, op. cit., 159-73. See also, J. L. Nelson, 'Women and the Word in the Earlier Middle Ages' in Sheils / Wood (eds), op. cit., 76.

[23] Nineham, op. cit., 157, 208, states that wives were sometimes badly maltreated and subjected to savage brutality. This possibility was implicit in Augustine's insistence on the need for coercion within the husband-wife relationship – noted in chapter 3.

[24] See W. Rösener, *Peasants in the Middle Ages* (Polity, Cambridge, 1992), particularly 169-90. She stresses the inferior legal position of peasant women and the right of the husband to inflict corporal punishment on the wife (183).

[25] British Museum Royal MS.6.E.vi (14th century) – Coulton, op. cit., 3.119. Geoffrey de la Tour-Landry, says that 'Men can chastise their wives with fear and strokes' (ibid., 3.116).

[26] See K. Moxey, *Peasants, Warriors and Wives* (University of Chicago Press, Chicago, 1989), 113-20.

However, social position is never solely created by theoretical notions or by past or current authority, of course. In fact, one of the other most pervasive influences[27] in the medieval period for the continued subjugation of wives was the persistent tradition of misogynism and, particularly, its theological depreciation of women, together with its attendant literature. This 'chorus of contempt'[28] can be traced back (theologically[29]) at least as far as Jerome's pamphlets on the fickleness of women, in general. Indeed, his *Adversus Iovinianum* became the basic medieval textbook for antifeminism.[30] With their negative attitude towards women, these works came to be widely read, imitated and represented by the mainstream of medieval thought.[31] From the thirteenth century, for example, *Hali Meidenhad*, following Jerome, reads,

---

[27] By this phrase we intend to suggest that there are other factors which, in the interests of space, will not be touched upon in this study. One example is that of sociological pressure. Herhily, art. cit., 125, states that there was *a need* for a strong protector of the family in an age when plagues, famines, wars, economic troubles, social upheavals, and so on, threatened the welfare and even the survival of households. Another factor was the negative attitude of common preachers of the day who were generally pessimistic about marriage - see F. Bottomley, *Attitudes to the Body in Western Christendom* (Lepus, London, 1979), 124.

[28] The apt phrase is from B. J. van der Walt, 'Women and Marriage in the Middle Ages, in Calvin and in our own time' in idem (ed.), *John Calvin's Institutes: His Opus Magnum* (Potchefstroom University for Christian Higher Education, Potchefstroom, 1986), 188.

[29] It had its roots in classical antiquity - see McLaughlin, art. cit., 251-5.

[30] One quotation is perhaps sufficient to grasp the tone of Jerome's understanding: 'Woman is the gate of the devil, the path of wickedness, the sting of the serpent, in a word a perilous object' (quoted in F. Heer, *The Medieval World*, Cardinal, London, 1962, 318). See also, Brooke, *The Medieval Idea of Marriage*, 62.

[31] See B. M. Bolton, '*Vitae Matrum*: A Further Aspect of the *Frauebfrage*' in D. Baker (ed.), *Medieval Women* (Blackwell, Oxford, 1978), 253-4; K. Jeay, 'Sexuality and Family in Fifteenth Century France: Are Literary Sources a Mask or a Mirror?', *JFH* 4 (1979), 328-45, particularly 328-31. An infamous medieval example is that of *Malleus Maleficarium*, published by two Dominicans (Heinrich Kramer and Jacobus Sprenger) as late as 1486. They say, for example, that, 'When a woman is alone, she thinks evil' (quoted by S. Dowell / L. Hurcombe, *Dispossessed Daughters of Eve*, SPCK, London, 1987, 101. See also, 142, fn. 15). Other examples are cited by McLaughlin, art. cit., 251-5.

> Now thou art wedded, and from so high estate alighted so low ... into the filth of the flesh, into the manner of a beast, into the thraldom of a man, and into the sorrows of the world. ... She, much against her will, must suffer his will, often with great misery.[32]

However, Jerome's most popular disciple, in the medieval period, was Peter Damian [1007-1072]. According to Brooke, he had 'a quite exceptional horror of human sexuality' and stood out amongst his contemporaries for his reluctance to accept the institution of marriage as being within God's good intention. He understood that it was permitted, but only 'by some curious and incomprehensible mystery of the divine providence' and only in order to continue humanity's existence.[33] Procreation was the single, profitable use to which women could be put within a marriage dominated by the husband.

It is clear that women were confronted by ideas detrimental to themselves, governed by a thoroughly masculine theology. Yet, this grim negativity towards women was not the sole strand of thought throughout the period, of course. Alongside the misogynistic current there co-existed a more positive one. That is, increasingly, there were those who defended the position of women, even within the household. This eventually gave rise to the humanist writers of the fourteenth and fifteenth centuries who often esteemed marriage and praised the joy of living with a good wife (*mulier bona*) in domestic happiness.[34] It resulted, most significantly, in the works of Erasmus.[35] But, we should notice that even comparative champions of women still insisted on their weakness and the need for their subjection.

---

[32] Amt, op. cit., 91, 92.

[33] Brooke, *The Medieval Idea of Marriage*, 73. See also, I. K. Resnick, 'Peter Damian on the Restoration of Virginity: a Problem for Medieval Theology', *JTS* 39 (1988), 125-34.

[34] Herhily, *Medieval Households*, 116-17, cites Coluccio Salutati, Leonardo Bruni and Francesco Barbaro, for example. He quotes Bruni: 'Man is a social animal [*L'uomo è animal civile*], as all philosophers agree; the fundamental union, which by its multiplication creates the city, is that of husband and wife. Nothing can be accomplished where this union does not exist. And this love alone is natural, legitimate, and allowed.'

[35] See, particularly, *Encomium Matrimonii* in J.-C. Margolin (ed.), *Opera Omnia Desiderii Erasmi Roterodami* (North Holland Publishing Co., Amsterdam, 1975), 1.5, 385-416.

One conspicuous example of this is Christine de Pisan [1364-c.1430]. Though Gottlieb speaks anachronistically of her as a feminist, it is obvious why she does.[36] In her writing, Christine de Pisan defends women against misogynism with great vigour and propounds the idea that the ideal marriage *must* include loyalty, kindness and wisdom on the man's part. Yet, importantly, she does not believe in equal capacities, nor does she demand equal opportunities. In fact, even within her 'feminist' programme, she stresses the need for domestic and social hierarchical structure – repeating the idea that the husband is the head of the household and that the subjugated wife should be obedient to him. She also lays great stress on the value that fulfilling one's obligations had in the sight of God. Apparently, the reason for this is that she wants to guarantee order and stability in society.

So what we find, then, is a balance of continuity and change. The mainstream ecclesiastical and theological thinkers of the period[37] follow Jerome, and to a certain extent Augustine, in a disparagement of women.[38] Conversely, throughout the millennium, others seek to raise the status of wives. However,

---

[36] See B. Gottlieb, 'The Problem of Feminism in the Fifteenth Century', in J. Kirshner / S. F. Wemple (eds), *Women in the Medieval World* (Blackwell, Oxford, 1987), 337-64. Gottlieb defines 'feminism' as 'thinking about women and feeling that they deserve better in the world' (359). See also, Amt, op. cit., 163-5, where she excerpts part of de Pisan's, *The Treasure of the City Ladies, or, The Book of Three Virtues* (1405).

[37] We stress *ecclesiastical and theological* thinkers because the courtly love tradition cannot be included in this chapter. It arose, largely, in defiance of the church and, though it elevated women, it affirmed the value of romantic (not religious) love and glorified sexual relations in which women (not men) had the upper hand. See R. Miles, *The Woman's History of the World* (Michael Joseph, London, 1988), 68 – she cites Beatriz de Diaz, Eleanor de Aquitaine and Marie de France. According to Southern, op. cit., 2.311-12, 'The growth of romantic and erotic literature only strengthened belief in the moral and social dangers of feminine wantonness.' R. Bainton, *The Reformation of the Sixteenth Century* (Hodder and Stoughton, London, 1963), 258, calls medieval and sixteenth century romantic love, 'the art of adultery'. See also, B. Gottlieb, *The Family in the Western World* (OUP, Oxford, 1993), 101; Heer, op. cit., 153-92.

[38] The disparagement of women continues into the Reformation period and beyond. See Moxey, op. cit., 101-26. Moxey, an art historian, focuses on art work of the fifteenth and sixteenth centuries – for example, Albrecht Giockendon's broadsheet, *There is no Greater Treasure Here on Earth Than an Obedient Wife who Covets Honor* (Nuremberg, 1533) with the woodcut by Erhard Schön (101-10). He sees these as 'visual metaphors' of the period which reveal the misogynism of the age.

both groups emphasize the patristic concept of *ordo* reflected in social order, and in the family in particular. Even those who would liberate women from the male misogynist tradition and maltreatment are adamant that hierarchical order is crucial for the maintenance of society. In this, both groups continue the stress on the essential importance of order as the foundational idea behind the family's well-being. Specifically, the hierarchical order of the husband and wife is fundamental to that relationship. The medieval period emphasizes that the husband is the head of the household, the wife is (and has to remain) subservient to him.

SEXUAL AMBIVALENCE

The attitude of the age towards sexual intercourse within marriage is all part of its sharp dichotomy between spirit and flesh and its distrust of the latter. Medieval theologians, in general, follow the harsher conclusions of Jerome, rather than those of Augustine, in condemning sex for pleasure alone; although there is considerable disagreement between them over the degree of sin involved in satisfying sexual desire or in pursuing sexual pleasure for its own sake.[39] Generally, there appear only two alternatives for them: either coitus is for a purpose - *viz.* that of procreation - or it is no better than sinful concupiscence.[40] As we noted in the previous chapter, this appears to be an implication of Augustine's ambivalent thinking. The Fall, and the consequent sinfulness of humanity, makes concupiscence part of its makeup and daily temptation. Able to reduce man to the level of animals, it has the potential to disrupt social order and stability and, therefore, it should be restrained. In an extreme and cryptic manner, Bernard of Clairvaux, for example, cautions his monks that,

---

[39] T. N. Tentler, *Sin and Confession on the Eve of the Reformation* (Princeton University Press, Princeton, 1977), 165-7, shows that medieval theology was inordinately concerned with the sexual in relation to sin.

[40] Nineham, op. cit., 159, concludes that, 'the church's teaching of our period treated sexual relationships as simply a matter of physical pleasure - to be avoided - or simply as a technique of reproduction on a biological level'.

To be always with a woman and not to have sexual relations with her is more difficult than to raise the dead. You cannot do the less difficult; do you think that I will believe that you can do what is more difficult?[41]

One of the harshest exponents of an extreme sexual negativity is Peter Damian. He has an exceptionally acute sense of sin, particularly as it expresses itself in the sexual relationships of men and women. He believes that even those getting married at best only cover their own lust and that God reserves the highest places in heaven for those who avoid sexual relations. To believe thus is to disparage women and marriage – which he does in favour of celibacy.

There were those who would teach a more positive sexuality, however. Thus, there open up two strands in the twelfth century: one which sees virginity as better than marriage (especially, extolling virginity *within* marriage); the other emphasizing that the husband and wife both have duties and rights within the sexual experience of their relationship.

At the other end of the spectrum of thought from Damian stands Peter Abelard [1079-1142] and his followers; notably (for our purposes) Gratian and Peter Lombard.[42] With these the medieval period sees an increasingly positive attitude towards marriage and marital sex, though, at best, the teaching still remains ambivalent.

Although the experience of Heloise and Abelard's affair is somewhat unique,[43] their teaching on love and sexuality becomes an important facet of the Middle Age's understanding of marriage. Abelard's thinking on sexual sin is significant, for he is

---

[41] *Sermones in Cantica canticorum*, 65.2.4 – quoted by Brundage, op. cit., 251.

[42] On Gratian and Lombard, generally, see D. E. Luscombe, *The School of Peter Abelard* (CUP, Cambridge, 1970), 214-23, 261-80, respectively.

[43] The affair, itself, is summarised in outline by R. A. Tucker, 'Heloise and Abelard's Tumultuous Affair', *CH* 10 (1991), 28-30. Their letters are translated by B. Radice, *The Letters of Abelard and Heloise* (Penguin, Harmondsworth, 1974) – see, particularly, 109-58. These are cited as *Letters*, throughout. We are following Brooke, *The Medieval Idea of Marriage*, 91, 93-102, in taking the letters as authentic in all essentials – contrary to B. Schmeidler, 'Die Briefwechsel zwischen Abälard und Heloïse eine Fälschung?', *AKG* 11 (1913-14), 1-30 and also, Heer, op. cit., 109. Generally, see Brooke, op. cit., 93-118; idem, *Europe in the Central Middle Ages*, 457-65.

'almost alone in the period in denying the intrinsic sinfulness of sexual relations and in maintaining that sexual intercourse is both natural and beneficial'.[44] In this, Abelard argues against Augustine's insistence that *all* sexual desire (post-Fall) is necessarily sinful: '[I]t is not the temptations of lust that are sinful. Morality here depends upon whether the ruling bias of the will overcomes these temptations or yields to them.' He continues, 'Sin arises only when one suffers oneself to be drawn by those fleshly solicitations into transgression of the divine law.' For Abelard, the merit of virtue consists in the fact that believers do God's will, though they are 'in conflict with themselves'.[45] But, the divine will within marriage is that sexual intercourse takes place. Abelard is quite clear that carnal pleasure and the desire for it is human (in the sense of being natural). It is also unavoidable and it can be without sin. 'To say that intercourse should be done with no pleasure is to say it is not to be done at all.'[46] Both Abelard and Heloise stress the selflessness of love — that it is a mutual self-giving, a complete sacrifice to the other.[47]

However, their ambivalence becomes obvious, for despite these positive emphases, Abelard still concurs with Augustine's conclusion that marriage is a cure for incontinence. He agrees too with his teaching on the shame attendant on the independent movement of the sexual organs.[48] Indeed, he commends philosophers for their restraint in not marrying; that is, in not allowing themselves to be distracted by a wife.[49] Heloise, for her part, repeats the traditional understanding of the weakness of women, the precariousness of their salvation and their inherent inferiority in relation to their male counterparts.[50] Brooke, rightly, points out that Heloise's taking the veil shows, in a very traditional manner, that her will was wholly subject to that of

---

[44] Brundage, op. cit., 187. See also, Tentler, op. cit., 167.

[45] Quoted by R. E. O. White, *The Changing Continuity of Christian Ethics* (Paternoster, Exeter, 1981), 2.120.

[46] Abelard's *Ethica* in D. E. Luscombe (trans.), *Peter Abelard's Ethics* (Clarendon, Oxford, 1971), 20-21.

[47] Heloise says, 'A woman who prefers a rich to a poor husband, or who yearns for his goods rather than himself, may not reckon herself other than *corrupt (venalem)*', *Letters*, 114. See also, ibid. 261-4.

[48] *Letters*, 154-5, 147-8, respectively.

[49] See Abelard's *Theologia Christiana* in J. R. McCullam (trans.), *Abelard's Christian Theology* (Blackwell, Oxford, 1948), 64-5.

[50] Brooke, op. cit., 114; *Letters*, 127, 137-8.

Abelard.⁵¹ Nevertheless, however conventional they remain, their understanding of marriage gives prominence to conjugal love and singles out the importance of sexual intercourse within the husband-wife relationship.

Others of the period, also, stress the importance of companionship and conjugal love, of course. Hugh St Victor, for example, says of the married couple,

> The two shall become one soul [*in corde uno*] ... each shall be to the other as a same self, in all sincere love, all careful solicitude, every kindness of affection, in constant compassion, unflagging consolation, and faithful devotedness. ... [E]ach no longer lives for himself, but for the other. ... Such are the good things of marriage and the happiness of those who love chaste companionship.⁵²

Abelard's follower, Gratian, does the same in a different context. The question that he seeks to answer is, 'What constitutes a legal marriage?' Though all in the twelfth century were basically clear that marriage consisted in the three goods of *fides, proles and sacramentum* (following Augustine), it was not so obvious at what point the relationship became a marriage. Gratian's definition⁵³ establishes two things: marriage is a sacrament⁵⁴ and it is made by the partners.

Gratian grounds his understanding on Augustine. In his *Decretum*, he builds a theory of marriage in which the basic idea

---

⁵¹ Ibid., 108.

⁵² PL 176.859-60 – quoted by Brooke, *The Medieval Idea of Marriage*, 278-9. See also Hugh St Victor, *Summa Sententiarum Tract*, 4, 5, cap. 7 in PL 176, col. 126; Lombard, *Sententiae*, 2.174; Aquinas, ST II-II, q. 27, art. 7 – cited by Herhily, *Woman, Family and Society*, 125, fn. 52; 126, 129, respectively. Also, *Serm Luke 10:27*, by Bernardino of Sienna (1427), extracted in Coulton, op. cit., 1.217-29.

⁵³ Gratian works this out in *Concordia discordantium canonum* (c.1140), later known as Gratian's *Decretum*. See, particularly, Brundage, op. cit., 229-55. Excerpts of the *Decretum* are to be found in Amt, op. cit., 79-83; that is, cases 27 [q.2], 30 [q.5] and 32 [q.2].

⁵⁴ For Gratian, the sacramental nature of marriage denoted its indissolubility (after Augustine); the bond, itself, and the mystical significance of symbolizing Christ's union with the Church. With Peter Lombard the number of sacraments was established at seven: *baptismus, confirmatio, panis benedictionis, id est eucharistia, poenitentia, extrema unctio, ordo, coniugium* – see Lombard's *Sententiae in IV Libris Distincae* (Collegii S. Bonaventurae Ad Claras Aquas, Rome, 1971), 4.Dist. 2. See also, D. O'Callaghan, 'Marriage as a Sacrament', *Concilium* 5 (1970), 101-10; Delhaye, art. cit., 85-6.

is that union between man and woman is part of natural law. Legal marriage becomes a two-stage process: the initiation (with the words of promise signifying consent) and the completion (consummation in the physical act – *copula carnalis*) which made it indissoluble.[55] 'Coitus without consent is no marriage; nor is an exchange of consent that is not followed by intercourse.'[56] In this way, he assigns a principal role to sexual union within the husband-wife relationship. Sexual intercourse is both a duty and a right. In fact, Brundage says that this 'parity in respect to the conjugal debt was Gratian's most emphatic venture in the direction of a doctrine of equality between the sexes'.[57] Despite this, although he speaks of the social bond (*sociale vinculum*) of marriage, he speaks very little of conjugal love.[58] He also retains Augustine's understanding that the main purpose of marriage is procreation (although he allows for sensual pleasure in intercourse) and its secondary function is that it is a remedy against sin (*remedium peccati*).

EXCURSUS: AQUINAS ON MARRIAGE

We turn, now, to a brief *excursus* on Aquinas (1224-1274) to see the subject of medieval marriage in a typical and a more protracted example. In this way, we will see two things: first, we will examine how Augustine's teaching is distilled into the understanding of an equally androcentric, medieval writer and, second, we will discern the principles already delineated in an

---

[55] Amt, op. cit., 79-80. Peter Lombard found Gratian's definition to be unsatisfactory for if consummation was necessary for marriage, the legitimacy of Mary and Joseph's would be put into doubt. Therefore, he suggested that the words explicitly stating that the couple take each other as man and wife (*verba de praesenti*) were sufficient.

[56] Brundage, op. cit., 236. Aquinas, on the other hand, argues that marriage exists from the promise (*sponsione*), not the marriage act. However, the former promises (*spondet*) the latter. See ST III suppl., q.44, art.1, where he explains that the joining of bodies and minds is the *result* of marriage: '...*coniunctio autem corporum vel animorum ad matrimonium consequitur*'. See also, q.43, art.1.

[57] Ibid., 242 – see fn. 58.
[58] Ibid., 239.

orthodox and representative theologian, before moving on to examine the reformers.

Aquinas' thinking on marriage begins, traditionally, with the presupposition that people are created gregarious beings. It is natural for them to live in community. They are inclined to connubial union[59] and therefore marriage, itself, is natural – in the sense of being given at creation.[60] Nevertheless, marriage is inferior to virginity, largely, because of its worldly preoccupation.

Aquinas suggests that virginity is directed chiefly to spiritual good. However, 'marriage is directed to the good of the body, namely the bodily increase of the human race,[61] and belongs to the active life, since the man and woman who embrace the married life have to think on the things of the world.'[62]

He accepts Augustine's three goods of marriage – *fides, proles, sacramentum* – but he does so saying that they are excuses for sexual activity, rendering it inoffensive.[63] He stresses the priority of procreation over against the others, broadening the definition (as Augustine) to include both having children and raising them. It is an obligation imposed on the parents by nature (*officium naturae*).[64]

In examining Augustine we discovered that his foundational teaching of the divinely given nature of marriage had specific implications. So, too, in the thinking of Aquinas. First, if God instituted marriage, then it must be fundamentally good and, second, if procreation is its main purpose, then the sexual act, necessary for procreation, must be discerned as something other than entirely sinful.

---

[59] These and other natural, general principles (*in universali*) could not be eliminated from the human heart – see ST I-II, q.94, art.6; q.71, art.2; q.95, art.2. Unless otherwise indicated, we refer to Aquinas' work in *Sancti Thomae de Aquino: Summa Theologiciae* (Editiones Paulinae, Rome, 1962) and, in translation, *Summa Theologica*, volume 3 (Benziger Brothers, New York, 1948), *The Summa Theologica of St Thomas Aquinas*, volumes 13 and 19 (Burns, Oates and Washbourne, London, 1921, 1922).

[60] See, for example, ST III suppl., q.41, art.1; q.50, art.1; ST II-II, q.154, art.2. Because marriage is given at creation, Aquinas accepts that of unbelievers – ST III suppl., q.59, art.2.

[61] '...*coniugium autem ordinatur ad bonum corporis, quod est corporalis multiplicatio generis humani*'.

[62] ST II-II, q.152, art.4.

[63] See Børresen, op. cit., 326.

[64] See ST III, suppl., q.42, art.2; q.49, art.2; q.65, art.1; q.67, art.1.

In fact, Aquinas goes a step further back and argues from God's creation of humanity's physicality:

> If we suppose the corporeal nature [*nature corporalis*] to be created by the good God, we cannot hold that those things which pertain to the preservation of the corporeal nature and to which nature inclines, are altogether evil [*sint universaliter mala*], wherefore, since the inclination to beget an offspring ... is from nature, it is impossible to maintain that the act of begetting children is altogether unlawful [*universaliter illicitus*].[65]

The problem that Aquinas runs into is that he wishes to maintain the conventional, Augustinian teaching that there is sin inherent in intercourse – even within marriage. The shamefulness that inevitably accompanies the act has to do with the original punishment of Adam in which the 'lower members' do not obey reason. It is in this sense that sin is excused by 'the marriage blessing'.[66] He says, that since 'in matrimony man receives by divine institution the faculty to use his wife for the begetting of children, he also receives the grace without which he cannot becomingly do so'.[67]

What is *forbidden*, then, is enjoyment as an end in itself. Aquinas acknowledges that pleasure inevitably accompanies coitus,[68] but insists that present guilt will be avoided if the intention of the act is reasonable:

> Now the pleasure attaching to the marriage act, while it is most intense in point of quantity, does not go beyond the bounds previously appointed by reason before the commencement of the

---

[65] ST III suppl., q.41, art.3.

[66] Ibid. See also, ST II-II, q.151, art.4.

[67] '*Unde, cum in matrimonio detur homini ex divina institutione facultas utendi uxore sua ad procreationem prolis, datur etiam gratia sine qua id convenienter facere non posset*' (ST III suppl., q.42, art.3).

[68] Aquinas speaks of sexual intercourse as 'the greatest bodily pleasure' (ST II-II, q.152, art.1). Børresen, op. cit., 187, suggests that Aquinas' originality appears in the idea that enjoyment (*delectatio*) was greater in the primitive condition than it is now – a point of view that separates him from Augustine. However, it is hypothetical, as (according to Aquinas) intercourse did not take place in Eden.

act, although reason is unable to regulate them during the pleasure, itself.[69]

The bounds agreed before commencement are that the husband and wife must come together for procreation and/or paying the conjugal debt to one another. The criterion of sexual morality is, therefore, tied up with these functions.

If the chief purpose of marriage is procreation, it also exists as a remedy for concupiscence. Passionate, irrational sexual desire is a result of the Fall and the postlapsarian, sexual drive is insatiable and well-nigh irresistible. 'Now, lust consists essentially in exceeding the order and mode of reason in the matter of venereal acts. Wherefore, without doubt, lust is a sin.'[70] It is in this context of humanity's potential disorder that marriage becomes a *remedium peccati*. This is its secondary usefulness and in this is its sacramental character. Defining sacrament as 'a sanctifying remedy [*remedium sanctitatis*] against sin offered to man under sensible signs', Aquinas concludes that marriage is a sacrament.[71] It signifies both its indivisibility and the union of Christ and the Church. Marriage, also, importantly, neutralizes concupiscence, through both partners carrying out their sexual functions in a way that is controlled by reason and by sustained conjugal fidelity.[72]

---

[69] '*Deleciatio autem quae fit in actu matrimoniali, quamvis sit intensissima secundum quantitatem non tatem excedit limites sibi a ratione praefixos ante principium suum: quamvis in ipsa delectatione ratio eos ordinare non possit*' (ST III suppl., q.49, art.4). See also, q.64, art.7; q.65, art.1; q.67, art.1. '[T]o make use of sexual intercourse on account of its inherent pleasure, *without reference to the end for which nature intended it*, is to act against nature' (ibid., q.65, art.3, emphasis added).

[70] ST II-II, q.153, art.3. See ST III suppl., q.49, art.l. See also, McLaughlin, art. cit., 224. It is significant that Aquinas defines moral virtue as consisting in things that pertain to a person directed by their reason or to someone acting moderately – 'A sin in human acts, is that which is against the order of reason [*contra ordinem rationis*]' (ST II-II, q.153, art.2). See also, ST I-II, q.64, art.1; ST II-II, q.168, art.1; q.154, art.1; q.155, art.1; q.164, art.1, art.5; q.141, art.4; q.151, art.1; q.160, art.1.

[71] ST III suppl. q.42, art.1. See also, ST III suppl., q.45, art.2.

[72] ST III suppl., q.44, art.3; q.48, art.1; q.49, art.2. See also, *Summa contra Gentiles*, 123, 124 – cited by L. S. Cahill, *Between the Sexes* (Fortress, Philadelphia, 1985), 106. Børresen, op. cit., 247, says that, 'The grace of the sacrament acts on the evil of concupiscence by stifling it at its root, thus making sexual activity lawful and inoffensive.' See also, 326

Through this brief study of Aquinas' understanding of marriage, we already observe similar problems to those which relate to Augustine's thinking. For example, the heavy stress on the primacy of procreation has, at least, two attendant weaknesses. It diminishes the probability of further elucidation of marital love and it restricts Aquinas' appreciation of the function of women, almost exclusively, to that of the 'inferior' or auxiliary purpose of motherhood.

First, though Aquinas certainly speaks of companionship and love between the marriage partners, he relegates it to a third position behind marriage's essential and primary end (*viz.* procreation) and its secondary purpose of curbing concupiscence. He speaks of the growth of conjugal love as 'the accidental [essential] end of matrimony',[73] but the friendship that he envisages is, inevitably, impaired because it remains between a superior and an inferior. He differentiates between physical sex and spiritual love and as a result, as McLaughlin argues, what is lacking 'is the conception of a truly mutual I-Thou relationship within marriage'. Nowhere, in Aquinas, do we find the concept of sexual union as an outward sign of conjugal love or fidelity.[74] Coitus, in marriage, then, takes on the basic instrumental role of the procreation of children, but not the affirmative role of signifying and maintaining love – the relationship is defined from the former tenet.

Second, as with Augustine, Aquinas' perception of woman is inherently bound to his restrictive view of her procreative function. Woman's existence is essentially related to the reproduction of humanity. The sole purpose of woman as a 'helpmate' is to assist man in the work of generation, not to help him in anything else, for in all other areas he would be better assisted by another man. Børresen sums this up in the following words:

---

[73] ST III suppl., q.54, art.3. Aquinas uses 'accidental' in the sense of an essential property of the relationship, but, nevertheless, speaks of conjugal love as being, in some way, inferior to the other two ends of marriage. See also, ST III suppl., q.56, art.1; *SCG* 3/II, 123.6 – cited by Cahill, op. cit., 113. Børresen's conclusion is that 'in all his teaching about marriage there is hardly a word about love between married partners' (op. cit., 295).

[74] McLaughlin, art. cit., 229. He writes this despite the fact that he believes that making marriage a sacrament implies raising it from the level of mere animality to a focus of religious and personal meaning (228). Cahill, op. cit., 113, suggests that Aquinas downplays the intimacy and love between the spouses.

In her position as helper in the process of procreation, woman is, therefore, subordinated to man, considered as the superior sex. For thus, the distinction of the sexes signifies that woman is different from man. The manner in which the female body was formed is interpreted in this sense of subordination. The end of woman's existence as *mulier* is her function as helpmate.[75]

In this interpretation, Aquinas takes over the Augustinian understanding of Genesis, accepting that Adam and Eve's relationship is a norm for moral theology. He presumes that Eve's nature, function and *raison d'être* become those of every subsequent wife.[76]

Within the realm of procreation woman is said to be inferior to man. She must assume an auxiliary role in conformity with the inferiority of her body.[77] The man is pre-eminent as the 'material principle'. In him is the embryo *in potentia*, he has the active, superior part. The woman plays the passive, inferior role.[78] This means that woman is viewed from a perspective of mere instrumentality, as an aid to reproduction. Nonetheless, even in this limited context of sexual intercourse, there is a great deal of ambivalence, for Aquinas speaks of both inequality and of equivalence between the spouses.

For instance, Børresen stresses Aquinas' teaching on mutual sexual debt between the husband and wife; but even this is an ambivalent area. He *does* teach mutuality; for example, he speaks of each receiving 'power over the other in reference to carnal intercourse'.[79] However, in discussing the explicit question of whether the husband and wife are equal in the marriage act, Aquinas answers in an uncertain manner. He says that their equivalence is that they are mutually bound to pay the marital

---

[75] Børresen, op. cit., 171.

[76] See ST I, q.92, art.1-4. See also P. K. Jewett, *Man as Male and Female* (Eerdmans, Grand Rapids, 1975), 62-7, for a liberationist's commentary on this section of the *Summa Theologiae*.

[77] See L. Dewan, 'St. Thomas and Creation', *Dionysius* 15 (1991), 81-90; F. F. Centore, 'Thomism and the Female as seen in the *Summa Theologiae*', *Angelicum* 67 (1990), 37-56.

[78] ST III suppl., q.58, art.2.

[79] ST III suppl., q.48, art.1. See also ibid., q.49, art.3; q.58, art.1; Børresen, op. cit., 261-71.

debt; but he puts this into a wider, qualifying context that effectively destroys the reality of that equivalence. He says that

> [H]usband and wife are not equal in marriage; neither as regards the marriage act, wherein the more noble part is due to the husband, nor as regards the household management, wherein the wife is ruled and the husband rules. ... [T]hey are both bound one to another ... that is, they are not equal absolutely.[80]

Within this context, citing Augustine, Aquinas states that the father is more important than the mother.[81] However, the woman's delegated duty is to nurture and raise the children thus born – again, though, he qualifies the comment:

> *Although the father ranks above the mother,* the mother has more to do with the offspring than the father has. Or we may say that woman was made chiefly in order to be man's helpmate in relation to the offspring, whereas the man was not made for this purpose. Wherefore, the mother has a closer relation to the nature of marriage than the father has.[82]

Procreational inferiority suggests a more fundamental presupposition. For Aquinas, as for Augustine, woman is ontologically (*per definitionem*) inferior; man is, by nature, superior.[83] The superiority of the husband is based on two things: on the purpose for which the woman was created and on the manner of her creation. Børresen is right in suggesting that it is because the man is considered as the *exemplum* of humanity, that

---

[80] ST III suppl., q.64, art.5. In ibid., art.1 Aquinas has already qualified his comments: '[S]ince the wife has power over her husband only in relation to the generative power and not in relation to things directed to the preservation of the individual, the husband is bound to pay the debt to his wife, in matters pertaining to the begetting of children, with due regard, however, to his own welfare.'

[81] ST III suppl., q.44, art.2 – citing Augustine's *Contra Faustum Manichaean*, 19.26. See also *Summa contra Gentiles*, III. 122 – cited by McLaughlin, art. cit., 223.

[82] Ibid. – emphasis added. Generally, his stress is that the mother is mainly responsible for the child's upbringing, but occasionally he speaks of the father's joint-responsibility – e.g. ST III suppl., q.59, art.1.

[83] '*Vir naturaliter supereminet feminae*' – ST II-II, q.177, art.2 (cited by Børresen, op. cit., 173. See 174-7.)

the woman (obviously differing from him) is compared unfavourably with him.[84] For instance, he has more of 'the good of reason', she is weaker and more easily deceived.[85] At creation, Adam was 'more perfect' than Eve.[86]

With this essential inequality there is posited a social one in which the husband is to rule and the wife to obey. The submissive status of women is considered as natural, *a priori*. This, again, is traditional philosophical and theological thought, which, previously, Augustine had espoused and, later, the Reformers were to reaffirm. The wife has been subject to the husband in the social order since creation – that is, more pointedly, since *before* the Fall.[87] In a significant paragraph, quoted by Paul Jewett, Aquinas makes this clear:

> Subjection is twofold. One is servile, by virtue of which a superior makes use of a subject for his own benefit, and this kind of subjection began after sin. There is another kind of subjection, which is called economic or civil, whereby the superior makes use of his subjects for their own benefit and good; and this kind of subjection existed even before sin. For good order would have been wanting in the human family if some were not governed by others wiser than themselves. So by such a kind of subjection woman is naturally subject to man.[88]

A number of points may be noted from this passage. First, hierarchical familial order is inherent in the created *ordo*. It is God's intention for man to rule and for woman to be ruled, *for woman's own well-being*. Second, Aquinas, here, implicitly states that man rules because he is wiser than woman – or, perhaps, that he has been made wiser in order to rule. Either way, woman's fundamental inferiority is thereby assumed. Third, though the woman's subjugation belongs to the order of creation, it has been

---

[84] Ibid., 195, 329. She says that 'the androcentrism that belongs to the order of creation is ... transposed into the relationship between husband and wife' (333).

[85] '*Quia plus habet de rationis bono*' – ST III suppl., q.62, art.4; ST II-II, q.165, art.2, respectively.

[86] ST II-II, q. 163, art.4.

[87] ST II-II, q.164, art.2.

[88] Jewett, op. cit., 63. See also, Børresen, op. cit., 171, citing ST I, q.92, art.2.

aggravated by sin and the divine punishment.⁸⁹ The wife is to be subjected to her husband's authority against her own will – this is part of the divine judgement on Eve's sin.⁹⁰

From this passage, two things can be stated about Aquinas' methodology, as well. The order of creation, from which he appears to work as a foundational, fixed point, is essentially man-centred or male-orientated. From what has been shown of his teaching on the inherent inferiority of women (simply because *they are not men*), we can also argue that woman's subjection in a hierarchical social and familial order is bound up with her femaleness.⁹¹ But, further, because Aquinas' ethics of the husband-wife relationship conform to what he conceives to be the laws of nature, he derives what humans essentially are from empirical observation as much as from anything else. The 'naturalness' of woman's subjection is gleaned as much from the experience of his own community (with its obsession with hierarchical order) as from his continuance of the Augustinian theological tradition.⁹² He seems to have an idea of what 'good order' presently is and reads that back into prelapsarian Eden (as paradigmatic) and, further, into the divine purpose for the domestic structure.

There is, then, a hierarchical arrangement of husband and wife *as spouses* (in domestic relationship) and of man and woman *considered together* (in social relationship). However, as an individual human being (*homo*) possessing the *imago Dei* or as a believer in Christ, the woman is equivalent to the man. That is, in a general way, the subjection of woman corresponds to the order of creation, her equivalence to the order of salvation. There is inevitable tension between the two in a world dominated by the former, but in which the latter already operates.⁹³ But, again, the

---

⁸⁹ Børresen, op. cit., 214, argues that this becomes 'domination by the stronger over the weaker'.

⁹⁰ ST II-II, q.164, art.2. Following Genesis and Augustine (he cites *GnL* 11.42 earlier, at q.163, art.4) Aquinas also includes in the punishment the problems associated with the procreation of children – in which he incorporates weariness in carrying the child, pain in the birth and the troubles involved in its upbringing.

⁹¹ McLaughlin, art. cit., 218: '[I]t seems to be the woman's body that is the ultimate source of her inferiority and *subjection to the male*' (emphasis added).

⁹² See Cahill, op. cit., 107.

⁹³ Børresen, op. cit., 335, 338, respectively.

proposed equivalence has to be qualified: it is not simple equality. Børresen, correctly, argues that the woman's dignity belongs to her, not inherently but by reason of her identification with man on the spiritual level: that is, 'Equivalence is linked to her capacity to surmount her essentially feminine and different character.'[94]

CONCLUSION

What stands out most prominently from this short résumé of the Middle Ages' understanding of the husband-wife relationship is a clear androcentrism. Even in those who are not so misogynist (as in Abelard or Aquinas, for example) the social world and created order are man-centred and male-orientated. Man is the *exemplum* of humanity, woman is not. She is measured against him, her existence and worth against his and, generally, she is found to be wanting. This is somewhat circular becoming particularly apparent in her role in procreation, for it is here that she is defined. She is inferior because her body is different to the man's; it is different because she has an instrumental or auxiliary role. She is *his* helpmate; it is never the other way round. This shows her to be inferior.

Therefore, following the Augustinian emphases, the period stresses the crucial significance of *ordo* – in which, in the domestic context, the husband remains solidly as the head of the family, the wife continues to be his subordinate. This is assumed, not argued. The husband is thought to be superior both by intrinsic nature and by social status; conversely, she is thought to be fundamentally inferior on both counts. Generally, this was believed to be an immutable, God-given fact of social existence. The implication, throughout, is that a recognition of the hierarchical organization of the family represents a willingness to obey God's intention.

As with Augustine, the possibility of social egalitarianism springing from the believer's new status in Christ, is not realised. Many state women's equality in their common standing in the faith, but this did not affect the political order. The spiritual sameness of men and women, therefore, stands in opposition to

---

[94] Ibid., 339.

their inherent and social difference. Nevertheless, there is, generally, understood to be an equivalence in some areas of the husband-wife relationship (for example, mutual fidelity, the conjugal debt). However, as we observed in the thought of Aquinas, these are so heavily qualified by inegalitarian comment that they diminish in importance.

In the sexual realm, the relationship of the spouses is not really enhanced very much. With a current of negative thinking, on the one hand, and traditional belief in procreation as the primary reason for marriage, on the other (together with marriage as a remedy against lust, as a second), there was not a great deal written about conjugal love and companionship. Indeed, when this is prioritized (as with Abelard and Heloise, for example) the other, more negative, conventional ideas accompany it to its detriment. Generally, two things reduce any realistic possibility of the consideration of the significance of coitus to the maintenance and growth of mutual love. The first is that shame and guilt are believed to accompany sexual intercourse and the second is an emphasis on the moral worth of the act being dependent on rational reasoning at its commencement. Intercourse is considered instrumental in procreation, but not affirmative of the couple's love. When companionship or friendship do become themes, they invariably come within the context of hierarchical superiority and inferiority.

Of course, it is a moot question whether the position of women deteriorated during the period. The likely answer is that, in fact, it did.[95] However, what we have discerned is enough to counter a *purely* negative view of the medieval period in its understanding of marriage. Lehmann's conclusion that the Middle Ages is 'a stranglehold of negativity' is a caricature, as is Harrison's that the period delivered 'an antisexual, antifemale, antisensual heritage' to succeeding generations.[96] What we can

---

[95] Herhily, art. cit., 125, suggests that women's status did deteriorate. Gies / Gies, op. cit., 270, say that, generally, they did suffer a diminution of status (see also, idem, *Women in the Middle Ages*, 230); while Brundage, op. cit., 227, states that wives and daughters in the twelfth century, in particular, became increasingly marginalized. See also, Heer, op. cit., 313.

[96] P. L. Lehmann, *Ethics in a Christian Context* (SCM, London, 1963), 136; B. W. Harrison, 'Human Sexuality and Mutuality' in J. L. Weidman (ed.),

say, however, is that the period conspicuously failed to solve the problem of woman's place in society and bequeathed that failure to the next age. A significant part of the difficulty is the inherent ambivalence in much of its comment, in which equivalence (sometimes, grudgingly) given to the woman appears to be taken back in a dogmatic reassertion of her inferiority and the ancillary nature of her role and duty. This has been seen, by one writer, as the church's attempt to do justice to the equivalence while assuming and reinforcing the subjection.[97] But, it is questionable whether the equality demanded by the gospel should not have more affect than that. Should individuals be able to live in domestic community without the constraints of sexual stereotyping or hierarchical power-relations?[98]

Another aspect of the difficulty is the rather static and detached model of society and family, generally, presented during the age. The teaching on domestic relationships is conventional and as a result rather sterile and hardly likely to engender any fundamental reform. Instead, the individual is obliged to submit to the prevailing social order and the traditional, hierarchical, domestic structure.

With these conclusions in mind, we turn to the Reformers to examine their view of marriage and the husband-wife relationship, specifically. We will discern in them features already espoused by the Augustinian tradition which they follow. However, their emphases and the nuances of their thought will be seen to be somewhat different.

Christian Feminism: Visions of a New Humanity (Harper and Row, San Francisco, 1994), 144, respectively.

[97] McLaughlin, art. cit., 221. See also, 232.

[98] Ibid., 257. McLaughlin's conclusion is worth noting: To say that 'a specific order and precedence was assigned by divine fiat to man and woman, which order we are yet bound to maintain', is 'static, ahistorical, hierarchical, Platonizing in its assumption of ontologically fixed relationships between the sexes' (259). Jordan, op. cit., 5, rightly claims that an acid test in writing on woman's equivalence is 'the extent to which woman's spiritual equality is seen to entail a correlative political status'.

III MARRIAGE IN LUTHER

CHAPTER 5

MARRIAGE AND THE TEMPORAL KINGDOM

The introductory chapter indicated and outlined the debate surrounding both Luther and Calvin's views on the husband and wife relationship. Chapters 3 and 4 examined the traditional, Augustinian concept of the marital union, by way of background – discerning and exploring three basic characteristics: *viz.* the importance of order, sexual negativity and androcentrism. We now turn to a detailed analysis of the writing of both Luther and Calvin in order to establish the theological undergirding of their teaching on marriage. The method of each of the analyses is identical. First, we outline a more general theological matrix in which to read the particular ethical teaching of marriage, and then proceed to a closer examination of the husband and wife relationship within that framework. Lastly, we turn to an enquiry into each Reformer's exposition of the principal scriptural passages, in order to discern the inter-relationship between theological emphases and exegesis at that point.

In general terms, it will be found that both Luther and Calvin teach that marriage is a divinely given vocation. They are found to be basically traditional. Both insist on a hierarchical understanding of the husband-wife relationship. Both seek to soften any implicit harshness by an emphasis on mutuality and love. There are different nuances, of course. The chief one is that, whereas Luther stresses marriage as a vocation, Calvin appears to emphasize the purpose of marriage as something God uses to keep societal order. Therefore, in chapters 5 to 7 the study establishes Luther's doctrine of vocation as determinative of his view of the marital relationship. On the other hand, the chapters on Calvin (8-10) concentrate on his conception of order (*ordo*) as regulative of his ideas on that relationship. It will be observed, however, that both are ultimately and traditionally concerned with order in society – Luther's teaching, after all, is that vocation is a control of behaviour in the community. Yet, as far as we are able to discern, Luther seems to emphasize the *nature*, Calvin the *function* of marriage.

Turning to Luther, we find that he came to the subject of marriage with a few persistent themes. Lisa Cahill lists the goodness of creation, the radical nature of the effects of sin, faith as the essence of Christian living, God's grace and the centrality of suffering in the believer's existence in the world.[1] We might add Christian liberty, freedom of conscience, and the almost overwhelming sense that men and women stand daily on trial before God and before their neighbour. But nothing is more fundamental to an understanding of Luther's thought on marriage and the husband-wife relationship than his teaching on vocation (*Beruf, vocatio*). With its emphasis on the grace of God to the individual within community and on their personal response by faith, the Reformation generally demanded the correlative principle of evangelical lifestyle before the saving God, in Christ and by the power of the Holy Spirit. That lifestyle was firmly rooted, by Luther, in God's calling of the individual within society to that person's own vocation.

The thrust of this chapter, then, is that Luther's teaching on vocation is determinative for his understanding of the relationship between the spouses. That is, to gain an adequate grasp of what Luther teaches concerning the hierarchical arrangement of husband and wife, it is necessary to locate that concept in the broader, theological and social context of *vocatio*. To put this as a question: How does his idea of vocation, within the temporal realm of God's authority, relate to Luther's view of marriage and the concrete relationship between the spouses?

The following seeks to establish a matrix of theological thought in which we may read Luther's concept of the marriage relationship. It will be found that Luther's perception of present

---

[1] L. S. Cahill, *Between the Sexes* (Fortress, Philadelphia, 1985), 123.

reality is framed within his teaching on the two kingdoms of God's rule. First, the relationship between them is explored, relative to their similarities. Luther teaches that both originate in God, both have the common purpose of sustaining people in an ordered society countering their own sin and the onslaughts of the devil. The examination then moves to a consideration of the significant differences between the two kingdoms. In so doing, it shows that the believer inhabits the temporal kingdom in which inequality between persons is fundamental. The implications are then drawn. If marriage, as a vocation, is located in the temporal kingdom, it must reflect the nature of that reality. The chapter, therefore, shows that vocation originates with God, is part of his control of society and has inherent inequality between its members. If this is so, of course, then marriage itself will demonstrate these characteristics.

THE TWO KINGDOMS

Together with other Reformers, Luther evidences *Angst* (*anxietas*) concerning the predominance of sin, disorder and disruption in the society of his own generation. Although perhaps not as clearly pronounced in Luther's writing as in Calvin's, it is there.[2] For Luther, this is directly attributable to humanity's sinfulness and to Satan's malicious activity and is measured against its opposite – God's authoritative ordering of the world and his preservation of it until the Last Day. God preserves and maintains everything (including government and authority in the world) by the same power that made the world out of nothing and now continues its existence.[3] Luther never tires of this emphasis. Despite the ramifications of the Fall, the natural and societal order of God's creation is preserved by God's continuous activity. He is concerned with its order (*ordo*). This is central to the Reformer's ethics: it is the traditional starting point.

---

[2] See, for example, *Comm. Ps.* 101:4, LW 13.190 [WA 51.236]; *Comm. Gal.* 3:19 (1535), LW 26.307-8 [WA 40.478]; *Comm. Gen.* 7:1, LW 2.83 [WA 42.320]; 19:5, LW 3.255 [WA 43.58].

[3] See *Comm. Ps.* 102:25, LW 14.186 [WA 18.515]; 118:2, LW 14.52 [WA 31.77]; 82:1, LW 13.45 [WA 31¹.192].

According to Luther, God oversees the world of humanity in two distinct ways: through both the spiritual rule (*das geistliche Reich / Regiment*) and the worldly, or temporal rule (*das weltliche Reich / Regiment*). In asserting the existence of both, Luther insists on beginning from the perspective of God's authoritative regulation. There is, undoubtedly, ambiguity in Luther's language.[4] But, from the viewpoint of this study, we note that when Luther employs the term *das weltliche Regiment* in its *primary* sense of temporal or natural order, in it, 'he embraces the whole external order of society and all the institutions and callings of man's natural life'[5] – including those in the household. This is the instrument of the continuous, providential, ordering activity of God in the world. In Luther's thought this is distinct from and parallel to *das geistliche Regiment* which designates the order of redemption, of the Word and of the Spirit. This is *regnum fidei* introduced by Christ – the spiritual kingdom of God. The essence of the latter is that it directs people vertically towards God, the former directs them horizontally towards one another.[6]

However, an emphasis on the antithesis between the two, although important, actually belies the strong relationship between them.[7] Therefore, before we turn to the distinguishing

---

[4] For example, Luther's use of such words as *Reich, Regiment, Welt* and *Weltliche* is highly elastic. See W. D. J. Cargill Thompson, 'The "Two Kingdoms" and the "Two *Regiments*": Some Problems of Luther's *Zwei-Reiche Lehre*' in C. M. Dugmore (ed.), *Studies in the Reformation: Luther to Hooker* (Athlone, London, 1980), 42-59. He observes that the term *Reich* [Latin *regnum*] can mean 'kingdom' [realm] or 'office' [authority]. *Regiment* [Latin equivalent, *gubernatio*] basically means 'rule' or 'government'. Both, however, denote 'two ways in which God governs mankind or two orders of government' (44).

[5] Ibid., 54.

[6] *Comm. Ps* 101:5, LW 13.197 [WA 51.241]. In this way he developed the Augustinian teaching of two cities and the medieval doctrine of the two estates in which the clergy and the laity were made distinct as 'spiritual' and 'temporal'. See A. E. McGrath, *Reformation Thought* (Blackwell, Oxford, 1989), 142; T. F. Torrance, 'The Eschatology of Faith: Martin Luther' in G. Yule (ed.), *Luther: Theologian for Catholics and Protestants* (T&T Clark, Edinburgh, 1985), 145-213; particularly, 152-65; G. Rupp, *The Righteousness of God: Luther Studies* (Hodder and Stoughton, London, 1968), 286-309; E. W. Gritsch, *Martin – God's Court Jester: Luther in Retrospect* (Fortress, Philadelphia, 1983), 113-17; J. M. Tonkin, 'Luther's Interpretation of Secular Reality', *JRH* 6/2 (1970-71), 133-51; G. Ebeling, *Luther: An Introduction to His Thought* (Collins, London, 1970), 175-209.

[7] A. MacIntyre, *A Short History of Ethics* (Macmillan, New York, 1966), 126, for example, exaggerates the autonomy of the temporal realm.

marks that are particularly pertinent to the present study, it is necessary to see the two authorities in their relational context. Our interpretation of Luther's vocational understanding of the husband-wife relationship depends on seeing the differences between the spiritual and temporal realms *within* the context of their correlation because Luther is at pains, not only to see them as separate, but also to emphasize their common origin in God and their common purpose in God's ordering of societal peace. The vocation of marriage shares in the commonality as well as the differences.

Commonality between the Kingdoms

As noted, there are clearly significant differences between the kingdoms, but there are also salient points of contact between them. Scholars see the relationship in different ways. Ebeling, for example, though qualifying the idea later in his work, suggests that we see the two kingdoms as two concentric circles. He states that, '[W]e do no more than draw two circles which, with this same point as their centre and the world and God as their respective radii, include everything that exists.' The two realms of authority 'coincide and yet remain separate'.[8] For Torrance, the eschatological perspective that Luther maintained throughout his life keeps the two kingdoms 'differentiated and yet unified'. Thompson suggests that they are not antithetical, but complementary,[9] Gustaf Wingren that they are not in opposition to one another, but in reality that they exist side by side.[10] There are several reasons for holding to this sort of analysis of Luther's two governments.

The common origin of the two kingdoms

Luther holds that the origin of both kingdoms is God. Both derive their existence from the Creator of all things. That is, they are related primarily because of their inception in both the mind and the creative activity of God. From this point of view, both are part of God's original creation and not simply a result of the Fall (though they *are* modified in the light of Adam's sin). This means

---

[8] Ebeling, op. cit., 177, 191, respectively.
[9] Torrance, op. cit., 156, 165; Cargill Thompson, op. cit., 46.
[10] G. Wingren, *Luther on Vocation* (Muhlenberg, Philadelphia, 1957), 85.

that God is not only the author of spiritual reality, but also of temporal existence. In this context, Luther divides God's government into three basic institutions[11] – the church,[12] the family and the state. Commenting on Genesis 2:16-17, he shows how the church was established first, then the government of the home and the state, in that order. The church comes into being as the Lord speaks to Adam in the garden. The family exists at the creation of Eve and civil government (as a remedy, in contrast to human society which was formed at Eve's creation) only when the pair rebel against God.[13] Luther speaks of the church as God's priority within the overall scheme of things:

> [T]oday the world stands and empires are preserved for no other reason than that God gathers a church for himself in the midst of a perverse nation. For God has no concern for the state and the household except for the sake of the church.[14]

By the phrase, 'no concern for the state and the household', Luther refers to *ultimate, not* temporal concern. Elsewhere he is clear on God's intimate involvement with both the family and with civil government. But here, in this context, he stresses God's eternal concern. In terms of temporal priorities, things are significantly different. This is so not only because, logically, a whole community is merely the sum of many households,[15] but also, as Luther repeatedly emphasizes, the family is the source from which the other two originate. Family, epitomized by the married pair, is the oldest of all the estates (*Stände*). Indeed,

---

[11] E. L. Long, *A Survey of Christian Ethics* (OUP, New York, 1967), 186-90, suggests four institutions – family, state, church and daily employment. It is true that Luther speaks a great deal about daily employment as a calling before God, but he often subsumes it under the state or the family. See also, J. R. Loeschen, *The Divine Community* (SCJ publishers, Kirksville, 1981), 59.

[12] It is interesting to note that P. Althaus, *The Ethics of Martin Luther* (Fortress, Philadelphia, 1972), 45, 56, 66-8, 79, does not include the church in worldly orders because he stresses too much the opposition between the two kingdoms.

[13] *Comm. Gen.* 2:16-17, LW 1.103 [WA 42.79]. Also, *Comm. Gen.* 2:18, LW 1.115 [WA 42.87]; 6:13, LW 2.64 [WA 42.307].

[14] *Comm. Gen.* 43.1-5, LW 7.348-9 [WA 44.559]. See *Comm. Gen.* 19:15, LW 3.279 [WA 43.74]; 18:15, LW 3.217 [WA 43.30]. See also, P. Meinhold, 'Society in Transition in the Age of the Reformation', *SCJ* 3 (1972), 35-6.

[15] LW 45.328 [WA 15.370]. See also, *Comm. Gen.* 18:13-14, LW 3.214 [WA 43.28]; 19:15, LW 3.253-4 [WA 43.58]; *Comm. Ps.* 68:12, LW 13.13 [WA 8.14].

'heaven and earth with all that is in them were created for the sake of the married estate, which is the fountainhead of all other estates'.[16]

Both spiritual and temporal governments originate with God, then. In all their complexity of being and function, he is the source of their existence and continuance. Over and through each he directly exercises his final sovereignty. As Pannenberg observes, Luther 'regarded both the spiritual power and the secular as God's ways of exercising his rule, and not as powers entrusted to humans'.[17]

The common purpose of the two kingdoms

It is apparent that in Luther's theology God not only created both governments but he also sustains them, and, on one level at least, for a similar, important purpose – that is, the maintenance of order, the preservation of peace. In the continuous, providential working of God he preserves the peace necessary for mankind's existence. This emphasis retains the traditional stress on the significance of *ordo*. God maintains order through both the spiritual and the temporal governments.[18] In the spiritual kingdom, God works through the Spirit and the Word to teach righteousness, love and obedience,[19] to maintain peace with himself, to bring harmony about between enemies. In the temporal kingdom and in its societal aspect, particularly, Luther insists that God is neither less active, nor less personally involved in seeking to protect the common fabric of human society.[20] It is God who creates society: it is not a matter of

---

[16] *Comm. John* 1:13, LW 22.91 [WA 46.615]. Luther's commentary on Genesis is full of such statements: *Comm. Gen.* 4:1, LW 1.240 [WA 42.178]; 9:1, LW 2.131 [WA 42.354]; 16:1-2, LW 3.43 [WA 42.579]; 18:9, LW 3.202 [WA 43.579]; 24:10-11, LW 4.259 [WA 43.321]; 28:1-2, LW 5.189 [WA 43.558]; 37:12-14, LW 6.347 [WA 44.259-60], etc. See also, LW 51.154 [WA 30^1.76], and his sermon preached at the marriage of Sigismund von Lindenau, LW 51.358 [WA 49.797-8].

[17] W. Pannenberg, 'Luther's Doctrine of the Two Kingdoms' in idem., *Ethics* (Westminster / Search, Philadelphia / London, 1981), 112-31. He further points out that Luther's idea of two realms derives from Augustine; the concept of two ways in which God rules from the medieval theory of two forces in Christendom – one spiritual, the other secular. 'Luther's original contribution ... is his bringing together these two lines of thought' (117).

[18] *Comm. Ps.* 101:5, LW 13.195 [WA 51.239-340].

[19] *The Estate of Marriage* (1522), LW 45.31 [WA 10^2.288].

[20] *Comm. Gen.* 43:1-5, LW 7.312 [WA 44.530].

human ingenuity or determination, but it is God who appoints and preserves everything in the temporal as in the spiritual realm.[21]

In the social order, God seeks peace and the preservation of mankind through the setting up of institutions and the arrangement of society by his Word and command. These would include the familial callings of husband, wife and parents. Simply put, the stability of family life is the ideal beginning and foundation for the stability of society.[22] God daily maintains external societal peace and a satisfactory life in community through his worldly government. It is within this context that the concept of vocation (for example, that of marriage) is to be seen.

However, a question is naturally raised by this brief outline of Luther's thought. Why is restraint and order necessary in the world God has created? Luther's answer appears to divide into two parts. It is necessary because of humanity's continuing sin and because of Satan's opposition. The former gives insight into Luther's postlapsarian anthropology, the latter reveals something of his eschatological perspective as he tries to make sense of the society in which he lives. Both reveal something of the nature of the context of the vocation of marriage.

1. Purpose in relation to sin. God's purpose in exercising both realms of his authority is similar in relation to mankind's sin, because through them both he seeks to confront that sin directly. He does so by the gospel or by the law. In this area of thought, they are merely 'two different ways in which God encounters the sinful world', as Ebeling observes.[23] Luther believes that humanity's sin needs to be confronted by the righteous God if his purposes are to be achieved in human society.

---

[21] *Comm. Ps.* 82:1, LW 13.46 [WA 31^1.193-4]; LW 13.44 [WA 31^1.191-2], respectively.

[22] Institutions would also include the civil stations of magistrate, lord, subject and servant and the ecclesiastical ones of church order. See R. Po-Chia Hsia, *Social Discipline in the Reformation* (Routledge, London, 1989), particularly, 143-7; C. J. Blaisdell, 'The Matrix of Reform: Women in the Lutheran and Calvinist Movements' in R. L. Greaves, *Triumph Over Silence* (Greenwood, Westport Connecticut, 1985), 20; *Comm. Ps.* 111:3, LW 13.358 [WA 31^1.399-400].

[23] Ebeling, op. cit., 184-5.

Sin, itself, entered the world through Adam and Eve's fall from grace.[24] The root of that sin and of subsequent impiety is unbelief, doubt, abandoning of the Word of God and, ultimately, rebellion against a genuine relationship with the Creator. Through that original sin all people were tainted and corrupted; the whole human race was destroyed, the 'flesh [became] ... overwhelmed by the leprosy of lust [*carnis lepram*]'.[25] For Luther, a major problem is that human nature will always be the same, thus perpetuating the need for God's intervention in anger as well as in grace;[26] that is, through the law as well as through the gospel. That is not to say that Luther considered the law's function of promoting order to be its primary one. That is always subordinate to its work of disturbing men and women with the intention of driving them to Christ and salvation. However, the law's societal task of the preservation of order and its repressive work against disorder is of crucial importance to this present examination.[27]

As a consequence of rebellion, all men and women are unable to restrain sin by their own efforts. Indeed, Luther draws this pessimistic, universal conclusion from his study of Genesis 6: '[W]ithout the Holy Spirit and without grace man can do nothing but sin and goes on endlessly from sin to sin'.[28] Being, now, wholly ignorant of God, men and women have become blinded by

---

[24] See, for example, *Comm. Gen.* 3:1, LW 1.149 [WA 42 .112]; 3:6, LW 1.162 [WA 42.122].

[25] *Comm. Gen.* 1:28, LW 1.71 [WA 42.53]. See also, *Comm. Ps.* 8:3, LW 12.121 [WA 45.220-21]; *Comm. Deut.* 1:20, LW 9.21 [WA 14.557]; *Comm. Gen.* 21:20-21, LW 4.70 [WA 43.185]; *Comm. Ps.* 51:5, LW 14.169 [WA 18.500]; T. N. Tentler, *Sin and Confession on the Eve of the Reformation* (Princeton University Press, Princeton, 1977), 165-7.

[26] *Comm. Hos.* 9:10, LW 18.50 [WA 13.45]; *Comm. Jonah* 2:2, LW 19.73 [WA 13.224].

[27] See, for example, LW 26.441-2 [WA 40^1.664-5]. J. M. Gustafson, *Protestant and Roman Catholic Ethics* (SCM, London, 1979), 13, describes the Reformer's societal concept of law in this context as, 'a dike against the chaos Luther saw threatening community'. See also, idem, *Christ and the Moral Law* (Chicago University Press, Chicago, 1976), 123; Wingren, op. cit., 62; D. Wright, 'The Ethical Use of the Old Testament in Luther and Calvin: A Comparison', *SJT* 36 (1983), 463-86; E. L. Long, Jr, 'Soteriological Implications of Norm and Context' in G. H. Outka / P. Ramsey (eds), *Norm and Context in Christian Ethics* (SCM, London, 1969), 265-95, particularly 277-8.

[28] *Comm. Gen.* 6:5, LW 2.40 [WA 42.290]. He cites Ps. 14:2-3; Rom. 3:10, 11:32; Ps. 116:11; 1 John 15:5. See also, LW 45.45 [WA 10^2.300].

sin, full of guilt and subsequent anxiety and 'fleshly' by nature.[29] In Luther's forceful words from his commentary on Psalm 51:[30]

> Through the Fall his will, understanding, and all natural powers were so corrupted that man was no longer whole, but was diverted by sin [*sed incurvatus per peccatum*], lost his correct judgement before God, and thought everything perversely against the will and law of God.

This has significant implications for the vocation of marriage, for if mankind's nature is so fallen, then their relations with others are going to be affected in an equally adverse manner. In his commentary on Romans, Luther shows how this sinfulness and fallenness affects people and their relations with others in society and the family. People have become so curved in upon themselves (*in-curvatus in se*)[31] that they use everything and everyone for their own egotistic purposes. This is natural, given the Fall – 'a natural wickedness and a natural sinfulness'.[32]

In their curvedness, people continually put things as priorities before the true God as idols that pamper to their own egoism. It is significant that the Reformer includes in a list of such idols, family, relatives, children, wife, parents – together with riches, power, honours, friends, health, strength, beauty, talent, intellect, wisdom, spiritual good (such as righteousness, devotion, gifts of the Spirit and meditation).[33]

---

[29] *Comm. Deut.* 4:2, LW 9.51 [WA 14.585]; *Comm. Rom.* 6:13, LW 25.320 [WA 56.332].

[30] LW 12.307 [WA 40^2. 323-4].

[31] Note *Comm. Ps.* 51:1-2, LW 12.308-9 [WA 40^2.323-4]: '*Sed per lapsum postea corrupta est voluntas, intellectus et omnia naturalia, ita ut homo non amplius sit integer, sed incurvatus per peccatum, ut qui amisit iudicium rectum coram Deo et omnia perverse statuit contra voluntatem et legem Dei...*'. Here we find Luther's characteristic teaching concerning humanity's sinfulness before (*coram*) God.

[32] *Comm. Rom.* 8:3, LW 25.345 [WA 56.355-6]. See also, *Comm. Rom.* 5:4, LW 25.291 [WA 56.305]; 6:6, LW 25.313 [WA 56.525]. A. Nygren, *Agape and Eros* (SPCK, London, 1953), 485-6, fn. 3, compares Luther's understanding to that of Augustine in the following way: 'For Augustine, sin consists in the fact that man is bent down to earth (*curvatus*); and Luther, too, can say that sinful man is "*curvatus*". But this means for Luther something different; it means that man is egocentric, that his will is determined always by his own interest and so is bent upon itself (*in-curvatus in se*).'

[33] *Comm. Rom* 8:7, *LW* 25.351 [WA 56.361-2].

It is clear from this that Luther understands postlapsarian men and women to be inherently selfish and that they naturally seek to use other people (even husband or wife) to their own advantage. Such is sinful humanity without the grace of God that changes the nature of things. Yet even Christians experience this selfishness, for they are in the flesh in the limited sense that remnants of sin remain.

It is to this reality of sin and its pervasive disorderliness in regenerate and unregenerate alike that both governments speak. The spiritual government (with its internal rule of the Spirit,[34] its inner peace and freedom and reforming ability) seeks to mould the Christian after Christ by changing the man from within. Thus life is 'a life of *being healed* from sin, it is not a life of sinlessness, with the cure completed and perfect health attained. The church is the inn and the infirmary for those who are sick and in need of being made well'.[35] The temporal government, on the other hand, seeks to curb and to restrain the continuing sinfulness of the believer and the inherent sinfulness of those outside of Christ, by law, by arrangement, by social order, by threat and by punishment of sin. Political and social institutions are, therefore, a kind of emergency measure against sin.[36] These keep a check on behaviour through such 'offices' as the magistrates, lords, parents, teachers, husbands and the like, and the continued subjection of their lower relational counterparts – subjects, servants, children, students, wives and so on.

This is significant for Luther's concept of vocation in which inequality of position is intrinsic and, also, his teaching on the necessity of marriage to avoid sin. Husband and wife, by postlapsarian nature, are sinful people and have been placed within that marital relationship by God as a control to that sin – both in relation to their sexuality and their inherent selfishness. Marriage is said to remedy the former. A true understanding of their hierarchical positions should help in the latter.

2. Purpose in relation to the devil. As God's purpose in exercising two realms of authority is related to sin, so it is to the unceasing,

---

[34] On *the* transforming power of the Holy Spirit in a believer's life, see *Comm. Isa.* 9:4, LW 16.99 [WA 31².69-70]. See also, W. H. Wagner, 'Luther and the Positive Use of the Law', *JRH* 11/1 (1980-81), 45-63.

[35] *Comm. Rom.* 4:7, LW 25.262-3 [WA 56.275] – emphasis added.

[36] See Pannenberg, op. cit., 129.

malevolent work of the devil during what Luther believed to be the last days. This widely accepted aspect of Luther's thinking is cogently argued by Oberman, for example, and is well documented.[37] It needs to be taken into account in our examination of the two kingdoms and of Luther's teaching regarding the marriage relationship. Here, his moral teaching becomes, what has been appropriately called, 'survival ethics in dangerous times'.[38] It is within this apocalyptic framework that he understands the nature and purpose of marriage.

It is clear that, together with many of his generation, Luther believes himself to be at the end of the last days. He holds an apocalyptic view of history that gives him a sense of living on the very edge of the age.[39] Oberman speaks of the Reformer as 'Luther

---

[37] See, particularly, H. A. Oberman, *Luther: Man Between God and the Devil* (Fontana, London, 1993), 43-4, 67-80, 297; idem, '*Teufelsdreck*: Eschatology and Scatology in the "Old" Luther' in idem, *The Impact of the Reformation* (T&T Clark, Edinburgh, 1994), 51-68 and, in the same volume, 'The Impact of the Reformation: Problems and Perspectives', 194-8. Other scholars disagree with this interpretation of the Reformer. Oberman, himself, cites B. Lohse, 'Luthers Selbsteinschätzung' in P. Manns (ed.), *Martin Luther: Reformator und Vater im Glauben: Referate aus der Vortragsreihe des Instituts für Europäische Geschichte Mainz* (Stuttgart, 1985), 118-33 and B. Moeller, 'Was wurde in der Frühzeit der Reformation in den deutschen Städten gepredigt?', *ARG* 75 (1984), 176-93. The former does not accept Luther's theology as apocalyptic; the latter argues that it is not merely a characteristic of Luther, but of the early leaders of the City Reformation, generally. But, see also, Wingren, op. cit., 78-161; Althaus, op. cit., 161-8; D. R. Reid, 'Luther, Münster and the Last Day: Eschatological Hope, Apocalyptic Expectation', *MQR* 69 (1995), particularly, 57-64. R. Barnes, *Prophecy and Gnosis: Apocalypticism in the Wake of the Lutheran Reformation* (Stanford University Press, Stanford, 1988), 4, says that Luther 'took over common eschatological views ... sifted them and applied them with an unprecedented explicitness to the events of his day. ... Everything pointed to the Coming Day of Redemption.'

[38] Oberman, *Luther: Man between God and the Devil*, 79.

[39] In fact, Luther's thinking here appears to work at two levels. On the one hand, he is clear that the last days are called such, 'not because of the shortness of the time, but because of the nature of the teaching'. That is, the teaching after the resurrection of Christ and the formation of the church (that is, the gospel) is the last *new* teaching that the church will receive (*Comm. 1 John* 2:18, LW 30.251 [WA 20.667]). On the other hand, he holds parallel to this and increasingly that these are the last days, in the sense that Christ's Second Coming is due at any moment, as it were. See also, Torrance, art. cit., 154-5; S. H. Hendrix, *Luther and the Papacy: Stages in the Reformation Conflict* (Fortress, Philadelphia, 1981), 150-52.

the Apocalyptic'.⁴⁰ His writing and preaching is littered with reference to the closeness of the Last Day. Characteristically, in 1532, for example, he says that, 'The Last Day is at hand. My calendar has run out.'⁴¹ He describes the world in this context, in typically expressive language, as 'an old wornout coat ... which soon has to be changed'.⁴² The Reformer believed the end to be close partly because of signs that he interpreted as portents of Christ's return – for example, certain apparitions reported in 1529; a solar eclipse, followed by a heat wave as late as 1540.⁴³ But there were more pertinent reasons for his view.

In his mature commentary on Genesis, Luther extracts from the biblical narrative of the flood a doctrine of what happens before the wrath of God destroys mankind. He sees it as a paradigm for the Day of Christ's return. First, God raises up holy men, full of the Holy Spirit, to instruct and to reprove the world. Second, the world, blinded by ιebellion and impiety, indulges more persistently in sins with greater zeal. He states, 'That was what happened at the beginning of the world [i.e., in Noah's day] and *we see that the same thing is happening now at the end of the*

---

⁴⁰ Oberman, 'The Impact of the Reformation', 194. See also, H. Preuss, *Die Vorstellungen vom Antichrist im späten Mittelalter, bei Luther und in der konfessionellen Polemik* (C. J. Hinrichsehe Buchhandlung, Leipzig, 1906). See also M. Parsons, 'The Apocalyptic Luther: His Noahic Self-Understanding', *JETS* 44 (2001) 627-45.

⁴¹ January 1, 1532, LW 54.134 [WA Tr. 2.33]. See also, for example, LW 54.440-41 [WA Tr. 5.205]; *Comm. 1 Pet.* 1:5, LW 30.16 [WA 12.271]; *Comm. 2 Pet.* 3:3, LW 30.193 [WA 14.66]; *Comm. Hos.* 12:9, LW 18.67 [WA 33.424]; to the Elector, Frederick, Wartburg, between Jan. 13-19, 1519, LW 48.103-6 [WA Br. 1.306-8].

⁴² To James Propst [Wittenberg] Dec. 5, 1544, LW 50.245 [WA Br. 10.554]. See also, to King Christian of Denmark [Wittenberg] April 14, 1545, LW 50.251 [WA Br. 11.70]; *Comm. Gen.* 34:1-2, LW 6.188 [WA 44.140]; April 11, 1539, LW 54.346 [WA Tr. 4.339]; LW 54.101 [WA Tr. 1.262-4]; LW 48.111-15 [WA Br. 1.359-60]; LW 48.215-17 [WA Br. 2.332-3]; LW 49.13 [WA Br. 2.568]; *Comm. Gen.* 49:16-18, LW 8.283 [WA 44.786-7]; LW 35.136-40 [WA 10².77-80].

⁴³ To Wenceslas Link [Wittenberg] March 7, 1529, LW 49.216 [WA Br. 5.28]; to Mrs M. Luther [Eisenach] July 16, 1540, LW 50.218-20 [WA Br. 9.174-5]. H. H. Kramm, *The Theology of Martin Luther* (James Clarke, London, 1947), 103, mentions that when astronomers predicted a great flood in 1524 Luther hoped that it would signify the Last Day, and Torrance, art. cit., 155, suggests that Luther worked in haste during 1530 in case the second advent occurred. See also, *Comm. Gen.* 6:1-2, LW 2.13 [WA 42.271].

world.'⁴⁴ This, Luther explicates regarding his own time and, importantly, regarding his own teaching ministry and the social application of the Word. Therefore, the godlessness that Luther saw around him was a sure sign of the end of the age. The world was going its own way against God, inclined to hell and its own damnation; it 'is deteriorating from day to day. But it was the deterioration of morals that was the surest indication of impending ruin.'⁴⁵

In this worsening context the preacher's responsibility was to preach Christ and to apply the gospel in such a way that lives were changed and followers were strengthened against Satan's attacks. Both doctrine and conduct were to be directed to the expectation of the Last Day and of eternal life. This is the emphasis that carried with it the mandate to rebuke current sins.⁴⁶ This Luther attempted in the area of the relationship between the spouses. Against the backdrop of deteriorating morals and the activity of the devil, the Reformer saw in this the fact that in his age 'everything begins to be restored, as if that day of the restoration of all things were near'.⁴⁷

This is very significant for the present study. It shows that the subject of marriage – both its nature and purpose – is to be interpreted within the apparently increasing sinfulness of men and women exactly at the time in which the work of Satan (*opus diaboli*) is to oppose the work of God. He is thought to do this directly in tempting people to misuse vocation, in seeking to gain allegiance from followers of Christ.⁴⁸ Satan tries to lure men and

---

⁴⁴ *Comm. Gen.* 6:1-2, LW 2.13 [WA 42.271] – emphasis added.

⁴⁵ *Comm. Gen.* 3:17-19, LW 1.206 [WA 42.154 – *Mundus enim de die in diem magis degenerat*]. See also, *Comm. Gen.* 9:26, LW 2.175 [WA 42.385]; to Wenceslas Link, [Wittenberg] June 20, 1543, LW 50.241-4 [WA Br. 10.335]; *Comm. 2 Pet.* 3:3, LW 30.193 [WA 14.66]; LW 36.225 [WA 8.559]; LW 43.67-9 [WA 10².58-9]. See particularly, M. U. Edwards, Jr, *Luther and the False Brethren* (Stanford University Press, Stanford, 1975), 181-3.

⁴⁶ *Comm. Isa.* 9:8, LW 16.102 [WA 31².72]. See also, preface to *Comm. Hab.*, LW I9.153 [WA 13.351].

⁴⁷ The prefatory letter to *Comm. Deut.*, LW 9.6 [WA 14.499]. See also, *Comm. 1 Pet.* 1:20, LW 30.38 [WA 12.293]; LW 43.174-5 [WA 30².705]. As this relates specifically to marriage, see LW 54.177 [WA Tr. 3.40]; *Comm. Gen.* 2:22, LW 1.135 [WA 42. 101]; LW 47.52 [WA 30³.317].

⁴⁸ Luther states, '[T]he estate of marriage does not set well with the devil, because it is God's good will and work [*es ist gottis werck und gutter wille*]' (*The Estate of Marriage*, (1522), LW 45.37-8 [WA 10². 294]).

women away from the teaching and application of the Word of God, as he did with their first parents. He attempts to indoctrinate them with lies.[49] He seeks what Luther calls *Werckheiligen* (work-saints)[50] – those who count on and boast of their own righteousness and live without God and outside of salvation. Opposed to this, God uses both governments against Satan; he presses his opposition both as gospel and as law.

On the one hand God exercises his spiritual government to win believers from the clutches of the devil and to set them upon lives which are pleasing before him: lives which will be most clearly seen in application in the social and familial (and ecclesiastical) spheres of their existence. Indeed, part of the evidence of God's re-creative and renewing work in the believer is that he casts off self-chosen and self-important works and performs the tasks given him by God in his vocation in the world.[51] On the other hand, God exercises his temporal government to limit and to restrict the advances of Satan by the preservation of order and social arrangement. Gritsch puts it as follows: 'The secular order battles the kingdom of Satan with law and order; the spiritual government nourishes Christians with Word and sacrament.' Thompson, on the other hand, sees the realms as weapons which God 'employs in his struggle against the *regnum diaboli*'.[52] In the temporal realm, at least, he does this largely through vocation.

Commonality in relation to divine love and natural law

It is apparent from Luther's writing that the two governments of God's rule connect in a more complex way than simply in their origin and purpose. There are two elements of what we might call inner connection between them that need to be noticed. The first concerns the love of God, which is common to both.

---

[49] *Comm. 1 Cor.* 15:33, LW 28.163 [WA 36.621]. See *Comm. Ps.* 90:17, LW 13.137 [WA 40³.588]; the preface to *Comm. Jonah*, LW 19.35 [WA 13.186]. On Luther's teaching regarding Satan's activity against the vocations that God has established, see particularly, Oberman, *Luther: Man between God and the Devil*, 78-161.

[50] *Comm. John* 3:13, LW 22.330 [WA 47.58].

[51] *Comm. Gal.* 6:15 (1535), LW 27.140 [WA 40².179].

[52] Gritsch, op. cit., 117; Cargill Thompson, op. cit., 48, respectively.

Gustaf Wingren summarizes this juxtaposition from two different perspectives. First, he speaks of the vertical plane – that is, the situation looked at from God's perspective. Then, he analyses the horizontal plane of humanity's understanding and experience.[53] The former perspective sees the two governments as expressions of God's love towards fallen men and women; God's positive, creative work going on in his world. In this context, people are seen as God's 'co-workers' and ministers as preachers of forgiveness. The latter perspective on the two governments shows people pondering their tasks in the world and being forced to ask the question, 'What does God want of me?' In vocation and calling, people are tangibly made aware of God's requirements by both the law and the gospel.

There is a great deal to be said for this interpretation. Certainly, it demonstrates the connection between the two spheres of God's authority by showing that their purpose, though not identical, is to drive people to a continual awareness of the God before whom they stand and to cause them to realize their life's calling before him. And, as we have previously seen, both the temporal and the spiritual governments are affirmations of the love of God. Through their joint, though separate, ministry they seek to regain something of that which was lost by Adam – genuine, spiritual peace with the Creator, through Christ, and (as far as possible in this life) order and peace within societal relationships. The former will naturally express itself in the latter. Their aim is substantially to reverse the effects of the Fall within the spiritual, societal and temporal spheres of existence. Consequently, in writing on Psalm 101, Luther speaks of the tasks of the two governments as they are concretized within society and concludes,

> The spiritual government or authority should direct the people vertically toward God that they may *do right* and be saved; just so the secular government should direct the people horizontally toward one another, seeing to it that body, property, honour, wife, child, house, home, and all manner of goods *remain in peace* and security and are blessed on earth.[54]

---

[53] Wingren, op. cit., 27-8.
[54] *Comm. Ps.* 101:5, LW 13.197 [WA 51.241] – emphasis added. See also, for example, *Comm. Gen.* 2:7, LW 1.84 [WA 42.63].

In singling out Philip Melanchthon among the Reformers as natural law's chief proponent, Lang stresses that for Luther's theology the concept was 'to play merely a secondary, incidental part'.[55] This may be substantially true. Nevertheless, Luther teaches that natural law (*lex naturae, lex naturalis*), together with natural reason, determines what duties are required within vocation in the temporal realm. In this sense, it is expressive of God's will.

He states that earthly matters have been subjected to natural reason. This occurred at creation when God spoke to Adam saying, 'Have dominion over the earth' and its effect is permanent. It is an inherent part of the creative order.[56] It is inherent, not simply because God commanded, but also because he empowered humanity to maintain that life by implanting the principle within their nature and writing it upon their heart.[57] Luther repeatedly shows marriage, for instance, to be subjected to natural reason and law.[58]

It is in answer to the question, 'How does this relate to the gospel and the commands of Scripture?' that we discover a juxtaposition between the spiritual realm (in which the Word and the gospel rule) and the temporal realm (in which reason and natural law hold sway). The fact is that, because Luther holds both kingdoms to be governed by God and not to be completely separate, the visible and outward realm must listen to the gospel as it is 'through the Word of God that the heavenly realm is made relevant to the earthly'.[59] Love, set forth and applied in the Word, ought to regulate and permeate all secular activities. Luther relates life in the world to the highest moral order (the *communio sanctorum*) and, therefore, the moralizing influence of the kingdom of Christ is at work in the world.

So, referring to the temporal realm of government, the Reformer can state that 'everything must be most securely

---

[55] A. Lang, 'The Reformation and Natural Law' in W. P. Armstrong (ed.), *Calvin and the Reformation* (Baker, Grand Rapids, 1980), 56-98. See *Comm. Ps.* 101:1, LW 13.161 [WA 51.212].

[56] To the Elector [Coburg] August 26, 1530, LW 49.411 [WA Br. 5.574]; *Comm. Ps.* 111:3, LW 13.369 [WA 31^1.409-10].

[57] *Comm. John* 15:5, LW 24.228 [WA 45.669].

[58] See, for example, *Comm. Matt.* 5:31-2, LW 21.93 [WA 32.376-7]; *On Marriage Matters*, LW 46.269-70 [WA 30^3.208].

[59] Torrance, art. cit., 166. See also, Wingren, op. cit., 44, 151-4.

established on the basis of God's Word'.[60] As Torrance explains, he can employ this language because, for Luther, 'the Word addresses itself critically ... to every ordinance and aspect of human life in this world, calling them in question and refashioning them in accordance with their true end and authority'.[61] After all, Luther would maintain that they are and remain *God's* ordinances. To put the situation the other way, the gospel confirms and establishes the creation ordinances of God.[62] So it is by the grace of God and through the Word that he restores marriage to what it ought to be, for example.[63] However, on the other hand, from the reverse perspective, natural law and reason is that implanted understanding of what God requires. And, although distorted by sin and impaired,

> when we look at natural law, we see how right and universal the commandments are. They require nothing toward God or our neighbour but that which anyone would want to see done, either from a divine or from a human point of view.[64]

Of course, as we shall see, Christians understand increasingly more clearly what the Lord requires and voluntarily fulfils that requirement through the Holy Spirit by whom they are endowed.[65] Thus, Luther can speak of marriage, for instance, as a matter of both divine and natural law. However, if they conflict in

---

[60] *Comm. Isa.* 49:9, LW 17.143 [WA 31².374].

[61] Torrance, art. cit., 166.

[62] *Comm. Tit.* 1:6, LW 29.20 [WA 25.19]; *Comm. Isa.* 46:4, LW 17.139 [WA 31².370-71]; LW 33.52 [WA 18.626].

[63] *Tischreden* [2867ᵇ] LW 54.177 [WA Tr. 3.40].

[64] LW 43.16 [WA 10².379]. See also, the preface to *Notes on Ecclesiastes*, LW 15.5 [WA 20.8]; *Comm. Gen.* 35:9-10, LW 6.262 [WA 44.194-5]. It is important to note that Luther never places natural reason alongside the Word of God as a final court of ethical appeal, as is suggested, for example, by R. E. O. White, *The Changing Continuity of Christian Ethics* (Paternoster, Exeter, 1981), 2.328. See B. A. Gerrish, *The Old Protestantism and the New* (T&T Clark, Edinburgh, 1982), 51-8; A. C. George, 'Martin Luther's Doctrine of Sanctification with Special Reference to the Formula "*Simul Iustus et Peccator*"' (unpublished doctoral thesis, Westminster Theological Seminary, Philadelphia, 1982), 120-48, 160-66; H. Blocher, 'Luther et la Bible', *RRéf* 35 (1984), 41-55; J. M. Headley, 'The Reformation as Crisis in the Understanding of Tradition', *ARG* 78 (1987), 5-22; *Comm. Gen.* 2:21, LW 1.122 [WA 42.92].

[65] See, for example, *Comm. Isa.* 9:4, LW 16.99 [WA 31².69-70].

a given situation, then divine law has the priority.⁶⁶ Therefore, in positing two governments, the spiritual and the temporal, within the context of his own ethical teaching, Luther is 'seeking to use the second for the fruitful implementation of the ethical decisions inspired by the first'.⁶⁷

A consideration of the commonality between the two kingdoms of God's rule has made a significant contribution to our understanding of marriage and the husband-wife relationship in Luther's theology. It has revealed that marriage, as a vocation in the earthly realm has its origin in God's institution, not in humanity's. One of its major purposes, in terms of its societal role, is to maintain order and peace. Its true function is to reflect something of the gospel within a sinful world. In that way it is inherently related to *both* kingdoms in Luther's thought, though this remains somewhat ambiguous. This is important because it shows, for example, why and how Luther refers marriage to both the temporal and the spiritual governments of God's authority while, at the same time, demanding that it is looked at as a creational, not a redemptive, ordinance of God. It is a gift of grace, not a means of grace. That is, it adds to our understanding of his affirmation that marriage is *not* a sacrament. It also makes sense of his insistence that the spouses consider God and his Word, within the context of what, on the face of it, is a worldly undertaking.

The Dichotomy between the Kingdoms

One problem with Luther's writing on the two governments is that he sometimes refers to these two orders of authority in such a way as to suggest an antithesis between them. A striking example appears in his correspondence to the Emperor, for example, where he comments that earthly things have *nothing* in

---

⁶⁶ To Robert Barnes [Wittenberg] September 3, 1531, LW 50.31-40 [WA Br. 6.178-82]. In this context, Luther actually says, 'if they *seem* to contradict' (emphasis added) and argues that the law of Moses is not strictly applicable to Gentiles, but that the Decalogue is reflected in natural law, anyway. See also, *Comm. 1 Tim.* 6:1, LW 28.361-2 [WA 26.104]. Luther often relates this principle to divorce, for example, see LW 51.160 [WA 30¹.85]; *Comm. 1 Cor.* 7: 10-11, LW 28.31-2 [WA 12.118-19]; *On Marriage Matters*, LW 46.277-8 [WA 30³.214-15]; *Comm. Gen.* 2:24, LW 1.138 [WA 42.104].

⁶⁷ Long, *A Survey*, 190.

common with eternal things and, later, in the treatise *On Marriage Matters*, that

> the two authorities or realms, the temporal and the spiritual, are [to be] kept distinct and separate from each other and that *each* is [to be] specifically instructed and restricted to its own task.[68]

Indeed, he asserts that the Christian church is not to be concerned with temporal life and secular government.[69] The spiritual realm is that of justification by grace, the temporal that of the external life (*externae vitae*) alone.[70] The former is essentially the age to come, the latter the age in which we now live.[71] The former sphere will be given to God in eternity, while the latter will be abolished by Christ at his Second Coming.[72] The one is internal, the other external,[73] and so on.[74]

---

[68] To the Emperor, Charles V, Friedberg, April 28, 1521 - LW 48.203-9 [WA Br. 2.307-10]; *On Marriage Matters* (1530), LW 46.266 - emphasis added [WA 30³.206], respectively. Also, *Comm. Matt.* 5:33-7, LW 21.99 [WA 32.382]; *Comm. Gal.* 2:20 (1535) LW 26.173 [WA 40¹.292].

[69] '...*dis zeitlich leben und weltlich Regiment*' (*Comm. John* 16:13, LW 24.360 [WA 46.56]). Indeed, in this context, Christ has no intention of interfering with it: '...*das Christus hie gar nichts wil reden inn das weltlich Regiment und ordnung*' (*Comm. Matt.* 5:33-7, LW 21.99 [WA 32.382]).

[70] *Comm. Isa.* 56:4, LW 17.262 [WA 31².463].

[71] *Comm. Heb.* 1:2, LW 29.110 [WA 57³.98]; *Comm. 1 Cor.* 15:24, LW 28.126-8 [WA 36.572].

[72] *Comm. 1 Cor.* 15:24, LW 28.126-7 [WA 36.572].

[73] LW 46.319 [WA 30³.247]. See also, *Comm. Jude*, v8, LW 30.213 [WA 14.88-9]; *Comm.1 Pet.* 1:10-12, LW 30.20 [WA 12.275-6].

[74] The basic differences may be conveniently tabulated as follows:

The temporal realm	The spiritual realm
- pertains to this life alone, 'earthly' (*terrenus*).	- pertains to eternal life, 'heavenly' (*coelestis*).
- this is relative to creation.	- this is primarily relative to redemption.
- belongs to this age.	- belongs to the age to come.
- is transient, it has an end.	- is eternal, without an end.
- directs people horizontally, towards others.	- directs vertically, towards God himself.
- the body belongs to the earthly kingdom.	- the conscience belongs to the spiritual kingdom.
- sin remains in its members.	- assured of God's forgiveness.
- concerned with bodily, external life.	- concerned with spiritual, internal life.

The apparent opposition between the two realms of God's authority seems to parallel the antagonism within the nature of a human being. As a person is a spiritual being with a soul having also a bodily nature, or flesh so, too, the world is divided into spiritual and secular realms.[75]

Therefore, while it is clear that Luther posits a connection between the two governments, it is also obvious that there are significant differences between them. Two of these differences are of particular importance to the present study as they give further understanding of Luther's doctrine of marriage. These differences are of 'habitancy' between the two kingdoms and the subject of *inaequalitas* in the secular realm.

The habitancy of the two kingdoms

Because the Reformer seems to hold the two governments at arm's length and, more significantly, because he sometimes uses

– to do with peace in society.	– to do with peace with God.
– relative to everybody.	– relative to believers alone.
– earthly blessings include: good government, household, to have children, peace, wealth, food, other physical advantages.	– spiritual blessings include: freedom from the law, sin and death; to be justified, made alive in Christ; to have a gracious God, confidence, a clear conscience, spiritual comfort, knowledge of Christ, the gift of prophecy, the Holy Spirit, the Scriptures, and to rejoice in God.
– subject to reason, common sense (*Vernunft*).	– subject to the Word of God (*Verbum Dei*) and the rule of the Holy Spirit.
– has external, transitory laws.	– has internal, eternal laws.
– dominated by force, compulsion, laws and authority over the outer man; the consequent restraint is God's *opus alienum* (his 'strange work').	– dominated by freedom and love for the inner man: this epitomizes God's *opus proprium* (his 'proper work').
– it is naturally hierarchical.	– all are intrinsically equal.

See Loeschen, op. cit., 56, fn. 9, who defines the two realms in terms of law and gospel and in relation to their function. Together with the passages already cited, see *Comm. Rom.* 6:6, LW 25.313 [WA 56.325-6]; *Comm. Gal.* 4:26 (1535), LW 26.440 [WA 40¹.662-3]; 3:10 (1535), LW 26.250-51 [WA 40¹.394]; *Comm. Zech.* 1:7, LW 20.171 [WA 23.513].

[75] LW 31.344 [WA 7.50]. See also, LW 25.166 [WA 56.185]; *Comm. Rom.* 7:18, LW 25.332 [WA 56.343]; 12:12, LW 25.434 [WA 56.442].

the terms *das weltliche Regiment* or *Reich* to denote the kingdom of Satan (*regnum diaboli*), he can give the impression that believers have nothing whatever to do with the temporal realm. They inhabit the Kingdom of God or of grace, not that of the devil and of sin. In this way, Luther appears to drive a wedge between the two realms.[76]

Obviously, a Christian *qua* Christian cannot be a member of the *regnum diaboli*. It is from this kingdom that they have been taken by God. Yet, in vocation, they are still a member of the secular realm. Thompson suggests that one solution is to see the believer as a person with two callings - a spiritual calling to salvation, together with one to a temporal office (*Amt*) or calling (*Beruf, vocatio*) in service to his neighbour. Gritsch adds the idea that as much as the temporal kingdom is to be equated with that of Satan's domain of activity, so much is it 'a vast prison of misery for the godly', though a paradise for the ungodly.[77]

The point is that the Christian seems to inhabit both governments, or kingdoms, in an ambiguous way. In the sense that he is in Christ he dwells in the spiritual kingdom, governed by the Word and the Holy Spirit. In that he remains sinful, he dwells in the temporal kingdom in which Satan is active and is ruled by reason and restraint. Thus he is a member of, and subject to, both governments - but certainly not in any straightforward or demarcated way. The unbeliever, on the other hand, is a member of only the temporal one. Indeed, in his later lectures on Galatians, Luther intimates that the physical blessings of this life and of its related kingdom are the unbeliever's only because he shares them with the Christian, for whom they are actually given.[78]

Ebeling comes to the problem in a way that is helpful to the present study. He finds a solution to the apparent tension in Luther's use of the preposition *coram* that he suggests is the key word for the Reformer's understanding of 'being'.[79] The preposition *coram* (*vor*) is translated in English as 'before', in the sense of 'before the face of' or 'in the sight of'. It is determinative of both place and time. Its importance is that (what Ebeling

---

[76] See, for example, *Comm. 1 Pet* .2:13-17, LW 30.76 [WA 12.330-31].
[77] Cargill Thompson, op. cit., 54-7; Gritsch, op. cit., 113, respectively.
[78] *Comm. Gal.* 3:10 (1535), LW 26.250-51 [WA 40.395].
[79] Ebeling, op. cit. - see chapter 12 for what follows.

terms) the 'coram-relationship' reveals that the fundamental situation of a man or woman is that of a person on trial. Intrinsic existence is *coram Deo*, carrying with it the forceful implication of being under the judgement of God and his Word. But *at the same time* a person's existence is *coram meipso* (in his own sight), *coram hominibus* (in the sight of others) and *coram mundo* (in the sight of the world). Ebeling, rightly, suggests that to exist before God and before people in this fundamental way is not to be presented with two possibilities or mutually exclusive choices, but to be within two relationships that are necessarily simultaneous.

Certainly, this accords with Luther's writing. In his commentary on the Sermon on the Mount, for example, he says that, just as a Christian is spiritual and subject only to Christ, he is *also* a secular person, a *Christen in relatione*, under obligation to others.[80] A little later he exhorts his readers, 'Just learn the difference between the two persons that a Christian must carry *simultaneously* on earth, because he lives in human society and has to make use of secular and imperial things.'[81] The believer is a member of both governments of God's authority because he belongs to both this age and the age to come.[82] The problem is that this could imply that Luther teaches two ethics – one for the Christian as a Christian, *per se*, the other for the Christian as a citizen of society. McGrath says that, 'Luther's social ethic seems to suggest that two totally different moralities exist side by side, a private Christian ethic ... and a public morality.'[83] However, this would be too simple an analysis for what has been shown to be a complex relationship between the two sides of the Christian's existence in the world. Ebeling is closer to the mark when he rejects a double moral standard: 'Both as a Christian and as a secular person, man has to act on one and the same basis: love.

---

[80] *Comm. Matt.* 5:38-42, LW 21.109 [WA 32.390].

[81] Ibid., LW 21.110 [WA 32.391] – emphasis added.

[82] See *Comm. Heb.* 1:2, LW 29.110 [WA 57^3.98]; *Comm. Gal.* 3:23, WA 40^1.525 (cited by Torrance, art. cit., 152); *Comm. Isa.* 52:6, LW 17.209 [WA 31^2.423].

[83] McGrath, op. cit., 143. Similarly, Gustafson, *Protestant and Roman Catholic Ethics*, 14-15, indicates two aspects of the moral life of the Christian; the one under civic use, in the orders of creation, the other under faith. Within the former, he is obliged to obey the moral law and to fulfil the duties of his office; within the latter, he acts out of gratitude for God's gift of grace.

The difference in the way love works in the two cases is due to a difference in the situation, in what has to be done for the sake of one's neighbour.'[84]

If the believer dwells in both kingdoms, on face value there appears little difference between the believer and the unbeliever within the realm of the worldly government. Both have their worldly tasks to do, both dwell under the scrutiny and judgement of God. Luther is evidently satisfied for the world to stand as neutral as the sphere of human vocation and activity[85] and for people to perform their duty before God as they will. However, the decisive difference between the believer standing *coram Deo* and the unbeliever, in a similar position, is basically twofold: the believer perceives what God has given and requires, and he brings faith to impinge on the way he carries out that task. The unbeliever does not.

These ideas are crucially important to the way in which Luther understands the vocation of marriage, for example. Believers look at marriage in a completely different light than do unbelievers. They understand that it is a divinely given creation ordinance and that it pleases God when his creatures value it highly and use it well. Unbelievers reason that it is unimportant in the same way that they do other duties that they find daily encumbering them. This is because they do not measure everything on the basis of the Word of God. This is true, not only of their perception of marriage, but of their comprehension of all the vocations and callings enjoined upon them. The opinion of the world is that they are unimportant, unimpressive and insignificant, with little real benefit.[86] The enlightened and renewed Christian, on the other hand, sees everything by faith.

The faith of the believer is never disembodied. It is given and operates, on one level, within the spiritual realm, but, on another, it is concretized in temporal life. The believer's morality is an

---

[84] Ebeling, op. cit., 208.

[85] It would be incorrect to say with W. Pauck, *From Luther to Tillich* (Harper and Row, San Francisco, 1984), 15, that the orders of the world, in themselves, were 'non-Christian'. Luther sees them as neutral; it is the incumbent who is either Christian or not.

[86] *Comm. Gen.* 13:14-15, LW 2.356 [WA 42.516]. See also, *Comm. Gen.* 13:13, LW 2.349 [WA 42.511]; *Comm. Ps.* 111:3, LW 13.358 [WA 31^1.399-400]; *Comm. Gal.* 4:6 (1535), LW 26.376 [WA 40^1.573]; 5:14 (1535), LW 27.56 [WA 40^2.70]; LW 45.39 [WA 10^2.295].

ethic of disposition (*Gesinnungsethik*) – believers live in the way they do because they are, by faith, the way they are. This is important because what would otherwise have been thought of as merely 'temporal' life is given the nature of spiritual reality through the faith that the believer brings to its duties and his own understanding and practice within it. Therefore, Luther speaks of the godly mother, for instance, being faithful in her duties,[87] through whom God shows 'how He works *heavenly and spiritual* things in things that are *carnal and earthly*'.[88] Likewise, parents who bring their children up responsibly, in faith, are told that it is a spiritual duty, not merely temporal. These activities, far from being merely worldly, are 'most excellent and most pleasing exercises of godliness toward God and man'. Men, who are godly, please the Lord – even if they are simply caring for flocks, fields, and 'stinking dunghills'. Indeed, the Reformer insists that such works are fruit of the Spirit, if they are performed in the Spirit and not merely in accordance with the flesh.[89] In this sense, then, it is at the interface of the believer's faith and life that spiritual reality impinges upon, and is regulative of, temporal existence.

'*Inaequalitas*' in the temporal kingdom

The second difference between the realms is that of relative status. According to Luther, all are equal within the spiritual government, but the temporal government is, *by definition*, the realm of intrinsic inequality. This is one of the most important differences between the two governments, for in it Luther continues the hierarchical tradition that we observed in Augustine and in the Middle Ages.

The first proposition to notice is that Luther says that it is God's will and his creative purpose that hierarchical distinctions between persons exist in *every* sphere of social life.[90] God wants people to observe differences of authority that he has established

---

[87] He lists milking cows and goats, bearing and rearing children.

[88] *Comm. Gen.* 30:2, LW 5.331 [WA 43.657] – emphasis added.

[89] See *Comm. Gen.* 37:12-14, LW 6.347 [WA 44.259-60]; *Comm. Gal.* 3:4 (1535), LW 26.217 [WA 40^1.348]. See also, *Comm. 1 Cor.* 7:17, LW 28.39 [WA 12.126]; *Comm. Gen.* 20:2, LW 3.322 [WA 43.106]; 41:16, LW 7.146 [WA 44.407]; 46:2-4, LW 8.82-3 [WA 44.639-40]; *Comm. Gal.* 5:15 (1535), LW 27.60-61 [WA 40^2.76].

[90] *Comm. Ps.* 101:1, LW 13.161 [WA 51.212]. See also, *Comm. Gen.* 41:45, LW 6.348 [WA 44.260].

– including the authority that puts the father *above* the child, the master *above* the servant, the ruler *above* the subject and the husband *above* his wife.[91] This hierarchical arrangement is not merely a way of fulfilling God's will in the abstract, as it were; but it is also necessary in order 'to serve human affairs'. By this, he generally means the preservation of societal peace and order.[92]

As previously intimated, this theme is related, in the Reformer's thinking, both to humanity's sinful and disorganizing tendencies and to the eschatological hope of Christ's return. Part of the sin of the original world, before Noah, was that it disorganized the hierarchical structure that God had set up in society. This was apparent largely in homes ruined by perverse lusts, but also in the state and in the church. Luther speaks of this in the context of his exposition of the reasons for God's anger before his judgement in the flood. His conclusion is very forceful, 'This world-wide corruption was the unavoidable result of the downfall of godliness and decency. Men were not only evil; they were utterly incorrigible.'[93]

In contrast to this, Luther sees the progress and application of reformation ideas, evidenced in a measure in the reinstatement of societal order and peace, as proof that within his own generation the restoration of all things is near.[94] One of the problems that he discerned, though, was that unbelievers still abused the consequent peace that they were afforded. Whereas Christians use peace for social and spiritual good, the unregenerate use it for their own wickedness.[95] Believers must remain in their vocation, therefore, both to facilitate peace and to prevent 'a disturbance and confusion of all social stations and of everything'. Above all else, in this context, the believer must be prevented from 'the dangerous abandoning

---

[91] *Comm. John* 1:13, LW 22.93 [WA 46.616]. See also, *Comm. Deut.* 15:1, LW 9.145 [WA 14.655].

[92] *Comm. Gen.* 41:45, LW 7.190 [WA 44.440]. In the context of the verse, Luther is speaking specifically of the magistrate-subject arrangement within society, but the comment applies generally to his thought. See also, *Comm. Deut.* 15:1, LW 9.145 [WA 14.655].

[93] *Comm. Gen.* 6:3, LW 2.31-2 [WA 42.284].

[94] See the prefatory letter, *Comm. Deut.*, LW 9.6 [WA 14.499].

[95] *Comm. 1 Tim.* 2:2, LW 28.259 [WA 26.33-4]. See also, *Comm. 1 Cor.* 15:24, LW 28.126-8 [WA 36.571-2].

of a calling, the abandonment which is never attempted without sin'.[96]

In this distinction between equality in the one kingdom and the inequality in the other, Luther differentiates between the person and the 'office'. That is, in the case of two Christian people in hierarchically different callings, for example, there is an essential, outward, social inequality between them, but also a fundamental, inward equality in Christ.[97] Therefore, no-one who comprehends God's purposes will believe, for instance, that the magistrate's position (office) is better in the sight of God than that of the subject, or a father's than that of the child. They may appear so (indeed, *they actually are*) within the social order, but the Lord considers the incumbents of these callings, first and foremost, as persons before him. Luther says, 'The difference there is among people in this life does not make different persons before God. God hears all alike – you in your menial state and another in his free state.'[98] The difference lies in the things that people *do* in the service of others, not in what they *are* in faith and their new existence in Christ (although, even for the Reformer, what they *do will* inevitably be interpretative of what they *are* in society). Speaking universally, he says, 'We all have one and the same God, and we are one in the unified worship of God, *even if our works* and *vocations are different*.'[99]

The significant passage, in the context of this study, is Galatians 3:28. It is significant for a number of reasons. It is significant because Luther explicates his own understanding of the equality and inequality within the governments from this

---

[96] *Comm. Gal.* 1:28 (1535), LW 26.357 [WA 40^1.547]; *Comm. Gen.* 16:11, LW 3.65 [WA 42.595], respectively. See also, *Comm. Gal.* 3:28 (1519), LW 27.281 [WA 2.531].

[97] This idea is clearly related to Luther's understanding of the priesthood of all believers, which title denotes, among other things, every believer's access to God, their ability to teach other Christians and to be pleasing to God in all that they do. In this all believers are equal before God. See, for example, *Comm. Ps.* 82:4, LW 13.65 [WA 31^1.211]; LW 39.235-8 [WA 8.251-4]; LW 31.355-7 [WA 7.57-9]; LW 36.138 [WA 8.486]; *Comm. 1 Pet.* 2:5, LW 30.55 [WA 12.309].

[98] *Comm. Gen.* 16:11, LW 3.65 [WA 42.595] – the use of the words 'menial' and 'free' is not insignificant, of course. See also, *Comm. Gal.* 5:15 (1535), LW 27.60-61 [WA 40^2.76], *Comm. John.* 1:13, LW 22.93-4 [WA 46.616]; to Margrave Albrecht [Wittenberg] December, 1523, LW 49.61-8 [WA Br. 3.214-19].

[99] *Comm. Gen.* 37:12-14, LW 6.348 [WA 44.260] – emphasis added. He speaks, specifically, of kings and slaves, men and women.

verse (and within his use of it). Also, his 'liberationist' contemporaries argued *their* position from that basis[100] and because the present liberationist/feminist interpretation of Christian ethics lays such weight upon it.

We have noted, previously, that Augustine (and the following tradition) held to inequality between the sexes and that he dismissed any possibility of change in that area – even from a reading of Galatians 3:28. Luther continued that tradition and appears to have strengthened his own support for it as he matured. That is, for him, the Pauline theology of Galatians is applied *only* in the area of the spiritual government of God's authority. For Luther, no argument for social equality can be raised on the basis of Galatians 3:28. This is made clear in his two series of lectures on Galatians. There is little material difference between the two expositions, but there appears to be a greater emphasis in the latter on the need to keep the order that God has ordained.

In the 1519 series,[101] Luther states that the probable context of Paul's words is the grasping of status by the recipients – particularly, those Jewish Christians who would not abandon the supposed benefits of their birthright. He interprets the apostle's conclusion: 'You are righteous, not because you are a Jew, and an observer of the law, but because by believing in Christ you have put on Christ.' He observes that it is a characteristic of people to make distinctions and rank. But the familiar Lutheran context here is that he supposes that they claim status *in order to gain salvation*. Later, he states that these things, 'do not make a Christian if they are present or an unbeliever if they are lacking'. That is neither the nature of distinguishing marks, nor the nature of redemption. On realizing the possible ethical and social implications that some might wish to draw from this, he then

---

[100] R. R. Ruether, *Sexism and God-Talk* (SCM, London, 1983), 35, states that, 'A host of ... popular movements in the late Middle Ages constantly came close to rediscovering a counter-cultural egalitarian Christianity opposed to the patriarchal and hierarchical Church.' See also, C. Jordan, *Renaissance Feminism* (Cornell University, Ithaca, 1990), particularly, chapter 2. Both W. P. de Boer, 'Calvin on the Role of Women' in D. E. Holwerda (ed.), *Exploring the Heritage of John Calvin* (Baker, Grand Rapids, 1976), 237 and R. H. Bainton, *Women of the Reformation in Germany and Italy* (Beacon, Boston, 1974), 55, mention the example of Katherine Zell in this respect.

[101] *Comm. Gal.* 3:28 (1519), LW 27.280-81 [WA 2.530-31].

makes the important distinction that these hierarchical rankings[102] must remain 'on account of the body'. However, they are removed in the Spirit through the unity of the faith. His own conclusion raises a question. He says,

> This alone is required, that we render to such persons service that is not contrary to the unity of faith but is in accordance with the unity of faith, *in order that the dissimilarity in outward station may not be stronger than the similarity in inward faith.*[103]

This is somewhat ambiguous. It is clear that he believes that inferiors should obey superiors, but is he suggesting that the mutuality between both should outweigh the social inequality between them so that the difference becomes cancelled out? This actually seems unlikely. Nowhere in this passage does he mention the love to be shown 'downward' by those in rank. When he returns to it some years later, he speaks with greater clarity on the distinction and with less emphasis on the possible similarities.

In 1535 he outlines the passage similarly, yet with slightly, but significantly, different emphases.[104] He still teaches that the Galatians are being tempted back to the law; but this time he spells out that the social stations are divinely ordained, that they are 'good creatures' of God and that they have wisdom, righteousness, devotion and authority. Having stated that, he emphasizes that they amount to nothing, in the matter of salvation. But, again, he outlines more thoroughly his idea in the social realm. Thus, the diligent, faithful work of slaves and free men within society, and men and women in the domestic sphere, counts for nothing in the realm of the spiritual government of God and avails nothing towards righteousness in God's sight.

His exhortation to hold to social hierarchical differentiation is more strongly put in 1535. 'There is, of course, a distinction among persons in the law and in the sight of the world; and *there must be one there,* but not in the sight of God, where all men are equal' (emphasis added).[105] Again, he states that, 'in the world and

---

[102] That is, Jew-Greek, free-slave, man-woman.
[103] Ibid., – emphasis added, LW 27.281 [WA 2.531].
[104] *Comm. Gal.* 3:28 (1535), LW 26.355-7 [WA 40².542-7].
[105] Significantly, he quotes Romans 3:23 here, 'For all alike have sinned...'.

according to the flesh there is a great difference and inequality among persons, and *this must be observed carefully*.[106]

He claims that if lower persons wished to change places with the upper, 'there would be a disturbance and confusion of all social stations and of everything'. Significantly, in a list of those possibilities he includes a woman wanting to be a man – by which he can only mean a woman wanting to usurp the man's role and place in the family and in society. So we see that the Reformer develops almost a defensive stance. Its primary teaching is to show that in Christ all are equal; yet his emphasis becomes both the rightness of social inequality in this life and the necessity to hold on to that, in both theory and practice.[107]

This point had been made clearly some years earlier. In his reply to the peasants[108] he alludes to the Galatians verse refuting their idea (as he interprets it) that all are now free in Christ and that, therefore, no-one should be a serf of anyone else. He declares, 'That is to make Christian freedom a completely physical matter.'[109] He fears that the article might make all men and women equal and that would turn the spiritual kingdom into a 'worldly, external kingdom'. He insists, 'A worldly kingdom cannot exist without inequality of persons.'

The way that Luther employs this verse in other contexts bears these conclusions out. In 'The Misuse of the Mass' he quotes Galatians 3:28, showing that the priesthood of believers is in the Spirit, alone.[110] He includes it in a similar context in his sermon on 1 Peter 2:5. He emphasizes that each one of the congregation is a priest and, in that sense, there is no distinction and no rank of authority. He applies this forcefully: 'You must not say, "This is a man or a woman; this is a servant or a master; this person is old

---

[106] Emphasis added. See also, *Comm. 1 Cor.* 15:24, LW 28.128 [WA 36.574].

[107] See also other allusions to the verse: *Comm. Gal.* 2:3-5: 5:19; 6:15. Notice, particularly, that at 6:15 he states that such things do not commend people to God.

[108] *Admonition to Peace. A Reply to the Twelve Articles of the Peasants in Swabia* (1525), LW 46.17-43 [WA 18.291-334].

[109] Ibid., LW 46.39 [WA 18.326-7]. Luther's conclusion seems both unwarranted and defensive. In the third article, the peasants acknowledge their need of rulers: 'God does not teach us that we should desire no rulers. ... Thus we willingly obey our chosen and appointed rulers in all Christian and appropriate matters.' LW 46.12.

[110] *The Misuse of the Mass* (1521), LW 36.138-9 [WA 8.486-7]. See also, *Comm. Zech.* 12:7, LW 20.326-7 [WA 23.646].

or young." They are all alike and only a spiritual people.' Yet, again, he feels the need to qualify his comment with the statement that wives have to obey their husbands and, therefore, cannot preach. And, though he has no fundamental problem with women preaching, *per se* (they may preach without men present), nevertheless he asserts that, '*God does not interfere with the [normal] arrangement.*'[111] Likewise, as he expounds 1 Corinthians 7, he quotes Galatians 3:28 to the effect that all are equal. In fact, in a daring emphasis he comments that 'a man is a woman *before God*' and likewise, 'a woman is a man *before God.*'[112]

However, in all his use of this important verse, Luther never makes an attempt to show a correlative, social application of the biblical idea that he has understood. The theological basis that continues to underline his approach to, and use of, the doctrine of the equality of believers is that the two kingdoms of God's rule are separate and, certainly, as far as salvation is concerned, irrelevant to each other.[113] But can this be strictly adhered to in the realm of ethics? We have already seen that the two kingdoms connect in origin, in purpose and in the way that the gospel informs the morality of the world. Luther states, too, that 'God wants the government of the world to be a symbol of true salvation.'[114] Though the context of Paul's verse, itself, lends weight to Luther's emphasis on redemptive status rather than on ethical categories, the Reformer's application appears to fall short of his own ideal. His use elsewhere implies a similar insistence.

Thus, he teaches emphatically that in the eternal government of God's rule all are equal, but that in the temporal government there exists a social hierarchy that has been established by God. He applies this with a disconcerting regularity in two basic ways. First, people must obey superiors. Therefore, in the realm of husband-wife relationship, for instance, 'though, inwardly we are all alike ... externally, God wants the husband to rule and the wife to be submissive to him'.[115] On another occasion he says that the

---

[111] *Comm. 1 Pet.* 2:5, LW 30.55 [WA 12.309] – emphasis added.

[112] *Comm. 1 Cor.* 7:22, LW 28.43-4 [WA 12.130] – emphasis added.

[113] See *Comm. Ps.* 2:12, LW 12.85 [WA 40.302].

[114] *Comm. Ps.* 101:5, LW 13.197 [WA 51.241].

[115] *Comm. 1 Pet.* 3:1-6, LW 30.92-3 [WA 12.347]. See also, *Comm. 1 Tim.* 2:13, LW 28.277-8 [WA 26.47]; *Comm. Tit.* 2:4, LW 29.55 [WA 25.44-5]; *Comm. Gen.* 17:12-13, LW 3.142 [WA 42.649].

husband is the 'sovereign lord of [his] wife'.[116] Second, no-one should exalt himself above his own position, nor above how God sees him in that position.

We have seen that Luther approaches his teaching on the marriage relationship, as he does his ethical teaching, generally, from the wider perspective of his doctrine of two kingdoms. We have noted that, for the Reformer, the temporal kingdom has its origin in God, the Creator; and that one of its purposes is the maintenance of society (both its order and its peace) through countering the effects of sin and the continuing activity of Satan. We further concluded that the Christian is an inhabitant of the temporal kingdom (as he is of the spiritual one) and that a characteristic of that kingdom in which he lives is an inherent inequality between its members. That is, the fact that Christians are entirely equal (spiritually) is irrelevant to the differences within the realm of social status. An examination of Luther's handling of Galatians 3:28 underlined this. He views the spiritual kingdom as of *no* consequence to social levelling in an ethical application of God's Word in the temporal kingdom. An examination of vocation, within Luther's theological ethics, is the next step to understanding his doctrine of marriage.

MARRIAGE AS WORLDLY VOCATION

Luther was not the only theologian of his generation emphasizing the importance of vocation or office within the temporal realm but, nevertheless, the concept is central to his thought.[117] A seminal work on this subject is Wingren's important book, *Luther on Vocation*. In it he shows that *vocatio*, in Luther's writing, means several things – the proclamation of the gospel, the work that each one does, a call to the office of preaching (with *vocatus*), and so on. The word *Beruf* has more than one connotation, as well. But, Luther never uses these words in reference to the work

---

[116] *Comm. 1 Cor.* 15:24, LW 28.128 [WA 36.573-4].

[117] See R. W. Scribner, 'The Social Thought of Erasmus', *JRH* 6 (1970-71), 3-26; L. Bakelant, 'Les Rapports de l'humanisme et de la Réforme', *RUB* 18 (1965-66), 264-82; R. E. O. White, op. cit., 172.

of an unbeliever. All, however, have station (*Stand*). Wingren defines a vocation as 'a "station" which is by nature helpful to others'.[118] He shows that nothing falls outside of 'station', 'office' or 'vocation' if it involves action in the world and a person's relationship to others around him. Thus, it belongs squarely to the present, worldly aspect of God's rule – it will come to an end. In that sense alone, therefore, hierarchical arrangement will be unnecessary in heaven.[119] He comments, 'Vocation belongs to this world, not to heaven, it is directed toward one's neighbour, not toward God.'[120]

Vocation is the particularization, or individualisation, of the temporal government of God's rule in the daily existence of the believer and, as such, it is defined in similar terms and with similar limits. For instance, as the origin of the temporal realm is in God, so vocation's origin is in God's will and institution.[121] Each station in life has been appointed and ordained by God's creative Word and command. And, because it has been established in this way, each person has been given a calling through which he is to serve God's purposes in society.[122] Luther refers to this idea in his commentary on Genesis 37:12-14, for example. Here, he comments on the divine institutions (*Ordnungen* or *Stände*). Together with 'citizen', 'prince', 'noble', he lists the category of 'woman'.[123] This is not so much because stations include biological categories, as such, but rather because

---

[118] Wingren, op. cit., 4. F. E. Cranz, *An Essay on the Development of Luther's Thought on Justice, Law and Society* (CUP, Cambridge, 1964), 155-8, draws attention to the development in Luther's thinking on 'calling' (*Beruf*) and 'estate' (*Stand*) in which development the two become virtually synonymous after about 1520. See also, G. D. Badcock, *The Way of Life: A Theology of Christian Vocation* (Eerdmans, Grand Rapids, 1998), 32-44.

[119] See *Comm. John* 15:4, LW 24.221 [WA 45.662]. See also, *Comm. 1 Cor.* 15:24, LW 28.126-8 [WA 36.571-2]. However, at 1 Cor. 15:27-8, LW 28.143 [WA 36.595], he comments, 'Persons, such as man and wife, will remain, and also the entire human race *as it was created*' – emphasis added. Here, he evidently means 'man and woman, without the implication of authority structure which attaches itself to the concept of 'wife'.

[120] Ibid., 10. See also, 166.

[121] This is clearly true of marriage: '*es ist gottis werck und gutter wille*' (*The Estate of Marriage*, LW 45.378 [WA 10².294]).

[122] See *Comm. Ps.* 111:3, LW 13.358 [WA 31¹.399-400]; *Comm. Gal.* 6:4 (1535), LW 27.120 [WA 40².153]; *Comm. Gen.* 7:1, LW 2.83 [WA 42.320]; 17:9, LW 3.128 [WA 42.639]; *Comm. Ps.* 82:6, LW 13.71 [WA 31¹.217].

[123] *Comm. Gen.* 37:12-14, LW 6.349 [WA 44.261].

biological categories, themselves, imply social relationship and duty within hierarchical structure – this is the divinely-given context of vocation. Vocation, then, is the realm of God's concern and activity. Certain things follow from this.

First, vocation is the sphere of God's concern and care for each individual. It is within a person's station that God oversees and governs his daily existence – nothing is too insignificant for his providential involvement. For example, in the context of the domestic economy, Luther states that God, 'cares about little, mediocre, and big things. He is the Creator and Governor of everything.'[124]

Second, and correlated with this, vocation is the sphere of God's control in the world. Pauck states that, 'It is merely the divinely controlled, natural world-order that is fulfilled in these offices.'[125] Luther teaches that estates and vocations have been established to preserve the social order and peace, by restrictions and controls.

> Where such stations operate as they should, there things go well in the world, and there is the very righteousness of God. But, where such stations are not maintained, it makes for unrighteousness.[126]

His use of the word 'righteousness' indicates stable, orderly and peaceful life in accordance with the will of God. Luther is anxious that if God did not preserve society in this way, 'no particle of right would last even for a moment'. If God did not check rebellion and maintain peace, people in lower relational positions would seek higher status, and, 'conditions would be worse among men than they are among the wild animals, where each devours the other; *for God did not give them such institutions*'.[127] In all of this, the preservation of the family structure is of primary importance. God wants peace and order to exist in the family and, through the family, in the community, as well. That is, marriage is conducive to the observance of law and order.[128]

---

[124] *Comm. Gen.* 30:2, LW 5.330 [WA 43.656]. See also, *Comm. Gen.* 29:31, LW 5.313-14 [WA 43.645].

[125] Pauck, op. cit., 15. See also, Wingren, op. cit., 8-10.

[126] *Comm. Ps.* 111:3, LW 13.358 [WA 31^1.399-400]. See also, *Comm. Isa.* 52:6, LW 17.209 [WA 31^2.423]; *Comm. Gen.* 7:1, LW 2.83 [WA 42.320].

[127] *Comm. Ps.* 111:3, LW 13.369 [WA 31^1.409] – emphasis added.

[128] *Comm. John* 1:13, LW 22.100 [WA 46.622]. See also, *Comm. 1 Pet.* 3:1-6,

Third, vocation is the sphere in which men and women partner God in genuine co-operation. It is concretely in the realm of calling, or vocation, that Luther speaks of God working through a person to fulfil his will, even in the ordinary duties of life. Wingren is perceptive on this.[129] He states that, 'The miraculous work of God and the daily toil of man join and grow together in a unity of *co-operation,* in the proper sense of the term. Our work in our vocation becomes a mask of God in a unique sense. 'Luther refers to this, for instance, in the realm of the *weltliche Regiment* and, specifically, in *das haus Regiment*. According to him, for example, God could easily rear children without parents but has ordained to accomplish it '*through* the parents and *with* the parents'. Similarly he could rule the household himself, but wills to do it *through* the householder (*Haushalter*).[130] Humanity's partnership or co-operation with God, is not directed toward God, but, rather, it is directed outward, towards their neighbour. It works 'horizontally' or 'downwards' in the temporal government and, therefore, in vocation, as well. Vocation is concerned with relationships with equals or with social inferiors or superiors, not primarily within relationship to God. For Christians, however, vocation is the sphere in which they put faith and love into practice.

Two specific applications are frequently made by Luther. First, he says that people should remain in their vocation and, secondly, that they should work hard and dutifully within it. By the former, Luther means that men and women must continue in their social station (not their occupation, as such), but it is difficult to escape the conclusion that often a social station is defined both by its position hierarchically and by its specific tasks and duties. For example, in the context of the possibility of a woman seeking to assume the role and position of her husband, Luther counters that she must not, 'because *everyone functions efficiently* in that for which he was created'.[131] Luther is quite explicit about this. Within the man-woman distinction he believes

---

LW 30.89 [WA 12.343]; introduction to *Comm. 1 Tim.* 2, LW 28.256 [WA 26.32].

[129] Wingren, op. cit., 196 – emphasis original. See *Comm. Gen.* 2:7, LW 1.84 [WA 42.63]; 19:20, LW 3.290 [WA 43.83]; 20:2, LW 3.321 [WA 43.105]; Rupp, op. cit., 300-308.

[130] *Comm. Zech.* 1:7, LW 20.171 [WA 23.513] – emphasis added. See also, *Comm. Eccl.* 2:3, LW 15.35 [WA 20.41-2].

[131] *Comm. Eccl.* 7:26, LW 15.131 [WA 20.149] – emphasis added.

that 'the male was not created for spinning; the woman was not created for warfare'. He continues, 'Let the proper station and task be attributed to each person. In this way let every creature serve in its own order and place.'[132]

By the latter application, Luther reminds his followers that vocation is demanding and that each person must fulfil it faithfully before God.[133] However, they should believe that labour in the Lord is never in vain. Indeed, their boast and joy is that, within legitimate vocation, they are pleasing to God.[134]

CONCLUSION

In attempting to establish a matrix of theological thought from which to understand Luther's ethical teaching on the husband-wife relationship, we have suggested that the starting point should be his doctrine of vocation within the concept of the two governments of God's rule. This is so because Luther clearly sees marriage as a vocation, instituted by God and behind that he sees vocation as the particularization of God's temporal government within the individual's worldly existence. The matrix and its relatedness to the present study may be summarized as follows:

1. God, as Creator and Sustainer, oversees the world of men and women in two distinct ways. He does so through both his spiritual and temporal rule. Broadly speaking, the former represents the Kingdom of Christ; the latter is God's rule of people within temporal callings and institutions.

2. Three particular areas of commonality between the realms of God's rule have been singled out as having direct concern with

---

[132] *Comm. Gal.* 3:19 (1535), LW 26.307-8 [WA 40.478]. It is in this sense that the Reformer speaks of the king, the mother, the father and the student as fulfilling their vocation or calling by governing, tending her baby, working and studying, respectively – *Comm. Gen.* 17:9, LW 3.128 [WA 42.639]. See also, *Comm. Gen.* 16:7-9, LW 3.62 [WA 42.593]; LW 27.120 [WA 40^2.153]; LW 40.391 [WA 30^3.524]; LW 21.258, 269 [WA 32.513, 523]; LW 15.151 [WA 20.163].

[133] See, for example, *Comm. Gen.* 18:9, LW 3.204 [WA 42.20-21]; 18:15, LW 3.217 [WA 43.30]; 37:12-14, LW 6.349 [WA 44.261]; *Comm. Gal.* 4:6 (1535), LW 26.376 [WA 40^1.573]; *Comm. Matt.* 7:21, LW 21.269 [WA 32.523].

[134] See *Comm. Gen.* 37:3, LW 6.325 [WA 44.242]; *Comm. 1 Cor.* 15:8-11, LW 28.92 [WA 36.521].

the topic under research. *a.* The source of both governments is God, himself. Ultimately, he is sovereign in both. This pinpoints divine authority, together with the basic unity of existence. *b.* The two governments have at least one common purpose. Through each, God establishes and maintains order and peace. Within the spiritual realm, that peace is directly related to the gospel, salvation in Christ and reconciliation with the Father. Within the temporal realm peace comes, largely, on a structural level through social ordering. We further noticed that the preservation of societal order is necessary because of two things. First, the sin and natural disorderliness of humanity and, second, Satan's malicious, destructive work. Against these, God employs both his temporal and his spiritual rule. The former employs regulative and controlling institutions (such as the state, the magistracy and the family) to keep order in the community. *c.* There is an inner connection between the two rules of God seen at the interface of natural law and gospel love. Love, set forth in the Word, should regulate all temporal activities. People are commanded to love and that command accords with what, at their best, they know is right. From another perspective the interface is actually the believer's faith, through which they seek to live spiritually and vocationally in the temporal world.

3. Two areas of major difference between the two rules were then established. *a.* The temporal government of God's rule speaks to both unbelievers and to the regenerate in their remaining sin. The spiritual government, on the other hand, speaks only to believers. The Christian (before God) has two callings – one to salvation, the other to vocation. *b.* A brief examination of Luther's understanding and use of Gal. 3:28 revealed that Luther teaches that within the spiritual government all are entirely equal in Christ, but that within the temporal government God has established the hierarchical arrangement of society. He has ordained distinctions of rank and inequality – distinctions that are permanent and unalterable.

4. Because vocation is the individualization of the temporal government, it has the characteristics of that government. Each vocation has its origin in God and has the purpose of God as its *raison d'être*. Each is the sphere of his concern and control. In each, humanity partnerships God in accomplishing his task.

If marriage is an example of a vocation, then it will demonstrate the characteristics outlined above. If this is so, then, perhaps, the husband-wife relationship itself will be largely defined within the parameters of this theological understanding. It is already questionable, given Luther's understanding of God's purposes within his temporal rule, whether he *could* have been very different in his definition of marriage and the relationship between the spouses. Indeed, as the study proceeds, we will find that, for Luther, the marital relationship comes directly from God – it is his institution and its underlying purpose (as vocation within the temporal realm) is to ensure societal order and peace. Furthermore, Luther sees the fundamental characteristic of the husband-wife relationship as a hierarchical structure, in keeping with God's general way of ordering society in and through vocation.

One question raised is whether Luther is *constrained* by his theological thinking or whether he pushes at the boundaries in order to apply his understanding in a more egalitarian way. What is the nature of the husband-wife relationship within a vocational understanding of marriage? This is, in a sense, the brief for the next two chapters. Chapter 6 will examine, more closely, Luther's teaching on the nature of marriage as a vocation and the way he employs traditional reasons for marrying in order to underline his own vocational framework in which to view the husband and wife relationship.

CHAPTER 6

MARRIAGE AS VOCATION

The previous chapter focused on the broad theological backdrop to Luther's understanding of marriage as a vocation in order to provide a doctrinal framework for his ethics of the husband and wife relationship. In this way, it showed the perspective from which his ethics of marriage proceeds. His teaching on the two kingdoms was shown to be essential in this. This is particularly so regarding his perception of the temporal government in which *vocatio* is divinely given. The qualities of the temporal government were then shown to be reflected in the particularization of that government; namely, in individual vocation.

Because marriage *is* a vocation in Luther's thought, the present chapter naturally proceeds to move from that general theological principle to examine the Reformer's more specific ethical application of it within the realm of marriage. It does so on two primary bases. First, it analyses Luther's understanding of the fundamental nature of marriage, given his 'creational logic'. Second, the discussion moves on to the question of how his vocational estimation of marriage permeates the traditional reasons for marrying which he often conventionally employs.

Almost in parenthesis, the chapter concludes with a brief consideration of Luther's own reluctance to get married. This is examined against the fact that the impulse and dynamic of his own theology and application is that everyone *should marry*. This comes as an answer to an obvious biographical question: If marriage is so important to Luther within the framework of his understanding of vocation, why does he seem to marry so unwillingly?

In Luther's understanding of worldly reality every station or vocation is important before God. Yet it is his conviction that, in the arrangements of the external life (*ordines externae vitae*), there is no higher office or estate than that of marriage. The only station that surpasses it is that of the ministry of the Word – not because it affects the status of the preacher, but because it concerns God and his work of salvation and restoration.[1]

Late in his own ministry, Luther states that the canonists have defined marriage as 'the union of male and female in accordance with the law of nature'. For the Reformer this is inadequate,[2] so he offers his own alternative,

> Marriage is the divinely instituted and lawful union of a man and a woman in the hope of offspring, or at least for the sake of avoiding fornication and sin, to the glory of God. Its ultimate purpose is to obey God and to be a remedy for sin; to call upon God; to desire, love and bring up children to the glory of God; to live with one's wife in the fear of the Lord; and to bear one's cross.[3]

The essential points of his own understanding of marriage remain fairly constant over his career. Some of them are hinted at in this definition – its divine origin, its purposes of obedience and remedy against sin, its position of importance before God.

MARRIAGE BEFORE GOD

Undoubtedly, the primary concern of Luther is that people understand that the origin of marriage is in the will of God and not humanity. This is important to establish because anything he says concerning the husband-wife relationship is based on what he presupposes here. The significance for the husband and wife relationship is immediately clear, for if the origin of the

---

[1] LW 45.154 [WA 12.241]; LW 45.46 [WA 10^2.301]; *Comm. Gen.* 18:11-12, LW 3.210 [WA 43.25]. See F. E. Cranz, *An Essay on the Development of Luther's Thought on Justice, Law and Society* (Harvard University Press, Cambridge, 1964), 153-9, 173-8.

[2] *Comm. Gen.* 24:1-4, LW 4.222 [WA 43.295].

[3] Ibid., LW 4.244 [WA 43.310]. See also, *Comm. Gen.* 28:1-2, LW 5.188 [WA 43.558].

institution of marriage is in the divine intention and its practice is related to his purposes, then it behoves both spouses to live as directed. That is, specifically, if (as Luther teaches) the husband and wife are to live together in hierarchical arrangement, then a weight of great seriousness is placed upon that imperative by its origin.

In keeping with his view that the whole of existence is divinely instituted, the Reformer teaches that marriage has its source in God's intention and activity. In his commentary on Genesis, for instance, he notes that after the creation of Eve God brings her to Adam, who 'does not snatch Eve of his own will'. These words echo those found in a sermon preached as early as 1519, where he says that, in the case of Adam,

> God creates for him a unique, special kind of wife out of his own flesh. He brings her to him, he gives her to him, and Adam agrees to accept her. Therefore, this is what marriage is.[4]

He concludes, elsewhere, that marriage is divinely instituted, speaking of it as an ordinance and creation of God.[5] By this, he envisages not only the original marriage, but every subsequent one. God institutes every marriage and matches every husband and wife – the paradigmatic nature of Adam and Eve's made that certain.[6] Luther rarely speaks of marriage as a covenant,[7] though he *can* speak with conviction of the responsibility of the spouses' marriage choice.[8] He prefers to discern its nature as one of the creational ordinances (*Schöpfungsordnungen*) of God, rather than in the will of a man and a woman. In that way, the relationship of husband and wife is basic to God's original

---

[4] *Comm. Gen.* 2:22, LW 1.134 [WA 42.100]; *The Estate of Marriage* (1519), LW 44.8 [WA 2.167], respectively.

[5] LW 54.31 [LW Tr. 1.98] – '*coniugium autem est ordinatio et creatura Dei.*' See also, *Comm. Matt.* 7:15, LW 21.257 [WA 32.512]; *On Marriage Matters*, LW 46.283 [WA 30³.219]; *The Estate of Marriage*, LW 45.37 [WA 10².294]; *Comm. Gal.* 3:2 (1535), LW 26.212 [WA 40¹.342]; *Comm. Gen.* 21:1-3, LW 4.6 [WA 43.140]; 24:55-61, LW 4.298 [WA 43.349]; 41:16, LW 7.146 [WA 44.407]; *Comm. John* 1:13, LW 22.93, 100 [WA 46.616, 622].

[6] See *Comm. Gen.* 24:50-52, LW 4.294-5 [WA 43.347-8]; LW 45.334 [WA 15.376].

[7] Two such occasions occur – *Comm. Mal.* 2:14, LW 18.405 [WA 13.689]; *Sermon on the Estate of Marriage*, LW 44.10-11 [WA 2.168].

[8] See, for example, *Comm. Gen.* 21:1-3, LW 4.6 [WA 43.140].

purpose. That is, marriage as a vocation is inherent in the temporal workings of God's rule. It is, 'a primal given factor in the divine creation'.[9]

There is a creational logic about the Reformer's thinking. In contemporary terms he would probably be designated an 'essentialist', believing as he does in an objective reality about sexuality which is constant and universal by nature or creation. In his *The Estate of Marriage*,[10] Luther grounds this on the creation of the first pair and states that 'God divided mankind into two classes, namely, male and female, or a he and a she.' His conclusion is that,

> Each one of us must have the kind of body God created for us. I cannot make myself a woman, nor can you make yourself a man; we do not have the power. But we are exactly as he created us: I am a man and you are a woman.[11]

The point that the Reformer makes is obvious enough. Having been created by God, either as male or female, each is fundamentally different and each is of value. But for Luther creation implies vocation and the differences between male and female are indicative of a demarcation in role and responsibility. That is, Luther teaches that the purpose of the creation of man and woman is that they enter into the vocation of marriage, which is an essential part of what it means to be human. In his comments on Genesis, Luther states, 'You were created *to be* a husband or a wife.'[12] This reveals what Luther believes to be the creational, prelapsarian condition in which everyone would have married. Now, after the Fall, there are those who *should not* marry because of the gift of celibacy, but they are few.[13] Therefore, because the majority have been created for the particular

---

[9] H. Bornkamm, *Luther in Mid-Career, 1521-1530* (Fortress, Philadelphia, 1983), 110.

[10] *The Estate of Marriage* (1522), LW 45.17-49 [WA 10².275-304], see particularly, 17-30 [275-87].

[11] Ibid., LW 45.17 [WA 275]. See also, LW 51.358-9 [WA 49.798-9]; LW 45.144 [WA 12.234].

[12] *Comm. Gen.* 30:22-4, LW 5.363 [WA 43.679] – emphasis added. See also, *On Marriage Matters* (1530), LW 46.283, 312-13 [WA 30³.219, 242]; *Comm. 1 Cor.* 15:3-7, LW 28.79 [WA 36.50].

[13] See, particularly, LW 51.359 [WA 49.799]. Also, LW 45.18 [WA 10².276]; *Comm. 1 Cor.* 7:1-2, LW 28.9-10 [WA 12.97-8]; LW 36.260 [WA 10².36].

vocation of marriage, both the man and the woman have their distinctive duties and roles which are inherent in that vocation. The man, on the one hand, is to be a husband and a father – he is designed for protecting and guarding. The woman, on the other hand, is to be a wife and a mother – she is designed 'for feeding, nourishing and taking pity'.[14] Luther is adamant, therefore, that both should be concerned about their own respective tasks, for which they were created.[15] Not only so, but each should be satisfied with God's individual calling. In marriage, 'a man can say: I thank God that I have been created a man by God; or a woman: I thank God that I have been created a woman'.[16]

In keeping with the notion of natural law as directional for vocation within the temporal government of God's authority, Luther teaches that man and woman, together, are not only given the responsibility of maintaining home-life and rearing children, but also that they are empowered by God to do so. That is, it is implanted in their nature and written in their hearts.[17]

This is most concretely seen in his view of the divine command to 'be fruitful and increase' (Gen. 1:28), that Luther sees as a command to everybody, not merely to Adam and Eve. In fact, he believes this to be more than a command – it is a divine ordinance that is more necessary to men and women than sleep, work, eating and drinking. Indeed, in a characteristic comment, he says that it is a nature or disposition, 'just as innate as the organs involved in it'.[18] Through it, God 'abides and rules within you'.

[J]ust as you cannot promise you will not be a man or a woman, so you cannot promise not to produce seed and multiply. It is a matter of God's ordinance (*Geschöpffe*), not your power.[19]

---

[14] *Comm. Isa.* 49:15, LW 17.183-4 [WA 31^2.404-5].

[15] See *Comm. Deut.* 22:1, LW 9.219-20 [WA 14.701]; *Comm. John* 8:12, LW 23.323 [WA 33.519]; LW 44.8 [WA 2.167].

[16] LW 51.360 [WA 49.799]. Given the close identification of task with gender, this sounds like a recipe for keeping the *status quo* without any continuing critical analysis and evaluation of the situation. Further comment on this will be made in the conclusion to the next chapter.

[17] See *Comm. John* 15:5, LW 24.228 [WA 45.669].

[18] *The Estate of Marriage*, LW 45.18 [WA 10^2.276].

[19] Ibid., LW 45.19 [WA 10^2.277]. See also, LW 45.144 [WA 12.234].

Marriage is not Redemptive

We have observed that marriage is divinely given at creation. This is the case, not merely for that first marriage but for every marital relationship thereafter. The logical consequence of this needs to be noted. As a creation ordinance of God, marriage is a 'worldly', temporal vocation. As such, the husband-wife relationship is to be entered into voluntarily,[20] openly,[21] in partnership with God,[22] according to both natural law and divine command,[23] and permanently.[24] Marriage is a public estate, the work and ordinance (*Werck und Orden*) of God within the temporal government of his rule. Its nature, therefore, is outward and physical. Its realm is *not* that of the church, but that of civil affairs.[25] Consequently, judgements concerning marriage and divorce are the prerogative of jurists and magistrates, in much the same way as they preside over matters regarding the commandment condemning murder. Luther says that marriage

> should be left to the lawyers and made subject to the secular government. For marriage is a rather secular and outward thing, having to do with women and children, house and home, and with other matters that belong to the realm of the government, all of which have been completely subjected to reason.[26]

The work of pastors, on the other hand, is to be limited to dealing with situations that cause problems of conscience. That is, in terms earlier used of a distinction between the two governments, the lawyers are to deal with the outward matters, the pastors are

---

[20] LW 46.304 [WA 30³.236]; *Tischreden* [5570ᵃ], LW 54.456 [WA Tr. 5.250].

[21] LW 45.390 [WA 15.167].

[22] In *On Marriage Matters* (1530), LW 46.277 [WA 30³.214], Luther writes that God joins man and woman together. Then he adds, by way of explanation, 'Joining *by God* means that which is done *by us* according to his Word and commandment' – emphasis added.

[23] *Comm. Gen.* 24:1-4, LW 4.222 [WA 43.295].

[24] LW 45.386 [WA 15.164]. See also, *Comm. Isa.* 56:4, LW 17.262 [WA 31².463]; LW 51.358 [WA 49.797-8].

[25] LW 54.315 [WA Tr. 4.111]. See also, LW 53.110-115 [WA 30³.74-80]; LW 54.305 [WA Tr. 4.52]; LW 54.363 [WA Tr. 4.445-6]; *Comm. Deut.* 16:18, LW 9.162 [WA 14.665].

[26] *Comm. Matt.* 5:31-2, LW 21.93 [WA 32.376-7]. See also, LW 54.66 [WA Tr.1.179-180].

to concern themselves with the inward.[27] Therefore, for example, the Reformer lays down general principles for evangelical pastors on matters of conscience regarding marriage, divorce and desertion in his work, *On Marriage Matters*. However, generally, he says, that it should be left to the temporal authorities, because, 'marriage is an external, worldly matter, like clothing and food, house and property, subject to temporal authority'. Indeed, pastors are to refuse to deal with marriage matters that are already adequately covered by temporal laws.[28]

Luther, therefore, teaches that marriage is part of the realm of creation rather than a part of the realm of redemption. In his *Sermon on the Estate of Marriage* (1519),[29] Luther follows a traditional teaching, speaking of marriage as a sacrament – signifying the union between the divine and human nature of Christ. The significance of his later understanding, however, is seen as early as 1520, when in his Latin treatise, *De Captivitate Babylonica Ecclesiae*,[30] Luther announces that marriage is no longer to be considered as a sacrament of the church.[31] For this conclusion, he suggests several reasons: *a.* The man who marries receives no special grace from God; *b.* Marriage is nowhere spoken of in terms of a sign of anything else, particularly of something spiritual; *c.* It has existed since the beginning of the world (it is creational); *d.* Marriage is found among unbelievers as well as the regenerate;[32] *e.* The word *sacramentum* denotes, not a sign of something sacred, but the secret, hidden thing, itself – the *mysterion*. Thus, he concludes that there are only two things worth calling 'sacraments': baptism and 'the bread'. 'Only in these two do we find both the divinely instituted sign and the promise of forgiveness of sins.'[33]

---

[27] LW 54.315 [WA Tr.4.111]. See also, H. White, *Social Criticism in Popular Religious Literature of the Sixteenth Century* (Octagon, New York, 1965), 180.

[28] LW 46.265, 266 [WA 30³.205, 206], respectively. See also, ibid., 318 [246].

[29] Sermon on the Estate of Marriage (1519), LW 44.10 [WA 2.168].

[30] *The Babylonian Captivity of the Church* (1520), LW 36.11-126 [WA 6.497-573].

[31] For a Catholic argument, contemporary with Luther, see J. Eck, *Enchiridion of Common Places* (Baker, Grand Rapids, 1979), 89-90.

[32] Indeed, he suggests that marriage is sometimes practised better among those who do not hold to its divine origin.

[33] *The Babylonian Captivity of the Church*, LW 36.124 [WA 571-2]. For the reasons outlined in the text, see ibid., 92-4 [550-51].

This final remark concerning the forgiveness of sins is crucial, of course. G. R. Evans says that medieval orthodoxy saw the sacraments as 'indispensable means' by which salvation was arrived at as an 'effect'. They were seen as a remedy against sin, in the salvific sense.[34] She further comments that what underlies the Reformer's theology, on the other hand, was 'a habit of looking for what "counts" in the forgiveness of sins, what "causes" salvation, what has "power to save"'.[35] Clearly, this could not be so for Luther's doctrine of marriage within his understanding of reality and of vocation, in particular. As a calling within God's temporal government, marriage is a channel of service. It has a welfare function, but it is not directly or indirectly relevant to a person's fundamental standing before God. Marriage is a restraint against sin and its selfishness, lust, disorderliness and disruptive tendency. But, in itself, it cannot be part of the redemptive process. It stands alongside the 'sacred' aspects of life, but it fails to bestow saving righteousness. Throughout his career, Luther is firm on the idea that marriage is not a contributory factor in salvation. If it were, then righteousness would come through works, not through grace.[36]

There is some debate on the question of whether the Reformer's teaching on this point raised or lowered the status of marriage. On the one hand, R. Phillips, for example, shows that the reformers, generally, denied the sacramentality of marriage and, thereby, any possibility of it conveying grace to the spouses. Yet, he claims that Luther raised the status of marriage. On the other hand, E. O. James speaks of marriage being 'reduced' to a civil contract, 'devoid of sacramental significance'.[37] Each judgement will appear right, depending on the foundational assumption of the critic. Each has an element of truth. However, strictly speaking, neither is entirely correct.

---

[34] G. R. Evans, *Problems of Authority in the Reformation Debates* (CUP, Cambridge, 1992), 144.

[35] Ibid., 115.

[36] See *Comm. Isa.* 56:4, LW 17.262 [WA 31^2.463]. See also, *Comm. Gal.* 2:20 (1535), LW 26.173 [WA 40$^{1.}$292]; LW 31.369 [WA 7.67].

[37] R. Phillips, *Putting Asunder* (CUP, Cambridge, 1988), 45; E. O. James, *Marriage and Society* (Hutchinson, London, 1952), 151, respectively. J. A. Brundage, *Law, Sex and Christian Society in Medieval Europe* (University of Chicago Press, Chicago, 1987), 556, also says that Luther demoted marriage from sacramental status.

Luther seeks neither to raise nor to lower the status of marriage. His intention is to put it into its proper place – according to both biblical doctrine (as he understands it) and his overall view of reality in the two governments of God's rule. Given all his presuppositions, how can marriage be a sacrament? If it is not, then people must recognize it for what it is – a station in which all (believers and unbelievers) are involved, within worldly existence; not a means of communicating God's saving grace. Therefore, he shifts the significance of marriage from redemptive to creational.[38] However, we note that to stress the vocational nature of marriage against any suggestion of a sacramental understanding is to reinforce a hierarchical understanding of the marital relationship. That is so, as we have seen, because vocation, within the temporal realm, *is hierarchical by nature*.

For Luther, to teach that marriage and the husband-wife relationship is intrinsically creational and part of temporal reality is *not* to say that he held it to be, somehow, 'unspiritual'. In the previous chapter we noted that, in one sense, it is at the interface of the believer's faith that 'spiritual' and 'temporal' reality connect. This happens most pertinently within his or her individual vocational existence in the world. Therefore, we now move to examine the husband-wife relationship as discerned by faith and lived out before God.

Marriage and the Recognition of Faith

Luther teaches that one of the distinguishing characteristics of believers is that they readily recognize the nature and importance of vocation. He defines this discernment (in the context of the subject of marriage) three years before his own marriage. It has four components: belief that marriage is divinely instituted; that God joins the couple together; that he ordains that they should have and bring up their children; and that everything involved in marriage, if accomplished through faith, is pleasing to God. In this, they are not to rely on feelings, but on knowledge of God's

---

[38] He says that 'marriage is not [even] conducive to salvation' (*Comm. John* 1:13, LW 22.100 [WA 46.622]). This position may be seen as part of a wider, contemporary secularization of society – on this, see J. Goody, *The Development of the Family in Europe* (CUP, Cambridge, 1983), 167.

desire.[39] A few years earlier he observes, 'What a truly noble, important, and blessed condition the estate of marriage is *if it is properly regarded!* What a truly pitiable, horrible, and dangerous condition it is *if it is not properly regarded!*'[40] The problem, as Luther sees it, is that the evil world of his day held marriage in such disrepute and so maligned it, that it is only by faith that the Christian can properly regard marriage in its vocational function in the society which God providentially orders and sustains.[41] They must, therefore, evaluate all occupations and stations solely on the basis of the Word of God.[42]

In a passage from *The Estate of Marriage* this is repeated and its significance is clearly seen.[43] Luther bemoans the disregard into which the subject of marriage has fallen; women are treated as though they are merely depraved, marriage as though it is nothing more than an unhappy estate. He continues,

> Now observe that when that clever harlot, our natural reason [*naturliche Vernunft*] ... takes a look at married life, she turns up her nose and says, 'Alas, must I rock the baby, wash its diapers, make its bed, smell its stench, stay up nights with it, take care of it when it cries, heal its rashes and sores, and on top of that care for my wife, provide for her, labor at my trade, etc. ... and whatever else

---

[39] *The Estate of Marriage*, LW 45.38-9 [WA 10². 294-5].

[40] *Sermon on the Estate of Marriage*, LW 44.13-14 [WA 2.170] – emphasis added. See also, to Nicholas Gerbel [Wartburg], November 1, 1521, LW 48.322 [WA Br. 2.398].

[41] At one point Luther cryptically remarks that the ungodly have 'the sun, moon, earth, water, air and everything that has been subjected to man. But because they are ungodly rather than godly, the sun is not the sun; and the moon, the earth, water, and air are not what they are.' How, then, can they be expected to recognize other works of God, such as marriage? (the preface, *Comm. Gal.* (1535), LW 27.148 [WA 40¹.36]). See also, LW 51.154 [WA 30¹.75-6]; LW 1.118 [WA 42.89]; M. Grossmann, *Humanism in Wittenberg, 1485-1517* (de Graff, Nieuwkoop, 1975), 59, 'Wittenberg scholars thought it to be in good humanistic taste to show contempt for women.' D. Herlihy, 'Did Women have a Renaissance?' in *Women, Family and Society in Medieval Europe* (Berghahn, Providence, 1995), 33-56, argues that by most social indicators women, especially elite women, were losing status, power and visibility as the Middle Ages progressed. Also, M. P. Fleischer, '"Are Women Human?" The Debate between Valens Acidalius and Simon Gediccus', *SCJ* 11 (1981), 107-21.

[42] *Comm. Matt.* 7:15, LW 21.257 [WA 32.512].

[43] LW 45.39-41 [WA 10².295-7]. Though this passage is long, it is worth quoting because of the considerably important points that it makes. However, it is not quoted in full – as indicated.

of bitterness and drudgery married life involves? What, should I make such a prisoner of myself?'

[At this point Luther comments that it might be better to be free – or even to be a priest or a nun!]

What then does Christian faith [*der Christlich glaube*] say to this? It opens its eyes, looks upon these insignificant, distasteful and despised duties in the Spirit, and is aware that they are adorned with divine approval. ... It says, 'O God, because I am certain that thou hast created me as a man and hast from my body begotten this child, I also know for a certainty that it meets with thy perfect pleasure. I confess to thee that I am not worthy to rock the little babe or wash its diapers, or to be entrusted with the care of the child or its mother. How is it that I, without any merit, have come to this distinction of being certain that I am serving thy creature and thy most precious will? O, how gladly will I do so, though the duties should be even more insignificant and despised. ... I am certain that it is thus pleasing in thy sight.'

A wife, too, should regard her duties in the same light, as she suckles the child, rocks and bathes it, and cares for it in other ways and as she busies herself with other duties and renders help and obedience to her husband.

[Emphasizing the mother's responsibility, he states that the wife should be willing to die in child-birth to do the duty of God.]

[W]hen a father goes ahead and washes diapers or performs some other mean task for his child, and someone ridicules him as an effeminate fool ... you tell me, which of the two is most keenly ridiculing the other? God, with all his angels and creatures, is smiling – not because that father is washing diapers, but because he is doing so in Christian faith. Those who sneer at him and see only the task but not the faith are ridiculing God with all his creatures, as the biggest fool on earth. Indeed, they are ridiculing themselves; with all their cleverness they are nothing but devil's fools.

Strauss cites this significant passage and concludes that Luther's attitude would be best summed up in the words, 'God made me; I am his servant; I comply with his wishes.'[44] But, surely, this is to

---

[44] Strauss, op. cit., 113. On the same passage, L. S. Cahill, *Between the Sexes* (Fortress, Philadelphia, 1985), 129, is nearer the mark when she says, more

miss the point. Here, in the example that Luther presents, is not, essentially, an ethic of servitude and obligation, but of a grateful response that comes from a recognition that one's vocation and its attendant tasks are generously bestowed by God.[45]

Although some of these will be examined in more detail later, it is useful to list one or two ideas that can be established by the passage, as they add to our understanding of Luther's doctrine of marriage as a vocation and of the husband-wife relationship:

a. On the one hand, we notice that it is natural reason or 'cleverness' that evaluates marriage as bitterness or drudgery in which the unregenerate feels imprisoned.[46] Natural reason is capable of discerning what to do in a calling, but it cannot recognize that calling for what it is in the wider context of reality. It lives altogether outside of the glory of God, not knowing him.[47] It is evident that Luther puts this down to the unbeliever's egotistic pride, which sees vocational tasks as obligatory. On the other hand, it is the person of faith who sees the identical tasks as entrusted to him by God. In human terms, the work still appears insignificant, distasteful and despised, but, in humility, he accepts them as necessary to the vocation that God has given him and, therefore, as pleasing to the Lord. Consequently, he will perform them with genuine joy and gratitude. The conclusion is that the worldly man sees 'only the task but not the faith'. Reason fails to recognize vocation; faith discerns its nature, its givenness and its privilege.

b. The fact that Luther sees the unregenerate man ridiculing the believing father as effeminate is interesting. It hints that the Reformer believes that it is natural reason and unbelief that demarcates the tasks of husband and wife in a strict and unbending way. Here, Luther depicts the father as employed in the duties usually caricatured as the female's tasks. This he does while maintaining his own tasks, of course. Yet, he rejoices in the parental duties. It is also clear from the passage that he performs

---

positively, that, 'Luther felicitously expresses ... elevated theological judgement in earthy, common-sense terms.'

[45] In the same way, elsewhere, Luther asks, 'Why should I not therefore freely, joyfully, with all my heart and with eager will do all things which I know are pleasing and acceptable to such a Father who has overwhelmed me with his inestimable riches?' (LW 31.367 [WA 7.65]).

[46] See also, *Comm. Gal.* 4:6 (1535), LW 26.376 [WA 40¹.573].

[47] '...*vivit plane extra gloriam Dei*' (LW 54.327 [WA Tr. 4.197]).

these tasks *within* the context of the hierarchical arrangement of marriage. The wife is said to render 'help and obedience to her husband'. As will be shown below, Luther, himself, caricatures the tasks of husband and wife in his patriarchal teaching, generally, but this passage and his own relationship with Kate give a slightly different perspective on this.

c. Luther affirms the centrality of faith. He shows that it is faith that makes the difference between the believer's and the unbeliever's response to his vocation. In this sense, vocational life is a spontaneous and concrete realization of faith, itself.[48] The Christian, living by the power of the Holy Spirit and with the transformed values of the Kingdom of God, realizes that every menial task in his vocation is a privilege that he is unworthy (before God) of performing. His rejoicing rests on three things: God's creation of him as a man, God's entrusting him with his tasks and the fact that all within his vocation of marriage is pleasing in God's sight.

Elsewhere, Luther asks, 'Now tell me, how can the heart have a greater good, joy and delight than in God, when one is certain that his estate, conduct, and work is pleasing to God?' [49]

Marriage in the Sight of God

Through his emphasis on faith in the vocation of marriage the Reformer stresses both the joy of calling, together with the seriousness of the task. Luther implies that marriage is never a trifling matter. Rather, it is the 'most serious and important matter in the whole world.'[50] A significant part of the reason for this is that, in keeping with its vocational nature, it is lived out *coram Deo*. But, within this area of his ethics there is a typically Lutheran ambiguity. On the one hand, the eschatological threat of the final judgement stands before every man and woman. On the other hand, the believer is judged, in Christ, to be already justified. Both ideas are indicative foci to his application.

---

[48] See LW 51.243-4 [WA 36.238-9]. See also, W. von Loewenich, *Martin Luther: The Man and his Work* (Augsburg, Minneapolis, 1986), 291-2.

[49] *The Estate of Marriage*, LW 45.38 [WA 10².295].

[50] *Comm. Gen.* 24:1-4, LW 4.221 [WA 43.294]. See also, LW 45.154 [WA 12.241].

Giving the husband and wife's vocational duties as an example, Luther states that, 'Nobody bears in mind that on Judgement Day God will demand from *everyone* an accounting of how he carried on his office (*Beruf*) or calling (*Stand*).'[51] This is in keeping with his persistent belief in the apocalyptic nature of existence in which vocations are lived out. However, for believers this is not to breed alarm as their faithful continuance within the ordinance or station (*Ordnung und Stande*) is enough to ensure God's pleasure on the Day of the Lord. He comments,'[T]he fact that you are married, as long as you are a Christian, will be a great glory and honour to you on the last day.' Indeed, elsewhere, he affirms this with characteristic exuberance, claiming that even if Christ returns to find a husband and wife engaged in sexual intercourse, they should not be afraid.[52] The fact is, they are maintaining their vocation into which they have been placed. However, the eschatological focus is only one side of living *coram Deo*.

Luther makes a great deal of the fact that when husbands and wives faithfully live within their vocation, God is pleased with every task they perform. This is the present focus of his ethics. As we have already seen, the reason for this is that the horizontal, relational dynamic of vocation forces men and women to live for others. In the case of marriage, for example, it causes the husband to live for the wife and the wife for the husband. Directing them to their partner, this takes them outside of themselves, makes them realise what little resources they have in themselves and compels them to live by faith in reliance on God.[53] In the important, related area of whether priests should take wives, for instance, Luther commends that they do so because it is right before God (*coram Deo*). That is enough, whether anyone agrees or not.[54]

---

[51] *Comm. John* 1: 13, LW 22.95 [WA 46.618] – emphasis added.

[52] LW 51.362 [WA 49.801]; LW 51.366 [WA 49.805], respectively. Also, *Comm. John* 15:4, LW 24.221 [WA 45.662], where he says that married couples will receive God's reward because of their faith within their vocational tasks.

[53] See G. Wingren, *Luther on Vocation* (Muhlenberg, Philadelphia, 1957), 32-3; B. A. Gerrish, *The Old Protestantism and the New* (T&T Clark, Edinburgh, 1982), 89, 314. fn. 104. In this context, D. Hampson, *Theology and Feminism* (Blackwell, Oxford, 1990), 127, suggests that Luther teaches that Christians live outside of themselves (*extra se*) in trust in God, in love for their neighbour. Also, LW 26.387 [WA 40^1.589]; LW 28.17-18 [WA 12.106].

[54] LW 36.102 [WA 6.557]. See also, LW 51.360 [WA 49.799, 800].

Marriage, by nature, and everything in marriage is pleasing in the sight of God, then, if the married couple are believers and perform their tasks in faith before him.[55] If this is so, then the man and woman need to trust in God and to show that trust by prayer at every turn. Consequently, they should pray when looking for the right spouse,[56] that the union will be one of the mind as well as the body, that ardent love will continue, for the grace necessary against the devil, the flesh and the world,[57] and against the troubles which are inevitable within the vocation of marriage.[58]

Marriage – 'a Cross-marked Vocation'[59]

A husband or wife's faith recognizes that, as a creational ordinance of God within the temporal government of his rule in society, marriage shares a characteristic of all other vocations within that rule; namely, that it brings with it misery, as well as delight. This is necessarily the case because it retains something of the original nature and purpose, while participating in the consequences of God's judgement upon Adam's sin and the subsequent curse on mankind. Margaret Miles speaks of this judgemental confrontation of Adam as 'the primal situation of human beings' and says that, in Luther's theology, it becomes, 'insistently existential'.[60] The day-to-day, ongoing relationship of two people who are *both* justified *and* sinful, who manifest the

---

[55] Together with the passages already cited, see also, *Comm. Isa.* 41:8, LW 17.39-40 [WA 31^2.291]; *Comm. John* 15:5, LW 24.231 [WA 45.671-2]; *Comm. Gen.* 37:12-14, LW 6.347, 349 [WA 44.259-60, 261]; LW 31.356-7 [WA 7.58-9]; LW 45.47 [WA 10^2.302]; *Comm. 1 Pet.*3:1-6, LW 30.90 [WA 12.344].

[56] *Comm. Gen.* 25:19-20, LW 4.335 [WA 43.377]. Also, LW 54.25 [WA Tr. 1.84]; LW 44.8 [WA 2.167]; *Comm. Gen.* 24:1-4, LW 4.225 [WA 43.297], 44:17, LW 7.367 [WA 44.573].

[57] LW 54.444 [WA Tr. 5.214]; *Comm. Gen.* 39:7-10, LW 7.85 [WA.3.63]; LW 46.305 [WA 30^3.236], respectively.

[58] *Comm. Gen.* 28:1-2, LW 5.190-91 [WA 43.559-60]. On the necessity of prayer within the context of vocation, generally, see Wingren, op. cit., 184-99. Also, *Comm. Eccl.* 2:3, LW 15.35 [WA 20.41-2]; *Comm. Gen.* 42:3-4, LW 7.221 [WA 44.463]; 44:17, LW 7.367 [WA 44.573].

[59] Wingren, op. cit., 57 – *mortificatio* within the social order.

[60] M. R. Miles, '"The Rope Breaks when it is Tightest": Luther on the Body, Consciousness and the Word', *HTR* 77:3-4 (1984), 239-58, particularly, 244.

two 'antagonistic components in man',[61] is bound to experience the unhappiness as well as the joy of present existence. The unbeliever overemphasizes the unhappiness, while the man or woman of faith is able to see both. However, the former *is* significant to them.

In his early work, *The Estate of Marriage*, Luther speaks of this with a sense of realism. In arguing against a contemporary, pessimistic attitude,[62] he states that he is sure that in all marriages there is suffering, labour and some bitterness, but, he is also certain that there is 'the inner, spiritual delight' that comes through faith.[63] What are some of the miseries that come to the husband and wife in their relationship? We can discern two broad areas in Luther's thinking. First, there is the *inner vexation*; that is, the trouble that comes from within the marriage. For example, Luther realizes that the initial love sometimes dies and that, subsequently, the spouses will find it difficult to get on with each other in their regret.[64] Then, there are the almost insurmountable problems related to having children and bringing them up together.[65] There is the trouble that a husband might find ruling his own household - his wife, children and servants.[66] And, of course, sin itself will cause difficulties in the relationship - sometimes sin of which the spouses, themselves, are not even aware.[67] Second, there are *external pressures*; that is, problems that come from outside, but which effectively impinge on the marriage relationship. These are as important to Luther as the former. He is concerned that marriage can bring poverty, for example, but he would not let the fear of this stand in the way of two

---

[61] Wingren, op. cit., 250.

[62] 'Eyn kurtze freud und lange unlust' (Brief is the joy, lasting the bitterness).

[63] *The Estate of Marriage* (1522), LW 45.42, 46 [WA 10².298, 301]. Luther often comments on the problems that marriages are bound to encounter, for example, *Comm. Eccl.* 7:1-2, LW 15.106 [WA 20.122-3]; *Comm. Matt.* 5:4, LW 21.17 [WA 32.311]; *Comm. Gen.* 2:15, LW 1.102 [WA 42.77]; 6:1-2, LW 2.8 [WA 42.267]; 28:1-2, LW 5.190-91 [WA 43.559-60]; 41:16, LW 7.146 [WA 44.407]. Augustine speaks in a similar way - see, for example, *DCD* 22.22 (ASW 2.497-501).

[64] *Comm. John* 15:9, LW 24.246 [WA 45.685]; LW 54.218 [WA Tr. 3.367-8].

[65] *Comm. Gen.* 30:22-4, LW 5.363 [WA 43.679].

[66] LW 45.154 [WA 12.241]. See also, *Comm. Gen.* 3:19, LW 1.213 [WA 42.159].

[67] *Comm. Gen.* 12:18-19, LW 2.319 [WA 42.490].

people getting married. This would be tantamount to a lack of confidence in God.⁶⁸ It is also clear that marriage, at least for some, brought persecution with it.⁶⁹ However, for Luther, the real external menace to marital relationship is the devil.

Marriage, as a temporal vocation given by God, is a prime target for spiritual battle. We saw, in the previous chapter, that this is part of the eschatological life-situation of married couples. Satan desires to take from marriage mutual love, respect, harmony and contentment. In this, he opposes God's rule and order, 'for the estate of marriage does not set well with the devil, [simply] because it is God's good will and work'.⁷⁰ Luther teaches that the devil wishes no-one to be married. Failing that, he brings contention and hatred into the situation and directly prompts men and women to lust and to commit adultery. He also tries to destroy women's honour before men and, generally, to bring about chaos in God's world and, particularly, in the familial realm.⁷¹

Yet, despite all of this, Luther emphasizes the positive perspective that comes from recognizing the true nature of marriage as a vocation lived before a God who cares. If, in marriage, trouble comes,

> What does it matter? Is it not better that I please God in this manner, that God hears me when I call upon Him, that He delivers me in misfortunes, and that He benefits me in various ways through

---

⁶⁸ To Nicholas Gerbel [Wartburg], November 1, 1521, LW 48.321-2 [WA Br. 2.397]; LW 45.47 [WA 10².302]. On the poverty of married, reformed pastors, generally, see S. Ozment, *The Age of Reform. 1250-1550* (Yale University Press, New York, 1980), 393-4.

⁶⁹ *Comm. 1 Cor.* 7:25-26, LW 28.49 [WA 12.134-5].

⁷⁰ '...es ist gottis werck und gutter wille' (*The Estate of Marriage*, LW 45.37 [WA 10².294]). I have added the word 'simply', giving, what I perceive to be the intention of the Reformer at this point.

⁷¹ See, for example, *Comm. Zech.* 1:7, LW 20.172 [WA 23.513-14]; LW 35.137-40 [WA 10².77-80]; LW 54.25 [WA 1.84]; to Staupitz [Wittenberg] June 27, 1522, LW 49.13 [WA Br. 2.568]; to John Rühel [Seeburg], May 4, 1525, LW 49.108-12 [WA Br. 3.480-82]; *On Marriage Matters*, LW 46.300-302, 305 [WA 30³.233-4, 236]; *Comm. John* 2:17, LW 22.233 [WA 46.743]; *Comm. Matt.* 5:27-30, LW 21.87 [WA 32.371-2]; *Comm. Gen.* 26:8, LW 5.33 [WA 43.451]; 39:7-10, LW 7.75-6 [WA 44.355-7]. See also, H. A. Oberman, *Luther. Man between God and the Devil* (Fontana, London, 1993); idem, 'Martin Luther' in E. Jungel / J. Wallman / W. Werbeck (eds), *Verifikationen Festschrift für Gerhard Ebeling 70. Geburtstag* (Mohr, Tübingen, 1982), 91-119; Wingren, op. cit., 78-161.

my life's companion, the pious wife whom I have joined to myself?'[72]

To summarize, Luther defines the fundamental nature of marriage from the perspective of creational logic. He teaches that God instituted marriage at creation to be a significant vocation within the temporal government. That is, the relationship that exists between the husband and the wife is not redemptive. It is involved with temporal existence, not with the communication of divine, saving grace. In keeping with its vocational nature, marriage is a restraint against sin's tendencies of disorder and disruption. Or, more positively, its purpose is to maintain societal order and peace. By this firm location of marriage into the temporal kingdom, the Reformer locks the institution into characteristics of that realm and forces it away from any real possibility of its relation to the social consequences of a spiritual equality in Christ. Its concern is 'this-worldly' in a way that precludes a familial egalitarian impulse.

Having asserted that much, we have seen that Luther stresses the importance of faith that recognises the privilege and joy of being a husband/father or wife/mother within vocation. Believers realise their responsibility – that each day in the marital relationship (with its bitterness and its pleasure) is a day before the judging, yet gracious, God. These characteristics of the nature of the husband-wife relationship stem directly from the Reformer's view of marriage as a vocation: characteristics that were outlined in the previous chapter. Much of this is traditional and little of it allows for mutuality or any sense of equality between the spouses, partly because of Luther's insistence on an intransigent order and partly because he defines roles and responsibilities on the basis of created *difference* between the male and female.

We now proceed to look at the traditional reasons for getting married as employed by Luther in order further to discern his view of the nature of the marital relationship within his concept of vocation. Clearly, the matters of sexual union, procreation and companionship bring the study more specifically to the dynamics of the relationship, itself.

---

[72] *Comm. Gen.* 21:1-3, LW 4.6 [WA 43.140]. See also, *Comm. Gen.* 24:1-4, LW 4.243 [WA 43.310]; *Comm. John* 14:24, LW 24.162 [WA 45.608].

TRADITIONAL REASONS FOR MARRYING

Luther speaks of marriage as consisting of three things: the natural desire for sex, the bringing to life of offspring, and life together with mutual fidelity.[73] In these, he says nothing unconventional. Indeed, as we have seen, they parallel Augustine's and the medieval understanding of marriage. However, within these purposes for marrying lie implications concerning the relationship between the husband and wife that Luther spells out in his works. This is so, because, on a secondary level, these are the grounds for that relationship.[74] However, they need to be examined within the concept of vocation in the government of God's rule against the criticism that has been levelled at the Reformer's ideas.

The Natural Desire for Sex

Luther says that a characteristic reason for marrying is simply the natural propensity that men and women have for sexual intercourse – by which he means that people have this as a result of their created constitution. However, as noted in the introductory chapter on Luther, this is one of the areas of Luther's ethics of marriage that is most criticized.[75] For example, J. B. Nelson suggests that a positive affirmation of sexuality evaded the Reformer.[76] One ethicist says that Luther was 'overshadowed by a grim negativity which found in marriage the one effective antidote to incontinence'.[77] Against the Reformer's teaching in this area, some feminist and liberationist scholars, in

---

[73] 'In coniugio sunt haec, quod sexus naturaliter appetitur, item generatio et proles, item cohabitatio et mutua fides' *Tischreden* ([185] 1532, LW 54.25 [WA Tr. 1.83-4]).

[74] On a primary level, God's intention is the ground for marriage.

[75] The other area is teaching on the hierarchical arrangement in marriage.

[76] J. B. Nelson, *Embodiment* (SPCK, London, 1979), 55. See also, for example, S. Bailey, *Common Sense About Sexual Ethics* (Victor Gollancz, London, 1962), 51-2; P. Althaus, *The Ethics of Martin Luther* (Fortress, Philadelphia, 1972), 84-5; R. S. Anderson, *On Being Human* (Eerdmans, Grand Rapids, 1982), 91, 137, 218-19; T. M. McDonough, *The Law and the Gospel in Luther* (OUP, Oxford, 1963), 27, 31, 72. H. Deniffle, *Luther et le lutheranisme* (Paris, 1913-16) 2.391-40.

[77] P. L. Lehmann, *Ethics in a Christian Context* (SCM, London, 1963), 134.

particular, are most scathing. M. S. Behrens, for example, sees in Luther's writing an inordinate emphasis upon woman simply as an instrument to be employed in curtailing sexual lust and feels, therefore, that she cannot over-emphasize his 'deep and pervasive negativity toward woman'. Similarly, Karen Armstrong states that the Reformer's view of sex was negative and unbiblical.[78] Her opinion is that he has no time for sex – sharing, as he did, Augustine's sexual neurosis. However, are these criticisms sustainable in the light of the evidence?

Lisa Cahill clearly discerns the problem in Luther's theology. But she wishes to see the Reformer's understanding more positively. Taking his comment that sexual intercourse is always sinful, she says that it raises several questions which need to be answered in the context of Luther's doctrines of original sin and humanity's restoration in Christ.[79] In this she is substantially correct, but, alternatively, we wish to suggest that there are two main factors to keep in mind. The first is that sexual desire is a gift of God, the Creator. The second is that the use of that gift has been tainted by the Fall. These will throw our discussion into the realm of Creation/Fall into which Luther seems to want to read his doctrine of marriage.

In examining Luther's doctrine of 'active sexuality', as it has been termed,[80] it is important to remember that he clearly teaches

---

[78] M. S. Behrens, 'Martin Luther's View of Women' (unpublished Masters thesis, Texas State University, 1973), 54, 65, 69; K. Armstrong, *The Gospel According to Woman* (Elm Tree, London, 1986), 7, 30-31, respectively. S. Selinger, *Calvin Against Himself* (Archon, Hamden, 1984), 29-30, 41-2, claims that, for Luther sin remained somehow rooted in sexuality, even though she says he broke with the medieval concept of sin which was inordinately concerned with the sexual. As we shall see, it is more precise to say that, for Luther, the *postlapsarian* experience of sexuality is rooted in sin.

[79] Cahill, op. cit., 124-6. As Cahill analyses it, the questions raised by Luther's assertion that sexual intercourse is never without sin, include the following: Why is the sexual act always sinful, if it is part of God's ordinance and command? Is God a cosmic utilitarian who commands sin that good may result? How can God command a sinful act, then 'excuse' it? Why is it in need of God's forgiveness if it is both commanded and the avenue through which the promise of creation is fulfilled? Is Luther articulating a theologically coherent position? Or, is it another instance of his disinterest in systematic thought? Is it a remnant of Augustinian and unbiblical negativity toward all sexual activity? The following pages, in the thrust of their argument, will intimate answers to these questions.

[80] Phillips, op. cit., 43. E. H. Schroeder, 'Family Ethos in the Light of the

that God, himself, has given men and women their sex-drive and mutual attraction. He did this at creation and his powerful, creative Word, implanted in everyone is, somehow, operative in men and women to form life by procreation. Men and women are incapable of resisting the drive of the sexual disposition which is part of their nature and which compels them to produce seed and to multiply. In stressing this aspect of the Reformer's teaching, Bornkamm remarks that it 'signified no capitulation to the irresistible sinfulness of human nature, as some have interpreted him. Rather, it is part of his teaching on creation which declares that nature...'.[81] The important point raised by Bornkamm's comment is that to start from the postlapsarian sexual drive is to begin at the wrong place. Luther's foundational doctrine is that the sexual desire of humanity is part of its created nature. Originally (that is, pre-Fall) it was without sin. Indeed, at creation and before the Fall there was no activity more excellent, except proclaiming the name of God.[82]

Although Luther seems to emphasize this more in his later ministry, even in an earlier work, *The Estate of Marriage* (1522), he insists that the sexual drive as an intrinsic part of the creation of humanity is a divine and natural ordinance[83] and is implanted and blessed by God. In 1532, he speaks of it again, together with the idea that even the attraction of a man for a woman is God's creation. Indeed, in his commentary on Titus, he states that because the physiognomy of man is itself God's creation, then the wife ought to enjoy her husband's body.[84] Presumably, the basic theological assumption behind this also allows it to be reversed and reciprocated. The husband ought to enjoy his wife's body,

---

Reformation' in O. E. Feucht (ed.), *Family Relationships and the Church* (Concordia, St. Louis, 1970), 101, speaks of this as marriage's 'dynamic operational character'.

[81] Bornkamm, op. cit., 111. See also, T. M. Safley, *Let no man put asunder. The control of marriage in the German Southwest. A comparative study, 1550-1600* (SCJ publishers, Kirksville, 1984), 182.

[82] *Comm. Gen.* 1:26, LW 1.56-7 [WA 42.42]; 2:16-17, LW 1.104 [WA 42.79]; 2:18, LW 1.117-18 [WA 42.89]; 2:23, LW 1.136 [WA 42.101-2]; 3:1, LW 1.142 [WA 42.106-7].

[83] '...dem gotlichen und naturlichen orden' (LW 45.22, 49 [WA 10^2.279, 304]). See also, *Comm. Gen.* 19:4-5, LW 3.255 [WA 43.57].

[84] '*Et appetitus ad mulierem est creatio Dei*' (LW 54.161 [WA Tr. 2.167]). See also, LW 54.158 [WA Tr. 2.150]; LW 54.324 [WA Tr. 4.171-2]; *Comm. Tit.* 2:4, LW 29.54 [WA 25.43-44].

too. He remarks that the phrase, 'Adam knew his Wife' (Gen. 4:1) is a very apt one because it expresses not an abstract knowledge, but feeling and experience: 'Adam knew Eve, his wife ... *as a woman.*'[85] Oberman remarks that, 'For Luther, God is so vitally present in the power of attraction between man and woman that he inspires the conjugal union and Himself constitutes the sexual bond of marriage.' This whole teaching is even more striking, if (as Oberman earlier suggests) this idea of God's intimate involvement in people's sexual drive was 'highly offensive in the sixteenth century'.[86]

The significant conclusion to be drawn from this is that, largely in contrast to his time, Luther spoke openly of the sexual drive and mutual attraction as being created, implanted and inspired by God. It is not, in itself, the result of sinfulness, nor is sexual intercourse sinful, *per se*. Here, then, is a positive affirmation of sex *as created by God*. In fact, according to the Reformer, God does not want sexual desire and mutual attraction 'to be despised as dishonorable. For it is a work of God in man's nature...'.[87] That is, it is fundamentally good, according to Luther's theology, because it is inherent in humanity's creation and in the continuing providential creativity of God, himself. As a part of a creational ordinance, sexual desire is reason enough for men and women to enter into the vocation of marriage. Indeed, they ought to do so.

However, this is only half of the current situation. If, in itself, marital sexual intercourse is not sinful, yet 'it is never without sin'.[88] The irresistible sex-drive is now tainted with sin and has become the overwhelming lust of both men and women.[89] The

---

[85] *Comm. Gen.* 4:1, LW 1.241 [WA 42.179] – emphasis added.

[86] Oberman, op. cit., 274, 273, respectively.

[87] *Comm. Gen.* 29:9-12, LW 5.282 [WA 43.623]. See also, *Comm. Gen.* 2:16-17, LW 1.104 [WA 42.79]; 49:3, LW 8.210 [WA 44.732].

[88] *Comm. 1 Cor.* 7:25-6, LW 28.49 [WA 12.135].

[89] There seems no good reason to agree with R. Marius, *Luther* (Quartet, London, 1975), 133, or with M. Wiesner, 'Luther and Women: The Death of Two Marys' in J. Obelkevich / L. Roper / R. Samuel, (eds), *Disciplines of Faith* (Routledge, London, 1987), 299, who each assert that Luther belied women's sex-drive to be stronger than that of men. Although this was a typically medieval idea, Luther evidences no such emphasis, as far as I am aware. See, *Sermon on the Estate of Marriage,* LW 44.8 [WA 2.167]; *Comm. 1 Cor.* 7:1-2, LW 28.11 [WA 12.99]; *Comm. Gen.* 26:8, LW 5.37 [WA 43.454]; 39:7-10, LW 7.75-6 [WA 44.355-6]; *Comm. Matt.* 5:27-30, LW 21.86 [WA 32.371]; LW 4.233 [WA 43.303].

fundamental disposition that remains becomes a passion of the flesh. The original sociability has become the arena for selfishness and egotism. With this comes another reason for marrying – the control and restraint of what sin has spoiled. Again, marriage as a vocation, within the realm of God's temporal authority, is seen as employed by God to restrain sin and disorder in society. This is part of the postlapsarian purpose of marriage. It is in *this* area that he appears to be pessimistic.

According to Luther, original sin is said to be the 'source of that familiar mad passion for sex'.[90] He puts this in a characteristic comment, 'the glory of the genitals was turned into the utmost disgrace' at the fall of Adam and Eve.[91] It is not surprising, therefore, that there is a continual refrain that goes through Luther's works that marriage is a remedy against sin.[92] The need for marriage, *in this context*, is a consequence of original sin, which manifests itself in lust of 'burning'. In telling comparisons, he likens sinful, sexual lust to sexual heat 'as the deer has it, as a harlot feels it toward adulterers'.[93] Luther believes that this lust is generally more prevalent among the young.

> [I]t often happens to pious young men and even women that, contrary to their own will they are seized by an intense sexual desire. When a person is seized by that desire, his whole being is captured by it, so that he sees, hears, and thinks about nothing else than what that desire suggests.

It is significant that in this context, he parallels sexual lust to other sinful passions, such as anger, anxiety, hatred and, later, he adds blasphemy.[94] In another passage, he links it to impatience

---

[90] *Comm. Gen.* 26:8, LW 5.33 [WA 43.451]. See also, *Comm. Gen.* 28:1-2, LW 5.189 [WA 43.559]; 38:16-18, LW 7.33 [WA 44.324].

[91] *Comm. Gen.*3:7, LW 1.168 [WA 42.126].

[92] E. W. Cocke, Jr, 'Luther's View of Marriage and Family', *RL* 42/1 (1973), 110, says, 'He reasoned that marriage held back the destructive flood of human sensuality and immorality.' Even as a remedy, of course, it is still a gift of God. See, for example, LW 54.270 [WA Tr. 3.607-8]; LW 54.294-5 [WA Tr. 4.10-11]; *Comm. Gen.* 6:1-2, LW 2.9 [WA 42.268].

[93] *Comm. Isa.* 57:5, LW 17.271 [WA 31^2.470].

[94] *Comm. Ps.* 90:7, LW 13.109 [WA 40^3.540, 541]. Later, he says, 'There resides in young people a smoldering fire of sexual desires... (*Sicut enim fomes libidinis est in adolescentibus...*)' (LW 13.114 [WA 40^3.548]). See also, *Comm. Gal.* 5:17 (1535), LW 27.74 [WA 40^2.93-4]; 5:19 (1535), LW 27.80 [WA 40^2.100].

and mental depression.[95] The significance lies in the fact that Luther is pessimistic, *not in singling out sexual desire*, as such, but because of the fact of the sin involved. His pastoral advice to such as suffer is that they should not despair of their salvation and that, through fervent prayer, walking in the Holy Spirit, Bible reading, hard work, temperance and fasting, they should resist the temptation.[96] When this becomes impossible, as generally it must (because sexual desire, outside of marriage, is unable to be restrained), then they are to marry, rather than 'to burn'. In marrying people put themselves under the restrictions of the Holy Spirit.[97] It is, therefore, an unfortunate reflection on Luther's society and, perhaps, his own reforming failure, that later in his pastoral ministry he comes, reluctantly, to the conclusion that sexual desire is so strong for many that 'not even marriage is an adequate remedy'.[98]

Two images pervade his writing on this subject. When he speaks of a young man or woman seeking to resist the temptation he uses the metaphor of battle. However, when speaking of sexual desire as a sin to be remedied by marriage, he employs the metaphor of sickness.[99] In this area, marriage seems to parallel the church in its work. In terms relevant to the whole framework of the two kingdoms and vocation in which this chapter is progressing, the temporal government of God's authority parallels the spiritual. One of the tasks of the spiritual government is to restore to health those caught up in it through

---

[95] *Comm. Gal.* 5:18 (1535), LW 27.78 [WA 40^2.98-9].

[96] See *Comm. Gen.* 25:19-20, LW 4.333-4 [WA 43.376-7].

[97] See, for example, LW 45.45 [WA 10^2.300]; *Comm. Gal.* 5:16 (1535), LW 27.69 [WA 40^2.88]. See also; LW 54.31 [WA Tr. 1.98]; LW 54.160-61 [WA Tr. 4.10-11]; LW 45.19, 36, 43 [WA 10^2.277, 292, 299]; *Comm. Tit.* 2:5, LW 29.55 [WA 25.45]; *Comm. Gal.* 5:22-3 (1535), LW 27.95 [WA 40^2.120]. The Reformer's understanding of marriage as a remedy against inevitable sin is an important reason in his argument against celibacy, in general. Unless the celibate is one of the exceptions that Jesus speaks of in Matthew's gospel, the consequence of not marrying *will be* sexual sin outside of marriage. This is probably not the place to discuss this, but, see the following: LW 45.141-158 [WA 12.232-44]; LW 35.136-40 [WA 10^2.77-80]; *The Estate of Marriage*, LW 45.18, 46-7 [WA 10^2.276, 302]; *On Marriage Matters*, LW 46.299 [WA 30^3.231]; *Comm. 1 Cor.* 7:1-2, LW 28.9-10 [WA 12.97-8]; LW 36.206 [WA 8.543-4]; *Comm. Gen.* 30:1, LW 5.323 [WA 43.651-2].

[98] *Comm. Gen.* 4: 1, LW 1.238 [WA 42.177].

[99] For example, '[I]f he cannot abstain let him take a wife; God has made that plaster for that sore' (*Table Talk* [715], Fount, London, 1995, 332).

Christ. So, in this context, Luther can say that, 'This life ... is one of being healed from sin, it is not a life of sinlessness, with the cure completed and perfect health attained. The church is the inn and infirmary for those who are sick and in need of being made well.'[100] On the other hand, in the temporal context, he can state that, 'Marriage is likened to a hospital for incurables which prevents inmates from falling into graver sin.'[101]

On the surface these two seem less than parallel. After all, the church cures from sin, yet the vocation of marriage only prevents worse consequences befalling the spouses. This difference could appear to be the difference between the two governments – the spiritual heals, the temporal simply restrains. At one level, this may well be the case. However, it is significant that, in the first passage, perfection is said to be attained only in heaven, life is '*being healed*'.[102] The second reference is an early comment (1519). It is from a passage that stresses the wickedness of present sexual desire over against that desire as first created. Much later, commenting on Genesis, Luther says that *through marriage* 'that hideous disease of the flesh is *healed* and the road is blocked to sin, lest it ensnare us...'. However, he still admits that it is 'a serious sickness', 'a kind of disease, ... frenzy and a fury'.[103] Perhaps his pastoral experience and his own marriage taught him to value, not only the preventative, but also the curative nature of marriage.

How does this 'work'? Luther only hints at an answer. To Nicholas Gerbel, he writes to encourage him that, by marriage, he has 'conquered' the uncleanness of celibacy.[104] Through it, the sexual desire, which would be unbridled, is controlled and channelled. The man who enjoys his own wife will be more likely to avoid fornication. That is, marriage is designed to end sexual frustration. More curatively, however, '[W]hatever remains of the flesh is devoured by faith. Therefore, it [marriage] is spiritual, for the spiritual sets us free from the corruption and the blemish of

---

[100] *Comm. Rom.* 4:7, LW 25.262-3 [WA 56.275]. Also, LW 26.233, 260, 403 [WA 40¹.369, 408, 613].

[101] *Sermon on the Estate of Marriage*, LW 44.9 [WA 2.168].

[102] He continues, 'But heaven is the palace of the healthy and the righteous.'

[103] *Comm. Gen.* 18:9, LW 3.202 [WA 43.19]; 25:19-20, LW 4.336 [WA 43.378]; 39:7-10, LW 7.79 [WA 44.358], respectively.

[104] To Nicholas Gerbel [Wartburg], November 1, 1521, LW 48.321-2 [WA Br. 2.397]. See also, *Comm. Gen.* 24:1-4, LW 4.222 [WA 43.295].

original sin.'¹⁰⁵ By 'spiritual' Luther refers to the fact that marriage, though a temporal vocation, is still closely related to the spiritual kingdom through the faith of the believer, who inhabits both realms. The morality inspired by the spiritual impacts upon and affects the temporal. The point is that marriage is God's way of restraining sin and of healing. Yet it falls short of being salvific.

This fairly positive reasoning seems also dominant in Luther's comments on sexual intercourse within marriage, though some would disagree. Bailey's conclusion is representative. He states that for Luther sexual intercourse was, at best, 'a regrettable but imperative necessity'.[106] But obviously, the problem that the Reformer wrestles with is the Augustinian one – the fact that coitus, though a gift of God, can never be without sin. That is the nature of the postlapsarian reality of marriage. That which *was* good is *now* tainted by the Fall.

Early in his ministry he appears reticent, speaking of sexual intercourse merely as 'a conjugal obligation', emphasizing that it comes through 'the wicked lust of the flesh, which nobody can do without'. He stresses that 'it is not reprehensible when expressed within marriage'. Indeed, it is a necessary part of the covenant. Even so, the husband must be careful to control himself and 'not make a sow's sty of his marriage'.[107] A little later he speaks more of the forgiving grace of God that permits and excuses the sin involved.[108] Luther notices that, outwardly speaking, marital intercourse is no different than harlotry. 'Yet the former is chaste and honorable under the forgiveness of sin and under the blessing, and is pleasing to God; the latter is shameful and condemned under the wrath of God.' Later, he remarks that dishonour is transformed into glory as the result of the pure grace of God.[109]

---

[105] *Comm. Gen.* 24:5-7, LW 4.252 [WA 43.316]. See also, *Comm. Matt.* 5:27-30, LW 21.86 [WA 32.371].

[106] Bailey, op. cit., 51-2. See also, Armstrong, op. cit., 7, 30-31.

[107] *Sermon on the Estate of Marriage* (1519), LW 44. 10, 11 [WA 2.168, 169], respectively. See also, *Comm. Gal.* 5:22 (1519), LW 27.378 [WA 2.596].

[108] *Comm. 1 Cor.* 7:3-4 (1523), LW 28.13 [WA 12.102]; *The Estate of Marriage*, LW 45.49 [WA 10².304]. Interestingly, Bucer was to go further in declaring it blasphemy to call marital intercourse sinful. See M. Bucer, *De Regno Christi* in F. Wendel (ed.), *Martini Buceri Opera Latina*, 15 (Université de France Press, Paris / C. Bertelsmann Verlag, Gütersloh, 1955), 2.46.

[109] LW 4.232 [WA 43.302]; ibid., 138 [306], respectively.

Towards the end of his ministry, he repeats the same ideas but adds a more positive conclusion, concerning procreation: '[T]hrough marriage God permits sexual intercourse. Not only does he cover the sin from which we are unable to abstain, but he also blesses the union between the male and the female.'[110]

Despite the inevitable presence of sin within the sexual relationship of the husband and wife, Luther, increasingly, wishes to hold to a confident hope in the grace of God. Although believers, together with their relationships, are tainted by sin and the image of God is corrupted in them as in all, yet, just as faith exists in the midst of doubt, so marriage is 'a blessing in a curse and chastity in lust'.[111] For believers living by faith and in the transforming power of the Holy Spirit, 'it is impossible ... not to do good works incessantly'.[112] He states categorically that 'the sexual union of husband and wife is ... most pleasing to God'. It has been created by him and occurs within the context of the vocation of marriage which, itself, is holy and pure. He further remarks that the sexual intercourse of husband and wife is a part of their vocational co-operation, or partnership, with God himself.[113]

In this, then, we see something of what Miles refers to in another context. She says that, in Luther's understanding, 'the body reflects and participates in the justification event'.[114] That is, believers are sinful (*Christiani sint peccatores*)[115] and, of course, Luther wants to affirm that with some passion. Yet, he also glories in the idea that '[T]he love of God toward us is stronger than the dirt that clings to us. Accordingly, although we are sinners, we do not lose our filial relation on account of our filthiness, nor do we fall from grace on account of our sin.'[116] However sinful the sexual relationship is between the husband and wife (*and it cannot avoid this*) they are justified before God, and Luther therefore accepts

---

[110] *Comm. Gen.* 16:4, LW 3.48 [WA 42.582]. This comes in the immediate context of speaking of human nature as both 'savage' and 'corrupt'.

[111] *Comm. Gen.* 2:18, LW 1.119 [WA 42.90].

[112] Quoted in McDonough, op. cit., 45. See also, LW 54.161 [WA Tr. 2.166]; *Comm. Gal.* 3:23 (1535), LW 26.340 [WA 40.524-5].

[113] See, for example, *Comm. Ps.* 110:3, LW 13.302 [WA 41.164-5].

[114] Miles, op. cit., 258.

[115] *Comm. Ps.* 51, LW 12.330, 348 [WA 40^2.356, 380]. Also, *Comm. Rom.* 12:2, LW 25.434 [WA 56.442].

[116] LW 54.70 [WA Tr. 1.189-90].

them as such. This is part and parcel of living within a vocation in Christ and *coram Deo.* Indeed, this is autobiographically underlined in Luther's own enjoyment of his wife: 'I go to bed each night with a beautiful woman and that is my Kate.'[117]

So, we observe that, rather than being overly negative and pessimistic concerning the sexual relationship between the spouses, Luther can actually openly proclaim his own sexuality. Both because the sexual relationship is a created gift of God and because in their fallenness no-one can restrain their sexual passion, Luther commends marriage to his followers. The reason itself is basically traditional, but he outlines it within the structure and context of vocation – lived out in faith before a gracious God. Given that theological framework, Luther's teaching is clearly positive, not negative.

The Bringing to Life of Offspring

The next two reasons that Luther posits for marriage need not detain us as long as the first. His second purpose of marriage is that the couple should have children. In looking at this, it needs to be remembered that the social importance of procreation in the sixteenth century cannot be over-emphasized. Together with getting married, procreation was one of the two significant events in a woman's life.[118] Luther, traditionally, understands the second purpose of marriage as more important than the first. He states throughout his ministry that people should marry to have children; though he continually emphasizes, not merely the birth, but also raising children in discipline and fear of the Lord.[119]

---

[117] Quoted by J. W. Zophy, 'We must have the dear ladies: Martin Luther and Women' in K. C. Sessions / P. N. Bebb (eds), *Pietas et Societas* (SCJ Publishers, Kirksville, 1985), 24.

[118] S. C. Karant-Nun, 'Continuity and Change: Some Effects of the Reformation on the Women of Zwickau', *SCJ* 12 (1982), 26.

[119] *Comm. Gen.* 28-1-2, LW 5.189 [WA 43.559]. Very early in his ministry, Luther claims that producing offspring is the purpose of marriage (*The Estate of Marriage* (1519), LW 44.12 [WA 2.167]) – but here he seems to be following traditional teaching. J. Cairncross, *After Polygamy was made a Sin* (Routledge and Kegan Paul, London, 1974), 2-7, claims that Luther's favourite text was 'Increase and multiply' (Gen. 1:28) and that the procreative aspect was *the* reason for marrying. This seems to draw too much from Luther's own use of the text. He certainly speaks of all three purposes of marriage, and perhaps

Therefore, as we have already seen, marriage is not only a *remedium peccati*, but is also a positive vehicle for God's creative activity. Luther never misses a chance to state its importance.[120] Even though the world believes that bringing forth children is merely a part of nature, or even an accident, Luther claims that God ordained marriage *for* procreation.[121] He says, 'The work of procreation is something good and holy that God has created; for it comes from God, who bestows His blessing on it.'[122] Not only that, but he created man and woman with the express purpose of procreation: man 'to beget fruit of his body'[123] and woman, to 'serve this purpose' of procreation.[124] It has often been noticed that, in passages on the subject, Luther seems to imply that woman is a tool or instrument for the use of man. He says, for example,

> We should love the female sex simply for the sake of offspring and procreation. It was created by God to serve this purpose, not for us to misuse it merely to satisfy lust. The structure of a woman's whole body bears this out. It has its own organs and members with which to conceive, nourish, and carry the fetus.

In another passage, he says that women are 'useful for procreation'.[125] It is understandable that these comments have had their critics. However, some underlying assumptions seem to be ignored in this criticism. First, the Reformer insists that men should love women for their procreative function, not because he

---

emphasizes the procreative one as the primary reason. Yet, it is not singled out by the Reformer in the way suggested.

[120] In Luther's *Sermon on the Estate of Marriage*, he says that procreation is the principal purpose for marriage: *'Das es frucht bringt, dan das ist das end und surnhemlich ampt der ehe'* ([WA 2.169], LW 44.12).

[121] See *Comm. John* 1:13, LW 27.100 [WA 46.622]; *Comm. Gen.* 9:1, LW 2.132 [WA 42.354]; 24:21-2, LW 4.276 [WA 43 333], 30:22-4, LW 5.363 [WA 43.679].

[122] *Comm. Gen.* 4:1, LW 1.237-8 [WA 42.177] – *'Opus generationis est creatura Dei bona et sancta, est enim ex Deo benedicente.'*

[123] LW 45.390 [WA 15.167].

[124] Of course, the words employed by Luther suggest the well-established, traditional teaching on the active/passive dichotomy between man and woman in producing offspring. See, for example, K. E. Børresen, *Subordination and Equivalence* (University Press of America, Washington, 1981), 41-3, 193-5. See also, Augustine, *DCD* 14.24.

[125] *Comm. Gen.* 29:16-20, LW 5.288-9 [WA 43.627]; *Comm. Gen.* 2:18, LW 1.115 [WA 42.87], respectively.

sees them as 'objects' to be used, but rather because, for Luther, the essential, physical nature of woman shows her creational purpose in the will of God. Again, this is inherent in his creational logic in relation to marriage. Also, this is contrasted with the purely selfish and lustful use of women. Second, Luther speaks in this way because he takes seriously and contemporaneously the command to 'Increase and multiply'. Therefore, the woman is 'useful', not so much to man, but to the creative purposes of God.

Again, the creational logic and the vocational nature of marriage are evident. Though humanity, generally, procreates on the basis of their natural reason, the powers of reproduction come initially from God and have not been revoked as a result of the Fall. Simply because procreation happens within the temporal and fallen vocation of marriage, it does not mean that the final cause of procreation is not God, himself.[126] After all, Luther would claim that marriage, in itself, is still good and permitted by God.[127] His purpose is to populate the whole world and in this men and women have a part to play. Not surprisingly, therefore, Noah, for example, is commended, not merely for saving the world 'spiritually' – in relation to God; but also for saving it physically – by procreation.[128]

In keeping with the vocational nature of marriage, the realm of procreation is an area in which people become partners of God in his creative activity. However natural the process may appear, Luther insists that the power comes from God's command – it happens 'through the potency of the Word which was uttered by God'. That is, Genesis 1:28, 'Be fruitful and multiply', is taken, not only as a command once delivered, but as a continually active and creative word of God.[129] In this context, in his Genesis commentary, Luther asks the mundane question whether God has better things to do. His answer is that this is one way in which the Lord cares for everyone, in their calling. God *could* create children without the husband and wife, but he chooses to do so

---

[126] LW 45.155 [WA 12.242]. See also, *The Estate of Marriage*, LW 45.18-19 [WA 10^2.276-7]; LW 43.88 [WA 15.88].

[127] *Comm. Ps.* 51, LW 12.348 [WA 40^2.380-83] – '*Nam coniugium est bona et licita et a Deo instituta.*'

[128] *Comm. Gen.* 6:9-10, LW 2.57 [WA 42.302]. See also, *Comm. Gen.* 9:1, LW 2.131 [WA 42.354]; 9:6, LW 2.142 [WA 42.362]; *Comm. Ps.* 45:8-9, LW 12.257 [WA 40^2.553]; *Comm. Deut.* 24:5, LW 9.241 [WA 14.714]; LW 51.359 [WA 49.799].

[129] *Comm. Gen.* 2:21, LW 1.128 [WA 42.96]; 21:1-3, LW 4.4 [WA 43.139].

through co-operation.¹³⁰ It happens on the principle that what God creates, he preserves.¹³¹ Indeed, Luther is so adamant that the procreation of children is a crucial task of men and women that he castigates Onan as deserving death for spilling his seed and as being worse than an adulterer or someone committing incest. Elsewhere, he comments that childbirth is pleasing to God even if the child is born out of wedlock.¹³²

In a discussion of the role of procreation in the marital ethics of the reformers, generally, Brundage concludes that, 'The virtue of sex in marriage ... was not that it led to procreation, but rather that it expressed and increased the couple's love for one another.'¹³³ According to him, then, procreation was a second-order virtue in married life. On a reading of Luther, this conclusion appears over-optimistic and, therefore, questionable. We have noted that within the context of marriage as a vocation, the horizontal relationship is vital, of course, and Luther *does* exalt in marital intercourse in the context of love-building. But what the Reformer *stresses* is the purpose of God in maintaining society, not the mutual love of the couple. Through marriage, then, God continues to preserve society by procreation. This is a sure sign of God's blessing because through it 'the human race and the very church of God are being rebuilt'.¹³⁴

Therefore, we see that procreation becomes a powerful reason for marrying as in this way the husband and wife, in their God-given vocational roles, can co-operate in the purposes of their Creator. Their relationship can be seen as one of partnership in both remedying sinful tendencies in each other and in the business of bringing children into the world and bringing them up before God. However, as we have observed, the two tasks (in themselves) can serve to underline procreational or remedial

---

¹³⁰ *Comm. Gen.* 29:31, LW 5.313-14 [WA 43.645]. The question arises at the point in Genesis where it is said that God opens Leah's womb. Luther uses the passage to show that God oversees and governs the domestic economy in every particular. Also, *Comm. Gen.* 46:28, LW 8.95 [WA 44.648].

¹³¹ *Comm. John* 1:3, LW 22.27 [WA 46.547]; LW 54.400 [WA Tr. 5.17]; *Comm. Ps.* 90:2, LW 13.91-2 [WA 40³.509]; *Comm. Gen.* 30:22-4, LW 5.359 [WA 43.676].

¹³² *Comm. Gen.* 38:9-10, LW 7.20-21 [WA 44.317]; LW 45.41 [WA 10².297], respectively. See also, *Comm. Gen.* 26:8, LW 5.37 [WA 43.454]. Augustine had stated the same thing – see, for example, *DgrC* 2.38 (ASW 5.250-51).

¹³³ Brundage, op. cit., 556.

¹³⁴ *Comm. Gen.* 17:10-11, LW 3.134 [WA 42.643].

aspects of marriage to the detriment of purely relational ones. If one marries in order to have children or to restrain sinful tendency, then any idea of mutual fellowship is (at least) pushed to third place. However, in this twofold task the husband and wife's relationship is to be one of mutuality. The next section briefly turns to this subject, before it is picked up again in the next chapter.

Life Together with Mutual Fidelity

Luther says very little on this in the specific context of relating reasons for marriage. However, Blaisdell claims that, beginning with Luther, 'There was a shift in thought about marriage away from the traditional emphasis on sexual intercourse solely for procreation and on marriage as a mere remedy for sexual incontinence.'[135] In fact, as we have noticed, this development had begun in the Middle Ages.

In 1519 Luther speaks of marriage as 'a covenant of fidelity' and states that, 'The whole basis and essence of marriage is that each gives himself or herself to the other, and they promise to remain faithful to each other and not give themselves to any other.' In this way, Luther says, marriage consists essentially in consent to one another.[136] His starting point is the paradigmatic joining of Adam to Eve in which he notes that Eve was created to be 'a companionable helpmeet'.[137] Again, based on the creational principle, the Reformer sees that God made man and woman so that they could be joined in marriage, 'with pleasure, willingly and gladly with all their hearts'. He says that the nature of marriage is 'an undivided relationship for life',[138] and its bond is love[139] – he speaks of 'mutual love, mutual play (fun?) and friendliness'.[140]

---

[135] C. J. Blaisdell, 'The Matrix of Reform: Women in the Lutheran and Calvinist Movements' in R. L. Greaves (ed.), *Triumph Over Silence* (Greenwood, Westport, 1985), 17.

[136] *Sermon on the Estate of Marriage*, LW 44. 10-11 [WA 2.168-9].

[137] Ibid., 8 [167].

[138] See *On Marriage Matters*, LW 46.312-14 [WA 30³.242-3].

[139] '...*vinculum matrimonii, amor scilicet*' (*Comm. Gen.* 16:6, LW 3.58 [WA 42.590]). See also *Comm. Isa.* 56:4, LW 17.262 [WA 31².463]: '*Honorabilis est status connubium et immaculatus thorus. Ita ut sint coniugati casti, amantes inter se, contenti suis coniugibus.*'

[140] '*Econtra si est mutuus amor, mutui lusus et blandiciae, id coniugium*

The concept of faithfulness is very important to Luther. In his *Sermons on the Ten Commandments*,[141] for example, he emphasizes this while showing that the determining commandment is, in fact, the first. If a believer rightly fears God, then he will remain faithful in his relationships with others. That is, the spiritual realm and the vertical relationship (*coram Deo*) impinges on the temporal, horizontal, vocational realm of marriage. That is part of the significance of the fact that God gives both husband and wife to each other. He rules both governments and, as we have seen, there is the juxtaposition between them that relates them both on the interface of the spiritual and temporal in the faith and life of the regenerate.

EXCURSUS: LUTHER'S RELUCTANCE TO MARRY

Having discussed Luther's understanding of the nature of marriage in its vocational and creational denotation, and having analysed the reasons that he gives for two people to enter into marriage, it is clear that the married estate is extremely significant within Luther's perception of the temporal kingdom. If this is so and if the Reformer underlines the three fundamentally traditional reasons for marriage in the manifest way that he does, it is instructive to note the way he reached the decision to marry and the reasons he gives for it. This is so because with regard to Luther's own marriage, we find a tension in his thinking. He seems to wrestle between the poles of circumstance and theological understanding.

He seems to approach marriage with a self-conscious measure of reluctance. For example, at one time he commented that the people of Wittenberg would not 'push a wife' on to him[142] and only a few months before his own wedding he wrote to his friend, Spalatin, that he had no intention of marrying.[143] Then

---

amatur et praedicatur passim ab omnibus' (*Comm. Gen.* 26:8, LW 5:32 [WA 43.450]).

[141] LW 51.154 [WA 30¹.75-6]. Also, *Comm. Gen.* 16:4, LW 3.48 [WA 42.58].

[142] To Spalatin [Wartburg], August 6, 1521, LW 48.290 [WA Br. 2.377]. See also, to Melanchthon [Wartburg], Sept. 9, 1521, LW 48.296-7 [WA Br. 2.382-6].

[143] To Spalatin [Wittenberg], Nov. 30, 1524, LW 49.92-4 [WA Br. 3.393-4].

again, in the year in which he married, he wrote that he had 'no thought of marriage at all' and, later, as he reflected over the course of events, that he had 'not been in the mood to get married'.[144] His own adamant teaching on the marital relationship would not lead us to expect personal reticence. In the light of his teaching, is there a discernible reason for this apparent inconsistency? Why was he so reluctant to go into marriage?

Although his motives were clearly complex, it is helpful to outline the possible reasons for his marriage. In a letter to Amsdorf[145] Luther outlines three primary ones. He wished to silence those who would scandal the gospel because of his relationship with Kate.[146] He wished to comply with his father's desire that the family name be passed on to another generation.[147] He wanted to live out his belief that marriage was a high calling from God – or, as William Lazareth puts it, 'as a public testimony of faith in witness of the restoration of marriage under God'. In this way, he also set an example to his followers.[148] In a letter to Rühel, he also speaks of his intention of spiting the devil.[149] Together with these, other factors played a part, of course. Many

---

[144] To Spalatin, [Wittenberg] April 6, 1525, LW 49.105 [WA Br. 3.475]. Two months later he wrote inviting Spalatin to the banquet – June 21, 1525, LW 49.115-16 [WA Br. 3.540]. See also, *Comm. Tit.* 1:6 (1527), LW 29.21 [WA 25.20].

[145] To Nicholas von Amsdorf [Wittenberg], June 21, 1525, LW 49.117 [WA Br. 3.541].

[146] See also, the letter he wrote to Amsdorf after his own wedding – [Wittenberg] June 21, 1525, LW 49.117 [WA Br. 3.541] – in which he states that he married suddenly 'to silence the evil mouths which are so used to complaining about me'. Again, he couples this reason with the desire to obey his father and to be an example to others. Also, *Tischreden* [3179ᵃ] LW 54.191-2 [WA Tr. 3.212].

[147] This reason seems to be over-stressed by R. H. Bainton, *Here I Stand* (Hodder and Stoughton, London, 1951), 287 and J. M. Todd, *Luther: A Life* (Hamish Hamilton, London, 1982), 261. Luther's father had always been determined to see Martin married – see, to Hans Luther [Wartburg], November 21, 1521, LW 48.331 [WA Br. 8.574].

[148] W. H. Lazareth, LW 44.xv. See also, Cocke, art. cit., 106; E. G. Schwiebert, *Luther and his Times* (Concordia, St Louis, 1950), 589; J. H. M. d'Aubigne, *The History of the Great Reformation* (Walther, London, 1841), 280, 282. The importance of the willingness of evangelical pastors to put their doctrine into practice by marrying is clearly brought out by L. J. Abray, *The People's Reformation* (Cornell University Press, New York, 1985), 216-20.

[149] To John Rühel [Seeburg], May 4, 1525, LW 49.111 [WA Br. 3.482]. This reason is singled out as the primary one by B. Lohse, *Martin Luther: An Introduction to his Life and Work* (T&T Clark, Edinburgh, 1987), 33 and by H. Daniel-Rops, *The Protestant Reformation* (Dent, London, 1961), 319.

of his associates and other reformers were getting married.¹⁵⁰ Some would have expected it of Luther; indeed, some encouraged him to marry – Spalatin and Argula von Grumbach among them.¹⁵¹ Von Loewenich senses that Luther longed for familiarity and security; Bainton suggests that he felt obliged by the situation.¹⁵² And, of course, Kate's own role in all of this should not be minimized. Having lodged her with Reichenbach, the city clerk of Wittenberg, Luther tried to marry her to either Jerome Baumgärtner of Nürnberg or to Casper Glantz, pastor of Orlamünde. But Katherine complained, saying that she would only be willing to marry either Amsdorf or Luther, himself. Certainly, for her to marry Luther would be a clear sign to others that she had fully accepted the doctrines of the Reformer and that he had accepted the implications of his own teaching. Yet, though the situation is complicated, there seems, in Luther, a genuine reluctance to marry.¹⁵³

Against this, we notice that, when it happened, Luther was certain that God had brought it about: 'God, in a wondrous way, threw me into matrimony.'¹⁵⁴ Believing, as he did, that God was

---

¹⁵⁰ Melanchthon, Agricola, and Bartolomaus had married as early as 1520; Bernhardi in 1521; Karlstadt, Justus Jonas and Bugenhagen in 1522; Wenceslas Link, Francis Lambert and Thomas Munster in 1523.

¹⁵¹ See, P. Matheson, *Argula von Grumbach. A Woman's Voice in the Reformation* (T&T Clark, Edinburgh, 1995), 23.

¹⁵² W. von Loewenich, op. cit., 283; R. H. Bainton, 'Luther' in J. Bodensieck (ed.), *The Encyclopedia of the Lutheran Church* (Augsburg, Minneapolis, 1965), 2.1356; idem, *The Reformation of the Sixteenth Century* (Hodder & Stoughton, London, 1963), 258. On other reasons, see M. U. Edwards, *Luther and the False Brethren* (Stanford University Press, Stanford, 1975), 71; Schwiebert, op. cit., 589; E. W. Gritsch, *Martin – God's Court Jester* (Fortress, Philadelphia, 1983), 61; G. Rupp, *The Righteousness of God* (Hodder and Stoughton, London, 1968), 351. See also, LW 49.105 [fn. 22], 111 [fn. 34], 115 [fn. 1].

¹⁵³ It also has to be noted that there was a reticence in Luther to marry Katherine, herself, because the match was not universally accepted by his friends and followers. Seven years later he said, 'If I had not married secretly, all my friends would have cried, "Not this woman but somebody else!"' (*Tischreden* [3179ª] LW 54.191-2 [WA Tr. 3.212]). Even Melanchthon was initially dispirited over the choice – see his letter to Camerarius in B. J. Kidd (ed.), *Documents Illustrative of the Continental Reformation* (Clarendon, Oxford, 1911), 179-80 and in translation in Todd, op. cit., 115-16. Luther's evident concern over the initial reaction can be gauged by his letter to Spalatin [Wittenberg], June 21, 1525 LW 49.115-16 [WA Br. 3.540], inviting him to his wedding in order that he might be assured of his friend's love.

¹⁵⁴ Quoted by Bornkamm, op. cit., 406.

involved in every circumstance, he held to the belief that God had willed his marriage despite his own reluctance. But, in fact, the situation is not quite that nebulous. The reason for his initial hesitancy, perhaps, emerges in his correspondence. For example, in a letter from 1524, Luther gives this clue,

> [T]he way I feel now and have felt thus far, I will not marry. It is not that I do not feel my flesh or sex, since I am neither wood nor stone, but my mind is far removed from marriage *since I expect the death and the punishment due to a heretic.*[155]

Even after his wedding, the Reformer states, merely, that he hopes to live for a little while longer.[156] In a letter to Link, in 1527, he comments that if he stays alive he will become a gardener![157] Therefore, it seems justifiable to assert that the reason for his reluctance is actually his overriding concern to protect any would-be wife from danger and the misery of sharing in his own peril, as he conjectured it. This is certainly the opinion of Gritsch, for example, who says that, 'Since the Edict of Worms had made him subject to the death penalty, he had no wish to expose a spouse and children to his own danger.'[158] Later, perhaps recollecting his own situation, in commenting on the Pauline idea of 'the present distress' (1 Cor. 7:25-6), Luther states that a good reason to remain *unmarried* is that, 'A Christian is always under the threat of persecution for the sake of the gospel, living in constant danger of losing his goods, his friends, and his life, and facing exile or execution.'[159]

But to Rühel, he writes, 'I have already had it in mind, *before departing this life*, to enter the married state, which I regard as commanded by God.'[160] Just ten days later (June 15, 1525) he was married. That is, finally, Luther's theology and his own understanding of biblical teaching won the day. Because God commanded it, he *would* marry. It is interesting to see that,

---

[155] To Spalatin [Wittenberg], November 30, 1524, LW 49.93 [WA Br. 3.393-4] – emphasis added.

[156] To Amsdorf [Wittenberg] June 21, 1525, LW 49.117 [WA Br. 3.541].

[157] To Link, December 29, 1527 – quoted by Bornkamm, op. cit., 413.

[158] Gritsch, op. cit., 60.

[159] *Comm. 1 Cor.*7:25-6, LW 28.49 [WA 12.134-5].

[160] Quoted by A. C. McGiffert, *Martin Luther: The Man and his Work* (Fisher Unwin, London, 1911), 277 – see 277-82.

despite Luther's clear-cut reasoning on the traditional purposes for marriage, when it came down to it he had to balance circumstance with understanding. However, for the Reformer, the latter was bound to hold sway. After all, misery and hardship are constituents of living in a God-given, temporal vocation.

CONCLUSION

The present chapter has examined Luther's doctrine of the nature of marriage in the light of his broader teaching on the temporal kingdom of God's rule.[161] There are two primary bases.

First, this has been done by examining the fundamental character of the marital relationship. We have observed that, as a consequence of his creational logic and vocational perspective on the nature and function of the marital state and relationship, he stresses several important characteristics. For instance, the relationship between the husband and the wife is clearly part of the temporal realm of this world, not of the eternal government of the Spirit. In this sense it has nothing inherently to do with the salvation of either spouse – it is vocational, not redemptive. Yet, despite this, its origin and purpose is in God's institution. He gives each person his or her partner, as he did for Adam in giving him Eve. More than that, he has given to each person the propensity to establish and to maintain family life. That is part of the created nature of humanity. But, on the other hand, even though the marital relationship is intrinsic to the temporal kingdom, it can only be discerned for what it is through faith. Faith sees it as a vocation, recognizes its bitterness and problems, its insignificant tasks and duties, yet rejoices in the privilege and in God's calling, nevertheless. Therefore, the vocation of being a husband or a wife, in relationship, is to be consciously lived in the sight of God – before whom everyone is accountable, both now and on the Day of Christ.

Second, the nature of marriage in Luther's thought has also been examined through a discussion of the reasons for which he commends marriage. Here it was found that he posits the three traditional reasons – of the sex-drive inherent in man and

---

[161] The broader perspective is discussed in chapter 5 of the present study.

woman, of the need to procreate and of companionship. It is significant that Luther reveals a positive approach to marital sexual intercourse, as such – fundamentally on the grounds that God created people experiencing sexual attraction and the drive to accompany it. The Reformer is certainly open about and positive of sexuality because it is a gift of God. Again, his creational logic demands this conclusion. However, Luther is aware that in postlapsarian existence sin has tainted *every act* of human beings – including the sexual one. It is at this point that the marital relationship becomes a remedy for sin – for both the man and the woman. In this context, Luther rests on the forgiving grace of God. When we turned to the subject of procreation, we found that, here too, his creational principle is of primary importance – men and women have been formed *in order to procreate*. Indeed, the power to create children originates from God's command. It was also discovered that the Reformer rests the concepts of faithfulness and mutuality in the marital relationship upon the fact that God made man and woman to complement each other in an 'undivided' way.

We have, therefore, narrowed down the subject from his broader theological basis (chapter 5) to a particular examination of his understanding of the nature of marriage and the husband and wife relationship. The following chapter expounds his teaching on and his approach to the major relevant texts of Scripture and his specific understanding of the hierarchical structure of the marital relationship.

CHAPTER 7

LUTHER, HIERARCHY AND MUTUAL LOVE

We have shown that Luther's teaching is that the husband-wife relationship is located in the temporal government of the two kingdoms. The temporal realm is particularized in vocation, in which the general characteristics of that kingdom are reflected. The study then moved on to demonstrate that the Reformer's understanding of the husband-wife relationship and the reasons that he gives for marrying are expressive of his creational and vocational perspective on marriage. In this chapter, the discussion proceeds to an analysis of his understanding of the key biblical passages on the subject of marriage and a closer examination of his concept of hierarchy within that relationship and of mutual love between the spouses.

LUTHER'S BIBLICAL EXPOSITION

We address the subject by looking at Luther's exposition of the major biblical passages, in the chronological order of his own ministry through them.[1] The purpose of this section is to explore Luther's understanding through his exegesis. It reveals the traditional emphases that we have picked up in the more systematic approach, but it develops that in so far as it shows that the Reformer expounds the texts from the theological

---

[1] That is, 1 Peter 3:1-7 (1522-23), 1 Corinthians 7 (1523), 1 Timothy 2:8-15 (1527-28), Genesis 1:26-3:24 (1535). There is no sustained, detailed exposition of Ephesians 5:22-33 in Luther's *corpus* as there is in Calvin's.

presuppositions outlined above. We discover that his exegesis is permeated by conventional teaching. This is often to the point of skewing the original intention or emphasis. His reading of the text is sometimes determined by a desire to see in it a hierarchicalism and a concept of order. However, he does qualify potential harshness by a traditional stress on mutual service and love.

I Peter 3:1-7[2]

It is significant that as Luther preaches on this passage, he dwells on Peter's insistence that women should remain submissive to their husbands, but minimizes the motivation behind the apostle's injunction, that this should be done to encourage the men to come to faith in Christ. He emphasizes the submissiveness that the apostle commands, but we notice that that characteristic is only one of three that Peter commends – the other two being a beautiful character and a freedom from fear.

At this point in his commentary he has already accepted Peter's teaching concerning slaves – recognizing them to be slaves, not merely servants. He accepts that according to their outward form of life they are in an inferior station (*Stand*), but says that this position and its inherent submissiveness is ordained by God.[3] This logic underlines his teaching on the wife's position, as well. Towards the conclusion, Luther spells out the hierarchical principle that he assumes and from which he has proceeded.

> For inwardly we are all alike; there is no difference between a man and a woman. Externally, however, God wants the husband to rule and the wife to be submissive to him (92-3 [347]).

By 'inwardly' Luther means that 'in Christ' both man and wife have been blessed, baptized and given faith. Spiritually, they are the same. However, 'externally' they live in a divinely-ordained, patriarchal relationship. The wife is said to serve her husband through her obedience. His is the right to rule. 'What he commands and orders, this should be done.' Luther gives three

---

[2] *Comm. 1 Pet.* 3:1-7, LW 30.87-93 [WA 12.341-7].
[3] *Comm.1 Pet.* 2:18-20, LW 30.81-4 [WA 12.336-9].

reasons for this: the husband might be brought to God by this behaviour, God desires peace in the household and this hierarchical order has been imposed as a punishment for sin. The first reflects Peter's reasoning, the others, though, are an intrusion into the text. In this, he appears to bring his own emphasis to the passage in hand. The apostle's specific purpose is to instruct wives to help them to bring unbelieving husbands to faith in Christ. Apparently they have already rejected the preaching of the gospel – hence, Peter's comment about the wives' behaviour winning the men 'without a word being said'. However, the Reformer applies the exhortation in a more general way to relate to all wives. He underlines this by stating that

> since at that time wives were commanded to be submissive to their husbands, *how much more this should be observed today* (87 [342] emphasis added).

Perhaps this last comment relates to his sense of the urgency of the period, either eschatologically or in relation to contemporary immorality, or, simply, to the momentum of reformation progress. Whichever it is, the emphasis is clear that wives must obey in the right attitude before God: '[T]hey should live as the husband rules'. It is certainly evident from this that the woman's social/familial position is measured and defined by her relationship to the husband. This, of course, is traditional Augustinian thinking.

Luther takes the opportunity to define the woman as a 'vessel or tool' that God uses to conceive, bear, feed, look after children and to manage the house. His creational logic is the foundation for this: 'God created her for this purpose and implanted this in her' (91 [346]). He is quick however to insist that man should regard himself as God's tool, too. Again, we are reminded of Luther's essentialism. But there is ambiguity here. Formerly, Luther has stated that the relative positions of husband and wife are the result of punishment, now he says that the wife's tasks, as part of the obedience that she owes the man, are themselves inherent in her creation. This ambiguity continually pervades the writing of the Reformer on this subject. However, he does feel it necessary to encourage the husband to treat his wife gently. He says, 'You must take care of her as you take care of another tool with which you work' (92 [346]).

In this context, generally, it is significant that Luther speaks of God using both man and woman as tools and, also, of the man using the woman as a tool – but not of the wife using the husband in this way. Clearly, because of the hierarchical arrangement and the nature of the wife's tasks, the husband is able to be in partnership with God in a way that the wife is not. However, by this unflattering image, Luther insists that the husband realize that his wife is to be treated considerately. He goes on to say that his authority should not be used arbitrarily, he should help, support, protect and treat his wife with kindness. 'At times you must be lenient, slacken the reins a bit, give in, and also accord your wife the honor that is her due' (92 [346]).[4]

He says that honour has been interpreted in different ways, but that he wants to define it as the husband's keeping in mind that his wife is also a believer, having been created by God. It is noteworthy that in this context Luther speaks of reciprocal honour. Unfortunately, he does not expand on his idea, nor does he say how it fits in with the other emphases – particularly, the husband's rule and the wife's submission.

I Corinthians 7[5]

In his commentary on 1 Corinthians 7 three recurring emphases stand out as particularly pertinent to our study – the comparison between marriage and celibacy, the dualistic characteristics of marriage before God, and the world and its utilitarian use against sin. These need not detain us long, but they do throw light on Luther's teaching on the husband-wife relationship.

Celibacy and marriage are compared in various ways. If one has the special grace to live a celibate life, it is happier and more rewarding. Yet, if one has not that grace, then singleness *must* become a life of sin and fornication (9-13 [97-101]). Therefore, 'Necessity orders that you marry.' The reason for this is twofold –

---

[4] Elsewhere, quoting 1 Pet. 3:7, Luther makes the point that there are two things that should encourage husbands to be gentle with their wives – their mutual creation and their access to God: 'Et hi sunt duo loci insignes ad corrigendam saevitiam maritorum, nempe si inspiciant uxores ut creaturam Dei et quae communem deum habeant' (*Comm. Mal.* 2:10 [WA 13.687] – LW 18.403).

[5] *Comm. 1 Cor.* 7, LW 28.9-56 [WA 12.88-142]. This short commentary was a wedding present for Luther's friend, Hans von Löser. Comments such as, 'It takes a brave man to take a wife!' (12 [101]) should be seen in this light.

God created the bodies of male and female to procreate and, since the Fall the flesh desires sexual gratification.[6] Here, again, we see the Reformer's creational logic. If that is how God created humanity in the beginning, that is how they remain. The Fall merely strengthens the sexual impulse to the point of incorrigibility. Marriage is a medicine for that (near) universal condition. It does for the man or woman who cannot contain their sexual desire, what celibacy does for those who can: it effectively removes sexual frustration, cares and distraction. On the other hand, marriage is said to be nothing (41 [130]).[7] Both are blessings for the present life alone, both fall within the temporal realm of reality. Therefore, Paul commends marriage (in so far as he does commend it), not because of virtue before God but, 'for its good and utility in this life' (54 [139]).[8]

Together with this, Luther insists on a dualistic way of looking at marriage. His conclusion is that 'marriage is a bound thing in this world but free before God' (55 [141]). In this he suggests his thinking on the two realms of God's authority. Again, he appears to drive a wedge between the spiritual and the temporal. He distinguishes between the freedom that believers have before God and the lack of freedom before others. Before God a man may marry or not. Indeed, before *him*,

> It would be of no importance ... if the husband were to leave his wife, for the body is not bound to God but made free by Him for all outward things and is only God's by virtue of inner faith.

In contrast, before others, 'these promises are to be kept'.[9] These ideas are a direct consequence of Luther's understanding of verses 22-24, where Paul speaks concerning the determinative call of God. The point that Luther makes, quoting Galatians 3:28, is

---

[6] *Comm. 1 Cor. 7*, LW 28.25-6 [WA 12.113].

[7] However, celibacy gives more time to read the Word of God daily, to pray, to preach and so on. In celibacy, a man can devote himself entirely to the Lord. On the other hand, in marriage a man is necessarily divided in his loyalties (*Comm. 1 Cor.* 7:32-4, LW 28.52-3 [WA 12.138-9]).

[8] *Comm.1 Cor. 7*, LW 28 34 [WA 12.12] – 'To a Christian, therefore, the entire world is holiness, purity, *utility*, and piety' (emphasis added). And again, 'In short: Better an unhappy marriage than unhappy chastity. Better a sour and difficult marriage than a sour and difficult chastity. Why? The latter is a sure loss; *the former can be of use*' (ibid., 30 [118] – emphasis added).

[9] LW 28.45-7 [WA 12.131-2] – emphasis added.

that everything is equal, 'One could even say: He who is called as a man is a woman before God. And she who is called as a woman is a man before God' (44 [130]). But then he stresses that the purchase of believers (τιμῆς ἠγοράσθητε) has no effect whatever in the social realm. 'These relationships are left intact, and God wants them maintained' (45 [131]). To some extent, of course, this is in line with the apostle's teaching, but the context for that is the Corinthians' insistence on freedom. On the other hand, Luther's writing is in the context of normal social arrangement and he insists that this remains as it is. Having quoted Galatians 3:28, he does not go further to see that the gospel might carry with it a necessary social correlative teaching in the realm of husband-wife relationship, for example. This is because Galatians 3:28 speaks only to the spiritual 'and takes place in our conscience' (45 [131]).

So, what of the relationship between husband and wife? Luther uses verses 3-4 to contrast 'the law of love' and fornication. Whereas the latter seeks its own pleasure and rules over the other, the former primarily serves the partner. Here, Luther shows the husband and wife to be so bound up with one another that, 'they cannot withdraw from the other even to fast or pray without the agreement of the partner' (14 [103]). That Luther stresses the fact that husband and wife are thus bound with each other is in agreement with the characteristic of marriage as a vocation in which the horizontal relationship is determinative. Therefore, he envisages a mutual concern for the relationship and a lack of egotistic dominance – perhaps, particularly, on the side of the man.

Emphasizing the distinction between the temporal and the spiritual, Luther applies Paul's comment that 'God's call is a call to live in peace' (v15),[10] to those who remain married to unbelievers, that they should leave the other to his own faith 'and commend the whole matter to God' (38 [125]). He continues, 'For no-one is driven or forced to believe; instead, God must draw him in grace.'[11] Later, he stresses the utility of marriage as temporary. Where Paul says that 'married men should be as if they had no

---

[10] The context for this phrase is probably that of the apostle's emphasis on keeping the peace with all men. His specific concern is that to keep the peace, those with unbelieving spouses should remain as they are. This is God's will (v.17) as well as an opportunity for the salvation of the spouse (v.16).

[11] See also, *Comm. Mal.* 2:10, LW 18.402 [WA 13.687].

wives' (v.29ᵇ), insisting that they now view things from a radically new perspective, Luther finds it necessary to stress, negatively, the utilitarian function of the relationship:

> This would mean having a wife as though I did not have one, *when in my heart I would rather remain unmarried*, but in order to avoid sin have found it necessary to have one (52 [138] – emphasis added).

Perhaps this reveals the Reformer's prejudice at the time. This was written two years before his own marriage and he was adamant, at that time, that he would not enter that estate. However, the interpretation does not do justice to the apostle's idea and imposes upon it something from outside. Luther's own emphasis on the freedom of individuals either to marry or not belies this.

His concluding advice is that it is well not to marry unless it is found to be necessary (55-6 [141-2]). In fact, this needs to be seen in the context of his further remarks that if God has not given the grace to live in chastity, then that person should not remain single. However, the implication of Luther's commentary on 1 Corinthians 7 is that the celibate state is 'better'. The major problem with Luther's approach to both 1 Peter and 1 Corinthians 7 is that he hardly stops to ask the question, 'Why?' Why does the apostle say what he says? In the next passage, however, Paul seems to define his own reasons.

1 Timothy 2:8-15[12]

Luther outlines three concerns of this passage: that the men should pray, that women should dress appropriately and that they should listen and not teach when men are present. That women do not pray in public,[13] the lifting of hands in prayer and women's decent dress, he acknowledges as 'custom', but the fact that women are not allowed to preach is a matter of more weight. Despite the fact that this subject is rather adjacent to the one under discussion, it bears relevance to Luther's view of women, in

---

[12] *Comm. 1 Tim.* 2:8-15, LW 28.270-80 [WA 26.42-9].

[13] Even in private prayer, the men are expected to begin to pray – women must wait before they commence (271 [42]).

comparison to men – particularly, because he applies it within the context of the husband and wife relationship.

For the Reformer, verses 11-15 relate to a second rule 'about controlling women in public' (276 [46]). (The first rule is that they must live with a zeal for piety and good works, not to overdress in luxury.)[14] Women must remain listeners, not teachers.[15] Luther is aware that the text speaks of 'men' (ἀνθρώπων - v.1) and 'woman' (γυνή - v.11). Interestingly, he questions why Paul should deprive women (*per se*) of authority, concluding that the apostle really means to say 'husband' and 'wife', and in this causes the domestic/familial sphere to control relationships within the ecclesiastical one. That is, Luther believes that because it is a given fact that husbands rule wives and that wives submit to husbands in the marital arrangement, that arrangement must hold everywhere where those same men and women are brought together publicly by God. Therefore, women must not have authority over men. Luther is not blind to the fact that some women *have* had authority in this way. He cites Queen Candace, Huldah, Deborah, Jael but later mistakenly claims that these were unmarried women (276-7 [46]). He also scathingly suggests that women wish to argue in church to have the priority, to be right, to have the last word and to appear wiser in public 'and in the home'. That aside, he allows for the *possibility* that God could raise up a woman to preach (280 [49]), but she would be *the exception* to a fixed rule.

Paul bases his conclusion concerning women's subjection on both an argument from sequence and from primal experience. Luther takes both of these to stress, not so much the penalty, but more the inherent superiority of man over woman and in that

---

[14] See also, *Comm. 1 Tim.* 5:11, LW 28.341-2 [WA 26.90].

[15] See R. A. Kelly, 'Luther's Use of 1 Corinthians 14' in J. E. Bradley / R. A. Muller (eds), *Church, Word and Spirit* (Eerdmans, Grand Rapids, 1987), 123-34; W. Pauck, *From Luther to Tillich* (Harper and Row, San Francisco, 1984), 14. See also, LW 40.388-91 [WA 30^3.522-5]; *Comm. Zech.* 3:12, LW 20.242 [WA 23.574-5]; *Comm. Isa.* 3:12, LW 16.45 [WA 31^2.32]; *Comm. Deut.* 22:1, LW 9.219-20 [WA 14.701]; *Tischreden* [2847^b] LW 54.174-5 [WA Tr. 3.26]; LW 51.296 [WA 47.765-6]; *Comm. Ps.* 82:4, LW 13.65 [WA 31^1.211]. Also, B. A. Gerrish, *The Old Protestantism and the New* (T&T Clark, Edinburgh, 1982), 90-117. For a contrasting situation in which women became important disseminators of reformation ideas partly as teachers, for example, see, S. M. Wyntjes, 'Women and Religious Choices in the Sixteenth Century Netherlands', *ARG* 75 (1984), 276-90.

he seems to impose his own idea on the text. Although he shows some unease about the logic of the argument, he speaks of Adam being superior to Eve by 'right of primogeniture' because what occurs first is 'most preferable' (278-9 [47]). Luther also takes Eve's being deceived to indicate Adam's superior wisdom and courage. This raises some questions. If Adam at creation was superior to Eve, were they ever equal? And, if so, in what way does Luther define this equality? Or, on the other hand, is Luther's own contradictoriness the cause of the ambiguity in his later writing – for example, his Genesis commentary? Also, if Adam was superior in wisdom, why did *he* fall into transgression? Luther's answer, that Adam simply wished to agree with and please his wife, only confuses the issue. His further claim that Adam had not understood the seriousness and significance of God's command destroys any appeal to greater wisdom.[16] Wherein, then, lies Adam's superior wisdom?[17]

However, having come to this conclusion, Luther insists that women are therefore to be subject and men are to have the dominance. Women are saved, not *by,* but for procreation (v.15). In this, they are to persevere in faith, modesty (*Vernünftig*) and responsibility.

---

[16] In an unguarded (and playful?) moment at the meal table, Luther remarks that Eve had persuaded Adam that he was lord over everything, even God. 'She spoiled everything' (*Tischreden* [2847b] LW 54.174-5 [WA Tr. 3.26]). He continues, 'We have you women to thank for that. With tricks and cunning women deceive men, as I, too, have experienced.'

[17] L. Scanzoni / N. Hardesty, *All We're Meant to Be* (Word, Waco, 1975), 32, claim that to speak of Eve as weaker in any way casts a slur on God's creation. But in principle, this argument does not really stand, simply because *it is possible* for God to create things in that way. The differences in terms of strength in created things is part of the variety of the created world. The difference in the physical nature of man and woman is, perhaps, part of that variety. Nevertheless, the question still remains: Does Genesis suggest that Eve was less wise or courageous than Adam at creation? Even Luther's faltering response to his own conclusions suggests that Genesis does not.

Genesis 1-3[18]

This huge portion of Luther's mature commentary on Genesis can only be examined here rather suggestively. Therefore, for convenience, Luther's exposition through these chapters can be divided into three areas, all of which address the subject of the husband-wife relationship: creation (1:26-2:7), marital union (2:15-2:25), transgression and penalty (3:1-25).

Creation (1:26-2:7)

Luther teaches that God is shown deliberating over Adam's creation as indicative of humanity's uniqueness above all other creatures. Part of this superiority is that each person is given the *imago Dei*. The Reformer argues that the *imago Dei* is not simply to be defined in terms of memory, intellect and will, although he later speaks of the image showing *itself through* enlightened reason, justice and wisdom.[19] And, though the concept of dominion as an aspect of the image is retained, Luther marginalizes it. For Luther, the image is not so much a faculty as a right relationship to God. Thompson defines it as a 'Christian's orientation to and disposition towards God'.[20] Indeed, Luther insists that it must be relationship, not merely attributes, because it has to be something unique to the creation of humanity (62 [46]). From its inception, that relationship is future-orientated. That is, Adam looked *forward* to the blessing of God. Luther says,

> But he [God] himself shapes him [Adam] according to his image as if he were God's partner and *one who would enjoy God's rest* (84 [63] – emphasis added).

---

[18] *Comm. Gen.* 1:26-3:24, LW 1.56-236 [WA 42.41-176]. For detailed studies of parts of this section, see D. F. Wright, 'Woman Before and After the Fall: a Comparison of Luther's and Calvin's Interpretation of Genesis 1-3', *Churchman* 2 (1984), 126-35; J. L. Thompson, *John Calvin and the Daughters of Sarah* (Librairie Droz, Geneva, 1992), 87-99, 128-59. See also, A. A. Miller, 'The Theologies of Luther and Boehme in the light of their Genesis Commentaries', *HTR* 63 (1970), 261-303.

[19] In the former comment, he argues specifically against the Augustinian tradition, speaking of it as mere 'speculation', though he commends the effort (60-61 [45-6]). However, these aspects still retain an importance in his understanding of the *imago Dei*. Mankind's wisdom, knowledge and justice show them to be μικρόκοσμος (see 66 [49]).

[20] Thompson, op. cit., 94.

And, later, he asserts that Adam

> has the hope of immortality, which the remaining living things do not have, *for* he carries in himself the image and similitude of God (87 [66] – emphasis added).

This is what gives Luther the eschatological framework evident in his comments on the first chapters of Genesis. But the image also carries with it both the knowledge of God's intention for humanity's daily life *and* the zeal to put that knowledge into action. That is, Luther's perception of the image is that it has twin implications – relationship to God *together with* a consequent holiness of life:

> My understanding of the image of God is this: that Adam had it in his being and that he not only *knew God* and believed He was good, but that he also *lived a life that was wholly good* (62 [47] – emphasis added).

A necessary conclusion follows. On the basis that the image primarily denotes relationship to God, Eve must have had the *imago Dei* just as Adam. She is said to have been 'similar to Adam so far as the image of God is concerned' (69 [51]). This is where the problem lies for Luther. He wishes to maintain that Eve is equal to Adam because that is the obvious implication; yet, somehow, he also wants to support the hierarchical concept of woman's inferiority. This results in the ambiguity which others have observed and variously explained. Wright, for example, holds that the Reformer believed Eve to be inferior from her creation.[21] He quotes Luther's comment,

> Although Eve was a most extraordinary creature ... she was nevertheless a woman. For as the sun is more excellent than the moon (although the moon, too, is an excellent body), so the woman, although she was a beautiful work of God, nevertheless was not the equal of the male in glory and prestige. This sex may not be excluded from any glory of the human creature, although it is inferior to the male sex.[22]

---

[21] See Wright, art. cit., 126-35.
[22] '...*ne ille sexus excludatur ab omni gloria humanae naturae, quamvis inferior sit masculino sexu*' (*Comm. Gen.* 1:27, LW 1.68-9 [WA 42.52]).

Two assertions are then made in the light of this paragraph. First, Luther had no textual basis for such a comment and, second, he contradicts himself, having already declared Eve to be a partaker of and sharer in the divine image.[23] In this, Wright depicts Luther's thought as a pendulum swinging backwards and forwards, from upholding woman's inferiority to that of her equality and back again. His conclusion is that Luther demotes *unfallen* woman to the moral inferior of man. One of the basic problems with this is that it seems to assume Luther's negative attitude. To accuse him of pendulum-thinking is legitimate. However, to claim that the pendulum finished in the negative position (strictly speaking) goes beyond the evidence which, at best, is confused.

In contrast, Thompson believes that, 'On balance, at least in his commentary on Genesis 1-3, the egalitarian statements seem to outnumber their counterparts.' Significantly, he continues, 'numbers notwithstanding, both his affirmations and his denials seem equally deliberate and intentional, despite their apparent irreconcilability'.[24] However, despite noting Luther's obvious contradictions, Thompson places him in the 'minority' position of holding to the prelapsarian equality of women.[25] He then seeks to explain the apparent commitment of Luther's stance. It might represent sincere support of the dignity of women – a nascent 'liberationist' theology. It is also possible that these statements are hyperbolic, signifying the depth of the woman's fall by exaggerating her original status. But both of these answers are rejected by Thompson, who adds a third possibility. Luther and the others might simply be projecting eschatological equality back into paradise. That is, he may espouse egalitarian theology at this point, not to dignify women, but as reflective of his view of Galatians 3:28. As Thompson points out, this preserves the

---

[23] As Wright further points out, Luther also unambiguously ascribes Eve's subjection to Adam to the penalty imposed by God after the Fall. See *Comm. Gen.* 2:18, LW 1.115 [WA 42.87].

[24] Thompson, op. cit., 142.

[25] The majority group includes Augustine, Ambrosiaster, Denis, Cajetan, Zwingli, Bullinger, Bucer, Martyr, Politus and Calvin. These commentators hold that the woman's lot worsened from that of submission to servitude at the Fall. Thompson places Luther in the minority group, together with Chrysostom, Oecolampadius, Brenz, and others. These speak of woman going from equality to servitude as a penalty for sin. See Thompson, op. cit., 137-44.

sincerity of Luther's statements and also, more importantly, draws the conclusion that *'the full equality of men and women is still counted a desideratum'*.[26]

There is a great deal to be said for Thompson's conclusion. However, the problem that we are left with is the contradictoriness between Luther's egalitarian statements and his comments that woman is inferior (particularly, in the light of his comments on Galatians 3:28, noted above). These ideas may have to be shelved as simply irreconcilable. But perhaps at least part of the answer lies in Luther's definition of the *imago Dei* in both men and women and, at the same time, his insistence that hierarchical theories stand in the temporal area of relationships – that is, in this case, between husbands and wives.

Time and again, Luther seeks to show women as spiritually equal (they are endowed with the *imago Dei*) but, at the same time, he seems to take that foundation away. For example, though he refuses to give the impression that God was excluding the woman 'from all the glory of the future life,'[27] he points out that she is a different, weaker creature than the man. Though she is extraordinary, 'she is nevertheless a woman', she is 'not the equal of the male in glory and prestige'. It is significant that, in explanation, Luther draws on a domestic illustration:

> In the household the woman is a partner in the management and has a common interest in the children and the property, and yet there is a great difference between the sexes. The male is like the sun in heaven, the female like the moon. ... [T]his sex may not be excluded from any glory of the human creature, although it is inferior to the male sex (69 [52]).[28]

---

[26] Ibid., 144 – emphasis original.

[27] This phrase, in itself, is suggestive of her possession of the *imago Dei*.

[28] Earlier, Luther had stated that the woman, at creation, had different physical members and that she had a *much* weaker nature (69 [51]). However, he refuses to speak of her as Aristotle had done, as 'a maimed man' (70 [53]). See also *Comm. Gen.* 1:27, LW 1.68-9 [WA 42.51]. Elsewhere, Luther emphasizes the weakness of women – see, for instance, *Comm. Nah.* 3:13-15, LW 18.311-13 [WA 13.391-2]; *Comm. Isa.* 19:16, LW 16.163-4 [WA 31^2.115]; *Comm. Deut.* 25:5, LW 9.248 [WA 14.718]; *Comm. Tit.* 2:3, LW 29.57 [WA 25.46]. However, he insists that, 'the sex must be kept distinct from its weakness' (*Comm. Eccl.* 7:26, LW 15.130 [WA 20.148-9]). He does not always comply with his own advice, of course.

As Lisa Cahill suggests, Luther appears to be working from the (Augustinian) presupposition that the standard of excellent humanity is man, not woman.[29] It seems that Luther is balancing two somewhat ill-fitting ideas – his theological perspective and his social requirement. On the one hand, because of his view of the divine image in male and female alike, he wishes to assert that Adam and Eve were equal as created and, on the other hand, that they were socially unequal. The man is superior, the woman inferior in social arrangement. Hence, there is the irreconcilable ambiguity in his position and, ultimately, the impossibility of saying which of the polarities he *most* believes. However, on this reading, it does seem clear that he is *not* content with an *unqualified* egalitarian position, even at creation.[30]

Marital union (2:15-25)

The Reformer employs the story of Eve's creation from the body of Adam to define marriage and to illustrate the relationship between husband and wife. He does so, stressing the 'usefulness' of sex and the 'equality' of the couple. First, he notes that God brought Eve to Adam as a 'kind of betrothal' (134 [100]). This reminds him that marriage and sexual activity (within marriage) are not optional, but are the word and command of God embodied in the natures of men and women. As such, marriage is a divine ordinance,[31] not of humanity's invention, and as such the man should accept his wife as God-given, in obedience, joy and 'an overwhelming passionate love' (136 [102]).

---

[29] L. S. Cahill, *Between the Sexes* (Fortress, Philadelphia, 1985), 126. Her further comment, that Luther goes beyond this in teaching woman's intrinsic equality, is perhaps over-optimistic. A reading of his Genesis commentary does not lead to this conclusion.

[30] It is instructive that as late as 1545 Luther published Freder's *Dialogus* that advocates only a *limited* equality between men and women. Freder does so by using the lowest common denominator. That is, he says that those things that can be negatively said about women can also be said about men. He still advocates the disjunction between feminine and masculine roles. This illustrates that even Luther's later followers were also not entirely comfortable with espousing an *unqualified* sexual equality. See S. H. Hendrix, 'Christianizing Domestic Relations: Women and Marriage in Johann Freder's *Dialogus dem Ehestand zu Ehren*', *SCJ* 23/2 (1992), 251-66. Also, G. Harkness, *Women in Church and Society* (Abingdon, Nashville, 1972), 83.

[31] *Comm. Gen.* 2:22, LW 134 [WA 42.101]. See also, *Comm. Gen.* 17:1, LW 3.97 [WA 42.617].

Emphasis also falls on the goodness and innocence of the sexual union of the first pair, particularly in comparison with what experience tells Luther of the present state of affairs. He says,

> There would not have been in him that detestable lust which is now in men, but there would have been *the innocent and pure love of sex toward sex*. Procreation would have taken place without any depravity, as *an act of obedience*.[32]

There still remains sexual desire, but it is now corrupted by sin (104-5 [79]).[33] In this context, Luther begins to speak of the woman as man's 'helper'. In a traditional emphasis on defining the woman's original helping role, he explains that Adam was unable to procreate on his own. Eve, therefore, is created 'useful' for procreation and 'the good of the human race'. For Luther, this is blatantly still true of women, but the reason for the wife's help has shifted a little. She is now 'an antidote and a medicine' and 'a remedy against the sin of fornication' (118 [89]). He admits that women are vital to life, not only for procreation and the increase of society, but also for companionship and protection.[34] He speaks of the wife in partnership with her husband, involving everything they have. Yet, again, she is measured in relation to him:

> [T]he wife shines *by reason of her husband's rays*. Whatever the husband has, this the wife has and possesses in its entirety. The result is that the husband differs from the wife in no other respect than in sex; *otherwise the woman is altogether* [certainly] *a man* [*alias mulier plane est vir*] – 1.137 [42.103] (emphases added).

---

[32] '...*fuisset simplex et purus amor sexus ad sexum*' (*Comm. Gen.* 2:16-17, LW 1.104 [WA 42.79] – emphasis added). The comment regarding prelapsarian procreation being 'an act of obedience' (*tanquam obedientia quaedam*) reminds us of the crucial and continuing importance with which Luther endowed that particular Edenic command.

[33] See also, *Comm. Gen.* 2:18, LW 1.117 [WA 42.89].

[34] Notice how Luther shifts from the concept of procreation to that of remedy, through the idea of companionship: 'Woman is needed not only to secure increase but also for companionship and for protection. ... In addition – and this is lamentable – woman is also necessary as an antidote against sin' (*Comm. Gen.* 2:18, LW 1.116).

It is significant that a sentence beginning with the husband as subject, turns at the crucial point to make the wife 'altogether a man'. At another point, the Reformer estimates the wife's value in relation to her husband's need. He admits that she must be thought of not only by what she *does*, but also by what she *is* – but for Luther, she is primarily 'medicine' against her husband's sinful sexual desire (116 [88]).

The interesting point about Luther's comments is that he refuses *at this juncture* to see the phrase, 'I will make a helper fit for him', as implying inferiority/superiority in the wife/husband relationship. Indeed, his stress is quite the reverse:

> Hence it follows that if the woman had not been deceived by the serpent and had not sinned, *she would have been the equal of Adam in all respects.... She was in no respect inferior to Adam* (115 [87] – emphasis added).

This contradicts other comments that he has made, but Luther's point here is in the context of exaggerating the consequences of the Fall. 'Eve was not like the woman of today; her state was far better and more excellent.' The imposition of subjection was the result of her sin. However, Luther still applies the biblical image of 'building' (Gen. 2:22)[35] to the wife of his own day. Luther finds three reasons for this: her part in procreation, because she (together with her husband) takes care of the home and, significantly, because the husband, himself, is 'built up' through spending time with her (133-4 [99-100]). Unfortunately, he does not develop this last idea. Nor does he notice the pair's *mutual* vulnerability, implied in Genesis 2:25, 'Both were naked, the man and his wife, but they had no feeling of shame.'[36]

Transgression and penalty (3:1-25)

The Fall narrative divides into two parts, the act of sin and God's judgement. In both, Luther primarily seeks to show the nature and awfulness of disobedience and the righteous, yet gracious,

---

[35] 'The rib he had taken out of the man the Lord God built up into a woman' (Gen. 2:22).

[36] See K. Lebacqz, 'Appropriate Vulnerability' in J. B. Nelson / S. P. Longfellow (eds), *Sexuality and the Sacred* (Mowbray, London, 1994), 256-61, particularly 259.

response of God.[37] In line with his own proposition – that the corruption of human nature should be emphasized on the basis that grace is devalued by minimizing sin (142 [107]) – this occurs within the context of the underlining of the depth of fallenness, against both the bliss of Edenic life and the hope of future blessing.

The Reformer defines Eve's sin as unbelief and an abandoning of God's Word. That is, at heart it is a letting go of the true God (*'incredulitas et aversio a Deo'*).[38] It is defined, therefore, largely, in terms of loss of relationship. In this it becomes typical of all sin. Two significant things proceed from Luther's approach.

First, he seeks to blame Eve and Adam disproportionately for the entrance of sin into humanity's experience. He is clear that Satan's ambition was to attack both, but that he chose the woman as his first target. In this, Luther is convinced, Satan attacked the *weak part* of humanity. Again, we find the contradictoriness of Luther's teaching.

> Although both were created equally righteous, nevertheless Adam had some advantage over Eve.... [I]n the perfect nature, the male somewhat excelled the female (151 [114]).

This is difficult to justify from the text, but undeterred, Luther states that if Satan had attacked Adam directly 'the victory would have been Adam's'. The problem that remains unresolved in Luther's treatment is that Adam *was* later tempted so easily by his wife. This does not so much make Adam stronger than Eve (which is basically Luther's point[39]) but it simply makes Eve cleverer than Satan!

---

[37] The emphasis on the grace of God is important in this context. Luther teaches that after the Fall Adam and Eve are called back into life by the grace of God. If they become an example of believers tempted away from God's Word, they also significantly illustrate the Lord's mercy to repentant sinners. See *Comm. Gen.* 3:2-3, LW 1.155-6 [WA 42.117]. Also, *Comm. Gen.* 3:15, LW 1.190 [WA 42.142]; 50:19-23, LW 8.331 [WA 44.823]. It is interesting that Augustine reveals a similar emphasis in his discussion of the Fall – *De peccatorum meritis...*, 2.55. See also, for example, Bucer's similar handling of David's sin and 'fall' in *Sacrorum Psalmorum libri quinque...* (John Heruagium, Basel, 1547), 330-34.

[38] *Comm. Gen.* 3:1, LW 1.146-7, 149 [WA 42.110-11, 112]; 3:3, LW 1.155 [WA 42.117]; 3:6, LW 1.162 [WA 42.122]. See also, *Comm. Deut.* 1:20, LW 9.21 [WA 14.557].

[39] It is true, however, that Luther blames *both* for the Fall. The man was

Second, while Luther believes that the Fall brought with it the violation of the entire Decalogue, overemphasis comes upon its consequences in the context of sexual union. In speaking of 'the manifold corruption of our nature', the Reformer relates this to deformity of the flesh, 'kindled with passion' (142 [106-7]). Intercourse would have taken place in public, but now it is done in secret; 'the glory of the genitals was turned into utmost disgrace'.[40] In dealing with the penalty for sin Luther speaks of Eve's punishment as twofold; that is, pain and subjection to her husband. By 'pain' Luther includes problems that women encounter in their menstrual cycles, pregnancy, giving birth and raising children. However, in his optimism he sees both pain and subjection within an eschatological context of hope and, therefore, the woman as 'truly happy and joyful [*laeta et hilaris*]'.[41] After all, she is not rejected by God (thus, keeping the hope of salvation), she remains a woman, she is not separated from her husband, nor deprived of the blessing of procreation or the 'glory of motherhood'.[42]

It is the second punishment (that is, submission to the husband) that relates more directly to the present study. Luther claims that the wife has been 'placed under the power' of her husband, though at creation she had been entirely free and equal to him.

> The rule remains with the husband, and the wife is compelled to obey him by God's command. He rules the home and the state, wages war, defends his possessions, tills the soil, builds, plants. ... The woman, on the other hand, is like a nail driven into the wall. She sits at home... (202 [151]).[43]

---

deceived by his wife *and by himself* because he was persuaded that, as Eve still lived, there was no punishment for sin (*Comm. Gen.* 3:12-13, LW 1.182 [WA 42.136]). See also, *Comm. 1 Tim.* 2:13, LW 28.278 [WA 26.47]. See also, Thompson, op. cit., 138-44.

[40] *Comm. Gen.* 3:7, LW 1.168 [WA 42.126].

[41] *Comm. Gen.* 3:6, LW 1.199 [WA 42.148]. That is because 'in those very punishments there shines forth His [God's] inexpressible mercy, which encourages Eve and gladdens her heart in the midst of her misfortunes' (ibid., 200 [149-50]).

[42] Ibid., 200. See also, *Comm. Gen.* 17:10-11, LW 3.134 [WA 42.643].

[43] Later, Luther sees Adam's naming of Eve as an indication of his power over her (*Comm. Gen.* 3:20, LW 1.219 [WA 42.163-4]). See also, *Tischreden*

This denies previous teaching concerning the woman's ontological inferiority and caricatures the role-relationship between her and her husband into typically sixteenth-century social patterns. It also seems to counter the concept of partnership that Luther has introduced earlier. The stress is on the deprivation of Eve's (that is, generally woman's) ability to administer and her total subjection. However, the biblical passage defines the result of sin against the backdrop of the positive, mutual interdependence intended between man and woman. Genesis 3:16 is a *prediction* of sinfulness, not a command to the first pair.[44]

Adam's punishment is, likewise, a burden to him. It is his duty to support his family, to rule, to instruct, 'and these things cannot be done without extraordinary trouble and very great effort' (203 [152]). 'Thus the husband *is forced* to perform a task which is not very pleasant or very successful.'[45] Again, he has the hope of resurrection. Indeed, the actual difficulty of the work that he has should encourage him that these things are only temporary.

A FIXED PATRIARCHY WITH MUTUALITY

We have noted that the relationship between husband and wife is that of inequality. This is so primarily because that relationship is vocational and reflects the inequality intrinsic to the temporal kingdom. The present chapter, examining the Reformer's exposition of the key texts on marriage, has shown that, for Luther, the New Testament passages seem to demon-

---

[2847b] LW 54.174-5 [WA Tr. 3.26]. Ruether, op. cit., 97-8, recognizes Eve's subjection as punishment for sin, then claims that 'Luther's use of the doctrine of the original equality with Adam does not become a source for theological re-evaluation of woman's historical subjection. On the contrary, it simply deepens the reproach of her as one whose sinfulness lost this original equality and merited the punishment of subjugation.' Unfortunately, this is true largely because Luther is more ambivalent on this than Ruether implies. His is not a clear, unambiguous teaching on woman's creational equality.

[44] See, for example, M. S. Van Leeuwen, 'The Christian Mind and the Challenge of Gender Relations' in Nelson / Longfellow (eds), op. cit., 120-30.

[45] *Comm. Gen.* 3:19, LW 1.211 [WA 42.157] – emphasis added.

strate and emphasize this hierarchically structured inequality. His handling of Genesis 1-3 largely reflects postlapsarian *experience* (which is hierarchical), rather than the intention of the text, which is to show something of the mutuality and correspondence of the couple in God's purposes. However, there have been hints that the structural relationship is to be tempered by mutual respect and love. We now turn in a more general way to this apparent and traditional qualification of domestic hierarchicalism.

Though the hierarchical order that Luther suggests is seen to be temporary, it is clear and uncompromising. The husband must rule his family, including his wife.[46] The wife, on her side, must serve and obey. Sarah becomes the example, *par excellence*.[47] In this, Luther stereotypes much of his application so that the roles of each are clearly defined and demarcated 'feminine' and 'masculine'. So, according to the Reformer, the wife enjoys staying home[48] and being in the kitchen, she is burdened with

---

[46] See, for example, *Notes on Ecclesiastes* 2:3, LW 15.35 [WA 20.41-2]; *Comm. Matt.* 5:1-2, LW 21.8 [WA 32.303]; introduction to *Comm. Ps.* 51, LW 12.311 [WA 40^2.328]; *Comm. Gen.* 24:62-7, LW 4.290 [WA 43.350]; 41:50, LW 7.206 [WA 44.452]; 49:4, LW 8.212 [WA 44.733]. The Reformer's letter to Roth, beginning with the sentence, 'Grace and peace in Christ, *and authority over your wife*' (emphasis added) has become notorious in this context. B. I. Murstein, *Love, Sex and Marriage Throughout the Ages* (Springer, New York, 1974), 182, speaks of it as 'a scathing denunciation of the failure to exercise masculine leadership'. However, the phrase should not necessarily be taken on face value – which, in practice, often means 'current value'; see B. Gottlieb, 'The Problem of Feminism in the Fifteenth Century' in J. Kirshner / S. F. Wemple (eds), *Women of the Medieval World* (Blackwell, Oxford, 1987), 340. The letter is full of irony. 'The phrase comes directly from Erasmus' *Coniugium*, which Roth had translated and published in 1524. Luther and Johannes Bugenhagen have then used this sarcastically against Roth in this letter, four years later.

[47] 'Ita Sara doceat de summis virtutibus sanctae et laudatae matrisfamilias' (*Comm. Gen.* 18:9, LW 3.200 [WA 43.18]). See also, *Comm. Gen.* 12:11-13, LW 2.296 [WA 42.473]; 16:1-2, LW 3.44-5 [WA 42.579-80]; 23:1-2, LW 4.194 [WA 43.275]; 26:8, LW 5.38 [WA 43.454-5]. Susan Dowell, 'One Unholy and Divided Trinity' in D. McEwan (ed.), *Women Experiencing Church* (Fowler Wright, Leominster, 1991), 157, points out that the minister's wife of the sixteenth century became 'the pilot model of the New Testament woman'. In fact, for Luther, the Old Testament wives of the patriarchs were more often the paradigmatic examples employed.

[48] Luther's comment is not entirely true, of course – even for the sixteenth-century. In fact, some women would have preferred to remain in convents where, at least, they were permitted a measure of self-regulation. See K. J. P.

family duties, childbirth and rearing and, if her husband allows, she takes charge of the household, preserving discipline and decency.[49] Significantly, Mary, having lost her soteriological role in Protestant Reformation theology, in that context becomes a clearer role-model and an example of humility for the wife, going about her usual household duties. Among these are milking cows, cooking, washing pots and kettles, sweeping the rooms, 'performing the work of maidservant or housemother in lowly and despised tasks'.[50] The husband, on the other hand, has overall charge, and is responsible for feeding,

---

Lowe, 'Female Strategies for Success in a Male-Ordered World: the Benedictine Convent of Le Murate in Florence in the 15th and Early 16th Centuries' in W. J. Sheils / D. Wood (eds), *Women in the Church* (Blackwell, Oxford, 1991), 209-21; M. U. Chrisman, 'Lay Response to the Protestant Reformation in Germany, 1520-1529' in P. Newman Brooks (ed.), *Reformation Principle and Practice* (Scholar, London, 1980), 42-3, 47-50; J. D. Douglass, *Women, Freedom and Calvin* (Westminster, Philadelphia, 1985), 101; J. Boswell, 'Homosexuality and Religious Life: A Historical Approach' in Nelson / Longfellow (eds), op. cit., 65; B. W. Harrison, 'Human Sexuality and Mutuality' in J. L. Weidman (ed.), *Christian Feminism* (Harper and Row, San Francisco, 1984), 144; S. M. Johnson, 'Luther's Reformation and (Un)holy Matrimony', *JFH* 17 (1992), 282; J. A. McNamara, 'Inside the Convent', *CHist* 10 (1991), 19-21. E. Cameron, *The European Reformation* (Clarendon, Oxford, 1991), 405, helpfully concludes that 'The Reformation simplified the structure of society, for men and women, by making domesticity the religious as well as the secular norm: whether women experienced more or less religious fulfilment in the re-spiritualized home surely depended on their family context, their own personalities, and those of their families.'

[49] *Comm. Tit.* 2:5, LW 29.56 [WA 25.43]; *Comm. Gen.* 24:26-28, LW 4.280 [WA 43.336]; 26:8, LW 5.31 [WA 43.450]; 30:2, LW 5.331 [WA 43.657]; 38:26, LW 7.45-6 [WA 44.334-5]; 47:5-6 – alluding to Prov. 31:10, LW 8.110 [WA 44.659]. Cahill, op. cit., 135, points out that Luther concedes, 'at least a shade of the joint-authority in human affairs that the Creator first intended them to inherit from Eve'. However, it was a delegated responsibility, it was given with respect to the household *by their husbands*. See *Comm. Isa.* 4:1, LW 16.50 [WA 31², 35]; *Comm. Gen.* 16:1-2, LW 3.44-5 [WA 42.579-80]; 24:1-4, LW 4.223 [WA 43.295]; 31:14-16, LW 6.15 [WA 44.10]. See also, P. A. Russell, *Lay Theology in the Reformation* (CUP, Cambridge, 1986), 189-211.

[50] *Commentary on the Magnificat* (Luke 1:49), LW 21.329 [WA 7.575]. See also, D. M. Webb, 'Woman and Home: The Domestic Setting of Late Medieval Spirituality' in W. J. Sheils / D. Wood (eds), *Women in the Church* (Blackwell, Oxford, 1990), 164-72; P. Newman Brooks, 'A Lily Ungilded? Martin Luther, the Virgin Mary and the Saints', *JRH* 13 (1984), 136-49, particularly 136-42; M. Burnotte, 'La Pensée Mariale de Jean Calvin', *RRef* 23 (1972), 188.

working, teaching,[51] and ruling in the family, in society and the church.[52]

The ambiguity that has been noted concerning the possibility of prefallen equality is further underlined in an examination of other passages. In his *Notes on Ecclesiastes*, for example, Luther says that woman 'was *created* ... to be subject to the man'. The man for his part is '*commanded* to govern and have rule over woman'.[53] This allows for a creational inequality – something underlined by a comment on Psalm 51, where he states that man's rule is something that had somehow been created *before man* in Paradise and was given him as a task by God's procreative command.[54] His later works show the same tendency. His *Commentary on 1 Corinthians 15* (1534), for instance, emphasizes the fact that all status is temporary and that 'a person's position ... *is* not something that was created'. Yet a little lower, speaking of the afterlife, he says, 'the creature will remain, the body of each one, both as male and female, an in the *same estate and position*'.[55] The logic of the Reformer's belief in the restoration of all things would seem to demand that if a creational equality ever existed it would be restored, if not in this life, at least in heaven.

---

[51] Luther employs the image of 'bishop' to encompass the husband's tasks of teaching and concern for the spiritual life of the household. Thus he speaks of Jacob's 'household church' (*domesticam Ecclesiam*) – see *Comm. Gen.* 34:1-2, LW 6.187 [WA 44.139]; 37:4, LW 6.325 [WA 44.243]; 49:4, LW 8.221 [WA 44.740]. One of the husband's tasks was to teach his wife the Scriptures. During 1535, Luther promised Kate 50 gulden if she finished reading the Bible before the Easter of the following year. She already knew the Psalms and had reached Deuteronomy. In a letter to Justus Jonas, Luther gives Kate's cryptic reply: 'I've read enough. I've heard enough. I know enough. Would to God I lived it!' (LW 49.107-9) See also, T. Wilson-Hayes, 'The Peaceful Apocalypse', *SCJ* 13 (1982), 77-89.

[52] *Comm.1 Tim.* 3:4, LW 28.288 [WA 26.54]; *Comm. Isa.* 4:1, LW 16.50 [WA 31^2.35]. See also, *Exposition of Psalm 127, for the Christians at Riga in Livonia* (1524), LW 45.317-37 [WA 15.360-78].

[53] *Notes on Ecclesiastes* 7:26, LW 15.130 [WA 20.148-9].

[54] Gen. 1:28, 'Be fruitful and increase' – *Comm. Ps.* 51, LW 12.311 [WA 40^2.328].

[55] *Comm. 1 Cor.* 15:35-38, LW 28.172-3 [WA 36.634-5] – emphasis added. He underlines this by commenting that the prophets and apostles 'will enjoy greater glory than others *as men*. Similarly, pious Sarah and Rachel will be before *other women*'. The fact that Luther feels it necessary to distinguish between the men and the women in heaven is significant. See also, *Comm. 1 Cor.* 15:24, LW 28.124 [WA 36.568]; *Comm. Ps.* 8:6 (1537), LW 12.133 [WA 45.242-3].

Yet, allowing for the ambiguity in his teaching, even this seems to evade him.

Even though Luther is, thus, overtly patriarchal, it seems a caricature simply to stereotype his familial teaching, as Jewett does, for example: 'Some must command ... some must obey.'[56] Other ideas and Luther's own experience qualify the harshness and apparent divisiveness within the arrangement – without ridding it of its inherent hierarchicalism, of course.

Although traditional, the most significant among these ideas is his teaching on marital love within hierarchical order. Discussing Luther's understanding, Nygren shows that he derived his idea from his perception of God's love in Christ that is always and by nature non-acquisitive. Luther, therefore, rejects all self-love and egoism.[57] As early as 1519, he distinguishes three kinds of love: false love which seeks only its own honour, natural love as between relatives or friends and married love 'over and above these'. This latter says, 'It is you I want, not what is yours: I want neither your silver nor your gold I want only you.'[58]

This love is created, implanted and commanded by God and is reciprocal between the spouses. Those intending to marry *should* love each other.[59] For the Reformer, there is nothing more desirable than the *mutual* love of husband and wife. He speaks of it as a miracle. Though it is true that Luther did not initially experience passionate love for his own wife, Kate, he realizes that

---

[56] P. K. Jewett, *Man as Male and Female* (Eerdmans, Grand Rapids, 1976), 131-2.

[57] A. Nygren, *Agape and Eros* (SPCK, London, 1953), ch. 6; particularly 681-720. His conclusion is that 'it is absolutely impossible to say that Luther had any tendency to minimize and depreciate love' (720). See also, L. Isherwood / D. McEwan, *Introducing Feminist Theology* (Sheffield Academic Press, Sheffield, 1993), 49; S. Heine, *Matriarchs, Goddesses and Images of God* (Augsburg, Minneapolis, 1989), 66-71. D. Maguire, *The Moral Choice* (Winston, Minneapolis, 1979), 93, on the other hand, suggests that Luther misses the point about self-love when he should attack 'egoistic self-love that gives a hierarchical and inherently hostile prominence above all other values'. However, this avoids the Reformer's own understanding of love and his application within his marital ethics. Clearly, Luther rejects any sense of hostility, *as fundamentally inherent within* the hierarchical order of marriage, although he concedes its presence as the result of sin.

[58] *A Sermon on the Estate of Marriage* (1519), LW 44.9 [WA 2.167-8]. See also, [717, 732] in Hazlett (trans.), *Table Talk*, 332, 336.

[59] *On Marriage Matters* (1530), LW 46.297-8 [WA 30³.230]; *Comm. Matt.* 7:15, LW 21.258 [WA 32.513]; *Comm. Gen.* 38:8, LW 7.19 [WA 44.315].

a relationship often begins with intensity. However, he warns that only through care and prayerful trust in God can it continue.[60] The importance of this is that within a predominantly vertical, familial arrangement in which the husband is *above* the wife, as a superior to an inferior, there is a qualifying emphasis on a horizontal relationship which centres on companionship.[61] Some would locate a problem here. Fuchs, for example, sees a tension between, 'the affirmation of the primacy of love as the foundation of the marital bond – a love which implies the recognition of the spiritual equality of man and woman before God and ... the need for maintaining a hierarchical order within the couple'.[62] However, as we have observed, it is doubtful whether Luther would have coupled spiritual equality and any thought of social inequality as a problem in this way. Nevertheless, Fuch's comment pinpoints something of the ambiguity in the Reformer's theology. Both emphases on inequality and mutual love are important to Luther. Both the horizontal and vertical perspectives of mutuality and hierarchy are inherent in his view of vocation. Significantly, Luther uses the closeness of husband and wife to show something of the intimacy of the believer's relationship to Christ.[63]

So, by way of application, Luther enjoins his followers, including married couples, to be as Christ (*alter Christus*) to their neighbour. He says, '[E]ach one should become as it were a Christ to the other that we may be Christs to one another and Christ may be the same in all, that is, that we may be truly Christians.'[64] This

---

[60] See, for example, *Comm. Gen.* 24:1-4, LW 4.247 [WA 43.313]; *Comm. Hos.* 2:19, LW 18.13 [WA 13.11]; *The Estate of Marriage*, LW 45.43 [WA 10^2.299]. See also, *Comm. Gen.* 19:31-33, LW 3.309 [WA 43.96]; 29:9-12, LW 5.281 [WA 43.632]; 29:23-25, LW 5.295, 300 [WA 43.632, 636]; *Comm. Deut.* 16:13, LW 9.74 [WA 14.616]; *Tischreden* [3530] LW 54.223 [WA Tr. 3.380]; to Nicholas Gerbel [Wartburg], November 1, 1521, LW 48.321 [WA Br. 2.397]. Of his own early love of Katherine, he writes, 'I feel neither passionate love nor burning for my spouse, but I cherish her' (letter to Nicholas von Amsdorf [Wittenberg], June 21, 1525, LW 49.117 [WA Br. 3.541]). See also, LW 34.41 [WA 30^2.323-4] and R. Marius, *Luther* (Quartet, London, 1975), 132.

[61] *Comm. Gen.* 2:18, LW 1.116-17 [WA 42.88]; 2:23, LW 1.137 [WA 42.103]; 20:11-13, LW 3.354 [WA 43.129-30]; 35:16-17, LW 6.269 [WA 44.199]; *Tischreden* [5524] LW 54.444 [WA Tr. 5.214]; LW 45.27 [WA 10^2.284].

[62] E. Fuchs, *Sexual Desire and Love* (James Clarke, Cambridge, 1983), 145.

[63] *Comm. Gal.* 1:2 (1535), LW 26.168 [WA 40.285].

[64] *The Freedom of the Christian* (1520), LW 31.367-8 [WA 7.66].

appears to have two consequences. First, each is to *serve* the other, having unselfish pleasure in the other's welfare. He says, for instance, 'It is the duty of the wife to serve her husband – *it is the duty of the husband to serve his wife.*'[65]

Second, love is to operate within the realm of forgiveness. Each must accept the other, despite faults, realizing everyone's proneness to sin. The Reformer applies this particularly, but not exclusively, to husbands.[66] He recognizes that they are conventionally harsh with, and contemptuous of their wives, but insists that they should not be tyrannical, nor dictatorial. Everything should be done with affection. That is, as Luther admits, 'the husband does have rule over his wife; not the kind of rule exercised over slaves, but the kind that the soul has over the body'.[67]

EXCURSUS: LUTHER'S MARRIAGE

Although this can only be briefly outlined, the other area of Luther studies that must inform our appraisal of his hierarchicalism is that of his own experience of marriage. It is one thing to expound principles on matrimony, but quite another to live them. We find that within those principles, Luther

---

[65] *Comm. 1 John* 3:7, LW 30.271 [WA 20.703] – emphasis added. See also, *Comm. John* 16:24, LW 24.399 [WA 46.90]; LW 31.369 [WA 7.67]. See G. H. Outka, 'Character, Conduct and the Love Commandment' in G. H. Outka / P. Ramsey (eds), *Norm and Context in Christian Ethics* (SCM, London, 1969), 37-66; E. L. Long, *A Survey of Christian Ethics* (OUP, New York, 1967), 132.

[66] *On Marriage Matters*, LW 46.312 [WA 30³.242]; *Comm. Matt.* 5:31-32, LW 21.98 [WA 32.380-81]; *Tischreden* [3178ª] LW 54.191 [WA Tr. 3.211]; *Tischreden* [3530] LW 54.223 [WA Tr. 3.380]; *Comm. Gen.* 26:8, LW 5.32 [WA 43.451] *Comm. Gal.* 6:2 (1535), LW 27.113-14 [WA 40².145]. R. Niebuhr, *Faith and History* (Nisbet, London, 1949), 226-8, overstates his conclusion on Luther's ethics. He speaks of the Reformer's concern as being essentially and entirely individualistic to the point of both obscuring humanity's moral and social meaning and *of evading their responsibility in relation to others*. We believe that a study of Luther's teaching on familial ethics shows this to be incorrect.

[67] *Comm. Gen.* 12:11-13, LW 2.296 [WA 42.474]. See *Comm. Gen.* 20:11-13, LW 3.354 [WA 43.129-30]; *Comm. Gal.* 6:3 (1535), LW 27.114 [WA 40².146]. Note *Comm. Mal.* 2:14, LW 18.404 [WA 13.689], which speaks of the husband clinging to his wife because she is a gift of God (*uxor donum Dei est*).

allowed flexibility in his own marriage. Indeed, C. Pearson rightly claims that Katherine, for whom Luther had initially so little desire, became a true love, a spiritual companion and a 'soul-friend'.[68]

Several things stand out as instructive of Luther's hierarchicalism in daily practice. First, it should be noted that Kate had what has been called 'a perceptible independence'.[69] She knew how to take on a leadership role beside her husband and he appears to have welcomed her doing so. In this, she looked after the considerable household. As Luther's letters show, she managed the servants,[70] did the buying and cooking,[71] looked after the hospitality,[72] attended to the finances and even saw to the remodelling of the building.[73] She became a 'business woman' in her own right.[74]

---

[68] C. Pearson, '"Line upon line: here a little, there a little."' Some letters of Martin Luther' in P. Newman Brooks, *Seven-Headed Luther* (Clarendon, Oxford, 1983), 275-310, particularly 286-90. It should be noted that few would speak of Kate as does Marius, op. cit., 185, who describes her as miserly, greedy, narrow, unimaginative, pretentious, overbearing and dictatorial, 'a typical *hausfrau* of the time'. For a more positive view generally, see, for example, E. J. Mall, *Kitty my Rib* (Concordia, St. Louis, 1959); Y. Davy, *Frau Luther* (Pacific, Mountain View, 1979); C. Schreiber, *Katherine, Wife of Luther* (Muhlenberg, Philadelphia, 1954); E. G. Schwiebert, *Luther and his Times* (Concordia, St Louis, 1950), 593; D. MacCuish, *Luther and his Katie* (Christian Focus Publications, Fearn, 1983). See also the significant article, J. C. Smith, 'Katherina von Bora through Five Centuries: A Historiography', *SCJ* 30 (1999), 745-74.

[69] H. A. Oberman, *Luther: Man between God and the Devil* (Fontana, London, 1993), 276.

[70] LW 50.48-50 [WA Br. 6.270-71]; LW 50.208-12 [WA Br. 9.168]. See also the following: *Comm. Gen.* 24:16-18, LW 4.269-70 [WA 43.329]; 38:26, LW 7.45-6 [WA 44.334-5].

[71] LW 50.93-7 [WA Br. 7.249-50].

[72] LW 50.125-30 [WA Br. 7.348-50].

[73] LW 50.213-17 [WA Br. 9.171-3].

[74] Katherine looked after the large gardens (Luther, himself, was considered a *Stadtbäuerlein* i.e. a farmer). She drove the wagon and bought and sold the cattle. See LW 50.107-9 [WA Br. 7.316-17]; LW 50.208 [WA Br. 12.168]. She tended the orchard, the fishpond and the barn; and, in later years, she acquired a farm at Zulsdorf and after Luther's death, at Wachsdorf. In this she epitomized a growing possibility for women of the period. See, for example, R. Jutte, 'Household and Family Life in Late Sixteenth Century Cologne: The Weinberg Family', *SCJ* 17 (1986), 165-82; M. Wiesner, 'Paltry Peddlers or Essential Merchants: Women in the Distributive Trades in Early Modern Nuremberg', *SCJ* 12 (1981), 3-14.

Second, Luther shows a substantial appreciation for Katherine's initiative and capabilities, speaking of her as his 'Lord Katie', 'doctor' or 'preacher'. These phrases have been variously interpreted. Loewenich and Bainton, for example, see them as an implication of her strong will which Luther had come to accept; whereas, Krodel refers them to Kate's importance to her husband. He sees it as 'a major comment on the relationship between husband and wife as Luther understood it'.[75] In fact, given a variety of such phrases, it seems clear that Luther uses them partly in jest, but partly in order to express his admiration for Kate. In one letter, for example, he writes, 'To my kind and dear mistress of the house ... a preacher, a brewer, a gardener, and *whatever else she is capable of doing.*' In another, it becomes, 'whatever she is capable of *being*'. He commends her, also, for her learning.[76]

Third, Luther's affection and love are apparent in his letters. The often repeated addresses, to 'my Katie'[77] and 'my beloved',[78] express this. In 1526, Luther states that because of Katherine he would not exchange his 'poverty for the riches of Croesus'.[79] The mutual love between them is also made obvious, on the one hand, through their humour and, on the other, by Luther's concern for Katherine's welfare.[80] On the former, Luther concludes, '[W]e

---

[75] W. von Loewenich, *Martin Luther The Man and his Work* (Augsburg, Minneapolis, 1986), 284; R. H. Bainton, *Women of the Reformation in Germany and Italy* (Beacon, Boston, 1974), 29. G. G. Krodel, LW 49.236, fn. 10.

[76] To Mrs. Martin Luther, [Zeitz] July 28, 1545, LW 50.277 [WA Br. 11.149]; to Mrs. Martin Luther, [Eisleben] Feb. 1, 1546, LW 50.290 [WA Br. 11.275], respectively – emphasis added. Also, LW 49.236-8 [WA Br. 5.154]; LW 50.80-81 [WA Br. 7.91]; LW 50.100 [WA Br. 7.251]; LW 49.264-7 [WA Br. 5.237]; LW 49.416-19 [WA Br. 5.608-9]; LW 50.48 [WA Br. 6.270]; LW 50.213 [WA Br. 9.171]; LW 50.277 [WA Br. 11.149-50]. See further, to Mrs. Martin Luther, [Eisleben] February 6, 1546, LW 50.300 [WA Br. 11.284]. Interestingly, Calvin also wants women taught religion – *Comm. Deut.* 31:12-13 (CO 24.231-2) – though he admits that, generally, they are not, because they 'are born for domestic offices' (*Comm. Ps.* 148:11-12 (CO 32.435)).

[77] For example, LW 49.165 [WA Br. 4.198]; LW 49.169 [WA Br. 4.222]; LW 49.180 [WA Br. 4.294].

[78] For example, LW 50.218 [WA Br. 9.174]; LW 49.416 [WA Br. 5.608].

[79] To Michael Stifel [Wittenberg] Aug. 11, 1526, LW 49.154 [WA Br. 4.109]. See also, Pearson, art. cit., 286-90.

[80] See LW 49.150-51 [WA Br. 4.73-4]; LW 50.305-6 [WA Br. 11.291]. Luther underlines the necessity of humour in marriage (*Comm. Gen.* 26:8, LW 5.31-7 [WA 43.450-54]). See also, *Tischreden* [1461] LW 54.153 [WA Tr. 2.105]. The

know that marriage is a sacred matter and that we are permitted to laugh and have fun with, to embrace, our wives, whether they are naked or not'.[81]

Notwithstanding, Carol Gilligan says that Luther is a primary example of someone who achieves great things in the world but has a diminished capacity for relationship, ignoring the people most closely around him. In this she is surely mistaken.[82] There is what Oberman has perceptively called, 'the intimacy of ... patriarchalism'.[83] Both sides of this apparent oxymoron are true. The hierarchical family arrangement is obvious in Luther's writing of his own marriage. He speaks, for instance, of Kate: '[S]he is well, by God's grace, *compliant and in every way obedient and obliging to me*, more than I had ever dared to hope'.[84] This probably reveals his own consciousness of her strong will as much as his intention to 'rule', but should not diminish the sense of warmth that is evident between them. Finally, Luther is encouraged by Kate's spiritual understanding and growth. He says that God speaks to him through her. He calls her 'preacher'.[85]

---

mutual concern is shown, for example, by Luther cutting short a letter he was writing in order to comfort Kate just prior to giving birth – LW 49.152-3 [WA Br. 4.87]. Certainly, their love is shown by both the tone and contents of Luther's will – see LW 34.295-7; also *Comm. Gen.* 48:22, LW 8.194 [WA 44.721]; *Tischreden* [1457] LW 54.153 [WA Tr. 1.72-3], and Kate's moving letter to her sister, two months after Luther's death: 'Who would not be sorrowful and mourn for so noble a man as was my dear lord? Truly I am so distressed I cannot tell the deep sorrow of my heart to anybody and I hardly know what to think or how to feel. I cannot eat or drink, nor can I sleep. If I had a principality or an empire it would never have cost me so much pain to lose them as I have now that our Lord God has taken from me this dear and precious man. God knows that for sorrow and weeping I can neither speak nor dictate this letter' (quoted by G. Rupp, *The Righteousness of God* (Hodder and Stoughton, London, 1968), 351).

[81] *Comm. Gen.* 26:8, LW 5.37 [WA 43.454].

[82] C. Gilligan, *In a Different Voice* (Harvard University Press, Cambridge, 1982), 155. For a more positive conclusion, see J. Lortz, *Die Reformation in Deutschland* (Herder, Freiburg, 1982), 1.409; E. Donnelly, 'The Personal Piety of Martin Luther', BT 243 (1983), 26; B. Lohse, *Martin Luther: An Introduction to his Life and Work* (T&T Clark, Edinburgh, 1987), 33 and, generally, H. Bornkamm, *Luther's World of Thought* (Concordia, St. Louis, 1958). See also, to Nicholas Hausmann [Wittenberg] August 5, 1528, LW 49.202-3 [WA Br. 4.511]; *Comm. Gen.* 23:1-2, LW 4.195 [WA 43.276-7]; 35:16-17, LW 6.269 [WA 44.199-200]; 37:34-36, LW 6.403-4 [WA 44.302].

[83] Oberman, op. cit., 280.

[84] LW 49.154 [WA Br. 4.109] – emphasis added.

[85] *Tischreden* [505] LW 54.89 [WA Tr. 1.229-30]. See also, LW 49.236 [WA

Though Luther teaches a definite subjection of wives to husbands in a somewhat medieval desire to maintain order (both in the home and in society), he qualifies the vertical pattern by his insistence on mutual love and by his example within his own relationship with Katherine. We need to draw our conclusions from the foregoing at this point.

CONCLUSION

The introductory chapter outlined two basic positions in regard to Luther's views of the husband-wife relationship. There are those who see his teaching as positive and to a slight extent, innovative. There are those whose opinions fall at the other extreme, who understand Luther's position as destructive of the value of marriage and· of the worth of women, in particular. Though the debate was found to be complex, we discovered, at least, three broad areas of concern. The foregoing chapters inform our conclusions and we observe that things are not straightforward. At this point, simply to draw our study of Luther's understanding to a temporary close, we summarize his theology of marriage under general headings. A more thorough, discursive conclusion needs to be presented in conjunction with the results of an exploration of Calvin's position.[86] For now, it is enough to offer the following ideas.

Luther's Traditionalism

It is clear that the Reformer is fundamentally conservative in his doctrine of marriage. As we have seen, he affirms the medieval concept of the importance of an ordered society, reflected in (and, in one sense, based upon) an ordered family. He believes in a social order that keeps check on behaviour, in which higher offices dominate their lower, relational counterparts. In this, he holds to a hierarchical and patriarchal structure of marriage and because he believes that the origin of such arrangement is in God's creational intention for mankind as part of his temporal

---

Br. 5.154]; LW 50.107-9 [WA Br. 7.316-17]; LW 50.300 [WA Br. 11.284].

[86] See chapter 11 of the present study.

government, he fully condones it, without qualification. So, if retaining and expounding a contemporary view of the spouses' relationship, which is inherently mistaken, is the same as furthering injustice (which, in this instance, it probably is), then Luther can be accused of so doing. Although it is *not* my agenda to uphold hierarchical teaching or to defend Luther at this point, we need to remember that he *is* a man of his time and must be seen against contemporary social and political understanding. It is also possible, having taken many out of convents and monasteries – insisting upon the right of nuns, monks and pastors to marry – that Luther asserted a strict order to militate against libertinism in this area of ethical practice. Such was the immorality that Luther discerned around him, that he preached discipline and order to counter it.

Against this, it is sometimes argued that Luther raises the role of women as wives and as mothers. But we have seen that Luther is actually reaffirming the value of the wife's duties *as her husband's subordinate.* It has been noted that because he defines the role-relationship between the husband and the wife vocationally he sees their respective tasks as intrinsic to that context. The problem is that the Reformer invariably seems to equate the person with the task. That God made, 'a he and a she' is indicative, for Luther, that he also created them for their respective vocation – the wife for her domestic duties; the husband for his tasks of leadership; the woman for subjection and obedience, the man for ruling and supporting. However, this demarcation of tasks is not a strictly regimental one, as we have observed.

Too often, perhaps, Luther defines the woman within her God-given vocation and responds to her in terms of his understanding of the spiritual referent (that is, to God) and not to the temporal one (that is, to herself). That is to say, he appears not so much to love his wife *for who she is in herself,* but rather because she is a gift of God to him – someone who is ultimately defined by the word 'helper'. Similarly, because he emphasizes that faith, alone, discerns the true vocational nature of marriage before God, he appears to exhort men to help wives with the despicable chores, more because that is pleasing to God, than because of outgoing love for them – for *who they are.* This, again, places Luther into conventional thinking in which, in a sense, theological understanding of the situation (however motivational that may be) appears to be vastly more significant than personal connection and interrelationship. He sets this almost exclusively in the context of love for and obligation to God, rather than in the corresponding context of love for and obligation to the wife, as a wife, as well. Authority, then, is set squarely in the hands of the husband in the patriarchal arrangement of the household. Therefore, in this area, liberationists would appear to have a case against Luther of maintaining traditional convention and values and, thereby, largely continuing a 'destructive' ethical doctrine, to the detriment of the woman.

Sexual Negativity

In the introduction we saw that Luther is accused by feminist writers of a wholly negative view of sex, even inside the bounds of marriage. This, they say, continues Augustine's despondent doctrine of coitus and emphasizes the Reformer's pessimistic theology of mankind-in-relation. However, our enquiry has called this interpretation into question at several important points. We have seen that Luther's teaching on sexual union is much more positive than it is often given credit for. This is due to several theological reasons that permeate from the Reformer's teaching on vocation. There is a tendency to begin examination of this point at the postlapsarian experience rather than at the prelapsarian creation of man and woman. But because marriage is a creational institution and remains within the worldly government, the place to begin is with Adam and Eve at creation. Therefore, sexual intercourse must have been a gift of God, before sin's entrance. It remains a gift of God to those within the legitimate vocation of marriage. Indeed, sexual desire and ability is implanted and inspired by God, as is the couple's reciprocal, sexual attraction. Luther is explicitly affirmative concerning God's good gift of sex, *per se*.

However, we also noted that, given the depravity that comes from that first disobedience, every present act of sexual intercourse (even within marriage) is tainted by sin. This has to be recognized within the fact that it is true of every sphere of human activity, of course. Luther certainly laments this fact, but refuses to hold merely a pessimistic view of it. He teaches that sexual union is necessary for three reasons: for procreation, for a remedy against sin and as a sign of companionship. It is because marriage is a vocation before God that these reasons take on such import. As we have discovered, vocation within the temporal realm seeks to reverse the effects of sin. Marriage (and legitimate sexual intercourse, specifically) seeks to counteract the egotistical and disordering potential of sexual sin and the attacks of Satan and to ease the necessarily troubled existence of believers in this apocalyptic time. In that this is the case, God not only permits and excuses, but he also blesses and becomes involved within marital sex. Here is one aspect of the vocational partnership between man and God.

Marital Inequality

By far the most ambiguous bone of contention is the question of whether Luther believed in woman's equality or not. Many of his critics suggest an uncompromising hierarchicalism in which the husband rules and the wife obeys. They accuse him of teaching a non-reciprocal relationship, and of not challenging the patriarchalism of his day.

At this point, Luther is at his most confusing. We noted that he fails to give any *unqualified* acceptance of woman's equality, even at creation. Though he seems to wish to do so (largely, because of his doctrine of the shared *imago Dei*), the total endorsement evades him. There is a great deal of contradictoriness in Luther's teaching. He seems to waver between his theology and his understanding of social requirement. That is, he wavers between the necessary corollary that men and women were created equal because both possessed the image of God in their relationship to him and his understanding of social reality in which a structured inequality is not only required, but also inherent.[87]

We further noted that two other considerations play an important role in Luther's thinking. First, he emphasizes that the

---

[87] Coming from a reasonably optimistic reading of Luther, Cahill, op. cit., 129-30, contends that Luther does not declaim merely to keep women in their place, but he does so to keep 'things as they are now' (130). That is, the Reformer subordinates women to men to retain the *status quo* of order in society – an order empirically observed. Her conclusion is materially in line with that of the present study, but her suggestion that this desire for order in society stems from Luther's refusal to define the differentiation of the sexes as characterized by the normativity that belongs to the order of nature, appears an incorrect basis on which to thus conclude.

woman's subjection to her husband is a result of the judgement of God upon Eve's sin – God commands it. Second, Luther expounds his view of the marriage relationship within the context of vocation. Because marriage is a vocation, the particularisation of the temporal realm of God's authority in the individual's familial existence, then inequality is intrinsic to its nature. This is God's way of keeping order in society. This is made evident in Luther's handling of key texts, in which he emphasizes (sometimes against the biblical purpose) that the woman's role is to be submissive to her husband, his is to rule the wife.

In this area, the importance of Galatians 3:28 has been identified. The Reformer sees the text as applying only to the spiritual realm, having nothing to do with the temporal, worldly one. Spiritually, all believers are entirely equal; socially, they are not. Therefore, seeking to define marriage as a temporal vocation, he refuses to take on board the possible implications of the Pauline text. What follows from this is his assertion that God requires hierarchical distinctions in society and that to seek change or equality is to rebel against God. We saw a hardening of application in his two series of lectures on the text in which a later shift of emphasis stresses the need to keep order.

Whether or not Luther believes in a prelapsarian equality (which is doubtful), he certainly teaches a clear patriarchal, hierarchicalism. This, he states, is the will of God. Understandably, he can be accused of perpetuating the ethics of inequality and of not challenging these social mores of both tradition and his own generation. Against those discussed in the introductory chapter who claim that Luther's understanding is nothing more than traditional, however, we need to remember two things. First, we have discovered several qualifying points in his theology. He teaches that within hierarchicalism marriage is a 'covenant of fidelity' in which each is to give himself or herself to the other. Each is to become another Christ (*alter Christus*) in serving and forgiving the other. Marital love is to be selfless. As we have seen, this is part of the nature of vocation – being the temporal realm in which Christian love regulates behaviour. Here, then, the moralizing influence of the Kingdom of God upon the temporal area of his authority is discerned. Therefore, Luther's application is often against a tyrannical, dictatorial dominance on the man's part. In this he develops a moral impulse less clearly present in Augustine and the Augustinian tradition.

Second, certainly, (at least as far as we are able to discern) his own example of married life with Kate seems to demonstrate a mutual and reciprocal intimacy together and a large measure of independence for his wife. However, it must be said that it remains questionable whether this particular relationship, as it appears in Luther's correspondence, was a result of *his* theological understanding and application, or of *her* strong will and personality. It is most likely that both played a part. Therefore, though we cannot totally excuse Luther for his patriarchalism we need to see this against the softening influences that came to impinge on his own understanding.

There again, against those who maintain that the Reformer's view is inherently destructive of the woman's status on the grounds that his thinking is either sexually negative or merely tyrannical, we have discovered that such an accusation (as it stands) will not bear the weight of the evidence. Luther's perception of sexuality within marriage is more positive than these scholars would outline and his teaching concerning love and mutuality (though, in some ways limited by his hierarchicalism) show his teaching to be genuinely concerned for the wife.

Luther could, and probably should, have questioned sixteenth-century marital hierarchicalism within his reforming programme. That he did not is largely due to his dualistic perception of reality, as spiritual (in which realm all Christians are equal) and as temporal (which is inherently hierarchical, in which inequality is a fundamental characteristic). Given this theological undergirding of the vocational nature of marriage within the latter realm, his ethical understanding of the relationship between the husband and wife was not likely to be significantly different from what it was. Luther's theology at this point remained traditional, yet it has a somewhat tenuous suggestion of innovative application in his own experience. Calvin's familial ethics, on the other hand, though conventional, appear (to some) suggestive of further theoretical change and are hailed as real or genuine progress. We now turn to an examination of Calvin's position and of this possible development.

IV MARRIAGE IN CALVIN

CHAPTER 8

MARRIAGE AND DIVINE ORDER

The following analysis of Calvin's teaching on marriage will keep our conclusions regarding Luther's doctrine in mind. In regard to Luther we have argued that he defines marriage as largely circumscribed by his concept of vocation. Vocation is an individualization of God's temporal ordering of society. In particular, chapter 5 demonstrated that Luther's view of the husband-wife relationship is best read within the wider, theological context of his understanding and teaching of the two kingdoms.

As a vocation marriage necessarily reflects the nature of the temporal kingdom. That is, its origin is in God's creational intention and its overall purpose is to preserve mankind, both in the procreative sense and in the context of the threat of sin and Satan against God's work of maintaining societal order and peace. Its inherent nature includes hierarchical inequality between the spouses. Chapter 6 pursued this argument by examining the characteristics and nature of marriage as a vocation. It was observed that marriage is temporal, not redemptive. This underlined the hierarchical nature of marriage. Yet, it requires faith in the partners to recognize marriage for what it is and to live before a gracious, but judging, God. Chapter 7 detailed the Reformer's particular teaching on the relationship that exists between the husband and wife. It did this, partly, through an examination of his exposition of the major biblical texts on the subject. We observed, in general terms, that it is to be unalterably patriarchal and hierarchical in character, but also noting that Luther seems to soften the edges of this arrangement by his emphasis on mutual love, respect and forgiveness. Nevertheless, generally, this is traditionally Augustinian.

In turning to Calvin, we find that much of what we have discovered in Luther is evident – the vocational nature of marriage, the threatening character of sin and immorality, the intrinsic inequality in the marital relationship, and so on. However, Calvin employs his doctrine of marriage much more emphatically to stress the need for order and control in society against what he believes to be the inevitable moral chaos if societal structure is removed.

As we noticed in the introductory chapter, there is an added aspect to the study of Calvin because recent revisionist studies have insisted that his idea of order is not static, but one which allows for differences in culture and time. They claim that if this is so, then Calvin's view on the place of women in society, generally, can be read as open to change and modification. That is, women may be able to gain much more freedom from the strictly hierarchical nature of structures like the church and family than a conventional reading of Calvin might allow. Consequently, this present chapter will need to review a number of contributions from scholars to further identify and clarify the importance of the concept of order in the Reformer's theology, before moving on to examine the Reformer's view of order as an underlying concept in his view of marriage. This will establish how he conceives of order and how it might affect his view of the structural arrangement within marriage. That is not to say that the present thesis necessarily singles out order as the centre of Calvin's theology and ethical thinking; it is not.

Such is the theocentric nature of his thought that the triune God, himself, is probably central to his ethics; yet the concept of order is axiomatic to that pivotal doctrine. Therefore, though accepting God's centrality to the Reformer's theology, it will be found to be helpful to work from the secondary concept of order – for reasons that will become evident.[1] This will be addressed

---

[1] Others have recognized the centrality of the doctrine of God in Calvin's ethics – for example, J. Rilliet, *Le Vrai Visage de Calvin* (Pensée / Privat, Toulouse, 1982), 98; P. Marcel, 'L'Humilité d'après Calvin', *R Réf* 11 (1960), 3; A. Ganoczy, *The Young Calvin* (T&T Clark, Edinburgh, 1987), 188; R. N. Carew-Hunt, *Calvin* (Centenary, London, 1933), 118 – or the divine-human relationship, for example, P. W. Butin, *Revelation, Redemption and Response* (OUP, New York, 1995).

against the backdrop of the present liberationist view which is found to be basically too optimistic and to be in error – though it asks significant questions and proposes an interesting perspective on Calvin. The following chapters will look specifically at the Reformer's teaching on marriage as the context for the husband-wife relationship and on the nature of that relationship itself – largely through examination of the key texts.

CALVIN, ORDER AND MARRIAGE

Through his teaching on vocation Luther comes to the subject of peace and order in society with an emphasis on order within the earthly realm of God's authority. Coming from a similar perspective, Calvin approaches the doctrine of marriage with an obsessive concern for order within society's diverse relationships. This general concern was seminally recognised by Joseph Bohatec who highlights Calvin's 'passion for order' (*Pathos der Ordnung*) which he discerns in the Reformer's desire for unity, harmony and order in society and the state, over against his contrasting fear of disorder and chaos. He further delineates Calvin's idea that it is through the church that order (specifically, *ordinationes Dei*) is restored in the historical realm.[2]

Acknowledging this, many proceed from a secondary principle: order (fn. 2); union with Christ – R. C. Doyle, 'The Context of Moral Decision-making in the Writings of John Calvin' (unpublished doctoral thesis, University of Aberdeen, 1981), 98; sanctification – F. Wendel, *Calvin. The Origins and Development of his Religious Thought* (Collins, London, 1965), 245; the covenant – J. F. Veninga, 'Covenant Theology and Ethics in the Thought of John Calvin and John Preston' (unpublished doctoral thesis, Rice University, 1974), 304; providence – E. Fuchs, *La Morale selon Calvin* (Les Éditions du Cerf, Paris, 1986), 27-39. R. C. Gamble, 'Current Trends in Calvin Research, 1982-1990' in W. H. Neuser (ed.), *Calvinus Sacrae Scripturae Professor* (Eerdmans, Grand Rapids, 1994), 106, says that most 'leading scholars today maintain that there is no one single key to unlock the door of Calvin's theology. There is a consensus that there is more than one centrally important theme or, to continue the key analogy, that some keys open more doors than others.'

[2] J. Bohatec, *Calvin und das Recht* (Buchdruck und Verlags-Anstalt, Feudingen, 1934). While not necessarily positing order as *the* governing principle, others see order as clearly central to specific aspects of Calvin's writing. In addition to those mentioned in subsequent footnotes, see F. L. Battles, '*Calculus Fidei*: Some Ruminations on the Structure of the Theology of John Calvin' in R. Benedetto (ed.), *Interpreting John Calvin* (Baker, Grand Rapids, 1996), 139-78; J. M. Gustafson,

Others have taken up Bohatec's reading of Calvin. For example, B. C. Milner takes the concept of order as a first principle in the Reformer's thought and relates it to the providential activity of God, pinpointing the opposition between order and *confusio* as an important characteristic of his theology. Milner's thesis is that Calvin teaches that God restores order in and through the creation and preservation of the church.[3] Somewhat more recently, R. C. Doyle has argued Christ's central importance in Calvin's ideas of order and its postlapsarian restoration. He proposes the motif of *coniunctio per Christum* as that which underlines all of Calvin's theological endeavour. In that context, the restoration of order comes through Christ's humiliation and exaltation. He is 'the special and necessary locus of this order'. The image of God is restored in Christ, thus enabling men and women to live godly lives, pleasing to their Creator.[4]

Two later, significant Calvin studies are worth mentioning at this juncture as they sharpen our understanding of the Reformer's concept of order from which he reads his theology of the husband-wife relationship. The first is Bouwsma's provocative and influential study, *John Calvin: A Sixteenth Century Portrait*. The other is Schreiner's published research thesis on the subject of natural order in the Reformer's thought.[5]

Theology and Ethics (Blackwell, Oxford, 1981), 166; P. L. Lehmann, *Ethics in a Christian Context* (SCM, London, 1963), 134; R. Prins, 'The Image of God in Man and the Restoration of Man in Jesus Christ', *SJT* 25 (1972), 32-44; M. L. Monheit, 'The ambition for an illustrious name: Humanism, Patronage, and Calvin's Doctrine of the Calling', *SCJ* 23 (1992), 278; C. A. M. Hall, 'With the Spirit's Sword' (unpublished doctoral thesis, Basel University, 1968), 49; L. W. Spitz, *The Protestant Reformation. 1517-1559* (Harper and Row, New York, 1985), 213. M. Mullett, *Calvin* (Routledge, London, 1989), 13, says that Calvin's passion for order lay 'deep in his personality, fostered ... by the whole of his education'. See also, J. D. Douglass, *Women, Freedom and Calvin* (Westminster, Philadelphia, 1985), ch. 2, who traces his doctrine of order to the late medieval voluntarism of Scotus and Occam, and to Stoicism and Augustine.

[3] B. C. Milner, *Calvin's Doctrine of the Church* (Brill, Leiden, 1970). On the principle of order, see particularly 12-45 and on the restoration of order through the church, see 46-70. See also, L. J. Richard, *The Spirituality of John Calvin* (John Knox, Atlanta, 1974), 111-26.

[4] Doyle, op. cit., 212, 414, respectively. For the concept of order, specifically, see 126-333. Also, Richard, op. cit., 135-6; R. S. Wallace, *Calvin's Doctrine of the Christian Life* (Oliver and Boyd, Edinburgh, 1969), 47.

[5] W. J. Bouwsma, *John Calvin. A Sixteenth Century Portrait* (OUP, New York, 1989); S. E. Schreiner, *The Theater of his Glory* (Labyrinth, Durham, North Carolina,

It is significant that Bouwsma, refusing to see a single underlying principle in Calvin's theology,[6] still centres much of his explication around the twin, antithetical concepts of order and disorder. In the context of the present study, however, the importance of Bouwsma's book is twofold. First, he draws Calvin's obsessive concern for order against the backdrop of the *Angst* that was characteristic of his age.[7] Calvin's anxiety, he says, can be seen clearly in two of the Reformer's most employed images: the abyss, that boundlessness and the horror of the unlimited; and, the labyrinth, which suggests powerlessness and alienation from God.[8] Second, and as a significant corollary to the former, Bouwsma shows that the Reformer (concerned to relieve fear) thinks in terms of 'cultural constructions' – boundary systems, patterns of control and order.[9] This is seen within a concept of 'cosmic order' and a tendency in Calvin to equate righteousness with control and sin with unrestraint.[10] In this Calvin is largely traditional, embedded within the spirituality of the Middle Ages.[11] It is within this important cluster of ideas that Bouwsma speaks of Calvin's doctrine of marriage as one of the institutions through which God

---

1991). H. A. Oberman, '*Initia Calvini*: The Matrix of Calvin's Reformation' in Neuser (ed.), op. cit., 127-40, speaks of Bouwsma's work as the most significant interpretation since that of François Wendel. Similarly, in the same volume, J. Hesselink, 'Reactions to Bouwsma's Portrait of "John Calvin"', 209-13, although noting less positive reviews, says that the book is 'a brilliant *tour de force*, quite unmatched in Calvin literature' (210). Much of what follows owes a debt to the perspective brought by Bouwsma.

[6] Ibid., 2.

[7] Ibid., 32. (see 32-65.) Also idem, 'Calvin and the Renaissance Crisis of Knowing', *CTJ* 17 (1982), 190-212.

[8] Ibid., 46-9. See, for example, *Inst* I.vi.1; *Comm. 1 Tim.* 6:7 (CO 52.326); *Comm. 1 Pet.* 1:14, 18 (CO 55.221, 224); *Comm. Ps.* 30:6 (CO 31.294).

[9] Ibid., 48. It is significant that W. Monter, 'Daily Life and the Reformed Church' in P. Chaunu (ed.), *The Reformation* (Alan Sutton, Gloucester, 1989), 245-7, confirms this from another perspective. Speaking of 'austerity' and 'sobriety' as key words to describe Geneva under Calvin, he shows them to be qualities 'that depended on both internal and external constraints, on self-discipline complemented by ecclesiastical discipline' (245). He cites marriage: 'The Reformed Church probably exercised stricter surveillance over marriage than its Catholic counterpart, even if they no longer considered it a sacrament' (247). See also, Battles, 'Against Luxury and License in Geneva: A Forgotten Fragment of Calvin [1546-47]' in R. Benedetto (ed.), op. cit., 319-41; Lehmann, op. cit., 134.

[10] Ibid., 50.

[11] Ibid., 3-4, 69, 73, 237-8.

seeks to stabilize society. Here, specifically, order begins with the hierarchical arrangement of the husband and wife. However, Bouwsma notes that this is made complicated by Calvin's opposite pole of thought; namely, that men and women are *spiritually* equal before God.

Similarly, Schreiner emphasizes Calvin's passionate quest for order, arguing that the motivating principle behind it is to be discerned in his view of providence. She states, 'Armed with his belief in providence, Calvin interpreted the cosmic and societal realms.'[12] As far as the present study is concerned, the significant contribution of this writer's thesis is her insistence that Calvin emphasizes the *instability* of nature and the consequent need for strong providence over both nature and societal arrangements. That is, reading Calvin's theology throws up an emphasis on the inherent instability of an order which requires the 'immediate, continual, and powerful presence of God'.[13] Order is contingent, subject, dependent and, at best, precarious. Therefore, in Calvin's view, an ordered society, including the political (*ad ordinem politicum*), domestic (*oeconomicum statum*) and conjugal (*ad ordinem coniugalem*) order, contributes to the present preservation and to the gradual restoration of an ordered world.[14]

The work of these scholars has provided a viable basis on which to examine and evaluate the doctrine of marriage within Calvin's *corpus*. In varying degrees, they have shown the traditional importance of the concept of order in his thinking and the way in which his view of the cosmic and creational order necessarily permeates his ethics of society and the conjugal arrangement of the home - largely, through his doctrine of providence. All of them emphasize Calvin's obsession with order and his fear of any alternative. It is clear that he looks to Christ and the activity of God to restore things to their God-intended order.

However, the relevance of these writers is not in this way exhausted, for it has been shown in the introductory chapter that their ideas have, somehow, become a foil to liberationist scholars who seek to define Calvin's view of order in a way that is less conventional. In this they seek to employ his writing to open the door to more liberty for women in society. For example, as we have

---

[12] Schreiner, op. cit., 3.
[13] Ibid., 23.
[14] Ibid., 110. On the restoration of a legitimate order, see 108-11.

seen, Biéler suggests that, for Calvin, social inequality is a contingent fact, 'historically conditioned and politically determined'.[15] Others follow him in stressing that the Reformer views social order and arrangement as fluid and changeable, rather than as fixed, static and unalterable. Bratt hesitates to affirm quite so much. He takes the implication from Calvin's writing on 1 Corinthians that the Reformer desires to go towards a limited liberation of women, yet is reluctant because of his own view of the laws of creation. De Boer also emphasizes that societal order is merely the ordering of outward things (*ordinem istum in rebus externis*) and not a fixed, timeless hierarchy of the created order.

Douglass, in particular, comes to her conclusion that Calvin allowed for more freedom for women than is usually accepted, interestingly, from the basis of her own examination of the Reformer's concept of order. She stresses that the importance of order in Calvin's theology is definitely to be viewed in its *purpose* or *intention*, not in its arrangement and structure. However, she discerns two perspectives: first, cosmic order, God's *ordinatio*, and, second, the humanly made ecclesiastical and political order. She admits that behind both lie God's providential care and the activity of the Spirit.[16] Because of this distinction, she claims that, 'Conformity to the order of nature ... is not an absolute command; it must always take into account God's purpose for that order.'[17] This means that societal order will vary in form according to the age and the culture in which it is set. It is not static, a fixed or rigid system, 'but one which is rooted in God's decree, an expression of the will of God'.[18] It is essentially a human order and, 'Human order is the result of human governance (*politia*) which must adapt to changing circumstances.' In other words, where Calvin uses the term 'inviolable' concerning societal order *he does not necessarily mean it.*[19] It may not definitely or always express a fixedness in the Reformer's thought.

---

[15] A. Biéler, 'Man and Woman in Calvin's Ethic', *RPW* 27 (1963), 359; idem, *L'homme et la femme dans la morale calviniste* (Labor et Fides, Geneva, 1961), 80. For precise details of others mentioned in this paragraph, see the introductory chapter.

[16] Douglass, op. cit., 24.

[17] Ibid., 29.

[18] Ibid., 36.

[19] Idem, 'Christian Freedom: What Calvin Learned at the School of Women', *CH* 53 (1984), 156.

This review implies a starting point for what follows. That is, having seen that Calvin's concept of order is of fundamental importance to understanding his relational ethics and, further, having noted that there are significantly different and polarized interpretations of what Calvin means by 'inviolability' in this context, the present chapter will examine the Reformer's view of 'order' as it impinges on his understanding of the husband-wife relationship.

Therefore, we turn to the idea of order as determinative for his social thinking. First, we observe the theocentric nature of order. Second, in line with the analysis of Luther, we seek to form a wider perspective in examining Calvin's understanding of the temporal realm and (because marriage is a temporal vocation), more specifically, upon the doctrine of vocation within that. In defining the temporal realm of God's authority, we will need to note the intrinsic inequality of that realm and its purpose in preserving and restoring order against the threat of sin and chaos. That gains a theological context in which to examine the husband-wife relationship, more specifically, in the next chapter.

Order in Calvin's Understanding of Marriage

Calvin's view of *ordo* is essentially traditional. First, order comes from God. The cosmos was created by the Word of God (*ex nihilo*) – the Spirit sustaining the unformed mass in God's creative work. Calvin, therefore, describes God as the 'Supreme Architect', or 'the Author of nature' as he wonders at the beautiful arrangement and variety in the universe. But, importantly, he discerns his *kingship* as he sees order manifested in the world.[20] Yet, everything is created and ordered according to the movement of God's grace, showing, not only his authority, but also his fatherly love towards mankind.[21] That is so because the basic perspective, as Doyle points out, is that the order of nature is anthropocentric in the

---

[20] *Comm. Ps.* 19:1 (CO 31.195); *Inst* II.i.10, III.iii.12; *Comm. Ps.* 24:2 (CO 31.244), respectively. See also, *Inst* I.v.1, I.xiv.21. The universe is a theatre displaying his glory – *Inst* IV.xiv.20, I.v.8, I.vi.2, II.vi.1, III.ix.2.

[21] See *Inst* I.xiv.2, I.xiv.20; *Comm. Gen.* 2:1 (CO 23.15-16). Also, *Inst* I.iii.3, II.viii.42; *Comm. Ezek.* 3:18 (CO 40.92); *Comm. Ps.* 8:1 (CO 31.87); *Serm. 1 Cor.* 11:11-16 (CO 49.740); *Comm. Gen.* 9:6 (CO 23.146); *Comm. Jonah* 1:13-14 (CO 43.226-7); *Comm. Mal.* 1:2-6 (CO 44.395-409); *Serm Job* 30:1-10 (CO 34.595-6), 35:8-11 (CO 35.240).

sense that, 'the whole order of this world is arranged and established for the purpose of conducing to the comfort and happiness of man'.[22] God's order is most clearly seen and culminates in the creation of mankind.[23]

Second, the work of creation is not merely a definitive past event. It is a *creatio continua* in its perpetuation in the present, providential and gracious working of God:

> [T]o make God a momentary creator, who once for all finished his work, would be cold and barren ... in that we see the presence of divine power shining as much in the continuing state of the universe as in its inception.[24]

So, providence is the continuing *administratio* of God.[25] It is on this point that Schreiner helpfully emphasizes the instability of the creation and, therefore, the need for a strong providence. However, the *ordre de nature* revealed to Calvin 'the regularity and continuity of creation' and the requirement of God's 'immediate, continual and powerful presence'.[26] The emphases on both the regularity and contingency of natural order are reflected in Calvin's doctrine of God's providential ordering of humanity, for (despite the Fall) it is still the centre and summit of God's creation and sustaining activity.[27] It is also worth noting that in primal humanity there existed an internal or moderated order in the parts of the

---

[22] Doyle, op. cit., 126. Also, *Inst* I.xiv.2, I.xvi.6; *Comm. Ps.* 8:6 (CO 31.92); *Comm. Acts* 14:17 (CO 48.327).

[23] *Inst* I.v.1-15, I.xv.1, III.xxiii.2. See B. M. G. Reardon, *Religious Thought in the Reformation* (Longman, London, 1981), 187.

[24] *Inst* I.xvi.1. See also, *De Aeterna Dei Praedestinatione*, CO 8.347.

[25] *Comm. Isa.* 37:16 (CO 36.626); *Comm. Acts* 17:28 (CO 48.416); *Comm. Ps.* 104:29 (CO 32.95). Calvin is careful to say that God continues his preserving work, not because mankind deserves it, but because God loves his own creation. See, for example, *Serm Deut.* 13:1-3 (CO 27.234); 28:1-4 (CO 27.488-9); *Serms Job* 10:7-15 (CO 33.483); 29:18-25 (CO 34.571-84); *Comm. Ezek.* 18:1-4 (CO 40.424).

[26] Schreiner, op. cit., 22, 23, respectively. *Comm. Ps.* 89:11-12 (CO 31.815) says, 'It belongs to God to maintain and govern whatever he has created.' See also, *Inst* I.v.2, I.xiv.21, I.v.5. Also, *Serm. 2 Sam.* 10:10-19 in *Sermons on Two Samuel, chapters 1-13* D. Kelly (trans.), (Banner of Truth, Edinburgh, 1992), 465-6, hereafter, cited simply as [Kelly]. Calvin's sermons on 2 Samuel are not in the volumes of the *Corpus Reformatorum*, but are to be found in *Supplementa Calviniana*. *Sermons Inédits* (Neukirchen, 1961f) - specifically, SC I.

[27] In this respect, Calvin, as Luther, employs the Renaissance cliché of man being μικρόκοσμος - a rare example of God's power, goodness and wisdom.

soul;[28] mankind in its ordered being represents or expresses the divine order.[29]

Because of humanity's centrality, providence extends to societal relationships and structures as it does to every other facet of created being and existence. In the same way that natural order remains at God's instigation, so social order is not humanity's prerogative, but God's – though mankind has a part to play in its continuance. Calvin stresses the former point in commenting on Psalm 127, for example, 'This psalm shows that the order of society, both political and domestic, is maintained *solely* by the blessing of God.'[30] This accords with his teaching on mankind's creation as a social animal for Calvin insists that each person is formed *for others*.[31] It also accords, therefore, with his view of society *rightly ordered*. Clearly, prelapsarian society would have been an ordered one, for the fact that mankind was originally made in the image of God, *ipso facto*, means that they would have lived in a right relationship with both God and persons-in-society in accordance with the order of God. In that context, Milner speaks of mankind's co-operation with God: 'the work of the Spirit and the *ordinatio Dei* conspire in the creation of the natural order ... and in the achievement *through man* of political order'.[32] Thus, in Calvin's words,

> This is truly ἀταξία [disorder], not to consider the purpose for which we were formed and not to order our lives with this end in view, *for it is only when we live in accordance with the rule of God that our life is set in order*.[33]

---

[28] '*Erat enim in singulis animae partibus temperatura quae suis numeris constabat*' (*Inst* I.v.3).

[29] See *Inst* I.v.3; *Comm. Gen.* 1:26 (CO 23.26-7). Also, *Comm Ps.* 8:6 (CO 31.92-3); 24:1 (CO 31.244); *Comm. Acts* 14:17 (CO 48.328); *Serm. Job* 10:7-15 (CO 33.481).

[30] *Comm. Ps.* 127:1-3 (CO 36.400) – emphasis added. See also, *Comm Dan.* 2:38 (CO 40.597); 4:17 (CO 40.663); *Comm. Rom.* 13:1 (CO 49.248-9); *Comm. Isa.* 24:1-3 (CO 36.400); *Comm. John* 5:17 (CO 47.111).

[31] *Comm. Gen.* 2:18 (CO 23.46) – '*Principium ergo generale est, conditum esse hominem, ut sit sociale animal.*' Doyle, op. cit., 134, speaks of it as 'mutual and other-person-centred community' (also, 333). Also, *Inst* II.ii.13; *Comm Gen.* 1:27 (CO 23.27); 2:21 (CO 23.48); *Comm. Matt.* 5:43 (CO 45.187); *Comm. Ps.* 127:1 (CO 32.321).

[32] Milner, op. cit., 43 – emphasis added. See also, Hall, op. cit. 49.

[33] *Comm. 2 Thess.* 3:6-10 (CO 52.211-12; *CNTC,* 8.416) – emphasis added.

It is noticeable, then, that for Calvin, as a Reformer in a time of crisis, 'order' means conformity to the divine will. That is, *ordo* indicates a practical order secured by obedience to God.

Marriage within 'Political' Jurisdiction

We have seen that Calvin teaches a view of divine providence that precludes nothing in its relation to humanity. The question is now raised as to how this is related to society and to social relationships.

We have shown that Luther held to a modified doctrine of two governments of God's rule in the world, the spiritual and the temporal. Calvin has no such clearly delineated doctrine of two kingdoms, but he adopts a similar perspective in that he draws a distinction between spiritual and political jurisdiction in society and within men and women. He discusses this in a number of contexts, notably in specifying the manner and boundaries of civil government and in distinguishing between civil and ecclesiastical jurisdiction. For example, in *Institutes* II.ii.13, in the context of mankind's universal understanding of 'earthly' things and their inadequate understanding of 'heavenly', Calvin explains the distinction between them in the following way:

> I call 'earthly things' those that *do not pertain to* God or his Kingdom, to true justice, or to the blessedness of the future life; but *which have their significance and relationship with regard to the present life* and are, in a sense, confined within its bounds. I call 'heavenly things' the pure knowledge of God, the nature of true righteousness, and the mysteries of the heavenly Kingdom.[34]

Calvin then states what sort of things each would include: 'The first class includes government, *household management*, all mechanical skills, and the liberal arts. In the second are the knowledge of God and of his will, and the rule by which we conform our lives to it.'[35]

The Reformer differentiates between the spiritual and temporal jurisdiction and, though he never disconnects the two, he sharply

---

[34] *Inst* II.ii.13 – emphasis added.
[35] Ibid.; emphasis added. He also suggests that people naturally tend to foster and to preserve society. See also, *Inst* III.xix.15, IV.x.5, IV.xx.1.

stresses their distinct independence.[36] He outlines this in his commentary on 1 Corinthians 11:3, where he defines the spiritual kingdom as that of the conscience and the mind, and the temporal kingdom as that of external arrangement, or structure and political decorum. In a similar passage in the *Institutes*, he describes the spiritual world within mankind as pertaining to the life of the soul/eternity, residing in the inner man and free, according to the Spirit. The political world within mankind, on the other hand, is concerned with the present day/outward behaviour, having not yet been released from bodily servitude.[37]

The purpose of the temporal realm is clear in the Reformer's thinking. Its primary task is to preserve the 'legitimate order' in the world; that is, the order that is the will and intention of God for mankind. It does so largely through structured institutions for, though the Reformer recognizes that there is variety and diversity in societal customs, he is convinced that at least, 'Some form of organization is necessary in all human society to foster peace and to maintain concord.'[38] It is in line with this that the Reformer commends even unbelievers' marriages, for instance. Though they do not acknowledge the author of their marriage, 'It [marriage] fulfils the function of preserving respectability in society and checking promiscuous desires. And so, because of those purposes, it is approved by God, *like other parts of social order* [*ordinis politici*].'[39] Thereby, he distinguishes between the *nature* of marriage and its abuse, hinting, significantly, that marriage is designed to preserve society.[40] In that way it reflects the purpose of the temporal government.

The structure and order that Calvin finds in society is reflective of the structural arrangement of the cosmos and of being, itself. He reads 1 Corinthians 11:3[41] hierarchically, seeing four gradations with

---

[36] *Inst* IV.xi.3. See W. van't Spijker, 'Bucer's Influence on Calvin: Church and Community' in D. F. Wright (ed.), *Martin Bucer. Reforming Church and Society* (CUP, Cambridge, 1994), 43-4.

[37] *Comm. 1 Cor.* 11:3 (CO 49.474-5); *Inst* III.xix.15, respectively. See also, *Inst* IV.xx.1-2, which is linked by Calvin with III.xix.15, which in substance formed the first part of chapter vi in the 1536 edition (OS I.223-80). It is therefore, in a real sense, a continuation of the former section. See *Inst* IV.xx.1, fn. 2.

[38] *Inst* IV.x.27. See Bouwsma, op. cit., 76.

[39] *Comm. 1 Cor.* 7:14 (CO 49.412; *CNTC,* 9.149) – emphasis added.

[40] See also, *Comm. Jer.* 7:34 (CO 37.706).

[41] In Calvin's French, 'le chef de tout homme, c'est Christ, et le chef de la femme, c'est l'homme, et le chef de Christ, c'est Dieu' (CO 57.431).

specific implications in the realm of authority: God, occupying the first place; Christ, submitting himself to the Father; man beneath Christ and woman below man. Because, like Luther, Calvin sets the order of marriage within *ordinem politicum*, he teaches that there is an inherent inequality in the structure of the household – man holds the authority in its government, woman is to be in subjection. This, he says, is *ordinem coniugalem* drawn from the very nature of things, persistent for this present life.[42] He draws the same conclusions in his sermon on Galatians 3:26-29, where he speaks of this diversity in the hierarchical structure, 'in worldly policy [*à la police de ce monde*]', as being an 'inviolable order' – one that cannot be dispensed with.[43]

For Calvin, the three significant institutions within society are the church, the state and the family. This was commonplace among the reformers and, previously, within medieval theology. With regard to the family, Calvin counts 'six status categories in the household, linked by three sorts of yoke: the yoke of marriage uniting husband and wife, the yoke binding parents and children, and the yoke connecting masters and servants'.[44] In other words, he holds to the order that he deems stipulated in the New Testament *Haustafeln*, literally understood. Here, order begins with the subordination of the wife and the parental control of the children.[45] Within this context, the Reformer speaks of the family as a church, as does Luther. But what is very significant is the fact that, whereas Luther's stress in employing this metaphor is on relationship and the spiritual importance of the man's teaching of the Word to his household, Calvin's emphasis is generally on organization and structure. So, for instance, in his comment on 1 Corinthians 16:19, regarding the church which meets in the house of Aquila and Prisca, he underlines the management of a Christian household. Despite the biblical context, he states that 'all families of the pious should be organized like so many little churches'. Similarly, at Genesis 17:12, he repeats the teaching that every believer's home should be a church. Here he comments even more

---

[42] See *Comm. 1 Cor.* 11:3 (CO 49.474-7).
[43] *Serm. Gal.* 3:26-9 (CO 50.567). Also, *Comm. Gen.* 21:20 (CO 23.305).
[44] Bouwsma, op. cit., 201. See also, *Serm. Job* 19:17-25 (CO 34.120).
[45] See *Comm. 1 Tim.* 2:13 (CO 52.276-7); *Comm 1 Cor.* 11:7 (CO 49.476); 14:34 (CO 49.533); *Comm Acts* 10:2 (CO 48.223); 16:15 (CO 48.378); 18:26 (CO 48.437); *Comm. Gen.* 18:6, 19 (CO 23.252, 258).

emphatically, '[I]f we desire *to prove our piety* we must labour that every one of us may have his house *ordered* in obedience to God.'[46]

It would appear then that, for Calvin, right ordering of the household (which is, itself, closely connected with faith and obedience) is actually *evidence* of right priorities, righteousness and godly living. As we have noted, pious ordering is hierarchical by nature and, therefore, conducive to inequality – an inequality which is clearly evidenced in the context of the husband-wife relationship. This was shown to be the case in Luther's thought. We turn now to this idea in Calvin's teaching.

HIERARCHY IN SOCIAL RELATIONS

In a similar way to Luther, Calvin claims that by creation everyone is, to some extent, equal (*pareils* – alike) because all are endowed with the image of God and are descended from Adam. In spiritual terms, all believers are equal, too. However, he teaches that in societal relationships there is a God-initiated inequality.[47] That is part and parcel of what Calvin seeks to protect in order to preserve society against confusion.

A God-given Inequality

Characteristically, Calvin stresses that it is God and not humanity who has created the temporal realm and also its inherent distinctions.[48] That is, God has ordained hierarchy in social relationships. In this he actively appoints and regulates all the arrangements of society by his providential activity. In this context, Calvin uses the image of a building that has been carefully constructed and divided into several compartments. God is its architect, yet it is described as a human ordination (*humana*

---

[46] *Comm. 1 Cor.* 16:19 (CO 49.571); *Comm. Gen.* 17:12 (CO 23.241), respectively – emphases added; cf. *Comm. Isa.* 38:19 (CO 36.662). On Luther, see, for example, LW 6.187, 325 [WA 44.139, 243]; LW 8.221 [WA 44.740].

[47] See *Serm. Deut.* 5:17 (CO 26.321); *Comm. Gal.* 3:28 (CO 50.222-3); *Comm. Ps.* 148:11-12 (CO 32.435).

[48] *Serm. Job* 19:17-25 (CO 34.115), 'Il est vray que nostre Seigneur a ordonné la police ... chacun sera en son degré...'. See also, *Comm. Dan.* 4:17 (CO 40.663), '...sed gubernet etiam humanum genus, et assignet cuique suum gradum vel locum'.

ordinatio), not because it is invented by mankind, but because it has been arranged and ordered for mankind.[49] Within that building there are gradations of distinction. There is a hierarchical structure. The simple reason for this is that God wishes it to be so.

Of the higher positions Calvin comments, '[T]he Lord has raised them to a degree superior in honour. For there is no authority, either of parents, princes, or governors of any kind, no empire and no honour, except by God's decree; *for it so pleased him to order the world.*'[50] Bluntly put, '[I]t is God who ordains superiority.' It is not chance, but a common and universal providential design and arrangement.[51] As a result, no-one is to erase the distinctions set in society – that, says Calvin, would be 'open war with God'.[52]

Galatians 3:28

If the Reformer holds to the notion of hierarchical arrangements within society, the question of what he makes of Galatians 3:28[53] is bound to arise, as it did in studying Luther's theology. It does so for identical reasons. First, it does so because of his use (or, lack of use) of this verse in his own understanding of the ethics of the relationships within society, and particularly within the familial sphere. And second, because the verse is so often seen as a biblical critique of patriarchal marriage, being employed against the Reformer by detractors of Calvin's views of marriage.

Calvin's commentary on the text[54] says very little of any significance to the present study. He simply repeats Luther's biblical emphasis that Paul is stressing that temporal distinctions between people (whether nation (*gentis*), condition, circumstance, sex or civil rank) make no difference *in terms of their salvation*, for Christ makes all believers one.

However, his sermon, examining this verse as Paul's conclusion to the matter of baptism,[55] fills out the thought in three points.

---

[49] *Comm. 1 Pet.* 2:13 (CO 55.247).
[50] *Catechismus Ecclesiae Genevensis* (1545), (OS 2.105-6) – emphasis added.
[51] *Serm. 2 Sam.* 3:26-39 [Kelly, 124]; *Comm. Ps.* 55:13 (CO 31.539), respectively. See also, *Serm. Gal.* 3:26-9 (CO 50.567-9).
[52] *Comm. Gen.* 38:26 (CO 23.500); *Comm. Rom.* 13:1 (CO 49.249).
[53] That is, 'There is no such thing as ... male and female.'
[54] *Comm. Gal.* 3:28 (CO 50.222-3).
[55] *Serm. Gal.* 3:26-9 (CO 50.566).

First, he repeats that there is no *religious* significance in the distinctions of society – salvation is based solely on God's goodness and mercy.[56] Second, Calvin states that the apostle deliberately intends *not* to do away with social inequality, and third, he makes the point that these distinctions are merely 'penultimate', that is, they will pass away with Christ's Second Coming.[57]

It is significant that Calvin, at least, recognizes that there *could be* a social implication to Paul's thought, but like Luther, he rejects this. He stresses that the apostle does not mean that there is *no* diversity at all; there clearly is in society – he lists magistrates and subjects, masters and servants, and, significantly, husbands and wives.[58] By listing it in this way he implies that present, empirical observation is enough to discern God's worldly order. This order (*la police de ce monde*) is *inviolable*; and he underlines this thought by asserting that Christ did not come to bring confusion, nor to abolish what the Father has established. What is important here is that he sees it as unalterable in the temporal realm. The Reformer's primary application of the text, in keeping with the exposition, is an exhortation to godliness and the need to continue in the heavenly kingdom, thus freely received through Christ. For our purposes, his secondary application at this point is significant; it is as stringent as that of Luther – the need to maintain the civil orders of this world.[59]

The use that Calvin makes of the text elsewhere is instructive. He employs it, directly, only three times in the *Institutes*, two of

---

[56] '*Si on demande la cause, ie di la vraye source et le fondement, il ne faut cercher sinon la pure bonté de Dieu, d'autant qu'il luy plaist d'avoir pitié de nous...*' (ibid., 559; cf. 68-9). See also, R. White, 'Women and the Teaching Office According to Calvin', *SJT* 47 (1994), 508.

[57] Ibid., particularly 567. The word 'penultimate', in this context, is John Thompson's (*John Calvin and the Daughters of Sarah*, Librairie Droz, Geneva, 1992, 157). He says that the majority of Calvin's sources and contemporaries ignore the potential social question altogether (154).

[58] At this point, Calvin seems to lay stress on domestic submission. It is also interesting that he moves from a theoretical knowledge of the establishment of order to an empirically observed structure as proof of that order. 'However, St. Paul does not mean that in regard to the established order of this world there is no diversity of rank. We know that there are servants and masters; there are magistrates and subjects; in the home there is the man who is the head and the woman who must be subject to him' (*Serm. Gal.* 3:26-29 (CO 50.567-8)).

[59] Ibid., 567-8, 569, respectively. See also, *Serm. Eph.* 2:13-15 (CO 51.399-412).

which make reference to the Jew and Gentile distinction (*Inst* II.xi.11, III.xxiii.10). The other passage (*Inst* IV.xx.1) is more significant, because its precise referent is the male/female distinction. His application is that the kingdom of Christ does not consist in the overthrow of social hierarchy or the establishment of egalitarian principles within society. It is not so much that Calvin sees no ethical implication in the verse, but, rather, that he actually rejects the possibility of a levelling implication within the context of social relationships. This is clear, again, in his comments on 1 Corinthians 11:3. The problem for Calvin is that in this text man appears to be placed hierarchically between Christ and the woman, which seems to indicate that he (not Christ) is the woman's 'head'. However, this could seem at variance with Paul's assertion that there is no difference between them (Gal. 3:28). The Reformer, therefore, is forced into the question of why the apostle makes this distinction at this point. His conventional answer is that it all depends on the context. When the apostle speaks of the lack of difference, he refers to man and woman within the spiritual kingdom in which individual distinctions (*les qualités externes*) are not regarded.

> When Paul says there is no difference between man and woman, he is speaking about the spiritual Kingdom of God, where the outward characteristics [*personae*], count for nothing, and are not taken into consideration, for it has nothing to do with the body, nothing to do with man's physical relationships with each other [*ad externam hominum societatem*], but it is concerned wholly with the spirit.[60]

But in 1 Corinthians 11:3, Paul reasons respecting outward propriety, not wishing to 'disturb civil order [*civilem ordinem*]'.

> Therefore, so far as spiritual union [*ad spiritualem coniunctionem*] is concerned, in the eyes of God, and inwardly in their conscience, Christ is the head of the man and woman without distinction, because in the spiritual realm, no consideration is given to male or female. On the other hand, as far as external connections and social

---

[60] *Comm. 1 Cor.* 11:3 (CO 49.474; *CNTC*, 9.229). In his sermon on the same passage, Calvin says, 'To be a child of God, ruled by his Holy Spirit and a participant in inheriting the Kingdom of Heaven, to pray to God, to be baptized, to come to the Lord's Supper – in none of these things are we permitted to distinguish between males and females...' (*Serm. 1 Cor.* 11:2-3 (CO 49.718-9)).

propriety are concerned, the male takes the lead from Christ, and the woman from the man, *so that they do not stand on the same level, but this inequality exists.*[61]

There are no references in Calvin to any direct societal application of Galatians 3:28, certainly not in the way that revisionists would wish to see. Perhaps the nearest he comes to it is in a sermon from his series on Deuteronomy where he uses the text to show that, because there are no distinctions in Christ, those in the lower ranks of the temporal hierarchies (including wives)[62] must not be abused. Yet, we notice, they remain in the lower ranks, of course.[63] The Reformer certainly employs the verse (together with v.27) in religious contexts,[64] showing its biblical emphasis, but rejecting any ethical implication of the text.

What this reveals to us is that the prism through which contemporary liberationists read biblical sexual and familial ethics is virtually of only theological and religious significance to Calvin. As he states it, the gospel did not come to change the common, social, and temporal relationships between people – including that between husband and wife. Indeed, for Calvin, as much as for Luther, social levelling in any concrete form is actually *wrong* and, therefore, *impermissible.*[65] The question naturally arises: Why is

---

[61] *Comm. 1 Cor.* 11:3 (CO 49.474; *CNTC,* 9.230) – emphasis added.

[62] It should be noticed, here, that Calvin speaks not only of *wives* in lower relational positions to husbands, but of *women to men.* His sermon on the passage makes this clear: 'Paul is not speaking here of individual persons, nor of an individual household. Rather he divides the human race into two parts. ... Thus there is the male and the female. I say this for the benefit of any unmarried man, lest he at any time abandon his privilege by nature, namely that he is the head. Of whom? Of women, for we must not pay attention to this only within a household, *but within the whole order that God has established in this world.* ... [A]s I have already said, this passage is not speaking of the individual person in particular, but of the whole sex inclusively' (*Serm. 1 Cor.* 11:4-10 (CO 49.730) – de Boer's translation, art. cit., 244, emphasis added).

[63] *Serm. Deut.* 5:13-15 (CO 26.295-308). It is probable that Calvin alludes to the verse in a similar way at other times in his sermons – for example, *Serm. Deut.* 15:16-23 (CO 27.350-64); 23:18-20 (CO 28.111-24).

[64] See, for example, *Concerning the Eternal Predestination of God* (James Clarke, Cambridge, 1982), 129; *Dilucida Explicatio,* in *LCC* 22, 278, 317; *Comm. Matt.* 22:11 (CO 45.401); *Comm. John* 20:22 (CO 47.438); *Comm Rom.* 6:4 (CO 49.105); 13:13 (CO 49.256); *Serm. Deut.* 20:10-18 (CO 27.616-28).

[65] *Serm. Eph.* 6:5-9 (CO 51.798). This judgement is the more remarkable for it surfaces in the context of Calvin's exposition of slavery in the New Testament and is

social equality, in any concrete way, not a *desideratum* for the Reformer? The answer, in part, is related to his concept of the causal connection between sin, its preponderance, and social disorder, to which we now turn.

THE PRESERVATION OF ORDER

Sin, Disorder and Social Peace

We have observed that Calvin's theology appears obsessed with the concept of order. Further, we have argued that Calvin employs the idea of order as a determinative factor in his understanding of social relationships. These are necessarily hierarchical. The defensive tenacity with which the Reformer holds on to this principle now causes us to examine the threat that he sees posed by sin to the order which he wishes to defend and maintain. This is necessary so that his understanding of marriage as a vocation can be seen in the context of its pragmatic purpose.

It is significant that when Calvin analyses the Fall he frequently does so in terms of the entrance of disorder into the world.[66] That is, he describes mankind's rebellion as introducing the forces of disorder that invade the world, overturning, perverting or destroying the very order of nature – the physical elements, mankind and, inevitably, society.[67] The Fall is overtly hostile to order of any kind. Consequently, Calvin speaks of it as 'the collapse of *the legitimate order* of nature'.[68] The opposition between order and *confusio*, thus, becomes a characteristic of the Reformer's thinking. In this sense, Monheit says that Calvin identifies vice 'with turbulent, disordered and unbounded passions, and opposes

---

given as a reason why the apostle left servitude untouched and did not advocate the manumission of slaves.

[66] *Serm. Eph* 6:5-9 (CO 51.798) – It is one of *'les fruits de la desobeissance et du peché de pere Adam'*.

[67] *Comm. Gen.* 3:1 (CO 23.55). Interestingly, Milner, op. cit., 37, states that when Calvin uses words like 'destruction' of the Fall, 'such language more nearly conveys his own feeling for the drastic nature of the occurrence than it provides a precise analysis'.

[68] *Comm. Ps.* 8:8-10 (CO 31.94-5) – emphasis added. See also, *Comm. Rom.* 8:21 (CO 49.153).

them to virtuous emotions that are calm, steady and ordered...'.[69] Part of this characteristic is the fact that Calvin uses the vocabulary of order/disorder regarding righteousness and sin, even though, as Bouwsma points out, this vocabulary is largely alien to biblical ideas.[70] Consequently, sin becomes almost synonymous with unrestraint and is related to the resultant social disorder and righteousness is virtually equated with control and related to subsequent order.[71]

As we have previously observed humanity is central to Calvin's scheme of things. After the Fall the consequences of rebellion are felt, not only by humanity itself, but throughout nature and society. On the one hand, that is personally, this is attested by the consequent disordering of the soul and the corresponding loss of spiritual understanding and relationship to God. People retain reason, but lose the soundness of mind and uprightness, which were theirs at creation.[72] It is true, of course, that Calvin has a concept of the continuing activity of the mind and will in fallen humanity; but, post-Fall, they cannot now move towards the good. Indeed, they are disposed towards sin.[73]

The imprisonment has at least two implications – both are of significance to the present study. First, as a consequence of Adam's rebellion, a person's whole nature is permeated by sin. Such is the corruption of humankind that sin clings to every part without exception.[74] Second, because the nature of mankind must show in their behaviour, Calvin emphasizes that sin (or,

---

[69] Monheit, art. cit., 278. See also, Milner, op. cit., 18. See, for instance, *Inst* I.xi.4; *Comm. Gen.* 3:1 (CO 23.52); *Comm. Jer.* 5:25 (CO 37.635); *Comm. Isa.* 3:5 (CO 36.83).

[70] See Bouwsma, op. cit., 34. He adds, by way of possible explanation, that 'confusion, unlike sin, can be remedied, at least symbolically, by various ordering devices at human disposal'. See *Comm. Isa.* 51:16 (CO 31.236); *Comm Jer.* 5:25 (CO 37.635); 18:1-6 (CO 38.293); *Comm Ps.* 30:6 (CO 31.294); 57:2 (CO 31.554).

[71] Bouwsma, op. cit., 35-6. See *Comm. Isa.* 3:24 (CO 36.93); *Comm. Acts* 28:6 (CO 48.561); *Comm. Ps.* 94:4 (CO 32.19); *Comm Jer.* 21:1 (CO 38.357); 32:16-18 (CO 38.387-90).

[72] The contrast, in Calvin, is not between faith and reason, but between faithful and unfaithful reasoning. See R. J. Mouw, *The God Who Commands* (University of Notre Dame Press, Notre Dame, 1990), 68-9.

[73] See *Inst* I.ii.1, I.v.4, II.ii.12, II.iii.5, II.xiv. See also, Schreiner, op. cit., 70; G. Harkness, *John Calvin. The Man and his Ethics* (Abingdon, New York, 1981), 79-80, 88.

[74] See *Inst* II.i.8-9, II.ii.12-17, II.iii.1-5, II.viii.1, IV.xv.10; *Comm. Gen.* 1:26 (CO 23.25); 3:1 (CO 23.52); *Comm. Ps.* 51:5 (CO 31.510); *Comm. Lev.* 12:1-2 (CO 24.312); *Comm. Rom.* 1:18 (CO 49.29); *Comm. Gal.* 1:4 (CO 50.170); *Comm. Col.* 1:20 (CO 52.88).

at least, sinfulness) is now, post-Fall, a constituent of every activity of men and women. Indeed, it is a governing factor in that activity because of the postlapsarian convergence of sin and the active nature of men and women as God created them. In other words, because humanity is now inherently active *and* sinful, they will necessarily show that sin by their actions. Moreover, Calvin teaches that, because of men and women's sinful nature, they are inclined to (even, impelled towards) evil.[75]

The postfallen sinfulness of people is typically depicted as immoderately expressed.[76] The Reformer speaks of 'those bold and *unbridled* impulses which *contend against God's control*.[77] That is, sinfulness tends towards social disruption and destabilization and, therefore, against the intentions of God, the Creator and the preserver of order. Furthermore, it is important to note that, though the *dominance* of sin is abolished in believers, nevertheless, sin remains. They can do nothing of any worth without the grace of God and the continuing power and help of the Holy Spirit.[78]

In the social sphere, mankind's sinfulness is characterized by moral disorder. That which was created having order has now fallen into moral chaos. Indeed, the Reformer implies that the opposite of the kingdom of God is disorder and confusion.[79] He states of mankind: 'persistent disorder and intemperance threaten, because these inclinations cannot be separated from such lack of restraint'.[80]

---

[75] See *Inst* II.iii.5, IV.xv.11. See also, *Inst* II.i.9, 11, II.iii.4; *Comm. Deut.* 13:7 (CO 24.360); *Comm. Matt.* 15:19 (CO 45.454); *Comm Eph.* 2:1-3 (CO 51.160-3); 4:19 (CO 51.206); 4:22-4 (CO 51.207-10).

[76] '...*quia semper intemperanter diffluat*'(*Comm. 1 John* 2:16 (CO 55.319)). See R. M. Kingdon, 'The Control of Morals in Calvin's Geneva' in L. P. Buck / J. W. Zophy (eds), *The Social History of the Reformation* (Ohio State University, Columbus, 1972), 3-16.

[77] *Inst* III.iii.12 – emphasis added.

[78] The *Institutes* makes this, together with the implication of sin's present potential, very clear. For Calvin, sin remains as a '*smouldering* cinder of evil'. He speaks of that 'inordinate desiring ... contend(ing) against righteousness' and says that every work of the believer is spotted with sin (*Inst* III.iii.10, 12; III.xiv.9). Against this, it is worth noting, however, that Calvin also insists that the Lord is pleased with the good works of believers because the Spirit works in them (*Inst* III.xvii.5).

[79] *Comm. Matt.* 6:10 (CO 45.197).

[80] *Inst* III.iii.12. See also, *Serm. Job* 24:19-25 (CO 34.397-8).

It is within this somewhat pessimistic understanding[81] – that the Reformer roots and establishes his doctrine of societal arrangement and, relevantly to the present study, his teaching on the husband-wife relationship. In this sense, Calvin's social ethics is a reflex response to his own fear of a chaos that continually threatens to engulf the community. Or, at least, his failure to question the accepted doctrine of hierarchicalism can be seen as a result of a greater desire to stabilize things in the society in which he lived. This is evident in Luther's theology, but it becomes more pronounced in Calvin.

In a sermon on Job, the Reformer speaks of the degeneration of society. He says,

> It is true that confusion is constantly increasing ... we must recognize that we are the cause of all the disorders in the world. ... If everyone would try to repress vices and iniquities and if, when there is evil, everyone tried to avoid it, God would certainly bless that response and we would have *a desirable order amongst ourselves*.[82]

Calvin's rather superficial attempt to make his listeners acknowledge their own involvement in the current moral confusion and to see their own responsibility in avoiding it belies his genuine and desperate fear that, if they do not respond, disorder will almost inevitably overrun society. Central to his response is the view of hierarchical arrangement within the society that he wishes to defend. So, he says, for instance, that mankind *could not continue* without hierarchical order. Indeed, according to Calvin, God preserves rank and the diversity of degrees in society in order that people might *survive*.[83] Therefore, more specifically, magistrates and judges (within their vocations) have been given the task to keep civil order and peace; husbands and wives (within their

---

[81] 'Calvin's dark vision of the contemporary world' (Bouwsma, op. cit., 63). See also, A. Biéler, *L'Humanisme Social de Calvin* (Labor et Fides, Geneva, 1961), 13-21; A. E. McGrath, *A Life of John Calvin* (Blackwell, Oxford, 1993), 43-7; idem, 'John Calvin and Late Medieval Thought. A Study in Late Medieval Influences upon Calvin's Theological Development', *ARG* 77 (1986), 58-79.

[82] *Serm. Job* 24:19-25 (CO 34.400) – Bouwsma's translation, emphasis added. See also, *Comm. Jer.* 31:22 (CO 38.678); *Comm. Ps.* 127 (CO 32.322).

[83] See *Serm. Gal.* 3:26-9 (CO 50.568). Also, *Comm. Isa.* 24:2 (CO 36.400); *Comm. 1 Cor.* 11:3 (CO 49.474); *Serm Eph.* 5:28-30 (CO 51.759-72); 6:1-4 (CO 51.787); *Serm. 2 Sam.* 4:5-12 [Kelly, 154-68].

vocations) to maintain familial order.[84] These are some of what Lehmann calls 'the providential and legal arrangements which God has ordained to check the anarchy and destructiveness of sin pending the slow and painful transformation of nature...'.[85] However, the Reformer's position is put in the following succinct way:

> Therefore, in summary, let us carefully note that *we cannot live together* here unless this order which God has established is holily kept, that is, unless we esteem and honour all those who possess authority [*superiorité*]. Without that, there would be one horrible confusion.[86]

For the purposes of the present study, the reference to the 'horrible confusion' can be clearly illustrated by reference to what Calvin says in this context concerning marriage and its violation. So, for instance, he places great weight on the continuance of marriage as a safeguard against moral and social disintegration. He says that God established marriage, 'in order to rid the world of *confusion*', and that, conversely, 'when the bond of marriage is broken ... the whole human society sinks into decay'.[87] For the Reformer, any violation of this important institution is worthy of divine vengeance,[88] for if marriage is destroyed, everything will end in anarchy.

It is small wonder, then, that in seeking to maintain a safe *status quo* within the community, Calvin is careful not to give any impression, whatever, that the normal patterns of societal life are open to change, modification, or even questioning. Firmly rooted

---

[84] *Serm. Deut.* 22:13-24 (CO 28.50).

[85] Lehmann, op. cit., 134. C. J. Vos, 'Calvin's View of Man in the Light of Gen. 2:15 or, Man: Earth's Servant or Lord' in A. J. van Rooy (ed.), *Calvinus Reformator* (University for Christian Higher Education, Potchefstroom, 1982), 139, is correct in saying that Calvin 'saw that the cohesiveness of society *does not lie* in well-defined tables of organization which include the mechanisms of enforcement' (emphasis added). He stresses that the cohesive nature of society comes from relationship. However, Calvin moves into discussion of mutual rule and reciprocity only after he has laid the ground-rules and established the necessity for the structures in which that reciprocity can flourish. This is why we are outlining the structures and their role in his view of an ordered society before reflecting on Calvin's teaching on the husband-wife relationship.

[86] *Serm. Deut.* 5:16 (Farley, 139) – emphasis added.

[87] *Serm. Deut.* 22:13-24 (CO 28.48-9); *Comm. Gen.* 31:50 (CO 23.433), respectively.

[88] See *Comm. Gen.* 26:16 (CO 23.362-3).

within this context is his fear of the threat of sin, disorder and social chaos – a threat that might be at least partially fulfilled, for example, if marriage is too lightly considered, or if the hierarchical arrangement is altered. In this, Calvin largely maintains a medieval notion of the world's order: it is natural, static, and it includes the existing and observable social structures within God's temporal ordering.[89] Thus, as Milner points out, the phrase *ordo politicus* becomes both descriptive of what things presently are, and normative with the connotation of how things ought to be and ought to remain.[90]

Although the conclusion to this present chapter will need to state this in more detail, it is worth noting at this point that the conclusion that Calvin leaves room for modification or change in the status of women in relation to men (and, specifically, wives in relation to their husbands) is unlikely. Not only are social relationships essentially an area of inequality, but also (as we have argued), Calvin holds to this view against a fear of this particular structural realm being destroyed by the dominance of sin in all levels of society. For Calvin to loosen his own perception of things would have taken a great deal more freedom and a great deal less defensiveness than he appears to have had at his disposal. As we now turn to his idea of vocation within the context of restraining the sinful tendencies of society, and then to the restoration of order in Christ's activity through the Spirit this will be further underlined.

The Individual's Responsibility – to Preserve Order

In examining Luther's teaching on vocation we noted that he stresses the horizontal relationship and its God-given utilitarian purpose of maintaining peace in the community. For him, vocation is the particularization of God's temporal government in the life of an individual. Calvin's idea of vocation is similar, but it seems to stem more naturally from the concept of God's initial spiritual calling of the person. It is most often employed with reference to the divine choosing of the elect. Indeed, McGrath emphasizes that Calvin's view of social *vocatio* is that it is inherently entailed in God's election to salvation. In Calvin's theology, *vocatio* 'expresses

---

[89] See McGrath, op. cit., 74-5.
[90] Milner, op. cit., 29.

primarily the fact that an individual has been elected by God, and only secondarily the worldly vocation (*un vocation juste et approuvée*) in which this calling finds expression'.[91] Calvin's emphasis falls heavily upon the idea of keeping practical, societal and familial order.

This is seen most clearly in the *Institutes*, Book three. Calvin stresses that the object of regeneration in believers is to confirm their adoption by living 'a rightly ordered life' [vi.1]. In the next two chapters, Calvin spells out that this pattern for the conduct of life (*Rationem vitae formande*) is to be modelled on God, himself [vi.2-3]. Later, the Reformer comes to the point at which he emphasizes that the Christian's life is to be a reflection of the calling he has received:

> [H]e [God] has appointed duties for every man in his particular way of life. And that no-one may thoughtlessly transgress his limits, he has named these various kinds of living 'callings'.[92]

He applies this initially to magistrates and then to heads of households, both of whom will confine themselves to their own duties, bearing with all the troubles involved because 'the burden was laid upon [them] by God'.

> [N]o task will be so sordid and base, provided you obey your calling in it, that it will not shine and be reckoned very precious in God's sight.[93]

Calvin's definition of 'calling' is revealing within this context. He says, 'We call vocation the duty to which God binds us.'[94] Elsewhere, he speaks of vocation as 'a lawful mode of life'[95] and, again, the sense of duty pervades his understanding. An integral link between 'vocation' as God's election to spiritual life and

---

[91] McGrath, op. cit., 251-2. (also, 241-2). See also, Harkness, op. cit., chapters 8-10; *Inst* III.ix.4. Also, G. D. Badcock, *The Way of Life: A Theology of Christian Vocation* (Eerdmans, Grand Rapids, 1998), 55-6.

[92] *Inst* III.x.6.

[93] Ibid. This is reminiscent of Luther, of course; but it lacks something of that Reformer's natural and theological warmth and exuberance. See, for example, LW 45.39-41 [WA 10².295-7].

[94] *Serm. 2 Sam.* 6:6-12 [Kelly, 246].

[95] '...*vocatio in scripturis est legitima vivendi ratio*' (*Comm. 1 Cor.* 7:20 (CO 49.415)).

'vocation' as the outworking of that life in society is established by Calvin in that way. For instance, he concludes explicitly in his commentary on 2 Peter 1:10, '[I]t is one proof that we have been really elected ... if a good conscience and integrity of life *correspond with* our profession of faith.'[96]

Apart from the fact that Calvin, characteristically, insists that it is God who calls men and women to vocation, there is clearly a twofold emphasis that seems to underline his thought. First, vocation is a duty for people to perform; second, vocation is that to which God 'binds' men and women. These two ideas are related to the fact that the Reformer defines and uses 'calling'/'vocation' with the purpose of stabilizing the social order. For instance, he says,

> The Lord bids each one of us in all life's actions to look to his calling. For he knows with what great restlessness human nature flames, with what fickleness it is borne hither and thither, how its ambition longs to embrace various things at once. Therefore, lest through our stupidity and rashness everything is turned topsy-turvy, he has appointed duties for every man in his particular way of life. And that no-one may thoughtlessly transgress his limits, he has named these various kinds of living 'callings'. *Therefore, each individual has his own kind of living assigned to him by the Lord as a sort of sentry post so that he may not heedlessly wander about throughout life.*[97]

Here we have two of the main characteristics: humanity's sinfulness tending towards individual and subsequently social instability, together with the divine appointment of vocations in which each person is kept under control and within limits. Consequently, one of the Reformer's constant applications is that everyone must persevere within the calling given to them by God.[98] Another persistent application is that men and women must not overstep the boundary lines of their particular vocation. Here,

---

[96] *Comm. 2 Pet.* 1:10 (CO 55.449) – emphasis added. *CNTC,* 12.333, translates the last comment: 'our profession of faith *should find its response* in a good conscience and an upright life' – emphasis added. Calvin says that the apostle 'uses "calling" here in the sense of result or evidence of election' (ibid.). See also, *Inst* III.xiv.19-20, III.xvii.1, 4-5, III.xxiv.4; *Comm. Matt.* 25:24 (CO 45.570).

[97] *Inst* III.x.6 – emphasis added.

[98] See, for example, *Serm. 2 Sam.* 5:6-12 [Kelly, 198]; *Comm. Col.* 3:18 (CO 52.125). See also, Fuchs, op. cit., 83.

Calvin certainly seems aware that some might positively advocate going beyond or even redefining the limits of vocation. So, on preaching about the story of the ill-fated Uzzah reaching out to steady the ark of God and his subsequent death, for example, he applies the particular situation in a general principle (as he almost invariably does):

> Let us note that we must undertake nothing outside of our vocation. For what might seem a virtue to us will be considered vice before God *if we go beyond our limits*.[99]

Later, he locates the reason behind people assuming to go beyond their vocation as that of pride. Therefore, he exhorts his congregation in the following way,

> In sum, *let us be modest enough* to pay attention to that to which God calls us, which he strictly requires from us and which belongs to our office. Let everyone openly devote himself to it, so that we will not go beyond our boundaries *like wild horses*.[100]

The latter italicized phrase is an important simile, giving the sense that it is a person's pride which leads to being out of control. Part of the remedy for this pride and, therefore, part of the maintenance of social order is to foster modesty and humility (*modestia et humilitate*)[101] and to live in moderation (*moderatio*) within one's calling. It is this self-control that Bouwsma terms a component of Calvin's 'boundary maintenance in the realm of ethics'.[102] In a sense, this is part of the inner boundary, the self-imposed restrictions of a believer within his calling. There are external boundaries, as well, such as the implied threat of the judgement of God in the history of Uzzah's death. This is an implication from which he does not shy away, employing it elsewhere in order to

---

[99] *Serm. 2 Sam.* 6:1-12 [Kelly, 246] – emphasis added.

[100] Ibid.; emphases added. Elsewhere, he speaks of those who exalt themselves within their callings as being 'inflated with arrogance' and as refusing to turn to God – *Comm. Ps.* 127 (CO 32.322).

[101] See *Catechismus Ecclesiae Genevensis* (OS 2.104). Here, Calvin initially applies the terms 'modesty and humility' to parents, but then he widens the application to apply to all within vocation.

[102] Bouwsma, op. cit., 89; see 88-9.

further encourage his hearers to conform to the standards that he considers set by vocation.[103]

Calvin defines the way the community is divided into 'so many yokes' in vocational terms. That is, each 'yoke' entails two mutually-obligated callings; for example, within the household, the husband and wife, the parents and children, the masters and servants.[104] In doing this, he asserts the vocational nature of marriage[105] and therefore Calvin speaks of the hierarchical arrangement of marriage not only as *'l'ordre naturel'*, but also as *'l'ordre de Dieu'*. In doing this he sets up the boundary that must be respected. Thus, for instance, for the wife to argue against this arrangement is to complain against God, not against the husband. Though out of biblical context, Calvin employs the imagery of God being the potter and of men and women being the clay. Because this is so manifestly the case, he exhorts people (and in this case, women) to be content with the way things are.[106] Indeed, the obedience of wives to their husbands 'forms a part of civil or social subjection'.[107] Again, though he is clear that men and women are, for various reasons, disinclined to shoulder their responsibilities, it remains the vocational duty of the wife, for instance, to do the housework – this is her obligation and a sacrifice that is acceptable to God. Likewise, the Reformer speaks of 'the duty of motherhood'.[108]

Calvin's application that people should retain modesty within their vocation, more often than not comes to the person in the lower hierarchical position, as Stauffer has pointed out.[109] Therefore, it comes to the wife more often than it does to the husband. In his comments on Genesis 18, for instance, Calvin singles out Sarah as an example of *modestia*. Part and parcel of it is her respect and obedience to her husband. Sarah's example shows

---

[103] *Serm. Job* 31:9-15 (CO 34.660) – Calvin persuades people to persevere in following their vocation and adds that in so doing everyone would glorify God, 'the great Lord and Master, who is the common Judge of all [*qui est le Iuge common de tous*].'

[104] *Comm. Eph.* 5:22-4 (CO 51.222) – '*Porro oeconomia tribus quasi iugis constat, in quibus mutua est partium obligatio.*'

[105] See, for example, *Comm. Matt.* 19:11 (CO 45.533); *Inst* II.viii.42, III.x.6; *Comm. 1 Cor.* 7:20 (CO 49.415).

[106] *Serm. 1 Tim.* 2:12-14 (CO 53.211, 212).

[107] '*...partes sunt subiectiones politicae*' (*Comm. 1 Pet.* 2:13 (CO 55.247)).

[108] See *Serm. 2 Sam.* 6:1-7 [Kelly, 239]; *Serm. Deut.* 5:18 (CO 26.345); *Serm. 1 Tim.* 2:13-15 (CO 53.228-9); *Comm. 1 Cor.* 7:20 (CO 49.415).

[109] R. Stauffer, 'Un Calvin inconnu: le prédicateur de Genève', *BHPF* 4 (1978), 197.

that other women should be obedient and towards their own husbands. 'Many women, indeed, without difficulty, give their husbands this title ["lord"], when yet they do not scruple to bring them under rule, by their imperious pride.'[110]

Because the application pivots about the use of the word 'lord', it is clear that modesty, from the wife's perspective in the marital context, includes accepting the limits of her own *vocatio* and acquiescing in the hierarchical assumptions of Calvin's theology. In another place, the Reformer speaks, more strongly, of modesty as including the wife yielding to her husband's commands.[111] This, for Calvin, is simply part of the natural order of things; an order being presently restored by Christ in and through his people.

The Restoration of Order through Christ

We have observed that, for Calvin, order is precarious to say the least. On the one hand, it is entirely contingent on the direct and effectual, providential activity of God for its continuance. On the other hand, order is substantially threatened by the forces of sin and disorder in society. In the midst of this overall context, believers seek by faith to maintain order, largely through the stability of their calling – within which they need to persevere and restrict themselves. We noted that marriage is one of these restrictive, stabilizing vocations in society. However, this is not the whole story – there is a dynamic element to Calvin's understanding of order and this comes in trinitarian activity, but predominantly in the person and the eschatological work of Christ.[112] As Schreiner puts it, 'Not surprisingly, Calvin saw [the] reconstitution or "renovation of the world" (Acts 3:21) as a restoration to order.'[113] Thus, he teaches that all things are going to be restored to order by God,[114] through the means of the gospel,[115] progressively and

---

[110] *Comm. Gen.* 18:2 (CO 23.253).

[111] *Comm. Matt.* 19:5 (CO 45.529). See also, *Serm. Tit.* 2:3-5 (CO 54.511).

[112] Butin, op. cit., 68, rightly insists, 'The Christological centre of Calvin's doctrine of the restoration of the divine image in human beings is firmly set within a more comprehensively trinitarian matrix that renders possible the application of the divine pattern in Christ to the rest of humanity' (see 67-9).

[113] Schreiner, op. cit., 108.

[114] See *Comm Eph.* 1:10 (CO 51.151); 5:30 (CO 51.225-6); *Serm. Eph.* 1:10 (CO 51.283-96); *Comm. 1 Cor.* 15:21-2 (CO 49.545-6).

[115] *Comm. Acts* 15:16 (CO 48.355); *Comm. Isa.* 2:4 (CO 36.64).

gradually,[116] through the work of the Spirit of Christ. This restoration of a lost order is said to be God's purpose in redemption and sanctification through Christ's humiliation and exaltation.[117]

In the present, everything is brought back to 'a fixed order by Christ'.[118] However, in terms of its future reference, this is significant for the believer's present faith and hope, within the context of the social disorder and chaos threatened and caused by sin:

> If, therefore, at the present time we see much confusion in the world, let us lift up our hearts and be revived by the hope that Christ shall one day come and restore all things.[119]

This exhortation is firmly based on the belief that all will be 'restored to the legitimate order [*legitimum ordinem*]' at the Second Coming of Christ.[120] This, then, is the grand, teleological perspective of Calvin's theology of order. Christocentricity is a major factor in his indicative thinking, but it is also a familiar theme in the Reformer's moral imperatives – for it is in Christ, alone, that the new humanity is created.

In Christ, believers become part of the restoration of order.[121] This is so on two accounts. First, it is so because of the restoration of order through the renewal of the image of God in the believer. Second, it is so because the renewal of the image results

---

[116] *Comm. 2 Cor.* 3:18 (CO 50.46); *Comm. 1 Cor.* 15:49 (CO 560); *Comm. Gen.* 1:26 (CO 23.25); *Inst* I.xv.4.

[117] *Comm. 1 Cor.* 11:4 (CO 49.475); *Inst* I.xv.4. See also, *Comm Gen.* 3:6 (CO 23.59); 3:22 (CO 23.78); *Comm Ps.* 2:4 (CO 31.44); 8:5 (CO 31.91); *Comm. Dan.* 7:17-18 (CO 41.65-8); *Comm. Rom.* 8:21 (CO 49.153); *Comm. Matt.* 10:37 (CO 45.293); *Inst* II.ii.27; *Serm Eph.* 3:9-12 (CO 51.459-74); 4:23-26 (CO 51.617-30).

[118] *Comm. Eph.* 1:10 (CO 51.151). See also, *Serm. Gal.* 3:26-29 (CO 50.568). The Reformer does not elaborate here on *when* this was established by God – whether at creation or at the Fall (as a result of or in response to Adam's rebellion). Elsewhere, however, Calvin says that Christ brings 'everything to its state and order ... to its first origin [*primam originem*]' (*Comm. Isa.* 65:25 (CO 37.434)).

[119] *Comm. Acts* 3:21 (CO 48.72-3; *CNTC*, 6.103). Significantly, Calvin (speaking in what has become the 'already/notyet' dichotomy of theological thought) had already stated that Christ *has restored* all things, 'as far as the power to achieve this and the cause of it are concerned; but the effect of it is not yet fully seen, therefore that restoration is still in process of completion, and so too our redemption' (ibid.).

[120] *Comm. John* 12:31 (CO 47.293).

[121] Doyle, op. cit., 325, 349.

in the restoration of order in society, largely, through the establishment and preservation of the community of renewed men and women – that is, the church. These two ideas need to be outlined together at this point in order to understand the movement of the Reformer's thought.

Renewal of the *Imago Dei*

Calvin connects the idea of the restoration of the original order to that of the image of God in humanity as part of his doctrine of sanctification. He states that,

> Adam was at first created in the image of God, so that he might reflect, as in a mirror, the righteousness of God. But the image, having been wiped out by sin, must now be restored in Christ. *The regeneration of the godly is indeed ... nothing else than the reformation of the image of God in them.*[122]

However, the question of what the phrase *imago Dei* represents in Calvin's theology has a long history and its answer is not unimportant to the present study, which understands it to be defined in a comprehensive way,[123] with reference to relationship, order and a resultant stability.

First, we notice that Calvin suggests that the image is, somehow, still to be found in everyone:

> If it is objected, that the image of God in human nature [*Dei imaginem in humana natura*] was removed by the sin of Adam; we must admit

---

[122] *Comm. Eph.* 4:24 (CO 51.208; *CNTC*, 11.191) – emphasis added. Also, *Inst* I.xv.4, III.vi.3; *Comm. John* 17:11 (CO 47.381). For Calvin, sanctification is the gradual restoration of order in the soul or the renewal of the *imago Dei* in regenerate man – see *Comm. Col.* 3:10 (CO 52.121); *Comm. 1 Cor.* 15:44-50 (CO 49.559-60). See also, Wallace, op. cit., 106-7; Richard, op. cit., 111-16.

[123] Recently, scholars have stressed the comprehensiveness of the term, rather than polarising to the relational or the facultative aspects – that is, everything and anything (including relationship with God) that sets humanity apart from the rest of God's creation is, in this sense, part or reflective of the *imago Dei*. See B. A. Gerrish, *The Old Protestantism and the New* (T&T Clark, Edinburgh, 1982), 150-59; idem, 'The Mirror of God's Goodness: Man in the Theology of Calvin', *CTQ* 45 (1981), 211-22; T. F. Torrance, *Calvin's Doctrine of Man* (Lutterworth, London, 1949), 36, 71; Thompson, op. cit., 65-107. See also, Richard, op. cit., 112; Prins, art. cit., 33; Douglass, op. cit., 25.

that it was sadly deformed [*misere deformatam*], yet in such a way that certain lineaments of it still appear.[124]

Though he does not say exactly what *does* remain, he speaks of righteousness (*justitia*), moral uprightness (*rectitudo*) and the freedom of choosing what is good as having been lost. Having related the *imago Dei* to mankind's original participation in God,[125] Calvin visualizes this as lost and with that loss comes slavery to sin, the inability to serve God and, as previously noted, a resultant personal and social disorder.

Second, we note that there are two dogmatic foci for the Reformer's thinking – the original creation and, taking precedence, the person of Jesus Christ in whom the image is being restored. Calvin insists that the way we know anything of the image is by comprehending that which is being restored in us through the gospel, by Christ.[126] Wallace, helpfully, puts this into societal terms: 'Calvin believed that what happens when humanity is redeemed in Christ gives us a true picture of what was meant to happen originally in society in its natural form. For grace always tends to reveal and restore the original form of nature.'[127] However, it is clear that the individual takes priority (at least, chronologically) at this point in Calvin's thought and that society's restoration is a consequence of the social nature of men and women, restored in Christ.[128] Hall suggests that, 'The true importance of man's original perfection for Calvin becomes clear when he equates it with the *imago Dei* in man. ... For man to reflect the glory of God, to be in the *imago Dei*, then, really means for man

---

[124] *Comm. Jas* 3:9 (CO 55.411; *CNTC*, 3.292). He continues, 'Righteousness, equity, the freedom to seek after good, these things have gone; but many gifts are left to us, by which we are superior to beasts.'

[125] *Inst* II.ii.1.

[126] See, for example, *Inst* I.xv.4, II.xii.6-7, III.iii.9; *Comm. Col.* 3:10 (CO 52.121); *Comm. 1 Cor.* 11:7 (CO 49.476); *Serm. 1 Cor.* 11:11-16 (CO 49.737-50); *Comm. Gen.* 1:26 (CO 23.25).

[127] R. S. Wallace, *Calvin, Geneva and the Reformation* (Scottish Academic Press, Edinburgh, 1988), 117.

[128] This is the equivalent of Luther's doctrine, of course. We noticed in the previous chapter that for Luther the primary denotation of the *imago Dei* is relationship to God, with its consequent holiness of life. Similarly for Calvin its restoration, internally, is characterized by integrity and the right ordering of the soul and, externally, by peace and the proper ordering of society in general. This reflects conventional and Augustinian teaching.

to live wholly in accordance with the order of God, in right relationship with God and all of creation.'[129]

Third, if men and women are personally renewed, by Christ, then social relationships and peace will flourish and society will gradually be restored to order. That is, an ordered individual life necessarily contributes to the gradual restoration of an ordered community. This is so because the image of God expresses itself through order, which is not something static and engraved *on* people, but is expressed dynamically *by* them. This is in relation to themselves, in relation to the household and in service to others[130] – living in thankful response to God's grace in Christ. This inevitably takes place in the church, which becomes 'the embryo of an entirely new world'[131] where relationships go back to the original purpose, order and design of God. This nascent society is an ordered one, which seeks to combat the destructive forces within mankind and society.

Finally, Calvin builds his social ethics (including his teaching on marriage) partly on the continuance and restoration of the image of God in people because, in that restoration, they are being returned to the nature that God intended – a nature that endures in remnant-form in everyone. Calvin bases this, largely, on two texts, Genesis 2:18 and Romans 2:14-15. From the former, depicting the social nature of mankind, he deduces that natural law (*lex naturae*) and reason are inherently theirs by creation:

> [S]ince man is by nature a social animal, he tends through instinct to foster and preserve society. Consequently, we observe that there

---

[129] Hall, op. cit., 48-9, respectively.

[130] See *Serm. 1 Tim.* 3:3-5 (CO 53.271-82); *Comm. Gen.* 2:18 (CO 23.46). In the context of the restoration of society, Biéler, *L'Humanisme Social de Calvin*, 94, stresses that, 'L'éthique sociale du Reformateur est une éthique dynamique.'

[131] Biéler, op. cit., 23. He further stresses that Calvin does not so much envisage the restoration of mere individuals but, rather, the restoration of society 'in the diverse forms of its existence' (26). See also, Milner, op. cit., 46-70, on the restoration of order through the establishment and preservation of the church. His later conclusion is worth quoting: '[T]he conception of the church as the restoration of order in the world means that the church cannot be thought of apart from the world, or as a secure corner of redemption in it. That is so, because the order which is being restored in the church is nothing else than the restoration of the *imago Dei* in man, and the three spheres of order are interrelated. The restoration of man will thus entail the restoration of order in the world' (195).

exist in all men's minds universal impressions of a certain fair dealing and order.[132]

From the latter, the Reformer reasons that every nation knows basic laws within which they limit themselves and that there is an inward law,[133] 'a natural light of righteousness', or, at least, preconceptions (προλήψεις) implanted within the hearts of men.[134] Calvin draws two conclusions from this: first, although natural law only affords a faint idea of what God requires, everyone can distinguish sufficiently between right and wrong for a basic conduct in life and, second, no-one is without excuse before God.[135]

Restoration, Natural Law and Natural Order

We previously noted that Luther held to a similar understanding of natural law and, in the same way, the concept of natural law is part of what Calvin understands as *ordo naturae*, given at creation.[136] Although Lang overstates his position in saying that, for Calvin, natural law had 'almost no importance at all', it is true to say that his doctrine is imprecise.[137] It remains of secondary importance. His doctrines of Scripture as externally normative and of the renovation of men and women in the image of God necessitate this. Nevertheless, he speaks of the primal knowledge to which the order of nature would have led if Adam had retained his original position before God.[138] This remains in everyone in remnant form.

---

[132] *Inst* II.ii.13.

[133] '...dictat lex illa interior' (*Inst* II.viii.1).

[134] *Comm. Rom.* 2:14-15 (CO 49.37).

[135] *Inst* II.viii.1, II.ii.22, respectively. See also, *Inst* I.v.5, III.xix.15, IV.x.3; *Comm. Deut.* 5:18 / *Exod.* 20:14 (CO 24.261); *Comm. Deut.* 13:6 (CO 24.359).

[136] Luther's teaching is found throughout his writing, but see particularly, LW 49.411 [WA Br 5.574]; *Comm. Ps.* 111:3, LW 13.369 [WA 31¹.409-10]; *Comm. John* 15:5, LW 24.228 [WA 45.669]. Bohatec, op. cit., 4, says that natural law indicates 'the laws which rule and condition actual being and occurrences in the universe ... as well as *the unalterable necessities of social and political life*' (emphasis added).

[137] A. Lang, 'The Reformation and Natural Law' in W. P. Armstrong (ed.), *Calvin and the Reformation* (Baker, Grand Rapids, 1980), 56-98, particularly 72. See also, Schreiner, op. cit., 73-9, who sees the Reformer as exploring society by means of his doctrine – not so much proposing a doctrine of natural law, but rather using it (as an extension of his doctrine of providence) 'as a way to explain the continuation of society after the devastating effects of the Fall' (79).

[138] See *Inst* I.ii-v. Also, *Serm. Job* 31:1-4 (CO 34.631); *Serm. Deut.* 19:14-15 (CO 27.568); *Serm. 1 Tim.* 5:4-5 (CO 53.456).

Thus, in that sense, natural law still has a normative though restricted, value for mankind in Calvin's theology. Now, recreated humanity in Christ has both a natural sense of ethical behaviour and also the objective and normative inscripturated law of God to confirm, to supplement and, in a way, to supersede their own inadequate understanding of what God requires.[139] At times, the Reformer almost identifies the natural law and the divine moral law. The latter then becomes a 'clearer witness' of what remains obscure in the former, which is at times depicted as being nothing else than 'a testimony of natural law and of the conscience – a conscience which God has engraved upon the minds of men'.[140] Bouwsma speaks of the law, in this sense, as 'given to induce God's order into people's living'.[141] Certainly, what *is* central to Calvin's thinking is that God's will comes for mankind's obedience through natural law and/or scripture.

Although we cannot now pursue this in detail, we note that Calvin employs this concept of natural law in his relational ethics. It is sufficient to list some examples to show that if all people (simply by natural law) know an ethical particular to be obvious, then believers certainly have no excuse for not holding to it as prescribed – not *only* by natural reason, but *also* by the direct teaching of Scripture.[142] Calvin teaches that Christians in being restored to the *imago Dei* in Christ have their understanding of God's intention heightened by the Holy Spirit[143] and should conform all the more to his purposes for ordered societal relationships.

---

[139] Gerrish, op. cit., 59, is right to emphasize that, although Calvin apparently has two sources of knowing God and his will, only Scripture is of 'immediate normative importance'.

[140] *Inst* II.viii.1, IV.xx.15, respectively. Also, *Serm. Deut.* 19:14-15 (CO 27.568); *Comm. Ps.* 119:52 (CO 32.236); *Comm. John* 1:5, 9 (CO 47.5, 8). This is traditional thinking – natural law is given written form as its divine formulation. See also, Schreiner, op. cit., 78; Gustafson, op. cit., 166.

[141] Bouwsma, op. cit., 179. See *Comm. Deut.* 11:1 (CO 24.237); *Serm. Deut.* 11:1 (CO 27.72-84); *Comm Luke* 1:6 (CO 45.9); 2:41 (CO 45.105); *Comm. Matt.* 7:1 (CO 45.213); *Comm. Rom.* 7:23 (CO 49.133-4).

[142] The Reformer's logic in this is much the same as Luther's. As we have noticed, Luther holds that the Christian, having a vague sense of right and wrong through natural law, becomes more clear about what God requires of the believer through the renewing activity of God and the further, continuing work of the Holy Spirit.

[143] *Inst* II.i.9, II.ii.27.

According to Calvin, ties between family members are firmly grounded in the law of nature and are universally recognized through natural reason.[144] This is so because *ordinem coniugalem* is a concomitant part of the creational nature of mankind. But Calvin goes further than simply saying, in general terms, that group integrity and cohesiveness is natural. He includes a number of details. For instance, he says that by natural law people know that the hierarchical structure of the family group (*that presently pertains*) accords with the natural order;[145] that a husband has a right *over* his wife;[146] that the place of women is to stay quietly at home;[147] that wives must be obedient to their husbands,[148] being their helpers;[149] that children are under an obligation to parents as 'a perpetual law of nature';[150] that parents must be obeyed;[151] that a couple must be of similar age to get married[152] and that family members should not be suspicious of each other, which in itself would destroy natural order.[153] Any violation of this order is opposed, not only to God's command, but also to nature itself.

The point is that the original bonds within the familial context are engraved in the laws of nature and should, therefore, be understandable by all people – even without the aid of special divine revelation. In this way, natural law should function as an internal restraint which fosters order in society. What is even more important for the present study is that because these things are shown to be within *l'ordre naturel*[154] Calvin asserts them to be inviolable – that is, *unalterable* by men and women.

---

[144] *Comm. 1 Cor.* 7:37 (CO 49.425); *Comm. 1 Tim.* 5:8 (CO 52.309); *Serm. Deut.* 21:18-21 (CO 27.686-7); *Serm Eph.* 5:31-33 (CO 51.774); 6:1-4 (CO 51.788); *Comm. Ps.* 50:20 (CO 31.506).

[145] See *Serm. Gal.* 3:26-29 (CO 50.567); *Comm. Gen.* 2:18 (CO 23.46).

[146] *Comm. Num.* 30:1-17 (CO 24.572).

[147] '...*et natura ipsa dictat*' (*Comm. Gen.* 34:1-19 (CO 23.456)).

[148] *Comm. 1 Pet.* 2:18 (CO 55.247); *Serm. Eph.* 5:31-33 (CO 51.771).

[149] *Comm. Gen.* 2:18 (CO 23.46).

[150] *Comm. Exod.* 20:12 / *Deut.* 5:16 (CO 24.603-4). See also, *Comm. Eph.* 5:31 (CO 51.226).

[151] '[N]ature prescribes and dictates' (*Comm. Gen.* 21:20 (CO 23.305)). Also, *Comm. Jer.* 29:6 (CO 38.586); *Comm. 1 Cor.* 7:36 (CO 49.425); *Serm. Eph.* 6:1-4 (CO 51.787); *Comm. Heb.* 12:9 (CO 55.175).

[152] *Comm. Lev.* 21:13 (CO 24.454).

[153] '...*perverti totum ordinem naturae*' (*Comm. Mic.* 7:5-6 (CO 43.409)).

[154] In his preaching, particularly, Calvin uses the synonyms, *l'ordre de nature, l'ordre de Dieu, Dieu l'ordonne, Dieu ... commande* – see, for example, *Serm. 1 Tim.* 2:12-14 (CO 53.211); *Serm. Tit.* 2:3-5 (CO 54.515-16).

This is particularly clear from the Reformer's commentary on Levitcus 18:6, on the subject of incest. It is significant because he moves from the particular case to the general principle regarding natural law. He says,

> [T]his was part of the political constitution [*ordinis politici*] which God established for his ancient people. ... [W]hatever is prescribed here is deduced from the source of rectitude itself, and *from the natural feelings implanted in us by Him*.[155]

In other words, God commands what is already obligated by natural law: 'What is natural cannot be abrogated by any consent or custom ... [since it] is founded on the general principle of all laws, *which is perpetual and inviolable*.' He continues,

> If this discipline were founded on the utility of a single people, or on the custom of a particular time, or on a present necessity, or on any other circumstances, the laws deduced from it might be abrogated for new reasons, or their observance might be dispensed with in regard to particular persons, by special privileges; but since, in their enactment, the *perpetual decency of nature* was alone regarded, not even a dispensation of them would be permissible.[156]

What is noticeable is the extent to which Calvin strives to emphasize the point. Neither consent, local custom, usefulness, time, nor even momentary necessity is allowed to cancel that which is obvious from natural law and backed up by God's direct command. He further stresses this by stating that even among Gentiles this law was counted as indissoluble, 'as if implanted and engraved on the hearts of men'.

The dictates of natural law are unalterable by men or women, if only because to do away with them would be to jeopardize an essential part of what it means to be human, made in the image of

---

[155] *Comm. Lev.* 18:6 (CO 24.661) – emphasis added: '*ex ipso rectitudinis fonte sensuque nobis divinitus ingenito esse sumptum.*'

[156] Ibid., 662 (emphasis added): '*Si doctrina haec vel in unius populi utilitate, vel in usu certi temporis, vel in praesenti necessitate, vel in aliis circumstantiis fundata esset, abrogari possent leges inde elicitae novis de causis, aut solvi posset earum observatio in certis personis, privilegio singulari: verum quia in illis ferendis tantum spectata fuit perpetua naturae honestas, ne dispensatio quidem esset tolerabilis.*'

God. Inherent to people possessing the *imago Dei* is that they know something (however slight, post-Fall) of the moral requirements of God. Common sense tells us as much.[157] Another reason for their unalterableness is that Calvin rejects the idea of a mere orderliness, in favour of stressing the constancy of God's will within nature.[158]

These are significant points for our study. It has already been shown that among the things that Calvin includes in the necessities of natural law are such specific ideas as the hierarchical arrangement of the husband-wife relationship and the woman's subservient place in the home, which nature itself dictates.

However, it must not be concluded from this that Calvin sought exact uniformity in localized detail and activity. He is well aware that in practice things may vary in form. Yet the umbrella-rule of natural law (now, in renewed human beings, supported by the moral law of God's command) is 'the true and eternal rule of righteousness, prescribed for men of *all nations and times*, who wish to conform their lives to God's will'. God would have natural order 'remain in force to the end of the world'.[159] However, Calvin, reluctantly, allows for exceptions. Thompson concludes that the Reformer shows 'an unusually negative attitude toward exceptional women in the Bible'.[160] He certainly does not allow exceptions if that would mean contravening moral law and he stresses that exceptions are the products of God's activity, not man's long-term or contingency planning.[161]

---

[157] *Comm. Gen.* 1:28 (CO 23.29) – '*illa est naturae quam inviolabilem esse dictat communis sensus.*'

[158] *Inst* I.xvi.3-5.

[159] *Inst* IV.xx.15; *Serm. Eph.* 5:31-3 (CO 51.775), respectively – see also, 771-4.

[160] Thompson, op. cit., 277-8. The Reformer makes this clear, for example, in his comments on Deborah's extraordinary leadership, 'Extraordinary acts done by God do not overturn the ordinary rules of government [*communem politiam*] by which he intended that we should be bound' (*Comm. 1 Tim.* 2:12 (CO 52.276)). He further emphasizes the distinction in his sermon, '[W]e must make a difference between *common order* which God will have to be observed amongst men for a rule [*pour regle*], and that which is done after a strange manner [*d'une façon estrange*], and not usually' (*Serm. 1 Tim.* 2:13-15 (CO 53.221) – emphasis added).

[161] In his commentary on Isaiah he states that the degrees of social pre-eminence are lawful and are not usually set aside (*neque aliter confundi* [thrown into disorder] *solere*), 'unless the Lord determines to chastise his people with dreadful vengeance...' (*Comm. Isa.* 24:1-3 (CO 36.400)).

Thompson's research thesis has clearly demonstrated that Calvin's view of women in exceptional roles is that they *are exceptional* and, in that sense, he stresses both their uniqueness and inimitability.[162] Thompson's handling of that particular subject is entirely adequate and need not be rehearsed here, but it does impinge on our understanding of the Reformer's doctrine of the unchangeableness of what natural law demands. The present work underlines and complements Thompson's work and, in a more general way, shows that Calvin will only consider temporary exceptions to general rules. 'Necessity may suspend the rule, but there is no hint that the rule is ever changed.' Indeed, Calvin sometimes sees it necessary to protect the rule against the exception.[163] This applies to the relationship between the husband and his wife and the characteristic roles of the wife as mother and housekeeper – these are unalterable rules, according to Calvin, which are fixed by natural law within the creational nature of mankind and repeated in scriptural command.

CONCLUSION

In examining the broad range of Calvin's theological *corpus*, in order to form an understanding of the preconceptions and theological assumptions with which Calvin approaches the subject of marriage, the present chapter has shown that his concept of order is a determinative factor in his social and ethical ideas. This is so because his thinking begins with a creative God of order, concerned for humanity's welfare, demonstrated in his providential activity in the world and in society. God's purpose is to preserve 'legitimate order' within the realm of the community. He does so, largely, through structured institutions – primarily, the church, the state and the family. Calvin's view of the husband-wife relationship is determined by his concept of social order.

We have observed that one intrinsic characteristic of social relationships is inequality. Although, to some extent everyone is

---

[162] Thompson, op. cit., particularly 161-267.
[163] Ibid., 274. See *Comm. 1 Cor.* 11:10 (CO 49.476); *Comm. 1 Tim.* 2:12 (CO 52.276); *Serm. 1 Tim.* 2:12-14 (CO 53.209-22); *Comm Acts* 18:26 (CO 48.437); 21:9 (CO 48.477); *Comm. Gen.* 21:10 (CO 23.301).

equal (having descended from Adam) and, certainly all believers are equal in Christ. Nevertheless, within societal relationships there is a fundamentally given inequality that prevails amongst men, and between men and women. In other words, for Calvin, social order is *always* hierarchical. There are always superior positions, counterbalanced by inferior ones. Marriage reflects this in its hierarchical arrangement – the husband has the superior position, he is to rule as the head or leader; the wife has an inferior status and is to be an obedient helper.

We have also noted that the Reformer holds to the idea of order and hierarchical arrangement somewhat tenaciously. He seems obsessed with the concept. This is so because he believes that sin and a resultant disorder threatens to destroy the order and social peace that is precariously maintained through God's providence and mankind's obedience. Against this threat, Calvin is desperate to defend the order that he sees as vital to mankind's existence in the world. Therefore, he looks upon a person's vocation as crucial in the fight against social chaos. It is through vocations, such as marriage, that individuals have the responsibility to preserve order. His theology of vocation, therefore, stresses duty, responsibility and the demand for perseverance, with the purpose of stabilizing society and the social order. Marriage takes on that purpose, securing the *status quo* – but only if each partner knows his or her place and remains within it.

Finally, the chapter showed the Reformer's eschatological hope – that true and perfect order will finally be and is presently being restored in and through the person and work of Christ. The restoration of order in society is seen to be accomplished through the renewal of the *imago Dei* in recreated men and women and the creation of a new community (the church) through which society regains its order and stability in the purposes of God. Having defined the *imago Dei* largely in dynamic, relational terms, it has been shown that because humanity is in the image of God, it has natural law and reason as part of what it means to be a human being, distinct from the rest of creation. Therefore, through the restoration of the *imago Dei* (with the ethical implications of that idea) comes a restoration of order through relationship with God and mankind's response of thankfulness. Here we noticed, by way of example, that an essential part of what Calvin believed to be entailed in the idea of natural law is that the husband and wife live in a hierarchical structure and that the woman's place is in the home as the man's helper. These two specific features were shown, then, to be unalterable in Calvin's view and application.

We noted in this chapter's introduction that several liberationist writers have developed an idea of the Reformer allowing for more freedom for women in the church and the family. Biéler's conclusion, which is characteristic of this group, is that, 'In Calvin's view, social inequality of married people was a contingent fact, historically conditioned and politically determined, whereas their spiritual equality was inherent and unchangeable.[164] We noted that others have followed suit, among them Bratt, de Boer, and (notably) Jane Douglass. However, the idea of the Reformer's more 'liberationist' perspective on the status of women (within the structure of marriage) has to be seriously questioned and called into doubt as an over-optimistic interpretation. This is so, for the following reasons, already delineated in this chapter.

First, though it is true that Calvin emphasizes the *purpose* of social order, rather than its mere arrangement, it has been shown that he conceives of that purpose to be one of stabilizing society and maintaining a safe *status quo* within the community. Douglass herself concedes this much, yet concludes that Calvin speaks as such only 'as the Reformation took institutional form'.[165] But she advances no evidence for this and it is more likely, from the present reading of Calvin, that this was his consistent view. Indeed, we have seen that his understanding of vocation commits people to a responsible maintaining of their position with the intention that the fragile social order is not disrupted. The position of the wife in relation to her husband is, therefore, not in question, nor is it open to change in Calvin's understanding of the purpose of order within society.

Second, we noted that Calvin is clear that inherent to the institution of marriage is inequality between its members. There is much that is empirically discerned in the Reformer's concept here, of course; but the point is that as he discerns God's intention, both through natural reason and the Scriptures, he is certain that the relationship between the spouses is and *is to remain* hierarchical and patriarchal by nature. The inherent order of the husband and wife in their marital relationship is determined as much by nature

---

[164] Biéler, art. cit., 359.
[165] J. D. Douglass, 'Christian Freedom: What Calvin Learned from the School of Women', *CH* 53 (1984), 172.

and biology as by God's direct command. It is thus not susceptible to change.[166] Significantly, that the husband and wife are spiritually equal is of little significance to their social relationship: an examination of Calvin's exposition and use of Galatians 3:28, for example, made that all too evident. Calvin's concept of the renewed humanity does not create a new order of family.

Third, it needs to be remembered that, according to Calvin, the Fall (together with its continuing consequences) is threatening to social relationships. The opposition between order and confusion is characteristic of the Reformer's thinking and the pervasiveness of this antithesis in his writing would indicate (at the very least) that it is unlikely that he would endanger God's order for the community by allowing for change in such a fundamental area as that of the relationship between the husband and wife. Indeed, we noted, in this area that he singles out the esteem that is due to those in a position of authority (*superiorité*) as being of utmost importance to the defence of society. Calvin is careful not to give any impression that normal patterns of societal life are open to change or modification.

Finally, in his discussion of the restoration of order, Calvin shows that the renewal of the *imago Dei* is crucial. Within this comprehensive concept of the image, we found that he includes humanity's primitive understanding of God's righteousness being restored by Christ. Natural law and natural reason are of significance to his theology of order in that humanity is being restored to the original nature that they possessed at creation. However, it is natural law that teaches society that the marriage relationship is fundamentally hierarchical and that the woman is to be in subjection to her husband. Calvin believes this to be evident in every culture and clearly taught in the Scriptures. But more than that, the logic of Calvin's use of natural law, at this juncture, is that what it teaches shows that these specific features, discovered in his own ethical understanding, are unalterable – and by that, he seems really to mean *unchangeable* by man or woman. On that basis, woman's marital status of inequality *is a fixed point* in the order that God establishes for society.

Broadly speaking, in his doctrine of marriage and the marital relationship Calvin espouses that which we discovered in Luther.

---

[166] R. S. Anderson / D. B. Guernsey, *On Being Family: A Social Theology of the Family* (Eerdmans, Grand Rapids, 1985), 15.

He certainly teaches a definite patriarchal hierarchicalism – it is the will of God, it helps to stabilize society, it is inherently part of the natural order of things. We noted, however, that Luther tends to soften the corners of the teaching by an insistence on mutuality, love and forgiveness. The following chapter examines Calvin's teaching on the husband-wife relationship in more detail, to gain a clearer understanding of what his hierarchicalism means and how it 'works', and to show in what ways, if any, he promotes the position of wives *within hierarchicalism*.

CHAPTER 9

THE NATURE OF MARRIAGE

In a general way, the previous chapter sought to locate Calvin's theology of marriage and teaching on the husband-wife relationship in the context of his concept of order. We have seen that the concept of order is a determinative factor in Calvin's theology and ethics. The world is divinely ruled in such a way that the relationships between men and between men and women are under providential ordering and command. Its purpose is to regulate and to maintain order in society.

Calvin follows Luther's idea of the vocational nature of marriage, but it has been observed that he emphasizes the notion of order-maintenance more as an obsessive requirement to preserve social peace and coherence. As with Luther, Calvin teaches the natural and fundamental *inequality* that exists between people in social relationships. Because this is so, we now move nearer to the heart of his teaching on marriage by tracing his thought on the motives traditionally given for marrying. In this way, we proceed from the general outline of his governing ideas to a more specific consideration of the marriage context in which the husband-wife relationship is to be defined and practised. It will be seen that his conventional use of the three purposes for marriage fits well into his concept of safeguarding order in society. It will also give further general information concerning what he considers to be the true nature of marriage.

In the parallel chapter on Luther[1] we were able to conclude with a biographical question on the Reformer's personal reluctance to marry – a reluctance which seemed, on the face of it, to run

---

[1] See chapter 6 of the present work.

counter to his own theology of marriage and his own advice to others. However, in turning to Calvin, no similar excursus is possible, simply because Calvin's *persona* remains, largely and intentionally, hidden behind his works. However, some of what little information is available will be employed within the main body of the chapter. The next chapter will take the final step of examining the Reformer's exposition of the scriptural passages on the husband-wife relationship to determine further his views on the subject, before drawing to a close.

However, before turning to the purposes of marriage as employed by Calvin, it is necessary to give further consideration to his view of marriage as a secular vocation. If sin's character is to threaten the stability and order of the community,[2] then it is the contrary nature of vocation to minimalize the detrimental effects of that sin. More particularly, if marriage is a vocation, as Calvin insists, then its purpose will be seen to be related to the sinfulness of the husband and the wife and that sin's potential to disrupt the divinely-appointed order of the community through promoting disorder in the family.

MARRIAGE IN THE *ORDO CREATIONIS*

As with Luther, Calvin employs the three conventional reasons given for marriage. However, these are put within the context of his theology of sin, of vocation and the consequent need for order. Simply put, for Calvin, marriage as a remedy contends against natural (that is sinful), promiscuous lust that would militate against society's wellbeing. Marrying in order to procreate runs counter to the tendency to see sexual activity as disengaged from the legitimate roles of having and raising children. Marrying for the purpose of companionship forms the ordered and well-regulated context for the other two to remain viable. Therefore, in order to comprehend Calvin's views on the purpose of marriage, two ideas need to be held side by side at this juncture: his view of the pervasive and continuing activity of sin and his understanding of the restraining function of marriage as a vocation.

---

[2] See chapter 8 of the present study.

Calvin removes marriage from its sacramental status. In doing so, he presents a similar ambivalence towards marriage in his insistence that it is a temporal vocation, together with his emphasis on its important spiritual significance.

Calvin writes on the sacraments in the *Institutes*, Book Four, particularly, chapters 14-19. Early on, he defines a sacrament as 'a sign of the covenant' confirming God's goodness, inducing faith in the believer.[3] Largely on the grounds of this definition he disregards confirmation, penance, extreme unction, orders and marriage from the traditional list – retaining only Baptism and the Eucharist as divinely appointed sacraments.[4] The Reformer argues from several perspectives to conclude that marriage is not a sacrament. Historically, it was not assumed to be so until the time of Gregory VII; exegetically, the concept of *sacramentum*, or, more precisely, *mysterium*, in Ephesians 5:28, refers, not to the husband and wife relationship, but rather to the relationship between Christ and the church; philologically, the translator should have kept *mysterium*, and not replaced it with *sacramentum*, which has now given the wrong impression. And, logically, if the Roman Church maintains that in a sacrament the grace of God is conferred and they teach that marriage is a sacrament, then they should be consistent. They should say, first, that the Holy Spirit is present in the act of sexual intercourse – which they deny – and, second, that priests should marry – which they disallow.

As Calvin sees it the question is, 'Has marriage been appointed as a sacred symbol of the grace of God to declare and represent to us something spiritual...?'[5] The answer is a definite, 'No!' In the

---

[3] *Inst* IV.xiv.5.

[4] See, particularly, *Inst* IV.xix.4-34. See also, *Inst* IV.xiv.8-9, 19; *De Necessitate Reformandae Ecclesiae* (CO 6.457-534). At *Inst* IV.xiv.1, Calvin gives two definitions of a sacrament: 'An outward sign by which the Lord seals on our consciences the promises of his goodwill towards us in order to sustain the weakness of our faith; and we in turn attest our piety toward him in the presence of the Lord and of his angels and before men.' And shorter: 'a testimony of divine grace toward us, confirmed by an outward sign, with mutual attestation of our piety toward him'. See also, *Confession de la Foy*, 1537 (OS 1.422-3); *Catechismus Ecclesiae Genevensis*, 1545 (OS 2.130); *Comm. John* 20:22 (CO 47.438); *Comm. 1 Cor.* 7:36-38 (CO 49.424-6); *Serm. Gal.* 1:22-2:2 (CO 50.351-64). See also, Beze's argument in *Tractationum Theologicarium* (Joannis Crispini, Geneva, 1570-82) 1.24, 49.

[5] *Comm. Eph.* 5:31-33 (CO 51.227). See also, *Serm. Eph.* 5:31-33 (CO 51.773). Calvin teaches that Paul includes in sacraments 'the communicating of Christ' – *Inst* IV.xiv.7.

Reformer's opinion, marriage is a good, even a holy, ordinance established by God at the creation of man and woman. He says that it is the same, in that respect, as farming, building, cobbling and so on – lawful ordinances or vocations of God, but *not* sacraments. Calvin maintains Luther's assertion that marriage is a worldly ordinance and that it forms part of the temporal ordering of things. As such, it is a constituent of the *ordinem creationis*. Calvin is aware that marriage is a principal part of human life.[6]

> [A]mong the offices pertaining to human society [*humanae societatis*], this is the principal and as it were the most sacred, that a man should cleave to his wife [*ut vir uxori suae adhaereat*].[7]

We can say that, on the one hand, from the perspective of the man and woman's initiative and experience, marriage is a contract[8] or a covenant, which they enter by mutual agreement and consent (*mutuo consensu*).[9] In this, Calvin emphasizes the mutual obligation to faithfulness – he asserts that, 'the marriage vow was a promise to remain'.[10] Each partner is obligated to offer continuing fidelity to the other. On the other hand, from the converse perspective of God's initiative in marriage, it is a heavenly calling or vocation (*coelesti vocatione*)[11] and a divine institution (*divinae*

---

[6] *Comm. Gen.* 21:20 (CO 23.305).

[7] *Comm. Gen.* 2:24 (CO 23.50). See also, *Comm. Mal.* 2:14 (CO 44.451) where he singles out seriousness concerning marriage partnership as that which indicates 'integrity and a sense of religion': '*Si qua est in hominibus integritas et religio, debet certe in coniugio vigere*'. Also, *Serm. Deut.* 22:13-24 (CO 28.48-9).

[8] *Comm. Hos.* 2:19-20 (CO 42.248-52); *Comm. Josh.* 15:16 (CO 25.528-9).

[9] *Serm. Deut.* 24:1-6 (CO 28.150); *Comm. Deut.* 22:22 / *Lev.* 20:10 (CO 24.648); *Comm. John* 8:1-11 (CO 47.191). Cf. *Comm. Matt.* 5:31 / *Luke* 16:18 (CO 45.180); *Comm. Gen.* 24:57, 67 (CO 23.339, 340); 29:27 (CO 23.403). On the grounds that marriage can only be established by mutual consent – ibid., 404. Although mutual consent is crucial to entering marriage, the authority of parents is also to have prominence – *Comm. Gen.* 21:20 (CO 23.305); 24:57 (CO 23.339); *Comm. Jer.* 29:6 (CO 38.586). See also, J. R. Watt, 'The Marriage Laws Calvin Drafted for Geneva' in W. H. Neuser (ed.), *Calvinus Sacrae Scripturae Professor* (Eerdmans, Grand Rapids, 1994), 247.

[10] *Comm. Ex.* 2:18 (CO 24.31).

[11] *Comm. Matt.* 19:11 (CO 45.533); *Comm. 1 Cor.* 7:20 (CO 49.415); *Serm. 1 Tim.* 2:13-15 (*sa vocation* – CO 53.229); *Inst* III.x.6; *Comm. Exod.* 2:1 (CO 24.21). W. J. Bouwsma, 'Calvin and the Dilemma of Hypocrisy' in P. de Klerk (ed.), *Calvin and Christian Ethics* (Calvin Studies Society, Grand Rapids, 1987), 6, appears to be correct in suggesting that Calvin commends the doctrine of vocation, 'on the

institutionis).¹² In this Calvin stresses not only the true nature of marriage, but also God's creative and sustaining right to establish marriage, to call men and women into it and to be involved in its day-to-day outworking. In other words, God is intimately involved in marriage as an institution and, also, in every individual marriage-relationship contracted in society. When a marriage takes place God is involved: he presides over the union, his authority joins the man and his wife together, their promises are spoken before him and in his name, he requires a mutual pledge of faithfulness from both, he sanctions the alliance. In daily experience, the husband and wife need to work at their continuing relationship *through* the work of the Holy Spirit.¹³ Speaking of the Old Testament history of the patriarch, Joseph, Calvin states,

> [W]e know that the sanctity of marriage is here commended to us ... whereby the Lord would declare himself to be the maintainer of matrimonial fidelity. ... For he is a surety between the man and his wife, and demands mutual chastity from each.¹⁴

For Calvin, as for Luther before him, the first marriage becomes a perpetual law (*lege inviolabili*) and a blessing of God. God both commands people to marry and also commands the form of that relationship.¹⁵ Something of the joint divine-human co-operation in marriage is seen in the paradigmatic example of Adam and Eve. Calvin stresses that the man (Adam) did not choose his wife (Eve), but he *did*, actively, receive her from God. In this Calvin clearly recognizes both God as the author of marriage and man's responsibility in that area of experience.¹⁶

---

ground that it provided a remedy for the anxiety otherwise likely to surround activity in [an increasingly mobile] society'.

¹² *Comm. 1 Cor.* 6:15-20 (CO 49.398); 7:1 (CO 49.401); *Comm. Matt.* 19:5 (CO 45.528); *Inst* II.viii.41, IV.xix.34; *Serm. Deut.* 22:13-24 (CO 28.48). See also, *Lausanne Articles* (1536), article ix, LCC.22, 36. Although this work was prepared by Farel, Calvin supported the articles.

¹³ *Comm. Mal.* 2:14 (CO 44.452); *Serm. Deut.* 21:15-17 (CO 27.666). Also, *Serm. 2 Sam.* 9:1-13 [Kelly, 437].

¹⁴ *Comm. Gen.* 39:7 (CO 23.505).

¹⁵ *Inst* II.viii.41; *Comm. Matt.* 19:7, 12 (CO 45.529, 534); *De Scandalis* (OS 2.230); *La Forme des Prieres et chantz ecclesiastiques*, 1542-43 (OS 2.52). See also, *Serm. 2 Sam.* 13:15-25 [Kelly, 630-31].

¹⁶ *Comm. Gen.* 2:22 (CO 23.49, 50).

The significant point is Calvin's understanding of the underlying purpose of marriage in the overall, societal intentions of God. If God is the author of marriage, then the ongoing obligation and responsibility of men and women is to use that institution for God's purpose in the world. We have seen that the Reformer teaches that the overall purpose of vocations (of which marriage is one) is to restrain sin and, consequently, to maintain order in the temporal realm. He stresses, particularly, the vocational nature of marriage and the restraining influence it is intended to have against potential societal disorder. Marriages were established by God 'to rid the world of confusion'; even those of unbelievers (who refuse to acknowledge God), 'serve to maintain decency and order' in the community, and serve to restrain illicit desire.[17] Without proper marriages, 'no holiness can continue to exist in the world'.[18]

In a general sense, then, the institution of marriage (in a postlapsarian world) is divinely given to humankind as a remedy, or a restraint, against the influence and inroads of sin and disorder. Given the Reformer's understanding of the continuing activity and unrestrainedness of sin, which we noted in the previous chapter, it is clear that marriage *is* God's gracious provision against the would-be ravages of sin and disorder in society. This is so even though it is not the conveyor of saving grace; that is, it is *not* of sacramental significance.

Suzanne Selinger, understandably, goes as far as to call marriage in Calvin's thought, 'an intervention, like Christ's, to save mankind, despite man's nature'. She continues, 'It is a major example of man's total dependence upon God in his post-Fall condition.'[19]

This outline of Calvin's thought on the nature of marriage and its overall purpose of societal order-maintenance in the intention of God, increases our own understanding of one or two secondary emphases that become apparent on reading the Reformer's *corpus*. These can be briefly delineated at this juncture, before we turn directly to the three traditional purposes of marriage that Calvin adopts. What is obvious, from this, is that Calvin wishes his

---

[17] *Serm. Deut.* 22:13-24 (CO 28.48-49); *Comm. 1 Cor.* 7:14 (CO 49.412), respectively.

[18] *Comm. John* 8:1-11 (CO 47.191).

[19] S. Selinger, *Calvin Against Himself* (Archon, Hamden, 1984), 96. Calvin comments that the conjugal relationship works to his salvation, not his destruction – *Comm. Gen.* 2:18 (CO 23.46).

followers to see the social importance of marriage and to retain a sense of its strict orderliness, over against the destabilizing tendencies of (what he sees as) the general and popular disparaging view of marriage and the husband-wife relationship. In practice, more often than not, he believes there is disharmony between the spouses – 'husbands and wives are always quarrelling and disagreeing [*en riotte et en discord*]'.[20] Against this prevalent, socially-threatening attitude and lifestyle, the Reformer emphasizes certain stipulations to bring order and peace in the community through the stable relationship of the husband and wife.

First, Calvin stresses, time and again, the people who should get married and those who should not. For example, men and women with a definite calling from the Lord to celibacy should not marry, though those who have no such calling (and here he indicates the vast majority) *must* marry. The former have been released from marriage 'through special grace'. Their celibacy is a gift of God – a gift, not given to the body of the church as a whole, but given to only 'a few of its members'. Conversely, the majority would be contending against both God and nature if they sought to remain celibate.[21] Then again, people who do marry should be roughly the same age as each other. This general principle seems to him to be dictated by both nature and reason (*quae a natura et sensu dictatur*). He asserts that to apply this principle would be to maintain modesty and propriety – two important characteristics in Calvin's view of well-regulated, societal behaviour. Indeed, if an old man should marry a young woman, for instance, he would be exposing himself to a great number of personal troubles and to general, social ridicule.[22] No-one should marry foreign women until

---

[20] *Serm. Eph.* 5:28-30 (CO 51.763). See also, *Serm. Deut.* 28:29-35 (CO 28.408-20, particularly, 409-10).

[21] The remark by J. A. Brundage, *Law, Sex and Christian Society in Medieval Europe* (University of Chicago Press, Chicago, 1987), 555, is to the point: according to the Reformer, 'Marriage was the greater good, benevolent and conducive to holiness, while celibacy was a rare condition, always morally suspect, which usually led to unhappiness and sin' (that is, in those not thus gifted). He adds that, in effect, Calvin stood the standard Roman view on its head. See *Inst* II.viii.42. The subject of celibacy is too large and beyond the scope of the present study for a detailed examination at this juncture. However, as it relates to the present point, see the following, *Inst* IV.xii.22-28; *Comm. Matt.* 19:11-12 (CO 45.533); *Comm. 1 Cor.* 7:20 (CO 49.415).

[22] *Comm. Lev.* 21:13 (CO 24.454). He blames Abraham for taking another wife in his old age, as 'unworthy of his gravity' – *Comm. Gen.* 25:1 (CO 23.342).

they have renounced their 'wicked superstitions', that is their heathen religion and all that goes with it. Interestingly, he teaches that, although people in his time are not bound to this specific, Old Testament observance, yet the rule (*ratio*) still holds good.[23] Also, infatuation and lust must never constitute the reason for marriage – on this, he is emphatic.[24] He writes to Farel of his own aversion to this, 'I am none of these insane lovers who embrace also the vices of those they are in love with, where they are smitten at first sight with a fine figure.'[25]

Second, he stresses the seriousness of getting married. He insists, for instance, that some solemn, public testimony to marriage should be practised. Indeed, on the basis of 'la dignité et excellence de l'estat de Mariage' and upon scriptural evidence, this is said to be necessary. In fact, it is God's will.[26] In this context, the wedding ceremony is to reflect the worldly nature of marriage, while it is also to maintain its spiritual significance. And it is to be conducted with order and seriousness (*tenant ordre et gravité convenable à Chrétiens*). Calvin stipulates that the ceremony, though it is *not* a spiritual matter, should begin with spiritual songs, it should include a sermon and be followed by the Eucharist. Though he emphasizes that it is a civil matter, the ceremony should be conducted by ministers of the gospel, not by magistrates.[27] The impression given by these requirements is, therefore, that marriage should be considered as important and as

---

[23] *Comm. Deut.* 21:10-13 (CO 24.354) – see, generally, 352-4. The French significantly adds, 'Pour s'envelopper en leur impiété' [CTS, 2.70]. See also, *Serm. Deut.* 21:10-14 (CO 27.657-9); *Comm. 2 Cor.* 6:14 (CO 50.81). In relation to this, he shows concern when Viret proposes to marry someone Calvin judges to be spiritually unsuitable. He discourages Viret from, what he terms, 'the unholy alliance' on the grounds that it will lead to unhappiness. See Calvin's letter to Monsieur de Falais, 4 July (1546) in *Tracts and Letters* in H. Beveridge / J. Bonnet (eds), *Selected Works of John Calvin* (Baker, Grand Rapids, 1983), 5.63-4 and discouraging letters to Viret himself – 13 July (1546), 15 July (1546), ibid., 5.65-9.

[24] See, for example, Calvin's letter to Farel, 19 May (1539), ibid., 4.141.

[25] Ibid. However, Calvin insists that choosing a wife because of her elegance or beauty is not necessarily sin (*non simpliciter peccabit*), 'provided reason maintains the ascendancy, and holds the wantonness of passion in subjection' – *Comm. Gen.* 29:18 (CO 23.402).

[26] *La Forme des Prieres et chantz ecclesiastiques*, 1542-43 (OS 2.50) – he insists on 'bon et decent ordre' (51); *Comm. Gen.* 24:59 (CO 23.339), respectively.

[27] *Les ordonnances ecclesiastiques*, 1541 (OS 2.345-55). See also, G. Harkness, *John Calvin: The Man and his Ethics* (Abingdon, New York, 1981), 138.

the converging point of temporal reality and spiritual significance. It is, after all, a temporal vocation, graciously instituted by God.[28]

Third, Calvin follows Luther's stress on the inherent indissolubility of the marriage bond. In a characteristic statement, he says,

> God has declared once for all, that the bond of union between husband and wife is closer than that of parents and children; wherefore, if a son cannot shake off the paternal yoke [*iugum patris*], no cause can permit the dissolution of the connection which a man has with his wife.[29]

Elsewhere, he applies this idea to those in his congregations, 'The connection which God has ordained must always remain firm and steadfast.' Furthermore, he underlines the responsibility and obligation of both the husband and the wife to maintain conjugal association and fidelity.[30] In Selinger's words '[T]he indissolubility of the bonds of marriage clearly appeals to his [Calvin's] sense of order; he likes the stability implied in the idea of mutual help and obligations.'[31]

As a conclusion to this brief outline, it should be observed that the immediate context for Calvin's understanding of the purpose of marriage, generally, is in the experience and social convergence of two opposed things: *viz*, the pervasiveness and continuing activity

---

[28] Occasionally, Calvin fails to follow the implications of his own teaching. This is so, for example, when he seems to put commercial considerations before the importance of the marriage ordinance. See *Comm. Exod.* 21:1-6 (CO 24.700-701) – pointed out by D. F. Wright, 'Calvin's Pentateuchal Criticism: Equity, Hardness of Heart, and Divine Accommodation in the Mosaic Harmony Commentary', *CTJ* 21 (1986), 41.

[29] *Comm. Deut.* 24:1-4 (CO 24.658). There are many references to this, but see, particularly, *Comm. Gen.* 5:2 (*'constitui sub una persona'* – CO 23.105); *Comm. Matt.* 5:31 (*'eus tamel nodo indissolubili eos adstringit'* – CO 45.180); 10:35 (CO 45.293); 19:3-4 (man and wife make one whole man [*integrum hominem*] – CO 45.528); *Comm. 1 Cor.* 6:15-20 (CO 49.400); 7:10 (*'insolubile vinculum'* – CO 49.409); 7:39 (CO 49.427); *Serm Deut.* 22:13-24 (CO 28.46); *Serm. Eph.* 5:22-6 (CO 51.736); 5:28-30 (CO 51.764-5); *Serm. 2 Sam.* 5:13-15 [Kelly, 203].

[30] *Serm. Deut.* 24:1-4 (CO 28.151). As noted in chapter 8, any violation of marriage is contrary to both nature and the law of God. So divorce, for example, is said to be 'directly repugnant to the first institution of God [*primae Dei institutioni*] from whence a perpetual and inviolable rule [*perpetua et inviolabilis est regula*] is to be sought' (*Comm. Deut.* 24:1-4 (CO 24.657)).

[31] Selinger, op. cit., 96.

of sin, and the restraint and control of vocation. The previous chapter demonstrated that Calvin teaches that because of Adam's original sin every person is necessarily polluted by sin, which manifests itself (if unrestrained) in immoderate behaviour. Every part and activity of man and woman is affected by sin. In its outworking, this is true of unbelievers, particularly; but it is also the case that Christians are tempted in that way, too. One vulnerable area is that of relationships between people and, particularly, relationships in which sexuality may play a part. Alongside this pessimistic emphasis on the potential unrestrainedness of sin, Calvin teaches that God has established vocations within which people are given conduct-boundaries through duty and obligation. Marriage is such a vocation. Through it, on the one hand, God seeks to limit the destabilizing influence of sin and, on the other hand, to establish and to maintain order in society. What we find is that Calvin emphasizes those things that are seen to fulfil the requirement of communal stability, underlining his commitment to social order.

TRADITIONAL REASONS FOR MARRYING

The Reformer speaks in traditional manner of three reasons for marrying – as a remedy against man and woman's unbridled sexual desire and lust (it is a *remedium peccati*), for the legitimate conception and raising of children and as the social, vocational context for men and women to enjoy companionship together. Although Calvin says considerably less on the purposes of marriage than Luther, the reasons he gives exactly parallel Luther's reasons[32] and are the conventional purposes that the medieval church would have listed.[33]

It is sometimes said that companionship is the primary purpose for marriage in Calvin's thinking. Biéler, for example, highlights this against the traditional teaching that saw procreation as the chief reason, saying that Calvin's theology put the fulfilment of the human person – male and female – as its priority in this

---

[32] See chapter 6 of the present study.
[33] See chapter 4 of the present study.

context.[34] In a similar way, Douglass concludes that, in Calvin, 'The shifting of priority in marriage away from procreation or prevention of sin to the mutual cherishing of husband and wife and their help to one another does represent significant change in the understanding of marriage.'[35] Jewett also asserts that in the Reformer's thinking the primary purpose of marriage is social. He states that the wife 'was not given the man as a "remedy", the comrade merely of his bedchamber, but to share life with him as his inseparable companion'. Jewett commends Calvin for being on higher ground than Luther.[36]

However, it should be noticed that this general conclusion seems largely unwarranted and optimistic. While it is true, for instance, that unlike the majority of his contemporaries Calvin does emphasize companionship in his commentary on Genesis 2:18,[37] it will be argued in the following chapter that the Reformer stresses the inherent sociability (and, therefore, companionship) of the original pair, not as an end in itself, but as a stable and ordered context in which procreation (together with the raising of children[38]) is to be undertaken. As such, it is a paradigm for those who follow. It also needs to be noted that Calvin himself is rather more flexible than these writers would suggest. For instance, in his commentary on 1 Corinthians he asserts the (theoretical) priority of procreation as a reason for marriage, while at the same time

---

[34] A. Biéler, 'Man and Woman in Calvin's Ethic', *RPW* 27 (1963), 358; idem, *L'Homme et la Femme dans la Morale Calviniste* (Labor et Fides, Geneva, 1961), 89.

[35] J. D. Douglass, *Women, Freedom and Calvin* (Westminster, Philadelphia, 1985), 86. See also, for example, B. J. van der Walt, 'Woman and Marriage in the Middle Ages, in Calvin and in our own time' in idem (ed.), *John Calvin's Institutes: His Opus Magnum* (Potchefstroom University for Christian Higher Education, Potchefstroom, 1986), 213-14.

[36] P. K. Jewett, *Man as Male and Female* (Eerdmans, Grand Rapids, 1976), 67. Despite Jewett's overemphasis, he is nearer the mark than Harkness, op. cit., 135, who says that, in her opinion, '[N]either Calvin nor Luther ever speak of marriage as an institution established for the mutual companionship of husband and wife.' See also, M. A. Farley, 'Sexual Ethics' in J. B. Nelson / S. P. Longfellow (eds), *Sexuality and the Sacred* (Mowbray, London, 1994), 63.

[37] *Comm. Gen.* 2:18 (CO 23.46). See J. L. Thompson, *John Calvin and the Daughters of Sarah* (Librairie Droz, Geneva, 1992), 120.

[38] As we shall see later, Calvin follows Luther in stressing the logical and practical connection between marriage for the purpose of procreation and the continuing necessity of raising the children thus born. This was the traditional way of expanding on the idea.

insisting on the pragmatic or practical priority of its remedial character in the context of the sinfulness of human beings.[39]

The previous chapters on Luther have also demonstrated that his view and his practice show a great deal of emphasis on companionship in marriage. Calvin was not the first to stress it, nor, indeed, was Luther. It had been present in both Augustine's understanding and that of the mainstream of medieval theologians. However, we have already noted that Luther's understanding of companionship is a limited one – limited, partly by his theology of hierarchicalism within marriage and his strict patriarchalism. It will be seen that Calvin's is no broader. Indeed, it may even have been *more* limited by his obsessive need for order and stability, together with his fear of its opposite. In the light of Calvin's writing and intention, the conclusions reached by Biéler, Douglass, Jewett and others, seem to be anachronistic.

The general principle that Calvin seems to follow in his discussion of the purposes of marriage is that which he, himself, outlines in another context in the *Institutes*, '[T]he use of God's gifts is not wrongly directed when it is referred to that end to which the Author himself created and destined them for us, since he created them for our good, not for our ruin.'[40] What, then, are the purposes for which God gives the institution of marriage, for which men and women may legitimately use it?

A Remedy against Unbridled Lust

It has often been pointed out that Calvin, as Luther, has a very negative view of sex and sensuality, which forces him to emphasize the traditional purpose of marriage as a remedy against the sin of unbridled lust. For instance, in *Calvin Against Himself* (1984), Suzanne Selinger speaks of Calvin's 'censorious attitude toward sexuality and anything that can be associated with it', and of 'the absolutism of his censoriousness'.[41] Part of the thesis of her work is to suggest that the Reformer had a character disorder, a neurosis[42] and that as a result his concept of human nature is more 'extremely and directly sexually determined than

---

[39] *Comm. 1 Cor.* 7:9 (CO 49.408).
[40] *Inst* III.x.2.
[41] Selinger, op. cit., 72.
[42] Ibid., 74. (See also, Bouwsma, op. cit., 80.)

Luther's'.[43] Indeed, according to her examination of Calvin's writing, he saw sex and sexuality as merely sordid.[44] Two years later, in *The Gospel According to Woman*, Karen Armstrong generally took the same position, emphasizing Calvin's apparently Augustinian, anti-sexual neurosis.[45] This is manifested in a negative attitude towards sexuality and marriage, which, she says, he took 'right into the heart of the Reformation'.[46] Calvin is said to have held 'sex as a concupiscent and irrepressible force against which man was helpless'.[47]

It has to be said that there is some truth in this criticism. Calvin, generally, evidences a negative attitude towards sex, even within the marriage relationship. Therefore, his writing does make such criticism reasonably plausible. However, it is important to get the balance right. It will be remembered that in examining Luther at this point,[48] the present study argued that to begin at the Reformer's theology of postlapsarian experience is to start at the wrong place. It was found that, against Luther's apparently dominantly negative approach to sex, his more positive view of divinely given, prelapsarian sexuality and sex had to be taken into account, as did his understanding of the present, covering grace of God. Indeed, at the conclusion, we discovered that Luther was relatively open about sexuality, in general, and about his own sexuality in particular. The following brief discussion argues a similar case for Calvin – but we need to take into account his natural reticence and his own ambivalence on the topic.[49]

It is important to notice that the Reformer holds that at creation humankind was made perfect. That is, not only was their soul well-ordered, but so also was their physical being. Calvin clearly asserts the theological proposition that, 'Our bodies are, in

---

[43] Ibid., 42-3.

[44] Ibid., 85-6, 95.

[45] K. Armstrong, *The Gospel According to Woman* (Elm Tree Books, London, 1986), 273, 278, respectively.

[46] Ibid., 25. See also, 7.

[47] Ibid., 278. This judgement is sometimes levelled at Luther as well. See P. L. Lehmann, *Ethics in a Christian Context* (SCM, London, 1963), 135; B. J. Murstein, *Love, Sex and Marriage through the Ages* (Springer, New York, 1974), 179.

[48] See chapter 6 of the present study.

[49] We need, also, to take into account the lack of occasional writing on the subject of marriage, of course.

their essence, good creatures of God.[50] This is necessarily the case, for the body (together with both sensuality and the ability to reproduce) is part of the originally created perfection of Adam and Eve.[51] Furthermore, he speaks of sexual intercourse between the husband and wife, at that time, as 'that pure and lawful method of increase which God ordained from the beginning'.[52] His conclusion on Adam and Eve *as created*, then, is that, 'our parents had nothing in themselves which was unbecoming *until they were defiled with sin*'.[53] It is the Reformer's conventional understanding of the contradictoriness of present life-experience (implied in the italicized clause) which forces Calvin into a pessimism and a resultant ambivalence in his writing. This is well summed up in Bouwsma's words:

> Thoughts of the body, especially when associated with sensuality, could produce in his rhetoric sudden reversals in which he would switch within a single paragraph from wonder at the miracle of human reproduction to a sense of the body as 'ordure and contagion' and of the procreative act as 'a shameful thing one does not mention'. [54]

The major element in his thinking at this point of rejection concerns the postlapsarian reality and unrestrainedness of sin in every activity of human life. No human activity is altogether blameless before the righteous God.[55] Therefore, it would be mistaken to single out sexual intercourse as *the* area in which sin is uncontrolled. Yet, clearly, Calvin teaches that sexual desire and activity is *one* sphere (and an important one) in which the sinfulness of *both* men and women[56] would be out of control if some restraint were not put upon it. For Calvin, as for Luther before him, marriage (qualified by moderation) is that restraint.

---

[50] *Serm. Job* 5:11-16 (CO 33.728). See also, *Comm. Ps.* 139:15 (CO 32.381); *Comm. 1 Tim.* 5:23 (CO 52.319); *Comm. John* 4:32 (CO 47.93); *Comm. Col.* 2:23 (CO 52.115).
[51] *Comm. Gen.* 3:6 (CO 23.59).
[52] *Comm. Gen.* 1:28 (CO 23.28).
[53] *Comm. Gen.* 2:25 (CO 23.52) – emphasis added.
[54] W. J. Bouwsma, *John Calvin: A Sixteenth Century Portrait* (CUP, New York, 1988), 80. He cites *Serm. Job* 10:7-15 (CO 33.483); *Comm. Gen.* 9:23 (CO 23.151).
[55] *Inst* III.xiv.9.
[56] See, for example, *Serm. 2 Sam.* 12:7-12 [Kelly, 537]; *Serm. Deut.* 5:18 (CO 26.341-2).

In preaching on the Old Testament story of the rape of Tamar (2 Samuel 13:1-14), for example, Calvin says that our lust and passions are terrible beasts and very difficult to keep under control.[57] It is characteristic of the Reformer that he takes an exceptional act of rape to infer the general sinfulness of everyone. The animal imagery is significant, too. Calvin often resorts to it in the context of his discussions on the sinfulness of men and women. By it, in the present context, he implies at least two things. First, the sinful, sexual lust of people is untameable.[58] That which we found in Calvin's thinking to be true of sin, in general – that it always tends to be excessive or immoderate – is, *ipso facto*, true of sexual sinfulness, in particular. By his emphasis on the pervasiveness and the uncontrolledness of sexual sin Calvin underlines the idea that, *without control*, sexual sin can only deteriorate into personal disorderliness and, if permitted, eventually into social chaos.[59]

Second, as a beast needs bridling to curb its activity, so the sinful, sexual inclination of men and women needs control from without. That is, sexual desire and activity requires restrictive parameters in which to work as closely to God's intention as possible in postlapsarian experience. Simply put, marriage forms that control. Negatively, it restrains lust; positively, it maintains decency[60] – that is its purpose in this context. In Calvin's often-repeated word, it is the divinely-appointed 'remedy'.[61] Therefore, marriage is an aid given by God, 'it helps men handle the weakness and corruption into which they have fallen ... in order to avoid fornication'.[62]

---

[57] *Serm. 2 Sam.* 13:1-14 [Kelly, 616].

[58] *Serm.. Deut.* 21:10-14 (CO 27.652, 662); 21:15-17 (CO 27.664); *De Scandalis* (OS 2.230); *Comm. Ps.* 14:3 (CO 31.138); *Comm. Isa.* 3:5 (CO 36.83); *Inst* II.ii.24, II.viii.41, IV.xiii.3, 17.

[59] See *Serm. 2 Sam.* 1:21-7 [Kelly, 32]; 2:1-7 [Kelly, 59]; *Comm. Heb.* 13:4 (CO 55.188); *Comm. 1 John* 2 16 (CO 55.319).

[60] *Comm. 1 Cor.* 7:14 (CO 49.412).

[61] As with Luther, Calvin can employ the idea of medicine to the institution of marriage – see *Serm. Matt.* 19:10 (CO 45.532). However, in this context, Calvin often uses the idea of divine remedy – see *Serm. Deut.* 5:18 ('*le remede que Dieu leur assigne*' – CO 26.342-3); *Inst* II.viii.42,43, IV.xiii.17 (citing 1 Cor. 7:9); *Comm. 1 Cor* 7:1 (CO 49.400); 7:2 (CO 49.402); 7:9 (CO 49.408); 7:29 (CO 49.420); *Comm. 1 Pet.* 3:4 (CO 55.254); *Comm. Heb.* 13:4 (CO 55.188); *Serm. 1 Tim* 3:1-4 (CO 53.245-8); *De Scandalis* (OS 2.230).

[62] *Serm. 2 Sam.* 12:7-12 [Kelly, 537]. On the same page, Calvin insists that he

Calvin says that for people to feel heat in itself is natural and not wrong. But to 'burn' (using the apostle's image – 1 Corinthians 7:9[63]) means that a person is out of control. At that stage, the Reformer claims that the feelings and inclination 'cannot be extinguished except by marriage'.[64] Unbridled lust needs to be kept in check 'by the bridle of marriage', promiscuous desires must be avoided, by 'the true way of escape'.[65]

Given Calvin's largely pessimistic theology of fallen humanity and his teaching on the sovereign graciousness of God, it is little wonder that his writing is ambivalent on the subject of marriage. On the one hand, he speaks of the shame and indecency of the (legitimate) cohabitation of a husband and wife and the impurity of marital, sexual intercourse.[66] On the other hand, he rejoices that, in reality, the indulgent God covers that sin:

> [W]hen a man lives honourably with his wife in the fear of God, although their lawful intimate relationship might be disgraceful [*honteuse-timide*], nevertheless neither before God, nor his angels, is such a relationship shameful. ... The mantle of marriage exists to sanctify what is defiled and profane; it serves to cleanse what used to be soiled and dirty in itself.[67]

It is noticeable that the husband has to be living 'honourably' with his wife, in the fear of God – that is, in faith and in the recognition of his *vocatio*. By the word 'honourably' it is reasonable to assume that he has in mind, in part, the concept of moderation or controlledness, for he often urges husbands (in particular) to this.[68] In his sermon on Deuteronomy 22:13-24, for instance, he says that marriage is holy and honourable *in so far as* the bed is dedicated to God, and the spouses are joined in his name.[69] In another passage he states that God actually blesses *'de societale coniungali'* – when

---

means women, too. See also, *Serm. Deut.* 24:1-6 (CO 28.159).

[63] See *Comm. 1 Cor.* 7:9 (CO 49.408); *Comm. Luke* 1:23 (CO 45.21); *Inst* IV.xii.24.
[64] *Comm. 1 Cor.* 7:9 (CO 49.409). See also, *Inst* II.viii.43.
[65] *De Scandalis* (OS 2.230); *Comm. Heb.* 13:4 (CO 55.187), respectively.
[66] *Comm. Lev.* 12:1-2 (CO 24.312).
[67] *Serm. Deut.* 5:18 (CO 26.343) – Farley's translation [Farley, 179-80]. Elsewhere: '[T]he sanctity of marriage covers what otherwise might be imputed to blame, and purifies the very defilements of our guilty nature. Whence it is plain that marriage ... has nothing disgraceful about it' (*Comm. Lev.* 2:1-2 (CO 24.312)).
[68] See *Comm. Gen.* 2:22 (CO 23.49); 19:18 (CO 23.402). Also, *Inst* 1.xv.3.
[69] *Serm. Deut.* 22:13-24 (CO 28.48).

the bodies of both the husband and the wife are dedicated to his glory.[70]

> And, certainly, the sanctity of marriage [*coniugii sanctitas*] demands that men and women should not live like cattle; but that, having pledged their mutual faith, and invoked the name of God, they might dwell with each other.[71]

Surprisingly perhaps, Bouwsma points out that Calvin deals with sexual attraction 'with a touch of romantic feeling'.[72] It is interesting and somewhat significant that of the passages Bouwsma cites, two (Jer. 3:4; Dan. 2:11) express the Reformer's comprehension of the love of God through the imagery of romantic love. A third (Gen. 2:11) relates to Abraham and Sarah in old age and the final one (Gen. 9:18 – concerned with Jacob and Rachel) is heavily qualified by the following lengthy and characteristic application:

> Only excess is to be guarded against, and so much the more diligently, because it is difficult so to restrain affections of this kind, that they do not prevail to the stifling of reason. Therefore, he who shall be induced to choose a wife because of the elegance of her form will not necessarily sin, *provided reason always maintains the ascendancy, and holds the wantonness of passion in subjection.*[73]

Bouwsma, also, suggests that Calvin teaches that there is genuine pleasure in the sexual act.[74] This is certainly true.

---

[70] *Comm. 1 Cor.* 6:15-20 (CO 49.398). See also, *Inst* II.viii.44, where Calvin encourages married people not to pollute marriage, 'with uncontrolled and dissolute lust'.

[71] *Comm. Gen.* 24:67 (CO 23.340-41).

[72] Bouwsma, op. cit., 137. He cites *Comm. Jer.* 3:4 (CO 37.550); *Comm. Dan.* 11:38-9 (CO 41.271-8); *Comm. Gen.* 12:11 (CO 23.183); 29:18 (CO 23.402). Bouwsma claims that 'Every aspect of human sexuality, for Calvin, was valuable and moving' (137).

[73] *Comm. Gen.* 29:18 (CO 23.402) – emphasis added. L. Stone, *The Family, Sex and Marriage in England. 1500-1800* (Penguin, Harmondsworth, 1979), 314, says of Calvin's teaching that, 'All passionate love-making was sinful, regardless of whether it took place inside or outside marriage.' This is to distort the Reformer's understanding, for he believed that passion could (and should) be controlled, but that it remained passion, nonetheless. Calvin's fear was of excessive, unreserved passion. See, in contrast to Stone, T. George, *Theology of the Reformers* (Broadman, Nashville, 1988), 184.

[74] Bouwsma, op. cit., 137. He cites *Comm. Deut.* 24:5 (CO 24.652).

On the Old Testament stipulation that a newly-wed should not go to war for a year (Deut. 24:5), Calvin remarks that God, 'allows them to enjoy themselves'.[75] The context is important, too, for the Reformer infers that the sexual physicalness between the spouses, as much as their being together, generally, will foster love and a mutual confidence between them.[76] However, again, we need to note the comments appended. First, he says that the husband and wife learn, thereby, to be faithful, not promiscuous (evidently, with an eye to the man going to war after the first year). Second, he stresses, within this context, that sin must, of necessity, affect their sexual intercourse – yet, he affirms that God pardons it, covering it with 'a veil of holy matrimony'. Of course, Bouwsma is right to allude to these passages in the way that he does, but they should not be taken as demonstrating Calvin's *unqualified* presentation of romantic love and intercourse. He remains uneasy about the 'pleasurable concomitants of the sexual act'.[77] Calvin's underlying agenda is apparent in the contexts which seem, on the surface, most positive – that is, he stresses the pervasiveness of sin, the need for disciplined and well-ordered lives and the gracious pardon of God.

In a sense, Calvin's thesis at this point is *both* negative and positive. On the one hand, in that he seeks to underline the present sinfulness of fallen men and women and the threatening pervasiveness of that sin, he must stress postlapsarian helplessness in the face of sexual desire and inclination. It cannot be restrained without aid. On the other hand, in that he wishes to delineate the undeserved grace of God in *every* situation, he must stress the remedy of marriage as a divine gift. Marriage's purpose (at least, in this context) is to help to establish, maintain and, ultimately, to restore order in both personal behaviour and within

---

[75] Biéler, op. cit., 60-61, suggests that Calvin's emphasis is that people should use *the remedy* with joy. See also, Lehmann, op. cit., 135.

[76] Brundage, op. cit., 556, suggests that for the Reformer the virtue of married sexual intercourse, generally, was that it expressed and increased the couple's love for one another. This passage (*Comm. Deut.* 24:5) is a rare, specific incident of that idea in Calvin's writing. However, Brundage further contrasts what he sees to be Calvin's view with the traditional concept that the virtue of such intercourse was, in fact, procreation. The contrast will not hold, simply because Calvin's common emphases are on marriage as a remedy and for procreation; not so much on companionship and the growth of the spouses' love.

[77] Lehmann, op. cit., 135.

society. As we have seen, this is the nature of vocation in the divine purpose.

Calvin's sermon on Deuteronomy 5:18 sums up most of what has been said.[78] There, alluding to Paul's opinion that it is better to marry than to burn (1 Cor. 7:9), the Reformer says that the inclination to sexual activity in both men and women is a natural one, but that it has been corrupted because of Adam's sin. It is now 'a great distance from the excellent dignity' that God gave to mankind at the beginning. It has become a vice. He further reminds his congregation that *all* unrestraint of the flesh is 'sin and damnable'. But his emphasis falls on the idea that through divine grace marriage is a remedy for everyone who cannot control themselves:

> Although God was pleased to leave this mark of iniquity in us, yet he appoints a convenient remedy for it. ... [The inherent sin] shall not be imputed to us before God, if it is covered with marriage.[79]

His direct application is characteristic of the Reformer. He insists that people have to learn to be humble, 'to receive the yoke of marriage'[80] in the knowledge that this in itself is a sacrifice which is acceptable before God. Elsewhere, he encourages others to take refuge in the remedy offered.[81] This accords with his teaching, in several other places, that believers should allow God to possess bodies as well as souls to his glory (*ad gloriam Dei*); and that love for the Lord is to be reflected in every part of life – the areas of love and sexual intercourse not excluded.[82]

This brief outline has raised some significant points related to the husband-wife relationship in this broad area of sexuality. Calvin clearly teaches an equality between men and women as far as sexual sinfulness is concerned. Though good at creation, sexuality fell with every other aspect of humanity's being. Therefore, both men

---

[78] *Serm. Deut.* 5:18 (CO 26.334-46, particularly 341-2).

[79] *Serm. Deut.* 5:18 (CO 26.341-2).

[80] It is worth noting, incidentally, that the image of the yoke implies external control and is a favourite with Calvin, particularly in his social ethics and understanding of the vocational nature of the family.

[81] *Inst* IV.xiii.17 – again, alluding to *1 Cor.* 7:9.

[82] See, for example, *Serm. Deut.* 5:4-7 (CO 26.247-57, particularly 257), *Comm. 1 Cor.* 6:20 (CO 49.400) and *Serm. Deut.* 5:8-10 (CO 26.268), *Comm. 1 Cor.* 10:31 (CO 49.471), respectively.

and women have a tendency to uncontrolledness – both need the remedy of marriage in order to live decently and to restrain promiscuity. That is, they both need marriage to maintain order in their relationships. On the other hand, Calvin's positive teaching is that God is gracious enough to cover the sin involved, even in marital sex. So, marriage is a remedy against unbridled lust, if it is used correctly.

The Legitimate Procreation of Children

The second purpose that Calvin puts forward for marriage is that it forms the legitimate context for the procreation of children. Pre-Fall, this would have been the main purpose, 'nature dictates that the propagation of offspring is the special end of marriage'.[83] However, Calvin generally seems to infer that in the post-Fall period, for practical reasons, the control of unbridled lust is its chief purpose. Certainly, the former has the chronological precedence. Consequently, marriage with the intention of procreating is vitally important to the Reformer. This was both a traditional reason and also one which reflected the social importance of family in the sixteenth century.[84]

Much of what Calvin says regarding this reason for marriage is a repetition of Luther's main concerns in the same area. So, Calvin stresses the importance of both having children and of bringing them up before God. The two are bound together within parental calling.[85] The Reformer forcefully argues that God should have central significance in all of this, after all, procreation is *his* purpose for marriage. Adam and Eve were formed with the express purpose of having offspring.[86] In this, Calvin wishes to glory in both the all-pervasive power of God and divine grace.

---

[83] '*...propagationem sobolis esse proprium coniugii finem*' – *Comm. Gen.*24:59 (CO 23.339); contra, Biéler, op. cit., 89, 91-2. See also, *Comm. Gen.* 1:28 (CO 23.28); 16:1 (CO 23.222); *Comm. Jer.* 16:1-4 (CO 38.238); *Comm. Matt.* 22:30 / *Mark* 12:25 (CO 45.454).

[84] See S. C. Karant-Nunn, 'Continuity and Change: Some Effects of the Reformation on the Women of Zwickau', *SCJ* 12 (1982), 26. As in previous centuries, getting married and bearing children were still the two significant events in most women's life-experience in the sixteenth century. The whole idea also accords with the developing theory of the Middle Ages – see chapter 4 of the present work.

[85] *Comm. 1 Tim.* 2:15 (CO 52.277-8).

[86] *Comm. Gen.* 1:28 (CO 23.28). See also, *Comm. Gen.* 16:1 (CO 23.222).

Calvin stresses the naturalness of conception and of childbirth and that these occurrences are *not* miracles because God has implanted the power of procreation in men and women as an intrinsic part of their created humanness.[87] He is quite clear that the woman has an active role to play in the generation of children. On the one hand, he agrees with those who deem her gamete material only to be a passive force in conception. But, on the other hand, he does not wish to discriminate against her.[88]

Nevertheless, he underlines the converse idea that it is God who gives offspring – this is an element of his continuing providential care of humanity.[89] So, babies are conceived by God's grace, even if they are illegitimately conceived.[90] Every child born is a testimony to the secret, powerful and incomprehensible working of God in and through the union of men and women.[91] Arguing a creationist doctrine, he says,

---

[87] *Inst* I.xvi.7; *Comm. Gen.* 21:1 (CO 23.296); *Comm. Isa.* 7:14 (CO 36.154).

[88] *Inst* II.xiii.3. This argument occurs in Calvin's disagreement with those who would say that Christ, specifically, took his body from nothing rather than from the woman. In general, following the Aristotelian idea that the man had the active 'material principle', it was believed that while both parents were necessary for procreation, only the father has procreative seed. The woman merely has passive matter or 'passive force'. On the basis of the male's preferential status, Calvin says that it is sufficiently well known that 'as far as the political order is concerned' descent is reckoned by the male sex. But his conclusion on the physicality of conception, formation and birth, however, is that Christ did come physically from Mary (*Inst.* II.xiii.4). See J. Irwin, 'Embryology and the Incarnation: A Sixteenth Century Debate', *SCJ* 9 (1978), 93-104; K. E. Børresen, *Subordination and Equivalence* (University Press of America, Washington, 1981), 41-3, 193-5; C. Jordan, *Renaissance Feminism* (Cornell University Press, Ithaca, 1990), 29-34; R. A. Holbrooke, *The English Family. 1450-1700* (Longman, London, 1985), 96-7; *Comm. Gen.* 21:2 (CO 23.297). See also, Augustine, *DCD* 14.24.

[89] Ibid. Also, *Comm. Gen.* 24:3 (CO 23.331); 30:2 (CO 23.408); 34:4 (CO 23.457); *Comm. Ps.* 22:9-10 (CO 31.226).

[90] *Comm. 1 Sam.* 1:19-20 (CO 29.274); *Comm. Gen.* 25:21 (CO 23.347); *Comm. Ps.* 71:6 (CO 31.655); 113:9 (CO 32.179); 127:3 (CO 32.324); *Serm. 2 Sam.* 6:20-23 [Kelly, 293]; 11:14-27 [ibid., 517]; 12:13-14 [ibid., 579]. In *Comm. Gen.* 9:1 (CO 23.143) Calvin states that the blessing of God in childbirth is in some way extended to illegitimate conception; yet he speaks of it as 'impure fruitfulness'. Augustine also taught this – see for example, *DgrC* 2.38 (ASW 5.250-51).

[91] *Comm. Gen.* 29:31 (CO 23.404); 30:2 (CO 23.408); *Comm. Ps.* 22:9-10 (CO 31.226); 71:6 (CO 31.655); 139:13-15 (CO 32.380-81); *Serms Deut.* 8:14-20 (CO 26.624-37); 28:2-8 (CO 28.358-71). See also, Bouwsma, op. cit., 162-76.

> When God has created a human creature in the womb of the mother, it has as yet no soul; on the contrary we know that while the creature is shaped in the womb of the mother, God breathes into it a soul and certainly then there is a seed of life.[92]

In other words, because God commanded men and women to increase and multiply, it is *their* responsibility to pursue that divine intention through sexual intercourse, but it is, simultaneously, altogether God's initiative to 'put forth his own power, to fulfil what he has said'.[93] For Calvin, as for Luther, marriage is a positive vehicle for God's gracious, creative activity in the lives of men and women. It is not, intrinsically, a *remedium peccati*. It becomes that at the fall of Adam and Eve.

Together with the more limited and specific purpose of procreation, itself, almost invariably, comes the wider intention of raising the children thus born. This is important, for with it Calvin seeks to emphasize the vocational duties of both parents and children in keeping order in the family and thus in society.

Procreation is God's method of propagating the species, with the purpose of preserving the human race,[94] or of safeguarding society.[95] He does this through the hierarchical structure of the parent/child relationship. Having brought children into the world, parents have the obligation of raising them before God, in faith and discipline. The husband and wife, then, are obliged to have children in the respectable and stable context of marriage. They are also obliged to train their children, to teach them the importance of societal order and peace and to keep them under strict control within the household and in the community. In this way societal peace is preserved. It is noticeable that, commenting on Ephesians 6:1-4, Calvin's reason for this responsibility is that children are so apt to become capricious, 'it requires frequent admonition and restraint'. In his sermon on the same passage, he adds, significantly, that 'it is just as if they were fully bent on abolishing the whole order of nature'.[96]

---

[92] *Serm. Job* 3:11 (CO 33.162).
[93] *Comm. Gen.* 21:1 (CO 23.296).
[94] '...*coniugium est conservation generis humani*' - *Comm. Jer.* 16:1-4 (CO 38.238).
[95] '...*ad conservationem societatis humanae*' - *Comm. Jer.*7:34 (CO 37.706). See also, *Comm. Gen.* 24:59 (CO 23.339).
[96] *Comm. Eph.* 6:1-4 (CO 51.229); *Serm. Eph.* 6:1-4 (CO 51.787), respectively. The

However, it needs to be added, on the more positive side, that parents are to be gentle and not tyrannical. They are to treat their children with 'self-control and fair dealing'.[97] Above all, they are to teach them to live lives honouring to God, giving them to Christ.[98] This comes through example, teaching and admonition.[99] He says, for instance,

> Let parents undertake to nourish, govern, and teach their children committed to them by God, not provoking their minds with cruelty or turning them against their parents ... but cherishing and embracing their children with such gentleness and kindness as becomes their character as parents.

By the last phrase ('their character as parents') Calvin apparently intends the character of *their vocation* as parents.[100] Significantly, elsewhere, the Reformer insists that only if the father and mother fulfil their vocational roles in this area is the law to be 'maintained in vigour by perpetual succession'. Indeed, if the structural arrangement of authority and submission is not perpetuated in this way, he says, 'human society [itself] cannot be maintained in its integrity'.[101] It is evident, then, that marriage is the legitimate context for procreation. But Calvin goes further in saying that the resultant family structural relationships have the role of maintaining moral uprightness in society – including the concept of societal order.

Reformer's allusion to the order of nature reflects what he has previously said concerning the hierarchical relationship between the parents and children. Children are under a double obligation, both because of *l'ordre naturel* and also because of God's divine command (*Dieu nous declare*) – (CO 51.785). Also, *Comm. Gen.* 21:20 (CO 23.305); 24:3 (CO 23.331); 34:4 (CO 23.457).

[97] *Comm. Josh.* 15:16 (CO 25.528-9); *Comm. Gen.* 24:57 (CO 23.339); 24:67 (CO 23.340); *Serm. Eph.* 6:1-4 (CO 51.783).

[98] See *Comm. Acts.* 16:14-18 (CO 48.377-82). In a letter to Viret, April 7 (1549), *Tracts and Letters,* 5.216-17, Calvin reports that his wife's last words regarding her children were, 'Assuredly, the principal thing is that they live a pious and holy life.'

[99] See for example, *Comm. 1 Thess.* 2:11-12 (CO 52.149-50); *Serm. 2 Sam.* 6:20-23 [Kelly, 280]; 8:9-18 [ibid., 427-9]; *Comm. Ps.* 78:3-4 (CO 31.722-3).

[100] *Inst* II.viii.46.

[101] *Comm. Deut.* 11:19 (CO 24.228-9), *Comm. Exod.* 20:12 / *Deut.*5:16 (CO 24.602), respectively. See also *Serm. Deut.* 6:4-9 (CO 26.432-44); 7:11-15 (CO 26.532-45); 11:16-21 (CO 27.109-21); 12:12-18 (CO 27.187-99).

Within the family and particularly within the husband-wife relationship, Calvin suggests that procreation has another, almost incidental, effect. He states that the bringing forth of offspring *'tends* to conciliate husbands to their wives'.[102] In his sermon on Job 19:17-25, the Reformer applies this as follows: 'When God blesses a marriage with descendants, that *ought* to increase the mutual affection to live in greater accord.'[103] It is clear by his use of the words 'tends' and 'ought' that, in practice, this is not always the case. But Calvin exhorts parents to love each other more *because* of their children. By implication from what has been said above, we may conjecture that the underlying reason for this is that of gratitude to God for his blessing on the marriage. From the husband's perspective, it may also reflect what he knows his wife has been through in her anguish of childbirth that draws love from him. Certainly, Calvin is at his most sensitive when contemplating that event.[104] However, these remain conjectures.

This brief consideration of Calvin's perspective on the second purpose for marriage addresses the subject of the present study in several ways. Not only do we find that he marvels at procreation,[105] but he also stresses man and woman's vocational role in the continuing process of both having and raising children. Although he does not emphasize the co-operation between the parents and God as Luther does, he infers an equality of obligation between the husband and wife before a God who is intimately involved in the whole event. Below, in the next section, this will need to be qualified by an examination of the respective roles of the father and mother, for it is the father who possesses higher authority and ultimate responsibility. Through having children and raising them in the right way, the husband and wife are maintaining and perpetuating societal order and, thus, fulfilling God's intention.

---

[102] *Comm. Gen.* 29:31 (CO 23.404) – emphasis added.

[103] *Serm. Job* 19:17-25 (CO 34.116) – emphasis added. In a way, that remains unspecified by Calvin, 'children confirm the love between husband and wife'.

[104] See, for example, his anxiety at Idelette's premature delivery – letter to Viret, July (1542) in *Tracts and Letters*, 4.335-6. Also, *Comm. 1 Thess.* 5:3 (CO 52.168); *Comm. Jer.*4:31 (CO 37.603-5); 13:21 (CO 38.169-70); 30:6 (CO 38.614-15); *Comm. Gen.* 12:11 (CO 23.183).

[105] Bouwsma, op. cit., 270, fn. 68, speaks of Calvin at times celebrating reproductivity. He cites both *Comm. Matt.* 21:16 (CO 45.583) and *Serm. Job* 19:17-25 (CO 34.116) as examples.

The Society of Two Reasonable Creatures[106]

Calvin addresses this conventional reason for marriage in much the same way as Luther and, again, with his own underlying emphasis on order or control in society. He emphasizes a mutual togetherness and love between the spouses, but he does so in the context of adamant teaching on a traditional, hierarchical structure between the husband and wife and on stereotypical roles.

Calvin adopts a creational logic, similar to that of Luther, to undergird his teaching on mutuality in the marriage relationship. Accordingly, God's created order, as it touches human beings (generally, as well as specifically in marriage), is a social design *necessarily* including a mutual partnership.[107] That is, at creation God appointed that this should be so in making of humanity, male and female – partners, companions, indeed, 'one whole man'. Thus each person is created a 'social animal [*sociale animal*]'.[108] Essential to the make-up of this social characteristic of human beings is a natural instinct 'to foster and preserve humanity'.[109] This becomes the man and woman's particular calling when they marry. Calvin says, 'The husband and wife live together in such a way as to cherish either the other no less than half himself.'[110]

The Reformer speaks of marriage in such terms as a 'holy friendship [*une amitié saincte*]', a 'friendship of life [*vitae societatem*]' and 'the society of two reasonable creatures [*la compagne de deux creatures humaines*]'.[111] Time and again, Calvin teaches that the husband and wife are mutual companions.[112] It is for this reason that Harkness' comment concerning the lack of

---

[106] *Serm. Deut.* 22:13-24 (CO 28.48): 'Il est question de la compagnie de deux creatures humaines ... compagnie à vie et à mort.'

[107] 'Active attention to co-operation and mutuality is, Calvin argues, entailed in the structure of humanity itself' (D. Little, 'Calvin and the Prospects for a Theory of Natural Law' in G. W. Outka / P. Ramsey (eds), *Norm and Context in Christian Ethics* (SCM, London, 1969), 179). Also, Biéler, op. cit., 36-9, 99.

[108] *Comm. Mal.* 2:14 (CO 44.453-6); *Comm. Gen.* 2:18 (CO 23.46), respectively. See also, *Comm. Gal.* 5:14 (CO 50.250); *Inst* II.iii.46; II.viii.41; *Comm. 1 Cor.* 6:15-20 (CO 49.398-400).

[109] *Inst* II.ii.13.

[110] *Comm. Matt.* 19:5 (CO 45.529; *CNTC*, 2.245). See also, *Serm. Eph.* 6:5-9 (CO 51.797).

[111] *Serm. Tit.* 2:3-5 (CO 54.516); *Comm. 1 Pet.* 3:1-7 (CO 55.256); *Serm. Deut.* 22:13-24 (CO 28.48), respectively.

[112] *Serm. Deut.* 24:1-6 (CO 28.149-63); *Serm. Eph.* 5:18-21 (CO 51.733); 5:31-3 (CO 51.779). See *Serm. Tit.* 2:3-5 (CO 54.516); *Serm. Deut.* 21:10-14 (CO 27.657-9).

teaching on companionship in Calvin is somewhat perplexing. She says, 'So far as I have been able to discover, neither Calvin nor Luther ever speak of marriage as an institution established for the mutual companionship of husband and wife, though they both say that the wife is given to be a helpmeet for her husband.'[113] Strangely, Karen Armstrong, who is generally extremely negative towards Calvin, concedes that his view of marriage includes the companionate element.[114] In fact, both Luther[115] and Calvin hold to companionship as a purpose for marriage, but they do so within their own terms of reference. Thus, Calvin stresses the companionate nature of the marriage relationship. He is logically bound to, of course, because of the nature of his understanding of the creational sociability of men and women.

The ethical corollary to the Reformer's teaching on companionship in the relationship between the spouses is to emphasize the practical importance of the mutual obligation to remain faithful to each other. Fidelity is a condition of marriage as God intended it to be.[116] Therefore, it is clearly an equal obligation of both the husband and the wife to remain faithful within their relationship together.[117] According to Calvin, faithfulness is maintained through mutual trust and love. On the former, Calvin says, 'If a man distrusts his wife ... it spreads a venom which corrupts the heart. And instead of winning peace, people lose it.'[118] It is significant that Calvin uses the concept of peace in the household. His concern stems both from his understanding of the pervasiveness and the destructive quality of sin and from his desire that peaceful order should prevail. On the latter, the Reformer speaks of a relationship that both exists and develops, that is closer than that between parents and children,[119] of harmony and consideration,[120] of love together with respect (*amor cum reverentia coniunctus*),[121] of the very opposite of egoistic self-love,[122] and (for

---

[113] Harkness, op. cit., 135.
[114] Armstrong, op. cit., 273.
[115] See chapter 6 of the present study.
[116] *Serm Deut.* 5:18 (CO 26.334-46); 24:1-6 (CO 28.150); *Comm. Ezek.* 16:8 (CO 40.342).
[117] *Comm. 1 Cor.* 7:4 (CO 49.403).
[118] *Serm. 2 Sam.* 10:1-12 [Kelly, 451-2].
[119] *Comm. Exod.* 2:1 (CO 24.21).
[120] *Serm. Eph.* 5:31-3 (CO 51.779).
[121] *Comm. 1 Pet.* 3:7 (CO 55.256).

the husband, at least) reflective of Christ's.[123] It is significant that his stress falls on peace, in the context of a well-ordered relationship as he comments on Genesis 2:18.

> Sweetest harmony would reign in marriage ... because the husband would look up with reverence to God; the wife in this would be a faithful assistant [*adiutrix*] to him; and both, with one consent, would cultivate a holy as well as a friendly and peaceful intercourse [*societatem*].[124]

It is generally true, as Selinger points out, that whereas Luther presents love as being Christ (*alter Christus*) to one's neighbour (including one's spouse), Calvin derives his notion of love from the second table of the Decalogue.[125] This appears to give Calvin's concept of love a reserve, largely missing in Luther. In keeping with its legal derivation, he also stresses that love has to be enjoined and controlled. Nevertheless, as far as we are able to tell, his own marriage to Idelette was more than a *mariage de convenance*. His grief over her death, though controlled, reveals the importance of their relationship together and his own love towards her.[126]

---

[122] *Inst* II.vii.6.

[123] *Inst* IV.xix.35.

[124] *Comm. Gen.* 2:18 (CO 23.47).

[125] Selinger, op. cit., 14, 102-4.

[126] This is an important subject in its own right, but one that cannot detain us at this point. It should be noted though, that several writers complain that Calvin's love for Idelette was less close than we are suggesting. For example, R. H. Bainton, *Women of the Reformation* (Beacon, Boston, 1974), 87, suggests that Calvin might as well have married a plank! See also, Murstein, op. cit., 179; F. Wendel, *Calvin: The Origins and Development of his Religious Thought* (Collins, London, 1965). However, the grief evidenced in his letters suggests the opposite – Calvin and his wife were close, he appears to have adored her. See correspondence to Viret, April 7 (1549) *Tracts and Letters* 5.216-17; to Farel, April 11 (1549), ibid., 217-19; to Richard Vauville, November (1555), ibid., 6.236-7. The fact that Calvin controls his grief reflects understanding of human nature and probably of God's passivity as well, but does not diminish its reality nor the love from which it springs. The Reformer teaches that godly men and women put a restraint upon their grief in case, 'like an unbroken horse' (the image of lack of control is significant, of course), 'by nourishing his grief, he might confirm himself in unsubdued impetuosity' – *Comm. Gen.* 37:35 (CO 23.490). See also, *Comm. Gen.* 23:2 (CO 23.321); 50:1 (CO 23.612); *Comm. Lam.* 3:51 (CO 39.598); *Comm. 1 Tim.* 1:6-7 (CO 53.254). Calvin limits the outworking of his personal grief in accordance with his own teaching. For a positive reading, see A. E. McGrath, *A Life of John Calvin* (Blackwell, Oxford:, 1993), 16; Bouwsma, op. cit.,

However, we note that companionship in marriage is not an end, in itself. Generally, it provides the legitimate context for sexual relations and the procreation of children. Calvin writes, '*the companionship of marriage* has been ordained as a necessary remedy to keep us from plunging into unbridled lust'.[127] It is companionship, primarily defined in terms of faithfulness and love, that is to be a help in restraining uncontrolled passion and fostering contentment in the husband and wife. Its spiritual purpose is, perhaps, to allow both spouses to gain access to God. For example, Calvin states that God brings spouses together, 'to be in love and concord (not grief and scorn) ... in order to pave the way to access to God'.[128]

How will this companionship reveal itself in everyday experience? In what context of relationship is it exercised? The teaching of Calvin is that mutual companionship is reflected in a voluntarily maintained, hierarchical marital structure. The wife will be willingly obedient to the husband, her head. The husband will be considerate towards his wife, his helper. So, in one passage, having defined marriage as a relationship in which each is to see the other as the half of themselves, he applies the idea to both:

> And the husband should rule, as the head of his wife [*ille vero sic imperet, ut caput sit uxoris*] not as a tyrant [*non tyrannus*]; and on her side, the wife should submit herself in modest obedience [*mulier vicissim modeste ad obsequia se submittat*].[129]

Two things are being stressed. Though he clearly teaches a patriarchal marital arrangement, its outworking is to be humanized by mutual love and respect. The significant point in Calvin's writing here is that companionship is simply defined by qualifying the hierarchical marital order. There is an order set by God which structures the family and which needs to be accepted by both the

---

23; R. N. Carew-Hunt, *Calvin* (Centenary, London, 1933), 101; J. H. Alexander, *Ladies of the Reformation* (Gospel Standard Strict Baptist Trust, Harpenden, 1978), 90-92.

[127] *Inst* II.viii.41. See also, *Comm. Gen.* 24:67 (CO 23.340-41).

[128] *Serm. Eph.* 5:31-3 (CO 51.779).

[129] *Comm. Matt.* 19:5 (CO 45.529; *CNTC*, 2.245). Elsewhere, he states that 'God established mankind according to this law: that the man maintain his position of head over the wife, and the wife, on the other hand, be a helper to the man; and so at the same time he bound both sexes together in a mutual bond' (*De Scandalis* (OS 2.230)). See also *Comm. Gen.* 2:18 (CO 23.46-7).

husband and the wife if true mutual companionship is to flourish. The order is, above all, a *useful* hierarchy; it maintains the divine economy (*oeconomiam*), it leads to 'good order and government (*ordre et police*)'.[130] The hierarchy begins with the recognition that at the apex of the structure is God or Christ.[131] Then, in domestic terms, it continues with the subjection of the wife. It is recognizably companionship when the spouses relate with consideration towards each other *within the given order*.[132] It is, therefore, a limited sense of companionship that Calvin actually advocates. In this context, it should be clear, on the one hand, that Calvin is speaking of a hierarchical authority and power that belongs to the husband, both by creation and by right. Being a husband is not merely a private phenomenon, it embodies an authority that is creational, religious and political, as well as familial.[133] On the other hand, he speaks of the woman's subjection as hers by creation and punishment. He speaks of the wife 'under the power' of her husband and of 'the right of the husband over the wife'.[134] Critics of Calvin's marital ideas justly complain of unequal power-relations.[135]

As we shall see, the Reformer seeks to soften the edges of his teaching, but nevertheless his hierarchical theory surfaces at times in his social application. For example, he emphasizes that because the woman loses her own name taking on her husband's at

---

[130] *Inst* II.viii.35; *Serm. Eph.* 5:22-26 (CO 51.737), respectively. See Bouwsma, op. cit., 194-203.

[131] *Comm. John* 19:25 (CO 47.417); *Comm. 1 Cor.* 7:34 (CO 49.423); *Serm. 2 Sam.* 13:25-39 [Kelly, 649-50]; *Comm Deut.* 13:6-11 (CO 27.250-51).

[132] *Comm. 1 Tim.* 2:13 (CO 52.276-7); *Comm. 1 Cor.* 11:7 (CO 49.476); 14:34 (CO 49.533); *Comm. Acts* 18:26 (CO 48.437); *Serm. Eph.* 5:31-3 (CO 51.771); *Comm. Isa.* 57:8 (CO 37.311). See also, *Comm. Lev.* 30:1-17 (CO 24.572); *Comm. Exod.* 20:12 / *Deut.* 5:16 (CO 24.602). It should be noted, at this point, that Calvin teaches a 'mutual submission' which will be examined in the next chapter. By 'mutual submission' he largely describes restraint and obligation *within individual* vocation for the good of the other. See, for example, *Comm. Eph.* 5:21 (CO 51.221); *Comm. 1 Pet.* 5:5 (CO 55.287).

[133] *Comm. Ps.* 101:7 (CO 32.59).

[134] *Comm. Num.* 30:1-17 (CO 24.572). See also, *Comm. Tit.* 3:1 (CO 52.425-6); *Inst* II.viii.35; *Comm. Exod.* 20:12 / *Deut.* 5:16 (CO 24.605).

[135] Even M. S. van Leeuwen (et al.), *After Eden* (Eerdmans, Grand Rapids, 1993), 219, though generally positive concerning Calvin, suggests that his teaching *could* be seen as 'punitive power-wielding'. On the complaint see, for example, R. Miles, *The Rites of Man* (Grafton, London, 1991), 129; idem, *The Woman's History of the World* (Michael Joseph, London, 1988), 112; Jordan, op. cit., 22.

marriage, she shows her own subject position and that he is the head. The veil that is worn at the wedding is somehow reflective of this too.[136] The husband retains the right to name children as a sign of his 'power and authority'.[137] The wife is sometimes spoken of as the husband's possession and property.[138] And again, on the subject of the rape of a wife, Calvin insists on the *man's* shame and distress, but says nothing of the woman's feelings.[139] These are characteristics which reflect sixteenth-century attitudes. It is a pity that the Reformer lacks a more rigorous application of gospel equality in these areas. This tends to be the case also in his teaching on respective roles, which remain stereotyped. Despite this, he seeks to humanize the basic structure.

The following passage, taken from the Reformer's comments on the visit of the three men to Abraham, illustrates his hierarchical application:

> Moses presents us with a beautiful picture of domestic government [*oeconomiae*]. Abraham runs, partly, to command what he would have done; and partly, to execute his own duty, as the master of the house. Sarah keeps within the tent; not to indulge in sloth,[140] but rather to take her own part also in the labour. The servants are all prompt to obey. Here is the sweet concord of a well-conducted family that could not have thus suddenly arisen, unless each had, by long practice, been accustomed to right discipline [*rectam disciplinam*].[141]

Significantly, both the husband and the wife have distinct and well-rehearsed duties that accord with their position in the familial hierarchy.

---

[136] *Comm. Isa.* 4:1 (CO 36.95).

[137] *Comm. Isa.* 7:14 (CO 36.157). The power and right, thus asserted, definitely does not belong to the woman: 'Scimus has partes semper tribui patri, ut nomen filio imponat. Hoc enim signum est iuris et potestatis patrum in filios: nec eadem autoritas ad mulieres pertinet.'

[138] For example, *Serm. Deut.* 20:2-9 (CO 27.602-16). This concept may lie behind Calvin's assertion that David, in taking Bathsheba, was engaging in 'an act of thievery' – *Serm. 2 Sam.* 11:1-5 [Kelly, 477].

[139] *Serm. 2 Sam.* 12:7-12 [Kelly, 542]; *Comm. Jer.* 8:10 (CO 38.12); *Comm. Gen.* 34:1 (CO 23.456).

[140] There is a hint elsewhere, that Calvin believes women, generally, to be less industrious than men – see *Comm. Lev.* 27:1-7 (CO 24.567-8).

[141] *Comm. Gen.* 18:6 (CO 23.252).

For his part, the man's chief marital obligation is to govern or to lead those under his authority in the household, including his wife.[142] Calvin sometimes uses the terms 'reign' and 'rule'.[143] He speaks of the husband as the 'lord of the wife' with the humanizing implication of protection.[144] However, as with Luther, he seeks to apply this patriarchal authority in a restrained and loving manner. The husband is to love his wife as himself,[145] to be content with and faithful to her,[146] to bear with her frailties,[147] correcting her faults with gentleness – while, at the same time, acknowledging his own.[148] Above all, the husband is not to abuse his position of authority, he is not to tyrannise his wife. In this, Calvin condemns the unreasonable exercise of power.[149] Apart from the fact that God commands otherwise, the significant basis for this is that women are not to be treated as nothing. They are companions and, in a sense, an egalitarian impulse may be discernible.[150] In this, we observe the Reformer's recognition of the naturally egotistical nature of sin and the need, in and through marriage, to control it and to maintain marital order. In a sermon he speaks of the spouses' obligations:

---

[142] See *Comm. Col.* 4:15 (CO 52.132) – the husband is to form his household 'in the likeness of a church'. He is to teach the household to live properly, the children are to be trained in the fear of God, to be kept in modesty and shown how to faithfully earn their living – *Serm. 2 Sam.* 8:9-18 [Kelly, 428-9]. On the image of the family as a church (*ut sit ecclesiae imago*), see *Comm. Acts* 16:14-18 (CO 48.378); *Comm. 1 Cor.* 16:19 (CO 49.571).

[143] See, for example, *Comm. Acts* 16:14-18 (CO 48.378). On the idea of governing, see *Comm. Ps.* 101:7 (CO 32.59); *Serm. 2 Sam.* 6:20-23 [Kelly, 280]; 9:1-13 [ibid., 437]; *Serm. Deut.* 22:13-24 (CO 28.49); *Comm. Gen.* 2:18 (CO 23.47).

[144] *Comm. Joel* 1:8 (CO 42.523).

[145] *Comm. Eph.* 5:28 (CO 51.225); *Serm. Deut.* 13:6-11 (CO 27.250-51); *Comm. Isa.* 6:11 (CO 36.139); *Serm. Job* 19:17-25 (CO 34.116).

[146] *Comm. Jer.* 2:33 (CO 37.538).

[147] *Serm. Deut.* 24:1-6 (CO 28.150).

[148] *Serm. Deut.* 21:15-17 (CO 27.666); 23:24-24:4 (CO 28.136-49); 24:1-6 (CO 28.161). This is to be the case *vice versa* as well: the wife gently corrects the husband's faults, acknowledging her own.

[149] On this generally, see *Comm. 1 Pet.* 5:3 (CO 55.286).

[150] *Serm. 1 Tim.* 2:12-14 (CO 53.217-18). See also, *Serm. Deut.* 22:13-24 (CO 28.41); *Serm. Job* 9:1-6 (CO 33.416); *Comm. Hos.* 3:1 (CO 42.257); *Comm. Matt.* 19:5 (CO 45.528); *Serm. Eph.* 5:22-6 (CO 51.741-2); *Comm. Col.* 3:18 (CO 52.126). Also, W. F. Graham, *The Constructive Revolutionary* (John Knox, Richmond, 1971), 154.

The husband will carry out his duty to live chastely with his wife, and even with all kindness, to support her *and foster peace and harmony in the household*. ... The wife also, when she remembers that she is joined in the name of God and that marriage is a sacred thing, will thus carry out her duty.[151]

Generally, the wife's vocational duty is to be the completion of the man,[152] as his helper (*adiutrix*).[153] In this, she is to be obedient to him in seeking to please him.[154] This entails governing the household (under her husband's authority and in the sight of God), being a 'keeper of the house'.[155] Two particular areas of obligation for the wife are those of raising and caring for the children and also doing the housework – both of which the Reformer sees as intrinsic parts of the woman's *vocatio*.

Certainly, the role of motherhood is the primary, specific calling of the wife.[156] Regarding this, Calvin shows warmth and some understanding of the woman's natural ability.

> What amazing affection does a mother feel towards her offspring, which she cherishes in her bosom, suckles on her breast, and watches

---

[151] *Serm. 2 Sam.* 9:1-13 [Kelly, 437] – emphasis added.

[152] *Comm Gen.* 2:18 (CO 23.47); 2:21 (CO 23.49); 38:8 (CO 23.495); *Comm. 1 Cor.* 7:1 (CO 49.401).

[153] Calvin wished for a wife who would be concerned for his physical wellbeing, particularly his health – to Farel May 19 (1539), *Tracts and Letters*, 4.141. On the necessity for this, see to Farel Oct. (1540), ibid., 4.204-8; to Bullinger, July 2 (1563), ibid., 7.320-23; to Bullinger, April 6 (1564), ibid., 7.362-3. This shows something of his realism and discretion in the face of his physical problems – see J. Rilliet, *Le Vrai Visage de Calvin* (Pensée / Privat, Toulouse, 1982), 90; F. W. Barton, *Calvin and the Duchess* (Westminster / John Knox, Louisville, 1989), 25 – *contra*, Murstein, op. cit., 179. After the death of Idelette, the Reformer wrote, 'From her I never experienced the slightest hindrance' – to Viret, April 7 (1549), *Tracts and Letters*, 5.216-17.

[154] *Comm. 1 Tim.* 2:12-13 (CO 52.276); *Serm. Deut.* 23:24-24:4 (CO 28.136-49); *Comm. Matt.* 19:5 (CO 45.529). Calvin says that Moses 'exhorts women [after the example of Sarah] ... to be obedient and well-behaved towards their own husbands' (*Comm. Gen.* 18:12 (CO 23.254)). The over-riding attitude that Calvin exhorts women to adopt is that of 'modesty' – see *Comm. Gen.* 24:64 (CO 23.340); *Comm. Exod.* 2:18 (CO 24.31); *Comm. Deut* 25:11-12 (CO 24.667); *Comm. Isa.* 4:1 (CO 36.94); *Comm. 1 Pet.* 3:3 (CO 55.254).

[155] See *Comm. Gen.* 34:1 (CO 23.456); *Serm. Deut.* 6:4-9 (CO 26.444); 22:13-24 – 'aider à gouverner une maison au nom de Dieu'. (CO 28.49); *Comm. Tit.* 2.4 (CO 52.420).

[156] *Comm. 1 Tim.* 2:5 (CO 52.277); *Comm. Isa.* 49:15 (CO 37.204).

over with tender care, so that she passes sleepless nights, wears herself out by continued anxiety, and forgets herself.[157]

Though the Reformer acknowledges that fathers also demonstrate great love to their children and anxiety when problems arise,[158] it is not to be compared with the mothers' love.[159] The woman's menial tasks - wiping, combing, dressing, nursing, feeding, disciplining and keeping the children in order - are of divine appointment and, therefore, form her sacrificial service to God.[160] Next to this, housework is considered of secondary importance, yet still significant and acceptable sacrifice before God. Calvin is specific:

> A woman, for instance, is doing well when she does her housework, makes up the bed, cleans the house, boils the pot, and governs the children: all of this is very appropriate.

He makes the point, as did Luther before him, that women should remain quietly at home - the apostle commends it, nature dictates it, women prefer it![161]

CONCLUSION

This chapter has presented Calvin's perception of the relationship between the husband and wife through an examination of the

---

[157] *Comm. Isa.* 49:15 (CO 37.204). See also, *Comm. Isa.* 42:14 (CO 37.69).

[158] See *Comm. 1 Cor.* 4:15 (CO 49.372). In a passage reminiscent of Luther, Calvin suggests that there are times when the father is the one to be awakened for the children. At such times he is to rejoice in God's calling and to be sacrificial and patient in the task - *Serm. 1 Tim.*2:13-15 (CO 53.229).

[159] He says that man's love is more hidden, the woman's more tender - *Serm. 2 Sam.* 1:21-7 [Kelly, 44].

[160] *Serm. 1 Tim.*2:13-15 (CO 53.228-9); *Serm. Tit.* 2:3-5 (CO 54.511). Women are to busy themselves with bringing up children - *Serm. Deut.* 6:4-7 (CO 26 444).

[161] *Serm. 2 Sam.* 6:1-6 [Kelly, 239]. Also, *Serm. Deut.* 5:18 (CO 26.334-6). Also, *Comm. Gen.* 34:1 (CO 23.456). The context of the story of the rape of Dinah makes this comment even more poignant: he says, 'She *ought* to have remained quietly at home' - emphasis added. Unfortunately, it also reveals a (typically male?) lack of understanding of the situation, in which Dinah (the victim) is by implication accused of wrongdoing. See also, *Comm. Mic.* 2:9 (CO 43.312); M. Parsons, 'Luther and Calvin on rape: Is the crime lost in the agenda?' *EQ* 74/2 (2002), 123-42.

reasons that he gives to encourage men and women to marry. We have observed that the reasons are conventional: that is, marriage is a remedy against unbridled lust, a legitimate context for the procreation of offspring and a genuine society between two reasonable creatures.

Given the immediate context in which the marital relationship exists in Calvin's thinking, it is clear that his emphasis underlines his fear of social (particularly, familial) disorder. This emerges, generally, from his overall, obsessive theological and social concern for order in society, detailed in chapter 8. His understanding of sin's pervasiveness and activity forms the underlying problem which marriage, in the intention of God, seeks to counter. Because sin permeates every part of the nature of men and women, because it infiltrates every element of their relationships and behaviour and itself vigorously tends to uncontrolledness, it is necessary for them to have a controlling context, a 'cultural construction'.[162] A well-ordered relationship between husband and wife fulfils that role in this context. It is not merely a voluntary institution (although, *it is that*), it is also God's way of promoting order and stability in the social arrangement of men and women. That is its divinely given task. Marriage, as a temporal vocation, restrains sin and maintains societal order.

It has been argued that Calvin holds a less negative view of sex and sexuality than is often suggested. If the discussion begins at his interpretation of sexual relations at creation (rather than in postlapsarian experience) then the general impression of his thinking is, at worst, only ambivalent. The Reformer can speak of sexual intercourse as pleasurable, he *can* allude to a genuine marital passion, but he only does so within a qualified context. As with Luther, he qualifies by comment on sin, but counters by a reminder of God's forgiving grace. In fact, he retains a negative element in his thinking, largely because of a pessimistic emphasis on sin that overshadows his comments. Sexual lust so easily gains uncontrolled momentum. Marriage allows the husband and wife to restrain promiscuity and excess, and to maintain familial order, *if* it is conducted in a God-honouring manner. Then, it becomes a *remedium peccati*.

We have found that marriage as a context for having children is stressed by Calvin in the wider sphere of both having and raising

---

[162] This is Bouwsma's useful phrase – op. cit., 48.

them. Children are God's creation and his intention for married couples. Parents have a vocational obligation to co-operate with God. The present chapter argued that Calvin's thinking in this area of having children resulted in two important conclusions. First, having and raising children issues in the preservation of a well-ordered humanity. Second, it also confirms and increases love between the spouses.

In the important area of the third purpose for marriage, we have maintained that, though companionship is vital to Calvin's concept of the husband-wife relationship, it is to be read in the context of two significant considerations. First, companionship (resting on the basis of a created sociability) is not an end in itself. It appears in Calvin's writing to be the context for remedying sin, for legitimate sexual relations and for having and raising offspring. Second, it forms the foundation for a voluntary, hierarchical marital arrangement, in which the husband rules his wife in love and the wife obeys with respect. In the same way as Luther, Calvin teaches a definite patriarchy which leaves the spouses in an *unequal* relationship, largely determined by concepts of power and authority, partly humanised by love. It has been noted that this, again, has the overall function of maintaining peace and social order.

We argued in chapter 8 that the concept of order is determinative for an understanding of Calvin's social ethics, generally, and of his teaching on the husband-wife relationship, in particular. Because the nature of sin and because the confrontational character of Satan's activity is to seek disorder, then the counter-character of *vocatio* is to restrain sin, to restrict its damage-potential and to preserve the order that God intends. Within this general context, it is the individual's vocational responsibility, before God, to maintain order. Chapter 8 hinted at the place of marriage within this scheme of things.

The present chapter has particularized that theme and has shown that, in Calvin's thought, within the context of sin and potential disorder the husband and wife relationship has a vital, societal part to play. The traditional purposes given for marriage lend weight to the Reformer's understanding that each pushed to a logical conclusion shows that the intrinsic reason for marriage is societal order-maintenance. This, in a conversely reciprocal manner, suggests the structural arrangement of the husband and wife relationship, for within this wider obsession for order lies a fundamental need of preserving the *status quo.*

The following chapter seeks to expound Calvin's reading and understanding of the major biblical texts to further examine his teaching on the marriage relationship, to explore his use of Scripture at this point and to see whether his concept of order is intrusive to his exposition.

CHAPTER 10

CALVIN, HIERARCHY AND MUTUAL LOVE

We have outlined Calvin's governing theological and social presuppositions (related to his concept of order) and, more specifically, his perspective on the traditional reasons for marriage. We have seen that Calvin teaches a fixed and permanent hierarchical arrangement between husband and wife, with the recurring emphases on marriage as a restraining institution and upon structure and obligation. We move, now, from the broader brushstrokes and more finely illustrate Calvin's concept of marriage from his own exposition of biblical texts. In this manner we will discover in what way the Reformer employs his theological assumptions in reading Scripture. We will find that the traditional emphases and theological assumptions are somewhat determinative. For example, his understanding of the Pauline emphases surfaces time and again, particularly in his exposition of Genesis 1-3. This, at times, makes his exegesis contrived and artificial. It will be found that the themes that come to the fore in his exposition are those of order and its maintenance, vocation and obligation, and the permanence of the hierarchical marital structure.

CALVIN'S BIBLICAL EXPOSITION

Although Calvin spoke on most of these texts somewhat later in his ministry, for convenience this section will address his thought in the chronological order of the publication of his earlier, Latin commentaries.[1] His preaching on these passages (as an application of his exposition and theology[2]) will also be taken into account.

I Corinthians 7[3]

Calvin approaches this passage in a similar way to Luther. He understands the words of the first verse[4] as the apostle's unsolicited advice, not as an idea from the Corinthians to which the apostle is responding. Largely on account of that, the general tenor of Calvin's writing at this point is that celibacy is to be preferred to marriage.[5] Given this underlying assumption, the Reformer speaks of the remedial characteristic of marriage, its practical and daily difficulties, and the mutuality between the husband and wife as intrinsic to the nature of that relationship.

According to Calvin, the Corinthians extolled celibacy to an excessive extent and, conversely, they abhorred marriage. The apostle's advice, then, is to teach that celibacy is good, but that most do not have the ability to abstain from sexual relations. Rather, they are urged on, incorrigibly, by 'promptings of the flesh' (402) and, therefore, should take the opportunity to escape inevitable sin – an escape afforded to them by marriage. Verse 9[6]

---

[1] That is, 1 Cor. 7, 11:2-16 and 14:33-5 (1546, sermons, 1555-6); Ephesians 5:21-33 (1548, sermons 1558); 1 Timothy 2:9-15 (1548, sermons 1554); Genesis 1-3 (1554, sermons 1559); 1 Peter 3:1-7 (1556). For the dating of both the Latin commentaries and the later, French sermons, see the following: T. H. L. Parker, *Calvin's Old Testament Commentaries* (T&T Clark, Edinburgh, 1986), 29; idem, *Calvin's New Testament Commentaries* (SCM, London, 1971), 153-63; idem, *Calvin's Preaching* (T&T Clark, Edinburgh, 1992); W. de Greef, *The Writings of John Calvin* (Baker, Grand Rapids, 1993), 237-41.

[2] See, B. W. Farley, 'John Calvin's Sermons on the Ten Commandments' (unpublished doctoral thesis, Union Theological Seminary, Richmond, 1976), 162; G. M. Sumner, 'The Style of John Calvin's Sermons' (unpublished B.Litt thesis, Oxford University, 1976), 248; A. E. McGrath, *Life of John Calvin* (Blackwell, Oxford, 1993), 145-7; *Serm. Deut.* 4:44-5:3 (CO 26.240-41); *Serm. 2 Sam.* 7:1-13 [Kelly, 298]; *Serm. Gal.* 1:15-18 (CO 50.339-52).

[3] *Comm. 1 Cor.* 7 (CO 49.400-427).

[4] That is, specifically, 'It is not good for a man to touch a woman.'

[5] *Comm. 1 Cor.* 7:8 (CO 49.407), for example. It is, perhaps, significant that eighteen months after his own wife's death he speaks of celibacy in preference to marriage – a celibacy which he, himself, is practising, 'not unwillingly' (*De Scandalis* (OS 2.229)).

[6] 'It is better to be married than to burn with desire.'

allows the Reformer to qualify what he has written regarding the priority of celibacy.

> Although Paul advises them to abstain from marriage, he always speaks conditionally – 'if it is possible', 'if they are capable of it'. But when the weakness of the flesh stands in the way of that freedom, he plainly directs them to marry, as if it were a matter about which there was no doubt at all.[7]

Having already stated that there is an excessiveness about all human affections (406), he defines 'burning' with the image of disease (424-6) and speaks of it, in an extreme way, as the complete inability to resist – the loss of control, the failure to withstand temptation. This inner lack corresponds to a loss of relationship with God (421).[8]

Calvin insists, however, that the remedial nature of marriage is not the only reason for getting married. In fact, *ideally*, the primary purpose is in order to have offspring; but, significantly, the avoidance of fornication becomes the main pragmatic reason for those who are liable to sin outside the institution of marriage. Thus, his extreme account of 'burning' and his insistence that marriage is primarily a remedy against such sin accord with his concepts of sin as disorder and of the vocation of marriage as a boundaried, controlling institution within which men and women can live an ordered and peaceful life.

Still seeking to be consistent with what he supposes to be Paul's preference for celibacy, the Reformer outlines the difficulties entailed in the marital estate.[9] In general, he shows a realistic understanding of these.[10] Calvin advises that,

---

[7] *Comm. 1 Cor.* 7:9 (CO 49.408; *CNTC,* 9.143).

[8] In other citations of this verse Calvin gives his opinion that the vast majority of people – both men and women – would fall under this category. See *Inst* II.viii.43, IV.xiii.17; *Serm. Deut.* 5:18 (CO 26.341-2).

[9] S. Selinger, *Calvin Against Himself* (Archon, Hamden, 1984), 59, suggests that, whereas Luther sees the struggles within marriage as necessary tragedy *in* life, Calvin speaks of them as a necessary mode *of* life. This is largely true. Whereas Luther seems to suggest that difficulties in marriage come upon a man or a woman, it appears to be part of Calvin's pessimistic thesis that these stem from the fallen nature of human beings and of the world in which they live. They are, somehow, inherent in the nature of things.

[10] He lists them as follows: '[T]he death of children or partner; quarrels, and little differences [between the husband and the wife], ... which result

> We must remember to distinguish between the unblemished ordinance of God [*puram Dei ordinationem*] and the punishments of sin, which came on the scene afterwards. For according to this distinction, it was good for a man to be joined to a wife, without anything to spoil it, and even now it is good but only to a degree, because the bitter is mixed with the sweet, on account of the curse of God.[11]

That is, Calvin teaches that the nature of marriage in the present is a mixture of bitterness and sweetness, of good and evil. That which is good is a remnant of what the institution would have been like if sin had never entered the world; that which is evil is part and parcel of what it means to live in postlapsarian existence. Calvin emphasizes that marriage is not merely a necessary evil, it is a temporal gift of God, which should be used correctly and enjoyed. In this, the Reformer widens the discussion, speaking of everything that God gives in the present.

He interprets verse 29,[12] not as eschatologically determined, but as indicating the shortness of a person's life and, characteristically, in a much more restrained way than Luther before him, addresses the believer, who ought not to be taken up with or repose in these things.[13] In respect of the present study, it is important to note that the major problem in marriage (as Calvin sees it here) is that believing husbands – feeling the sinfulness as well as the goodness of marriage, and with the possibility of being pulled simultaneously in the opposing directions of wife and God[14] – will become so anxious that they corrupt themselves with disorder / excess (ἀταξία) (422-3).

Throughout his exposition, the Reformer gives some indication of what he believes that marriage relationship to be in the light of the two emphases discussed above. He returns, in his comments on the first verse, to the creation narrative to stress that the

---

from being too fastidious; children's wrong-doing, the difficulty of bringing up a family, and similar things' (*Comm. 1 Cor.* 7:32 (CO 49.421; *CNTC,* 9.161)).

[11] *Comm. 1 Cor.* 7:1 (CO 49.402; *CNTC,* 9.136).

[12] 'The time we live in will not last long.'

[13] *Comm. 1 Cor.* 7:29 (CO 49.420). See also, *Inst* III.x.4, where, quoting verse 29, he says that Christians should use the world, but not be affected by it. Also, *Inst* III.x.1. As we noted earlier, Luther speaks with characteristic exuberance at this point – *Comm. 1 Cor.* 7:29, LW 28.52 (WA 12.138).

[14] On this subject, more fully, see *Serm. Deut.* 5:18 (CO 26.334-46).

goodness of marriage lies, as we have seen, in part, in that it completes something in man himself. Significantly, he does this with an important qualification.

> [W]here the wife is a help to her husband, making his life happy [*ad felicem vitam*], then that is in accordance with God's intention. For God so ordered it in the beginning that the man without a wife was half a man [*quasi dimidius homo*], as it were, and felt himself lacking in help which he particularly needed [*seque singulari et necessario auxilio*]; and the wife was, as it were, the completion of the man [*quasi viri complementum*].[15]

Two things seem to rest on this understanding. First, Calvin believes that the marriage bond is indissoluble (409-10, 427). In this context, then, he states that a marriage with an unbeliever is still necessarily a marriage and that it is therefore sacred and pure, for the piety of the one is sure to outweigh the impiety of the other. Similarly, a marriage between two unbelievers, neither acknowledging God as its author, is still pure on the grounds that it fulfils the function of preserving order and respectability within society. Therefore, says Calvin, '[I]t is approved by God, like the other parts of the social order [*ordinis politici*].'[16]

The idea of order and control within the community appears to be the bottom line for Calvin's appraisal of marriage. So, the doctrine of the indissolubility of marriage allows Calvin to affirm the inner nature of the institution (which is useful to his sense of order), while it also gives him a tool that is constructive to the continuance of that order within everyday, practical living. Actually, he is not entirely consistent in this, permitting a believer freedom from the bond of marriage (*liberari a vinculo coniugii*) if the unbelieving spouse leaves.[17] However, recognizing the possibility that allowing for an exception might destroy his argument for indissolubility, he asks, rather weakly, 'What connection can a pious wife any longer maintain with an unbelieving husband?'

---

[15] *Comm. 1 Cor.* 7:1 (CO 49.401; CNTC, 9.135).

[16] *Comm. 1 Cor.* 7:14 (CO 49.412; CNTC 9.149).

[17] Elsewhere, citing 1 Cor. 7:4, Calvin speaks of this in a fuller manner – *Serm. Deut.* 24:1-6 (CO 28.150-51). He says that the party leaving is breaking the conditions of fidelity and, therefore, 'the bond of marriage is untied' (150). The remaining partner is then free to remarry – for, if he [she] is constrained to divorce his [her] spouse 'must he [she] be punished?' (151).

(411)[18] It appears that his concern is not so much theoretical or doctrinal consistency, as his own need for an understanding of marriage that is likely to keep order in society.

The second thing that rests on his understanding of marriage comes to light in his comments regarding marital love and sexual relations. Presumably, because of his own and his readers' hierarchical presuppositions, the Reformer finds a need to question why the apostle puts the man and his wife on an equal footing in verse 4 in which Paul speaks of the body of both as not merely their own, but also each other's. The Reformer's question is full of implication. Calvin asks why Paul makes them equal in this, 'instead of requiring from the woman obedience and subjection'. Calvin is careful to point out their differences before responding to his own enquiry. 'The husband and wife, therefore, have different rights and duties in other things, but in the preservation of married faithfulness [*fide coniugali*], they are on an equal footing.'[19] It is an interesting question, that Calvin ignores, as to why the spouses should be less than equal in authority and duty and, yet, equal in their sexual relations. Calvin seems to miss the point of his own teaching that both have an equal obligation to maintain faithfulness within marriage and that this is one significant and obvious way to do it. Having already spoken of their mutual benevolence (*mutua benevolentia* – 402), Calvin now speaks of their joint responsibility to be 'helpful to each other's necessity'. However, at times, for short periods, they are to exercise mutual consent and abstinence in order to apply themselves to prayer and fasting.[20]

His final comment on the nature of marriage is that it is the 'law that declares the connection between the husband and wife to be indissoluble' (427). We judge, from the whole context, that he refers here to the law of nature (supplemented by and in agreement with the law of Scripture) which shows in the case of the husband

---

[18] Calvin's conclusions at this point throw up problems for his teaching on mixed marriages and a circular difficulty arises. Having taught that marriage is, by definition, indissoluble, the Reformer inconsistently gives this as an example of a marriage that can be dissolved. As we have seen, Calvin has already insisted that marriage between a believer and an unbeliever *is truly* a marriage, so the question quoted merely underlines the Reformer's problem. However, he appears unaware of the difficulty.

[19] *Comm. 1 Cor.* 7:4 (CO 49.403; *CNTC*, 9.137).

[20] *Comm. 1 Cor.* 7:5 (CO 49.403-5). *Inst* IV.xii.16 – Calvin believes that this verse means something demanding more serious attention than merely daily prayer.

and wife that they become one, as two halves joined become a whole.

In his commentary on 1 Corinthians 7, Calvin allows the wife an equality in sexual matters – particularly in the decision to abstain in order to exercise spiritual disciplines; in the ability to separate from a spouse who has deserted; and in an equality in mutual friendliness and love. The first, however, is given somewhat reticently. However, he does not question his own illustration of two halves becoming one whole, in terms of its possible implications regarding the equality of the two halves (husband and wife) and, in particular, as it relates to the status of the wife. This is probably the case for two major reasons: first, because, in Calvin's thinking (as in Luther's) it is the wife who is measured by her husband. It is the man who is incomplete without her help – that is, the situation is pictured, not as a mutual, reciprocal completing, but as the wife completing her husband. Second, behind everything in Calvin's exposition is the presupposition that men and women are in a hierarchical relationship – seen most pointedly in the fact that, before Calvin can allow the biblical comment concerning the similarity and equality within the sexual relationship, he finds it necessary to stress the differences of status and authority between the spouses in other areas (v.4 – 403). It is this idea of the difference in authority which is, ultimately, the sticking point in the Reformer's thinking. He imposes this presupposition on to the passage, underlining his own commitment to a hierarchical structure within the marriage relationship. When he turns his attention to 1 Corinthians 11, he broadens this out to envelop, not only those who are married, but also to women and men, *per se*.

I Corinthians 11:2-16[21]

A close study of Calvin's handling of this very difficult passage underlines our conclusion that the Reformer's over-riding presupposition is that women are intrinsically inferior to men. It develops the idea. This is shown to be an unalterable precept over against the localized customs and traditions of society that may change. However, this particular understanding is questioned by some revisionist interpreters of Calvin's thought. According

---

[21] *Comm. 1 Cor.* 11:2-16 (CO 49.473-79).

to Douglass, for example, it must be read very differently. Indeed, she turns the thing on its head, concluding that, 'Calvin has transformed this text[22] ... to his own satisfaction, from one of the foundation stones of a theological justification of women's subjection into support for women's greater freedom in the church.'[23] Generally, Douglass' explanation appears to be over-optimistic and a misreading of the Reformer at this point.

The idea dominating the Reformer's exposition is that of verse 3, 'while every man has Christ for his head, a woman's head is man, as Christ's head is God'.[24] Calvin interprets this as revealing a divinely-appointed arrangement, defined in terms of degrees of authority, in which God occupies the first place, Christ holds the second (having placed himself there as mediator), man and woman then follow, in that order. Again, we note that it is the concept of authority that pervades his hierarchical understanding. This order is laid down by God's eternal law in created structures (476). It is apparent that Calvin has in mind the concept of authority and status structure, and therefore of inequality, for he recognizes an inherent problem; that is, that this seems to contradict the apostle's other statement – that men and women are equal (Gal. 3:28). His answer is that men and women are spiritually equal, but are not socially so.[25]

> [A]s far as external connections and social propriety are concerned, the man takes his lead from Christ, and the woman from the man, so that they do not stand on the same level but this inequality [*inaequalitas*] exists.[26]

---

[22] 1 Cor. 11:7.

[23] J. D. Douglass, 'Christian Freedom: What Calvin Learned at the School of Women', *CH* 53 (1984), 166.

[24] Calvin's translation: 'le chef de tout homme, c'est Christ, et le chef de la femme, c'est l'homme, et le chef de Christ, c'est Dieu' – (CO 57.431).

[25] 'La police et l'ordre qui y est de la vie présente' – *Serm. 1 Cor.* 11:2-3 (CO 49.720). Also, ibid., 718-19.

[26] *Comm. 1 Cor.* 11:3 (CO 49.474; CNTC, 9.230): '*Ergo quantum ad spiritualem coniunctionem, coram Deo et intus in conscientia, Christus caput est viri ac mulieris absque discrimine: quia illic neque masculi neque feminae habetur respectus. Quantum ad externam compositionem et decorum politicum, Christum vir et virum mulier sequitur: ita ut non sit idem gradus, sed locum habeat inaequalitas ista.*'

This appears indisputable to Calvin, 'the civil order [*civilem ordinem*] and also the distinctions in honours' are left intact, 'for ordinary life cannot get on without these'.[27]

Having stated the principle, Calvin appears to expound the text with this as the determinative factor. Interestingly, he moves immediately into application regarding, not the church fellowship (as the biblical context might suggest), but marital relationships. According to him, a man must not cover his head because it would be a sign to others that he has relinquished his authority over his wife, he has allowed her to dominate and, importantly, the glory of God is somehow bound up with his authority.[28] The woman, on the contrary, must cover her head, for otherwise she would show contempt for her own head, namely, her husband. What is important, then, is not merely the fact of man's supremacy and woman's submission (although that much *is* certainly clear), but that this distinction should be concretized in social customs. Hierarchical structure of authority *must be apparent*.

This is a very significant point of interpretation because the revisionist understanding is that Calvin may here be opening doors for modification or change in the role and status of women. This position is based on the grounds that Calvin's exposition centres on Paul's insistence on custom and decorum, not so much on unalterable doctrine. Bratt, for example, suggests some 'soft spots' in Calvin's approach to the hierarchical structure – spots where he discerns some points of hesitancy and indications of flexibility. Bratt is able to do this because he holds that Calvin's chief argument is one of propriety (πρέπον), not doctrine as such.[29] Similarly, de Boer interprets the Reformer as relativizing Paul's argument. According to him, Calvin speaks of 'custom', not of created order, because the problem in Corinth arose from

---

[27] *Comm. 1 Cor.* 11:3 (CO 49.474; CNTC, 9.229) – emphasis added. '*Neque tamen civilem ordinem interea confundit, aut honorum distinctiones, quibus non potest carere communis haec vita.*'

[28] Also, he says that, somehow, the glory of Christ 'shines forth in the well-regulated order of marriage [*ordine coniugii*]' – (475).

[29] Bratt's conclusion is that 'we can go no further than to say that in Calvin's estimation the passages of 1 Corinthians, so frequently marshalled in favour of the traditional view, are not necessarily indicative of a timeless principle. ... [T]here is a qualified but definite supremacy of man and a qualified subjection of woman in the structure of human relationships' (J. H. Bratt, 'The Role and Status of Women in the Writings of John Calvin' in P. de Klerk (ed.), *Renaissance, Reformation and Resurgence*, Calvin Theological Seminary, Grand Rapids, 1976, 11).

a specific situation of disorderliness, not from their lack of doctrinal understanding. He says that because Calvin underlines the importance of culturally conditioned propriety, he also realizes that this is, at best, a very inadequate guide for perpetual application. Douglass, in her turn, concurs, saying that Calvin discerns the apostle's stress to be on *politia* (*police*), not on theological statements of women's inferiority.[30]

However, a careful examination of Calvin shows that the Reformer affirms a *fixed* hierarchical structure of authority. Indeed, this is his main emphasis – though not the apostle's. At the same time, Calvin allows for the possibility of change in the visible indication of the present application of that structure, in local churches and communities and at particular times. This is what he implies when asserting that if decorum is maintained, 'Paul requires nothing farther' (475). Again, at verses 14-16, Calvin makes the interesting point that the question of hair, *per se*, is not the problem – recognizing that it was not always a disgrace for men to wear long hair, for instance. But, he further asserts that what Paul speaks of became common use 'by universal consent and custom' (478). So, Calvin underlines the church's liberty in its variableness. He uses Paul's comment about 'tradition' (παραδόσεις – v.2) to say that every local church has the freedom to frame its own government as 'the Lord has not prescribed anything definite' (473),[31] and, more pertinently, he says that the covering as an emblem of authority is not necessarily a permanent token. But, what is unchangeable is the fact of social, hierarchical arrangement and the authority structure he discerns at 1 Corinthians 11:3. The decorum of both the husband and wife should indicate that to be so:

> For the man does honour to his head (Christ) by making it plain to everyone that he is independent; similarly the woman does so by showing that she is under subjection.[32]

This goes some way to explaining Calvin's interpretation of the idea of the *imago Dei*, mentioned in verse 7 of this chapter.

---

[30] W. P. de Boer, 'Calvin on the Role of Women' in D. E. Holwerda (ed.), *Exploring the Heritage of John Calvin* (Baker, Grand Rapids, 1976), 260-63; Douglass, art. cit., 161, respectively.

[31] '*Dominus nihil certi praescripserit.*'

[32] *Comm. 1 Cor.* 11:5 (CO 49.475; CNTC, 9.231).

There, Paul speaks of man as the image of God and implies that woman holds that same relationship to man – apparently corresponding to the structure of verse 3. Obviously, the Reformer is confronted with the question of why man and not woman is said to be in the image of God. His answer lies along the lines which have been seen to be his preoccupation to this point: that is, man is in the *imago Dei*, in the sense that he has both superiority (*superiore dignitatis gradu* – 476) and authority over the woman.

Calvin distinguishes between two definitions of the *imago Dei*, as Thompson illustrates.[33] First, there is the image in the sense of that which is given to all, regardless of gender.[34] Second, there is the image in man, specifically, relating to the *ordinem coniugalem* and pertaining to this *praesentem vitam* – the image as 'a visible and external representation of the divine glory'.[35] According to Calvin, the woman should feel honoured to be defined in relation to her husband![36]

Calvin then notes the apostle's two arguments for woman's submission; namely, her origin from man and her creation *for the sake of man* (vv.8-9). In his preaching he asserts that woman is merely a part and an accessory (*une parte et un accessoire*) of man – 'God forever established the man above the woman.'[37] His commentary stresses, again, that if she is subject, she should wear the token of submission. In his commentary, as in his sermon, the Reformer emphasizes that the apostle is speaking of *all* women, not merely those who are married. In this context he speaks of

---

[33] J. L. Thompson, '"*Creata ad Imaginem Dei, Licet Secundo Gradu*": Woman as the Image of God According to John Calvin', *HTR* 81 (1988), 125-44.

[34] *Serm. 1 Cor.* 11:4-10 (CO 49.726).

[35] Thompson, art. cit., 135. He speaks of Calvin's teaching at this point as 'an ambidextrous approach' (134). Elsewhere, Calvin explains that man alone is in the image of God in relation to the *ordinem politicum*, the *oeconomicum statum* and the *ordinem coniugalem* – *Inst* I.xv.1.

[36] *Comm. 1 Cor.* 11:7 (CO 49.476).

[37] For Calvin, the logic of the argument is irrefutable, 'Since the man preceded, and the woman came from him, is it not reasonable that she be thought of as a part and an accessory, and that she not push herself into first place? Does a branch seek to have greater prominence than the root or the trunk of a tree? A branch has emerged from the trunk. Does the branch vaunt itself as if the opposite were the case? ... [Therefore, God] forever established the man *above* the woman' (*Serm. 1 Cor.* 11:4-10 (CO 49.728-9) – emphasis added).

God's eternal law [*perpetuam Dei legem*], which has made the female sex subject to the authority of men. Therefore, all women are born to submit to the pre-eminence of the male sex.[38]

Calvin emphasizes this point in his sermon, speaking as a pious woman to make the application.

> I am not one of those who wanders so far off as to know neither my end nor my present lot; rather, God has placed an obligation upon me. *As married,* I am to serve my husband and show him honour and reverence. *As unmarried,* I am to walk in the way of complete sobriety and modesty, acknowledging that men hold a superior station and that they must be the rulers.[39] Any woman who desires to exempt herself from this role forgets the very law of nature and perverts what God commands as necessary to observe.[40]

Earlier, he has spoken of this in the context of a divine, universal order (*l'ordre que Dieu à establi en ce monde* – 724). This does not seem to allow for modification or to suggest openness to change as has been suggested. It is extremely uncompromising.

Furthermore, it is interesting that in his commentary Calvin almost ignores the apostle's qualifying insistence on the inter-relatedness, interdependence and essential equality of the sexes (vv.11-12). Paul says that, 'In the Lord's fellowship woman is as essential to man as man to woman. If woman was made out of man, it is through woman that man now comes to be.' Almost as an aside, Calvin says that this comment is merely added for the woman's consolation and to encourage moderation and compassion in the man's legitimate use of his authority. Thus, he strongly emphasizes the woman's subordinate status and role, even as exegesis of a passage that seems to speak very differently.

> Let the man exercise his authority with moderation, and not ill-treat the woman, who has been given him as his companion. Let the woman be content in her position of subjection, and not feel indignant because she has to play second fiddle to the superior sex.[41]

---

[38] *Comm. 1 Cor.* 11:8-9 (CO 49. 477).
[39] '...que les hommes ont ce degré superieur, qu'il faut qu'il dominent'.
[40] *Serm. 1 Cor.* 11:2-3 (CO 49.730-31) – emphasis added.
[41] *Comm. 1 Cor.* 11:12 (CO 49.478; *CNTC,* 9.234). He continues, 'Otherwise they

The Reformer holds that woman, *as woman*, is inferior to man, *as man*. This, he says, is the unchangeable fact of creation. However, it is the visible token of the inferiority and consequent subjection (such as head-covering for example) which may be altered through historical and cultural change and evolution. His sermon on verses 2-3 makes this reasonably clear,

> Thus it is necessary ... that from time to time one establishes various ordinances which seem to be appropriate and which each one *makes use of in his own freedom*. But in all this, there is no question of adding something to the doctrine of faith, nor of making some laws put our souls in bondage [emphasis added].[42]

Although de Boer employs this paragraph in support of his argument that Calvin leaves doors open for modification to the status of women,[43] it appears that the Reformer has no such intention. What he wishes to convey is his insistence that, *though doctrine is unalterable*, outward signs and tokens may change in different cultures and times. However, those changing tokens still indicate an unalterable truth. Douglass' remark that what Calvin is interested in is *politia*, not a theological statement of woman's inferiority, is an optimistic oversimplification of what he says in both his commentary and his preaching. Indeed, her later comment that 'Calvin evidences little positive support for the traditional subordination of women'[44] can be seen, similarly, as a misreading of the Reformer's position. In fact, Calvin actually expresses his

---

will both throw off the yoke of God, who has made those differences in their positions, that they might be beneficial to them.' In fact, according to J. L. Thompson, *Calvin and the Daughters of Sarah* (Librairie Droz, Geneva, 1992), 110, among Calvin's contemporaries there appear to be no mediating positions on the issue of male headship. 'While some will moderate the application of the principle, urging men to compassion and patience, none question the principle itself or the hierarchical exegesis of the concept.' Calvin, then, fits into the main, contemporary stream of exegesis at this point.

[42] *'Il faut donc, quand l'Evangile se presche en quelque lieu, et qu'il se dresse une Eglise, qu'on mette quant et quant quelques ordonnances, qu'on cognoistra estre propres et que chacun en use en sa liberté: mais par cela (comme i'ay dit) il n'est point question de rien adiouster à la doctrine de la foy, ni aussi faire des loix qui mettent nos ames en servitude'* – Serm. *1 Cor.* 11:2-3 (CO 49.712). See also, *Inst* IV.x.29-30.

[43] de Boer, art. cit., 259.

[44] Douglass, art. cit., 161, 165 respectively.

opinion that women *are* inferior to men and that, therefore, they must remain in submission to them; that men *are* superior to women and that, consequently, they have authority and must rule. The practice of this hierarchical arrangement should be indicated by something that makes it clear – probably (but not necessarily) a head-covering or the lack of such, for female and male, respectively.

I Corinthians 14:33-35[45]

Though this short passage only tangentially touches upon the subject of the present thesis, Calvin's comments on it serve to confirm the preceding conclusions.

On the subject of women's silence in the gathered church the Reformer sets the context by asserting that the apostle is speaking only of church order in 'a duly regulated assembly'. He appears to allow that women *might* have to teach if exceptional circumstances demanded it – that is, where the church is not 'in working order' or 'properly organized'.[46] However, *as a norm* God does not permit women to hold public ecclesiastical office[47] and, therefore, he does not allow women to preach. Calvin offers a reason for this:

> [T]he task of teaching is one that belongs to someone with oversight, and is for that reason inconsistent with being in subjection. For how unsuitable [*indecorum*] it would be for a woman, who is in subjection to one of the members, to be in an authoritative position [preside[48]] over the whole body![49]

The exception previously spelled out by Calvin is now lost sight of in a host of comments which put a reluctant edge on his apparent generosity – women in all ages (*mulieres omnibus saeculis*), in all cultures, have never been allowed to rule. This is a dictate of common sense, natural reason and propriety. In other words, though Calvin insists that Paul is merely speaking of *externa politia*, of important matters,[50] this itself is a function of woman's

---

[45] *Comm. 1 Cor.* 14:33-5 (CO 49.532-3).
[46] Thompson, op. cit., 205.
[47] '...*publicam in ecclesia personam*'. See *Comm. Acts* 21:9 (CO 48.478).
[48] The French adds, 'Eust pre-eminence et authorité' – CTS, 468, fn. 2.
[49] *Comm. 1 Cor.* 14:34 (CO 49.533; *CNTC,* 9.306).
[50] I use the phrase 'important matters', in this context, in the way defined by

subordination to man established at creation and reiterated by God at the Fall. Though the outworking may alter in emergency situations, the underlying doctrinal foundation of a hierarchical structure between man and woman remains unchangeable. It is not a contingent truth.

Unfortunately, the Reformer's ambiguity becomes apparent and adds to the interpretative question. For example, he says, '[T]he discerning reader should take into account that the things Paul is dealing with here are indifferent, neither good nor bad; and that they are forbidden only because they work against seemliness and edification'.[51] This is a difficult passage, made the more ambiguous by what appears to be a contradictory one in his sermon on 1 Corinthians 11:2, where he speaks as if a church, having adopted certain ordinances, must not then change them.

> It is as if the Holy Spirit announces from heaven that this constancy is approved by God. ... And let us also note that this is said not only with respect to the main thing, namely doctrine, but even of those things which pertain to polity.[52]

The ambiguity of the former passage may not be finally resolved. Ultimately, it defies clear understanding *within the context of Calvin's explication* at this point and, therefore, certainty may elude us. However, taking both passages into account, he seems to be saying that a consistency in things that are not even vital to faith is approved by the Holy Spirit. If this is so, of course, it adds to the

---

Thompson, op. cit., 229-67, particularly 245, where he says that Calvin, in fact, treats women's silence more as an important matter than as a matter of *adiaphora* (that is, indifference). He defines an important matter as one that is explicitly taught in Scripture and is, therefore, not subject to revision or change. Nevertheless, it is not a matter that bears on salvation itself. In this, Thompson acknowledges his debt to D. A. Bowen, 'John Calvin's Ecclesiastical *Adiaphorism*: Distinguishing the "Indifferent", the "Essential" and the "Important" in his Thought and Practice, 1547-1559' (unpublished doctoral thesis, Vanderbilt University, 1985).

[51] *Comm. 1 Cor.* 14:33-5 (CO 49.533): '*Interea prudentis lectoris est expendere, res, de quibus hic agitur, esse medias et indifferentes, in quibus nihil sit illicitum nisi quod decoro et aedificationi adversatur.*'

[52] *Serm. 1 Cor.* 11:2 (CO 49.712). Thompson, op. cit., 221, also notes the problem: 'Here again is the tension. On the one hand, Calvin highlights the freedom we have in polity and its local variability. On the other hand, Paul's traditions and instructions are more than merely his own advice – they represent the intention of the Lord, and they are not to be changed.'

impression already gained that Calvin is determined to keep order in the church and society. However, it is not altogether surprising that Douglass and de Boer, for example, use the former passage to assert that the Reformer's intention is to qualify the apostle's teaching and to interpret it as applying only to a local situation.[53] However, on the evidence of the wider exposition, of the underlying doctrine of hierarchical arrangement, of the Reformer's stress on man's authority and, finally, of his apparent reluctance to permit women to speak even in exceptional cases, this seems unlikely. As noted, he apparently offers limited freedom in theory, only to withdraw it in practice. In fact, therefore, it seems more possible that the reformer (though admittedly ambiguous here) is saying that Paul wishes the church to behave in a seemly manner and *in Calvin's opinion* it is decidedly *without* seemliness for women to take authority and to teach in a mixed congregation. The reason for this is simply that, by nature, women are inferior to men and are to be in subjection to them.[54] Again, the teaching that is *unalterable* is that men are to rule and women are to be in submission. Exceptions do not alter the foundational, structural fact.

Ephesians 5:21-33[55]

This passage, expounded at length in both his commentary and his sermons, presents the Reformer's teaching and application of Paul's words in some detail. The whole exposition hangs on Calvin's interpretation of the idea of mutual submission (v.21 - ὑποτασσόμενοι ἀλλήλοις)[56] from which he moves to a description of how that works out in practice from, first, the wife's and second, the husband's perspective and vocational obligation.

Calvin's underlying proposition is that it is God who has bound all people together. The necessary corollary to this creational notion is that each should be in loving subjection to the other. He

---

[53] Douglass, art. cit., 161; de Boer, art. cit., 260-61, respectively.

[54] de Boer, art. cit., 263, suggests that the 'humanity' test comes closest to Calvin's own position: that is, 'Do what is the most humane.' This is to be rejected on the grounds that it simply does not work – Calvin defines 'humanity' by what he considers to be biblical and *hierarchical* theology.

[55] *Comm. Eph.* 5:21-33 (CO 51.221-7).

[56] Calvin's translation: 'Soyez subietz les uns aux autres en la crainte de Dieu' (CO 57.490).

says, 'Where love reigns, mutual services will be rendered.'[57] He defines 'subjection', in this context, as serving or assisting another, or as acting for another's good, with its reverse side of being disinterested in personal advantage [732]. Ultimately, it is the humble realization of the communality of mankind [734].

This mutual obligation has strongest application to the closer ties, according to respective callings, in which the community is divided into so many yokes (222 [735]).[58] Calvin sees the household, for instance, as divided into six different classes, arranged into three hierarchically defined pairs: the husband and wife, parents and children, masters and servants.[59] Each individual of each pair is to assist the other within the guidelines and boundaries of his, or her, own *vocatio* – this is mutual subjection. The significant characteristic of this is that the one who has the authority within the pair does not, thereby, relinquish his or her position within the hierarchical arrangement, but maintains it while assisting the person on the lower relational level. Order is in that way perpetuated.

> For is it not subjection that the husband supports the frailty of his wife, and is prudent enough not to use rigour towards her as his companion [*sa compagne*], and taking upon himself a part of her burden both in sickness and in health? Is that not a subjection? [733]

It is evident from this that 'subjection' includes humility and a willing acceptance of the responsibilities of *vocatio*. To the extent that what is done is for the wellbeing of those in lower relational positions, those higher in the structure are said to be in subjection.[60] That is, the husband, in this case, remains of higher rank and with authority, yet is 'under obligation to his wife'. Thus, each maintains his or her place; neither despises the order that God has established [735]. As Calvin moves on to the apostle's specific

---

[57] '*Ac ubicunque regnat caritas, illic mutua est servitus*' – *Comm. Eph.* 5:21 (CO 51.221). To reduce footnotes, the page numbers will be given in the text as above, but the sermon pagination will be in square brackets to distinguish it from the commentary references. Both commentary and sermons are found in CO 51.

[58] '*Porro oeconomia tribus quasi iugis constat, in quibus mutua est partium obligatio*' – *Comm. Eph.* 5:22 (CO 51.222).

[59] In this, he seeks to reflect the New Testament *Haustafeln*.

[60] See also, *Serm. Deut.* 5:16 (CO 26.309-21, particularly 313-14).

injunctions of verses 22-33, he does so with this definition of mutual subjection in mind.

First, Calvin turns his attention to the wives' relationship to their husbands. He maintains that, 'they cannot obey Christ without yielding obedience to their husbands' (222). The reason he gives is that the headship of man over his wife parallels that of Christ over his church. He interprets this as primarily indicating authority and rule.[61] His commentary makes the point, with the onus clearly on the wife:

> As Christ rules over his church for her salvation, so nothing yields more advantage or comfort to the wife than to be subject to her husband. To refuse that subjection, by means of which they might be saved, is to choose destruction.[62]

It seems likely that Calvin means to say that women are saved, not by (or through) subjection in itself, but through the faith and perseverance that maintain that subjection in obedience to God who has called the wife to that particular duty. Nevertheless, there is more than a strong hint of threat to those who see it differently.

In application, he stresses that the fear of God and the subjection that women owe to their husbands (*la subiection qu'elle doit à son mari*) are two conjoined and inseparable ideas (*deux choses inseparables*) [738]. The emphasis is that wives are to be under the rule of and in submission to, their husbands. God demands as much from them – this is their part in the practice of mutual subjection.

Second, Calvin speaks to the husbands.[63] At this point in his sermon, and largely against the emphasis of the whole, he is careful to exhort husbands to see their authority as 'companionship'

---

[61] In his preaching, for example, he draws the simple comparison: 'Ifit profits the church to have Christ rule; it must profit the wife to have the husband rule' [742].

[62] *Comm. Eph.* 5:23 (CO 51.222).

[63] This is not to suggest that Calvin ignores husbands while singling out wives in application (vv.22-6). He always preaches with an eye to all in the congregation and switches exhortation accordingly, refusing to allow any single group to become complacent when the Word is being expounded and applied. See Parker, *Calvin's Preaching*, 118; R. Stauffer, 'Un Calvin inconnu: le Prédicateur de Genève', *BHPF* 4 (1978), 192. The material has been arranged in this manner in order to facilitate study.

rather than as 'a kingship' and in this he softens the edges of his hierarchical teaching a little. Man's authority puts him under *more* obligation to be kind and supportive [740]. Primarily, the husband is Christ's representative, expressing something of Christ's extraordinary love (222). Though, that is not all. The necessity of loving one's wife goes back to *l'ordre naturel* and is also a specific application of the more general commandment to love one's neighbour as oneself [759-60]. With this complex motivation we see, again, Calvin's desire to link creational order, law and the restoration of order in Christ to his application of Scripture to the believer's daily life.

He does this by stressing both the man's duty before God and the need for order in society. Consequently, husbands are to consider what they *owe* to their wives [745], for even on verse 29[64] Calvin's emphasis is that Paul enforces the *obligations* of marriage (225). He says, '[I]f the husband intends to discharge his duty, and the wife similarly, both of them must have an eye to God (*regardent à Dieu*)' [779]. With the emphasis on duty comes a corresponding stress on the need for order in society. This appears most forcefully in his two sermons covering verses 28-33, in which he suggests that Paul takes his readers back to *l'ordre naturel* [759, 762]. If God established the order of marriage, then it is inviolable (both by law and nature) [764, 765] – neither can its ordered structure be changed. Calvin says that marriage is part of God's arrangement, part of 'the order that our Lord has set and will have to remain in force to the end of the world' [775].[65]

As with Luther, Calvin expounds an obvious creational principle – that mankind is composed of two kinds; namely, the male and the female [775]. Upon this principle the marital arrangement is clear. They are to be inseparably joined, the man having the superior position of authoritative headship and rule, and the woman maintaining the inferior one of submission and obedience: 'The husband is indeed the head, but the woman is the body. ... [T]he head has pre-eminence and [greater] dignity [*pre-eminence et dignité*] over the body...' [761]. In this way, Calvin underlines a hierarchical, patriarchal arrangement within marriage

---

[64] The point is that verse 29 speaks of Christ's love for the church: 'For no one hated his own body; on the contrary, he keeps it nourished and warm, *and that is how Christ treats the church...*' (emphasis added).

[65] See also, CO 51.766-7, 774.

consistently throughout his exposition. This structure does not exist for itself, however, but for the good and wellbeing of society. The husband's superiority will lead to and maintain good order and government (*ordre et police*) [740].

In contrast to the world's view of things,[66] Calvin teaches the importance of mutual love (225),[67] mutual honour [761], mutual submission [777] and companionship [779]. Principally, the husband and wife should be seeking to emulate the close relationship that Christ has with his church. In this, they each have their own exhortations to appropriate behaviour within the vocational and hierarchical understanding of marriage. That is, on the one hand, husbands must be kind – not harsh and tyrannical [740-41]; they must take the lead [764], supporting their wives, guiding them in the fear of God [763]. Wives, on the other hand, must be obedient (222), humble, pleasing to and helping their husbands [763]; they must be submissive, keeping the peace [771]. Something of the purpose of marriage is seen in this well-ordered arrangement [779].[68]

By its nature, Ephesians 5:21-33 presents Calvin with the possibility of outlining the characteristics of love and mutual regard that he believes to be the hall-marks of a biblically-defined marriage relationship. In this, he picks up the apostle's insistence on union and reciprocal obligation. However, in interpreting the idea of subjection (v.21) in the context of a fixed hierarchical structure, Calvin minimizes the point that the apostle seems to be making. Paul encourages each individual to make a personal and deliberate decision to give priority to the other person in the relationship. However, Calvin's exposition and preaching actually call for priority to be given to the form or structure of that relationship. He thus lessens the relational component by exaggerating the institutional

---

[66] In a similar way to Luther, Calvin laments what he believes to be the world's degradation of marriage. In practice, he sees few marriage relationships working as God would have them. Wives are generally dreadfully stubborn, proud, too talkative, drunkards and idle; and husbands, for their part, are irritable, niggardly, quarrelsome, gluttons, immoral, drunkards, having little regard for the ways of God [736].

[67] See also, *Inst* II.viii.18.

[68] He says, for example, 'The Lord joined them together [*associez ensemble*], in order that the husband could be a companion [*compagnon*] to his wife and receive her as part of himself, and the wife yield the degree of honour to her husband that belongs to him according to God, and submit to him, as to her head' [779].

one. That is, the Reformer introduces the concept of a fixed hierarchy between the husband and wife as the key to understanding the text – which it would appear not to be. However, again, the underlying assumption becomes the importance of order within society. The relational aspect remains secondary (though, admittedly important to Calvin) because it is seen as conducive to that concept of order. Nonetheless, Calvin softens the edges of his doctrine of marital hierarchicalism. But, one would have to say that he does so in a more restrained manner than Luther generally does. Of course, it could be questioned whether his restraint is a sign of theological reluctance, or whether it is simply reflective of his personality.

I Timothy 2:8-15[69]

In his examination of this passage, Calvin believes that Paul prescribes the manner in which men and women are to prepare for praying properly; namely, they are to come before the Lord in a godly way. For the men, this will be seen in their attitude, translated in practice to the lifting up of hands (v.8). For the women, however, it will be revealed in their humility and sobriety, translated in practice to both the appropriateness of their dress and to their behaviour in the context of the mixed church. (vv.9-15) In the limited space of his earlier commentary, the Reformer singles women out and appears quite negative about them; but he seems to soften this tendency in his later, fuller sermonic application of the passage.[70]

Instead of seeking to expound the specific, pastoral situation of the problem of wealthy women in Ephesus, Calvin, typically, generalizes insisting that extravagance in dress is 'a vice to which women are almost always prone' (275 [197]).[71] However, in his preaching, applying it particularly to the courts of the day, he also accuses men of such excess [201-2, 205]. Moreover, since clothing is an outward and indifferent matter and its appropriateness is largely subjectively evaluated, the Reformer deduces the rule that

---

[69] *Comm. 1 Tim.* 2:9-15 (CO 52.275-8).

[70] See *Serm. 1 Tim.* 2:9-11 (CO 53.197-210); 2:12-14 (CO 53.209-22); 2:13-15 (CO 53.221-32) – references to which will appear in square brackets.

[71] See also, *Serm. 2 Sam.* 1:21-7 [Kelly, 40-1]; *Comm. Gen.* 24:22 (CO 23.335-6); *Comm. Isa.* 3:16-26 (CO 36.91); *Comm. Jer.* 2:32-3 (CO 37.536); *Comm. Ezek.* 16:10-13 (CO 40.343-6).

it is the intention of such dress that defines its appropriateness. As he claims that the reason why women wear such excess is their love of being seen, revealing a deep-seated vanity (*la pompe et la vanité*) and ambition, Calvin characteristically exhorts them to moderation, modesty and sobriety.[72] His exposition makes it clear that modesty in appearance parallels modesty in behaviour. On the apostle's prohibition on women teaching (vv.11-12), therefore, Calvin asserts that women *must not* have the teaching office within a church – though she may teach at home.[73] Her creational function within the *genuinum naturae ordinem* is to be submissive to man.[74] The silence enjoined is to be expressive of that

---

[72] He comments, 'Without doubt the dress of an honourable and godly woman [*honestae et piae muleris*] ought to be different from that of a harlot [*meretricio*]' (*Comm. 1 Tim.* 2:10 (CO 52.275; *CNTC,* 10.216). See also, 200-201.)

[73] The context shows Calvin's views of women's inferior status within society: 'Paul is not taking from women their duty to instruct their family, but is only excluding them from the office of teaching [*a munere docendi*] which God has committed exclusively to men. ... The reason that women are prevented from teaching is that *it is not compatible with their status*, which is subject to men, whereas to teach *implies superior authority and status*. ... Thus he bids them be silent *within the limits of their sex*' (*Comm. 1 Tim.* 2:12 (CO 52.276) – emphasis added).

On the subject of women employed in tasks generally undertaken by men, see the following: on Miriam – *Comm. Exod.* 15:20 (CO 24.161); *Comm. Num.* 12:1 (CO 25.179) where, remarkably, the Reformer's conclusion appears to be that she only obtained the gift of prophecy to further ratify *her brother's* power; on women ruling and thus 'inverting the order of things' – *Comm. Isa.* 19:16 (CO 36.339); 27:11 (CO 36.458); on Priscilla, who taught only in private so as not to 'overthrow the law of God' – *Comm. Acts* 18:26 (CO 48.438) and *Acts* 21:9 (CO 48.477) on Philip's daughters prophesying. It may be significant that Calvin uses the word *ministra* (assistant), not διάκονος (deacon) with reference to Phoebe – *Comm. Rom.* 16:1-2 (CO 49.284). See also, R. White, 'Women and the Teaching Office According to Calvin', *SJT* 47 (1994), 489-509.

[74] The underlying assumption is related to the hierarchical authority structure: women 'are by nature [*quae natura*] born to obey' (*Comm. 1 Tim.* 2:12 (CO 52.276; *CNTC,* 10.217) – emphasis added.) Calvin continues, '[A]ll wise men have always rejected γυναικοκρατίαν, the government of women, as *an unnatural monstrosity*' – emphasis added. Later he insists on the foundational premise, 'woman was created ... to be a kind of appendage to the man on the express condition that she should be ready to obey him' (*Comm. 1 Tim.* 2:13 – de Boer's translation, art. cit., 242). There is a self-evidence about this, even the heathen would agree – nature, itself, teaches them. Calvin, therefore, asks, '[H]ow much more ought it to be amongst us? Now it is certain that women were never received to any public office. And who has hindered it or placed a restraint upon it, other than that God only has imprinted such a knowledge in nature, that although it be not otherwise

submission.⁷⁵ This is still the case, for Adam did not relinquish his right by his sin – that would have improperly made Eve's condition better than before (276). Furthermore, against the accusation that Deborah and other women seem to militate against this former rule, Calvin reluctantly concedes the possibility of exceptions, but remarks that, 'God's extraordinary acts do not annul the ordinary rules by which he wishes us to be bound.'⁷⁶ Again, we observe here that the under-girding doctrine is that of a permanent hierarchicalism. Exceptions in emergency circumstances may be granted (somewhat unwillingly and then only to shame the men), but they remain exceptions to the fixed rule.⁷⁷ Calvin insists on this argument so that these women are not so much an example to subsequent women, more a reprimand to men.⁷⁸

The apostle rests his argument for the prohibition (or woman's submission) on two premises from the narrative: Adam was created first and it was the woman who was directly deceived by Satan. Calvin sees these, as they stand, to be less than convincing.⁷⁹ He finds that he needs to substantiate them with further reasoning, or

---

taught, yet we know that it were an unseemly thing to have women govern men?' – *Serm. 1 Tim.* 2:12-14 (CO 53.209).

⁷⁵ It is interesting, then, that in his preaching Calvin takes the idea of submission (v.11) with a more general connotation to include an exhortation to men, who must *also* learn in submission. – *Serm. 1 Tim.* 2:9-11 (CO 53.206-7).

⁷⁶ *Comm. 1 Tim.* 2:12 (CO 52.276; *CNTC,* 10.217).

⁷⁷ 'We must make a difference between the normal order [*l'ordre commun*] which God will have to be observed amongst men for a rule [*pour regle*] and that which is done after a strange sort [*d'une façon estrange*], and not usually' – *Serm. 1 Tim.* 2:13-15 (CO 53.221). Interestingly, Thompson, op. cit., 24-5, makes the observation that, 'Calvin proves to be significantly *less open* to women in exceptional (read "leadership") roles than many of his predecessors and fellow commentators, and there is almost nothing in Calvin which is without precedent.' Also, ibid., 184.

⁷⁸ See also, *Comm. Ezek.* 13:17 (CO 40.288) – 'We know that the gift of prophecy is sometimes, though rarely, allowed to women, and there is no doubt that female prophets existed whenever God wished to brand men with a mark of ignominy as strongly as possible.' See also, *Comm. Exod.* 15:20 (CO 24.162); *Comm. Dan.* 5:10-11 (CO 40.706-8); *Comm. Matt.* 27:55 / *Mark* 15:40 (CO 45.785); *Comm. John* 20:18 (CO 47.435).

⁷⁹ The questioning of the adequacy of Paul's argument goes back at least as far as Chrysostom – *Hom.* 8.2 on Gen. 1:26; *Hom.* 13.3 on Gen. 2:7; cf. *Hom.* 9 on 1 Tim. 2:13 – cited by Thompson, op. cit., 114-15, fn. 14. Luther also showed some unease concerning the apostle's argument, as it stands, but concludes that Adam was superior to Eve 'by right of primogeniture', anyway. See *Comm. 1 Tim.* 2:13, LW 28.278-9 [WA 26.47].

to sustain them by broadening their base.[80] For example, admitting that the argument for priority from chronological sequence is 'not very strong' (276), the Reformer adds that it is not sequence alone but the fact that Eve was created second *in order to be an accessory* (*accessio*) to the man that is implied (277 [209-10] – emphasis added).[81] The external order of the present life was established at creation. Similarly, he infers that the apostle does not rest his argument entirely on the woman's transgression, but rather on the punishment of God following that transgression:

> Since the counsel she had given had been fatal, it was fitting that she should learn to depend upon the power and will of another. Since she had seduced the man from God's commandment, it was fitting that she should be deprived of all her freedom and placed under a yoke.[82]

The phrase 'all ... freedom' (*omni libertate*) is not to be misconstrued, suggesting that Eve had her own social, egalitarian independence at creation, only to lose it at the Fall. She has always been in subjection, but it was now to be 'less voluntary and agreeable than it had formerly been'. Present subjection is a continuing 'testimony to the anger of God' (277).

Calvin clearly sees the implication that if this is the case women may well sink into despair. Therefore, he argues that in v.15[83] the apostle seeks to comfort them. In the detail of this, Calvin's understanding differs somewhat from Luther's, in that the latter teaches that women are saved, not *by*, but *for* procreation; and the former focuses on the woman's duty in her vocation [229] leading to salvation. From Calvin's perspective, God offers the hope of salvation *if* the woman submits to her calling, in obedience to the obligations of her maternal *vocatio*. This is not the *cause* of salvation – that is by grace alone [224-5] – but it is the method *by which* God conducts women towards salvation, if they persevere in

---

[80] Ibid., 118.

[81] '...*puis que l'homme est creé pour le chef de la femme, et que la femme est une partie, et comme un accessoire de l'homme*'– *Serm. 1 Tim.* 2:13-15 (CO. 53.224). That is, God did not create two leaders of equal power, but added to the man an inferior aid (*adiumentum inferius*) – 277.

[82] *Comm. 1 Tim.* 2:14 (CO 52.277; *CNTC,* 10.217).

[83] 'Notwithstanding she will be saved in child-bearing, providing she continues in faith, love, and holiness, with modesty.'

faith and love (277-8).[84] This is an acceptable sacrifice and service [227, 228].[85]

In his examination of the biblical passage, Calvin has highlighted the social and familial structure of the husband-wife (or man-woman) relationship. He has done so, stressing that it is a hierarchically arranged one and that it is permanent.[86] Moreover, even though he finds cause to question the adequacy of the apostle's reasons for this, he alleviates the problem by forcing those reasons to imply a great deal more than they actually do. Throughout his exposition he emphasizes the inferiority of women and their natural, creational position of submission beneath their husbands.

Having said that, what is revealing is both the ambivalence that the Reformer shows towards women and the way in which he softens the stricter side of his teaching. On the one hand, Calvin seeks to encourage women by underlining their equality in the gospel [198], their excellence in possessing the *imago Dei* [212] and their share in salvation [224-5]. On the other hand, he speaks of them as 'poor frail creatures' [198] who are, generally, wont to be vain and immodest [197], inferior to men and naturally in subjection to them (276 [209-10]), merely an addition to them [224] and gullible. The underlying conviction is that this is their creational and vocational lot in life. Clearly, they need to be content with that.[87] Failure in this would be to reverse *l'ordre de nature*, to usurp authority, to bring utter confusion into the earthly realm (*l'estat de police terrestre*).[88]

However, the Reformer softens the application of that cluster of teaching. As we have already observed, in his preaching (unlike Luther at this point) Calvin applies to men that which he has applied most adamantly to women. He rebukes them also for

---

[84] The functions that they are expected to perform are stereotypical: running the household, busying themselves with the children – wiping, combing, dressing, nursing, being up night and day for them, feeding them – bearing it all patiently, though it seems menial and despised – *Serm. 1 Tim.* 2:13-15 (CO 53.228).

[85] In a short passage, reminiscent of Luther – LW 45.39-41 [WA 10^2.295-7] – Calvin encourages his congregation (including the men) to vocational duty on the basis that God and his angels look upon their faith in such action – *Serm. 1 Tim.* 2:13-15 (CO 53.229).

[86] '...aeterna et inviolabilis Dei institutio' – 277.

[87] Calvin uses the biblical images of God as potter and woman as the clay to enforce this conviction (*Serm. 1 Tim.* 2:12-14 (CO 53.212)).

[88] *Serm. 1 Tim.* 2:9-11 (CO 53.202, 207); 2:13-15 (CO 53.224), respectively.

dressing extravagantly; they too should listen in submission; God demands of them, as of mothers and wives, that they should perform the duties of their own vocation, and so on. Though he claims that men must rule and guide the family, they are deemed unworthy of it [215]; conversely, though women are forced to be submissive, the Lord has been gracious to them [216-17]. Within the husband and wife relationship, the men are encouraged to be selfless, not dictatorial – their wives are their companions and are not to be treated as nothing.[89] The couple must cherish each other in love, tenderness and peace [217]. Unfortunately, he is not explicit as to how this companionship is to be worked out, particularly within a hierarchical context. He even concedes that, in practice, the wife might be wiser than the husband in the context of the family and, if this is the case, she must govern the household in that wisdom.[90]

Again, we note that Calvin uses the passage to emphasize his understanding of the husband and wife relationship as a fixed and permanent part of the created order. The husband is to rule compassionately, the wife is to submit in faith. Above all, this reflects his concept of *vocatio* – with the backdrop of an ordered society in which each should remain content with his or her position. On the other hand, 1 Timothy 2:8-15 presents a problem in Paul's use of the Genesis account – a problem that Calvin does not confront. Nevertheless, as Calvin moves to the Genesis narrative, having examined Paul at so great a length, he draws upon the Pauline emphases.[91] That is, his conviction of the unity and the internal consistency of Scripture makes it possible for him to read Genesis (at least, partly) through the apostle.[92]

---

[89] *Serm. 1 Tim.* 2:12-14 (CO 53.216, 218-22).

[90] However, it should be noted that this applies only when there is a lack in the husband: '...*comme il pourra bien advenir qu'une femme en sa maison aura plus de prudence que son mari, et en usera pour gouverner sa famille*' – *Serm. 1 Tim.* 2:13-15 (CO 53.223). He cites Abigail (2 Sam. 25:14).

[91] As noted at the beginning of the chapter, by the time that Calvin came to comment on Genesis (1554) he had already commented on 1 Corinthians (1546), Ephesians (1548) and 1 Timothy (1548). Reading 1 Timothy as Pauline, the Reformer adopts the apostle's emphases in his exposition of Genesis. His sermons on the book of Genesis (1559) also post-date his sermons on the Pauline texts: 1555-6, 1558, 1554, respectively.

[92] See G. Harkness, *John Calvin: The Man and his Ethics* (Abingdon, New York, 1981), 66, 87; N. H. G. Robinson, *The Groundwork of Christian Ethics* (Collins,

Genesis 1:26-3:24[93]

Calvin emphasizes two distinctives in regard to the creation of humankind and the man-woman relationship. First, conventionally, he points out the social nature of human beings and, second, the hierarchical arrangement that exists between them in the domestic sphere. As Wright concludes, the former (stressing completeness, complementarity, mutual society and love) is Calvin's primary emphasis, the latter his secondary one. Wright later asserts that the Reformer speaks far more of marriage than of procreation and (specifically, in comparison to Luther) that, 'the interpersonal relationship clearly looms larger for Calvin'.[94] Nevertheless, it is not as clearly demarcated as it appears from Wright's summary; for, when the Reformer speaks of the sociability of the first pair (and, thereafter, ideally for all people) he has in mind this thought's inseparable connection to both the structural arrangement of the husband-wife relationship, and, importantly, the necessity of that sociability for the purpose of procreation. In other words, before Calvin can be commended (somewhat anachronistically) for his emphasis on the social nature and complementarity of the sexes, we need to realize that it appears from his exposition of the early chapters of Genesis that the social nature of human beings, itself, has a purpose – it is not an end in itself. Later, the story of humanity's fall underlines, for Calvin, the same two aspects of social nature and of the hierarchical structure of the marital relationship, but the stress falls on the important and drastic change that takes place within both.

Creation and union (Gen. 1:26-2:25)

Calvin reiterates Luther's insistence that when God deliberates (*consultationem adhibet*) concerning the original forming of humanity, he does so to reveal that in man is the excellence of his creation.[95] This is partly so because in him resides the *imago Dei*.

London, 1971), 20-21; G. F. Thomas, *Christian Ethics and Moral Philosophy* (Scribner's, New York, 1955), 134.

[93] *Comm. Gen.* 1:26-3:17 (CO 23.25-72).

[94] D. F. Wright, 'Woman Before and After the Fall: a Comparison of Luther's and Calvin's Interpretation of Genesis 1-3', *Ch* 98 (1984), 127-8, 130 respectively.

[95] *Comm. Gen.* 1:26 (CO 23.26-7). Also, *Comm. Gen.* 2:7 (CO 23.35). Calvin stresses that, despite the Fall, man is still the pre-eminent example (μικρόκοσμος) of divine wisdom, justice and goodness. Nevertheless, Calvin insists that the state

But, as we have already seen, Calvin is not terribly clear in his definition of the image of God. His principle of interpretation would seem to clarify the issue, for he asserts that what is restored in Christ[96] was obviously lost in Adam (26).[97] However, as the apostle's statement concerning the restoration of holiness and righteousness in the believer is considered a synecdoche by Calvin, the problem is not, thereby, clarified.[98] Therefore, in a comprehensive phrase, Calvin concludes that the image must be 'the perfection of our whole nature', an internal order – dominion also having a small part (*exigua*).[99]

The Reformer insists that God has given the *imago Dei* to man and woman, indiscriminately. In this, they appear to have a creational equality – they both represent *divinum ordinem*.[100] Yet, because of his assertion, Calvin is inevitably faced with the problem of Paul's, seemingly contradictory, comment that the man images God, whereas the woman merely images man (1 Corinthians 11:7). We have observed previously Calvin's answer to this difficulty.[101]

> Paul alludes only to the domestic relations. He, therefore, restricts the image of God to government, in which the man has superiority over the wife, and certainly he means nothing more than that man is superior in degree of honour.[102]

Two important things result from this dualistic approach to the woman's possession of the *imago Dei*. First, in answer to the

---

of humanity was not perfected in Adam and that it is conferred on believers by Christ, alone (he cites 1 Cor. 15:45). See also, *Serm. Gen.* 2 (Sept 23, 1559) *MS.Bod 740*, f38.

[96] See, for example, Col. 3:10, Eph. 4:23.

[97] He speaks of this again in the *Institutes* (I.v.4), saying that, 'What was primary in the renewing of God's image [*In renovatione imaginis Dei*] also held the highest place in the creation, itself.' See also, *Serm. Deut.* 5:13-15 (CO 26.295-308).

[98] Ultimately, what the likeness consists of is not identified by Calvin. See L. Anderson, 'The *imago Dei* Theme in John Calvin and Bernard of Clairvaux' in W. H. Neuser (ed.), *Calvinus Sacrae Scripturae Professor* (Eerdmans, Grand Rapids, 1994), 178-98, particularly 180-88.

[99] *Comm. Gen.* 1:26 (CO 23.26-27). Elsewhere, he says that, 'Whatever has to do with spiritual and eternal life is included in the image.' But, it is significant that the image implies an ethical component as well – Adam excelled in *everything good* – *Inst* I.xv.4. See also, *Comm. Gen.* 5:1 (CO 23.105).

[100] *Comm. Gen.* 1:26 (CO 23.27).

[101] See the section on 1 Corinthians 11:2-16 in the present chapter.

[102] *Comm. Gen.* 1:26 (CO 23.27). See also, *Inst* I.xv.4.

question whether the image actually pertains to women, logically, Calvin would have to answer in both the affirmative and the negative! Certainly, in terms of righteousness, spirituality and new creature-hood in Christ – that is, in its inner connotation – Calvin is bound to answer affirmatively. Women do possess the *imago Dei*. However, in the sense of the outer realm, the order of marriage – in terms of headship, eminence, superiority, authority and dominion – woman is excluded. In this context man alone possesses the image of God.[103] Second, although the Reformer is sure that women are endowed with the *imago Dei*, his explanation falls short of stating anything like equality between the sexes. In this, we find him qualifying any apparent egalitarian statements in his writing. 'Woman, *though* in the second degree [*secundo gradu*], was created in the image of God. Therefore, what was said in the creation of man belongs to the female sex' (46 – emphasis added).

It is within the context of such a heavily qualified statement that the Reformer's stress on the social nature of human beings is to be read. Bratt suggests that the woman is an image-bearer 'in a secondary degree', because, 'Presumably, she is one degree removed in that her dominion (an element germane to image-bearing) is not as extensive as that of the man.'[104] This is correct, but only as far as it goes. Its focus needs sharpening, for Calvin's judgement on woman relates more directly to his uncompromising belief in the lesser social status and, therefore, the inequality of the woman *measured against that of the man*. By implication, the man has the image in a primary degree in that his dominion is extensive and comprehensive, including his legitimate rule over the woman. The wife's dominion, on the other hand, is 'in the second degree' in that her dominion is limited, falling, as it does, under the headship and the jurisdiction of her husband. That is, even behind Calvin's concepts of complementarity and mutual love lies the insistence that woman is inferior (and that the man is, conversely, superior) and that the husband and wife live within a hierarchically structured, familial arrangement. This is an arrangement that is

---

[103] See Thompson, op. cit., 102-3. J. D. Douglass, *Women, Freedom and Calvin* (Westminster, Philadelphia, 1985), 61, states that, 'Eve's share in the image of God is not entirely equal.' She quotes Calvin's sermon on Job 3:3, 'It is true that the image of God is well imprinted on every person; but so is it true that the woman is inferior to man. It is necessary that we go along with these degrees which God has instituted in the order of nature.'

[104] Bratt, art. cit., 3.

somehow inherent in and reflective of their creation in the image of God. That is, it is normative for the husband-wife relationship.

On the words of Genesis 2:18, concerning the inappropriateness of Adam's initial solitariness, Calvin begins to outline his own emphasis on the sociability of humankind.[105] He does so in the context of the importance of procreation. The Reformer's understanding is that Moses explains the purpose of the divine creation of woman in terms of the necessity that there should be people who might cultivate mutual society between themselves (46). Before his stress on the social nature of humanity is interpreted to imply too much concerning the intimate nature of the union of husband and wife, its *qualifying* purpose must be briefly taken into account.

It is true that Calvin asides on the necessity of a man being content with his own wife (27) and on the need to remain faithful within marriage (28). But his primary teaching here is that the conjugal bond between Adam and Eve was formed 'for the production of offspring, in order that mankind might replenish the earth'.[106] Characteristically, then, he generalizes the application:

> God intends the human race to be multiplied by generation indeed, *but not as in brute animals, by promiscuous intercourse.* For he has joined the man to his wife that they might produce a divine, that is, a legitimate seed[107] (28 – emphasis added).

The underlying principle appears to be less that husbands and wives were formed sociable in order to get on together in mutual love (although, in a secondary way, Calvin does teach that, of course), but more, that men and women were created in this way to foster an ordered context in which to procreate. In the post-Fall experience of humanity, sociability safeguards an ordered context

---

[105] See CO 56.7. Calvin, elsewhere, states, 'As everyone knows, there is nothing more contrary to our nature than solitude' – quoted by R. Stauffer, *Dieu, la création et la providence dans la prédication de Calvin* (Lang, Berne, 1978), 252, fn. 318 and by Thompson, op. cit., 121. See also, *Serm. Gen.* 2 (Oct. 2, 1559), *MS.Bod 740*, ff46-52ᵛ.

[106] As noted in the previous chapter, to say with A. Biéler, *L'homme et la femme dans la morale calviniste* (Labor et Fides, Geneva, 1961), 89, that procreation is *not* the primary cause of marriage, but merely its consequence, is not close enough to Calvin's own position.

[107] '...*virum enim uxori coniunxit, ut divinum semen, hoc est legitimum, procrearent*'.

in which promiscuous, sexual passions would be restrained – while still allowing for God's command to have children (Gen. 1:28) to be put into effect.[108] This principle is apparent in Calvin's implied warning at this point,

> Let us then mark whom God addresses when he commands them to increase, and to whom he limits his benediction. Certainly, he does not give the reins to human passions, but, beginning at holy and chaste marriage, he proceeds to speak of the production of offspring.[109]

It is also apparent in his exhortation to husbands that they are to live modestly, not lasciviously, with their wives.[110] This would also explain his later comment that the conjugal life of man tends to his salvation, not to his destruction (46). The sexual drive of human beings is such that if they are not married they are bound to sin and to continue to sin outside of the God-given institution of marriage.

Within this context of thought, Calvin introduces the creation of woman. He argues on behalf of her rationality. He emphasizes that she shares a common dignity with her husband – in this sense she is 'nothing else than an addition [*accessio*] to the man' (46). This phrase does not carry any derogatory implication, but explains why God did not deliberate at the creation of Eve (Gen. 2:18-25). She needs no further eulogy from God. What he has already pronounced of man he also intends for the woman. In fact, Calvin, thereby, refutes those who take the biblical narrative at this point to imply woman's inferiority.

The woman is, both by God's prescription and by the order of nature, a helper of the man. She is 'as a companion and an associate to the man, to assist him to live well' (47). That is, the woman's function *is measured by the man's need*. Calvin defines a peaceful, well-ordered marriage in which the wife fulfils her role:

---

[108] Calvin makes the point that after the deluge, God did not permit promiscuous intercourse, but re-sanctioned the law of marriage – *Comm. Gen.* 9:1 (CO 23.143).

[109] *Comm. Gen.* 1:28 (CO 23.28).

[110] *Comm. Gen.* 2:22 (CO 23.49). See also, *Inst* IV.xiii.3; *Serm. Deut.* 23:24-24:4 (CO 28.136-49).

> [T]he husband would look up with reverence to God; the woman in this would be a faithful assistant [*adiutrix*– helper] to him; and both, with one consent, would cultivate a holy, as well as a friendly and peaceful intercourse [*societatem*] (47).

There is a clear enough echo of the underlying, hierarchical principle that Calvin finds in 1 Corinthians 11:7 in this idea. On the one hand, the husband knows himself to be directly beneath God (not Christ here, as such) – he looks up to God in reverence. On the other hand, the woman's person and role are directed with reference to the man. The influence of 1 Corinthians 11:7 is perceptible again later for Calvin says, 'Adam was taught to recognize himself in his wife, *as in a mirror.*'[111] Evidently, he reads the Genesis account within the framework of Pauline theology. The stress on the woman's role is repeated. In a brief application, Calvin exhorts wives to be careful to persevere in their divinely appointed vocation. Then, turning to husbands, he says,

> It is also the part of men to consider what they owe in return to the other half of their kind, for the obligation of both sexes is mutual,[112] and on this condition is the woman assigned as a help to the man, that he may fill the place of her head and leader (47).

So, although Calvin claims that Moses intended to note some equality between spouses, the singular equality that the Reformer appears to allow them (at this juncture) is a mutual obligation towards one another within, and defined by their respective, hierarchically conceived vocations.[113] The wife is to willingly submit herself to her husband, to help and assist him, because she was taken from him. The husband is to rule her with benevolence and modesty, because he is rendered complete in her (49). Such is to be the association of the human race (*humani generis coniunction*), even before the fall into sin.[114]

Some brief, preliminary conclusions on Genesis 1-2 are in order at this point. First, it is clear that Calvin sees the position and

---

[111] *Comm. Gen.* 2:21 (CO 23.49) – emphasis added.

[112] '...*mutua enim est utriusque sexus obligatio*'.

[113] See the section on Eph. 5:21-33 in the present chapter. It appears that Calvin's understanding of Eph. 5:21, concerning mutual subjection, has played a part in his exposition of Genesis at this point.

[114] *Comm. Gen.* 2:21 (CO 23.48).

roles of husband and wife as essentially unequal, though Genesis does not suggest this. Despite the fact that he outlines a creational equality (related to equal possession of the *imago Dei*), Calvin demonstrates a hierarchical understanding of marital relationships. With reference to his commentary on Genesis 1-3, Wright suggests that, 'We must note that Calvin nowhere uses Luther's language of inferiority.'[115] However, it is apparent from the foregoing argument that Calvin certainly holds the same position as the earlier Reformer in asserting the woman's basic, creational inferiority. In fact, he does so in a far less ambiguous manner than we discovered in Luther's writing.[116] Again, we observe that spiritual equality is not translated into a social equality.

Second, it is questionable whether a hierarchical structure of the husband-wife relationship can be posited from an examination of the Genesis account alone, as Calvin infers. Certainly, Calvin does not show anywhere that he gains the idea of order of rank or position as intrinsic to the creation of man and woman from a reading of the early chapters of Genesis.[117] Indeed, he appears to introduce the concepts of leadership and submission into the text from elsewhere. At Genesis 2:18, for instance, in contrast to Luther,[118] he allows the Hebrew word for 'helper' (*'ezer*) to come to mean 'subordinate assistant' or 'lesser helper' (*adiumentum inferius*),[119] when it could very easily be argued that the term, at

---

[115] Wright, art. cit., 128. See also, C. J. Blaisdell, 'The Matrix of Reform: Women in the Lutheran and Calvinist Movements' in R. L. Greaves (ed.), *Triumph over Silence* (Greenwood, Westport, 1985), 26.

[116] As suggested in chapter 7, Luther is very ambiguous on the question whether woman was created inferior to man or whether she became so in God's judgement against her sin. We have argued that the *probability* is that he never accepted an *unqualified* equality, even at creation. On the other hand, as it has been observed in the present chapter, Calvin teaches a definite creational inequality between man and woman.

[117] There is no hint of structural hierarchy in Gen. 1:27 or 2:18, for example. Rather, the idea seems to be that of discernment. On this see, for example, G. W. Ramsey, 'Is Name-Giving an Act of Domination in Genesis 2:23 and Elsewhere?', *CBQ* 50 (1988) 24-35; M. S. van Leeuwen, 'The Christian Mind and the Challenge of Gender Relations' in J. B. Nelson / S. P. Longfellow (eds), *Sexuality and the Sacred* (Mowbray, London, 1994), 120-30.

[118] *Comm. Gen.* 2:18, LW 1.115 [WA 42.87].

[119] *Comm. Gen.* 2:18 (CO 23.46). Thompson, op. cit., 118-19, helpfully points out that the traditional and contemporary interpretation of the word 'helper' (*'ezer*) was to underline inferiority/mutuality. Accordingly, Ambrose, Augustine, Aquinas, Cajetan, Erasmus all see the main connotation as having the husband's children,

this point, implies man's *lack* and *need,* and woman's *ability* to fulfil that deficit – not, *his* leadership and *her* subordination. It has also been noted that Calvin's understanding of 1 Corinthians 11:7 plays a perceptible part in his interpretation.[120] Indeed, Douglass suggests that Calvin is haunted by the text.[121] Because of his use of it, his exposition appears somewhat contrived, resting as it does on a foundational preconception of a hierarchical principle in marriage.[122]

Third, though there is an emphasis on companionship and complementarity (particularly at Gen. 2:18), Calvin outlines this, not as an end in itself but as a suitable, ordered context of relationship in which legitimate procreation can take place. In other words, if anything, companionship is subordinate to mankind's obedience to the command to increase in number. The idea of companionship appears to function, not for its own sake and importance, but as very much secondary to its perceived purpose of order-maintenance.

Fourth, it is noticeable that there is a contrast between Luther and Calvin's handling of the passage. According to Wright, 'Calvin ... gives greater prominence than Luther to the social and interpersonal, rather than the strictly sexual, dimensions of the relationships in which woman and wife are involved.'[123] It is true that Luther speaks a great deal concerning sexual matters. However, as we noted, his intention is to emphasize, not sexuality, itself, but rather, the *usefulness* of sexual desire and activity *for procreation*.[124] In contrast, Calvin speaks little of conjugal sex, but stresses the in-built sociability of men and women, together with its *usefulness for procreation.* It would seem, then, that they come

---

whereas Zwingli, Pellican, Martyr, Bucer, Capito, Musculus see it as implying the wife's obedience.

[120] Parker, *Calvin's Preaching,* 91-2, suggests that Calvin looks to New Testament authors for confirmation, rather than injecting their thinking into the Old Testament. This may be generally the case, but it certainly appears otherwise at this point.

[121] Douglass, op. cit., 63; idem, art. cit., 165.

[122] de Boer, art. cit., 245, 'For Calvin, the man is not subject to the woman – such would be an upsetting of the created order. The man is head, leader, ruler; he holds a superior position. The woman is to serve him, obey him, and be his lesser help. Calvin is confident that this is the very order of creation. *He hasn't noted how little the creation account, itself, supports him in this*' (emphasis added).

[123] Wright, art. cit., 133.

[124] See, for example, *Comm. Gen.* 2:16-17, LW 1.104 [WA 42.79].

at the same emphasis on the primary significance of procreation from two different perspectives – perhaps indicating nothing more telling than Calvin's natural reticence and sobriety as compared to Luther's greater openness.

Sin and judgement (Gen. 3:1-24)

We have underlined that the Reformer's two emphases that pervade his account of Adam and Eve's creation and union together are the social nature of mankind and the hierarchical structure of the husband-wife relationship. Naturally, as Calvin turns to the narrative of the Fall and God's subsequent judgement, he registers a fundamental change in both.

Calvin's deliberation on the temptation and sin of Eve (Gen. 3:1-7) signals his understanding of her original inferiority. But it must be said that within that he attempts to underline Adam's own responsibility. Regarding the woman's fall, he says,

> [T]he craftiness of Satan betrays itself in this, that he does not directly assail the man, but approaches him ... in the person of his wife (52).

Two implications concerning woman's original status are to be drawn from this. First, we note that Satan actually desires *Adam's* downfall and attacks *him* through his wife. The man is his primary target – not the woman – probably because it is the man who, in his created being, most fully images God. Second, Satan channels his attack through Eve because she is the weaker part of humanity.[125] This is 'an invidious method of attack' which seeks to subvert the order established by God, bringing 'dreadful confusion ... into the whole world' (52). Interestingly, though, the Reformer speaks of the prudence and courage that Eve, at first, displayed. However, when she begins to waver, Satan sees the breach open and seizes upon the woman's doubt (58). In this description, Calvin implies that Eve was too inquisitive or too ambitious, but he softens this by reference to its pervasiveness in the present time.[126]

---

[125] This accords with Luther's treatment of the same passage of course – see LW 1.151 [WA 42.114]. Luther further elucidates in stressing that, had Satan attacked Adam, the man would have won the victory! However, it is typical that Calvin makes no such optimistic claim on behalf of Adam.

[126] *Comm. Gen.* 3:5 (CO 23.59). See also, *Comm. Gen.* 3:8 (CO 23.65).

While Luther's explanation centres on the loss of personal relationship to God and the perfection of Paradise,[127] Calvin's (while certainly implying that) stresses rebellion against the obligation enjoined upon man and woman as creatures. The significant thing is that Calvin underlines Adam's personal responsibility for his own downfall.[128] Though he attributes greater fault to Eve (because of her more direct experience) he does not exonerate Adam.

> [I]t was not only for the sake of complying with the wishes of his wife, that he transgressed the law laid down for him; but being drawn by her into fatal ambition [*exitialem ambitionem pertractus*], he became partaker of the same defection with her (60).

Here, Calvin insists that Adam is culpable for his own rebellion. Indeed, Adam obeyed his wife rather than God, he 'despised God for the sake of his wife' (72). As with Luther's interpretation, therefore, Eve's example and insinuations played a part; but Calvin rests the guilt for sin basically upon the man.[129] He does this largely to maintain the New Testament teaching on the representative headship of Adam, as against that of Christ. In other words, Calvin takes on the Pauline theology, but reverses its implication: what is now restored in Christ, was once lost in Adam (62).

In keeping with the Genesis account, Calvin teaches that sin of this magnitude deserves judgement from God. However, he insists that in this God acts like a physician, more than a judge.[130] It is here (Gen. 3:9-19) that he spells out the implications for the husband-wife relationship. The woman is punished in two ways. First, her life, principally in her role as a mother, is now to be one

---

[127] See chapter 5 of the present study.

[128] Douglass, op. cit., 47, makes the point with reference to the 1559 *Institutes*, that 'Calvin still passes by the traditional opportunity to castigate Eve for tempting Adam to sin.' However, it should be noticed that he says, elsewhere, that, 'We know where the perdition of men came from: it was from the woman!' – *Serm. 2 Sam.* 6:20-3 [Kelly, 284 – see also, 282].

[129] Elsewhere, he writes, 'Let Adam excuse himself as he may, saying that he was deceived by the enticements of the wife God gave him; *within himself* will be found the fatal poison of infidelity' (*De Aeterna dei Praedestinatione*, CO 8.314; LCC 22. 155 – emphasis added).

[130] *Comm. Gen.* 3:19 (CO 23.76). Eve is invited to repent, instructed in humility and warned against further sinning. See also, *Serm.* Gen. 3 (Oct. 7, 1559) *MS.Bod. 740*, ff. 84-91.

of pain and trouble. The second punishment is her subjection beneath her husband's authority. He explains that from the time of her punishment she 'would not be free and at her own command, but subject to the authority of her husband and dependent on his will' (72).

> Thus the woman, who had perversely exceeded her proper bounds, *is forced back to her own position*. She had, indeed, previously been subject to her husband, but that was a liberal and gentle subjection; now, however, she is cast into servitude.[131]

God now *compels* the woman back into her rightful, lower, hierarchical position under the authority of her husband.[132] The Fall is not the *material* cause for her subjection, that is rooted in creation. Her creational subjection is made more severe by the Fall. It becomes 'a double subjection'.[133]

Adam is punished too – and in a significant way in relation to the present study. Not only is the earth to manifest alienation from God, on man's account (vv.17-19), but *his relationship to his wife is to be altered*, as well. This is explicitly stated in the *Institutes*, in reference to Genesis 3, where the Reformer explains that man was initially created in a condition the nature of which would not allow him to live alone. Then, by the punishment meted out at the

---

[131] '...*nunc vero in servitutem coniicitur*' – *Comm. Gen.* 3:16 (CO 23.72) – emphasis added. It is noteworthy that Calvin concludes that the serpent was also returned to its original position, or state – in the dust of the ground. That is, order is re-established and punishment exacted.

[132] Calvin follows the majority position, teaching that the woman moved from submission to servitude at the Fall. Others holding that view: Augustine, *DGNI*, 11.37.50; Ambrosiaster, *Comm. 1 Cor.* 14:34; Denis, *Comm. Gen.* 3:16; Cajetan, *Comm. Gen.* 3:16; Zwingli, *Comm. Gen.* 3:12; Bucer, *Comm. Eph.* 5:23; Martyr, *Comm. Gen.* 3:16; Politus, *Comm. 1 Cor.* 11:10; *Comm. Eph.* 5:23; *Comm. 1 Tim.* 2:13. The minority position (including Chrysostom, for example) held that she moved from equality to servitude – see Thompson, op. cit., 137, fn. 84; 138. On Calvin's understanding that Eve's punishment put her back in her place, see *Comm. Gen.* 3:16 (CO 23.72); *Serm. Eph.* 5:22 (CO 51.737); *Serm. 1 Tim.* 2:12-14 (CO 53.216); *Comm. 1 Tim.* 2:14 (CO 52.277). M. R. Miles, 'Theology, Anthropology, and the Human Body in Calvin's *Institutes*', *HTR* 74 (1981), 309, suggests that the civil order which subordinates woman is 'symptomatic of the fallen condition of human beings'. Yet, as we see, the civil order simply returns the woman to her original position. In Calvin's estimation, she has *always* been subordinate.

[133] *Inst* II.viii.41 – quoted by Stauffer, op. cit., 210.

Fall, '*he has been still more subjected to this necessity*'.[134] It is, perhaps, ironic – given present critical focus on the woman's punishment – that Calvin teaches that the man, together with the woman, were forced into their original conditions – with the sense of compulsion. Both are now unwillingly fettered to their specific marital obligations. It is possible, too, that he implies a corollary to this – the natural (that is, sinful) response of both man and woman is to militate against this state of affairs.

In this way, Calvin shows that the Fall radically changed the husband-wife relationship from that which God had originally intended – though in this God is active, not passive: he 'pronounces, as if from his tribunal'.[135] It distorts the husband's legitimate exercise of authority – it is now possible for him to abuse his position in a tyrannical manner, making his wife little better than a slave. It impairs the wife's response to her proper status of submission – she is likely to flout the man's authority, feeling it to be oppressive. As we have seen, the hierarchical structure of marriage, for Calvin, is permanently binding.[136] But, nevertheless, the potential for sin and disorder has been introduced at the point of man's original rebellion and his subsequent tendency towards autonomy.

I Peter 3:1-7[137]

On examining this passage, Calvin, rightly, sees two exhortations to wives. First, he recognizes that they should submit to their husbands and, second, that they should dress appropriately. He approaches the text having already delineated a general assumption of hierarchical structure in marriage (1 Pet. 2:18 – 247). That is, he teaches that the characteristic of the husband's role is headship and of the wife's, submission. He says, specifically, that the latter

---

[134] Ibid. – emphasis added.

[135] *Comm. Gen.* 3:17 (CO 23.74) – quoted by Thompson, op. cit., 147, who comments that Calvin, as his contemporaries, sees the punishments as prescriptive, not descriptive. That is, the curse applies universally, deriving from God's command.

[136] Thompson, ibid., 152, concludes, 'For a woman to resist submission, then, is not to improve her condition but rather to resist the grace of God.' See *Serm. Eph.* 5:22-6 (CO 51.739).

[137] *Comm. 1 Pet.* 3:1-7 (CO 55.253-7).

is part of civil or social subjection[138] as much as that which exists for slaves in respect of their masters. Consequently, the Reformer outlines the apostle's first exhortation, characteristically stressing the woman's duty, rather than emphasizing the possibility of the unbelieving husband's salvation – as does the passage. He does this in such a way as to suggest that women, *in general*, are desirous of breaking free from the 'yoke' of marriage.[139] Thus, he gives a sense that his over-riding concern is actually that order and restraint may prevail.

> Since those who are married to men who are unbelievers *seem* to have more reason for shaking off the yoke, he expressly reminds them of their duty, and shows particular reasons why they ought to obey more faithfully, so that by their honesty they may attract their husbands to the faith. *If wives ought to obey ungodly husbands, those who have believing husbands ought to obey even more readily.*[140]

It is true that Calvin adds the incentive of possibly winning the husbands to Christ, but again his concern shows through. Wives of unbelievers *seem* to have the purpose of saving their husbands; but, clearly, beneath this there is a structural reason which wives of believers (without that apparent motivation) should be ready to comply with.

It would appear from the Reformer's later comments that he believes that familial order is, generally, delicately balanced. And, given the context, he largely places the onus for this on the shoulders of women. The weakness of the female sex causes them to be both timid and suspicious, turning their demeanour to sullenness as a kind of self-protection, 'lest by their subjection, they should be more reproachfully treated' (255). This, in turn, causes them to exaggerate trivial problems, bringing disruption to the family. Following Peter, Calvin introduces Sarah as exemplary

---

[138] '...*partes sunt subiectiones politicae*'.

[139] We have discussed the probable underlying theology behind this in our examination of Calvin's exposition of Gen. 1-3, above. Because the inner dynamic of the husband-wife relationship is now (post-Fall) centrifugal, both the man and woman will tend to work against God's institution of familial structure. The wife is Calvin's particular concern at 1 Pet. 3:1-6, of course.

[140] *Comm. 1 Pet.* 3:1 (CO 55.253; *CNTC*, 12.280) – emphases added.

– as one who 'knew the Lord's command to be subject'.[141] Peter's advice, then, is reduced to the following precept, where the idea of authority is of significance: 'Submit willingly to the authority of your husbands, and do not let fear prevent your obedience, as though your condition would be worse if you obeyed.'[142]

In his exposition, Calvin generalizes to underscore the point. Thus, for example, he prefers to see the idea of 'fear' (v.6) as a characteristic of women, generally, who fear for their own status and wellbeing. It appears to refer to newly converted, but naturally anxious wives in the specific and novel situation of living with husbands who do not, as yet, share their newly found faith. Also, he fails to see the possibility that an exhortation to first-century women to be subject to their husbands, *specifically in order to predispose them to the Christian faith*, may not be necessarily appropriate in other times and situations. But according to Calvin, the wife is subject to the husband, both by creation ordinance and by postlapsarian judgement. This, then, is applicable to all times and places – it is a fixed order in the world.[143] He also introduces the idea of the husband's authority as a biblical principle for marriage relationships.

The second apostolic exhortation is similarly addressed by Calvin. Peter encourages an inner peace and a gentle spirit in women, in contrast to an outward adornment of clothes and finery. Characteristically, Calvin deduces from the text (and from his reading of empirical evidence, no doubt[144]) that Peter's inference is that *all women* are naturally subject to an inclination towards vanity and excess. They seek to gain the attention of men, rather than being content to live in the sight of God, alone. Calvin gives two prerequisites of appropriate dress, it must be useful and

---

[141] However, see *Comm. Gen.* 20:16 (CO 23.294), where Calvin faults Sarah for her behaviour.

[142] *Comm. 1 Pet.* 3:6 (CO 55.255; *CNTC*, 12.282).

[143] Calvin had previously commented on the divinely appointed orderliness of society, as a building 'regularly formed and divided into several compartments': *'Deum mundi opificem non reliquisse humanum genus confusum, ut belluino more vivat: sed velut in aedificio rite disposito singulas partes suo loco esse distributas'* – *Comm. 1 Pet.* 2:13 (CO 55.244). Societal arrangement opposes confusion (disorder), is peculiar to humanity and is seen clearly in the domestic structure of husband and wife.

[144] On the empirical element in Calvin's ethical ideas, see D. Little, 'Calvin and the Prospects for a Christian Theory of Natural Law' in G. H. Outka / P. Ramsey (eds), *Norm and Context in Christian Ethics* (SCM, London, 1969), 175-97.

decent. Under the latter he subsumes the ideas of moderation and modesty – two important concepts in his thinking on self-restraint and order-maintenance, as already noted elsewhere. In application, Calvin says, 'We know what an outrageous being an imperious and a self-willed woman is.'[145]

The problem of disorder resulting from the attitude and behaviour of a strong-willed wife (seen, incidentally, in the clothes and finery she chooses to wear) is implied in these words and is re-introduced later in his exposition of verse 7.[146] Here, he speaks of the husbands' authority and 'dominion over their wives' (256), although Peter says nothing of this at this point. Calvin insists that men should bear with the difficulties brought upon them by their wives, but also that they should not be too lenient or indulgent, for they might thereby, inadvertently, foster foolishness in the women.

Later, he speaks of familial conflict and the need for peace. Significantly, employing an image of control, he says that both men and women have enough reason 'to quieten all domestic quarrels and strifes ... so in common life, generally, it ought to be as it were a bridle to check all contentions'.[147] Although Calvin stresses mutuality in honouring each other and covering each other's faults, he speaks somewhat disparagingly and, perhaps, patronizingly of women in this context – likening what he considers to be their inherent weakness to what he sees as the parallel inexperience (or naivety) of children. That consideration should give to husbands the ability to be gentle with their wives.

Having outlined some of the more negative ideas in Calvin's reading of 1 Peter 3:1-7, it should be admitted that he also seeks to be positive about the husband-wife relationship, *within* what he considers to be Peter's teaching of a permanent hierarchical principle. For instance, being careful to differentiate between the present, gracious gifts and spiritual ones, Calvin speaks of God wishing husbands and wives to seek equality between each other.

However, as we have seen, this has nothing whatever to do with their social status or present position. According to the Reformer, the gospel simply does not touch this area. Nevertheless,

---

[145] *Comm. 1 Pet.* 3:4 (CO 55.254-5; *CNTC*, 12.281).

[146] That is, 'In the same way, you husbands must show understanding in your married life: treat your wives with respect, not only because they are physically weaker, but also because God's gift of life is something you share together. Then your prayers will not be impeded.'

[147] *Comm. 1 Pet.* 3:7 (CO 55.257; *CNTC*, 12.284).

he remarks (as does the apostle) that they are equal in being co-heirs of spiritual life. He also presents married life as that of friendship and defends the necessity of reciprocal honour and respect in any genuine experience of married love. He says that Peter means

> husbands honour their wives ... [contempt] destroys fellowship of life [*vitae societatem*] ... we cannot really love any but those whom we esteem ... love must be connected with respect [*ut sit amor cum reverentia coniunctus*].[148]

However, generally, we see here that the Reformer introduces his own theological assumption of the fixedness of the hierarchical nature of marriage. He stresses both the husband's need to apply his authority over against his wife and the wife's need to curb her natural inclination to push against the restraints of her vocational status. Failure in either application might endanger marital order. As with Luther,[149] he presupposes a hierarchical principle and reads his own conclusions of rule and obedience into his application of the text. Though he speaks of the centrality of mutual respect and love, he does not expand on these ideas to show their compatibility with his emphasis on the wife's submission to an authoritative husband.

CONCLUSION

We have noted that in Calvin's exposition, he teaches a hierarchical structure of the husband-wife relationship. He appears to have gained this, largely, from his understanding of the Pauline passages. The arrangement he outlines centres on the concepts of authority and subsequent rule. For the Reformer, the hierarchical order is that the husband is the head, with the obligation to rule, and the wife is a subservient helper, with the obligation to obey. Two reasons are adduced for the wife's inferior position: that the woman was created from the man and for him, and that she was the one deceived. We have observed that Calvin is not entirely

---

[148] *Comm. 1 Pet.* 3:7 (CO 55.256; *CNTC*, 12.284).
[149] See *Comm. 1 Pet.* 3:1-7, LW 30.87-93 [WA 12.341-7].

content with Paul's reasoning at this point, but in shifting its base somewhat, is able to employ it to his own satisfaction.

This is not to say that Calvin never speaks of equality between the spouses. Indeed, he emphasizes the inherent creational dignity of them both, the fact that the woman has rationality and possesses the *imago Dei*. He also underlines the wife's spiritual equality in Christ. Within their relationship, the husband and wife have equal, vocational obligation towards each other and each belongs equally to each in the specific area of sexual intercourse. But any concept of spiritual equality found in Calvin's writing does not translate into social equality between men and women.

Three further considerations have been brought to our attention in the Reformer's commenting on the texts. First, he insists that the hierarchical arrangement has been instituted by God at creation. He emphasizes that the woman has always been inferior to the man and that she has always been in subjection. Although he reluctantly allows for exceptions, the idea that men rule women is an inviolable, foundational, structural fact. Previous to the Fall the arrangement was voluntary – that is, people were entirely willing within it. As a result of sin the situation is distorted. It became compulsory for both the woman (who naturally seeks to advance her own independence) and for the man (who is inclined both to rebel against being coupled with his wife and to have his way). As part of the law of God and of nature, patriarchalism is a fixed structure in society.

Second, the Reformer underlines that to rule and to be subservient is the vocational obligation of the husband and wife, respectively. In this, the person in the higher relational position has a duty towards the one in the lower rank and *vice versa*. Therefore, he defines the concept of mutual submission as assisting and serving each other *within the hierarchical structure*. However, it remains true that Calvin measures the woman's worth by her usefulness to fulfil the man's need – *she* completes *him, she* assists *him*. Rarely does the latter idea appear in the reverse sense.

Third, we have noticed that Calvin seeks to soften the rigorous hierarchical teaching in his application. He stresses that the husband and wife must cherish each other as mutual companions, that the man must not tyrannize his wife, and rather that he should be supportive, compassionate and considerate, and that the wife will be graciously saved if she perseveres in her calling of motherhood.

The present chapter has also shown that Calvin's idea of order in the husband-wife relationship underlies much of his exegesis, even when it needs introducing into the biblical passage. Consequently, his hierarchical theology surfaces in questioning Paul's comment on the sexual equality between the spouses (1 Cor. 7:4). It is his over-riding presupposition in considering the validity of head-covering for women (1 Cor. 11:2-16), the prohibition of their teaching in a mixed assembly (1 Tim. 2:8-15) and in his interpretation of Peter's comment concerning women's fear (1 Pet. 3:1-7). Furthermore, he introduces the concept of authority-structure where no such implication exists in the original, notably in his handling of Genesis 1:26-2:24 (but also, at 1 Pet. 3:7). Together with this, we have noted that the Reformer ignores the apostle's introduction of men and women's inter-relatedness and mutual dependence (1 Cor. 11:11-12) in an effort to support a neat, authority-based hierarchicalism from the passage.

Another strand of thought that permeates Calvin's reading of these passages is the concept of order-maintenance as a characteristic of the marital relationship. This is apparent in his comments on 1 Corinthians 7 in which he says a great deal about the context of the uncontrolledness of sexual sin and of marriage as a divinely given means of remedying the situation. But it is there implicitly, of course, in his teaching on the unalterableness of the created, ordered social structure that he posits in his expositions, as it is in his emphasis on the priority of the marital structure over and above the relationship, itself (Eph. 5:21-33). We noted, too, that in his comments on Genesis Calvin emphasizes the created sociability of men and women *within* the structured arrangement of the family. However, this social nature of human beings has a purpose beyond itself. It is the legitimate context in which to engage in sexual intercourse, to procreate and to raise children, while maintaining social peace and order.

The following chapter will recapitulate conclusions reached concerning the Reformers' views of the husband-wife relationship. We will do this briefly against the tradition they inherited and in a mutually comparative way to evaluate where the two Reformers agree and at what points they differ. It will be seen that their differences are largely a matter of *nuance*, rather than of theological or ethical divergence. Following that, the study will conclude with comment on some implications gained from the examination of reformational hierarchicalism in marriage.

V REFLECTION

CHAPTER 11

LUTHER, CALVIN AND MARRIAGE

In the conclusion to his work, *Theology of the Reformers*, Timothy George makes the following relevant comment:

> Reformation faith was concerned with the whole of life, not merely with the religious or spiritual sphere. This was true because the sovereign God of the Reformation was concerned with the whole human being, body, soul, mind, instincts, social relations, and political affiliations.[1]

He then singles out the major ethical contributions of Luther and Calvin as the notion of faith active in love and the concern for the sanctity of the temporal, respectively. In reality, these may not be able to be distinguished with such precision for each idea belongs to both Reformers – albeit, with different *nuances*. Nevertheless, underlying the social teaching of both Luther and Calvin is the strongly held presupposition that God is concerned and intimately involved with every area of a person's existence. As we have observed, this is nowhere more obviously the case than in the area of the relationship between the husband and wife.

In the introductory chapter of this study we outlined the present debate concerning Luther's and Calvin's views of marriage-relations and, particularly, the way in which that debate reads the

---

[1] T. George, *Theology of the Reformers* (Broadman, Nashville, 1988), 321.

Reformers on the status and role of the wife. The question is asked whether the basic impulse and perspective of each Reformer is primarily medieval or modern.

There appear to be three, broad approaches in answering this. The common approach is to interpret both Reformers as conservative in their understanding, maintaining the traditional, theological teaching of Augustine (primarily) and the perspective of the Middle Ages. It is argued that, together with this, there is an apparent softening of the hierarchical structure by an emphasis on love and companionship and a discernible shift away from the procreational and remedial aspects of marriage. We noted that, though the latter point is posited most emphatically with regard to Calvin's teaching, Luther is also given credit for it too.

Two other interpretations take the extreme positions around this central one. On the one hand, we found that some scholars read both Reformers in a negative manner. They complain that both demean the woman's status and conjugal role. They are said to do this in one of two ways. Either they do so by their strongly negative stress on the sinfulness of sexual intercourse and the functional nature of the woman's usefulness in both procreation and in remedying sexual sin. Or they do it by their insistence on and continuation of unequal power-relations between the spouses. Again, Augustine is singled out as the main, culpable forerunner; the Reformers apparently follow his teaching, which is based partly on his own neurotic sexual disgust.

On the other hand, we have shown that there are recent, influential scholars who argue that Calvin, specifically, suggests an openness to change in one of the areas in which the previous writers have discerned a strong negativity. That is, revisionists have interpreted Calvin as leaving a door open for modification to the wife's position, largely on the basis that the Reformer sees the inequality of man and woman as subject to change with circumstance and cultural conditions. This liberationist tendency – most fully and cogently argued by Jane Dempsey Douglass – argues on the basis that Calvin's understanding of *ordo* is not static and fixed as has usually been supposed. This position also posits a discernible shift away from the procreational and remedial purpose of marriage towards a companionate definition and experience.

The present work has taken the example of the marital relationship in the Reformers' teaching to examine these interpretations. Clearly, all three positions cannot be correct readings of the Reformers' view of marriage. They cannot both be degrading and negative of the wife's status and role (as one group suggests) *at the same time* as Calvin (specifically) shows genuine openness to modification in that area of social experience. Neither is it as simple as the central line of argument would appear, for we have seen that the Augustinian tradition is more positive and the Reformers are less innovative than its construal implies. That is, we are not simply contending that the clock is put back and that the common view of the Reformers is re-established, or that (contrary to some optimistic commentators) Luther and Calvin say what we would have expected them to say. Neither are we merely repeating John Thompson's finding that on the basis of Calvin's exegesis Douglass' conclusion must be repudiated in that, on balance, Calvin will not allow exceptions to overturn rules in relation to women's exceptional ecclesiastical roles.[2]

What we are arguing and the foregoing study has shown is that *Calvin is not open to change or modification with regard to the relationship of the husband and wife, and specifically in the status and position of the latter, under any circumstances.*

We have argued that on two bases. First, the wider theological matrix in which Calvin locates his understanding of marriage precludes any genuine possibility of openness to modification in women's status in society. In this, Calvin is similar to Luther whose own distinctive location of marriage within the temporal realm of God's rule will not allow for change either. However, it must be said that it is the case that, in the context of a continuing reformed and evangelical tradition,[3] *we would like* Calvin to be saying what Douglass maintains. We would like the Reformer to be more egalitarian and more open to social change in the manner of some of his contemporaries and, certainly, in a way that would form a direct precursor to late twentieth-century liberationist or feminist thought. Any such hint in his *corpus*, therefore, is liable to exaggeration and to an over-optimistic interpretation. Nonetheless, while finding the revisionist construal to be attractive, we have discovered that it does not hold up under the weight of the primary evidence.

---

[2] J. Thompson, *Calvin and the Daughters of Sarah* (Librairie Droz, Geneva, 1992).

[3] See J. M. Gustafson, *Theology and Ethics* (Blackwell, Oxford, 1981), chapter 4, particularly 163-78, in identifying this tradition.

Second, to argue in such a way as to suggest that Calvin is a latent liberationist is, simultaneously, to drive a wedge between him and Luther in the specific area of familial ethics. If such an interpretation were adopted, then the ethical understanding of Luther and Calvin (and the natural and theological impetus of that understanding) in relation to the marriage relationship would have to be found to be significantly different. We have noticed that this cannot realistically be shown to be the case. Calvin's view of the husband-wife relationship is significantly equivalent to Luther's. Basically, they both hold to conventional teaching. Calvin is as fundamentally traditional as Luther – and traditional teaching refuses to imply or allow any such equality in the conjugal sphere. Indeed, we have noticed that even those 'feminists' of the fifteenth and sixteenth centuries, willing to seek the good of women, are not generally willing to compromise a hierarchicalism that purports to keep societal peace and order.

We would suggest that much of what has been written until recently about Luther and Calvin on the marriage relationship suffers in one way or another. Conclusions have been presented either on too narrow a basis,[4] or on a misconception of Calvin's notion of order,[5] or from a provocative and unhelpful bias[6] and sometimes without due regard to the similarities between the two reformers. The present study has sought to redress the balance, largely, by employing the breadth of the Reformers' writing and in aligning the two adjacently together in a comparative manner.

In support of the conclusion of this thesis, we need, briefly, to review the two suggested bases: the wider theological location of the marital relationship and the similarities (together with the

---

[4] By this we intend such valuable, though limited, works as J. H. Bratt, 'The Role and Status of Woman in the Writings of John Calvin' in P. de Klerk (ed.), *Renaissance, Reformation, Resurgence* (Calvin Theological Seminary, Grand Rapids, 1976), 1-17 and W. P. de Boer, 'Calvin on the Role of Women' in D. E. Holwerda (ed.), *Exploring the Heritage of John Calvin* (Baker, Grand Rapids, 1976), 236-72 – both of whom take account of Calvin on 1 Corinthians, but very little else. Also, M. W. Wiesner, 'Luther and Women: The Death of the Two Marys' in J. Obelkevich / L. Roper / R. Samuel (eds), *Disciplines of Faith* (Routledge / Kegan Paul, London, 1987), 295-308 – who bases her conclusions on Luther's imagery alone.

[5] See the contributions of Jane Dempsey Douglass, for example – details in the bibliography.

[6] For example, M. S. Behrens, 'Martin Luther's View of Women' (unpublished Master's thesis, North Texas State University, 1973), betrays an unhelpful distrust (even, perhaps, dislike) of Luther.

differences) between the two men in the context of the tradition of which they form a part.

SUMMARY

Theological Location of Marriage

In general terms, Luther and Calvin both insist that God orders temporal existence and societal structure for the peace and continuance of mankind living in community. There are differences, of course, and the chief one is not insignificant. While the former reasons this through his notion of the two kingdoms of divine authority, the latter (having no such clearly delineated doctrine) does so, largely, through consideration of 'political' jurisdiction. Yet, however different the proposed wider context, both men conclude that this is part of a *creatio continua*, an instrument of the continuous providence of God. Its intention is that of preserving humanity against the disorder that would naturally and inevitably follow had God not committed himself to intimate involvement with mankind.

Within that wider matrix both Reformers locate marriage as, perhaps, the most important of the institutions divinely established at creation to maintain legitimate order in society – for in marriage man and woman together reflect something of the 'cosmic' order itself. In both Luther and, most pointedly, Calvin, marriage becomes a cultural construction or a pattern of control. That pattern or construction appears to be as fixed in shape as it is in purpose. Therefore, to be a husband (as head of the household) or to be a subservient wife is a God-given vocation, the keeping of which perpetuates God's intentions.

There are several implications, inherent in this fundamental cluster of ideas, that militate against any likelihood of Calvin (or Luther, for that matter) modifying their understanding of the position of women within the marital arrangement.

1. Both Reformers hold to a very pessimistic thesis of postlapsarian men and women. There are two problems that stem from this. The first problem is that both Luther and Calvin evidence a defensive, reflex response to the thought of men and women's sinfulness. We have observed that this is more

pronounced in John Calvin. But it is present in Luther's writing, too. Their failure to question woman's position would appear to be as much the result of a greater desire for stability as it is a continuance of a tradition or a result of exegesis – perhaps more. In different degrees, Luther and Calvin stress the opposition of man's sinfulness against the possibility of establishing and maintaining order in society and the family. Luther stresses the necessity of God's continuous intervention and confrontation with sin and pervasive disorderliness through both *das geistliche Reich* and *das weltliche Reich*. Calvin emphasizes the destabilizing and disruptive character of sin (both personally and socially) and his own fear of chaos and anarchy. Indeed, in response to this, he is obsessive in his requirement of order. In a society in crisis and within the Augustinian and medieval tradition of static social structures within God's ordering, both Reformers seek to maintain an ordered *status quo*.

The second problem is implied, in a different context, by James McClendon. He comments that the concepts of the Fall and original sin have been over-used by social thinkers and continues,

> This had the advantage of showing clearly the inevitable participation of each of us in the disorder of the world while providing a universal historical (or mythic) explanation of that participation. But these traditional concepts ... were inclined to an overly pessimistic account of human nature – *one that made little room for the life of redeemed discipleship celebrated in the New Testament*.[7]

As the present study has repeatedly observed, nothing of the New Testament teaching on mutual equality between the sexes in the social or familial spheres surfaces in the Reformers' writing. In fact, they both repudiate the possibility of a social levelling based on the spiritual equality regained through and in Christ – a spiritual equality that both, actually, espouse vigorously. Jordan is correct in stating that the acid test of a liberationist position (even a latent liberationist position!) is 'the extent to which woman's spiritual equality is seen to entail a correlative political status'.[8] That this is

---

[7] J. W. McClendon, *Systematic Theology: Ethics* (Abingdon, Nashville, 1986), 160-61 – emphasis added.

[8] C. Jordan, *Renaissance Feminism* (Cornell University, Ithaca, 1990), 5.

not the case in the Reformers' understanding of the husband and wife relationship is due, partly, to their teaching on the inevitable and fixed inequality within the temporal realm and, partly, to their strict teaching on callings in which each must remain *as they are*.[9] It is not surprising, then, that what is generally advocated in wives is *passive* virtue – modesty, humility, passivity, kindness, piety and, always, obedience.

2. The second implication that militates directly against any modification of the marriage-structure is, simply, that both Luther and Calvin teach a fixed, temporal inequality within the overall context of divine *ordo*. We noted that, in distinguishing between the two kingdoms of divine rule, Luther explicitly states that the spiritual realm is one of equality, whereas the temporal realm is inherently one of *inaequalitas*. Calvin makes the same clear distinction in his consideration of spiritual and political jurisdiction. Both Reformers emphasize that this is God's creational and continuing intention. Both insist that, because marriage is located within the secular realm, the subservient position of the wife is a fixed point in the order that God established and maintains. Significantly, both exhort their readers (or audience) not to erase distinctions, to remain in their present position and to obey their superiors.

Within this context, we noted that Luther and Calvin approach the important egalitarian text of Galatians 3:28 in a similar manner, applying it only to the spiritual realm in Christ. Indeed, between 1519 and 1535, Luther appears to harden his application and to refuse any possibility of social equality between the sexes deriving as an implication of the text. Calvin, on the other hand, actively rejects a social implication with a stress on the unalterableness of hierarchical distinctions. We noticed, too, that the Reformers, generally, follow this approach in passages in which they quote or cite this verse.

Importantly, this basic stance becomes determinative of and intrusive to much of their exegesis, as we have argued in chapters 7 and 10. This is certainly apparent in the Reformers' exposition of 1 Peter 3:1-7, in which they stress the wife's submissive position and the husband's authority and the marital structure, generally, over against the apostle's apparent intention. In commenting on 1

---

[9] See M. R. Miles, 'Theology, Anthropology, and the Human Body in Calvin's *Institutes*', *HTR* 74 (1981), 305.

Corinthians 7, it is implied again in Calvin's need to question the apostle's apparent egalitarian statement, that the man and woman are similarly indispensable to each other and, of course, in chapter 11 where Calvin stresses verse 3[10] in order to show that, while the sign of the hierarchical relationship may be modified according to culture or circumstance, the hierarchicalism that is signified thereby is a universally fixed point. Of course, this resurfaces in Calvin's writing on Ephesians 5:21-33 in which he comments that marital hierarchy does not exist for itself, but to maintain social order and in which there is a strong hint of threat (at least in his sermons) for those who disagree. In their understanding of Genesis 1-3, there is an apparent difference. Whereas for Calvin inequality is a creational distinction, we find Luther more ambiguous, struggling with the contrary desires, on the one hand, to assert woman's equality (in terms of possessing the *imago Dei*) and, on the other, to assert her inequality from a social perspective.

3. The third implication against significant change is that both Luther and Calvin allow natural law partly to determine the relative positions of husband and wife. However slight the role of natural law is within the Reformers' theology, its relevance cannot be mistaken. Both subject earthly matters to natural reason – given at creation, normative for everyone, but (somehow) superseded by Scripture and voluntarily fulfilled through the work of the Holy Spirit within the believer. In this subjection, Calvin (particularly) is very specific that the hierarchical structure of marriage (including the wife's subservience and her place in the home) is an inviolable law of nature.

The major problem, in relation to the present study, is that in this the family structure is primarily determined by nature and biology – how things appear to have been created – and *is thus not susceptible to change by any form of grace.*[11] The concept, therefore, lacks the inner dynamic to transform relationships within society (an idea to which we need to return in closing). As we have pointed out above, divine and natural laws seem to merge in thinking that justifies existing social practices. Because God had created nature and structured society, its present workings could

---

[10] That is, 'while every man has Christ for his head, a woman's head is man, as Christ's head is God'.

[11] See R. S. Anderson / D. B. Guernsey, *On Being Family* (Eerdmans, Grand Rapids, 1985), 15.

not be inimical to divine will. But as David Little suggests, in relation to Calvin, it must be shown that it is possible to move from a set of empirically-observed generalizations regarding how men and women *actually* relate and act to a set of prescriptions regarding how they *ought* to relate and act.[12] Instead, both Luther and Calvin presuppose the rightness of present hierarchical structure without question and read that (largely) through certain Pauline texts, into Genesis and further into the divine intention, itself. We have summarised something of this presupposition (in reviewing the second implication) as it permeates the Reformers' exegesis of key passages.

What we find, then, is that the wider theological matrix in which the Reformers locate their understanding of marriage needs to be considered if we are going to answer the specific question of Calvin's possible attitude to change in the husband and wife relationship. From the foregoing summary it is very unlikely (to say the least) that either Luther or Calvin would consider or anticipate modification in the wife's status or role. Their fundamental starting point of order in society – together with the implications outlined – altogether precludes this possibility. This has not been taken into account sufficiently by revisionists who propose Calvin as a latent liberationist.

The second issue not sufficiently considered by revisionists in the question of Calvin's more enlightened view is simply that to state that Calvin was open to change his teaching would be to separate him from Luther in his understanding of the husband and wife relationship. The present work has shown that this is clearly not possible – that in all significant points they agree. The following, brief summary of their teaching, against the Augustinian tradition, will make that clear.

The Husband-Wife Relationship

We can summarise the similarities that substantiate the second base of our argument in the following way:

1. The Augustinian tradition held to the ethically determining-concept of 'cosmic' order to which social arrangement should seek

---

[12] D. Little, 'Calvin and the Prospects for a Christian Theory of Natural Law' in G. H. Outka / P. Ramsey (eds), *Norm and Context in Christian Ethics* (SCM, London, 1969), 175-97, particularly 176.

to conform. Within the temporal realm (*civitas terrena*, for Augustine) there is an indispensable hierarchicalism in relationships. *Inaequalitas* is an essential principle of social reality. To remain within that is to engender harmony and order. We also noted that to be higher in the order is to be of inherently higher value. Within the structure of the married couple the husband is always in the higher relational position. Adam and Eve are posited as the paradigmatic couple as this structure is read into the Genesis account and it becomes a creational and inviolable axiom.

We need not elucidate further how Luther and Calvin follow this tradition. This has been shown above (under the first point in the Summary). Nevertheless, in following conventional teaching, the Reformers locked the husband-wife relationship into a theological/social context of essential inequality from which their own understanding would be unable to extricate the wife from her submissive position – even had they had been willing to do so.[13]

2. From this foundational idea the concept of the man as the *exemplum* of humanity naturally springs. Augustine measures the woman by the man. *She* is defined against *him*. And in this, the medieval period follows. We noted that Aquinas, for example, defines the woman (ontologically, *per definitionem*) and her role as inferior simply because she is not a man!

In the Reformers' thinking the prior creation of the man necessitates that the woman is defined against him. In Luther, this comes out, for example, in the way in which he defines the wife as a 'tool' to be employed by the husband and as a 'helper' both in procreative and remedial contexts. Calvin, holding to the same androcentric presupposition, reckons that the woman should feel honoured to be defined in relation to her husband and sees it working out in the fact that it is the man who is incomplete without the woman – the woman's function is measured by the man's need. In this, for both reformers (as we have observed) creation implies vocation and stereotypical roles.

3. If *ordo* is the determining principle and the man is the *exemplum* of humanity, it follows that in the family context he is, indisputably, the head of the household and his wife is his

---

[13] It is not insignificant, of course, that some of the more liberating voices of the Middle Ages – Peter Abelard, Heloise, Christine de Pisan and, later, Erasmus and others – though seeking a more positive understanding of women, were unwilling to break from a hierarchical social world-view.

subservient helper. We have shown that this is the case in the Augustinian tradition and the reformers' thinking. Augustine teaches that as a result of sin, natural (voluntary) hierarchy becomes mandatory. The dynamic of the marriage relationship changes in that both now want to control. Therefore, he advises the husband's use of coercion and even punishment. The Middle Ages, generally, with its misogynist convention (largely following Jerome) continued to assert this in its teaching.

However, the reformers consciously repudiated this extreme, exhorting gentleness. Nevertheless, they both emphasize the husband's authority and rule and the wife's submission and obedience as a creational command – although, as we pointed out, Luther's position is ambivalent. This emphasis permeates their exposition of scriptural passages; notably, Genesis 1-3, which reflects postlapsarian experience rather than creational interdependence and mutuality.[14] Both follow Augustine's teaching that the wife, for her part, is forced back to her original obedience and the husband, for his part, is compelled even more to live with and to rule his wife. Again the dynamic of the relationship is conceived as antagonistic.

4. Luther and Calvin are conventional in believing marriage to be essentially good, and in their teaching concerning its purposes. Augustine had enumerated three such purposes: *a.* (taking priority) a means of procreation, in which he included raising the children thus born, *b.* a guarantee of chastity, through which sexual intercourse is brought into an honest use and *c.* a (sacramental) bond of union, emphasizing marital indissolubility. Together with continuing discussion on the definition of the sacramentality of marriage, the medieval period maintained this tradition.

---

[14] By this we refer to the fact that both Luther and Calvin stress hierarchical relationship despite the fact that there appears to be no status connotations in the Genesis stories of creation. See P. Bird, 'Images of Women in the Old Testament' in Ruether (ed.), op. cit., 41-88, particularly 73. See also, M. S. van Leeuwen, 'The Christian Mind and the Challenge of Gender Relations' in J. B. Nelson / S. P. Longfellow (eds), *Sexuality and the Sacred* (Mowbray, London, 1994), 120-30 and, in the same volume, K. Lebacqz, 'Appropriate Vulnerability', 256-61. Also, J. F. Tuohey, 'The Gender Distinctions of Primeval History and a Christian Sexual Ethic', *HeyJ* 36 (1995), 173-89; A. Brenner, (ed.), *A Feminist Companion to Genesis* (Sheffield Academic Press, Sheffield, 1993), Part 1: 'At the start: Emblems of Gender Relations and Human Existence', 24-201.

a. The Reformers give procreation as the principle reason for marriage – but such is Calvin's concentration on sin and its control that he suggests that the remedial purpose of marriage now, pragmatically, takes the priority. Nevertheless, both Luther and Calvin stress the maintenance of social order through the family. However, we noted that there is an undeveloped hint that Calvin sees procreation as conciliatory for the spouses. Clearly, the woman is defined partly by her procreative role. Both, traditionally, define 'helper' in terms of having children. But in this area, Luther and Calvin differ slightly. Whereas Luther teaches that the woman is saved *for* procreation, Calvin (stressing vocational duty) teaches that she is saved *if she submits to her calling* as mother. We argued, also, that both come to the subject from different angles in their exegesis of Genesis. Luther stresses sexuality in the context of the importance of procreation, Calvin emphasizes sociability with the same end in view.

b. In relation to the remedial aspect of marriage and the overall context of sexuality and intercourse, Luther and Calvin continue traditional thinking, yet are, themselves, different in some respects.

We have noted in both the tradition and its continuance that there is a need to observe a conflict between the essentially good physical creation and the evil consequences of sin. Augustine's formative thought is that because God is good creation is good and because God is intimately involved in sexual intercourse, then it cannot be entirely evil. The sex drive is divinely appointed. Yet, in Augustine's understanding lust usurped the mind's control, resulting in personal and social disorder. We argued that the major problem with Augustine's position is that it results in coitus being defined as either procreational or concupiscential, but never, merely, a positive furthering and maintaining of marital love. Of course, with Augustine, we noted an obsessive disgust at the sexual members' movement – movement which to him seemed to prove the point of man's disorder and the consequent need for control.

Luther and Calvin certainly understand sexual intercourse to be essentially good – it is God-given, the sex drive and mutual attraction are parts of the created sociability of humanity. However, they teach that coitus is never without sin – not on the basis of singling out sexuality, though, but on the basis that no human activity is ever devoid of sin and it always needs restraint. The vocation of marriage, therefore, is seen to be that control.

Negatively, it restrains lust. Positively, it maintains decency. Both Reformers appear to be negative, then, but both *can* speak of sexual intercourse in a romantic manner. Calvin does this guardedly and with qualification. Luther proclaims it openly. At the base line, each reveals a confident hope in the grace of God to cover sin and their understanding appears to have taken the Augustinian tradition a little further in this direction.

c. The present study has made the point that Augustine speaks of companionship but spoils the comment by an insistence that if God wished man to have a companion he would have created another man – not a woman. Marital companionship, for him, indicates getting on with or tolerating the second best – not, so much, a divinely given opportunity to enjoy a partner.

Luther and Calvin stress the idea of companionship with a different emphasis. The former teaches that it is vital for the husband to see his wife as a companion, to give reciprocal honour in the vocational relationship that they share. We noted that as far as we can tell his own example, with his wife Kate, seems to indicate a flexible approach – but, at the end of the day, what he advocates is and (given his overall theology) has to be a friendship between unequals, a superior and an inferior.

For Calvin, on the other hand, the reason for companionship is to safeguard a stable, ordered context in which legitimate procreation can take place. He has a chance to develop a thorough view of companionship (in expounding Eph. 5:21, for example), but falls short of it because he stresses vocational duty and obligation, not mutual love and reciprocal esteem. He minimizes the apostle's point by emphasizing the structure, not the relationship. If there is a shift towards companionship, as some suggest, it is more a shift *away from* the negative attitude of Augustine, than towards a genuinely companionate view of marriage. For Luther and Calvin, companionship is defined largely in terms of a voluntary or willing acceptance of hierarchicalism. Thus, companionship fosters contentment in the wife and gentleness in the husband.

5. Lastly, both Reformers seek to humanize their hierarchical teaching – but even this is, generally, traditional. Augustine softens his doctrine by an emphasis on woman's equality in certain areas; for instance, her possession of the *imago Dei* at creation, its renewal by Christ in salvation and her endowment with rationality (though this latter idea remains ambiguous in his writing). Together with this, he stresses the need for mutual love (*caritas*)

between partners and a sense of mutual service, even from the higher to the lower.

The Reformers soften their teaching by allowing an inherent creational dignity together with an equality in the possession of the image of God. We noted, though, that Calvin has to define this in two ways in order to allow for Paul's ideas. Further softening comes about by teaching on spiritual equality, equal responsibility to maintain an ordered life within vocation, equal sexual obligation, mutual duty to remain faithful and so on. However, the man and his wife remain unequal partners in an over-riding patriarchal and hierarchical structure.

We noticed, too, that both Reformers soften this teaching by an exhortation to the spouses to love each other. Whereas Luther speaks of being *alter Christus* to one another in the context of forgiveness, Calvin derives his definition of love from the Decalogue and more characteristically speaks of duty and obligation. This appears to give Calvin's idea a reserve lacking in Luther's understanding.

THE SIGNIFICANCE OF THE STUDY

The similarities between Luther and Calvin in their teaching on the marriage relationship are not to be taken as exhaustive, of course. They are enough to show that, in general, the Reformers are in substantial agreement in their understanding. Also, the summary shows some of the areas in which they follow and are a part of the Augustinian tradition. This conclusion, in itself, is not entirely unexpected, of course. However, in defining the similarities in this way, by implication we have argued that these conventional factors have locked the Reformers' thinking into hierarchical formulation. Further, if this is the case with both Luther and Calvin, revisionists cannot divide the latter from the former in positing Calvin as a latent liberationist. Anyway, as we have shown, his own understanding of order and the implications derived from it are enough to preclude any genuine chance of modification or change in the relationship between the wife and her husband.

What we have discovered is that Luther and Calvin clearly teach that as one who possesses the *imago Dei* the woman is the equal of the man, but as one who lives in the temporal world she is and remains his inferior and subordinate. It is the latter concept that defines the husband-wife relationship. The wider theological matrix of order and its inherent social hierarchicalism determines that that should be so. It appears that the Reformers wish to reaffirm the values of the wife's vocational duties before God, but that they can only do so within that wider matrix.

Jane Dempsey Douglass' proposal that Calvin be viewed as a liberationist will not take the weight of the evidence. We cannot conclude a genuine possibility from one or two (more or less) ambiguous passages from the Reformer's work without seriously taking into account the wider theological context, nor his closeness in thought to both Luther and the Augustinian tradition.

But is there a useful alternative? Schuurman, for example, has suggested that, even as the perspective of Paul's letters eventually resulted in the demand for the manumission of slavery (though he did not advocate it himself), so Calvin's writing naturally leads to an egalitarian view of women (though he does not advocate this, himself).[15] The point is that in a similar manner to Paul's undermining of the institution of slavery, so Calvin (or more accurately, later-Calvinism) undermined patriarchal hierarchicalism in the husband and wife relationship. Schuurman says,

> [I]n a parallel manner, although early Calvinism did not overtly topple medieval hierarchicalism in political and ecclesiastical life, *in principle* it did so. ... [B]asic equality [in Calvinism] does oppose asymmetric social relations where some people cannot have authority simply because of their race, class or gender, and where the exercise of authority does not aim at and express mutual service.[16]

The point is well made, but it cannot stand without considerable qualification. First, consideration has to be given to an important factor, missing in Calvin, but present in Paul. That is, the fundamental impulse or trajectory of the apostle's understanding of the Christ-event is towards an equality of the sexes and, further, that impulse (outlined in Gal. 3:28, for instance) has to be transferred from the spiritual to the social realm. We have argued that Calvin was, categorically, unprepared to do this.

---

[15] See D. J. Schuurman, 'Humanity in Reformed and Feminist Perspectives: Collision or Correlation?', *CTJ* 27 (1992), 68-90.

[16] Ibid., 89-90 – emphasis added.

Second, because of the Reformer's own view of the unity of Scripture and his eschatological teaching on the restoration of all things, we might have expected him to start at Genesis 1-2 and to discern there an equivalence in the husband-wife relationship. That, then, would have been an equivalence that needs to be restored by Christ, through the gospel and within the context of the church – the new community. But he does not do this. He prefers to take Paul's more cultural statements and his own traditional belief in *ordo* into Genesis.

Third, Christian marital patriarchy, generally, flourishes only so long as both the patriarchal husbands and their subordinate wives *accept* the natural and theological justice of the relationship and of the norms within which it is exercised.[17] We have argued that Calvin is at pains to stress the theological and natural justification of patriarchy. He does this together with an equal emphasis on the belief that in maintaining hierarchy order is established and retained and the pervasiveness of sin is checked.[18]

Finally, the contemporary, reformed example of Karl Barth may draw a question mark on Schuurman's idea, for he hardly goes further than Calvin in his teaching on the marriage relationship.[19]

If we are not simply to reaffirm the value of the wife's duties as her husband's subordinate, there is only one viable option open to us. That is, it is necessary to reject the grounds upon which she

---

[17] L. Stone, *The Family, Sex and Marriage in England. 1500-1800* (Penguin, Harmondsworth, 1979), 109, states that, 'Willing acceptance of the legitimacy of the authority, together with a weakness of competing foci of power, are the keys to the whole [patriarchal] system.'

[18] See S. Motyer, 'The Relationship between Paul's Gospel of "All one in Christ" (Galatians 3:28) and the "Household Codes"', *VE* 19 (1989), 33-48, who argues for three discernible stages for the Christian church to take seriously the biblical teaching concerning slavery – he suggests acceptance, transformation and overthrow. However, even if these are transferred to the question of the husband-wife relationship (which in other contexts they may be), it is difficult to see where Calvin fits in. Again, presumably, the impulse towards overthrow *has to be present*. See also, Motyer's related essay, 'Expounding 1 Timothy 2:8-15', *VE* 24 (1994), 91-102.

[19] See P. S. Fiddes, 'The Status of Woman in the Thought of Karl Barth' in J. M. Soskice (ed.), *After Eve* (Collins, London, 1990), 138-55; P. K. Jewett, *Man as Male and Female* (Eerdmans, Grand Rapids, 1976), 37-46, 69-85; J. A. Romero, 'The Protestant Principle: A Woman's-Eye View of Barth and Tillich' in R. R. Ruether (ed.), *Religion and Sexism* (Simon and Schuster, New York, 1974), 319-40; M. W. Y. Wan, 'Authentic Humanity in the Theology of Paul Tillich and Karl Barth' (unpublished doctoral thesis, University of Oxford, 1984). For Barth's own theology, specifically, *CD* III/1, 290, 301-6, 326-7; III/4, 150, 163, 172-6.

has been assigned her role[20] and to discover a more biblical and gospel-affirming approach to the subject. Certainly, the liberationist writers on Calvin and many feminist scholars have pointed a way forward in this. We need to continue to evaluate historically located thought, such as that of the Reformers, principally against the impulses of the gospel. We need to remember our own ideological conditioning (for we all come to Scripture pre-committed) and to be open to having that commitment questioned by scriptural ideas, interpretation and impulses.[21]

In conclusion, it is worth noting that though the revisionist interpretation of Calvin's view of the husband-wife relationship is to be discounted, what they say has the value of pointing us beyond the Reformer to our present experience in a gender-reconciliatory way. What Luther and Calvin wished for was that those who believed biblical teaching also lived biblically oriented lives – in family, in society, in the church. Even if, on exegetical, hermeneutical and theological grounds, we reject hierarchical arrangement as the *necessary* structure for the husband and wife relationship, we could do no better than to imitate the Reformers' zeal for godly lives lived out *coram Deo* (to use Luther's often-repeated phrase).

Given a matrix of fundamental equality and friendship, genuinely restored in and through Christ, Christian spouses should be those who reveal something of the reality of the life-giving and life-affirming Spirit to the world in our day.

---

[20] See Jordan, op. cit., 13.
[21] See A. E. McGrath, *The Genesis of Doctrine* (Blackwell, Oxford, 1990), 81-102; W. M. Swartley, *Slavery, Sabbath, War and Woman* (Herald, Scottdale, 1983), 185; McClendon, op. cit., 17-75.

BIBLIOGRAPHY

Primary Sources

Abelard, P., *Ethica* in Luscombe, D. E. (ed.), *Peter Abelard's Ethics*, Clarendon Press, Oxford, 1971.

Aquinas, T., *Sancti Thomae de Aquino: Summa Theologiae*, Editiones Paulinae, Rome, 1962.

—— *Summa Theologica*, volume 3, Benziger Brothers, New York, 1948.

—— *The Summa Theologica of St. Thomas Aquinas*, volumes 13 & 19, Burns, Oates and Washbourne, London, 1921 & 1922.

Amt, E. (ed.), *Women's Lives in Medieval Europe. A Source Book*, Routledge Press, New York, 1993.

Augustine, *Augustine: Selected Works* in Schaff, P. (ed.), *A Select Library of the Nicene and Post Nicene Fathers*, volumes 1-8, The Christian Literature Company, Buffalo, 1886.

—— *Patrologiae cursus completus*, Latin series, volumes 32-46, Migne, J. P. (ed.), Faculties catholiques, Lille, 1952.

—— *Sancti Augustini* in *Corpus Christianorum*, Latin series, volumes 27-50A, Typographi Brepols Editores Pontificii, Turnholti, Belgium, 1967.

—— *The Confessions*, Boulding, M. (trans.), Hodder and Stoughton, London, 1997.

Beze, T., *Tractationum Theologicarum*, volumes 1-3, Joannis Crispini, Geneva, 1570-82.

Bucer, M., *A Brief Summary of Christian Doctrine* in Wright, D. F. (ed.), *Common Places*, Sutton Courtenay Press, Appleford, 1972, 75-94.

—— *De Regno Christi* in Wendel, F. (ed.), *Martini Buceri Opera Latina*, 15, University of France, Paris / C. Bertelsmann Verlag, Gulersloh, 1955.

—— *De Regno Christi* in Pauck, M. (ed.), *Melanchthon and Bucer* [Library of Christian Classics, volume 19], SCM, London, 1969.

—— *Sacrorum Psalmorum libri quinque...*, Ioan Heruagium, Basle, 1547.

—— *The Restoration of Lawful Ordination* in Wright, D. F. (ed.), *Common Places*, Sutton Courtenay Press, Appleford, 1972, 253-83.

Calvin, J., *New Testament Commentaries*, volumes 1-12, Torrance, D. / Torrance, T. F. (eds), Eerdmans, Grand Rapids, 1957-1970.

—— *Calvin's Sermons upon Genesis taken by a swifte writer as he preached them*, Denis Raguenier, 1559 - MS.Bod.740. [The Bodleian Library, Oxford.]

—— *Calvin's Tracts and Treatises*, Beveridge, H. (ed.), Oliver and Boyd, Edinburgh, 1958.

—— *Commentaires de M.Iean Caluin sur la concordance ou harmonie composée de trois euangelistes, ascauoir s.Matthieu, s.Marc et s.Luc. Item sur l'Euangile selon s.Iehan, et le second liure de s.Luc, dict les Actes des Apostres*, Geneva, 1564.

—— *Commentaires de M.Iean Caluin sur le liure des Pseaumes*, Imprime par Francois Estiene, Geneva, 1563.
—— *Commentaries*, volumes 1-22 [Calvin Translation Society], Baker Book House, Grand Rapids, 1989.
—— *Commentary on Seneca's Clementia*, Battles, F. L. (trans.), Brill, Leiden, 1969.
—— *Concerning the Eternal Predestination of God*, Reid, J. K. S. (trans.), James Clarke, Cambridge, 1961.
—— *Concerning Scandals*, Fraser, J. W. (trans.), St. Andrews Press, Edinburgh, 1978.
—— *Institutes of the Christian Religion*, volumes 1-4, Battles, F. L. (trans.), Westminster Press, Philadelphia, 1960.
—— *Institution de la Religion Chrestienne*, volumes 1-5, Benoit, J.-D. (ed.), Librairie Philosophique J. Vrin, Paris, 1957.
—— *Ioannis Calvini Opera quae supersunt omnia* in Baum, G. / Cunitz, E. / Reuss, E. (eds), *Corpus Reformatorum*, Schwetschke et Filium, Brunswick, 1863-1900.
—— *Johannis Calvini Opera Selecta*, volumes 1-5, Barth, P. / Scheuener, D. (eds), Chr. Kaiser, Monachii in Aedibus, 1952.
—— *Sermons from Job*, Nixon, L. (trans.), Baker Book House, Grand Rapids, 1980.
—— *Sermons of Maister Iohn Calvin upon the Booke of Job*, Golding, A. (trans.), Georgii Bishop, London, 1574 - facsimile reprint, Banner of Truth, Edinburgh, 1993.
—— *Sermons on Ephesians*, Golding, A. (trans.) - revised by Rawlinson, L. / Houghton, S. K., Banner of Truth, Edinburgh, 1973.7
—— *Sermons of M. Iohn Caluine vpon the Epistle of Saincte Paule to the Galathians*, H. Bynneman for L. Harison and G. Bishop, London, 1574.
—— *Sermons of I.Iohn Calvin vpon the fifth booke of Moses called Deuteronomie*, Golding, A. (trans.), H. Middleton for I. Harison, London, 1583 - facsimile reprint, Banner of Truth, Edinburgh, 1987.
—— *Sermons of Iohn Caluin on the epistles of S.Paule to Timothie and Titus*, G. Bishop and T. Woodcoke, London, 1579 - facsimile reprint, Banner of Truth, Edinburgh, 1983.
—— *Sermons on the Saving Work of Christ*, Nixon, L. (trans.), Evangelical Press, Welwyn, 1980.
—— *Sermons on the Ten Commandments*, Farley, B. W. (trans.), Baker Book House, Grand Rapids, 1980.
—— *Sermons on Two Samuel, chapters 1-13*, Kelly, D. (trans.), Banner of Truth, Edinburgh, 1992.
—— *Theological Treatises*, Reid, J. K. S. (trans.), [Library of Christian Classics, volume 22], Westminster Press, Philadelphia, 1964.
—— *Tracts and Letters* in Beveridge, H. / Bonnet, J. (eds), *Selected Works of John Calvin*, volumes 4-7, Baker Book House, Grand Rapids, 1983.
Clarke, E., *St. Augustine on Marriage and Sexuality*, Catholic University of America Press, Washington, 1996.
Coulton, G. G. (ed.), *Life in the Middle Ages*, volumes 1-4, Cambridge University Press, Cambridge, 1967.

Eck, J., *Enchiridion of Common Places*, Battles, F. L. (trans.), Baker Book House, Grand Rapids, 1979.

Erasmus, D., *Encomivm Matrimonii* in Margolin, J.-C. (ed.), *Opera Omnia, Desiderii Erasmi Roterdami. Recognita et adnotatione critica instructa notisqve illvstrata*, North Holland Publishing Company, Amsterdam, 1975, volume 5, 385-416.

Hughes, P. E. (ed.), *The Register of the Company of Pastors of Geneva in the Time of Calvin*, Eerdmans, Grand Rapids, 1966.

Kidd, B. J. (ed.), *Documents Illustrative of the Continental Reformation*, Clarendon Press, Oxford, 1911.

Lombard, P., *Sententiae in IV Libris Distinctae*, Collegii S. Bonaventurae Ad Claras Aquas, Rome, 1971.

Luther, M., *D.Martin Luthers Werke. Kritische Gesamtausgabe*, Hermann Böhlaus Nachfolger, Weimar, 1883-1987.

—— *Luther's Works* [American Edition], volumes 1-55, Concordia, St. Louis / Fortress Press, Philadelphia, 1955-1986.

Principal individual works employed:

Comfort for women who have had a miscarriage (1542), Raun, J. (trans.), LW 43.247-50 [WA 53.205-8].

Commentary on 1 Corinthians 7 (1523), Sittler, E. (trans.), LW 28.1-58 [WA 26.1-120].

Exhortation to the Knights of the Teutonic Order, that they lay aside false chastity and assume the true chastity of wedlock (1523), Lambert, W. A. / Brandt, W. I. (trans.), LW 45.141-58 [WA 12.232-44].

Exposition of Psalm 127, for the Christians at Riga in Livonia (1524), Brandt, W. I. (trans.), LW 45.317-37 [WA 15.360-78].

How God rescued an honorable nun (1524), Bertram M. H. (trans.), LW 43.85-96 [WA 15.89-94].

Lectures on Deuteronomy (1525), Caemmerer, R. R. (trans.), LW 9 [WA 14.497-744].

Lectures on Galatians (1519), Jungkuntz, R. (trans.), LW 27 [WA 2.443-618].

Lectures on Galatians (1535), Pelikan, J. (trans.), LW 26 [WA 40^1.16-601, 40^2.1-184].

Lectures on Genesis (1535-45), Schick, G. V. / Pahl, P. D. (trans.), LW 1-8 [WA 42-44].

Lectures on Isaiah (1527), Bouman, H. (trans.) LW 16-17 [WA 31^2].

Lectures on 1 Timothy (1527-28), Dinda, R. J. (trans.), LW 28.215-384 [WA 26.1-120].

Lectures on Romans (1515-17), Tillmanns, W. G. / Preus, J. A. O. (trans.), LW 25.133-524 [WA 56.156-528].

Lectures on the Minor Prophets (1524-27), Dinda, R. J. (trans.), LW 18-20 [WA 13].

Letters (1507-46), Krodel, G. G. (trans.), LW 48-50 [WA.Br 1-12].

Luther's Small Catechism, Concordia, St. Louis, 1943.

Notes on Ecclesiastes, Pelikan, J. (trans.), LW 15 [WA 20.7-203].

On Marriage Matters (1530), Ahrens, F. C. (trans.), LW 46.265-320 [WA 30^3.205-48].

Sermon on the Estate of Marriage (1519), Atkinson, J. (trans.), *LW* 44.7-14 [*WA* 2.166-71].

Sermon Preached at the Marriage of Sigismund von Lindenau in Merseburg, Heb 13:4 (Aug 4.1545), Doberstein, J. W. (trans.), LW 51.357-67 [WA 49.797-805].

Sermons on the Gospel of John (1537), Bertram, M. H. (trans.), *LW* 22-24 [*WA* 33, 45.465-733, 47].

Sermons on 1 Peter (1523), Bertram, M. H. (trans.), *LW* 30.3-145 [*WA* 12.259-399].

Tabletalk, Tappert, T. G. (trans.), *LW* 54 [*WA.Tr* 1-6; *WA* 48.365-719].

Table Talk, Hazlett, W. (trans.), Fount, London, 1995.

Ten Sermons on the Catechism (1528), Doberstein, J. W. (trans.), *LW* 51.137-93 [*WA* 30^1.57-122].

That parents should neither compel nor hinder the marriage of their children, and that children should not become engaged without their parents' consent (1524), Brandt, W. I. (trans.), LW 45.385-93 [WA 15.163-9].

The Babylonian Captivity of the Church (1520), Steinhäuser, A. T. W. / Ahrens, F. C. / Wentz, A. R. (trans.), *LW* 36.11-126 [*WA* 6.497-573].

The Estate of Marriage (1522), Brandt, W. I. (trans.), *LW* 45.17-49 [*WA* 10^2.275-304].

Migne, J.-P. (ed.), *Patrologiae cursus completus*, Latin series, volumes 32-46, Faculties catholiques, Lille, 1952.

Milton, J., 'The Judgement of Martin Bucer Touching Divorce' in *The Complete Prose Works of John Milton*, volume 2, Oxford University Press, London, 1959, 447-77.

Noll, M. A. (ed.), *Confessions and Catechisms of the Reformation*, Apollos, Leicester, 1991.

Radice, B. (ed.), *The Letters of Abelard and Heloise*, Penguin, Harmondsworth, 1974.

Secondary Works

Abray, L. J., *The People's Reformation*, Cornell University Press, New York, 1985.

Adeney, B. T., *Strange Virtues*, Apollo, Leicester, 1995.

Alexander, J. H., *Ladies of the Reformation*, Gospel Standard Strict Baptist Trust, Harpenden, 1978.

Allen, J. L., *Love and Conflict*, Abingdon Press, Nashville, 1984.

Althaus, P, *The Divine Command*, Fortress Press, Philadelphia, 1966.

—— *The Ethics of Martin Luther*, Fortress Press, Philadelphia, 1972.

—— *The Theology of Martin Luther*, Fortress Press, Philadelphia, 1966.

Alvarez, A., *Life After Marriage*, MacMillan, London, 1982.

Anderson, L., 'The *imago Dei* theme in John Calvin and Bernard of Clairvaux' in Neuser, W. H. (ed.), *Calvinus Sacrae Scripturae Professor*, Eerdmans, Grand Rapids, 1994, 178-98.

Anderson, M., 'John Calvin: Biblical Preacher (1539-1564)', *Scottish Journal of Theology* 42 (1989), 167-81.

Anderson, R. S. [with Guernsey, D. B.], *On Being Family*, Eerdmans, Grand Rapids, 1985.

On Being Human, Eerdmans, Grand Rapids, 1982.
Armstrong, K., *The Gospel According to Woman*, Elm Tree Books, London, 1986.
Arnold, M., *Les femmes dans la correspondance de Luther*, University of France Press, Paris, 1998.
Aubigne, J. H. M., *The History of the Great Reformation*, Walther, London, 1841.
Badcock, G. D., *The Way of Life: A Theology of Christian Vocation*, Eerdmans, Grand Rapids, 1998.
Bailey, S., *Common Sense about Sexual Ethics: A Christian View*, Victor Gollancz, London, 1962.
Bainton, R. H., *Here I Stand*, Hodder and Stoughton, London, 1951.
—— 'Luther' in Bodensieck, J. (ed.), *The Encyclopedia of the Lutheran Church*, Augsburg, Minneapolis, 1965, 2.1356.
—— 'The Immoralities of the Patriarchs according to the Exegesis of the Late Middle Ages and of the Reformation', *Harvard Theological Review* 23 (1930), 39-49.
—— *The Reformation of the Sixteenth Century*, Hodder and Stoughton, London, 1963.
—— *Women of the Reformation in Germany and Italy*, Beacon Press, Boston, 1974.
Bakelant, L., 'Les Rapports de l'humanisme et de la Réforme', *Revue de l'Université de Bruxelles* 18 (1965-1966), 264-82.
Baldwin, C. M., 'Marriage in Calvin's Sermons' in Schnucker, R. V. (ed.), *Calviniana: Ideas and Influence of Jean Calvin*, Sixteenth Century Journal Publishers, Kirksville, 1988, 121-9.
Barth, K., *Church Dogmatics*, volumes 1-4, T&T Clark, Edinburgh, 1936-77.
Barton, F. W., *Calvin and the Duchess*, Westminster / John Knox, Louisville, 1989.
Battles, F. L., '*Calculus Fidei*: Some Ruminations on the Structure of the Theology of John Calvin' in Benedetto, R. (ed.), *Interpreting John Calvin*, Baker Book House, Grand Rapids, 1996, 139-78.
—— 'Against Luxury and License in Geneva: A Forgotten Fragment of Calvin [1546-47]' in Benedetto, R. (ed.), *Interpreting John Calvin*, Baker Book House, Grand Rapids, 1996, 319-41.
Bavel, J. van., 'Augustine's View of women', *Augustiniana* 39 (1989), 5-53.
Beach, W. / Niebuhr, H. R., *Christian Ethics: Sources of the Living Tradition*, Ronald Press, New York, 1955.
Behrens, M. S., 'Martin Luther's view of Women' (unpublished Masters thesis, North Texas State University, 1973).
Bennett, J. M., 'Feminism and History', *Gender and History* 1 (1989), 251-72.
Women in the Medieval English Countryside, Oxford University Press, Oxford, 1987.
Benoit, J. D., 'Calvin, the Letter Writer' in Duffield, G. E. (ed.), *John Calvin*, Sutton Courtenay Press, Appleford, 1966, 67-101.
Betzig, L., 'Medieval Monogamy', *Journal of Family History* 20 (1995) 181-216.
Biéler, A., *L'homme et la femme dans la morale calviniste: la doctrine réformée sur l'amour, le mariage, le célibat, le divorce, l'adultère et la prostitution, considerée dans son cadre historique*, Labor et Fides, Geneva, 1961.
L'Humanisme Social de Calvin, Labor et Fides, Geneva, 1961.

—— 'Man and Woman in Calvin's Ethic', *The Reformed and Presbyterian World* 27 (1963), 357-63 [also published as 'Mann und Frau in Calvins Ethik', *Der deutsche Hugenott* 28 (1964), 69-74].

Bigham, T. J. / Mollegen, A. T, 'The Christian Ethic' in Battenhouse, R. W. (ed.), *A Companion to the Study of St. Augustine*, Oxford University Press, New York, 1955, 371-97.

Biller, P., 'The Common Woman in the Western Churches in the Thirteenth and Early Fourteenth Centuries' in Sheils, W. J. / Wood, D. (eds), *Women in the Church*, Blackwell, Oxford, 1990, 127-57.

Bird, P., 'Images of Women in the Old Testament' in Ruether, R. R. (ed.), *Religion and Sexism*, Simon and Schuster, New York, 1974, 41-88.

Blaisdell, C. J., 'Calvin's and Loyola's Letters to Women' in Schnucher, R. V. (ed.), *Calviniana: Ideas and Influence of Jean Calvin*, Sixteenth Century Publishers, Kirksville, 1988, 235-53.

—— 'Calvin's Letters to Women: The Courting of Ladies in High Places', *Sixteenth Century Journal* 13 (1982), 67-85.

—— 'The Matrix of Reform: Women in the Lutheran and Calvinist Movements' in Greaves, R. L. (ed.), *Triumph Over Silence: Women in Protestant History*, Greenwood Press, Westport, Connecticut, 1985, 13-44.

Blocher, H., 'Luther et la Bible', *La Revue Réformée* 35 (1984), 41-55.

Boer, W. P. de., 'Calvin on the Role of Women' in Holwerda, D. E. (ed.), *Exploring the Heritage of John Calvin*, Baker Book House, Grand Rapids, 1976, 236-72.

Boft, L., 'The Sacrament of Marriage', *Concilium* 7 (1973), 22-33.

Bohatec, J., *Calvin und das Recht*, Buchdruck und Verlags-Anstalt, Feudingen, 1934.

Bolton, B., '*Vitae Matrum:* a further aspect of the *Frauenfrage*' in Baker, D. (ed.), *Medieval Women*, Blackwell, Oxford, 1978, 253-73.

Bornkamm, H., *Luther in Mid-Career. 1521-1530*, Fortress Press, Philadelphia, 1983.

—— *Luther's World of Thought*, Concordia, St. Louis, 1958.

Børresen, K. E., *Subordination and Equivalence: The Nature and Role of Woman in Augustine and Thomas Aquinas*, University Press of America, Washington, 1981.

Boswell, J., 'Homosexuality and the Religious Life. A Historical Approach' in Nelson, J. B. / Longfellow, S. P. (eds), *Sexuality and the Sacred*, Mowbray, London, 1994, 361-73.

Bottomley, F., *Attitudes to the Body in Western Christendom*, Lepus Press, London, 1979.

Bouwsma, W. J., 'Calvin and the Dilemma of Hypocrisy' in de Klerk, P. (ed.), *Calvin and Christian Ethics*, Calvin Studies Society, Grand Rapids, 1987.

—— 'Calvin and the Renaissance Crisis of Knowing', *Calvin Theological Journal* 17 (1982), 190-212.

—— *John Calvin: A Sixteenth Century Portrait*, Oxford University Press, New York, 1988.

Boyer, C., *Calvin et Luther. Accords et différences*, Universitá Gregoriana Editrice, Rome, 1973.

Bratt, J. H., 'The Role and Status of Woman in the Writings of John Calvin' in de Klerk, P. (ed.), *Renaissance, Reformation, Resurgence*, Calvin Theological Seminary, Grand Rapids, 1976, 1-17.
Brenner, A. (ed.), *A Feminist Companion to Genesis*, Sheffield Academic Press, Sheffield, 1993 – part 1, 'At the start: Emblems of Gender Relations and Human Existence', 24-201.
Brooke, C., *Europe in the Central Middle Ages*, Longman, London, 1987.
—— *The Medieval Idea of Marriage*, Oxford University Press, Oxford, 1991.
—— [with Brooke, R.] *Popular Religion in the Middle Ages*, Thames and Hudson, London, 1985.
—— *The Structure of Medieval Society*, Thames and Hudson, London, 1971.
Brooks, P. N., 'A Lily Ungilded? Martin Luther, the Virgin Mary and the Saints', *JRH* 13 (1984), 136-49.
Brown, P., *Augustine of Hippo*, Faber and Faber, London, 1967.
—— *The Body and Society. Men, Women and Sexual Renunciation in Early Christianity*, Faber and Faber, London, 1990.
Brundage, J. A., 'Concubinage and Marriage in Medieval Canon Law', *Journal of Medieval History* 1 (1975), 1-17.
—— *Law, Sex and Christian Society in Medieval Europe*, University of Chicago Press, Chicago, 1987.
Burnotte, M., 'La Pensée Mariale de Jean Calvin', *La Revue Réformée* 23 (1972), 185-91.
Burrus, V., 'The Heretical Woman as Symbol in Alexander, Athanasius, Epiphanius, and Jerome', *HTR* 84 (1991), 229-48.
Burton, A., '"History" is Now: feminist theory and the production of historical feminisms', *Women's History Review* 1 (1992), 25-38.
Butin, P. W., *Revelation, Redemption, and Response. Calvin's Trinitarian Understanding of the Divine-Human Relationship*, Oxford University Press, Oxford, 1995.
Cahill, L. S., *Between the Sexes*, Fortress Press, Philadelphia, 1985.
Cairncross, J., *After Polygamy was made a Sin*, Routledge / Kegan Paul, London, 1974.
Cameron, E., *The European Reformation*, Clarendon Press, Oxford, 1991.
Carew-Hunt, R. N., *Calvin*, Centenary Press, London, 1933.
Cargill Thompson, W. D. J., 'The "Two Kingdoms" and the "Two Regiments": Some Problems of Luther's *Zwei-Reiche Lehre*' in Dugmore, C. W. (ed.), *Studies in the Reformation: Luther to Hooker*, The Athlone Press, London, 1980, 42-59. [First published in *Journal of Theological Studies* 20 (1969), 164-85.]
Carr, A. E., *Transforming Grace*, Harper and Row, San Francisco, 1990.
Centore, F. F., 'Thomism and the Female Body as seen in the *Summa Theologiae*', *Angelicum* 67 (1990), 37-56.
Chadwick, H., *Augustine*, Oxford University Press, Oxford, 1986.
Chaunu, P., *Église, Culture et Societé: Essais sur Réforme et Contre-Réforme*, Société d'Édition d'Enseignement Supérieur, Paris, 1981.
Chrisman, M. U., *Strasbourg and the Reform*, Yale University Press, New Haven, 1967.

—— 'Lay Response to the Protestant Reformation in Germany, 1520-1528' in Newman-Brooks, P. (ed.), *Reformation Principle and Practice*, Scholars Press, London, 1980, 33-52.

Church, F. F., 'Sex and Salvation in Tertullian', *HTR* 68 (1975), 83-101.

Clanton, J. A., *In Whose Image? God and Gender*, SCM, London, 1990.

Clark, E. / Richardson, H., 'Luther and the Protestant Reformation: From Nun to Parson's Wife' in idem, (eds), *Women and Religion*, Harper and Row, New York, 1977, 133-48.

Clark, M. T., *Augustine*, Geoffrey Chapman, London, 1994.

Cocke, W. E., 'Luther's View of Marriage and Family', *Religion in Life* 42 (1973), 103-16.

Cottret, B., *Calvin. A Biography*, Eerdmans / T&T Clark, Grand Rapids, Mich. / Edinburgh, 2000.

Coudert, A. P., 'The Myth of the Improved Status of Protestant Women: The Case of the Witchcraze' in Brink, J. R. / Coudert, A. P. / Horowitz, M. C. (eds), *The Politics of Gender in Early Modern Europe*, Sixteenth Century Journal Publishers, Kirksville, 1989, 61-89.

Counts, W. M., 'The Nature of Man and the Christian's Self-Esteem', *Journal of Psychology and Theology* 1 (1973), 28-44.

Cranz, F. E., *An Essay on the Development of Luther's Thought on Justice, Law and Society*, Harvard University Press, Cambridge, 1964.

Crawford, J. R., 'Calvin and the Priesthood of all Believers', *Scottish Journal of Theology* 21 (1968), 145-56.

Crawford, P., *Women and Reformation in England. 1500-1720*, Routledge, London, 1993.

Daly, M., *Beyond God the Father*, The Women's Press, London, 1986.

Daniel-Rops, H., *The Protestant Reformation*, Dent, London, 1961.

Davy, Y., *Frau Luther*, Pacific Press, Mountain View: California, 1979.

Deane, H. A., *The Political and Social Ideas of St. Augustine*, Columbia Press, New York, 1966.

Delhaye, P., 'La Morale des Pères', *Seminarium* 3 (1971), 623-37.

—— 'The Development of the Medieval Church's Teaching on Marriage', *Concilium* 5 (1970), 83-8.

Dewan, L., 'St. Thomas, Aristotle and Creation', *Dionysius* 15 (1991), 81-90.

Dickens, A. G., *Reformation and Society in Sixteenth Century Europe*, Thames and Hudson, London, 1966.

Donelly, E., 'The Personal Piety of Martin Luther', *The Banner of Truth* 243 (1983), 19-28.

Douglass, J. D., 'Calvin's Use of Metaphorical Language for God: God as Enemy and God as Mother', *Archiv für Reformationsgeschichte* 77 (1986), 126-40.

—— 'Christian Freedom: What Calvin Learned at the School of Women', *Church History* 53 (1984), 155-73.

—— 'The Image of God in Humanity: A Comparison of Calvin's Teachings in 1536 and 1559' in Furcha, E. J. (ed.), *In Honor of John Calvin, 1509-1564*, FRS / ASC, Montreal, 1987, 175-203.

—— 'Women and the Continental Reformation' in Ruether, R. R. (ed.), *Religion and Sexism*, Simon and Schuster, New York, 1974, 292-318.

—— *Women, Freedom and Calvin*, Westminster Press, Philadelphia, 1985.

Doumergue, E., *Le caractère de Calvin, l'homme, le système, l'Eglise, l'Estat*, Slatkine Reprints, Geneva, 1970.

Dowell, S. [with Hurcombe, L.], *Dispossessed Daughters of Eve*, SPCK, London, 1987.

—— 'One Unholy and Divided Trinity' in McEwan, D. (ed.), *Women Experiencing Church*, Gracewing / Fowler Wright, Leominster, 1991, 153-60.

—— *They two shall be One: Monogamy in History and Religion*, Collins, London, 1990.

Dowsett, R., 'Womanhood and Feminism', *Scottish Bulletin of Evangelical Theology* 10 (1992), 80-93.

Doyle, P. M., 'Women and Religion: Psychological and Cultural Implications' in Ruether, R. R. (ed.), *Religion and Sexism*, Simon and Schuster, New York, 1974, 15-40.

Doyle, R. C., 'The Context of Moral Decision-Making in the Writings of John Calvin. Christological Ethics of Eschatological Order' (unpublished doctoral thesis, University of Aberdeen, 1981).

Driver, S. D., 'The Development of Jerome's Views on the Ascetic Life', *Recherches de Théologie Ancienne et Médiévale* 62 (1995), 44-70.

Duby, G., *Love and Marriage in the Middle Ages*, Polity Press, Chicago, 1994.

Duggan, L. G., 'Fear and Confession on the Eve of the Reformation', *Archiv für Reformationsgeschichte* 75 (1984), 153-75.

—— 'The Unresponsiveness of the Late Medieval Church: A Reconsideration', *Sixteenth Century Journal* 9 (1978), 3-26.

Ebeling, G., *Luther: An Introduction to his Thought*, Collins, London, 1970.

Edwards, M. U. Jr, *Luther and the False Brethren*, Stanford University Press, Stanford: California, 1975.

Ellis, E. E., *Pauline Theology: Ministry and Society*, Eerdmans, Grand Rapids, 1989.

Engel, M. P., *John Calvin's Perspectival Anthropology*, Scholars Press, Decatur, 1988) See also, under her maiden name, Potter, 'Gender Equality and Gender Hierarchy in Calvin's Theology', *Signs* 2 (1986), 725-39.

Evans, G. R., *Problems of Authority in the Reformation Debates*, Cambridge University Press, Cambridge, 1992.

Evans, M., *Woman in the Bible*, Paternoster Press, Exeter, 1983.

Eugene, T. M., 'While Love is Unfashionable: Ethical Implications of Black Spirituality and Sexuality' in Nelson, J. B. / Longfellow, S. P. (eds), *Sexuality and the Sacred*, Mowbray, London, 1994, 105-12.

Farley, B. W., 'John Calvin's Sermons on the Ten Commandments; translated, edited and critically introduced' (unpublished doctoral thesis, Union Theological Seminary, Richmond, Virginia, 1976).

Farley, M. A., 'Sexual Ethics' in Nelson, J. B. / Longfellow, S. P. (eds), *Sexuality and the Sacred*, Mowbray, London, 1994, 54-67.

Fiddes, P. S., 'The Status of Woman in the Thought of Karl Barth' in Soskice, J. M. (ed.), *After Eve*, Collins, London, 1990, 138-55.

Finch, A. J., 'Sexual Relations and Marriage in Later Medieval Normandy', *Journal of Ecclesiastical History* 47 (1996), 236-56.

Fischer, D., 'L'élément historique dans la prédication de Calvin. Un aspect original de l'homilétique du Réformateur', *Revue d'Histoire et de Philosophie Religieuses* (1984), 365-86.

Flandrin, J. L., *Families in Former Times: Kinship, Household and Sexuality*, Cambridge University Press, Cambridge, 1979.

Fleischer, M. P., '"Are Women Human?" The Debate of 1595 between Valens Acidalius and Simon Gediccus', *Sixteenth Century Journal* 11 (1981), 107-21.

Fuchs, E., *Sexual Desire and Love*, James Clarke, Cambridge, 1983.

—— *La Morale selon Calvin*, Les Éditions du Cerf, Paris, 1986.

Gamble, R. C., 'Current Trends in Calvin Research, 1982-1990' in Neuser, W. H. (ed.), *Calvinus Sacrae Scripturae Professor*, Eerdmans, Grand Rapids, 1994, 91-112.

Ganoczy, A., *The Young Calvin*, T&T Clark, Edinburgh, 1987.

George, A. C., 'Martin Luther's Doctrine of Sanctification with special reference to the Formula "*Simul Iustus et Peccator*": A Study in Luther's Lectures on Romans and Galatians' (unpublished doctoral thesis, Westminster Theological Seminary, Philadelphia, 1982).

George, T., *Theology of the Reformers*, Broadman Press, Nashville, 1988.

Gerrish, B. A., 'John Calvin on Luther' in Pelikan, J. (ed.), *Interpreters of Luther*, Fortress Press, Philadelphia, 1968, 67-96.

—— 'The Mirror of God's Goodness: Man in the Theology of Calvin', *Concordia Theological Quarterly* 45 (1981), 211-22.

—— *The Old Protestantism and the New: Essays on the Reformation Heritage*, T&T Clark, Edinburgh, 1982.

Gibson, J., 'Could Christ Have Been Born a Woman? A Medieval Debate', *Journal for Feminist Studies in Religion* 8 (1992), 65-82.

Gies, F / Gies, J., 'Life in a Medieval Village: From birth to death, a peasant woman's difficult life intersected by the church', *Christian History* 10 (1991), 16-18.

—— *Marriage and the Family in the Middle Ages*, Harper and Row, New York, 1987.

—— *Women in the Middle Ages*, Harper Perennial, New York, 1980.

Gilligan, C., *In a Different Voice: Psychological Theory and Women's Development*, Harvard University Press, Cambridge: Mass, 1982.

Gittins, D., *The Family in Question: Changing Households and Familiar Ideologies*, Macmillan, Basingstoke, 1985.

Goody, J., *The Development of the Family and Marriage in Europe*, Cambridge University Press, Cambridge, 1983.

Gottlieb, B. T., *The Family in the Western World*, Oxford University Press, Oxford, 1993.

—— 'The Problem of Feminism in the Fifteenth Century' in Kirshner, J. / Wemple, S. F. (eds), *Women of the Medieval World*, Blackwell, Oxford, 1987, 337-64.

Gould, G., 'The Contribution of the Church Fathers' in Rodd, C. S. (ed.), *New Occasions Teach New Duties?*, T&T Clark, Edinburgh, 1995, 35-46.

—— 'Women in the Writings of the Fathers: Language, Belief and Reality' in Sheils, W. J. / Wood, D. (eds), *Women in the Church*, Blackwell, Oxford, 1990, 1-13.

Graham, W. F., *The Constructive Revolutionary*, John Knox Press, Richmond, 1971.
Greef, W. de., *The Writings of John Calvin*, Baker Book House, Grand Rapids, 1993.
Green, V. H. H., *Luther and the Reformation*, Batsford Press, London, 1964.
Grey, M., *Redeeming the Dream*, SPCK, London, 1989.
Grimm, H. J., 'Luther's Contribution to Sixteenth Century Organization of Poor Relief', *Archiv für Reformationsgeschichte* 61 (1970), 222-33.
—— 'Social Forces in the German Reformation', *Church History* 31 (1962), 3-13.
Gritsch, E. W., *Martin - God's Court Jester: Luther in Retrospect*, Fortress Press, Philadelphia, 1983.
Grosshans, H. P., *Luther*, Fount, London, 1997.
Grossmann, M., *Humanism in Wittenberg. 1485-1517*, de Graff, Nieuwkoop, 1975.
Guerdan, R., *La vie quotidienne a Geneve au temps de Calvin*, Hachette, Paris, 1973.
Gustafson, J. M., *Christ and the Moral Life*, University of Chicago Press, Chicago, 1976.
—— *Protestant and Roman Catholic Ethics*, SCM, London, 1979.
—— *Theology and Ethics*, Blackwell, Oxford, 1981.
Haile, H. G., *Luther - An Experiment in Biography*, Sheldon Press, London, 1981.
Halkin, L. E., *Erasmus - A Critical Biography*, Blackwell, Oxford, 1994.
Hall, C. A. M., 'With the Spirit's Sword' (unpublished doctoral thesis, University of Basel, 1968).
Hamilton, B., *Religion in the Medieval West*, Edward Arnold, London, 1986.
Hampson, D., *Theology and Feminism*, Blackwell, Oxford, 1990.
Harkness, G., *John Calvin: The Man and his Ethics*, Abingdon Press, New York, 1981.
—— *Women in Church and Society*, Abingdon Press, Nashville, 1958.
Harrington, J. F., *Reordering Marriage and Society in Reformation Germany*, Cambridge University Press, Cambridge, 1999.
Harris, B. J., 'Women and Politics in Early Tudor England', *Historical Journal* 33 (1970), 259-81.
Harrison, B. W., 'Human Sexuality and Mutuality' in Weidman, J. L. (ed.), *Christian Feminism: Visions of a New Humanity*, Harper and Row, San Francisco, 1984, 141-57.
Hay, D., *The Medieval Centuries*, Methuen Press, London, 1964.
Haytor, M., 'The New Eve in Christ: The Use and Abuse of the Bible in the Debate about Women's Ministry' (unpublished doctoral thesis, University of Oxford, 1985).
Headley, J. M., 'The Reformation as Crisis in the Understanding of Tradition', *Archiv für Reformationsgeschichte* 78 (1987), 5-22.
Heer, F., *The Medieval World*, Cardinal Press, London, 1962.
Heine, S., *Matriarchs, Goddesses and Images of God*, Augsburg Press, Minneapolis, 1989.
Hendrix, S. H., 'Christianizing Domestic Relations: Women and Marriage in Johann Freder's *Dialogus dem Ehestand zu Ehren*', *Sixteenth Century Journal* 23 (1992), 251-66.

—— *Luther and the Papacy: Stages in a Reformation Conflict*, Fortress Press, Philadelphia, 1981.
Herlihy, D., *Medieval Households*, Harvard University Press, Cambridge, 1985.
—— 'The Making of the Medieval Family: Symmetry, Structure and Sentiment', *Journal of Family History* 8 (1983), 116-30.
—— 'Did Women have a Renaissance?' in *Women, Family and Society in Medieval Europe*, Berghahn Books, Providence, 1995, 33-56 [reprinted from *Medievalia et Humanistica* (1985), 1-22].
—— 'Family' in *Women, Family and Society in Medieval Europe*, 113-34 [reprinted from The American Historical Review 96 (1991), 1-15].
—— 'The Family and Religious Ideologies in Medieval Europe' in *Women, Family and Society in Medieval Europe*, 154-73 [reprinted from *Journal of Family History* 12 (1987), 3-17].
Hesselink, J., 'Reactions to Bouwsma's Portrait of John Calvin' in Neuser, W. H. (ed.), *Calvinus Sacrae Scripturae Professor*, Eerdmans, Grand Rapids, 1994, 209-13.
Heyward, C., 'Notes on Historical Grounding: Beyond Sexual Essentialism' in Nelson, J. B. / Longfellow, S. P. (eds), *Sexuality and the Sacred*, Mowbray, London, 1994, 9-18.
Hodgkinson, L., *Unholy Matrimony*, Columbus Press, London, 1988.
Höpfl, H., *The Christian Polity of John Calvin*, Cambridge University Press, Cambridge, 1985.
Houlbrooke, R. A., *The English Family. 1450-1700*, Longman Press, London, 1984.
Hsia, R. Po-Chia., *Social Discipline in the Reformation*, Routledge Press, London, 1989.
Huizinga, J., *The Waning of the Middle Ages. A Study of the Forms of Life, Thought and Art in France and the Netherlands in the 14th and 15th Centuries*, Penguin, Harmondsworth, 1955.
Irwin, J. L., 'Embryology and the Incarnation: A Sixteenth Century Debate', *Sixteenth Century Journal* 9 (1978), 93-104.
—— 'Society and the Sexes' in Ozment, S. (ed.), *Reformation Europe: A Guide to Research*, Centre for Reformation Research, St. Louis, 1982, 343-59.
—— *Womanhood in Radical Protestantism. 1525-1675*, Edwin Mellen Press, New York, 1979.
Isherwood, L. / McEwan, D., *Introducing Feminist Theology*, Scottish Academic Press, Sheffield, 1993.
Ishida, Y., 'Luther, the Pastor' in Lindberg, C. (ed.), *Piety, Politics and Ethics*, Sixteenth Century Journal Publishers, Kirksville, 1984, 27-37.
James, E. O., *Marriage and Society*, Hutchinson Press, London, 1952.
Jeay, M., 'Sexuality and Family in Fifteenth Century France: Are Literary Sources a Mask or a Mirror?', *Journal of Family History* 4 (1979), 328-45.
Jewett, P. K., *Man as Male and Female*, Eerdmans, Grand Rapids, 1976.
Johnson, S. L., 'Role Distinctions in the Church. Gal 3:28' in Piper, J. / Grudem, W. (eds), *Recovering Biblical Manhood and Womanhood*, Crossway Press, Wheaton, 1991, 154-64.
Johnson, S. M., 'Luther's Reformation and (Un)holy Matrimony', *Journal of Family History* 17 (1992), 271-88.

Jordan, C., *Renaissance Feminism: Literary Texts and Political Models*, Cornell University Press, Ithaca, 1990.
Jutte, R., 'Household and Family Life in Late Sixteenth Century Cologne: The Weinberg Family', *Sixteenth Century Journal* 17 (1986), 165-82.
Karant-Nunn, S. C., 'Continuity and Change: Some of the Effects of the Reformation on the Women of Zwickau', *Sixteenth Century Journal* 12 (1982), 17-42.
—— 'The Transmission of Luther's Teachings on Women and Matrimony: The Case of Zwickau', *Archiv für Reformations-geschichte* 77 (1986), 31-46.
—— 'The Women of the Saxon Silver Mines' in Marshall, S. (ed.), *Women in Reformation and Counter-Reformation Europe*, Indiana University Press, Indianapolis, 1989, 29-46.
Kelly, J., 'Early Feminist Theory and the *Querelles des Femmes*, 1400-1789', *Signs* 8 (1982), 4-28.
Kelly, R. A., 'Luther's Use of 1 Corinthians 14' in Bradley, J. E. / Muller, R. A. (eds), *Church, Word and Spirit*, Eerdmans, Grand Rapids, 1987, 123-34.
Kingdon, R. M., *Adultery and Divorce in Calvin's Geneva*, Harvard University Press, Cambridge: Mass., 1995.
—— 'The Control of Morals in Calvin's Geneva' in Buck, L. P. / Zophy, J. W. (eds), *The Social History of the Reformation*, Ohio State University Press, Columbus, 1972, 3-16.
—— 'The First Calvinist Divorce' in Mentzer, R. A. (ed.), *Sin and the Calvinists. Morals Control and the Consistory in the Reformed Tradition*, Sixteenth Century Journal Publishers, Kirksville: Miss, 1994, 1-14.
Kittleson, J., *Luther the Reformer: The Story of the Man and his Career*, Augsburg Press, Minneapolis, 1986.
—— 'Successes and Failures in the German Reformation: The Report from Strasbourg', *Archiv für Reformationsgeschichte* 73 (1982), 153-74.
Kolb, R., *Martin Luther as Prophet, Teacher and Hero*, Baker Book House, Grand Rapids, 1999.
Kramm, H. H., *The Theology of Martin Luther*, James Clarke, London, 1947.
Kreck, W., 'Parole et Esprit salon Calvin', *Revue d'Histoire et de Philosophie Religieuses* (1960), 215-28.
Lacey, T. A., *Marriage in Church and State*, SPCK, London, 1947.
Lambert, M., *Medieval Heresy*, Blackwell, Oxford, 1994.
Lane, A. N. S., 'Calvin's Use of the Fathers and the Medievals', *Calvin Theological Journal* 16 (1981), 149-205.
Lang, A., 'The Reformation and Natural Law' in Armstrong, W. P. (ed.), *Calvin and the Reformation*, Baker Book House, Grand Rapids, 1980, 56-98.
Laporte, J., *The Role of Women in Early Christianity*, Edwin Mellen Press, New York, 1982.
Laslett, P., 'The Comparative History of Household and Family', *Journal of Social History* 4 (1970), 75-87.
Lazareth, W. H., 'Introduction to "The Christian in Society"' in Atkinson, J. (ed.), *Luther's Works*, volume 44, Fortress Press, Philadelphia, 1966, xi-xvi.
—— *Luther on the Christian Home*, Muhlenberg Press, Philadelphia, 1960.
Lebacqz, K., 'Appropriate Vulnerability' in Nelson, J. B. / Longfellow, S. P. (eds), *Sexuality and the Sacred*, Mowbray, London, 1994, 256-61.

Leeuwen, M. S. van., 'The Christian Mind and the Challenge of Gender Relations' in Nelson, J. B. / Longfellow, S. P. (eds), *Sexuality and the Sacred*, Mowbray, London, 1994, 120-30.

—— [et al.] *After Eden: Facing the Challenge of Gender Reconciliation*, Eerdmans, Grand Rapids, 1993.

Lehmann, P. L., *Ethics in a Christian Context*, SCM, London, 1963.

—— 'The Anti-Pelagian Writings' in Battenhouse, R. W. (ed.), *A Companion to the Study of St. Augustine*, OUP, New York, 1955, 203-34.

Lemaître, A., *Calvin et Luther*, Éditions Labor et Fides, Geneva, 1959.

Lerner, G., *The Creation of Patriarchy*, Oxford University Press, Oxford, 1986.

Levi, A., 'Humanist Reform in Sixteenth Century France', *Heythrop Journal* 6 (1965), 447-64.

Lienhard, M., 'La Réforme de Luther et l'Europe: Succès ou Échec?', *Revue d'Histoire et de Philosophie Religieuses* 75 (1995), 113-21.

Lindberg, C., *The European Reformations*, Blackwell, Oxford, 1996.

—— '"There should be no beggars among Christians": Karlstadt, Luther and the Origin of Protestant Poor Relief', *Church History* (1977), 313-34.

Linder, R. D., 'Calvinism and Humanism: The First Generation', *Church History* 44 (1975), 167-81.

Little, D., 'Calvin and the Prospects for a Christian Theory of Natural Law' in Outka, G. H. / Ramsey, P. (eds), *Norm and Context in Christian Ethics*, SCM, London, 1969, 175-97.

Loeschen, J. R., *The Divine Community. Trinity, Church and Ethics in Reformation Theologies*, Sixteenth Century Journal Publishers, Kirksville, 1981.

Loewenich, W. von., *Martin Luther: The Man and his Work*, Augsburg Press, Minneapolis, 1986.

Lohse, B., *Martin Luther: An Introduction to his Life and Work*, T&T Clark, Edinburgh, 1987.

Long, E. L. Jr, *A Survey of Christian Ethics*, Oxford University Press, New York, 1967.

—— 'Sociological Implications of Norm and Context' in Outka, G. H. / Ramsey, P. (eds), *Norm and Context in Christian Ethics*, SCM, London, 1969, 265-95.

Lortz, J., *Die Reformation in Deutschland*, Herder, Freiburg, 1982.

Lowe, K. J. P., 'Female strategies for success in a male-ordered world: the Benedictine convent of Le Murate in Florence in the 15th and early 16th centuries' in Sheils, W. J. / Wood, D. (eds), *Women in the Church*, Blackwell, Oxford, 1990, 209-21.

Luscombe, D. E., *The School of Peter Abelard*, Cambridge University Press, Cambridge, 1970.

Maclean, I., *The Renaissance Notion of Woman*, Cambridge University Press, Cambridge, 1980.

Mall, E. J., *Kitty, my Rib*, Concordia Press, St. Louis, 1959.

Mancha, R., 'The Woman's Authority: Calvin to Edwards', *Journal of Christian Reconstruction* 6 (1979-80), 86-98.

Mann, G. A., '*Simul Iustus et Peccator*: Luther's Paradigm of the Christian Life and Systematic Principle' (unpublished doctoral thesis, Drew University, 1988).

Marcel, P., 'L'Humilité d'après Calvin', *La Revue Réformée* 11 (1960), 1-38.
Margolin, J.-C., 'La notion de dignité humaine selon Erasme de Rotterdam' in Kirk, J. (ed.), *Humanism and Reform*, Blackwell, Oxford, 1991, 37-56.
Marius, R., *Luther*, Quartet Press, London, 1975.
Markus, R. A., *Saeculum: History and Society in the Theology of St. Augustine*, Cambridge University Press, Cambridge, 1970.
Matheson, P., *Argula von Grumbach. A Woman's Voice in the Reformation*, T&T Clark, Edinburgh, 1995.
—— 'A Reformation for Women? Sin, Grace and Gender in the Writings of Argula von Grumbach', *Scottish Journal of Theology* 49 (1996), 39-55.
—— *The Imaginative World of the Reformation*, T&T Clark, Edinburgh, 2000.
MacCuish, D., *Luther and his Katie*, Christian Focus Publications, Fearn, 1999.
MacIntyre, A., *After Virtue*, University of Notre Dame Press, Notre Dame, 1984.
—— *A Short History of Ethics*, Macmillan, New York, 1966.
Maguire, D., *The Moral Choice*, Winston Press, Minneapolis, 1979.
Malone, M. T., *Women and Christianity*, volumes 1 &2, Columba Press, Blackrock: Co. Dublin, 2000 / 2001.
Martin, F., *Call Me Blessed: The Emerging Christian Woman*, Eerdmans, Grand Rapids, 1988.
McClendon, J. W., *Systematic Theology*, volume 1, *Ethics*, Abingdon Press, Nashville, 1986.
McCool, G. A., 'The Ambrosian Origin of St. Augustine's Theology of the Image of God in Man', *Theological Studies* 20 (1959), 62-81.
McDonough, T. M., *The Law and the Gospel in Luther*, Oxford University Press, Oxford, 1963.
McGiffert, A. C., *Martin Luther: The Man and his Work*, Fisher Unwin, London, 1911.
McGowen, R. J., 'Augustine's Spiritual Equality: The Allegory of Man and Woman with Regard to *Imago Dei*', *Revue des Études Augustinienne* 33 (1987), 255-64.
McGrath, A. E., *A Life of John Calvin*, Blackwell, Oxford, 1993.
—— 'John Calvin and Late Medieval Thought. A Study in Late Medieval Influences upon Calvin's Theological Development', *Archiv für Reformationsgeschichte* 77 (1986), 58-79.
—— *Reformation Thought*, Blackwell, Oxford, 1989.
—— *The Genesis of Doctrine*, Blackwell, Oxford, 1990.
McLaughlin, E. C., 'Equality of Souls, Inequality of Sexes: Woman in Medieval Theology in Ruether, R. R. (ed.), *Religion and Sexism: Images in the Jewish and Christian Tradition*, Simon and Schuster, New York, 1974, 213-66.
McNamara, J. A., 'Inside the Convent', *Church History* 10 (1991), 19-21.
—— 'The Reformation' in Rodd, C. S. (ed.), *New Occasions Teach New Duties?*, T&T Clark, Edinburgh, 1995, 47-60.
McNutt, J., 'Martin Luther as Human Being: reflections from a distance', *Churchman* 108 (1994), 265-70.
Meinhold, P., 'Society in Transition in the Age of the Reformation', *Sixteenth Century Journal* 3 (1972), 25-36.
Miles, M. R., 'Theology, Anthropology, and the Human Body in Calvin's *Institutes*', *Harvard Theological Review* 74 (1981), 303-24.

—— '"The Rope Breaks When it is Tightest": Luther on the Body, Consciousness and the Word', *Harvard Theological Review* 77 (1984), 239-58.

Miles, R., *The Rites of Man. Love, Sex and Death in the Making of Man*, Grafton Press, London, 1991.

—— *The Women's History of the World*, Michael Joseph Press, London, 1988.

Miller, A. A., 'The Theologies of Luther and Boehme in the Light of their Genesis Commentaries', *Harvard Theological Review* 63 (1970), 261-303.

Milner, B. C., *Calvin's Doctrine of the Church*, Brill, Leiden, 1970.

Monheit, M. L., 'The ambition for an illustrious name: Humanism, Patronage, and Calvin's Doctrine of the Calling', *Sixteenth Century Journal* 23 (1992), 267-87.

Monter, W., 'Daily Life and the Reformed Church' in Chaunu, P. (ed.), *The Reformation*, Alan Sutton, Gloucester, 1989, 244-53.

Motyer, S., 'Expounding 1 Timothy 2:8-15', *Vox Evangelica* 24 (1994), 91-102.

—— 'The Relationship between Paul's Gospel of "All one in Christ Jesus" (Galatians 3:28) and the "Household Codes"', *Vox Evangelica* 19 (1989), 33-48.

Mouw, R. J., *The God who Commands*, University of Notre Dame Press, Notre Dame, 1990.

Moxey, K., *Peasants, Warriors and Wives. Popular Imagery in the Reformation*, University of Chicago Press, Chicago, 1989.

Mullett, M., *Calvin*, Routledge Press, London, 1989.

Murray, A., *Reason and Society in the Middle Ages*, Clarendon Press, Oxford, 1986.

Murstein, B. I., *Love, Sex and Marriage Through the Ages*, Springer Press, New York, 1974.

Nelson, J. B., *Embodiment*, SPCK, London, 1979.

—— *The Intimate Connection*, Westminster Press, Philadelphia, 1988.

Nelson, J. L., 'Women and the Word in the Earlier Middle Ages' in Sheils, W. J. / Wood, D. (eds), *Women in the Church*, Blackwell, Oxford, 1990, 53-78.

Neuser, W. H., 'Calvin's Verständis der Heiligen Schrift' in idem (ed.), *Calvinus Sacrae Scripturae Professor*, Eerdmans, Grand Rapids, 1994, 41-71.

Niebuhr, R., *Faith and History*, Nisbet Press, London, 1949.

Nineham, D., *Christianity Medieval and Modern. A Study in Religious Change*, SCM, London, 1993.

North, G., 'The Economic Thought of Luther and Calvin', *Journal of Christian Reconstruction* 1 (1975), 76-108.

Nygren, A., *Agape and Eros*, SPCK, London, 1953.

Oberman, H. A., '*Initia Calvini:* The Matrix of Calvin's Reformation' in Neuser, W. H. (ed.), *Calvinus Sacrae Scripturae Professor*, Eerdmans, Grand Rapids, 1994, 113-54.

—— *Luther: Man between God and the Devil*, Fontana Press, London, 1993.

—— 'Martin Luther' in Jungel, E. / Wallmann, J. / Werbeck, W. (eds), *Verifikationen Festchrift für Gerhard Ebeling 70, Geburtstag*, Mohr, Tübingen, 1982.

—— *Masters of the Reformation*, Cambridge University Press, Cambridge, 1981.

—— '*Teufelsdreck:* Eschatology and Scatology in the "Old" Luther' in *The Impact of the Reformation*, Eerdmans, Grand Rapids, 1994, 51-68 [reprinted from *SCJ* 19 (1988), 435-50].

—— 'The Impact of the Reformation: Problems and Perspectives' in *The Impact of the Reformation*, 173-200 [reprinted from Kouri, E. I. / Scott, T. (eds), *Politics and Society in Reformation Europe*, London: 1987), 3-31].

—— 'The Shape of Late Medieval Thought: The Birthpangs of the Modem Era' in Trinkaus, C. / Oberman, H. A. (eds), *The Pursuit of Holiness in Late Medieval and Renaissance Religion*, Brill, Leiden, 1974, 3-25.

—— 'The Virgin Mary in Evangelical Perspective' in *The Impact of the Reformation*, 225-52 [reprinted from *The Journal of Ecumenical Studies* 1 (1964), 271-98].

—— '*Via Antiqua* and *Via Moderna:* Late Medieval Prolegomena to Early Reformation Thought' in *The Impact of the Reformation*, 3-22 [reprinted from *Journal of the History of Ideas* 48 (1987), 23-40].

O'Callaghan, D., 'Marriage as Sacrament', *Concilium* 5 (1970), 101-10.

Oden, A., *In Her Words. Women's Writings in the History of Christian Thought*, SPCK, London, 1995.

O'Donovan, O., '*Usus* and *fructio* in Augustine', *Journal of Theological Studies* 33 (1982), 361-97.

Olsen, V. N., *The New Testament Logia on Divorce. A Study of Their Interpretation from Erasmus to Milton*, Mohr, Tübingen, 1971.

O'Rourke Boyle, M., 'Augustine in the Garden of Zeus: Lust, Love and Language', *Harvard Theological Review* 83 (1990), 117-39.

Osborn, E., *Ethical Patterns in Early Christian Thought*, Cambridge University Press, Cambridge, 1976.

Outka, G. H., 'Character, Conduct and the Love Commandment' in Outka, G. H. / Ramsey, P. (eds), *Norm and Context in Christian Ethics*, SCM, London, 1969, 37-66.

Ozment, S. E., *The Age of Reform. 1250-1550*, Yale University Press, New Haven, 1980.

—— *Protestants: The Birth of a Revolution*, Image Books, London, 1993.

—— *When Fathers Ruled: Family Life in Reformation Europe*, Cambridge University Press, Cambridge: Mass, 1983.

Pagels, E., 'The Politics of Paradise: Augustine's Exegesis of Genesis 1-3 versus that of John Chrysostom', *Harvard Theological Review* 78 (1985), 67-99.

Pannenberg, W., 'Luther's Doctrine of the Two Kingdoms' in *Ethics*, Westminster Press, Philadelphia, 1981, 112-31.

Parker, T. H. L., *Calvin: An Introduction to his Thought*, Geoffrey Chapman, London, 1995.

—— *Calvin's New Testament Commentaries*, SCM, London, 1971.

—— *Calvin's Old Testament Commentaries*, T&T Clark, Edinburgh, 1986.

—— *Calvin's Preaching*, T&T Clark, Edinburgh, 1992.

—— *John Calvin: a Biography*, Dent, London, 1975.

—— *John Calvin's Doctrine of the Knowledge of God*, Oliver and Boyd, Edinburgh, 1969.

Parsons, M., *Luther and Calvin on Old Testament Narratives. Reformation Thought and Narrative Text* (New York: Edwin Mellen Press, 2004).

—— 'Luther and Calvin on Rape: Is the Crime Lost in the Agenda?', *Evangelical Quarterly* 74 (2002), 123-142.

―― 'The Apocalyptic Luther: His Noahic Self-Understanding', *Journal of the Evangelical Theological Society* 44 (2001), 627-45.
Parvey, C. F., 'The Theology and Leadership of Women in the New Testament' in Ruether, R. R. (ed.), *Religion and Sexism*, Simon and Schuster, New York, 1974, 117-49.
Pauck, W., *From Luther to Tillich: The Reformers and their Heirs*, Harper and Row, San Francisco, 1984.
Paul, S. L., 'Patriarchal Anthropology: Spiritual Equality / Natural Subordination', *Ex Auditu* 13 (1997), 114-28.
Pearson, C., '"Line upon line: here a little, there a little." Some Letters of Martin Luther' in Newman-Brooks, P. (ed.), *Seven-Headed Luther*, Clarendon Press, Oxford, 1983, 275-310.
Perry, N. / Echeveria, L., *Under the Heel of Mary*, Routledge Press, London, 1986.
Pfeiffer, C. W., 'Heinrich Bullinger and Marriage' (unpublished doctoral thesis, St Louis University, 1981).
Piper, O., *The Christian Interpretation of Sex*, Nisbet Press, London, 1942.
Phillips, R., *Putting Asunder. A History of Divorce in Western Society*, Cambridge University Press, Cambridge, 1988.
Potter, G. R. / Greengrass, M., *John Calvin*, Edward Arnold Press, London, 1983.
Potter, M., 'Gender Equality and Gender Hierarchy in Calvin's Theology', *Signs* 2 (1986), 725-39. [See also, under Engel – her married name.]
Power, E., *Medieval People*, Methuen Press, London, 1929.
―― *Medieval Woman*, Cambridge University Press, Cambridge, 1975.
Preuss, H., *Die Vorstellungen vom Antichrist im späten Mittelalter, bei Luther und in der konfessionellen Polemik*, Hinrichsche Buchhandlung, Leipzig, 1906.
Price, R. M., 'The Distinctiveness of the Early Christian Sexual Ethics', *Heythrop Journal* 31 (1990), 257-76.
Primavesi, A., *From Apocalypse to Genesis*, Burns and Oates, Tunbridge Wells, 1991.
Prins, R., 'The Image of God in Adam and the Restoration of Man in Jesus Christ', *Scottish Journal of Theology* 25 (1972), 32-44.
Quistorp, H., *Calvin's Doctrine of the Last Things*, John Knox Press, Richmond, 1955.
Ramsey, G. W., 'Is Name-Giving an Act of Domination in Genesis 2:23 and Elsewhere?', *Catholic Biblical Quarterly* 50 (1988), 24-35.
Rearden, B. M. G., *Religious Thought in the Reformation*, Longman Press, London, 1981.
Reid, D. R., 'Luther, Munster and the Last Day: Eschatological Hope, Apocalyptic Expectation', *Mennonite Quarterly Review* 69 (1995), 53-74.
Resnick, I. M., 'Peter Damian on the restoration of virginity: a problem for medieval theology', *Journal of Theological Studies* 39 (1988), 125-34.
Richard, L. J., *The Spirituality of John Calvin*, John Knox Press, Atlanta, 1974.
Rilliet, J., *Le Vrai Visage de Calvin*, Pensée / Privat, Toulouse, 1982.
Robinson-Hammerstein, H., 'Luther and the Laity' in idem (ed.), *The Transmission of Ideas in the Lutheran Reformation*, Irish Academic Press, Dublin, 1989, 11-46.
Robinson, N. H. G., *The Groundwork of Christian Ethics*, Collins, London, 1971.

Roblack, H. C., 'Martin Luther and the Urban Social Experience' in Robinson-Hammerstein, H. (ed.), *The Transmission of Ideas in the Lutheran Reformation*, Irish Academic Press, Dublin, 1989, 65-82.

Roelker, N. L., 'The Role of Noblewomen in the French Reformation', *Archiv für Reformationsgeschichte* 63 (1972), 168-95.

—— 'The Appeal of Calvinism to French Noblewomen in the Sixteenth Century', *Journal of Interdisciplinary History* 2 (1972), 391-418.

Romero, J. A., 'The Protestant Principle: A Woman's-Eye View of Barth and Tillich' in Ruether, R. R. (ed.), *Religion and Sexism*, Simon and Schuster, New York, 1974, 319-40.

Roper, L., *The Holy Household: Women and Morals in Reformation Augsburg*, Clarendon Press, Oxford, 1989.

Rösener, W., *Peasants in the Middle Ages*, Polity Press, Cambridge, 1992.

Ruether, R. R., *Mary, The Feminine Face of the Church*, SCM, London, 1979.

—— 'Misogynism and virginal femininity in the Fathers of the Church' in idem (ed.), *Religion and Sexism*, Simon and Schuster, New York, 1974.

—— *Sexism and God-Talk*, SCM, London, 1983.

—— *Women and Redemption. A Theological History*, SCM, London, 1998.

—— *Women-Church: Theology and Practice*, Harper and Row, San Francisco, 1988.

Rupp, G., 'Protestant Spirituality in the First Age of the Reformation' in Cuming, G. J. / Baker, D. (eds), *Studies in Church History*, volume 8, Cambridge University Press, Cambridge, 1972, 155-70.

—— *The Righteousness of God: Luther Studies*, Hodder and Stoughton, London, 1968.

Russell, P. A., *Lay Theology in the Reformation*, Cambridge University Press, Cambridge, 1986.

—— '"Your sons and daughters shall prophesy..." (Joel 2:28). Common People and the Future of the Reformation in the Pamphlet Literature of South-Western Germany to 1525', *Archiv für Reformationsgeschichte* 74 (1983), 122-40.

Safley, T. M., *Let No Man Put Asunder: The Control of Marriage in the German Southwest. A Comparative Study, 1550-1600*, Sixteenth Century Publishers, Kirksville, 1984.

Scanzoni, L. / Hardesty, N., *All We're Meant to Be*, Word Press, Waco, 1975.

Schmeidler, B., 'Die Briefweschsel zwischen Abälard und Heloïse eine Fälschung?', *Archiv für Kulturgeschichte* 11 (1913-14), 1-30.

Schreiber, L., *Katherine, Wife of Luther*, Muhlenberg Press, Philadelphia, 1954.

Schreiner, S. E., *The Theater of his Glory: Nature and the Natural Order in the Thought of John Calvin*, Labyrinth Press, Durham: North Carolina, 1991.

Schroeder, E. H., 'Family Ethos in the Light of the Reformation' in Feucht, O. E. (ed.), *Family Relationships and the Church*, Concordia, St. Louis, 1970.

Schuurman, D. J., 'Humanity in Reformed and Feminist Perspectives: Collision or Correlation?', *Calvin Theological Journal* 27 (1992), 68-90.

Schwiebert, E. G., *Luther and his Times*, Concordia, St. Louis, 1950.

Scribner, R. W., 'Oral Culture and the Transmission of Reformation Ideas' in Robinson-Hammerstein, H. (ed.), *The Transmission of Ideas in the Lutheran Reformation*, Irish Academic Press, Dublin, 1989, 83-104.

—— *The German Reformation*, Humanities Press, Atlantic Highlands: New Jersey, 1986.
—— 'The Social Thought of Erasmus', *Journal of Religious History* 6 (1970-71), 3-26.
Selderhuis, H. J., *Marriage and Divorce in the Thought of Martin Bucer*, Thomas Jefferson University Press, Kirksville: Miss, 1999.
Selinger, S., *Calvin Against Himself: An Inquiry in Intellectual History*, Archon Press, Hamden: Connecticut, 1984.
Shaw, B. D., 'The Family in Late Antiquity - the Experience of Augustine', *Past and Present* 115 (1987), 3-51.
Siggins, I. D. K., *Luther*, Oliver and Boyd, Edinburgh, 1972.
—— 'Luther's Mother Margarethe', *Harvard Theological Review* 71 (1978), 125-50.
Simon, E., *Luther Alive: Martin Luther and the Making of the Reformation*, Hodder and Stoughton, London, 1968.
Smith, J. C., 'Katherina von Bora - through Five Centuries: A Historiography', *Sixteenth Century Journal* 30 (1999), 745-74.
Smits, L., *Saint Augustin dans l'ouvre de Calvin*, van Gorcum, Assen, 1957.
Snodgrass, K. R., 'Galatians 3:28 - Conundrum or Solution?' in Mickelsen, A. (ed.), *Authority and the Bible*, InterVarsity Press, Downers Grove, 1986, 161-81.
Somers, H., 'Image de Dieu: Les Sources de l'exégèse augustinienne', *Revue des Études Augustiniennes* 7 (1961), 105-25.
Southern, R. W., *Western Society and the Church in the Middle Ages*, Hodder and Stoughton, London, 1970.
Sowards, J. K., 'Erasmus and the Education of Women', *Sixteenth Century Journal* 13 (1982), 77-89.
Sparn, W., 'Preaching and the Course of the Reformation' in Robinson-Hammerstein, H. (ed.), *The Transmission of Ideas in the Lutheran Reformation*, Irish Academic Press, Dublin, 1989, 173-83.
Spijker, W.van't., 'Bucer's Influence on Calvin: Church and Community' in Wright, D. F. (ed.), *Martin Bucer. Reforming Church and Society*, Cambridge University Press, Cambridge, 1994, 32-44.
Spitz, L. W., 'Headwaters of the Reformation: *Studia Humanitatis, Luther Senior, et Initia Reformationis*' in Oberman, H. A. (ed.), *Luther and the Dawn of the Modern Era*, Brill, Leiden, 1974, 89-116.
—— *The Protestant Reformation. 1517-1559*, Harper and Row, New York, 1985.
Spykman, G. J., *Reformational Theology*, Eerdmans, Grand Rapids, 1992.
Stauffer, R., *Dieu, la création et la providence dans la prédication de Calvin*, Lang, Berne, 1978.
—— 'Un Calvin inconnu: le prédicateur de Genève', *Bulletin de l'Histoire du Protestantmise Francais* 4 (1978), 184-203.
—— *The Humanity of John Calvin*, Abingdon Press, Nashville, 1971.
Steinmetz, D., *Calvin in Context*, Oxford University Press, Oxford, 1995.
Stickleberger, E., *John Calvin*, T&T Clark, Edinburgh, 1959.
Stone, L., *The Family, Sex and Marriage in England. 1500-1800*, Penguin, Harmondsworth, 1979.
Storkey, E., *What's Right with Feminism?*, SPCK, London, 1985.

Strauss, G., *Luther's House of Learning: Indoctrination of the Young in the German Reformation*, Johns Hopkins University, Baltimore, 1978.
—— *Manifestations of Discontent in Germany on the Eve of the Reformation*, Indiana University Press, Indianapolis, 1971.
—— 'Reformation and Pedagogy: Educational Thought and Practice in the Lutheran Reformation' in Trinkaus, C. / Oberman, H. A. (eds), *The Pursuit of Holiness in Late Medieval and Renaissance Religion*, Brill, Leiden, 1974, 272-93.
—— 'Success and Failure in the German Reformation' in Dixon, C. S. (ed.), *The German Reformation*, Blackwell, Oxford, 1999, 221-57.
Stuard, S. M., 'The Chase after theory: Considering Medieval Women', *Gender and History* 4 (1992), 135-46.
Sumner, G. M., 'The Style of John Calvin's Sermons. 1549-1560' (unpublished BLitt thesis, Oxford, 1976).
Swartley, W. M., *Slavery, Sabbath, War and Women*, Herald Press, Scottdale, 1983.
Tamburello, D. E., *Union with Christ. John Calvin and the Mysticism of St. Bernard*, Westminster / John Knox Press, Louisville, 1994.
Tannahill, R., *Sex in History*, Hamish Hamilton Press, London, 1980.
Taylor, S. M., 'Sharing Within the Community of Saints: A Study of Luther's Ecclesiology', *American Baptist Quarterly* 14 (1995), 260-69.
Tentler, T. N., *Sin and Confession on the Eve of the Reformation*, University of Princeton Press, Princeton, 1977.
Thielicke, H., *The Ethics of Sex*, James Clarke, London, 1964.
Thomas, G. F., *Christian Ethics and Moral Philosophy*, Scribner's, New York, 1955.
Thompson, J. L., '"*Creata ad Imaginem Dei, Licet Secundo Gradu*": Woman as the Image of God According to John Calvin', *Harvard Theological Review* 81 (1988), 125-44.
—— *John Calvin and the Daughters of Sarah: Women in regular and exceptional roles in the exegesis of Calvin, his predecessors and his contemporaries*, Librairie Droz, Geneva, 1992.
Todd, J. M., *Luther. A Life*, Hamish Hamilton Press, London, 1982.
Tolley, B., *Pastors and Parishioners in Württemberg During the Late Reformation. 1581-1621*, Stanford University Press, Stanford, 1995.
Tonkin, J. M., 'Luther's Interpretation of Secular Reality', *Journal of Religious History* 6 (1970-71), 133-51.
Torrance, T. F., *Calvin's Doctrine of Man*, Lutterworth Press, London, 1949.
—— 'The Eschatology of Faith: Martin Luther' in Yule, G. (ed.), *Luther: Theologian for Catholics and Protestants*, T&T Clark, Edinburgh, 1985, 145-213.
Truc, G., *Histoire Illustrée de la Femme*, 2 volumes, Librairie Plon, Paris, 1940-41.
Tucker, R. A., 'Heloise and Abelard's Tumultuous Affair', *Christian History* 10 (1991), 28-30.
Tuohey, J. F., 'The Gender Distinctions of Primeval History and a Christian Sexual Ethic', *Heythrop Journal* 36 (1995), 173-89.
Veninga, J. F., 'Covenant Theology and Ethics in the Thought of John Calvin and John Preston' (unpublished doctoral thesis, Rice University, 1974).

Vos, C. J., 'Calvin's View of Man in the Light of Genesis 2:15 or Man: Earth's Servant or Lord' in Rooy, A. J. van. (ed.), *Calvinus Reformator*, Potchefstroom University for Christian Higher Education, Potchefstroom, 1982, 131-41.

Vos, L. A., 'Calvin and the Christian Self Image' in Holwerda, D. E. (ed.), *Exploring the Heritage of John Calvin*, Baker Book House, Grand Rapids, 1976, 76-109.

Wagner, W. H., 'Luther and the Positive Use of the Law', *Journal of Religious History* 11 (1980-81), 45-63.

Wallace, R. S., *Calvin, Geneva and the Reformation*, Scottish Academic Press, Edinburgh, 1988.

—— *Calvin's Doctrine of the Christian Life*, Oliver and Boyd, Edinburgh, 1959.

Walt, B. J. van der, 'Woman and Marriage in the Middle Ages, in Calvin and in our own time' in idem (ed.), *John Calvin's Institutes: His Opus Magnum*, Potchefstroom University for Christian Higher Education, Potchefstroom, 1986, 184-238.

Walters, D., 'The Reformation and the Transformation of Western Culture', *Journal of Christian Reconstruction* 2 (1975), 109-14.

Watt, J. R., 'The Marriage Laws Calvin Drafted for Geneva' in Neuser, W. H. (ed.), *Calvinus Sacrae Scripturae Professor*, Eerdmans, Grand Rapids, 1994, 245-55.

Webb, D. M., 'Woman and Home: The Domestic Setting of Late Medieval Spirituality' in Sheils, W. J. / Wood, D. (eds), *Women in the Church*, Blackwell, Oxford, 1990, 159-73.

Wendel, F., *Calvin et l'Humanisme*, University of France Press, Paris, 1976.

—— *Calvin: The Origins and Development of His Religious Thought*, Collins, London, 1965.

Whale, J. S., *The Protestant Tradition*, Cambridge University Press, Cambridge, 1955.

White, H., *Social Criticism in Popular Religious Literature of the Sixteenth Century*, Octagon Press, New York, 1965.

White, R., 'Women and the Teaching Office According to Calvin', *Scottish Journal of Theology* 47 (1994), 489-509.

White, R. E. O., *The Changing Continuity of Christian Ethics*, volume 2, Paternoster Press, Exeter, 1981.

Wiesner, M. W., 'Beyond Women and the Family: Towards a Gender Analysis of the Reformation', *Sixteenth Century Journal* 18 (1987), 311-22.

—— 'Luther and Women: The Death of the Two Marys' in Obelkevich, J. / Roper, L. / Samuel R. (eds), *Disciplines of Faith: Studies in Religion, Politics and Patriarchy*, Routledge / Kegan Paul, London, 1987, 295-308.

—— 'Nuns, Wives, and Mothers: Women and the Reformation in Germany' in Marshall, S. (ed.), *Women in Reformation and Counter-Reformation Europe*, Indiana University Press, Indianapolis, 1989, 8-28.

—— 'Paltry Peddlers or Essential Merchants: Women in the Distributive Trades in Early Modern Nuremberg', *Sixteenth Century Journal* 12 (1981), 3-14.

—— 'Women's Response to the Reformation' in Hsia, R. Po-Chia (ed.), *The German People and the Reformation*, Cornell University Press, Ithaca, 1988, 148-71.

Wiethaus, U., 'Sexuality, Gender, and the Body in Late Medieval Women's Spirituality. Cases from Germany and the Netherlands', *Journal for Feminist Studies of Religion* 7 (1991), 35-52.
Wilson-Hayes, T., 'The Peaceful Apocalypse', *Sixteenth Century Journal* 17 (1986), 131-43.
Wingren, G., *Luther on Vocation*, Muhlenberg Press, Philadelphia, 1957.
Winnett A. R., *The Church and Divorce*, Mowbray, London, 1968.
Wollasch, A., 'Eine adlige Familie des frühen Mittelalters', *Archiv für Kulturgeschichte* 39 (1957), 150-88.
Wright, D. F., 'Calvin's Pentateuchal Criticism: Equity, Hardness of Heart and Divine Accommodation in the Mosaic Harmony Commentary', *Calvin Theological Journal* 21 (1986), 33-50.
—— 'The Ethical Use of the Old Testament in Luther and Calvin: A Comparison', *Scottish Journal of Theology* (1983), 463-86.
—— 'Mary in the Reformers' in idem (ed.), *Chosen by God: Mary in Evangelical Perspective*, MarshallPickering, London, 1989, 161-83.
—— 'Woman Before and After the Fall: A Comparison of Luther's and Calvin's Interpretation of Genesis 1-3', *Churchman* (1984), 126-35.
Wyntjes, S. M., 'Women and Religious Choices in the Sixteenth Century Netherlands', *Archiv für Reformationsgeschichte* 75 (1984), 276-90.
—— 'Women in the Reformation Era' in Bridenthal, R. / Koonz, C. (eds), *Becoming Visible: Women in European History*, Houghton Mifflin Press, Boston, 1977, 165-91.
Yost, J. K., 'The Reformation Defence of Clerical Marriage in the Reigns of Henry VIII and Edward VI', *Church History* 7 (1981), 152-65.
Yule, G., 'Late Medieval Piety, Humanism and Luther's Theology' in Robbins, K. (ed.), *Studies in Church History*, volume 17, Blackwell, Oxford, 1981, 167-79.
Zappone, K., 'Is There a Feminist Ethic?' in Freyne, S. (ed.), *Ethics and the Christian*, Columba Press, Blackrock: Co. Dublin, 1991, 110-26.
Zimmerman, J. A. K., 'Christian Life in Luther and Calvin', *Lutheran Quarterly* 16 (1964), 222-30.
Zimbelman, E., *Human Sexuality and Evangelical Christians*, University Press of America, New York, 1985.
Zophy, J. W., 'We Must Have the Dear Ladies: Martin Luther and Women' in Sessions, K. C. / Bebb, P. N. (eds), *Pietas et Societas*, Sixteenth Century Journal Publishers, 1985, 141-50.

INDEX OF PROPER NAMES

Abelard, P., 88-90, 100, 345 n.13
Agrippa, C., 30, 32 n.96
Ambrose, 5, 324 n.119
Ambrosiaster, 190 n.25, 328 n.132
Angoulême, M. de, 32 n.96
Aquinas, T., 80, 91-100, 324 n.119
Aristotle, 65 n.82, 191 n.28
Augustine, 12, 13, 13 n.39, 21, 26, 31, 35, 42, 49-76, 78, 80, 81, 83 n.23, 86, 87, 89, 90, 91, 95, 99 n.90, 100, 112 n.32, 127, 130, 159, 160, 190 n.25, 195 n.37, 209, 211, 216 n.1, 267, 276 n.90, 324 n.119, 328 n.132, 337, 345, 346, 347, 348

Baumgärtner, J., 175
Beze, 258 n.4
Brenz, 190 n.25
Bucer, M., 2 n.2, 166 n.108, 190 n.25, 195 n.37, 325 n.119, 328 n.132
Bugenhagen, J., 198 n.46
Bullinger, H., 190 n.25

Cajetan, 190 n.25, 324 n.119, 328 n.132
Calvin, Idelette, 282 n.126, 287 n.153
Capito, 325 n.119
Chrysostom, 190 n.25, 314 n.79, 328 n.132

Damian, P., 85, 88
Dentière, M., 32 n.96, 39 n.4

Erasmus, D., 2 n.2, 85, 324 n.119, 345 n.13

Farel, 260 n.12, 263

Gerbel, N., 165
Glantz, C., 175
Gratian, 82, 83, 88, 90, 91
Grumbach, A. von, 175

Heloise, 88, 89, 345 n.13

Jerome, 12, 50, 84, 86, 87, 346

Lambert, F., 175 n.150
Levet, C., 32 n.96, 39 n.4
Link, W., 176
Lombard, P., 88, 91 n.55
Luther, Katherine, 44, 153, 168, 174, 175, 175 n.153, 200 n.51, 201, 203-7, 212, 348

Martyr, J., 190 n.25, 325 n.119, 328 n.132
Melanchthon, P., 119, 175 n.153
Münster, T., 175 n.150
Musculus, 325 n.119

Navarre, M. de, 39 n.4

Occam, 216 n.1
Oecolampadius, 190 n.25

Pellican, 325 n.119
Pisan, C. de, 86, 345 n.13
Politus, 190 n.25, 328 n.132

Rühel, 174, 176

Schön, E., 86 n.38
Scotus, 216 n.1
Spalatin, G., 173, 175

Valois, M. de, 30, 32 n.96

Zell, K., 30, 39 n.4, 130 n.100
Zwingli, 190 n.25, 325 n.119, 328 n.132

Modern Authors

Abray, L. J., 174 n.148
Adeney, B. T., 7 n.21

Ahme, E., 20 n.63
Alexander, J. H., 21 n.63, 23 n.65, 283 n.126
Althaus, P., 108 n.12, 114 n.37, 159 n.76
Alvarez, A., 14 n.42
Anderson, M., 45 n.18
Anderson, R. S., 159 n.76
Armstrong, B., 3 n.6
Armstrong, K., 4 n.9, 13, 13 n.38, 14, 14 n.41, 26, 37, 51 n.8, 68 n.94, 160, 160 n.78, 166 n.106, 268, 268 n.45, 281, 281 n.114
Arnold, M., 9 n.26

Badcock, G. D., 135 n.118, 237 n.91
Bailey, E., 159 n.76, 166, 166 n.106
Bainton, R., 2 n.5, 86 n.37, 130 n.100, 174 n.147, 175, 175 n.152, 205, 205 n.75, 282 n.126
Bakelant, L., 134 n.117
Baldwin, C. M., 6, 6 n.19, 45 n.18
Barnes, R., 114 n.37
Barth, K., 5-6, 5 n.12, 351, 351 n.19
Barton, F. W., 24 n.67, 282 n.153
Battles, F. L., 215 n.2, 217 n.9
Bavel, J. van, 50, 50 n.7, 57, 57 n.36, 60, 60 n.51, 65, 67 n.91
Behrens, M. S., 4 n.9, 6 n.16, 15-17, 16 n.48, 160, 160 n.78, 339 n.6
Bennet, J. M., 4 n.10, 29 n.86, 77 n.2, 82 n.17
Benoît, J. D., 45 n.19
Biéler, A., 6, 23 n.65, 27-8, 27 n.78, 34, 37, 219, 219 n.15, 245 n.130, 253, 253 n.164, 265, 266 n.34, 267, 273 n.75
Biller, P., 81 n.13
Blaisdell, C. J., 8, 10, 24, 24 n.67, 25, 172, 172 n.135, 324 n.115
Blocher, H., 120 n.64
Boer, W. P. de, 6 n.16, 30-31, 30 n.87, 31 n.91, 110 n.22, 130 n.100, 219, 253, 300, 301 n.30, 304, 304 n.43, 307, 307 n.54, 339 n.4
Bohatec, J., 215, 215 n.2, 246 n.136
Bornkamm, H., 144 n.9, 161, 161 n.81, 175 n.154, 206 n.82

Børresen, K., 50 n.4, 58 n.44, 60 n.55, 61, 61 n.58, 61 n.60, 64, 64 n.79, 66, 66 n.87, 68, 68 n.96, 70 n.104, 77 n.2, 92 n.63, 94 n.72, 95-6, 96 n.75, 96 n.79, 99 n.89, 100, 100 n.94, 169 n.124, 276 n.88
Boswell, J., 199 n.48
Bottomley, F., 50 n.6, 52, 52 n.10, 53 n.15, 67 n.93, 84 n.27
Bouwsma, W. J., 25 n.68, 42 n.11, 216-18, 216 n.5, 232, 232 n.70, 239, 239 n.102, 247, 247 n.141, 259 n.11, 269, 269 n.54, 272-3, 272 n.72, 282 n.126
Bratt, J. H., 6 n.16, 28, 28 n.82, 30, 219, 253, 300, 300 n.29, 320, 320 n.104, 339 n.4
Brooke, C., 50 n.3, 67 n.93, 72 n.2, 78 n.6, 80 n.9, 84 n.30, 85, 85 n.33, 88 n.43, 89, 89 n.50
Brown, P., 50 n.4, 60 n.53, 63 n.75, 65 n.82, 67 n.93, 68 n.94
Brundage, L. A., 13 n.36, 50 n.3, 50 n.5, 67 n.92, 68, 68 n.94, 77 n.2, 79, 79 n.8, 91, 91 n.56, 91 n.57, 148 n.7, 171, 171 n.133, 262 n.21, 273 n.76
Bücher, K., 20 n.63
Burnotte, M., 199 n.50
Burrus, V., 50 n.5
Burton, A., 4 n.10
Butin, P. W., 214 n.1, 241 n.112

Cahill, L., 56 n.32, 104, 104 n.1, 160, 160 n.79, 192, 192 n.29, 210 n.87
Cairncross, J., 168 n.119
Cameron, E., 199 n.48
Carew-Hunt, R. N., 214 n.1, 283 n.126
Cargill Thompson, W. D. J., 106 n.4, 117, 117 n.52, 124, 124 n.77
Carr, A. E., 15 n.45
Chadwick, H., 67 n.93
Chrisman, M. U., 2 n.4, 199 n.48
Clark, M. T., 49 n.2
Cocke, E. W., 20 n.63, 163 n.92
Coudert, A. P., 26 n.77
Cranz, F. E., 135 n.118, 142 n.1
Crawford, J. R., 32 n.94

Daly, M., 5 n.14, 15 n.45
Daniel-Rops, H., 174 n.149
Davy, Y., 204 n.68
Deane, H. A., 50 n.8, 67 n.93, 68 n.94
Denliffle, H., 159 n.79
Donnelly, E., 206 n.82
Douglass, J. D., 6 n.16, 18 n.57, 31-4, 31 n.92, 32 n.95, 73, 199 n.48, 216 n.1, 219, 243 n.123, 253, 253 n.165, 266, 266 n.35, 267, 299, 299 n.23, 301, 301 n.30, 304, 304 n.44, 307, 307 n.53, 320 n.103, 325, 327 n.128, 337, 350
Dowell, S., 68 n.94, 198 n.47
Dowsett, R., 15 n.45, 24 n.67
Doyle, P. M., 15 n.47
Doyle, R. C., 215 n.1, 216, 216 n.4, 220-21, 221 n.22
Driver, S. D., 50 n.5

Ebeling, G., 106 n.6, 107, 107 n.8, 110, 110 n.23, 124, 124 n.79
Edwards, M. U., 116 n.45, 175 n.152
Eßer, H. H., 34 n.105
Eugene, T. M., 22 n.64
Evans, G. R., 148, 148 n.34

Farley, M. A., 13 n.39, 45 n.18, 266 n.36, 293 n.2
Fiddes, P. S., 5 n.12, 351 n.19
Fischer, D., 45 n.18
Fleischer, M. P., 29 n.86, 150 n.41
Fuchs, E., 10 n.30, 75 n.118, 202, 202 n.62, 215 n.1

Gamble, R. C., 215 n.1
Ganoczy, A., 214 n.1
George, T., 19 n.60, 120 n.64, 272 n.73, 336
Gerrish, B. A., 120 n.64, 154 n.53, 186 n.15, 243 n.123, 247 n.139
Gies, F. / Gies, G., 77 n.2, 78 n.4, 78 n.5, 82 n.15
Gilligan, C., 206, 206 n.82
Gittins, D., 15 n.45
Goody, J., 149 n.38
Gottlieb, B., 29 n.86, 86, 86 n.36, 86 n.37, 198 n.46

Gould, G., 61 n.61, 65 n.82
Graham, W. F., 24, 24 n.66
Greef, W. de, 293 n.1
Green, V. H. H., 9 n.26
Grey, M., 15 n.45
Gritsch, E. W., 108 n.6, 117, 117 n.52, 124, 124 n.77, 175 n.152, 176, 176 n.158
Grossmann, M., 150 n.41
Gustafson, J. M., 111 n.27, 125 n.83, 215 n.2, 338, 338 n.3

Halkin, E., 2 n.2, 29 n.86
Hall, C. A. M., 216 n.1, 244, 245 n.129
Hamilton, B., 80 n.9
Hampson, D., 154 n.53
Hardesty, N., 187 n.17
Harkness, G., 27 n.77, 192 n.30, 232 n.73, 263 n.27, 280-81, 281 n.113, 317 n.92
Harrison, B. W., 15 n.47, 101, 101 n.96, 199 n.48
Hay, D., 80 n.9
Headley, J. M., 120 n.64
Heer, F., 50 n.6, 84 n.30, 86 n.37, 88 n.43
Hendrix, S. H., 114 n.39, 192 n.30
Herlihy, D., 62 n.69, 77 n.2, 78, 78 n.5, 85 n.34, 150 n.41
Hesselink, J., 217 n.5
Heyward, C., 7 n.22
Hodgkinson, L., 4 n.8
Höpfl, H., 42, 42 n.10
Houlbrooke, R. A., 82, 82 n.15, 276 n.88
Hsia, R. P-C., 110 n.22
Huizinga, J., 80 n.9

Irwin, J., 276 n.88
Ishida, Y., 43 n.13

James, E. O., 2 n.4, 148, 148 n.37
Jeay, K., 84 n.31
Jewett, P. K., 4 n.9, 5 n.12, 6 n.15, 15 n.44, 26, 26 n.73, 27 n.77, 37, 98, 98 n.88, 201, 201 n.56, 266, 266 n.36, 267, 351 n.19
Johnson, S. M., 2 n.3, 199 n.48

Jordan, C., 15 n.45, 20, 20 n.61, 29 n.86, 130 n.100, 276 n.88, 284 n.135, 341, 352 n.20
Jutte, R., 204 n.74

Kamerou, W., 20 n.63
Karant-Nunn, S. C., 6 n.16, 10, 10 n.28, 168 n.118, 275 n.84
Kelly, J., 29 n.86
Kelly, R. A., 186 n.15
Kingdon, R. M., 233 n.76
Kittleson, J., 43 n.13
Kramm, H. H., 115 n.3
Kreiger, L., 15 n.45
Krodel, G. G., 205, 205 n.75

Lambert, M., 81 n.13
Lang, A., 119, 119 n.55, 246, 246 n.137
Lazareth, W. H., 6, 6 n.17, 20 n.63, 174, 174 n.148
Leeuwen, M. S. van, 197 n.44, 284 n.135, 324 n.117, 346 n.14
Lehmann, P., 13, 13 n.37, 67 n.93, 101, 101 n.96, 159 n.77, 216 n.1, 217 n.9, 235, 235 n.85, 268 n.47, 273 n.75
Lerner, G., 15 n.45, 27 n.77
Lienhard, M., 2 n.3
Loeschen, J. R., 108 n.11, 123 n.74
Loewenich, W. von, 2 n.4, 175, 175 n.152, 205, 205 n.75
Lohse, B., 114 n.37, 174 n.149, 206 n.82
Long, E. L. Jr, 11 n.27, 108 n.11, 121 n.67, 203 n.65
Lowe, K. J. P., 198 n.48
Luscombe, D. E., 88 n.42

MacCuish, D., 21 n.63, 204 n.68
MacIntyre, A., 106 n.7
Mall, E. J., 204 n.68
Mancha, R., 23 n.65
Marcel, P., 214 n.1
Marcus, R. A., 62 n.66
Marius, R., 162 n.89, 202 n.60
Matheson, P., 4 n.10, 175 n.151
McClendon, J. W., 341, 341 n.7
McDonough, T. M., 159 n.76

McGiffert, A. C., 176 n.160
McGowen, R. J., 50 n.4, 65 n.85
McGrath, A. E., 3, 3 n.6, 106 n.6, 125, 125 n.83, 236, 236 n.89, 237 n.91, 282 n.126, 293 n.2, 352 n.21
McLaughlin, E. C., 6 n.14, 77 n.2, 84 n.29, 84 n.31, 95, 95 n.74, 102 n.97
McNamara, J. A., 199 n.48
McNutt, J., 42 n.11
Meinhold, P., 108 n.14
Miles, R., 14 n.40, 27 n.77, 51 n.8, 86 n.37, 155, 155 n.60, 167, 167 n.113, 284 n.135
Miller, A. A., 188 n.18
Milner, B. C., 216, 216 n.3, 222, 222 n.32, 231 n.67, 232 n.69, 236, 236 n.90, 245 n.131
Moeller, B., 114 n.37
Monheit, M. L., 216 n.1, 231, 232 n.69
Monter, W., 217 n.9
Motyer, S., 351 n.18
Mouw, R. J., 232 n.72
Moxey, K., 83 n.26, 86 n.38
Mullett, M., 216 n.1
Murstein, B. I., 198 n.46, 268 n.47, 282 n.126, 287 n.153

Nelson, J. B., 7 n.22, 22 n.64, 159, 159 n.76
Newman Brooks, P., 199 n.50
Niebuhr, R., 203 n.66
Nineham, D., 50 n.3, 80 n.9, 81, 81 n.11, 83 n.23, 87 n.40
Nygren, A., 112 n.32, 201, 201 n.57

Oberman, H. A., 114, 114 n.37, 115 n.40, 117 n.49, 157 n.71, 162, 162 n.86, 204 n.69, 206, 206 n.83, 217 n.5
O'Callaghan, D., 90 n.54
Olsen, V. N., 7 n.20
Osborn, E., 52 n.10
Outka, G. H., 203 n.65
Ozment, S., 1, 1 n.2, 21 n.63, 157 n.68, 157 n.71

Pagels, E., 55 n.23, 61 n.60, 68 n.94

Pannenberg, W., 109, 109 n.17, 113 n.36
Parker, T. H. L., 42 n.11, 44 n.17, 45 n.18, 293 n.1, 309 n.63, 325 n.120
Parsons, M., 115 n.40, 288 n.161
Pauck, W., 126 n.86, 136, 136 n.125, 186 n.15
Paul, S. L., 5 n.13, 50 n.4
Pearson, C., 204, 204 n.68
Pfeiffer, C. W., 7 n.20
Phillips, R., 148, 148 n.37, 160 n.80
Piper, O. A., 2 n.4
Potter, M., 6 n.16, 25, 25 n.69
Power, E., 82 n.18
Preuss, H., 115 n.40
Primavesi, A., 14 n.43, 15 n.47
Prins, R., 216 n.1, 243 n.123

Radice, B., 88 n.43
Reardon, B. M. G., 221 n.23
Reid, D. R., 114 n.37
Richard, L. J., 243 n.122
Rilliet, J., 214 n.1, 287 n.153
Robinson, N. H. G., 317 n.92
Roelker, N. L., 34 n.105
Romero, J. A., 5 n.12, 5 n.14, 351 n.19
Roper, L., 19 n.58
Rösener, W., 83 n.24
Ruether, R. R., 4 n.9, 5 n.14, 14, 15 n.44, 26, 26 n.73, 51, 51 n.9, 66 n.8, 75, 75 n.118, 130 n.100, 197 n.43
Rupp, D. R., 106 n.6, 175 n.152
Russell, P. A., 199 n.49

Safley, T. M., 38 n.2, 161 n.81
Scanzoni, L., 187 n.17
Schlabach, G. W., 58 n.43
Schmeidler, B., 88 n.43
Schreiber, C., 204 n.68
Schreiner, S., 216 n.5, 218, 221, 221 n.26, 241, 241 n.113, 246 n.137, 247 n.140
Schroeder, E. H., 160 n.80
Schuurman, D. J., 350, 350 n.15
Schwiebert, E. G., 20 n.63, 175 n.152, 204 n.68
Scribner, R. W., 43 n.13, 134 n.117
Selderhuis, H. J., 7 n.20

Selinger, S., 160 n.78, 261, 261 n.19, 264, 264 n.31, 267, 267 n.41, 282, 282 n.125, 294 n.9
Shaw, B. D., 49 n.2, 54 n.17, 61, 61 n.61
Siggins, I. D. K., 2 n.4, 10–11, 10 n.31, 11 n.35, 18 n.57
Simon, E., 20 n.63
Smith, J. C., 204 n.68
Somers, H., 65 n.85
Sparn, W., 43 n.13
Stauffer, R., 26 n.73, 42 n.11, 240, 240 n.109, 309 n.63
Steinmetz, D., 42, 42 n.11, 44 n.17
Stickleberger, E., 23 n.65
Stone, L., 15 n.45, 272 n.73, 351 n.17
Storkey, E., 9 n.26
Strauss, G., 151, 151 n.44
Southern R. W., 81, 81 n.10, 86 n.37
Spijker, W. van 't, 224 n.36
Spitz, L. W., 216 n.1
Strauss, G., 2 n.5
Stuard, S. M., 4 n.10
Sumner, G. M., 45 n.18, 293 n.2
Swartley, W. M., 352 n.21

Tamburello, D. E., 42 n.11
Tentler, T. N., 87 n.39, 111 n.25
Thomas, G. F., 318 n.92
Thompson, J. L., 5 n.11, 6 n.16, 32 n.96, 33 n.100, 34 n.105, 38, 38 n.1, 188, 188 n.18, 190, 190 n.24, 191, 228 n.57, 243 n.123, 250, 250 n.160, 251, 266 n.37, 302, 302 n.33, 314 n.77, 320 n.103, 328 n.132, 338, 338 n.2
Todd, J. M., 174 n.147
Tolley, B., 2 n.5
Tonkin, J. M., 106 n.6
Torrance, T. F., 106 n.6, 107, 107 n.9, 114 n.39, 115 n.43, 119 n.59, 120, 120 n.62, 243 n.123
Tucker, R. A., 88 n.43

Veninga, J. F., 215 n.1
Vos, C. J., 235 n.85

Wagner, W. H., 113 n.34

Wallace, R. S., 244, 244 n.127
Walt, B. J. van der, 6, 6 n.19, 34 n.105, 84 n.28, 266 n.35
Wan, M. W. Y., 5 n.12, 351 n.19
Webb, D. M., 77 n.2, 83 n.22, 199 n.50
Wendel, F., 215 n.1, 282 n.126
Whale, J. S., 32 n.94
White, H., 147 n.27
White, R., 42 n.11, 228 n.56, 313 n.73
White, R. E. O., 89 n.45, 120 n.64, 134 n.117
Wiesner, M., 4 n.9, 4 n.10, 5, 5 n.14, 6 n.16, 16 n.48, 17-19, 17 n.53, 19 n.58, 20 n.63, 37, 162 n.89, 204 n.74, 339 n.4
Wiethaus, U., 81 n.13
Wilson-Hayes, T., 200 n.51
Wingren, G., 107, 107 n.10, 11 n.27, 114 n.37, 117, 118 n.53, 119 n.59, 134, 135 n.118, 137, 137 n.129, 154 n.53, 156 n.61, 157 n.71
Wright, D. F., 11 n.27, 188 n.18, 189, 189 n.21, 190 n.23, 264 n.28, 318, 318 n.94, 325
Wyntjes, S. M., 186 n.15

Zophy, J. W., 168 n.117

SCRIPTURE INDEX

Genesis
1–3 188–97, 293 n.1, 343, 346
1:26–2:7 188–92
1:26–2:25 318–26
1:26–2:24 335
1:26–3:24 318–29
1:27–8 64, 324 n.117
1:28 145, 168 n.119, 170–71, 200, 200 n.54, 322
2:11 272
2:15–25 192–4
2:16–17 108
2:18 245–6, 266, 282, 321, 324 n.117
2:18–24 64
2:22 194
2:25 194
2 29
3:1–24 326–9
3:1–25 194–7
3:7 72 n.113
3:16 197
4:1 162
6 111, 115–16
9:18 272
17:12 225–6
18 240
18:6 285
37:12–14 135–6
41:45 128, 128 n.92

Leviticus
18:6 249

Deuteronomy
22:13–24 271
24:5 273, 273 n.76

2 Samuel
13:1–14 270

Job
3:3 320 n.103
19:17–25 279
24:19–25 234 n.82
31:9–15 240 n.103

Psalms
51 112, 200
101 118
127 222

Isaiah
24:1–3 250 n.161

Jeremiah
3:4 272

Daniel
2:11 272

Acts
3:21 241

Romans
2:14–15 245–6
8:10 59

1 Corinthians
7 133, 182–5, 293–8, 293 n.1, 335, 343
7:3–4 184
7:4 296 n.17, 335
7:9 271, 274
7:22–4 183
7:25–6 176
7:29 295 n.13
11:2 306
11:2–16 293 n.1, 298–305, 335
11:3 224–5, 229–30
11:7 65, 319, 323, 325
11:11–12 335
14:33–5 293 n.1, 305–7
15 184
16:19 225

Galatians
3:26–9 225
3:28 20, 59–60, 81, 129–32, 139, 183–4, 190–91, 211, 227–31, 254, 299, 342, 350

Ephesians
5:21 323 n.113, 348
5:21–33 293 n.1, 307–12, 335, 343
5:28 258
6:1–4 277

1 Timothy
2:8–15 185–7, 293 n.1, 312–18, 335
2:11–15 186
2:13 313 n.74
2:15 187
5:8 62 n.66

1 Peter
2:5 132
2:18 329
3:1–7 180–82, 329–33, 335, 342
3:7 182 n.4

2 Peter
1:10 238

SUBJECT INDEX

Abraham, 262 n.22, 272, 285
'active sexuality', 160–61
Adam, 20, 22, 30 n.89, 51, 53, 56, 60, 68, 69, 69 n.100, 93, 96, 98, 107, 108, 111, 118, 119, 143, 155, 162, 163, 172, 177, 187, 187 n.16, 195, 209, 226, 232, 242 n.118, 243, 246, 252, 260, 265, 269, 274, 275, 314, 319, 321, 326, 345
alter Christus, 202–3, 211, 282, 349
anxiety (*Angst*), 105, 112, 217, 288, 295
Aquila, 225
authority, 28, 61, 62, 73, 74, 82, 83, 99, 127, 128, 182, 186, 198 n.46, 209, 225, 227, 235, 254, 278, 284, 285, 286, 297, 299–300, 303, 305, 309, 316, 328, 331, 332, 342, 346

calling (see 'vocation')
Candace, 186
celibacy, 32, 56, 88, 144, 164, 165, 182, 183, 185, 262, 293, 293 n.5
Christ, 17, 18, 22, 24, 57, 58–9, 74, 113, 118, 124, 128, 129, 130, 153, 160, 168, 180, 181, 201, 202–3, 216, 218, 227, 228, 236, 241–4, 247, 252, 254, 258, 261, 278, 284, 299, 309, 310, 311, 319, 320, 323, 327, 330, 341, 348, 350, 351, 352
Christ's return, 115, 122
civitas Dei, 54–5
civitas terrena, 54–5, 345
cognitio Dei, 25
cognitio hominis, 25
companionship, 8, 9, 21, 22, 26, 41, 46, 47, 63–4, 74, 76, 90, 95, 101, 157–8, 178, 193, 193 n.34, 202, 204, 209, 257, 266, 267, 280–88, 290, 309, 311, 317, 325, 334, 337, 348
confusion (*confusio*), 216, 226, 228, 231, 233, 234, 235

conscience, 146–7, 184, 224
consummation (*copula carnalis*), 91
coram Deo, 124–5, 129, 153–5, 168, 173, 177, 331, 352
creation, 17, 20, 22, 24, 25, 28, 30 n.89, 53, 65, 67, 69, 80, 92–9, 104, 107, 160, 161, 187 n.17, 188–92, 220–22, 232, 244, 246, 252, 259, 268, 280, 284, 289, 306, 315, 318–26, 340, 345; ordinances, 120, 121, 126, 143, 146, 155, 161, 162, 209, 331
creational logic, 46, 144, 158, 170, 177, 181, 183, 280
curse, 9, 155
custom, 30, 185, 249, 298, 300, 301

Deborah, 186, 314
devil, the, 18, 18 n.56, 105, 113–17, 123–5, 139, 155, 157, 174, 195, 210, 213, 290, 314, 326
divorce, 30, 147, 264 n.30

equality, 13, 14, 22, 24, 25, 28, 30, 31, 35, 52, 65, 66, 74, 75, 99, 101, 102, 129, 132, 133, 187, 189, 190, 191–2, 195, 200, 210, 218, 226, 252, 274, 286, 297, 298, 299, 316, 319, 324, 333, 334, 341, 343, 352
Eve, 19 n.58, 22, 30 n.89, 51, 53, 60, 69, 69 n.100, 96, 98, 108, 111, 143, 162, 163, 172, 177, 187, 187 n.16, 189–92, 195, 209, 260, 269, 275, 314, 315, 321, 322, 326, 345

faith, 104, 126–7, 129, 131, 149–53, 155, 156, 158, 165, 167, 168, 177, 180, 181, 208, 213, 226, 241, 242, 258
Fall, the, 19 n.58, 22, 24, 56, 57, 61, 65 n.84, 72, 87, 94, 105, 107, 112, 118, 144, 160, 161, 166, 170, 183, 187, 194–7, 221, 231, 232, 242 n.118,

246 n.137, 254, 306, 315, 318, 326–9, 341
family, the, 1, 2 n.3, 10, 32, 54, 62, 108, 110, 214, 225, 283, 317, 335, 352
feminist studies, 4; writers, 7, 209
freedom, 23, 27, 33, 35, 40, 46, 48, 59, 81, 104, 132, 183, 184, 185, 219, 236, 244, 296, 299, 301, 304
friendship, 41, 50, 57, 59–67, 78, 280, 298, 333, 348, 352

Geneva, 33, 217 n.9
God, 19, 214, 237, 260; grace of, 1, 60, 65, 67, 104, 113, 120, 148, 149, 158, 166, 167, 178, 184, 195 n.37, 206, 213, 220, 244, 245, 261, 268, 271, 275, 276, 289, 315, 343; love of, 117–18, 201, 220
gospel, the, 5, 7, 20, 60, 102, 110, 111, 116, 118, 119, 120, 121, 133, 174, 181, 184, 230, 241, 285, 316, 351, 352

harmony, 1, 53–5, 109, 281–2, 287
headship, 24, 25
hierarchicalism, 4, 9, 21, 61, 127, 131–2, 136, 210, 211, 255, 267, 312, 314, 335, 339, 343, 345, 348, 350
hierarchy, 7, 34, 59–67, 81, 143, 179, 180, 198–203, 226, 277, 280, 283–4, 298, 312, 346
Holy Spirit, 104, 106, 109, 113, 115, 120, 124, 127, 131, 132, 151, 153, 164, 167, 177, 219, 220, 222, 224, 229 n.60, 233, 236, 242, 247, 247 n.142, 258, 260, 306, 343, 352
household management, 9
Huldah, 186

idols, 112
image of God (*imago Dei*), 30, 39, 51, 51 n.9, 65, 67, 74, 81, 99, 167, 188, 188 n.19, 190, 191, 210, 216, 226, 242–6, 247, 250, 252, 254, 318, 334, 343, 348, 349
incest, 171
in-curvatus in se, 112

inequality (*inaequalitas*), 14, 15, 22, 28, 31, 35, 39, 81, 96–9, 105, 127–34, 197, 200, 210–12, 214, 219, 225, 226–7, 230, 236, 252, 253, 256, 290, 299, 320, 342, 345
inferiority, 64–7, 74, 252, 298, 304, 305, 316, 320, 322, 326, 333, 343, 345, 350
Institutes, the, 3, 42, 44, 44 n.17, 45, 228–9, 233 n.78

Jacob, 272
Jael, 186
Joseph, 260

kingdom of God, 211, 223, 229, 233

law, 110, 118, 282, 297, 334, 343
Last Day, the, 114–15
leadership, 28
Leah, 171 n.130
liberationist position, 12, 14, 20, 29 n.86, 215, 218, 230, 253, 300, 337; theology, 190
lust, 9, 12, 16, 18, 47, 58, 67, 68, 71, 88, 94, 111, 148, 157, 160, 162, 163, 169, 193, 257, 263, 265, 270, 271, 283, 289, 347

marriage, 1, 3, 4, 10, 79; clerical, 1, 1 n.2, 79; medieval, 77–102; sacrament of, 90, 94
Mary and Martha, 17
medieval church, 9; theology, 21
metaphorical language, 11, 18–19, 18 n.57, 164–5, 217, 225, 226–7, 239, 240, 270, 294
Middle Ages, the, 24, 26, 27, 34, 35, 50, 52, 76, 77, 79, 81, 101, 127, 172, 217, 275 n.84, 337, 346
Miriam, 313 n.73
misogyny, 37, 50, 84, 85, 100
moderation (*moderatio*), 239, 269, 271, 303, 313, 332
motherhood, 17
mutual confidence, 273; faithfulness, 7, 159, 172–3, 178, 211, 281, 297; love, 8, 21, 23, 34, 50, 62, 63–4,

101, 171, 172, 179, 180, 198, 201, 202, 205, 207, 211, 259, 280, 293, 318, 320, 333, 348; obligation, 67, 281, 297, 308, 323; servitude, 61 n.59; submission, 284 n.132, 307-8, 311; vulnerability, 194
mutuality, 37, 42, 75, 89, 103, 198, 212, 280, 293, 332, 346
mysterion, 147, 258

natural law, 119-20, 139, 145, 146, 245, 246-51, 254
natural reason, 150, 152, 170
Noah, 115, 128, 170

Onan, 171
order (*ordo*), 22, 31, 33, 34, 35, 37, 40-41, 47, 52-5, 59, 63, 65, 73, 74, 80-87, 98, 100, 103-4, 105, 109, 117, 118, 121, 128, 136, 139, 140, 158, 180, 207, 211, 213, 214-51, 236-43, 246-51, 257, 280, 289, 291, 296, 308, 310, 337, 342, 345-6, 349
original sin, 160, 163, 166

parental authority, 30
partnership, 9, 197, 210, 280
patriarchy, 4, 7, 10, 14-23, 37, 197-203, 210, 267, 283, 290, 334, 351
penalty (see 'punishment')
Phoebe, 313 n.73
physical abuse, 83
politia, 33, 219, 304
poverty, 156
prayer, 57, 155, 164, 185 n.13, 297 n.20, 312
preachers, 116, 118, 142
priesthood of believers, 32, 129 n.97, 132
Prisca / Priscilla, 225, 313 n.73
procreation, 9, 12, 13, 16, 26, 32, 34, 46, 47, 56-7, 64, 69, 70, 74, 75, 85, 87, 91, 92, 94, 100, 101, 142, 158, 161, 167, 168-72, 178, 187, 193, 194, 196, 209, 257, 265, 266, 275-9, 283, 289, 315, 318, 321, 325, 337, 347
propriety, 30, 229, 305

punishment, 72, 74, 181, 190 n.25, 194-7, 211, 295, 326-9

querelle des femmes, 29 n.86, 39

Rachel, 200 n.55, 272
rape, 270, 285, 288 n.161
Rebecca, 82
Reciprocal honour, 182
Reformation, the, 1, 5, 7, 13, 26, 27, 253, 268, 336; theology of, 14, 128
remedy against sin (*remedium peccati*), 32, 34, 57, 91, 94, 113, 142, 148, 163, 169, 171, 178, 209, 257, 261, 265, 267-75, 277, 283, 309, 317, 337, 347
righteousness, 109, 136, 148, 226, 232, 244 n.124, 246, 319
rule, 60, 180, 182, 186, 196, 203, 305, 309, 317, 323, 333, 346
Ruth, 82

sacrament, 32 n.95, 58, 121, 147-8, 149, 258, 258 n.4
Sarah, 82, 198, 200 n.55, 240-41, 272, 287 n.154, 330-31
Satan (see devil, the)
Scripture, 9, 21, 23, 35, 44 n.17, 46
sex, 8, 13, 46, 68, 160, 163, 209, 268, 289, 325
sexual incontinence, 10
sexual intercourse, 9, 13, 51, 58, 68, 69, 70-71, 75, 87-91, 92, 93, 160, 162, 166, 167, 178, 192, 196, 209, 258, 269, 271, 273, 289
sexual need, 14, 161-2, 193
sexual negativity, 12-14
sin, 51, 54, 55, 56, 59, 60, 68, 69-71, 73, 87, 104, 110, 111-12, 156, 162-3, 164, 166, 167, 178, 181, 190 n.25, 193, 195-7, 203, 211, 213, 217, 231-6, 238, 243, 252, 257, 261, 265, 281, 286, 289, 293, 295, 322, 341, 351
spiritual battle, 156-7
spiritual realm, 106, 109, 113, 117, 122, 122 n.74, 130, 131, 138, 211, 224, 342

status quo, 7, 18, 20, 29 n.86, 60, 81, 145 n.16, 210 n.87, 235, 252, 291
subjection, 17, 34, 39, 60, 66, 84, 102, 186, 194, 196, 207, 211, 225, 240, 284, 299, 304, 309, 316, 328, 330
submission, 180, 182, 186, 190 n.25, 196, 300, 302, 305, 309, 316, 329, 342, 346
subordination, 15, 20, 28, 33, 60, 67, 100, 225
superiority, 74, 186, 187, 188, 192, 202, 227, 252, 303, 311

temporal realm, 45, 46, 104, 106 n.7, 109, 113, 117, 122, 122 n.74, 132, 133, 138, 145, 146, 148, 155, 157, 158, 173, 177, 183, 197, 207–8, 211, 236, 342
two cities, 54
two kingdoms, 45, 105–34, 138, 149, 164, 173, 213, 223–4, 340

unequal power-relations, 7, 7 n.22, 8, 102, 337; structure, 37

vocation (*vocatio*), 14, 24, 38, 45, 46, 81, 103–4, 105, 110, 112, 113, 116, 117, 118, 119, 121, 124, 126, 128, 129, 134–8, 141–58, 159, 163, 164, 167, 168, 170, 177, 184, 208, 209, 211, 213, 231, 236–8, 241, 252, 257, 258, 259, 261, 265, 278, 280, 308, 287, 289, 294, 308, 340, 345, 347

Wittenberg, 173
woman's evil, 16; inferiority, 16, 32, 37, 40, 82, 89, 95, 96–9, 100, 102, 113, 189, 192, 202
women's (wives') roles, 10, 11, 12, 19, 22, 145, 208, 337; status, 10, 11, 12, 18, 22, 23, 26–7, 83, 86, 212, 320, 332, 337
Word of God, 3, 19, 109, 110, 111, 117, 119, 124, 126, 135, 150, 195, 220

Zwickau, 10

www.ingramcontent.com/pod-product-compliance
Lightning Source LLC
Chambersburg PA
CBHW071419290426
44108CB00014B/1892